H.J. de Blij

University of South Florida, St. Petersburg

HUMAN GEOGRAPHY
Culture, Society, and Space
Fifth Edition

JOHN WILEY & SONS, INC.

New York   Chichester   Brisbane   Toronto   Singapore

ACQUISITIONS EDITOR Frank Lyman
SENIOR MARKETING MANAGER Catherine Faduska
SENIOR PRODUCTION MANAGER Linda Muriello
SENIOR PRODUCTION EDITOR Jeanine Furino
DESIGN SUPERVISOR Ann Marie Renzi
MANUFACTURING MANAGER Mark Cirillo
PHOTO ASSOCIATE Michelle Orlans
ILLUSTRATION EDITOR Edward Starr
TEXT AND COVER DESIGN Nancy Field
COVER PHOTO David Turnley/Black Star

This book was set in ITC Garamond Light by University Graphics and
printed and bound by Von Hoffmann Press. The cover was printed by Lehigh Press.

Library of Congress Cataloging in Publication Data:
De Blij, Harm J.
    Human geography : culture, society, and space / H. J. de Blij. —
5th ed.
        p. cm.
    ISBN 0-471-03914-4
    1. Human geography.   I. Title.
    GF41.D4   1995   95-35568
    304.2—dc20   CIP

Printed in the United States of America

10 9 8 7 6 5 4 3 2

PREFACE

Over the twenty-year lifetime of this book, the world has changed substantially, and so has the discipline of geography. Natural environments are changing, these changes influenced by human action. Transculturation energizes a multicultural world of shrinking functional distances. Economic developments transform whole regions. Global and regional political frameworks are buckling as that cornerstone of the international system, the state, loses relevance.

Geographers chronicle, analyze, and often predict such changes. The old image of place-name and product-list geography has finally faded in the bright light of modernization, of satellite imagery and computer cartography, of Geographic Information Systems and spatial analysis. But geography's overarching, encompassing character has not changed.

In the broadest possible terms, the discipline of geography consists of two subdisciplines: human geography and physical (natural) geography. Each of these, in turn, consists of several fields. Physical geography incorporates such diverse fields as climatology, geomorphology, aspects of biogeography, glaciology, and much more. Human geography, too, is wide ranging and diverse and includes, among other areas, cultural geography, economic geography, urban geography, and political geography. Rarely is any of these fields studied in isolation. When physical geographers study glaciers or coastlines to understand the natural processes at work, their conclusions also tell us about these areas as places of human habitation and impact. When human geographers study cities, they often do so with reference to the physical landscape on which the urban area lies, and the role this physical stage has played in the city's evolution. This relationship between human endeavor and natural setting forms one of the discipline's unifying themes.

Another such bond lies in the spatial perspective: physical *and* human geographers depend on it to formulate their research questions, and to look for answers. Maps, representing spatial information, are therefore indispensable to geography.

When a book is entitled *Human Geography*, that title reveals its emphasis, not the whole story of its contents. Nor could it cover all the many fields of human geography itself; there is much more to this part of the discipline than one book or one course could convey. But *Human Geography* does comprise the core of one of geography's major dimensions, as reflected also by its subtitle, *culture, society,* and *space*.

This fifth edition retains the structure of the fourth, which divided the book into 12 parts and 43 (now 40) comparatively short chapters. Each part addresses a prominent field of human geography, and each chapter focuses upon a particular aspect of that field. A course outline need not cover every one of these topics. This creates greater flexibility in the use of *Human Geography*.

Once again a number of perceptive reviewers recommended changes I have incorporated in this new edition. Readers will note that the technical material on map projections and other cartographic issues has been moved to the ancillaries. This is part of a new arrangement in which these appendices collectively form a set of what I have called *Resources*. These resources include not only this discussion of mapmaking, but also the new glossary, the bibliographies relating to each part of the book, the (also new) table of demographic data, and the index.

Many readers commented favorably on the sometimes provocative

iii

At Issue statements that open each part, and these have been modified, where appropriate, to link geography to events or conditions affecting the human world today. I took all photographs, including the part openers, and the captions are taken directly from my field notes written at each site. The *Author's Video Link*, an innovation in this edition, connects topics discussed in the text to segments from the television program "Good Morning America" in which these matters also were addressed. The number given in each "link" refers to the six tapes dated 1990 (1) to 1995 (6). The title of each segment appears on the cassette. Another new feature in this edition is the listing of salient points in *Geographica* form at the beginning of each chapter. These entries summarize important realities, developments, and trends to be discussed in the chapter that follows.

As readers familiar with earlier editions will recognize, considerable revision of the text marks this fifth edition, despite the retention of the book's fundamental structure. Part 5 was revised extensively; Part 9 was shortened considerably; the order of chapters in Part 11 permitted a more rational discussion of economic geography and development. These and many other changes were based on the advice not only of formal reviewers but also of colleagues and students who wrote me to comment on the fourth edition in the course of their encounter with it.

I acknowledge with gratitude the work of the following reviewers:

Prof. Reuel Hanks
Kennesaw State College, Kennesaw, Georgia

Prof. Keith Harries
University of Maryland, Baltimore County, Maryland

Prof. Brian F. Harrison
Clatsop Community College, Astoria, Oregon

Prof. Andrew Herod
University of Georgia, Athens, Georgia

Prof. Vandana Kohli
California State University, Bakersfield, California

Prof. Ian MacLachlan
The University of Lethbridge, Alberta, Canada

Prof. Glenn R. Miller
Bridgewater State College, Bridgewater, Massachusetts

Prof. Bimal K. Paul
Kansas State University, Manhattan, Kansas

Prof. Deborah Paulson
University of Wyoming, Laramie, Wyoming

Prof. Roger W. Stump
State University of New York, Albany, New York

I also thank my friend and colleague Dr. Peter O. Muller, Chair of the Department of Geography at the University of Miami in Coral Gables, Florida, which was my academic home until my resignation in December, 1994; he has contributed materially to this project in several ways, and co-authored the third edition. As always he provided me with information and data while this work was in progress, and he gave generously of his time in making suggestions and recommendations.

Once again I am indebted to Dr. Alan C. G. Best, now of Lincoln, Nebraska, who controlled the transition of this book from manuscript to printed page. He verified the editing, checked the galleys, read the pages, corrected the map numbers, assembled and supplemented the glossary, updated the bibliography, and in addition acted as perceptive reviewer and adviser. I am deeply grateful to him.

At John Wiley & Sons, I had the good fortune of benefiting from the hard work and dedication of a team of more than a dozen people. Frank Lyman, Wiley's Geography Editor, set admirable standards of efficiency in every conceivable way, from writing schedules to review timing and from photo selection to supplement production. Jeanine Furino, the Senior Production Editor, did a magnificent job with a manuscript that had its problems, and never lost her gentle good humor; there were no difficulties that could not be resolved. Edward Starr, Illustration Editor, made it possible for me to use the 1995 demographic data on the world maps by waiting, almost literally, to the last minute for that information to be published; his careful attention to detail is evident from every map in this book. The cartography was expertly performed by Don Larsen and his team at Mapping Specialists in Madison, Wisconsin. Catherine Faduska, Senior Marketing Manager, took an active interest in this book even before it was completed, to plan her campaign on its behalf.

The attractive layout of this book resulted from the fine work of Ann Marie Renzi, Designer, who was confronted by a daunting range of "features" to incorporate on the page. As always, Stella Kupferberg, Director of Photo Research, gave special attention to this book, and advised me on the photos from my collection that would reproduce best on the printed page.

Senior Production Manager Linda Muriello supervised the entire process in which my manuscript was converted into printed pages; Ishaya Monokoff, Director of the Illustration Department, made possible the tight scheduling of the map program. The Design Manager, Maddy Lesure, has seen several editions of this book; this is its most attractive version yet. Michelle Orlans, Photo Associate, made sure that my photographs were recorded, processed, and returned, which is no small order in the case of a book as lavlishly illustrated as this.

Beth Brooks, Assistant to the Geography Editor, handled countless details ranging from travel arrangements to review processing and from manuscript reproduction to correspondence relating to this book, and she was truly indispensable to the project.

Manufacturing Operations Director Susan Stetzer and Manufacturing Manager Mark Cirillo ensured the on-time and handsome appearance of this book. And last but not least, the important supplements are the result of the expert work of Supplements Editor Jennifer Brady.

I am deeply grateful to every member of this superb Wiley team, and consider it an honor to have had the benefit of their involvement in this project.

As always, my greatest thanks go to my wife, Bonnie, whose enthusiastic participation in every facet of this migratory geographer's life has made that life, quite simply, worth living.

H. J. de Blij
Boca Grande, Florida
June 1995

For Bob and Karla

CONTENTS

1

INTRODUCTION: GEOGRAPHY AND HUMAN GEOGRAPHY

Over the past 15 years or so (you have probably seen the newspaper headlines) something called "geographic illiteracy" has begun to come to national attention in the United States—and not just in the United States, but in other countries as well. Various tests and polls have proven that many of us do not know much about the geographic layout of our world. This was revealed primarily through answers given by randomly selected people to questions about the world map or the map of their own country. Such questions, to professional geographers, often seemed trivial. True, a significant percentage of the respondents in the United States could not locate the Pacific Ocean. Many could not even identify New York State on an outline map of the United States. Such results certainly suggest that we do not have a clear picture of the way our world is laid out, but something else is strongly indicated: by not even knowing where the most important things are located (countries, cities, resources, rivers, mountains, and deserts), we lose a valuable instant

frame of reference for communication. To put this in geographic language, a weak **mental map** is a huge disadvantage for anyone functioning in our interconnected world. But a weak mental map is not strengthened by memorizing names of places for their own sake any more than a weak historical perspective is improved by rote memorization of dates and associ-

ated events. Knowing where things are is just the beginning, a little like knowing some introductory vocabulary when you start studying a foreign language. Knowing *why* places and things are where they are, *what* their location means in past, present, and future, and *how* their location affects other places— all this brings us much closer to what geography is about.

Geographica

- **Physical and Human Geography are two great branches of the discipline.**

- **Geography during the twentieth century has been marked by four durable traditions.**

- **The National Geographic Society in the 1980s introduced a five-theme framework for geography.**

- **The spatial perspective is geography's unifying bond.**

- **The map is geography's powerful ally.**

Note that we just referred to places *and things*. This book is mainly about places and their human inhabitants, and how the world has become organized, and in many places transformed, by human activity. But make no mistake: there is more to geography than **human geography**. The other half of geography consists of a group of fields usually called **physical geography**. Actually, a better name for this group would be **natural geography**, because it deals not only with mountains, glaciers, coastlines, and climates, but also with soils, plants, and animals. As we will see, it often is difficult to discuss human geography without also referring to the physical stage on which the human drama is being played out. However, our focus will be on human geography. Although it represents only part of the discipline, human geography embodies several individual fields (Fig. 1-1).

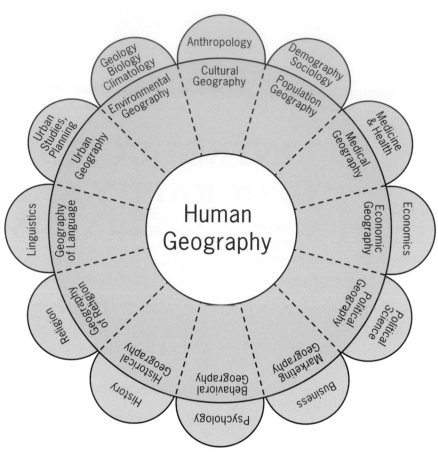

FIGURE 1–1   A schematic diagram showing the relationships among the fields of human geography and related fields outside the discipline. From author's sketch.

THE TYING BOND

If geography deals with so many aspects of our world, ranging from people and places to coastlines and climates, what do the facets of this wide-ranging discipline have in common? The answer lies in a term that often is used most effectively as an adjective: *spatial*. Whether they are human geographers or physical geographers, virtually all geographers are interested in the way places and things are laid out, organized, and arranged on the surface of the Earth. Sometimes a particular spatial arrangement of certain human activities or conditions leads geographers to raise questions as to how this has come about, and what processes are at work. In such instances, the spatial pattern already is evident, and the search is on for an explanation. But at other times, the spatial arrangement may not be evident at all and must be discov-

ered before it can lead to answers. As we will see in our discussions on medical geography, the mapping of the distribution of people afflicted by certain illnesses has led directly to the sources of the illnesses and thus to remedies against them. Medical geography is just one part of human geography in which spatial analysis has practical application.

The spatial arrangement of things is not a monopoly of human geography, however. Physical and human geographers are drawn together because they have a similar way of looking at the world, although their gazes are focused on different areas. Early in this century a climatologist, Alfred Wegener, became convinced—based on decades of observation—that the

jigsaw-like fit of the continental landmasses on opposite sides of the North and South Atlantic Oceans could not be a matter of chance. He marshaled a vast array of geographical and geological evidence, most of it spatial in nature, and on this basis proposed a hypothesis of continental drift. His theory was that the continental landmasses were once united as a giant supercontinent that later broke apart. Wegener's geographic hypothesis, based on the spatial layout of the physical world he knew so well, set the direction for the geological research that was (a half century later) to lead to the discovery of plate tectonics and crustal spreading, the mechanism that drives the continents apart.

Human and physical geographers thus share this particular spatial perspective, this way of looking at the world's—and the Earth's—layout. So the language of geography is not only the language of places and things, but also a whole vocabulary of spatial terms, many of which will become familiar (though occasionally from a new viewpoint) as we proceed. Some of these terms already have been used: **location** is one, and **pattern**, and **distribution** are others. In due course we will become familiar with others, making geographic communication in the pages that follow not only easier but also more efficient and accurate.

Author's Video Link
↓
1
Geographically
Speaking—Overview

TRADITIONS

Before we begin our journey through the world of human geography, we should equip ourselves with some insights into the traditions and themes that have developed in this wide-ranging discipline. With its spatial perspective and its human as well as physical contexts, geography seems to be an all-encompassing, but ill-defined, field. In fact, some geographers have spent their entire careers trying to define the nature of geography, to identify what is, and what is not, scholarly geographic work. Fortunately, these philosophical debates need not concern us here, but we will have occasion to refer to some of the long-term legacies and customs that have developed in geography.

As long ago as 1964, a University of Chicago geographer, W. D. Pattison, published an article in the *Journal of Geography* entitled "The

Four Traditions of Geography." In that much-debated publication, Pattison identified four areas in which geographic research, teaching, and other activity were so concentrated that they could be designated as traditions within the discipline. These four traditions were:

1. An earth-science tradition, represented by many decades of work in physical (natural) geography;
2. A culture-environment tradition, in which the dominant questions have to do with the relationships between human societies and their natural environments;
3. A locational tradition, the spatial unifying theme referred to previously; and
4. An area-analysis tradition, which at the time was represented mainly by studies in regional geography.

Today, more than three decades later, geography is a much more complex discipline. But the strands of the traditions Pattison identified are still there. As noted previously, physical geography (the **earth-science** tradition) remains one of the cornerstones of the discipline. Physical geographers report on the processes, cycles, and systems that modify the natural world. They interpret the landscape, analyze it, and predict how it changes. Although the focus is on the physical world, what physical geographers learn is often of urgent importance to the Earth's human inhabitants. When they study the silting of a delta, the movement of a glacier, the carving of a shoreline, or the shifting of a dune, physical geographers help us to better comprehend the changing nature of our world. As we will see, our study of human geography cannot be carried out without frequent reference to what physical geographers have learned about soil fertility, climatic patterns, river dynamics, and so on.

The **culture-environment** tradition has a difficult, even controversial, history. This tradition encompasses a wide range of topics, some of them quite straightforward (for example, the impact of deforestation on traditional society in the Amazon region or in Zaïre). But more complicated questions have proven risky for reasons that will be discussed in Part 6 of this book. Many years ago, some geographers were tempted to generalize about the relationships between the natural environment (mainly climate) and the level of technological development of societies, concluding that the natural environment is a determinant for progress. This led to assumptions about predictable advantages and disadvantages, which were misused by demagogues. For a long time, the culture-environment tradition was burdened by criticism that was often unfair. Yet, societies and cultures evolve and develop on a physical-environmental stage that has much to do with their properties, patterns, and prospects. The old questions are still there, and modern techniques of analysis have ushered in a new age for this geographic tradition.

What Professor Pattison described as the locational tradition lies at the heart of all geography, because this is the spatial focus of the discipline. This dimension of geography has experienced explosive growth during the past three decades, especially in areas of human geography. The methods of gathering data have expanded almost unimaginably, from Earth satellite recording to sophisticated electronic sampling. Methods of analysis also have changed, so that geographers now deal with unprecedented quantities of data.

Location theory has become a modern element of human geography, seeking answers to a wide range of questions—some of them theoretical, others highly practical:

Why are villages, towns, and cities spaced the way they are? Given a market of a certain size and wealth, where in the surrounding countryside should particular products be grown or raised? What would be the best position for a new shopping center, given existing urban patterns?

The fourth tradition, area analysis, also has undergone a transformation without losing its heritage in classical geography. In the early 1960s, area analysis primarily still involved the description of areas and regions. Regional geography of a more sophisticated type still forms an important part of the discipline. But the area-analysis tradition also has given rise to **regional science**, the application of modern spatial analytical techniques to regional problems and issues. In whatever form it exists and whatever it is called, regional study will survive as one of those threads that make geography what it is. James Michener, the author, once wrote that whenever he started a new book, he prepared himself by turning first to the works written by regional geographers about the area where the action was to occur. Geography's regional dimension is, indeed, one of its permanent traditions.

THEMES

During the 1980s, when concern in the United States about geographic illiteracy was rising, several organizations began campaigns to reintroduce geography in the country's school systems, where the field had been badly eroded. In fact, many students had come to college without ever having taken a course in geography!

Leading these campaigns was the National Geographic Society, and this organization's contribution went beyond the financial: it published a document entitled *Maps, the Landscape, and Fundamental*

Themes in Geography (1986). Several million copies of this publication were disseminated to the schools, and the "Five Themes" became, for many students, a first acquaintance with geography.

Three of the Five Themes correspond to traditions identified previously: location, human-environment interaction, and regions. These durable traditions continue to anchor geography, as we will see in the pages that follow.

In addition to these three traditional themes, the National Geographic Society's publication identified two others. The fourth theme is represented by the simple word **Place**. All places on the surface of the Earth have distinguishing human and physical characteristics, and it is one of the purposes of geography to study places and to understand how they function. The fifth theme is called **Movement**, the mobility of people, goods, and ideas. Interactions of many kinds shape the human geography of the world, and understanding these is another key to geography.

The National Geographic Society's Five Themes of 1986 have much in common with the Four Traditions of 1964, with one important exception: their neglect of physical geography. We should remember this in our current focus on human geography: we deal here with only part of a discipline that is bound *not* by a set of facts, but by a perspective that applies to the physical as well as the human world.

USING THE SPATIAL PERSPECTIVE

There is no better way to demonstrate the insights gained through spatial analysis than using maps. Maps and geography are practically synonymous, and mapmaking is as

old as geography itself. (For details on cartography, see Resource A at the end of this book). Maps are used to wage war, to make political propaganda, to solve medical problems, to locate shopping centers, to bring relief to refugees, to warn of natural hazards—in short, for countless purposes.

And yet we sometimes fail to see what the map tells us. Here is an example involving the breakdown of the former Soviet Union as it affected the Baltic republics in the empire's western flank. Estonia, Latvia, and Lithuania were in the forefront of the growing movement toward independence for all Soviet republics. News reports in the United States in 1989 often referred to "the Baltics" as if these were three geographically similar territories whose problems, as they moved toward sovereignty, would be the same. Then, late that year, television viewers were treated to the remarkable spectacle of the last Soviet leader, Mikhail Gorbachev, arguing with a crowd of angry citizens by the side of his official car, in the street in the Lithuanian capital of Vilnius. The President pleaded with the Lithuanians to slow their drive toward independence. The citizens were not persuaded. It was a tense scene, and our television commentators referred to this presidential attempt as an effort to defuse the independence fervor in "the Baltics."

Author's Video Link
↓
3
The Baltic States

But the geographical question was: Why did President Gorbachev choose Lithuania to make his point, rather than Estonia or Latvia? Why Vilnius rather than Tallinn or Riga? None of the political commentators noted it, but the reason could be

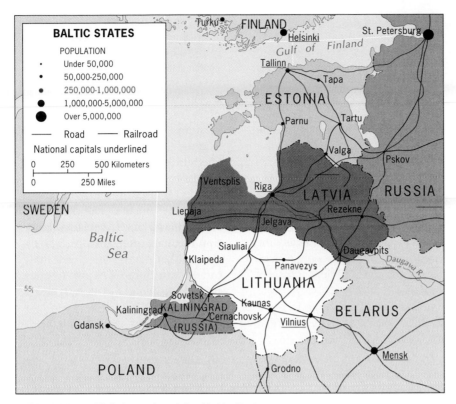

FIGURE 1–2 Kaliningrad and the Baltic States.

seen on the map (Fig. 1-2). There is quite a difference between Estonia and Latvia on the one hand, and Lithuania on the other, when it comes to the Baltic coast they share. Estonia and Latvia extend from the Russian border to the sea, but Lithuania has something different. A small corner of territory belonging to Russia lies between southern Lithuania and the Baltic coast. Make Lithuania independent, and that corner of Russia is cut off from the interior—from Russia, from the (former) Soviet Union, from the Commonwealth of Independent States, or from whatever Slavic-dominated entity exists inland.

As we look at the map in more detail, we note that this Russian outlier (*exclave* is the geographic term for such a small area separated from a country's mainland) is not just a small corner of insignificant territory. On its coast lies a port with the name of Kaliningrad, also

the name of the area as a whole. This port is a major military naval base, a key strategic link in the former Soviet chain of bases. Cut if off from the Russian interior, and its military value is much diminished. The Russians always worried about their warm-water ports, and losing one as important as Kaliningrad was no minor problem for President Gorbachev. So he came to Lithuania to argue for restraint.

The Russians (then Soviets) wanted this former German port as part of the settlement of World War II. They got not only Königsberg (its former German name) but also about 6000 square miles (15,540 square kilometers) around the city, which had been heavily damaged by wartime bombing. The Soviets exiled or executed the remaining Germans, brought in Russians, and rebuilt the military facilities into a major center for fleet and army operations. While Lithuania was part of the Soviet empire, access from

land presented no problem. But an independent Lithuania would mean that the Russians would have to travel overland through foreign territory to reach Kaliningrad. When President Gorbachev was trying to get his reforms approved by the Soviet congress, he saw no way the representatives would allow the "fragmentation" of the Soviet Union.

As we now know, events overtook President Gorbachev, and Estonia, Latvia, and Lithuania did become independent in 1991—but not before the American Secretary of State, James Baker, referred to them as "little Finlands" on Russia's western border. As the issue of independence was being discussed in Moscow, Secretary Baker asked, during a news conference, if it would not be better to have three "little Finlands" on Russia's rim than to engage in a struggle over their continued membership in the Soviet Union. But look at the map again: these are not, and are unlikely ever to become, small versions of the Finnish state to the north. We would need additional maps to prove it, but they would show that, unlike Finland, the "Baltic states" have substantial Russian minorities in their populations; their raw materials for industry come from the former Soviet Union; their products are best distributed to Russian consumers; and they have very limited domestic resources and few international connections. Finland has managed to establish an economy linked to, but not dependent upon, its giant neighbor. Like it or not, the economic fate of the so-called Baltic states will for a long time to come be bound up with the former Soviet Union. Their "Finlandization" will not happen overnight, if ever.

The map suggests why, and as these examples illustrate, maps are uniquely helpful in explaining and understanding major developments in the world of today. In this book, we will come across many instances of their productive use. To begin, let us see how maps relate to the geographic traditions and themes identified earlier.

MAPS AND LOCATIONS

The theme (and long-term tradition) of location is fundamental to geography. Maps tell us where places are located with respect to other places. However, there is more to this than first meets the eye. True, maps provide the locations of places in terms of the Earth's latitude-longitude grid, but it really means very little to know that Chicago lies at 41 degrees, 53 minutes North Latitude and 87 degrees, 38 minutes West Longitude. Those data identify Chicago's **absolute location**. They become interesting when compared to other absolute locations, but for our purposes are not useful for much else. By checking a map, we can determine that Chicago lies approximately at the same latitude as Madrid, Spain, and Beijing, China, and (this might surprise you) at the same longitude as the Galapagos Islands in the Pacific Ocean. So the coordinates of absolute location are mainly useful in the determination of exact distances and directions.

The **relative location** of a place is a very different matter. This is its location relative to other distributions. Take the case of Chicago, once again. Where does Chicago lie in relation to Lake Michigan, its important waterway; to Milwaukee, its not-too-distant neighbor; to the mineral resources and farmlands of the Midwest; or to the road and railroad networks that form the arteries of the heart of the country? All of these could be represented on maps. Note that a vast system of roads and railroads converges on Chicago from all parts of the surrounding region (Fig. 1-3). This means that the city's interconnec-

tions with the region around it are exceptionally efficient. Whether you wanted to distribute something from Chicago into the four states that lie within 60 miles (100 kilometers) around it, or reach the Chicago market from some place in the region, surface communications are readily available. What the map does not show is Chicago's role as a hub of airline transportation. As geographers who study cities (urban geographers) say, Chicago has great **centrality**. Centrality is a function of relative location, vis-à-vis other urban places, resources, productive farmlands, and efficient transport linkages.

Whereas the absolute location of a place does not change, its relative

location is subject to constant modification. Chicago was always an important city in the interior of North America, but its relative location changed markedly when the St. Lawrence Seaway was opened in 1959, and the city acquired a direct maritime connection to the North Atlantic Ocean. Although the seaway closes in the winter when ice blocks navigation, Chicago can be reached by ocean-going vessels during the remainder of the year. As an inland port, its relative location changed substantially. Ships that could once get no closer than the eastern ports of North America now dock in sight of downtown Chicago's skyline.

An especially dramatic change in

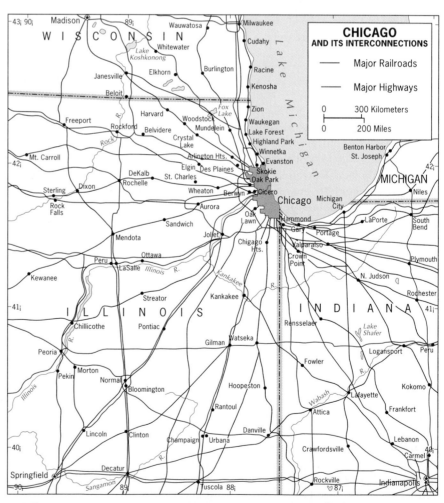

FIGURE 1–3 Surface communication lines converging on Chicago.

relative location has affected an entire country, Japan, during the past century. As late as the mid-nineteenth century, Japan was an isolated, remote, closed island country off the East Asian coast. When the Japanese decided to modernize, during the last third of that century, they chose Britain as their model (which is why they still drive on the left side of the road in Japan). However, Japan was half a world removed from Europe, the center of the industrial world at the time. Then during the twentieth century, America took this position from the Europeans, and now Japan lay directly across the Pacific from the newly powerful market. Today, Japan's relative location is changing again as China becomes a growing trading partner, right across the East China Sea, and Russia beckons across the Sea of Japan. Japan has gone from remote isolation to global hub—but its absolute location never changed!

MAPS AND PLACES

Maps demonstrate a vital rule of geography: that places on the Earth have their own distinctive properties that, taken together, give each of these places its own character.

No place is exactly like another, and a map is the best way to prove this. Geographers study both the physical and human properties of places. The Earth's surface, its elevation and relief, slopes and drainage, soils, natural plants, and atmospheric conditions (climate and weather) form the physical setting. The use of this setting, in the form of settlement layout, population patterns, transport networks, land use, and other activity creates the human imprint. Together, these physical and human features constitute the overall geographic character of a particular place.

Author's Video Link
↓
5
The Power of Maps

Therefore, geographers have a special interest in the quality of places. Whether it's a fishing village on China's coast or a bustling Arab town, geographers want to know how the people have implanted their traditions on that locale, why they have done it there, what sustains them now, and how they interact with the outside world (Fig. 1-4). It is impossible, of course, to study all these aspects at once, so geographers tend to specialize in

certain features of places. Some study the street layout and architecture of a town; others concentrate on the transport systems that serve it. Still others focus on the business and industry that sustain the local economy. In the process, a kind of geographic overview of the place emerges. If you were to become a professional geographer and found yourself assigned to study, say, the growth of suburbs around Santiago, the capital of Chile, you would first read what geographers (and others) had already written about that city. With the many specialized maps they had prepared, you would be in a good position to be well informed before you ever set foot in the field.

MAPS AND ENVIRONMENTAL ISSUES

Throughout this book, the human-environment theme emerges time and again. Human geography, whether economic, political, urban, agricultural, or in whatever other context, cannot be studied without reference to the physical, natural environment in which the action takes (and has taken) place. In the course of our journey we will look

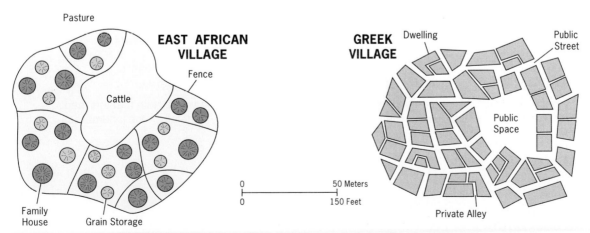

FIGURE 1–4 Contrasting village forms in Africa and Europe. From author's sketch.

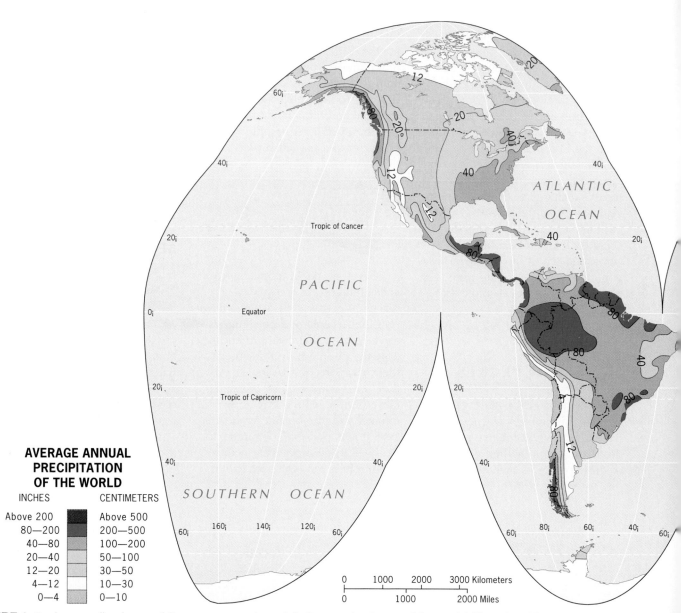

**AVERAGE ANNUAL
PRECIPITATION
OF THE WORLD**

INCHES		CENTIMETERS
Above 200		Above 500
80—200		200—500
40—80		100—200
20—40		50—100
12—20		30—50
4—12		10—30
0—4		0—10

FIGURE 1–5   A generalized map of the mean annual precipitation received around the world. Note that this map projection (see Resource A) is interrupted in the oceans, allowing for maximum clarity of detail on the landmasses.

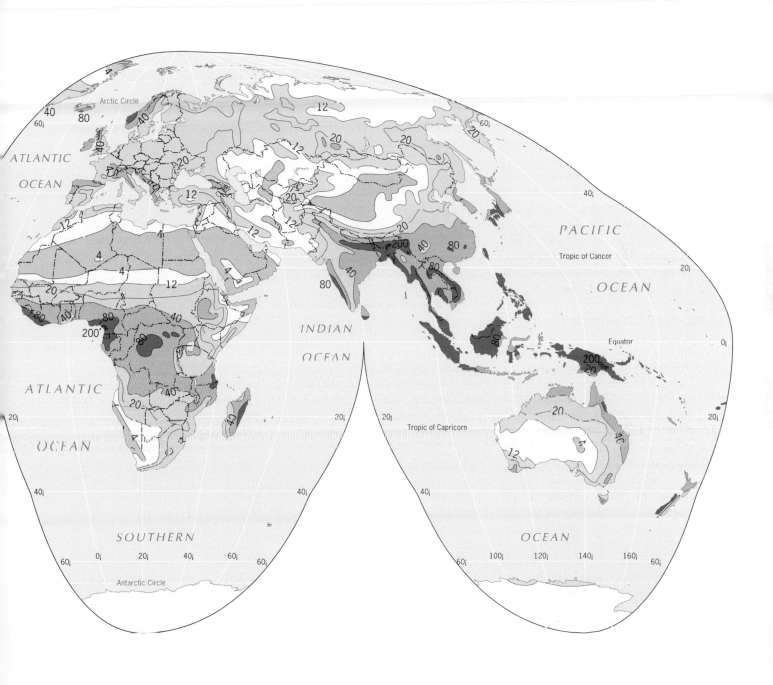

at maps of acid rain distribution, deforestation, river basins, ice ages, and other aspects of the natural environment. Some of these maps will raise as many questions as they answer: If Bangladesh faces certain disaster from cyclones that can kill hundreds of thousands, why do people continue to inhabit low-lying ground in the most dangerous areas? Is the southward spread of the Sahara in West Africa a natural phenomenon, or are people and their livestock responsible for this devastating process? If the Amazonian rain forest in Brazil and adjacent countries continues to be destroyed at present rates, what will happen to the rainfall pattern there?

In Part 1 we will take a closer look at past and present global environments, but it is useful now to consider a map of one vital ingredient in our Earthly existence: water. On the preceding pages is a map of the mean annual precipitation of the world (Fig. 1-5). Note the prevalence of dry conditions over much of the globe, from inner Asia to western Africa to central Australia. As the Earth's human population grows, the demands on this limited supply of water also increase. Drought-caused famines have struck many areas in vulnerable parts of the world, including the northeastern corner of South America, the southern margins of the Sahara in Africa, and south-central Asia. Often such death-dealing droughts cause people to seek relief elsewhere, creating migration streams that cause further dislocation in neighboring zones. For example, thousands of people and their livestock, fleeing from the last drought in West Africa, migrated southward into the moister savannalands of coastal countries. There cattle trampled crops and destroyed harvests, and the result was armed conflict between the local farmers and the invading migrants.

Water shortages, however, are

not confined to desert-edge grazing lands in remote corners of the world. Water rationing became a fact of life in California in the early 1990s, yet people continue to move not only into California but also into other water-deficient areas of the Southwest. As Figure 1-5 suggests, the prospect for water supply in a burgeoning world is worrisome. Expensive desalinization plants, using ocean water and modeled after those in use on the Arabian shore of the Persian Gulf, are making their appearance in California. But their capacity is a drop in the proverbial bucket.

The map of world precipitation emphasizes the importance, in the global scheme of things, of the Atlantic Ocean. Note that except for South Asia and Southeast Asia, the moistest areas of the world lie clustered against Atlantic shores, from water-warmed Western Europe to Amazonian South America, and from the southeastern United States to west and equatorial Africa. These regions owe most of their annual water supply to the Atlantic Ocean, whose slowly circulating waters bring warmth and moisture to wind-wafted areas from Britain to Brazil. Even the peaks of the Andes Mountains in *western* South America, and the densely populated highlands of *eastern* Africa, get most of their snow and rain not from the neighboring Pacific and Indian Oceans, but from the faraway Atlantic. It is another lesson that a map tells far more than mere distribution.

MAPS AND HUMAN MOBILITY

It is one thing to map static features, such as existing patterns and distributions or the locations of cities and towns, but it is quite

another to represent movement on the map. Yet movement is a central theme of geography. Whether it is the movement of goods from factories to markets, the flow of oil from Arabian wells to American consumers, or the migration of people from one region to another, movement must be recorded on maps and interpreted.

To map movement, cartographers use many symbols. For example, you can represent the numbers of travelers on key highways or major airline routes through arrows of varying width, the widths of the arrows revealing the comparative quantities of traffic (Fig. 1-6). Such maps show at a glance the intensity of movement along certain routes, and more careful examination reveals the actual numbers or volumes involved.

But there are times when it is not so much the actual volume, but mainly the direction of movement that matters most. Often it is the movement of ideas, notions, and innovations that matters, but such movement cannot be quantified. The geographic term for this is **diffusion**, the spread of such ideas or knowledge from their sources or origins to areas where they are adopted. Much as we would like to, we often cannot measure such diffusion quantitatively, but we *can* trace its direction. So some maps representing this process have arrows that are meant to reflect direction only, not volume.

Maps showing movement of various kinds are among the most interesting in geography. In the chapter on medical geography, you will find a series of maps that shows, by means of arrows, the routes of invasion of a dreaded illness of the nineteenth century, cholera. At the time, no one knew what caused cholera; people died by the hundreds of thousands. But others were somehow spared. As it turned out, a map was the key to

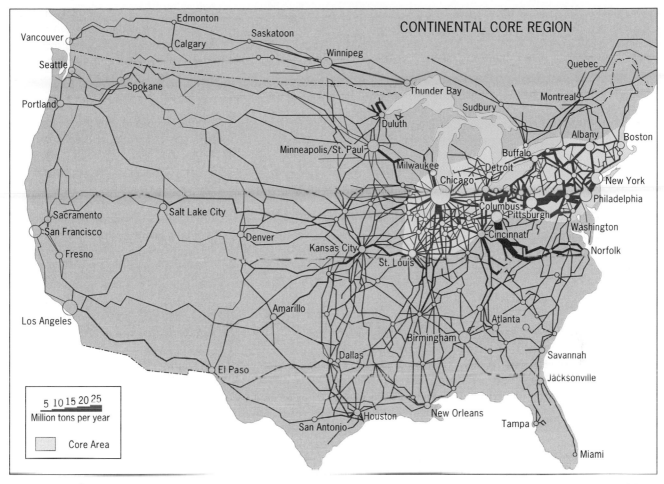

FIGURE 1-6 The comparative amount of freight carried on major North American railroads can be quickly assessed from this map.

the answer, and a medical geographer solved the problem. Today, the search is on for protection against another dreaded disease affecting millions, AIDS. And again, medical geographers are using maps to help.

REGIONS ON THE MAP

Throughout this book, we will use regions, and the regional concept, to clarify what is being discussed. Actually, we use some form of the regional idea all the time, even in everyday conversation. When you plan a vacation in "the Rockies," or

a hiking trip in New England, or a cruise in the Caribbean, you use regional notions to convey what you have in mind. Regions, used this way, are informal frames of reference.

In geography, the regional concept is, of course, more specific. To refer to "the Rockies" as a perceived region summarizes what is prominent about this region: steep slopes, high relief, dramatic mountain scenery, snow-capped peaks, and ski slopes. But as a geographer you might be asked to *define* and *delimit* a Rocky Mountains region. Exactly where are the boundaries of "the Rockies"? In some places the answer is easily found as the

mountains rise suddenly from the adjacent Great Plains (another region!). But elsewhere the mountainous terrain develops gradually; the plains become hilly and the slopes become steeper. Where, and on what basis, do you draw the regional boundary?

To identify and delimit regions, therefore, we must establish *criteria* for them. Imagine that as an exercise in physical geography, you were asked to delimit the Amazon River Basin as a geographic region. There would be various ways to do this: you might use vegetation distribution, soil properties, slope angles, or drainage patterns. Submitting your results, you would first

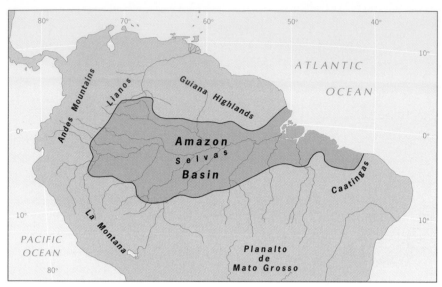

FIGURE 1–7 The Amazon Basin as a region defined by catchment area and topography.

state the basis on which you mapped the region, and then produce the resulting map. On a small scale, the map might resemble Figure 1-7, which uses drainage lines and defines the Amazon Basin by all the rivers and their tributaries that ultimately drain into this great South American river.

Thus we know that all regions have: **area**, that is, they all have some defined spatial extent; **location**, in that all regions lie somewhere on the Earth's surface; and limits or **boundaries**, which are sometimes obvious and evident on the ground, and sometimes not, and are often based on specifically chosen criteria.

Regions have two other properties, but these are not common to all. Some regions are marked by a visible uniformity, for example a desert basin marked by severe aridity, sandy surface, and steep surrounding mountain slopes. Such a homogeneous region is called a **formal region** in geographic usage. Formal regions also are defined by cultural (as opposed to physical) criteria. A region within which French is spoken by, say, 90

percent of the population or more, also is a formal region. A **functional region**, on the other hand, is the product of interactions, of movement of various kinds. A city, for example, has a surrounding region within which workers

commute, either to the downtown area or to subsidiary centers such as office parks and shopping malls (Fig. 1-8). That entire urban area, defined by those people moving toward and within it, is a functional region. Thus a functional region is a spatial system, its boundaries defined by the limits of that system.

Finally, regions must be seen in a vertical order or **hierarchy**. The French-speaking region to which we referred earlier is a region within a larger region, namely, Western Europe. Western Europe, in turn, is a region of the European geographic realm. All regions are positioned on a ladder of size and importance.

Regions, therefore, are ways of organizing ourselves geographically. They represent a form of spatial classification, a means of handling large amounts of information that must be generalized to make sense. As you will find, the regional concept is an indispensable aid in our journey through human geography.

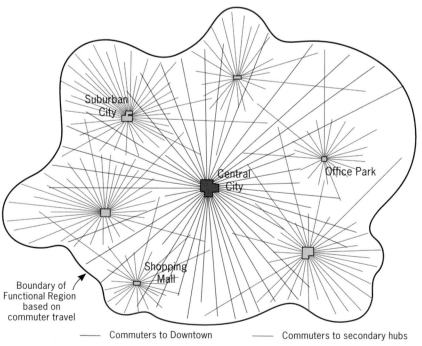

FIGURE 1–8 Commuter travel patterns in an urban area. From author's sketch.

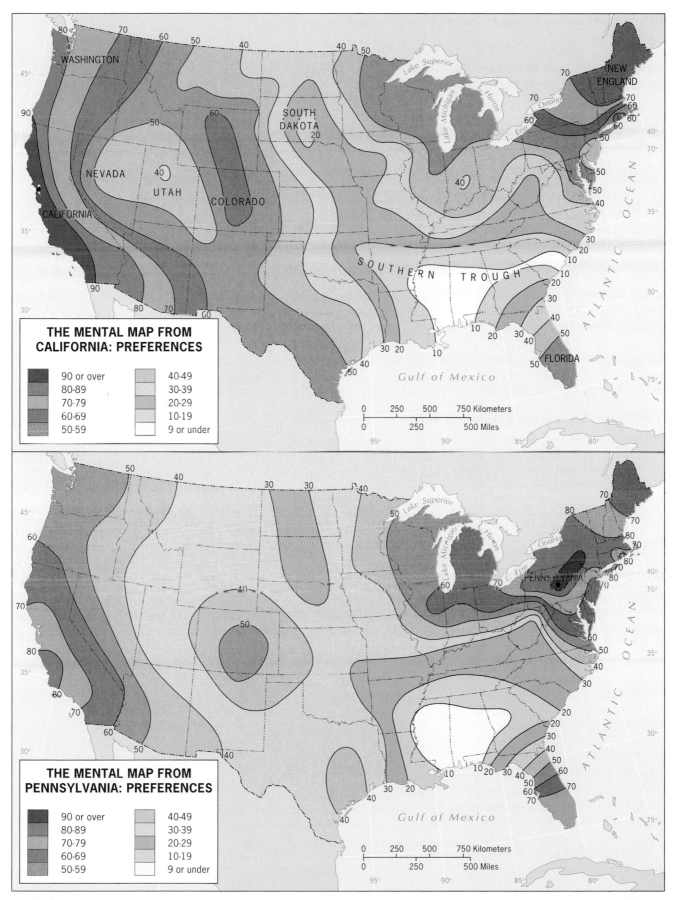

FIGURE 1–9 Where Californians and Pennsylvanians would prefer to live. From P. R. Gould and R. White, *Mental Maps* (Harmondsworth: Penguin Books, 1974), pp. 94 and 99. Redrawn by permission of the publisher.

13

MAPS IN THE MIND

This book deals with the human world from a spatial perspective, but let us recognize an important bias: whether we like it or not, we see and study things from our particular viewpoint, which is shaped by our cultural environment. No matter how hard we try to be objective, our view of the world and its problems (geographic and otherwise) is not the same as the view from Africa or China. Certainly, a map of mountain ranges or known oil reserves might look the same whether drawn in China or America, but when we study more subjective things—culture and tradition, politics, or development—we may have quite a different outlook. Take, for example, a standard picture of a major city in another country, such as Mexico (Mexico City) or Kenya (Nairobi). Such a picture is likely to show the modern, high-rise buildings of the "downtown" area, the heart of those cities. However, the fact is that the great majority of the people of Mexico City and Nairobi (and dozens of other large cities) live their lives in modest, often inadequate dwellings in vast, sprawling housing tracts that surround the urban core. For many of these people, the skyscrapers of the central city are irrelevant, and city life is a battle for survival in quite a different environment. Shouldn't a "typical" picture of Mexico City or Nairobi show *that* image, rather than the downtown area?

Thus it is important to realize that our study of the human world contains some cultural bias, no matter how hard we try to see alternate viewpoints. As you get to know geographers, you will find that they tend to be drawn to the field partly because of their interest in, and respect for, other societies and cultures. That, however, does not provide us with immunity from bias or insensitivity. After all, human geography deals with population growth and control, race and religion, economic development, and political institutions. These can be touchy subjects.

MENTAL MAPS

Imagine that you are in a seminar discussion on the political geography of Southern Africa, but there is no wall map to which you can refer. What is your frame of reference? Obviously, the countries of the region: South Africa, Namibia, Swaziland, Lesotho, Botswana, Zimbabwe, and their neighbors. As you speak, you will use the map that is in your mind, the **mental map** of that part of the world. That mental map has developed over your years of looking at wall maps, atlas maps, maps in books, magazines, and newspapers. The more accurate your mental map is, the better your seminar contributions will be.

Mental maps are a fundamental part of one's general knowledge; we use them constantly. If someone were to call you now to suggest that you go to the theater, a mental map would come to mind: the hallway, the front door, the walk to your car, the lane on the highway to choose in order to be prepared for the left turn you must make, where you would prefer to park, and so forth. If your mental map is vague, you need a city map to find your way, because a vague mental map may cause you to lose your way. That, of course, would be a minor matter, easily corrected. However, if the issue is more serious than a trip to the theater, and a large number of people are poorly informed (including, perhaps, their government representatives), vague mental maps can lead to policy mistakes of greater consequence.

ENVIRONMENTAL PERCEPTION

Mental maps (also called cognitive maps) are derived from visual observation of the real world (your city or town, college campus, shopping center) and from the scrutiny and study of printed maps. Sights are supplemented by sounds and smells, and the total impression is called our **environmental perception**. This is the impression that generates our mental map.

Since geographers are interested in both the physical world and the human organization of it, environmental perception is a popular geographic topic. We have perceptions of places we know by personal experience, but we also carry images of places we have never visited. What shapes these perceptions? To what extent are they accurate or distorted? In a fascinating book entitled *Mental Maps* (1982), geographers Peter Gould and Rodney White begin by asking the following question: If you could presently move to any place of your choice, without any of the usual financial and other obstacles, where would you like to live? (For their respondents' answers, see Fig. 1-9.) Perhaps you would select a location you perceive as attractive, but have never personally experienced. However, the actual environment may turn out to be quite different from your perception of it.

A crucial part of our perception of a place lies in its layout, that is, its spatial arrangement and organization. To know the location of a country (whether it is Laos or Afghanistan or Bolivia) is only a beginning. From maps we can gain impressions of topography and relief, climate and weather, the quality of roads, the layout of villages and towns, and countless other conditions—without ever having been there. The map is our window on the world.

KEY TERMS

Absolute Location	Map
Area	Mental Map
Boundary	Movement
Centrality	Pattern
Culture-Environment	Physical (Natural) Geography
Diffusion	Place
Distribution	Regional Science
Earth-Science	Regions (formal, functional)
Environmental Perception	Relative Location
Hierarchy	Spatial Perspective
Human Geography	Themes
Location (absolute, relative)	Traditions
Location Theory	

An East African landscape. Was this the landscape to which humanity awakened?

PART ONE

ENVIRONMENT AND HUMANITY

At Issue

Humans have an attachment to territory, a fondness that is often intense and passionate. This territorial imperative, as some scholars describe it, can engender conflict between neighbors and among societies that sense a violation of their living space. At another level, people's affection for territory has an environmental dimension. Geographers call this penchant topophilia, the love of familiar topography; biologists refer to it as biophilia. At issue: are territorial compulsion and environmental propensity encoded in our genes, accruing from millions of years of experience and accommodation? Can our behavior be better understood and interpreted in this long-term geographic context?

PART ONE

2

THE EARTH AS HUMANITY'S HOME

From the surface of the moon, our Earth, as seen by America's first lunar astronauts, was a pearl of bright colors in a black sky. Great swirls of white clouds partly veiled blue oceans and brown-gray continents. Emerald-green patches of land drew the eye to the oases of life on Earth. The glistening white snows of the polar regions really did look like ice caps, as textbooks call them. It was a lesson in geography no ordinary Earthling had ever had, and may not soon have again (see box, "Apollo's Promise Betrayed").

The photographs taken on that lunar mission have become commonplace in the media. Again and again, we see the Earth from space—in books and journals, in advertising, and on television and film. What of the geography lesson, however? How well do we remember just how small our Earth really is, how thin that layer of clouds, and how tiny those specks of life-giving green? Nearly 6 billion people depend on the air, water, and land of this small planet. The term *spaceship earth* came into use to signify the finiteness of these and other resources. However, the real

Geographica

- The geologic past has relevance to the geographic present.

- The Earth presently is in the grip of the Late Cenozoic Ice Age.

- The Earth's modern human geography has evolved entirely during the current Holocene warm spell.

- Environmental change is humanity's constant companion.

- Technological progress notwithstanding, terrain and climate continue to influence the distribution of human activity.

meaning of this notion did not seem to strike home. The triumph of technology that sent the astronauts to the moon was not followed by a victory on earth. Weapons of mass destruction were manufactured in growing quantities, resource exploitation intensified, and air, water, and soil absorbed increasing amounts of pollutants, raising fears for the planet's environmental future.

A CHANGING EARTH

From the moon, the astronauts saw our Earth for an instant in its 5-billion-year history. They saw an Earth on which the oceans' blue was the dominant color because approximately 70 percent of its surface is water. They saw landmasses colored gray and brown because more than 70 percent of the land surface is desert, steppe, rock, or otherwise

APOLLO'S PROMISE BETRAYED

In the early evening of July 20, 1969, virtually the entire United States (and much of the Western world) paused to witness on television, or to hear on radio, an event of surpassing importance: the first landing on the Moon. We saw, heard, and felt it all, the tense descent of the vehicle, which set down on the very edge of a crater with 17 seconds of maneuvering fuel remaining, the relief at the words "The Eagle Has Landed," the emergence of space-suited astronauts Armstrong and Aldrin, and the awe at the first words spoken to Earth from another place in space. It was a historic moment, and we envisaged moon bases, Mars voyages, and space exploration in the years ahead.

But now, more than a quarter of a century later, the **Apollo Moon Program** looks like a dead end, and the Saturn 5 rocket engines (described by those who know space technology as the greatest machines ever built) roar no more. Those same experts say that we could not even duplicate the feat of July 1969 today, with existing technology. President Kennedy's exhortation to "put a man on the Moon in this decade and return him safely to Earth" galvanized public opinion and energized Congress, but even before the end of that decade, even before Apollo orbited the Moon, his successors were cutting budgets and canceling missions. The **National Aeronautics and Space Administration (NASA)**, symbol of engineering excellence and global technological supremacy, was reduced to a shuttle program that would make space travel routine, dependable, cheap, and safe. It turned out to be none of these things; in the meantime, Congress bickered over funds to sustain an orbiting space station that would grow by accretion.

But the Earth already had a space station, and its name is Moon. Opponents of space exploration argue that dollars spent on a revived space program would be better spent on social programs on Earth, but those who remember the 1960s recall the social impact of Apollo. A nation at war in Vietnam and at war with itself, divided over ideology, racial issues, crime, and poverty, was temporarily healed, revived by Apollo. It was America at its best, taking a "giant leap for mankind," in Armstrong's words, that promised a postwar frontier in space, a unifying, inspiring goal for the future.

Later that evening, we stood outside, looking anew at the Moon, awestruck, hoping the return would be safe, talking of the next mission and who would go. No one believed that those pictures of the rising Earth over the lunar landscape would be the last in our lifetimes.

---

sparsely vegetated. The swirls of clouds seemed thin because the atmosphere that envelops our planet is so shallow. Our globe was described as an oasis of life, but, as in any oasis, the environment is fragile and subject to damage and destruction.

What the astronauts could not see in that moment of revelation was the changeable nature of the Earth's environments. If they had

stood on the moon's surface just 20,000 years earlier (not long, given the age of our planet), they would have seen larger ice caps, huge ice sheets in North America and Eurasia, lower sea levels, and very different continental outlines. If they had been there 20 million years ago, the continents themselves would have been in locations quite different from those of today.

So what the astronauts saw was

a still frame in a moving picture: the Earth at a moment in time. They saw an Earth with small ice caps and large oceans, continents with flooded margins, and an Earth warmer than it has been for much of the past 3 million years. During these past 3 million years, and for some time previously, the Earth has been in an ice age, the Late Cenozoic Ice Age, as physical geographers call it. During this ice age, the most recent of several in the Earth's history, the global temperature has decreased repeatedly, causing the polar ice caps to expand, and ice sheets to form over high latitudes. When it was cold, these ice sheets pushed relentlessly into lower latitudes, scouring the rocky surface and carrying millions of tons of debris as they expanded. In highlands, such as the Rocky Mountains and Europe's Alps, great Alpine glaciers filled the valleys once occupied by streams, and the whole landscape was practically buried under ice and snow. It was a frigid time, and the Earth's livable space was much reduced. Animals and plants migrated to warmer latitudes, but many died out, deprived of suitable environments. Other animals and plants managed to adjust and even thrive, and the biological map changed repeatedly.

The ice covered much land in the Northern Hemisphere, as Figure 2-1 shows, and in the Southern Hemisphere it not only buried Antarctica, but extended far northward on the Southern Ocean. However, it was in the northern lands where the impact was greatest. Virtually all of Canada, the whole Great Lakes region, and the Northeast of the United States were icebound. Note, on the map, that a corridor in Alaska remained ice-free. (It is believed that this may have been an avenue for human immigration from Asia into North America.) Also note the large glaciers in the high mountains of the West.

The whole world looked differ-

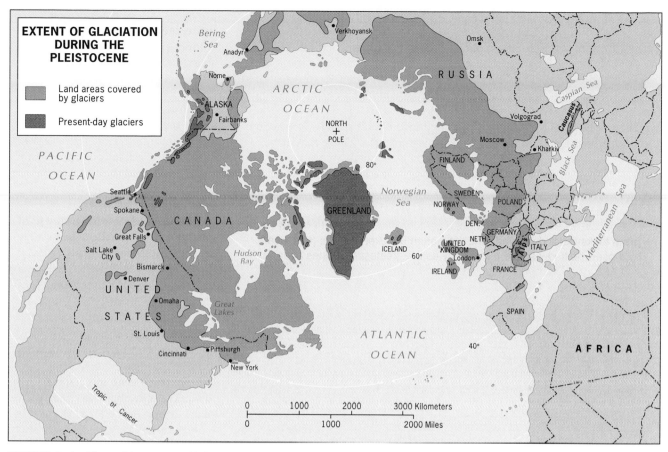

FIGURE 2–1 The evidence on which this map is based includes glacial deposits and the marks of glaciers' erosion on bedrock.

ent. In fact, the continental outlines are shown on this map for reference only. They did not look like this when the ice was at its maximum. Sea levels were lower, since so much water was taken up in the ice. The Mediterranean Sea was more shallow. Possibly the myth of a submerged Atlantis, the lost continent, was born when the ice melted and the Mediterranean rose to flood human settlements.

TIME AND SPACE

To get a clearer picture of the complicated interrelationships among environmental change, human evolution, and Earth history, we should be familiar with what we might call the "calendar" of geologic time (Table 2-1). Just as we name the days of the week and the months of the year, and number the years and centuries, Earthly time has been divided into stages. Analyses of rocks and fossils have led to the division of the last billion years of Earth history into three great *eras*: the Paleozoic, the oldest, dating from about 220 million years and older; the middle era, or Mesozoic, from about 220 to 65 million years ago; and the Cenozoic, the era that began approximately 65 million years ago and still continues. The boundary between the Mesozoic and the Cenozoic has become quite famous as the so-called **K/T boundary**, a sharp transition marking the extinction of many animals and plants, including the great dinosaurs. The cause of this widespread extinction is being debated by scientists, a growing majority of whom prefer the theory that our planet was struck by a giant meteor, with calamitous consequences for all life.

Geologic eras are in turn divided into *periods*. The last period of the Mesozoic era was the Cretaceous, and the first period of the Cenozoic was the Tertiary (hence the corruption into the K/T boundary). The Tertiary Period covers most of the Cenozoic era, ending only about 3 million years ago to give way to the present period, the Quaternary.

Periods, finally, are divided into *epochs*. The Quaternary period, of only about 3 million years' duration, is divided into the Pleistocene and the Holocene (or Recent) epochs.

The Tertiary period is divided into five epochs. We now know that the **Late Cenozoic Ice Age** began during the late Tertiary, perhaps even before the Pliocene epoch. But the ice age reached its climax during the Pleistocene epoch, and many scientists continue to call it the Pleistocene (rather than the Late Cenozoic) Ice Age.

How many times the Pleistocene ice has expanded and contracted over the past several million years is still a scientific question without an absolute answer. To reconstruct the ice age, physical geographers have studied the crushed and powdered rock debris left behind by the successive advances of the ice sheets. Geologists have researched the oxygen content of the permanent ice of the ice caps to identify periods of comparatively cold and warm climate. There may have been as many as two dozen icy periods, some more severe than others. What is certain is that each cold period, or **glaciation**, was followed by a warmer time, when the ice melted and balmier climates prevailed. These warmer periods, or **interglaciations**, saw plants and animals occupy the newly vacated areas, only to be thrown back again by the ice of a new glaciation.

The astronauts saw our Earth during an interglaciation. The Earth today is warm and living space is large. Not much more than 12,000 years ago, a glacial period was still in progress, and winter was "permanent" as far south as the Ohio River. Where Chicago now lies, conditions were similar to those of northern Siberia today. However, the most recent warming trend came quickly, and the ice and snow melted as far north as Alaska. Today, Canada, Norway, Sweden, and Finland have balmy, mild summers—however short—at least in comparison with what prevailed just thousands of years ago.

As we will note in Chapter 3, the evolution of humankind has taken place during times of great environmental variation. The center stage for this momentous development lay in eastern Africa, a region not affected by the ice sheets—but certainly affected by the glacial cold that swept the globe during glacial times. We should remember that global cooling not only spreads the great ice sheets from polar areas into lower latitudes; it also affects mountains and highlands, even near the equator. Today, Africa's tallest mountain, Kilimanjaro, has permanent ice and snow on its crest, although it lies in sight of the equator. During a glaciation, the ice on Kilimanjaro (and the other high mountains on the East African plateau) increased in volume and size, creating ice caps and glaciers that moved far downslope. Warm tropical weather changed to much colder conditions on the adjacent plains. Lake levels dropped, forests died out, and animals migrated away in search of survival. Our distant ancestors also saw their survival threatened. From fossil evi-

---

TABLE 2-1 Stages in Earth History

Era[a]	Period[b]	MYA	Epoch
Cenozoic	Quaternary		Holocene (Recent)[c]
		3	Pleistocene
	Tertiary	6	Pliocene
		25	Miocene
		40	Oligocene
		60	Eocene
			Paleocene
Mesozoic	K/T Boundary	65	
	Cretaceous	130	
	Jurassic	190	
	Triassic	220	
Paleozoic	Permian	270	
	Pennsylvanian	310	
	Mississippian	350	
	Devonian	400	
	Silurian	440	
	Ordovician	500	
	Cambrian	625	
	Precambrian	↓	

[a]The numbers represent millions of years ago and are very approximate, even for the Tertiary Period.
[b]The second half of the Cenozoic Era has been marked by the onset of a global ice age that prevailed throughout the Quaternary Period.
[c]The Holocene Epoch is merely the latest of many interglaciations (warm periods) during this ice age, and has lasted only about 10,000 years.

dence we know that some of the early branches of our family tree died out. Certain ancestors were better equipped to overcome the rigors of changing environments than others.

HOLOCENE HUMANITY

Table 2-1 refers to the most recent 10,000 years of Earth history as the **Holocene epoch**, thus differentiating it from the **Pleistocene epoch** that preceded it. However, there is no evidence that this so-called new epoch is, in fact, a new stage in the environmental history of our planet. All the evidence indicates that the Holocene epoch is really the most recent (indeed, the current) inter-glaciation of the continuing Late Cenozoic Ice Age.

The Holocene epoch merits distinction not because of its geological qualities, but because of its cultural-geographical characteristics. Compared to other epochs millions of years in duration, the Holocene has lasted only about 10,000 years. But within that short time, humanity did what it had not done during previous interglaciations. In the wake of the retreating ice and in the comfort of a warming planet, an incredible drama began: plants and animals were domesticated, agriculture developed, and surpluses were stored for future use; villages grew larger, towns and cities emerged, and political organization became increasingly complex; inventions multiplied, and tools were more efficient. Certain communities thrived and expanded, sometimes at the expense of others. Religious ideas appeared. The spiral leading toward states and empires, and colonial realms and global power struggles, had begun.

Another spiral also began: that of population numbers. No one

knows, of course, how many people lived on Earth at the beginning of the Holocene epoch. Perhaps there were 4 million, or possibly as many as 8 million. Throughout the Pleistocene, these numbers had grown and declined with the varying fortunes of our early ancestors. During the Holocene epoch, however, growth began—slowly at first, then ever faster. Modern humanity is indeed the product of the Holocene epoch.

During the Holocene, our Earth changed as never before, not because of geologic forces, but because of the imprint of humanity. As we will see, that imprint has become ever stronger. Especially during the past two centuries, the Earth has been transformed by the expansion of the human population and the impact of human activities. Not all of this impact has had negative results: hillslopes have been carefully terraced and made productive; wild, flood-prone rivers have been controlled and their floodplains converted into fertile farmlands; land has even been reclaimed from the sea and made livable. However, the Earth, especially during the twentieth century, has begun to strain under the requirements of the growing human population. Soil erosion is more severe than ever. Rivers, lakes, and even parts of the oceans are polluted. Gases of many kinds are spewed into the atmosphere with uncertain consequences. Raw materials (fuels, ores) are used up at an ever faster rate, and the search for additional resources poses new dangers. As humanity and its activities expand, nature recedes. Many species of animals and plants are becoming extinct, and we may never know what role some of them might have played in sciences such as medicine and plant physiology. Our need to dispose of wastes (many of them hazardous or poisonous) has led to the con-

tamination of drinking water and the fouling of the air we breathe.

HUMAN GEOGRAPHY AND NATURAL ENVIRONMENT

As we noted in the Introduction, the relationship between human society and the natural environment constitutes a leading theme in the whole discipline of geography. This theme is especially central to cultural geography, for reasons we have already begun to explore. The emergence of *Homo Sapiens* from a series of predecessors may have spanned 6 million years or more, but the expansion of humanity to unprecedented numbers has taken only two centuries, the last 200 years of the Holocene. With this expansion has come an unprecedented impact on the natural environment—local, regional, even global.

We should be aware, therefore, of two kinds of change that can affect elements of our natural environment. We have reason to believe that the present, warm Holocene will not last forever. Some climatologists have suggested that our interglaciation may soon come to an end (see Chapter 3)—soon, not in geologic terms, but in human-historic terms. This natural swing between cold glaciation and warm interglaciation is nature's grand design. But now, the human impact on the natural environment is taking on powerful dimensions. Scientists are in agreement that people and their industries are pouring so much pollution into the atmosphere that global environments may be modified as a result. The loss of high-altitude ozone, for example, is attributed to the

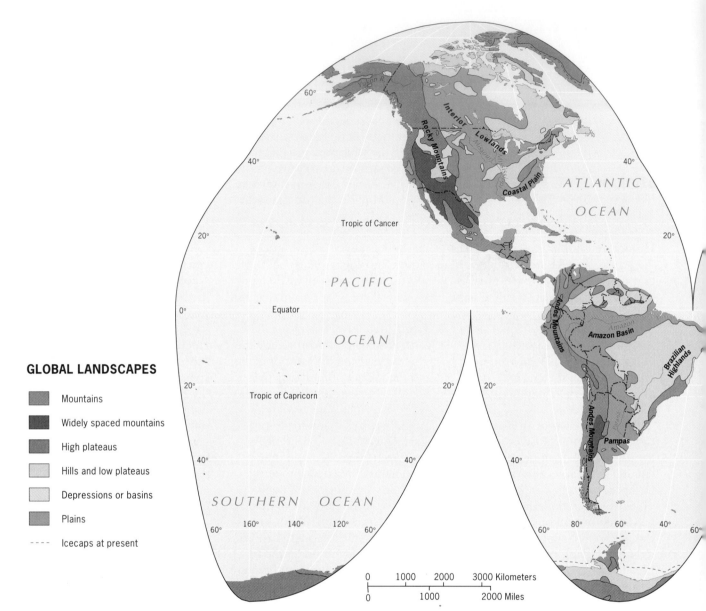

GLOBAL LANDSCAPES

- Mountains
- Widely spaced mountains
- High plateaus
- Hills and low plateaus
- Depressions or basins
- Plains
- - - - - Icecaps at present

0   1000   2000   3000 Kilometers

0   1000   2000 Miles

FIGURE 2–2 Despite centuries of technological progress, the influence of terrain as an element of the overall natural environment still is reflected in world population distribution. Mountains and high plateaus do not generally support large or dense population clusters.

emanation of chlorofluorocarbons (CFCs) from air conditioners and other equipment; as the ultraviolet-radiation filtering by the diminished ozone layer weakens, plants, animals, and people are affected by overexposure. Photosynthesis is impaired, skin cancer rates increase, and eye problems multiply.

During the 1980s, many scientists warned that growing atmospheric pollution was creating an enhanced **greenhouse-warming effect** in the atmosphere, which might lead

to global temperature increases, rapid melting of the remaining glaciers, and rising sea levels. But while there was some evidence of a temporary warming trend in some regions of the world, other areas did not record any warming. The spatial evidence for *global* warming was weak, and geographers predicted that the greenhouse-warming furor would pass.

Geographers did not, however, ignore the evidence that global environments were experiencing

wider fluctuations, greater deviations from the norm. The regional warming that led to the greenhouse concern was only one of these variations. In the Pacific Ocean, **El Niño Southern Oscillation (ENSO)** events, involving perturbations of water circulation, occurred with greater frequency and had wider impact; ENSO events were correlated with floods in Texas and droughts in Africa. During a short span of time, North America experienced a hundred-year storm, a

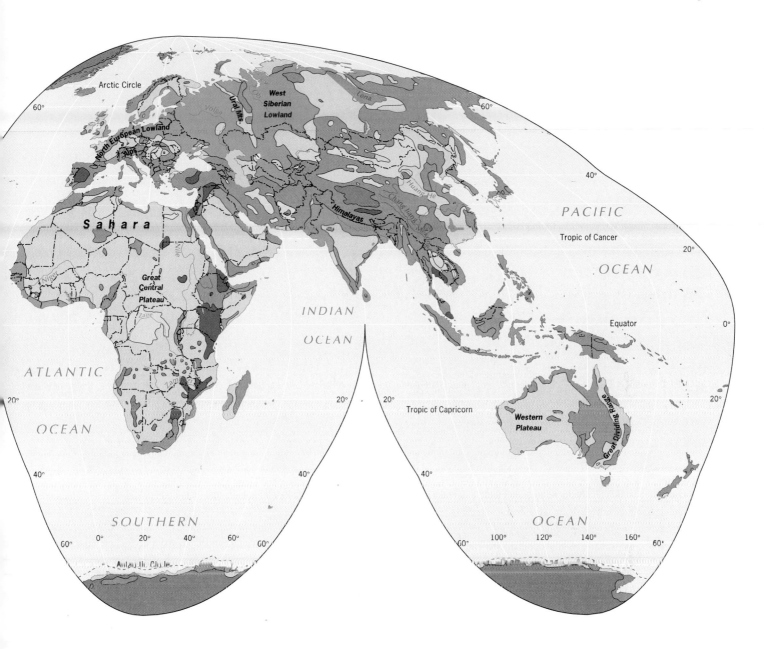

blizzard of the century, and a flood of the millennium.

Is it possible that our continuing and growing pollution of the atmosphere is contributing to these environmental extremes? Or are these wide variations of climate an early warning that a major environmental reversal lies ahead? At present we cannot answer these questions, but one thing is certain: our befouling of the atmosphere *can* interfere with natural changes the Earth has in store for us, and we should seek ways to limit and reduce it.

Author's Video Link
↓
5
Greenhouse Effect

Whatever the course of events, it has become clear that we should be prepared for environmental challenges. Two good ways to begin this preparation are with an awareness of the layout of the habitable world, that is, its geography, and with an appreciation of the possible directions change might take. We

deal with the first challenge in this chapter and with the second in Chapter 3.

LAND AND SPACE

The pages that conclude this chapter present three important maps, each containing information on the habitable space on our planet. It is hardly necessary to remind ourselves that only about 30 percent of the surface of the Earth consists of land, but Figure 2-2 emphasizes how much of this 30 percent is incapable of sustaining dense human

WORLD CLIMATES
After Köppen–Geiger

A HUMID EQUATORIAL CLIMATE

- **Af** No dry season
- **Am** Short dry season
- **Aw** Dry winter

B DRY CLIMATE

- **BS** Semiarid
- **BW** Arid

} h=hot
k=cold

C HUMID TEMPERATE CLIMATE

- **Cf** No dry season
- **Cw** Dry winter
- **Cs** Dry summer

D HUMID COLD CLIMATE

- **Df** No dry season
- **Dw** Dry winter

} a=hot
summer
b=cool
summer
c=short, cool
summer
d=very cold
winter

E COLD POLAR CLIMATE

- **E** Tundra and ice

H HIGHLAND CLIMATE

- **H** Unclassified highlands

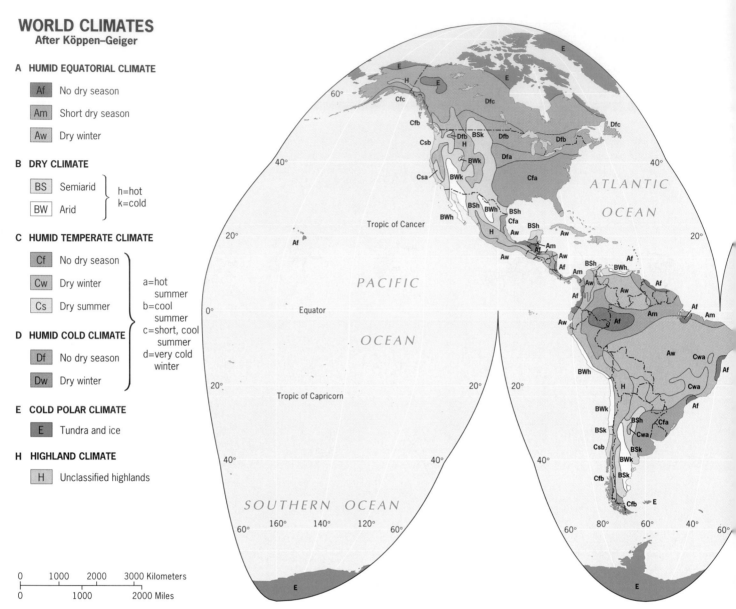

FIGURE 2–3 The Köppen map of world climates as modified by R. Geiger. These, of course, are macroclimatic regions; microclimates are set within these, but cannot be shown at this scale.

populations. Much of the land surface of the Earth is mountainous and rugged, including the great arc of mountains that extends from the Atlas in North Africa through the Caucasus and the Himalayas into China and Southeast Asia. Certainly, mountains *can* sustain people in sizeable clusters (the Inca Empire was a mountain-based state in the Andes of South America), but generally mountains do not support

populations comparable to those in river basins and plains, where accessibility, circulation, and movement of people and goods are less impeded by relief. In Part 2, where we focus on the present population distribution and density, Chapter 6 contains a map (Fig. 6-1) which, when compared with Figure 2-2, clearly reveals the sparseness of population in the mountainous regions of the globe.

High plateaus also tend to support sparse populations. It is no coincidence that the entire continent of Africa, much of which is plateau surface, sustains fewer people than the single country of India. The elevation of high plateaus can make living conditions difficult (for example on the plateau of Tibet [Xizang] in China). Severe erosion can create problems similar to those presented by mountainous terrain,

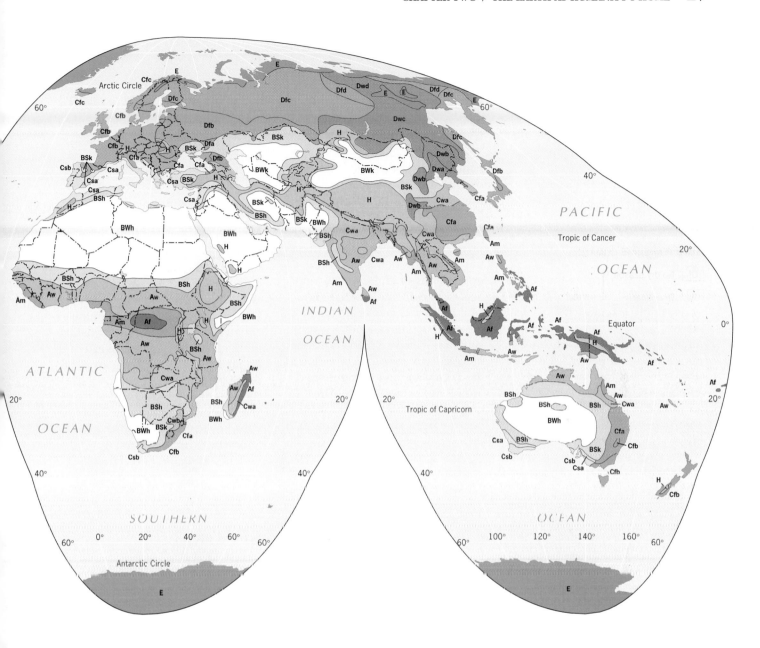

as in Ethiopia, the country previously known as *Abyss*inia. Again, the high-plateau regions stand out as low-population areas.

LAND AND CLIMATE

All the weather factors combined— the sweep of the sun's energy, the rotation of the Earth, the circulation of the oceans, the movement of weather systems in alternate zones, the rush of air in jet streams—produce a pattern of climates that may,

on the map, look complicated at first but is actually remarkably simple. This is one of those maps that's worth a million words, because it allows us, at a glance, to determine what climate and weather are like anywhere on Earth.

We owe this remarkable map to the work of Wladimir Köppen (1846–1940), who devised a scheme to classify the world's climates based on indices of temperature and precipitation. Since his time, many efforts have been made to

improve on Köppen's classification and regionalization of climates, but nearly a century after its creation, and despite the greater accuracy of climatic data today, it has stood the test of time (Fig. 2-3).

Köppen's map displays the present distribution of **climatic regions** across the planet. The legend looks complicated, but it really is not; here is one of those maps worth spending some time on. For our purposes, it is enough to get a sense of the distribution of the major types of climate. The letter categories in the legend give a clear indication of the conditions they represent.

The (A) climates are hot or very warm and generally humid. The subdivisions are quite familiar: the "no dry season" (Af) regions are also called *Equatorial Rainforest* regions. The "short dry season" (Am) climate is known to us as the *Monsoon* climate. And if you can envisage an African savanna, you know what the Aw *(Savanna)* designation means.

Once you realize that the yellow and light beige colors on the map represent dry climates (BW, *Desert* and BS, *Steppe*), it becomes clear how much of our world is sub-humid, always in need of water. And, as we will note later, some very large population clusters have developed in these water-deficient regions, especially at lower (therefore, warmer) latitudes. The world faces a long-term water crisis, and the Köppen map helps explain why.

The C climates also have familiar names. The Cf climate, marked by a dark green color, prevails over the Southeastern United States. If you know the local weather in Atlanta or Nashville or Jacksonville, you understand why this climate is often called "humid temperate." It's moist, and it doesn't get as cold as it does in Canada or as warm (continuously, anyway) as in the Amazon Basin. Now, if you have experienced this kind of climate, then the map gives you a pretty good idea of what it's like in much of eastern China, in southeastern Australia, and in a large part of southeastern South America.

The "dry summer" C climates are known as the *Mediterranean* climates (the small s in Cs means that summers are dry). This mild climate occurs not only around the Mediterranean Sea, and thus in the famous wine countries of France, Italy, and Spain, but also in California, Chile, South Africa's Cape, and southern parts of Australia. So you know what to expect, weatherwise, in Rome, San Francisco, Santiago, Cape Town, and Adelaide!

Poleward of the C climates, the planet gets rather cold. Note that the D climates dominate over the upper Midwest and Canada, but it gets even colder in Siberia! The "milder" D climates (here the key is the small a, which denotes a warm summer) have very limited extent in Eurasia. Winters are very cold in all the D climates and outright frigid (and long) in the Dfb and Dfc regions. The latter, in fact, merge into the polar climates, where tundra and ice prevail.

The climate map, like the landscape map, reflects the limitations of our habitable Earth. Vast areas of the landmasses are extremely arid or frigid, or excessively hot and humid to sustain large populations that depend directly on the land for their sustenance. And despite our technological advances, many hundreds of millions of people still live off the land they till.

Figure 2-3, like Figure 2-1, is a still photo of a changing pattern. When the conditions shown in Figure 2-1 prevailed, the habitable zone of the Earth was much narrower, and polar (E) climates reached as far south as the central Great Plains of the (present) United States and the Alpine slopes of southern Europe. Today the Earth is much warmer, but it will not remain so warm forever. Before long, the Köppen map will look quite different.

Author's Video Link
↓
❶
Geographically Speaking: Physical Geography

The three world maps displayed in Chapters 1 and 2 provide a good gauge of the nature of the physical stage on which the events described in the remainder of this book take place. For example, our discussion will turn to such entities as Nigeria (Africa's most populous country) and Quebec (the Canadian province where separatism is a popular sentiment). At a glance, it is possible to deduce the terrain, the climate, and the precipitation there, and thus obtain some notion of what environments are like. This information can be useful in understanding the human geography.

KEY TERMS

Apollo Moon Program
Climatic Regions
ENSO (El Niño Southern Oscillation)
Geologic Eras
Glaciation
Greenhouse (Enhanced) Warming Effect
Holocene Epoch
Interglaciation
K/T Boundary
Late Cenozoic Ice Age
NASA (National Aeronautics and Space Administration)
Pleistocene Epoch

3

CHANGEABLE GLOBAL ENVIRONMENTS

During the 1950s and throughout the 1960s, the weather in most of North America and in much of Europe was marked by cold winters and cool summers. Snow fell in Chicago as early as the second week of September 1957, and in the following winter Lake Michigan was more icebound than it had been in living memory.

By the early 1960s, scientific articles began to carry an ominous message: the series of cold winters, late spring seasons, and shortened growing seasons not only marked the end of a half century of slow but measurable global warming, but it also presaged something worse. The Earth might be getting ready for a return to the ice age. Maps appeared in newspapers suggesting how the Earth's living space might shrink as a result. As high-latitude glaciers were going to expand, sea-level would drop, so that land lost to the ice in frigid areas would be partially replaced on newly exposed **continental shelves** (offshore land submerged under shallow water) at lower latitudes. But this would not be enough to offset the loss. Massive dislocation might result. Crops would fail, and hunger and starvation loomed. A

Geographica

- The second half of the twentieth century has witnessed two environmental debates: the "icehouse" issue of the 1950s/1960s and the "greenhouse" question of the 1980s/1990s.

- "Global" climatic trends often display persistent regional exceptions.

- Ice ages, including the current Late Cenozoic Ice Age, consist of irregular cycles-within-cycles of alternate cooling and warming.

- Climatic reversals (from warming to cooling and vice versa) appear to be heralded by periods of marked weather extremes.

- The Little Ice Age, commencing during the early thirteenth century, ended a long warming phase and plunged Europe into chaos and famine.

memorable BBC television program hosted by a prominent scholar showed how fast the climatic transition might occur; at its conclusion, even as the host warned of what might lie ahead, snow began to fall on his lectern, on the stage—*inside* the studio!

Some of the scientists who did research on this cooling phenomenon did not share the concern of the majority. They argued that climatic swings of this kind had

occurred before and would happen again. Furthermore, they found that the severe cold recorded in the Northern Hemisphere was not always matched south of the equator. Winters in Australia and southern South America were relatively mild. Summers were warm. Spatially, there was nothing "global" about the cooling that had northerners so worried.

By the 1970s, the environmental pendulum had begun to swing the

From the Field Notes

❝ As we flew over the ice sheet, I imagined that this is what much of the world—at higher latitudes and altitudes—must have looked like during the most recent advance of the Late Cenozoic Ice Age. Whole expanses of continent, plateaus, plains, hills, as well as mountains, lay buried under thousands of feet of ice, only the highest crests protruding. It must have been a cold, forbidding world of climatic extremes in which only the most adaptable of our ancestors survived. ❞

other way. Memories of extreme winters faded. Things returned to normal.

And then, as we all know, the 1980s brought another environmental alert: the Earth was warming at a measurable, increasing rate. But this time it was not the Earth but humanity that was believed to be responsible. The atmosphere functions like a greenhouse, allowing light rays from the sun to penetrate but trapping heat from Earth and preventing its escape. It is a natural process, but it can be modified by human intervention. Pollution from factories, automobiles, and other sources was held responsible for a general warming of the Earth, an enhanced greenhouse effect with postulated consequences ranging from the drying up of farmlands to the drowning of coastal zones because of melting ice and rising sea levels. Alarmed political leaders assigned millions of dollars of research funds to scientific organizations seeking to confirm this threat to the world's natural environments, and steps were taken to reduce some of the underlying causes. Exceptionally warm summer temperatures (and high annual averages) recorded during 1987 and 1988 in areas of the Northern Hemisphere seemed to prove that "greenhouse" warming was under way. Overall, the 1980s was reported to be the warmest decade since recordkeeping began. Ceaseless befouling of the atmosphere, in growing quantity ever since the onset of the Industrial Revolution, finally seemed to have its inevitable consequence.

But not all scholars were convinced that the observed temperatures were due to atmospheric pollution, or that the warmth of the 1980s constituted the beginning of any long-term trend. Some dissidents argued that the global record is too incomplete, the observed warming trend too regional and too brief, and the available evidence too weak to postulate anything so comprehensive as a coming century of greenhouse warming. Geographers reminded their colleagues of the cooling episode 30 years earlier and found that—again—the observed "global" trends had regional rather than worldwide expression. During the supposedly warmest decade in recorded history, Southern Hemisphere regions again bucked the trend, recording several cool summers and unusually cold winters.

Whatever the human contribution to the climatic cycles that our instruments record, there is no doubt that the forces of nature are the dominant forces of change. The public debate over the merits of the **greenhouse-enhanced warming theory** that was in vogue during the 1980s and early 1990s resulted in greater awareness of the environmental uncertainties we confront, and this in itself was a positive outcome. And, as we noted in Chapter 2, even if long-term global warming is not in the offing, this does not mean that we should worry less about atmospheric pollution. Whether recent temperature observations reflect a natural cycle, human-induced warming, or both, steps must be taken to reduce the emissions of damaging gases into the air.

CYCLES OF NATURE

The greenhouse issue has helped focus attention on a circumstance that has much to do with the appearance and evolution of humanity on this Earth: the rapid and apparently unpredictable changes that characterize global and regional environments. If a time traveler could visit our planet during the late Mesozoic, say 100 million years ago, and could return to the present, that traveler would be astonished at the contrasts between then and now. Then, the Earth was warm and moist, even at higher latitudes such as those of Labrador (northern Canada) and Patagonia (southern Argentina). Leafy forests thrived, and biodiversity was enormous. Returning now, our visitor would be amazed that so luxuriant, warm, and moist a planet could turn so cold, dry, and, over vast stretches, barren.

But as we know, had the traveler come back just 25,000 years earlier, things would have looked even worse. At least the ice sheets that then covered North America and northern Eurasia have withdrawn now, and Earthly living space is much larger than it was at that time.

All this reminds us that the Earth's environments change in cycles, some long-term and others of shorter duration. There are cycles within cycles that make understanding (let alone predicting) the process difficult. We do not yet understand why, about 40 million years ago, the Earth began to slowly cool. That cooling trend continued throughout the Oligocene and Miocene epochs, smothering Antarctica's plant and animal life and creating an ever-growing ice sheet on that polar continent.

It is interesting to note that the previous period of global cooling and glaciation, the Dwyka glaciation that occurred more than 200 million years ago, happened when the great supercontinent, Pangaea, was about to break up into smaller landmasses that became the continents as we know them today. Some scientists are now suggesting that the outward movement of these continents, carried on tectonic plates of the crust, is slowing down and may soon (in geologic terms) stop. Could it be that the onset *and* the ending of phases of continental drift are accompanied by periods of global glaciation?

Whatever the answer, it is clear

that permanent ice began building on the polar continent of Antarctica some 40 million years ago, and from then on ever-greater climatic swings affected the Earth. But let us recall the state of terrestrial life at that time. This (the Cenozoic Era) was the age of mammals, and the great extinction of dinosaurs had already taken place. The earliest primates (animals characterized by their ability to grasp objects with their fingers and/or toes) had appeared about 10 million years later, and they were exposed to the Miocene cooling. Forests dominated the landscape, and these early primates, like most land animals, were forest dwellers.

But the Earth was changing, and not only because of global cooling. Near the end of the Miocene, the Mediterranean Sea dried up because plate movement closed the Strait of Gibraltar, but soon the Strait opened again and water from the Atlantic Ocean filled its basin once more. About 4 million years ago, the landmasses of North and South America were connected by a land bridge (again created by plate movement) that closed off a wide channel that had existed where Central America lies now. While that channel was open, warm waters from the Pacific Ocean flowed into the Atlantic, warming higher latitudes as they circulated northward. When the Central American land bridge formed, the Atlantic was cut off, and it is believed that this contributed to the rapid cooling of the Arctic, perhaps starting the Late Cenozoic Ice Age in full force.

ANCIENT ECOSYSTEMS

Whatever the underlying causes, it is certain that the slow Miocene cooling gave way to much colder conditions shortly after the beginning of the Pliocene Epoch. This heralded the beginning of the ice

age, variously called the Late Cenozoic, Plio-Pleistocene, or simply the Pleistocene Ice Age. But how can climates of 5 million years ago and even more be reconstructed? The answer lies in muds on the ocean floors that contain layers of tiny fossil shells of organisms called foraminifera. These layers of shells contain varying concentrations of an oxygen isotope, oxygen-18. Shells in some layers have more than others. When climatic conditions cause the ocean surface to cool, more of this oxygen isotope is bound up in the foraminifera's shells; when it warms again, the shells' oxygen-18 concentrations decrease. Thus a series of layers of foraminifera shells can reveal alternate cooling and warming phases of the ocean surface, and provide a calendar of temperature changes.

Since these tiny ocean shells have lain in undisturbed, deep-ocean beds ever since they sank to the bottom, confidence in what they reveal is quite high. And what they reveal is that the gradual cooling throughout the Miocene became a more rapid cooling not long after the Pliocene-Miocene transition, between 6 and 5 million years ago, and that this, in turn, was followed by an even more severe cooling between 3 and 2.5 million years ago. This latter drop in global temperatures approximates the beginning of the Pleistocene part of the current ice age, with its dramatic advances of great ice sheets and their ensuing withdrawals.

We will return to the Pleistocene story shortly, but it is important to keep in mind that glaciation is not exclusively a polar or high-latitude event. In the next chapter, our attention will be focused on eastern Africa, where the great drama of human evolution gathered momentum during the Pleistocene. Although Africa lies astride the equator, the continent did not escape the impact of the ice age into which the rest of the Earth was plunged. The tall mountains of East Africa acquired ice caps that grew downward as the regional climate cooled. Cycles of weather became more varied and more rigorous, and most importantly, the region became drier than it had been for many millions of years. The dense, leafy, moist, warm forest environments, in which the existing primates had lived, gave way to a kind of savanna-like grassland similar to that prevailing over much of East Africa today; fossil and pollen evidence confirm this change. As we will see in the next chapter, tree-dwelling primates faced an ecological challenge that exterminated some and strengthened others.

GLACIATION CYCLES

Until the secrets of global temperature change during the Late Cenozoic were unlocked through the analysis of ocean deposits, the history of the Pleistocene was reconstructed from landscape evidence and from sediments deposited where the glaciers had spread. Glaciers carve telltale marks into the rocks over which they move, and they grind boulders into fine silt. Much of the landscape of Canada consists of hard, crystalline rocks scraped bare by great ice sheets. Much of the U.S. Midwest is covered by pulverized rock named **till**, laid down by those same glaciers.

After a glacial advance or glaciation, a warm period (such as the one we are experiencing now) begins with **deglaciation**. As the ice melts, some of the powdered rock it contains is blown away by winds and deposited elsewhere in the form of a layer of **loess**. Now the warm interglaciation is in full swing, and soil develops on the till. When the next glaciation brings the ice back, the till, loess, and soil are

evidence that a glacial cycle has occurred.

For a long time, scientists could only use such depositionary evidence as they tried to reconstruct the Late Cenozoic Ice Age, and under the circumstances they did remarkably well. It has been known for many decades that Pleistocene ice advanced and retreated a number of times. The evidence from North America and from Europe suggested that there were at least four such episodes. But over the past several years, there have been repeated technical breakthroughs, among which the analysis of ocean deposits is only one. Both long-range and shorter-term cycles are now much better understood.

From the Field Notes

❝ Flying over the Rocky Mountains on the route from Salt Lake City to Denver, you can see topography showing all the signs of glaciation. But now the ice is gone and the valley floors show evidence of human habitation. But just ten thousand years ago, this landscape would have looked like that on page 30! ❞

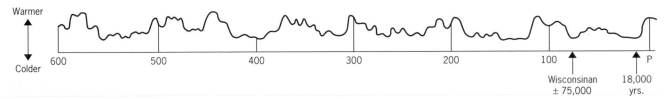

FIGURE 3–1 A composite of seven assessments of temperature changes over the past 600,000 years.

LONG-TERM GLACIATION

As noted earlier, we know that the Earth experienced a significant cooling phase between 6 and 5 million years ago, and a more abrupt one between 3 and 2.5 million years ago, which should now be regarded as the onset of the **Pleistocene Epoch**. Within the Pleistocene, there have been many advances and withdrawals of the ice, not just four. Some of the glaciations were colder and longer than others; interglaciations also have varied in duration and intensity. The data indicate that more than 25 advances of the ice have taken place since the severe cooling that occurred more than 2.5 million years ago, so that there has been a glaciation, on average, every 90,000 to 100,000 years. The temperature fluctuations and ice advances over the most recent 600,000 years are shown in generalized form in Figure 3-1, which is a composite of several versions published in recent years. The most recent series of glaciations remains collectively known as the **Wisconsinan Glaciation**, and it is marked by the steep decline in temperature about 75,000 to 80,000 years ago. Just 18,000 years ago, the Wisconsinan glaciers covered most of northern North America. Now is a good time for another thoughtful look at Figure 2-1 (page 21).

Figure 3-1 should alert us to an uncomfortable reality: the cold periods over the past 600,000 years have been long; the warm interglaciations relatively short. Conditions such as those familiar to us today have been infrequent and brief, and

our Holocene warm spell, already in progress for some 15,000 years, now has lasted longer than many others. So what is our future: greenhouse or icehouse?

SHORT-TERM GLACIATION

Modern human civilization has evolved entirely in the wake of the retreat of the last of the Wisconsinan glaciers, a brief period even in the context of the Pleistocene. But we should not conclude that the Holocene interglaciation has been, or will for its remainder be, a time of steady conditions or stable environments. The warming phase after about 18,000 years ago produced many short-term variations: the warming process was by no means continuous. At least once, it is believed, so much frigid icewater from the melting glaciers poured into the North Atlantic Ocean that water temperatures dropped sharply—and briefly caused a return to colder conditions on land. Between 12,000 and 6,000 years ago, atmospheric conditions favored higher rainfall, especially in tropical areas, and lake levels in Africa and Asia rose.

Various new and modified dating and measuring techniques have enhanced the picture of climate and weather during our present interglaciation, and all have told an environmental story that one report described as a "roller coaster." In Europe, the sequence of environmental events may have been approximately as suggested in Fig. 3-2 (A) to (C). About 14,000 years ago, ice still covered all of Scandi-

navia and most of Britain; present-day France and Germany were tundra-like, and the south resembled conditions in, say, Ontario today. By 10,000 years ago, the northern ice sheets had become confined to Scandinavia, tundra conditions had been driven northward, and a temperate climate prevailed in Mediterranean areas. And by 6000 years ago, the map begins to resemble what we saw in Figure 2-3. None of this, however, happened smoothly or evenly. Periods of cooling and warming alternated even as the prevailing trend continued.

What do we know about the past 1,000 years? Now our calibrations become even more precise, as tree-ring analyses are added to other methods of investigation. Again, the story is one of considerable variation *and* regional contrast. The past millennium encompasses a cooling phase known as the **Little Ice Age**. In her book *The Little Ice Age* (1988), Jean M. Grove describes what happened:

For several hundred years climatic conditions in Europe had been kind; there were few poor harvests and famines were infrequent. The pack ice in the Arctic lay to the north and long sea voyages could be made in the small craft then in use . . . Icelanders made their first trip to Greenland about AD 982 and later they reached the Canadian Arctic and may even have penetrated the North West Passage. Grain was grown in Iceland and even in Greenland; the northern fisheries flourished and in main-

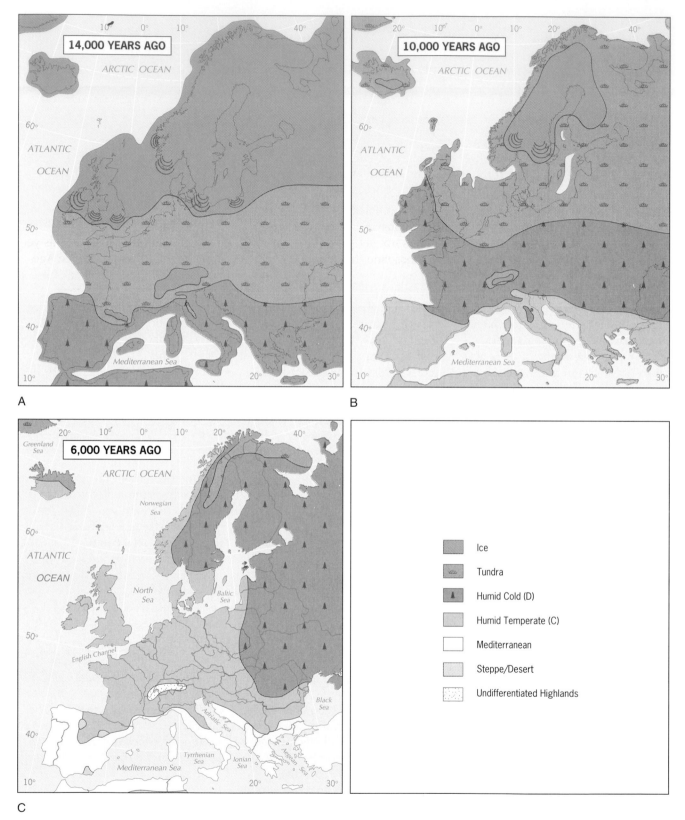

FIGURE 3–2 Europe during the Holocene. Author's approximation from descriptive and computer-generated sources.

land Europe vineyards were in production 500 kilometers (300 miles) north of their present limits.

The beneficent times came to an end. Sea ice and stormier seas made the passages between Norway, Iceland and Greenland more difficult after AD *1200; the last report of a voyage to Vinland was made in 1347. Life in Greenland became harder; the people were cut off from Iceland and eventually disappeared from history toward the end of the fifteenth century. Grain would no longer ripen in Iceland, first in the north and later in the south and east . . . life became tougher for fishermen as well as for farmers. In mainland Europe, disastrous harvests were experienced in the latter part of the thirteenth and in the early fourteenth century . . . extremes of weather were greater, with severe winters and unusually hot or wet summers (pp. 1–2).*

The onset of the Little Ice Age occurred in the thirteenth century, and it continued during the fourteenth. Then came an interval of more moderate conditions, but another cool period followed from the mid-sixteenth to the mid-nineteenth centuries. Since the 1870s, the Earth has been warming up gradually, although conditions do not yet appear to be as warm as they were a thousand years ago, during the warm period described by Grove, called the **Medieval Optimum**.

Author's Video Link
↓
③
Original Viking
Voyagers

Although there is no doubt that a significant, double-phase cooling affected the Earth between the thirteenth and the nineteenth centuries, it also is clear that the effects of this cooling were not felt equally in all parts of the world. Tree-ring research in Scandinavia, for example,

indicates that the impact of the Little Ice Age came later and lasted less than in Western Europe; it seems to have affected the weather significantly only from about 1560 to 1660. On the other hand, the Medieval Optimum does not seem to have warmed northern Sweden when the Vikings were sailing the northern seas: Sweden stayed much colder.

The lessons from this research are several. First, environmental fluctuations are nature's design, so that it is not yet possible to establish a baseline that would distinguish natural variation from human-induced climate change. Second, the varying impacts of the Little Ice Age *and* the Medieval Optimum indicate the risk in extrapolating from regional observations to global conclusions. And third, the Little Ice Age, like the Late Cenozoic Ice Age as a whole, may not be over; further cooling phases

may lie ahead. Coupled with the prospect that the Holocene interglaciation may come to a close at any time (given its duration as of A.D. 2000), it is appropriate to couple any concern for greenhouse warming with some consideration of alternate scenarios.

AVERAGES AND AMPLITUDES

If the greenhouse prospect is as yet unproven, and post–Little Ice Age warming is largely a natural phenomenon that may presage a further cooling phase, and if Holocene conditions should begin to change, what will be the environmental signals?

Research indicates that environmental swings of this kind are preceded by weather extremes, and it is the number, incidence, and dis-

From the Field Notes

❝ Some countries have to take the enhanced greenhouse–warming warning more seriously than others. As we approached the Maldives (in the Indian Ocean south of India), the islands lay like lilypads on the surface of a pond. No part of this country's natural surface lies more than 6 feet (less than 2 meters) above sea level. The upper floors of the buildings in the capital, Male, form the Maldives' highest points. Almost any rise in sea level would threaten this outpost. ❞

tribution of these extremes that we should monitor. A place that has an average annual temperature of 60° F may have a normal annual temperature range from 90° in summer to 30° in winter. If those amplitudes rose from these data to 110° in summer and 10° in winter, the average would remain about the same . . . but the extremes would be much greater. And if there is yet insufficient global, consistent evidence for greenhouse-caused warming, there is ample indication that extreme variations *are* affecting global environments, from more frequent El Niño effects to more persistent droughts. Apparently conflicting signals come from everywhere: retreating Arctic ice, severe Canadian spring cold, hurricane-force destruction in Britain, and unprecedented Australian drought. Consider the record over just the half decade of the 1990s: unprecedented floods in the U.S. Midwest and South, extremely severe blizzards and storms in the East; the highest temperatures on record in southern Pakistan and western India; the latest iceberg sightings ever in the western Atlantic; the most powerful hurricane ever recorded in the central Pacific. Most significant are the oceanic perturbations, which may be the most sensitive systems of all.

THE HUMAN PRESENCE

The emergence of humanity on this Earth took place during a time of great environmental variation. As we will see in the next chapter, the evolutionary tree that eventually yielded modern humans was a complex, multibranched tree, many of whose limbs and branches died out. We do not yet know the exact role of environmental fluctuations in this process, but there is no doubt that the environment's challenges defeated some and stimulated others.

One of the most interesting problems now facing us is the timing and the routes of the hominid as well as the human outmigrations from Africa. How do the routes and the dates fit what we know about the global environment? For example, there is ample evidence of human habitation in Europe *before* the last (Wisconsinan) glaciation. Our distant ancestors obviously migrated into higher latitudes when interglaciation prevailed, and were driven away by the next glaciation.

The arrival of the earliest people in the Americas still is a matter for debate. The oldest firm evidence, many scholars believe, dates this immigration as recently as 12,000 years ago. As the last Wisconsinan glaciers withdrew, these people are believed to have come across the land bridge from Siberia to Alaska and then migrated southward. Their culture, the **Clovis culture**, included big-game hunting with finely made, fluted arrowheads. These arrowheads, first found near Clovis, New Mexico, have been found by archaeologists along a trail that seems to confirm the date and place of these early Americans' entry. But other researchers believe that the first immigrants arrived many thousands of years earlier. Research in Chile has produced evidence of older occupation, which would mean that any Bering-to-Alaska crossing would have taken place even earlier.

The problem that arises, of course, is that the Wisconsinan ice sheets were in full development, say 40,000 years ago. As Figure 3-1 shows, it was not quite as cold as it was 18,000 years ago, but Alaska and Canada would have been inhospitable nevertheless. What would have impelled people to undertake the journey at such a daunting time? One possibility is this: when the glaciers form, much water is converted into ice, and sea levels drop. That may have created, during the mid-Wisconsinan, a coastal ledge along the western shore of northern North America, an inviting route for hunting-and-fishing migrants.

The issue is not settled, and there are geographers who take still another view: those ancient Chilean settlements may have been populated by travelers who came not across the Siberian-Alaskan land bridge, but across the Pacific Ocean on canoes and rafts, much as Polynesians dispersed much later. Correlating the human dissemination with the environmental pulse is a critical geographic task that lies ahead.

KEY TERMS

Clovis Culture
Continental Shelf
Glaciation Cycles
Deglaciation
Greenhouse (Enhanced) Warming
Little Ice Age
Loess
Medieval Optimum
Pleistocene Epoch
Till
Wisconsinan Glaciation

4

HUMAN ORIGINS
AND DISPERSALS

It is one of the rules of biology that plants and animals—all living things—have *niches*, places or areas on or near the Earth's surface that best support their survival. A niche may be very small, even microscopic for the smallest organisms. It can also be so large that it constitutes a geographic region and becomes a *range*. The African elephant, for example, has a range that extends from South Africa to the Sudan, encompassing habitats that vary from dry bushland to equatorial rainforest. China's panda, on the other hand, has a comparatively small niche in the bamboo-clothed, misty mountain slopes of a tiny part of Asia. We commonly associate animals with their niches: the *mountain* gorilla of East Africa, the *polar* bear of Arctic habitats, the *snow* leopard of the Himalayas, the *desert* fox of interior Asia.

No species has ever ranged as widely over the Earth as **Homo sapiens** (modern humans). No species has ever competed so vigorously with others for space, food, water, and other resources of life. Long before modern humans made their appearance, **hominids** (predecessors of *H. sapiens*) had spread widely across Eurasia from their African sources, but these hominids did not have the tools, technology, or adaptability to overpower the animals with which they shared their habitats. Nor could they sustain themselves in every environment. But the emergence of *H. sapiens* transformed the Earth. In a fraction of time, humans multiplied into the billions, invaded virtually every corner of the world, exterminated thousands of animals and plants, and exploited an ever-expanding array of resources to feed, house, and enrich their growing numbers. Today, there are fears that the human explosion is leading to irreversible damage to the global

Geographica

- **Eastern Africa, from Ethiopia through Kenya and Tanzania to South Africa, was the scene of the transition from Australopithecenes to Hominids to *Homo sapiens*.**

- **Environmental changes appear to have played a key role in the evolutionary sequence; some lineages adapted and survived, others could not.**

- **After more than a million years of dispersal from their African source area, Hominids never reached either the Americas or Australia, although they got as far as the Yellow River and Java.**

- ***Homo sapiens* may have evolved quite rapidly in East Africa as recently as 200,000 years ago, and swiftly expanded and migrated into Eurasia, eliminating their Hominid contemporaries.**

- ***Homo sapiens* reached Australia about 55,000 years ago and the Americas as recently as 13,000 years ago. Evidence for earlier arrival (in South America) exists but remains controversial.**

environmental balance. That this should be possible, less than 200,000 years after the rise of our species, within 10,000 years after the beginnings of agriculture and urbanization, and barely 200 years after the onset of the industrial revolution, is as astounding as it is disturbing.

HUMAN ORIGINS

This much is certain: human **evolution** has been a complex process of development, virtually all of which took place in Africa. It is a process that has spanned the past 6 million years of Earth's history, or about the last one-tenth of 1 percent of the planet's existence. Comparing this to the lifetime of a person exactly 20 years old, human evolution would have begun *one week* before that person's twentieth birthday. And the presence of the product of that process, modern *Homo sapiens*, proportionately extends over just the last 4 hours of that lifetime.

The past 6 million years, we noted in the previous chapter, span the Plio-Pleistocene Ice Age. Wherever and however hominids evolved, they were challenged by changing environments—even in Africa, far from the polar icecaps and sheet glaciers that spread over higher latitudes time and again. Even today, when the Earth is experiencing a warm interglaciation, snow and ice cover the crests of East Africa's highest mountains (Fig. 4-1). When Pleistocene glaciations pushed ice sheets over northern North America and Eurasia, the glaciers on Mounts Kilimanjaro and Kenya also grew and spread downslope. Lush forest gave way to dry grasslands, warm lake waters chilled, rivers dwindled, and cold winds swept the East African highlands. When the glaciations waned and the glaciers receded, African habitats became warmer and wet-

ter, the forests grew back, and opportunities for life expanded. Time and again during the late Pliocene and Pleistocene, the natural environment presented alternations of challenge and opportunity. The niches occupied by hominids, and the primates with whom they shared their habitats, did not afford permanent security. Some species could adapt; others migrated and found niches in which they could survive; others succumbed.

We should not assume that environmental variations were the sole driving force in the evolutionary process. But there is no doubt that Plio-Pleistocene climatic reversals played a role in human evolution. When hominids eventually migrated from Africa into other realms of the Old World, it happened when environmental conditions favored such long-distance, interregional movement. Much later, when *H. sapiens* migrated into North America and Australia, environment again was a factor. An ice-free corridor may have facilitated movement through Alaska into North America. Lowered sea level during a late Pleistocene

glaciation enabled people to cross from New Guinea into Australia.

Thus the process of evolution occurred on a changing physical stage. Actually, it is better to speak of process*es* of evolution, because human evolution was not a linear sequence of development from primate to hominid to human. For many years after the first hominid remains were found, the search was on for the so-called "missing link," the key skull in the human fossil record that would incontrovertibly link apes to humans. We now know that such a connector does not exist. The **Neanderthals**, named after the site in Germany where their bones were first discovered, long were regarded as transitional from earlier forms to our modern humans. They were dense-boned, thick-skulled people who were very muscular and rugged, and they managed to survive an advance of the Pleistocene glaciers in their European habitat during their occupancy, probably lasting from 100,000 to about 35,000 years ago.

Additional fossil finds seemed to

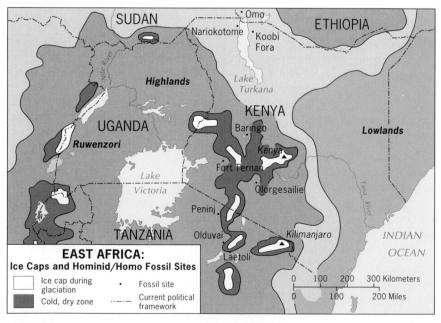

FIGURE 4—1 This is what East Africa's environments may have been during a glaciation.

indicate that younger skeletons had smaller teeth, narrower faces, and lighter bone structures, and were indeed transitional to modern humans. But more recent research and analysis suggests that the Neanderthals were not after all, ancestors of modern humans, but contemporaries—and competitors—who were exterminated when modern *H. sapiens* migrated from Africa into the Middle East (where Neanderthals also lived) and Europe. Therefore, what had appeared to be an evolutionary sequence turned out to be an instance of earlier branching, of simultaneous development, a struggle for primacy, and the eventual success of modern humans over Neanderthals.

PLACE AND TIME

If the search for a "missing link" has been called off because no such single connector between apes and humans has ever existed, the quest for another linkage continues. Even while questions about human evolution over the past several hundred thousand years are being answered, the story of the Miocene epoch, when primates emerged among the Earth's mammals, remains shrouded in mystery. Paleontologists have identified a cat-like (and housecat-size) animal from the preceding epoch, the Oligocene, as the first known primate, based on its ape-like teeth and its monkey-like limbs. This small primate lived more than 30 million years ago in the forests of North Africa, which is why it is called *Aegyptopithecus*.

During the tens of millions of years that followed, the biological order of primates (which includes prosimians such as Madagascar's lemurs, monkeys such as baboons, apes such as the chimpanzee, and humans) must have expanded and diversified, but the record of this momentous development is poor. By the time the fossil sequence is reestablished, we are well into the Pliocene, a mere 5 million years ago.

It may not be a coincidence that this matches approximately with the onset of the Plio-Pleistocene Ice Age. Perhaps the Miocene primates remained forest dwellers until their habitats and niches shrank or disappeared as global climates cooled and dried out. This may have forced survivors onto the savanna-like grasslands that replaced the forest habitats—surviving apes whose fossil bones, skulls, and teeth we now study for clues about their lives and environments.

From the Field Notes

❝ After traveling through the dense forest in the eastern Chyulu Hills we reached the open savanna country below. When our distant ancestors inhabited East Africa, the vegetation was forest not unlike that of Chyulu; but as global climate changed, so the forest gave way to the open savanna. This sequence happened several times during the Pleistocene, and survival depended upon adaptability. ❞ (Note: the albino giraffe amid the savanna was one of the most extraordinary sights recorded over a period of nearly 50 years in Africa; without its natural color, its chances of survival were slight, but it had reached adulthood.)

Early Discoveries

The first significant fossil finds occurred not in Africa, but in Eurasia. Neanderthal fossils, as we noted, were found in Europe as long ago as the 1850s. In 1894, a Dutch surgeon, who was working in what was then the Dutch East Indies (now Indonesia), reported on his discovery of, as the title of his series of books put it, "a human-like transitional form from Java." The **Java Ape Man**, as this find became known, had a flattened skull and a small brain, but a century ago Dr. Eugene Du Bois had no doubt regarding its position in the sequence of human evolution.

The Neanderthal finds in Europe and other factors led scientists to conclude that human evolution occurred in central Asia, from where it

From the Field Notes

❝ In this cave near China's capital, Beijing, were discovered the fossil bones and teeth of Peking Man, one of the most significant finds ever made. Now the question is: are modern East Asians descended from Peking Man and his contemporaries, or did a much later wave of *Homo sapiens* arrive from Africa to vanquish their predecessors? Whatever the answer, it is noteworthy that the site of China's modern capital may have been inhabited for more than a half million years. ❞

was believed hominids radiated outward into other areas of Eurasia and into Africa, Australia, and the Americas. When in the 1920s a cave near Beijing, China, began to yield the remains of a larger-brained hominid, this hypothesis seemed confirmed. **"Peking Man,"** as this Chinese representative was called, appeared more advanced and therefore younger than the Java Ape Man. Unfortunately, modern testing of the bones will not be possible. In 1941, when the Japanese invasion of China was imminent, the fossils were crated and hastily despatched to the United States. The crate was lost and has never been recovered.

While virtually all attention was centered on Eurasia, a discovery was made in Africa that was the beginning of the end of the central Asia hypothesis. In South Africa, a cave being excavated for lime had for some time been yielding bones, mostly the remains of baboons. Anthropologist Raymond Dart had asked the workers at the Taung cave to keep an eye out for fossil skulls and to send him any that might be found. In 1924, a box of fossils sent to Dart contained a petrified skull that was no baboon. The anthropologist instantly knew that he held in his hand, in his words, "one of the most significant finds ever made in the history of anthropology." The skull was that of a young child, probably five or six years old at the time of its death. It sat on the spine in such a way that the child would have walked upright, unlike baboons. The teeth were human-like and did not resemble those of monkeys. Dart named the Taung child *Australopithecus africanus*, southern ape of Africa, and proclaimed it a human ancestor.

Dart's assignment of a new genus **(Australopithecus)** and species *(africanus)* to the Taung child's skull was not approved by all anthropologists. Was this just a malformed chimpanzee? Was it re-

ally older than the Java Ape Man? But additional finds in South Africa soon proved that the Taung child was no isolated individual. At the Sterkfontein cave, not far from Johannesburg, anthropologist Robert Broom identified additional skulls and other remains that matched Dart's discovery. These confirmed that *A. africanus* was a species that occupied South Africa's highveld regionally, that it was bipedal, and that it was not an ape or monkey. A key branch of the evolutionary tree had been identified and named.

How old is *A. africanus*? The Taung and Sterkfontein individuals probably lived between 2.5 and 3 million years ago. But they are not the oldest representatives of the *Australopithecus* genus known to us today. Almost 50 years to the day after the discovery of the Taung child in South Africa, anthropologist Donald Johanson, surveying in Ethiopia, found an assemblage of bones that turned out to constitute about 40 percent of the skeleton of a single individual. This was an adult female, about 3′8″ (1.1 m) tall, who weighed about 65 lb (30 kg). The anthropologists concluded that Lucy (as she was called, after a Beatles' song popular at the time, in 1974) was of the same genus as the Taung child, but not of the same species. Lucy represented *A. afarensis*, perhaps 3.25 million years old. Again, not all anthropologists agreed that a separate species designation was warranted for Lucy, but all agreed on her great age and significance. Only a few fragments of bones have ever been discovered that suggest bipedality existing even longer—nearly 4 million years. Clearly, the dawn of the walking apes goes far back, possibly 5 to 7 million years.

East African Sources

No region of the world has yielded as many significant fossil remains of apes, hominids, and humans as East Africa. Beginning in the 1950s, discoveries at Laetoli and Olduvai in

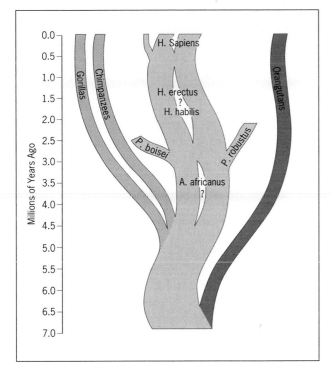

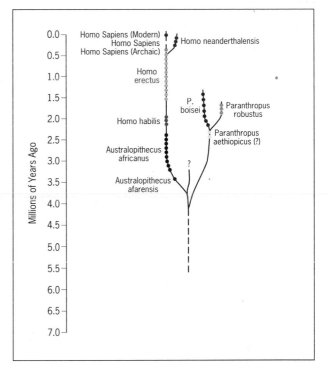

FIGURE 4-2 New data continue to change constructions of the evolutionary "tree." These two versions undoubtedly will change again; note that both regard the Neanderthals as offshoots from the *H. sapiens* lineage.

Tanzania, and the Lake Turkana area near the border between Kenya and Ethiopia (and other places as well) not only confirmed what had been found in South Africa decades earlier, but also expanded the evolutionary "tree" (Fig. 4-2). The South African finds had suggested that *Australopithecus* was represented by two species, not just *africanus*. *A. africanus* was smaller and more slender in structure than a larger-boned, more rugged species that had been called *A. robustus*. Later, researchers in East Africa, notably Louis, Mary, and Richard Leakey, found even more brawny specimens of what appeared to be *A. robustus*. To account for the differences between *A. africanus* and the more robust individuals, some anthropologists suggested that the former was an omnivore, eating animals as well as plants, whereas the latter were herbivores, or plant eaters only.

Additional field work in East Africa turned up an even more massive form than *A. robustus*, ini-

tially called *A. boisei*. The first specimen was found by Mary Leakey at Olduvai in strata dated as 1.8 million years old. So different was this species from *A. africanus* that anthropologists disagreed over their relationship. At present, the prevailing view is that while *A. afarensis* and *A. africanus* are links in the sequence leading to modern humans, *A. robustus* and *A. boisei* belong to an evolutionary dead end and should be assigned their own genus: *Paranthropus*. In Figure 4-2, note that these two species are placed on a branch diverging from that connecting *Australopithecus* to later hominids.

Why did the representatives of *Paranthropus* die out? The appearance of a new, powerful competitor for its food resources probably indicated the end of their lineage. East Africa's fossil sites prove that the genus *Homo* had entered the stage.

Tools and Teeth

One of the topics of debate concerning the discoveries of the

various species of *Australopithecus* has to do with the possibility that individuals belonging to this genus might have been users of simple tools. Field workers pointed to assemblages of fractured rocks and broken bones that lay in and near the caves and other sites where hominid fossil finds were made. Were the rocks deliberately broken by our distant ancestors, to be used as tools? Were the bones splintered for similar purposes? Or did these rocks and bones fracture by natural processes? Such questions are not always easy to answer, and thus arose the science of **taphonomy**, the study of assemblages of fossil remains and the circumstances prevailing during and after the organisms' deaths.

Among the most useful indicators of the ways our distant ancestors lived are the teeth found among the fossil remains. First, the teeth provide an indication of the speed with which *Australopithecus* children matured. Apes mature on a faster schedule than humans, and the teeth of the South African specimens indicate that *Australopithecus* was on a much faster maturation schedule than humans. Second, teeth reveal much about the diet of their owners. The transition from forest life to savanna life that preceded the rise of *Australopithecus* was accompanied by a change in dentition. The large canine teeth shrank in size, front teeth became smaller, and the amount of tooth enamel increased. Anthropologists believe that these developments came just before the emergence of bipedal walking and may, in fact, have facilitated this momentous adaptation of the earliest apes.

Teeth can reveal much more than bone fragments do. When Davidson Black identified Peking Man in 1927, he concluded the existence of this hominid from the discovery of a single tooth. He predicted that fragments of skull and bone would be found at the site, and later excavations located them. But that lone tooth had been enough to herald the reality of this hominid—whether or not the bones were found.

Australopithecus walked on two feet but does not seem to have used tools. At least this genus apparently did not *fashion* tools. There is a lively debate as to whether these hominids might have used sticks and stones and bones, which they probably did. But the first tool makers appear to have been members of the genus *Homo*, between 2 and 2.5 million years ago. One piece of evidence is taphonomic: where fossils of *Australopithecus* are found, there are no chipped stone tools, but where *Australopithecus* and *Homo* are found together, stone tools also occur. Importantly, skeletons of *Homo* show a significant increase in brain size and a further reduction in tooth size (especially the back teeth). Not only the size of the brain, but also the shape of the interior skull now change. Some specialists suggest that this modifi-

cation shows that the early members of the genus *Homo* could utter sounds that probably constituted the first signs of speech.

But the first species of *Homo* is named after its stone-toolmaking ability: **Homo habilis** or "Handy Man." Two million years ago in East Africa, *H. habilis* was a contemporary of *Paranthropus robustus*. This may have been a time when the region was again cooling from a resurgence of the Pleistocene glaciers, and drought affected many areas. The impact of the glaciation can be seen in the animal-fossil record: old species disappear, and modern plains animals such as the kudu, waterbuck, and drought-adapted oryx make their appearance. It must have been a difficult time for the robust *Paranthropus*. Environmental change and competition from the tool-wielding *H. habilis* indicated the end of this lineage.

If the evolutionary line of *P. robustus* and *boisei* now reached dead ends, the connection between *Homo* and *A. afarensis* and *africanus* is by no means clear; the fossil record still is incomplete. The problem is that *H. habilis* is not yet sufficiently represented in the fossil record, and some supposed *H. habilis* bones have been variously interpreted by anthropologists. Thus a crucial period of human evolution is not well understood.

In 1984, a discovery was made by the Kenyan anthropologist Kamoya Kimeu that confirmed an important evolutionary step. At a fossil site called Nariokotome, Kimeu found parts of what proved to be the most complete hominid skeleton found anywhere. Based on various dating methods, this skeleton is believed to be more than 1.5 million years old. Nariokotome Man, as it is called, leaves no doubt about his differentiation from earlier forms. When measurements of brain size, skeletal parts, and teeth were made, it became clear that this was a close relative of Java Man

and Peking Man, of the genus *Homo* and the species *erectus*. From the campsites and caves where **H. erectus** lived, it was found that this species had learned not only to make stone tools, but also to control fire and cook food. Undoubtedly, these hominids had more advanced speech than *H. habilis*, lived in small communities, and migrated far and wide over Eurasia.

HUMAN DISPERSAL

The migration of *H. erectus* from Africa into Eurasia did not, however, begin during the lifetime of Nariokotome Man. In fact, it did not begin until more than a half-million years later. The Nariokotome individual, as we noted, lived about 1.6 million years ago. The emigration of *H. erectus* from Africa did not begin until 1 million years ago. Why did it happen? In all probability this was the first time that our genus experienced the pressures of regional overpopulation. With its ability to communicate, to live cooperatively, to use tools, and to escape narrow niches and exceed formerly limiting ranges, *H. erectus* exploited the available resources more intensively than any predecessors did. When that happened, groups would move on to another area, and progressively farther afield. Eventually, population growth and communal needs drove some members into what is today the Arabian Peninsula, crossing the Red Sea when glaciation again lowered sea levels and natural bridges widened. Now *H. erectus* ventured into the Middle East, into Asia south of the Himalayas, into Southeast Asia, and into China. Consider this: after more than 4,600,000,000 years of Earth history, *Homo* entered Eurasia for the first time in just the past *1 million* years!

On this, anthropologists and archeologists are in agreement. But exactly how *H. erectus* was succeeded by our own species, *H. sapiens*, remains a much-debated issue. In fact, there is no general consensus on how the racial groups of modern humanity (see Chapter 5) evolved. Given what we know about *Anthropithecus* several million years ago, one would expect that the most recent 1 million years would be much clearer in the fossil record. But that is not the case, in part because dating methods have not provided absolute, reliable ages for the available fossils (see box, "Old Bones, New Tales").

HOMO SAPIENS EMERGES

Even the relationships between *H. erectus*, *H. sapiens*, and the racial mosaic of modern humanity are uncertain. At present there are two quite different theories to explain what happened when *Homo erectus* dispersed from Africa and later species of *Homo sapiens* evolved. These are the so-called Out of Africa model and the Regional Continuity model.

Out of Africa

According to this theory, modern humans originated in Africa (as all their predecessors did), establishing themselves first, and then, like *H. erectus* previously, spreading into Eurasia. There they eliminated *H. erectus* and whatever successors that genus might have had, including the Neanderthals whose remains are found in the Middle East and Europe. Once established, *Homo sapiens* differentiated into the geographical racial groups of modern Eurasia and Africa. All this occurred within the past 200,000 years, so humanity's racial groups result from very recent evolution.

Regional Continuity

This theory suggests that the emigration from Africa by *H. erectus* 1 million years ago led to the formation of regional communities from

OLD BONES, NEW TALES

As long as paleontology (the study of animal and plant fossils) and paleo-anthropology (focusing on hominid and human fossil remains) have existed as sciences, researchers have drawn their conclusions about the development of organisms and the evolution of humans from the sizes, shapes, and forms of skulls, bones, and other preserved remnants of once-living things. Often, scientists disagreed over their interpretations. What might to one scholar appear to be an entirely new hominid could, to another researcher, seem to be a mere variant of an established one.

During the past 15 years or so, paleoanthropology and archeology have been revolutionized by three new methods of analysis that come from molecular biology, physics, and computer science, respectively. Obviously, the best way to solve evolutionary problems is to *date* the fossils, to establish their absolute age. But dating methods have not been satisfactory. A long-established method, carbon-14 dating, measures the time it has taken for carbon atoms in bone to undergo radiactive decay—but that method, even with its current refinements, is reliable only to about 40,000 years ago. Another method, potassium-argon dating, covers the period beginning around 300,000 years ago and older. This leaves a crucial gap in the evolution of humanity.

Two of the new techniques come from solid-state physics. Thermoluminescence (TL) and Electron-Spin Resonance (ESR) measure the time that has passed since the bones were laid down by determining changes in the bones' microscopic crystal structures caused by radiation. Such radiation, generated by decaying radium and thorium, creates gaps in the crystal trellises in the bones. The rate at which these holes are formed is assumed to be constant, and the larger the number of holes and gaps in the trellis, the older a skull or bone will be. If these techniques prove dependable, they will enable scientists to determine the ages of fossils as old as 1 million years.

The third technique is known as mitochondrial deoxyribonucleic acid (DNA) analysis. This is an outgrowth of the field referred to as "genetic fingerprinting" and is used to calculate the divergence of species over time—and their convergence in history. Based on this work, researchers in the late 1980s arrived at a newsworthy conclusion: early modern humans may have derived from a single woman who lived in Africa about 200,000 years ago. She began a wave of expansion that carried *H. sapiens* over much of Africa and Eurasia, where they overcame the older populations that long had been living there. In a relatively short time, the hegemony of modern humans was established.

This **"Eve Theory"** was much in vogue during the late 1980s, but recently doubts have been cast on its fundamental assumptions. Evidence in support of it and other information that tends to undermine it continue to be presented. As of mid-1995, however, the theory still had not been conclusively disproven.

Obviously, the new technology is not without its detractors. Some scientists argue that the margins of error in TL and ESR calculations still are two great to permit their acceptance. Others fault the mitochondrial DNA analysis because it contains assumptions about a mutation rate that may not be valid. Whatever the outcome of this debate, paleoanthropology and archeology will never be the same again.

which local evolution took place, eventually leading to the human racial groups of Eurasia. According to this model, the Neanderthals of Europe and the Middle East would indeed be forerunners of modern

THOSE MALIGNED NEANDERTHALS

The word *Neanderthal* sometimes is used to describe a modern person perceived to be crude, uncivilized, or socially primitive. In cartoons, Neanderthals are pictured as ape-like cave dwellers who wield tree-limb clubs and drag their spouses by their long hair during family disputes.

But archeologists report that reality was quite different. There is evidence that Neanderthal communities cared for their sick and for the aged and infirm. Skeletal remains prove that some individuals were so badly ill with arthritis that they must have been carried along as the community moved. Others had virtually no teeth left when they died, so they were unable to chew, and probably were unable to help with the hunting and gathering. Yet they were supported by their companions.

The Neanderthals also were the earliest people known to have buried their dead, apparently with some ritual. Graveyards contain skeletons buried along with tools and other items (such as animal skulls and bones), suggesting that the Neanderthals may have had notions of a hereafter.

The tools made by the Neanderthals reveal an eye for beauty as well as function. During their 70,000-year heyday, their tools show remarkable refinement. And despite their limited technology, they were able to hold their own through western Eurasia's challenging environmental swings. Given our present capacity for destructiveness and violence, we should perhaps revise our view of those "crude" Neanderthals.

Homo sapiens. Those who prefer the Out of Africa model believe that the Neanderthals may have been successors of *H. erectus,* but not direct ancestors of modern *H. sapiens.* Rather, they argue, modern *H. sapiens* emerged from Africa, better adapted and more skilled than the Neanderthals, whom they exterminated over a period of several tens of thousands of years (see box, "Those Maligned Neanderthals").

Note that our reference is to "modern" *H. sapiens,* not just *H. sapiens.* Just as there is a (still somewhat doubtful) differentiation between *H. habilis* and *H. erectus,* so the species *H. sapiens* is divided (on grounds that may shift when better dating and other information become available) into an "old" form: *H. sapiens* (archaic), *H. sapiens* (Neanderthal), and *H. sapiens* (modern). Modern *H. sapiens* often is identified as *H. sapiens sapiens.* Not all anthropologists are satisfied

that this is an appropriate classification, but it is commonly used anyway.

Until fossil finds can be analyzed and dated with greater precision and certainty, arguments of this kind will continue. In this context, the problem of drawing conclusions from skeletal anatomies (referred to earlier in this chapter) is especially evident. To some scholars, a skull, tooth, or bone may appear intermediate between, say, Neanderthal and modern *H. sapiens;* to others the same fossils may seem to represent a member of one or the other. Exact and incontrovertible dating will not solve all the problems, but it will be a crucial aid.

TECHNOLOGY

And often the past is not revealed by bones at all, but by accumulations of stone tools. As we noted

earlier, the earliest beginnings of tool-making cannot yet be precisely dated, but it is known that stone tools were made and used for hundreds of thousands of years before the emergence of modern humans. This long, early period, when communities subsisted on hunting and gathering, and when fire was already in use, is known as the Old Stone Age or the **Paleolithic** period. Animals small and large were hunted and caught in various ways—by trapping them or by forcing them over a steep, deathly scarp, for example. Once killed, the carcasses would be butchered on the spot with the use of sharp-edged stone tools—those made of flint were the best—that could skin even thick-hided animals such as elephants and buffaloes. Because the stone tools would quickly become dull, the butchers constantly sharpened them by chipping off flakes to expose new edges. Many stone-tool sites contain hundreds of used tools and flakes. If such a site can be dated geologically, then we may conclude that the toolmakers were present there at that time, whether or not their bones remain.

The Paleolithic probably began about 2 million years ago, when *H. habilis* and *H. erectus* used stone tools as they spread across vast areas of Eurasia. In Western Europe, one of the oldest known sites lies in the Massif Central of France, where animal bones and tools have been found in a layer dated at 930,000 years. *Homo erectus* lived here then; we do not have the hominid bones to prove it, but we do have the tools.

The Paleolithic is divided into Lower, Middle, and Upper phases. The Lower Paleolithic, which lasted until about 200,000 years ago, includes the stone-tool workings of *H. habilis* and *H. erectus.* The Middle Paleolithic refers to the period from 200,000 to about 40,000 years ago, when archaic *H. sapiens* improved the tool-making technology and produced more efficient utensils. But much more diversification occurred during the Upper Paleolithic, from about 40,000 to 10,000 years ago, when anatomically modern *H. sapiens* made sophisticated stone tools as well as other implements fashioned from bone. Cutters, scrapers, spearpoints, harpoon heads, even needles have been found among the Upper Paleolithic tool kits left behind by early modern humans in Europe.

The Paleolithic is followed by the **Mesolithic**, the Middle Stone Age, the period when the most recent glaciers of the Plio-Pleistocene Ice Age advanced and retreated, causing major environmental changes in Europe. The environmental swings led to considerable cultural adaptation by the people who depended on the plant and animal life of the region. Stone and bone tools became still more specialized and sophisticated, and clothes were fashioned from animal skins. Communities grew larger, and their settlements began to take on some aspects of permanence. Animals became less plentiful, and there was greater dependence on plants and on fish.

The last phase of the Stone Age, the **Neolithic**, was a momentous period in the development of humanity, the time of animal domestication, the production of food rather than just the gathering of it, the artificial selection of certain plants and animals for propagation, and the diversification of tool-making industries. The weaving of textiles, smelting of metals, and making of building materials changed peoples' way of life in crucial respects. The New Stone Age was in fact a Neolithic Revolution, and anthropologists refer to it as such.

We should keep in mind that the transition from Mesolithic to Neolithic circumstances was not a regional phenomenon, but a local one. Just as there are technologically "developed" and "underdeveloped" societies today, so the Neolithic Revolution came earlier to some Eurasian communities of *H. sapiens* than to others. As we will note later, communities in certain areas progressed rapidly to become more diverse and culturally complex, while others remained for many centuries unaffected by the Neolithic transformation. So unlike the geologic time scale, which is as absolute as dating allows, the period of the Stone Age are relative. Indeed, some indigenous peoples, remote from the mainstream of modern times, continued to live very much like Stone Age peoples even after the Industrial Revolution. It was, of course, a matter of geography.

FACING THE CHALLENGE

When *Homo sapiens* began its momentous migration out of Africa, perhaps as long as 200,000 years ago, climatic swings were not the only challenge faced by the migrating groups that followed routes probably pioneered by Hominids before them. Even by geologic standards, 200,000 years is a substantial stretch of time, and chances are that our planet experienced some major events after our distant ancestors left their African home. Just as we are subject to earthquakes and volcanic eruptions, storms and floods, so were they—but their numbers were miniscule, and their preparedness minimal.

If theories about the geography of human evolution are correct, *H. sapiens* became familiar with such threats very early on. Humanity arose in the shadows of active volcanoes on the highlands of East Africa. Our ancestors endured eruptions, ashfalls, lahars, and other assaults. We know this because some of their oldest campgrounds have been found under lava and ash.

One of the gravest threats to human survival may have occurred about 73,500 years ago, when a gigantic volcanic eruption blew up the (now) Indonesian island of Sumbawa. This, the so-called Toba eruption, is by far the largest eruption known to have occurred over the past half million years. It was 1000 times as large as the Mount St. Helens eruption of 1980 and 100 times larger than the infamous 1883 eruption of Krakatoa. The Toba eruption threw a huge quantity of ash, dust, and rocks into the air—so much that the cloud of dust orbited the Earth, obscured the Sun, and created a prolonged series of **volcanic winters** in the years that followed. Scientists calculate that temperatures in the Northern Hemisphere were between 5°C and 15°C (11°F and 33°F) colder than they already were in the frosty middle latitudes, and overall global temperatures dropped by 3°C and 5°C (6°F and 11°F). Cold summers and frigid winters persisted for years, probably for decades.

The Toba eruption, as Figure 3-1 reminds us, occurred just after the start of an exceptionally cold phase of the Wisconsinan glaciation. Our migrating ancestors, therefore, faced a double threat, and it is believed that many communities succumbed. Anthropologists refer to the time following the Toba eruption as an "evolutionary bottleneck," because the corridors of survival were nearly closed off and *H. sapiens* (and their predecessors alike) suffered large numbers of deaths.

How far had migration carried *H. sapiens* when this cataclysmic event occurred? We do not yet know, but it is perhaps reasonable to assume, given the extraordinary cold to which the migrants were exposed after a lengthy and warm interglaciation, that those moving eastward were driven south: into

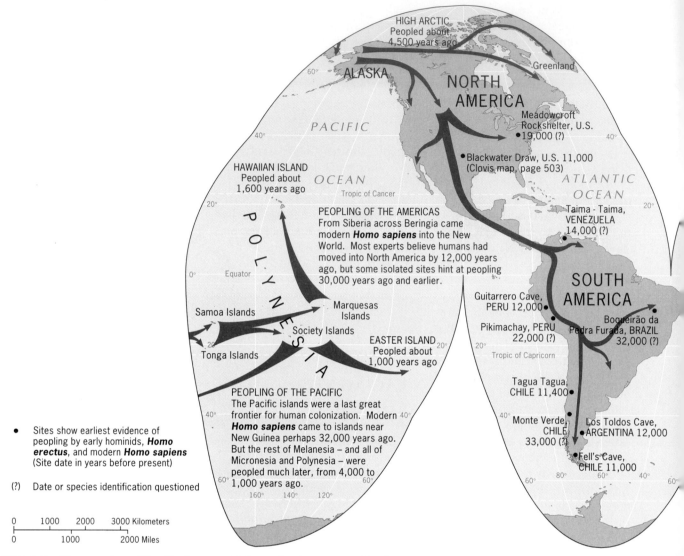

FIGURE 4–3 The peopling of the Earth: recent information is cartographically represented on a map published in the *National Geographic Magazine,* Vol. 174, No. 4, October, 1988, pp. 436–437.

the Indian peninsula, into Malaysia, perhaps even into Indonesia (the growth of the Wisconsinan glaciers lowered sealevel and connected many islands). That happens to be the approximate latitude of the Toba volcano, so their environment was severely affected. It is no exaggeration to say that, in the face of the twin threats of glaciation and eruption, humanity's very existence was in the balance.

It also is possible that the Toba eruption contributed to the demise of *H. sapiens'* competitors. While it probably is true that *H. sapiens* overpowered and eliminated Hominids and Neanderthals with whom they came into contact, nature may have lent a hand. If humans had difficulty surviving during the "evolutionary bottleneck," less adaptable contemporaries undoubtedly fared even worse.

As we note below, the timing and the routes of dispersal from Africa into Eurasia and beyond still are being reconstructed. Whenever we secure a fossil location and a reliable date, we should ask the geographical question: What was the environment like at the site, at the time? Eventually, the record will tell us how our ancestors and predecessors faced the challenge of changing climates and catastrophic events.

ROUTES OF DISPERSAL

All the evidence indicates that *H. erectus* never reached the Americas, so that its dispersal from Africa

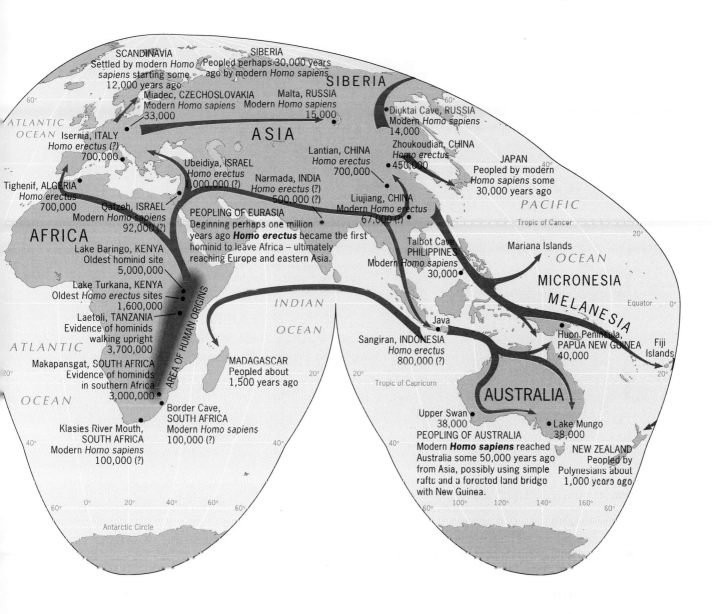

remained confined to the Eurasian landmass and the islands of present-day Indonesia as far east as Java. This is noteworthy because, as we noted, *H. erectus* is known to have lived at relatively high latitudes in eastern Asia as early as 500,000 years ago, which means that it experienced several warm interglaciations that must have opened the land route to America later used by *H. sapiens*. Apparently, *H. erectus* did not follow the retreating ice northward; in any case, the Americas lay untouched

by hominids. When *H. sapiens* entered the scene, its expansion, too, went no farther than Eurasia for tens of thousands of years.

BEYOND EURASIA

The past 100,000 years have witnessed the emergence and demise of the Neanderthals, the rise of modern *H. sapiens*, and the final act in the emigration process that started from Africa about a million years ago. Until perhaps 50,000 years ago, the entire drama of hu-

man evolution had played itself out on the Eurasian stage. But then began the last significant migrations of humans before the development of modern civilization.

Again we should view these movements in environmental context, although the sequence of events is far from clear. Possibly the invasion of Australia, from present-day Indonesia and New Guinea, happened first. Still another lowering of global sea level, resulting from an expansion of the glaciers during the last of the pre-Holocene

From the Field Notes

❝ In Auckland, New Zealand, the National Museum's Maori exhibit includes one of the Polynesians' oceangoing canoes that could accommodate as many as 200 rowers. Did Pacific seafarers reach South American shores thousands of years before East Asians crossed the Bering Strait? ❞

glaciations, facilitated entry into Australia and Tasmania across the Torres and Bass Straits. Recent research has put this immigration at 50,000 to 55,000 years ago. There is no record of *H. erectus* having reached Australia. Remarkably, there also is no record of modern *H. sapiens* having entered New Zealand until little more than 1000 years ago, when the Maori made their first landfalls on these islands.

The penetration of North America, which is comparatively recent, is still not well understood. It is almost inconceivable that the

Americas were unaffected by the momentous events occurring in Africa and later in Eurasia for millions of years, and that the first entrants were modern humans less than 40,000 years ago. As noted in Chapter 3, not only the timing but also the route of this immigration remains uncertain. The logical track is from Siberia, across the Bering Strait into Alaska, and then southward into North America, across the Middle American land bridge, and into South America. But the record of this path is weak. It has even been suggested that a lowered sea level

may have created an exposed, shelf-like platform adjacent to present-day Alaska and British Columbia, facilitating movement along the North American shore; but the evidence has been erased by a subsequent rise in sea level. It also has been suggested that the Americas were reached by East Asians across the Pacific Ocean. Most anthropologists and cultural geographers believe that the map drawn by the cultural geographer C. O. Sauer (Fig. 4-3) is essentially correct, and that future research will confirm the Alaskan route.

EARLY HUMANITY AND HUMAN GEOGRAPHY

When studying human geography, two realities should be uppermost in our minds: the impact of Plio-Pleistocene environmental changes on the evolution and distribution of our species, and the novelty of the modern human presence on Earth. Only one of our quintessential human qualities—walking upright—is several million years old. Other achievements, such as the use and control of fire, the hunting of animals and the gathering of other food resources, and the making of rudimentary tools, came much later. The story of this chapter begins 6 million years ago, but the key events in our human evolution occurred over the past 200,000 years, and many—the development of a large and complex brain, the use of sophisticated speech, and the capacity to symbolize—came even more recently. And despite these accomplishments, which happened not at once or in some sequence but as parts of a complex process in both time and place, we still were very much under nature's sway, even 15,000 years ago, when the glaciers were retreating once again and the Earth entered the present warm Holocene.

And in these 15 millennia, in that eyewink in Earth history, we have ended our dependence on niches and ranges, and have proven ourselves capable not only of conquering environmental limitations but also of destroying the environment itself. As we study the current growth of human population, our technological triumphs and convulsive conflicts, let us remember how recently we emerged from a primeval past.

KEY TERMS

Australopithecus
Eve Theory
Evolution
Hominids
Homo erectus
Homo habilis
Homo sapiens
Java Ape Man

Mesolithic
Neanderthals
Neolithic
Paleolithic
Peking Man
Taphonomy
Volcanic Winter

5

ORGANIZING HUMANITY

After more than 30 glaciations and ensuing deglaciations, and after more than 2.5 million years of environmental alternations, the present warm period opened much the same as preceding periods. Humans of the Paleolithic period (the earliest and longest stage of the Stone Age, marking the period when simple stone tools were made and fire was used) lived in scattered groups and depended on hunting and gathering for their survival. As had happened before, the retreat of the ice expanded living space and widened the range of environments confronting the moving bands. But there was no paucity of wildlife to be hunted, fish to be caught, or edible plants and fruits to be gathered. There is evidence that goods (such as cured animal skins for clothing, flint and obsidian weapons and tools, and foods) were traded. Nevertheless, a map of the human population of 12,000 years ago would show mostly small, isolated groups of people numbering perhaps 20 to 60 members, their cultures diverging as a result of contrasting ecological settings.

Although survival was the

Geographica

- The innovation of plant and animal domestication may have occurred nearly simultaneously in areas as far removed as the Middle East and Southeast Asia.

- The earliest states developed about 5500 years ago in the Middle East and southwestern Turkey.

- The First Agricultural Revolution's geographic expression was the Fertile Crescent.

- Human population numbers and pressure may have been the cause of the agricultural innovations that made the Holocene different from all previous interglaciations.

principal objective of those hunting-and-gathering communities, there *was* time for other things. From the cave-wall paintings of European Paleolithic groups, we have learned how and what the people hunted, which weapons were in use, and other aspects of their culture. In addition to art, there were local developments in language, religion, and custom (such as burial of the dead). Recent research shows that hunting (sometimes accompanied by deliberate burning of grassland or forest to drive herds of reindeer, bison, or other prey) often went far beyond what the community needed, and destroyed vast numbers of plains and forest animals. Something akin to the destruction of the present Amazon rainforest occurred as migrating, more numerous, and more efficient hunters exterminated whole species of animals, large and small, in North America, Eurasia, and Africa.

A DIFFERENT EPOCH

This picture of the early Holocene is not fundamentally different from earlier warm periods of the late Pleistocene; there seems to have been little to foreshadow the momentous events soon to come. But the Holocene proved to be unique for many reasons.

Long before the revolutionary changes of modern times began, some hunter-gatherer groups probably were using plants in ways not practiced before. The notion that useful plants could be protected by pulling weeds away from them added a new dimension of food production to hunter-gatherer clans. But a patch of food-producing plants could not move with nomadic communities, so the idea of plant care is likely to have taken hold around stable, long-term settlements, where food from other sources was assured.

PLANT DOMESTICATION

The simple caring for plants that yield desired products is not the same as **plant domestication** and

organized, planned farming, but it was an important, contributing idea. We should note that the inhabitants of western and central Europe and the immigrating Clovis-culture North Americans were not the only inhabitants of the northern landmasses, certainly not in Eurasia. Human groups lived under widely diverse environments, and they learned to exploit the opportunities of these various environments in diverse ways. The domestication of root crops, plants that grow as tubers in the tropics (such as manioc or cassava, yams, and sweet potatoes) is not the same as the sowing of seed for fields of barley or wheat under more temperate environments. So the domestication of plants took different paths in different places at different times—but it was a process unique to the Holocene, and one that was to transform patterns of livelihood.

Where did plant domestication arise? The cultural geographer C. O. Sauer, who spent a lifetime studying cultural origins and diffusion, suggested that southeastern Asia may have been the scene, more than 14,000 years ago, of the first

domestication of tropical plants. There, he argued, the combination of sedentary settlements, forest margins, and freshwater streams may have stimulted the earliest planned cultivation (Figure 5-1). A similar but later development may have taken place, he proposed, in northwestern South America.

The planned cultivation of seed plants is a more complex process, involving seed selection, sowing, watering, and well-timed harvesting. Again, the practice seems to have developed in more than one area and at different times. Some scholars believe that the Nile River Valley in North Africa was the scene of the first seed-plant domestication, but the majority view is that the crucial developments took place in southwestern Asia, along the rim of the basin of the two major rivers of present-day Iraq, the Tigris and the **Euphrates**. This marked the beginning of what has been called the First Agricultural Revolution, and its geographic expression was the **Fertile Crescent**. The grain crops, wheat and barley, grew in the warming southwest Asian climate. When rainfall diminished as

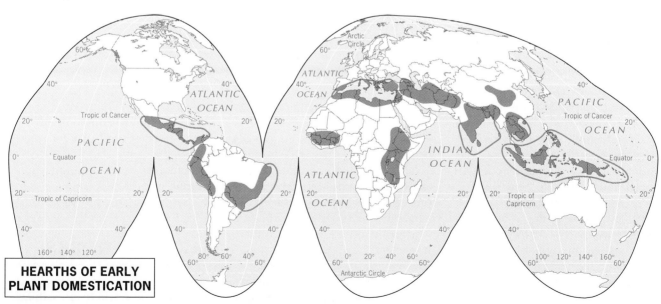

HEARTHS OF EARLY PLANT DOMESTICATION

FIGURE 5–1 Areas of earliest plant domestication, as postulated by C. O. Sauer. From J. E. Spencer & W. L. Thomas: *Introducing Cultural Geography* (New York: Wiley, 1973), p. 67.

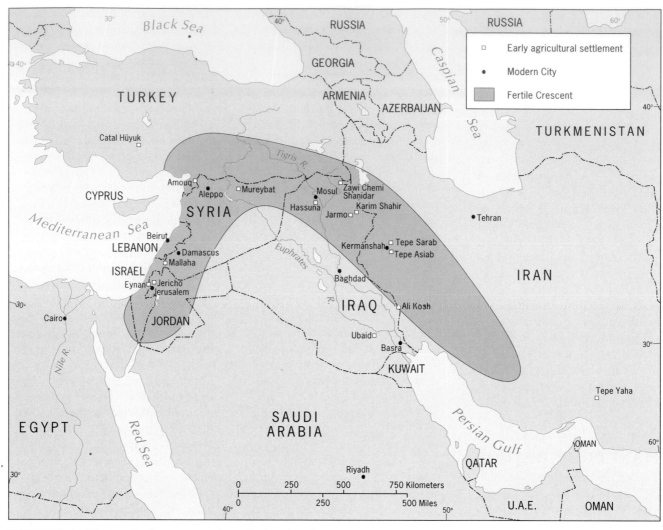

FIGURE 5–2 The Fertile Crescent, early agricultural settlements, and modern boundaries in southwest Asia.

the interglaciation wore on, the river-inundated plains of **Mesopotamia** provided alternate, irrigable fields for farming (Fig. 5-2). Food surpluses as had never been seen could now be stored for long-term distribution and use. The Agricultural Revolution heralded a social transformation.

ANIMAL DOMESTICATION

The domestication of animals appears to have taken place over the same period, also in different ways and different areas at different times. There was no shortage of species to use, and as with root-crop growing, the notion must have

presented itself quite naturally (see also Part 9, Chapter 27). Hungry animals foraged through garbage thrown near human settlements; orphaned young probably were adopted as pets; some wild animals were docile and easily penned up. Goats had been domesticated in the area of the Zagros Mountains as long as 10,000 years ago; sheep some 9500 years ago in Anatolia (Turkey); pigs and cattle shortly thereafter. The advantages of animal domestication—their use as beasts of burden, as a dependable meat source, and as providers of milk—stimulated the rapid diffusion of this idea throughout the inhabited world, and it gave the

sedentary farmers of southwestern Asia and elsewhere a new measure of security. Again, an idea that was probably not totally new to the Holocene (animals undoubtedly formed part of pre-Holocene human life as well) took on revolutionary form in the present epoch.

EARLY NETWORKS

The domestication of plants and animals made possible the stabilization of population over a large region for the first time in human history. A network of farm villages

FIGURE 5–3 The origins of what may be the world's oldest continuous civilization.

appeared across the area between the Mediterranean Sea, the Persian Gulf, the Caspian Sea, and the Black Sea about 10,000 years ago. These villages were not large by modern standards, but they contained hundreds of inhabitants, rather than the dozens in the nomadic hunter-gatherer settlements.

The implications of this transformation were far-reaching. In the emerging farm villages, there were people who were nonfarmers and who performed other work, including not only activities directly related to farming (toolmaking, bagging, transport) but also teaching, administration, and policing. Thus a social ladder, **social stratification**, developed. People in the villages became stratified into those with prestige, influence, and power (the *elite*), and lower classes engaged in production and provision.

And of course conflict and competition arose. Some villages were located advantageously and had more productive lands under their control; others were less fortunate. Stronger villages took control over weaker ones, and some of these stronger villages became regional centers. The transition from village to city was under way.

Just what stimulated the rise of cities in Southwest Asia is not yet certain. It may have been a combination of circumstances: prospering regional centers, strong militias, and the strength of numbers. Possibly the role of irrigation was crucial, because towns that controlled irrigation works could deny competitors water. Perhaps some villages grew stronger and larger because of technological inventions that enhanced their productivity and power. Some geographers believe that the rise of certain cities (and the decline of other places) was related to continuing climatic change. When the region's rainfall declined, towns on the Fertile Crescent's slopes, far from controllable river water, found themselves at a fatal disadvantage, leaving the river-basin towns to dominate the area. Whatever the cause(s), the spiral of urbanization had begun, eventually affecting all humanity, everywhere on Earth.

Although there can be no doubt regarding the primacy of the Southwest Asian region in the development of sedentary and irrigated agriculture, and the rise of villages and towns, we should remember that the dispersal of humans not only into Europe but also into East Asia, Australia, and more recently, into North and South America, had already taken place. We have been considering the period from about 10,000 to 5000 years ago, and important advances were being made elsewhere as well. In Africa, the Nile River Valley was a ribbon of agriculture. Rice-farming villages stood in Southeast Asia. And in China, momentous developments were occurring in the basin of the Chang and the Yellow (Huang) Rivers, where rice and millet farmers supplied villages in networks not totally dissimilar from those of Southwest Asia. On the North China Plain, there soon developed the historic heart of China, the Shang Dynasty, with its capital at Anyang and its core area in the confluence of the Huang and Wei Rivers (Fig. 5-3).

EARLY STATES

Even after the rise of the Fertile Crescent's villages, it would not yet have been possible to draw a map of the next stage of regional organization: the state. There were networks of farm settlements and established trade routes; fields and pastures marked the countryside, and some villages were growing larger. But political states, with capitals and boundaries and military forces, had not yet developed.

This next stage of human organization was not long in coming. The cities of the region (see box, "Ancient Babylon") became centers not only of political power and economic strength, but of religious dominance as well. Although there is no scholarly unanimity on the subject, there clearly is a relationship between the rise of powerful cities and the emergence of large and durable states. We will discuss the character of ancient cities in Part 10, but it is noteworthy that momentous politico-geographical developments followed the emergence of large cities. The **Sumerian state** arose in the lower reaches of Mesopotamia about the same time as Egypt was unified politically for the first time (Fig. 5-4). The state of Uruk developed on the southwest slopes of the Zagros Mountains in what is presently Iran. These states arose between 6000 and 5000 years ago, soon to be followed by Babylon (north of Sumer) and Assyria (a Tigris Valley state). Later the Hittites forged a state in Anatolia, but by this time Southwest Asia no longer had a monopoly over state development. Large and durable states had arisen in the Indus Valley (in present-day Pakistan) and in China, and the stage was set for the rise of Greek and Roman urban and political culture.

As we know, not only urban life but also the state idea spread worldwide, so that the planet's living space today is compartmentalized into over 200 states, dependencies, and other bounded territories. From a comparatively small number of migrating hunter-gatherer groups that just 12,000 years ago represented the most complex spatial-organizational system on Earth, we have reached a point where theirs is the simplest form, retained now by just a few surviving hunter-gatherer groups such as the San of Botswana's Kalahari Desert.

IMPRINTS OF ORGANIZATION

Time and again, over the past million years, deglaciation was followed by sustained interglaciation, and in the warmth of those interglaciations our hominid and human ancestors spread far and wide. They made their marks on the landscape: they burned forests, killed wildlife, built encampments, inhabited caves, and in some instances buried their dead. Their bone and stone tools are found, sometimes in large quantities, at fossil sites. But until the present interglaciation began, around 12,000 years ago, our ancestors had left only the slightest imprint on the Earth as a whole.

Indeed, the Holocene began with little indication that *this* interglaciation would be different. Perhaps this was so because, for the first time, humans living in more or less stable communities found themselves having to adapt to changing environments in various settings. People were living, for example, in the tundras and grasslands of northern Europe, following the migratory herds and killing for meat whenever they

ANCIENT BABYLON

Babylon was one of the largest and most powerful cities of antiquity, the capital of a powerful Mesopotamian state and the headquarters of formidable rulers, including Nebuchadnezzar's dynasty.

Situated on the Euphrates River in present-day Iraq, Babylon endured for nearly 2000 years (from 4100 B.P.) as a walled, fortified center endowed with temples, towers, and palaces. A bridge of stone and wood crossed the river, and docks accommodated the many boats that carried goods to and from what was, at the time, the world's largest city. Rising above the townscape was the tallest structure in Mesopotamian cities of the time: the **ziggurat**, or tower of the great temple. When Nebuchadnezzar ruled Babylon, he oversaw the building of the highest *ziggurat* yet constructed, to mark the temple of Marduk. The tower's base was 90 m (300 ft) square, and its height, in seven levels, reached more than 90 m as well. The uppermost level of the Babylonian *ziggurat* consisted of a magnificent temple glazed sky-blue. On the flat floodplain of the Euphrates, this symbol of power could be seen for many miles.

Babylon was laid out in a grid pattern, with wide and magnificently decorated processional roadways. Beyond the city's fortified walls lay a second line of defense, and between these were irrigated fields. Here, too, lay an artificial, terraced hill built and planted over an elaborate, vaulted foundation. When the Greeks of Alexander the Great conquered the city in 331 B.C., they called these "Hanging Gardens" one of the Seven Wonders of the World.

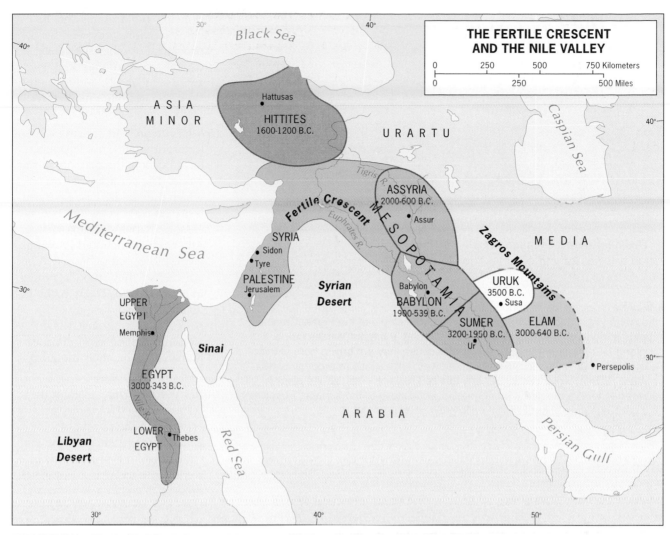

FIGURE 5-4 Ancient states in Mesopotamia and adjacent areas, and in the Nile Valley.

needed it. But the warming climate caused a northward shift of the tundras and the grasslands, and forests of pine, oak, and birch developed in their place. Some human groups moved northward, but others adapted to this new environment, where hunting was a more difficult proposition. Those who stayed learned to make new weapons, better suited to hunting in the woods. They also (their fossil teeth indicate) changed their diets. They collected wild grains, caught fish, and gathered mollusks. Importantly, they began to fashion better stone axes and were able to cut down trees. Now they could build log houses and hollow out trees for ca-

noes. Settlements took on the look of permanence.

But even then, toward the end of the Mesolithic (using this term as it applies to Europe and the Middle East), there really was no indication of what lay ahead. Had the Holocene interglaciation then come to a close, there would have been little to differentiate it from previous warm phases. Human communities remained small, and most still were migratory.

Human numbers, too, remained very small. There is no consensus because the data can be extrapolated in different ways, but approximately at the beginning of the Neolithic, some 10,000 years

ago, when animal and plant domestication commenced, the Earth's human population almost certainly was below six million. Although they had spread far and wide, humans occupied just a tiny fraction of the Earth's surface.

And yet the Holocene epoch witnessed the transformation of the world. Several theories have been proposed to explain why it happened *this* time; after all, humans were confronted by environmental change during previous interglaciations, and nothing comparable happened. In truth, there still is no satisfactory answer. Some historical geographers suggest that it was the result of comparatively rapid popu-

From the Field Notes

❝ Were it not for the telephone wires, this photo could represent a scene five thousand years ago. Short-stemmed wheat, the staple of the Fertile Crescent, stands at right; grapevines are in the foreground. If the grapevines do not conform to our image of neat rows, it is because they are grown here in the eastern Mediterranean in a time-honored way. High winds (a property of this climatic regime) would blow over any trellised rows of vines, so the plant is allowed to form a tangled knot of gnarled wood close to the surface, from which the grape-bearing shoots sprout each growing season. ❞

lation growth in the Middle East, which pushed people into less hospitable environs where they had to adapt or succumb. Adaptation led to animal and plant domestication, and this set in motion the First Agricultural Revolution with all it entailed. When we try to identify ways in which the early Holocene differed from the previous interglaciation (to help explain why matters took a new course this time), population contrasts do stand out. *Homo sapiens* was not nearly as numerous, nor as widely dispersed, during the previous warm phase.

Yet there were other areas where population numbers, at least in some locales, were substantial too—but where no revolutionary changes occurred. The special combination of conditions that was to propel the world into its modern age seems to have existed in but a few places. In that respect, the modern world still has vestiges of the old: even in this age of globali-

zation, there still are isolated peoples living a Neolithic existence.

As we approach the end of the Holocene, consider the human imprint on the Earth:

Farming. The First Agricultural Revolution has been followed by two more, one organizational and the other (still in progress) genetic. Entire regions of the Earth have been plowed, terraced, fenced, and carpeted by crops; huge herds of livestock graze on fields from Tierra del Fuego to Finland. No human activity transforms as much of the Earth's surface as farming does.

Administration. Whatever the rubric (politics, government, etc.), the world has been compartmentalized into more than 200 countries and other entities, heirs to the state idea that first arose about 5500 years ago. The modern state is a complex phenomenon, but on the ground its

principal political imprints include its capital city, its provincial or other subsidiary capitals, its heartland or core area (see Part 12), and its boundaries, the last often marked by walls, fences, or posts.

Urbanization. In a matter of centuries, urbanites, not villagers, have become the majority in this world. The earliest cities in which the Middle East gave rise less than 6000 years ago had successors (Babylon, Damascus, Athens) that anchored growing civilizations, but until the twentieth century they stood as rarities in a rural world. Today many individual cities house more people than entire nations do. Nothing symbolizes Holocene humanity as much as the great cities of modern time.

Industrialization. Even in the context of the Holocene (as opposed to the period of *H. sapiens'* presence or hominid evolution), industrialization as we know it today is a late development that changed the world. Industries existed 6000 years ago, and they spread worldwide; "preindustrial" India and Japan had major complexes of workshops that produced goods ranging from textiles to ceramics. The Industrial Revolution occurred little more than two centuries ago; it transformed manufacturing and incalculably expanded the demand for natural resources. From the great industrial complexes to the slag heaps at the mines, industrialization is etched in the landscape.

Transportation. Another symbol of humanity's Holocene imprint is the global network of transportation and communication routes and lines that crisscross the Earth's surface. Railroads, highways, ports, pipelines, airfields, power lines, and other attributes of the transportation age bear tangible witness to modern civilization; not even a new glaciation could erase all the evidence.

Population. Overshadowing all else is the almost unimaginable expansion of human population during the Holocene, especially during the epoch's most recent centuries. Today, *every month*, the Earth adds more people to its numbers than existed on the planet when the Holocene began. From 6 million the population has grown to 6 billion, a thousandfold increase, most of which has taken place in less than two centuries. In Part Two we begin our geographic look at the modern world by turning our attention to the population question.

KEY TERMS

Animal Domestication
Babylon
Euphrates
Fertile Crescent
Mesopotamia
Plant Domestication
Social Stratification
Sumerian State
Ziggurat

Shanghai's Nanjing Road mirrors China's massive population.

PART TWO

POPULATION AND SPACE

At Issue

The world's growing human population is poised to pass the six-billion mark, four times the number just one century ago. The rate of overall growth is declining, but the actual increase continues to exceed 90 million *per year*. Reducing this annual increment is an objective advocated vigorously by the wealthier, low-growth, Western countries. Improved living standards, they argue, can be achieved only by controlling the population explosion. Some poorer countries, notably China, have adopted policies designed to reduce their population growth rates. But a United Nations world population conference in 1994 revealed some deep disagreements among the participants. Many Islamic countries argued that population control of the kind advocated by Western nations violated Muslim precepts. (They found support in the Vatican, also represented at the conference.) Other countries argued that the high rate of consumption in the rich Western countries constitutes a larger problem than rapid population growth in poorer regions. In a lifetime, an American will consume 30 times as much as, say, a Bangladeshi of the world's food and other resources. So who should inhibit population growth? Should lowering the world's population growth rate be a global objective at all?

6

POPULATION: LOCATION, DISTRIBUTION, DENSITY

It is appropriate to study the growth and spread of the Earth's human population near the beginning of our journey, because virtually all else that follows flows from it. What lessons can we learn from population expansion during the twentieth century, and what do these lessons portend for the twenty-first?

What lies ahead is a study in staggering contrasts. Not only is the world's population unevenly distributed over the available land area of our globe (which constitutes below 30 percent of the total surface), but rates of growth differ from place to place. Often the areas that seem already overpopulated have the highest growth rates, dooming any hope for the improvement of living standards. In Bangladesh, an Iowa-sized country with more than 120 million inhabitants, people crowd on slivers of sand banks along the deltaic coast, where they face the wrath of death-dealing cyclones. In 1991, such a cyclone

Geographica

- **The world population is currently growing by about 100 million per year; the bulk of this growth is occurring in the world's poorer countries.**

- **The world's three largest population concentrations all lie on the Eurasian landmass, and the smallest of the three is the most highly developed and urbanized.**

- **Population data often are unreliable because of the high cost and organizational challenges of census taking.**

- **Population density can be measured on the basis of several different criteria, revealing contrasting aspects of a country's demography.**

killed more than 100,000 people, but as soon as the floodwaters had receded, the people came back to their hazardous abode. Already one of the world's poorest countries, Bangladesh adds about 3 million people to its population *every year*. Every 5 years, Bangladesh adds as

many people to its total population as inhabit all of Australia.

The fates and fortunes of regions and countries have been tied to their resources and environments, but in large measure they also are tied to their population numbers. Education, health conditions, food availability, and other elements of the quality of life are difficult to improve when the number of people is growing rapidly. This is a problem faced by many governments today, and as we will see later in Chapter 8, various solutions to population dilemmas have been tried in different parts of the world. Some have been very successful; others have failed almost totally. From the successes, we may learn how the world of the next century might cope with one its greatest challenges; the failures will serve as a warning of the risks.

ONE HUNDRED CENTURIES OF EVOLUTION

Humanity's modern evolution, as has been noted, has occurred during approximately the last 100 centuries. In those 10,000 years, people learned to domesticate livestock, cultivate crops, exploit resources, harness energy, build cities, create industries, combat diseases, and venture into space. Also during that period, the earth's human population increased from a few million to an anticipated 6.3 billion by the year 2000 (see box, "How Reliable Are Population Data?").

This expansion of human population did not occur at a slow or a steady rate. After nearly 99 centuries of relatively slow growth, the last century has witnessed an unprecedented explosion of population, and there are few signs that this process is slowing down. During the mid-1990s, about 100 million people were being added to our already crowded world every year—over 8 million per month, more than 270,000 per day, over 11,000 every hour. Furthermore, most of the world's newborn arrive

HOW RELIABLE ARE POPULATION DATA?

When the United States conducted its periodic population **census** in 1990 and the results began to be published, there was an uproar from several quarters. Mayors of major cities insisted that the census had undercounted their populations, to great financial disadvantage during coming years. Governors complained that undependable state figures could cost their states representation in Washington. Independent observers found that the census had been carried out well, but that as many as 2 million people may have been missed.

If a comparatively prosperous country such as the United States has problems mounting an accurate census, imagine what is faced in less-well-off countries. The cost, organization, and reporting of a census is more than many countries can afford or handle.

World population is monitored by several agencies. Official statistics, assembled and reported by national governments, are recorded by the United Nations. The U.S. Census Bureau also gathers global population data. The World Bank and the Population Reference Bureau are among other organizations that conduct research and report on world population.

The population data published by these and other organizations frequently are inconsistent. In this and the following chapters, it has been necessary to select those figures deemed most nearly correct, based on available sources. If you examine various statistical tables in detail, inconsistencies will inevitably emerge. Growth rates and other vital statistics, data on food availability, health conditions, and incomes are at times informed estimates rather than hard facts. Thus you should consider the figures used in these chapters to have been carefully assessed, but they are still subject to substantial margins of error.

in areas of the world where health care facilities are inadequate, food is insufficient, diets are deficient, and other conditions are inimical to their well-being or even their survival.

Why have such circumstances not contributed to a sharp decline in the growth of population? If people are faced with starvation in parts of Asia and areas of Africa, and others are malnourished even in the Western Hemisphere (in Haiti, for example), why does the population explosion of the twentieth century continue? Will the rate of population growth eventually decline? Can new sources of food be found and developed? These and

other questions will be addressed in the following pages.

OUR INTERCONNECTED WORLD

In the United States and Canada, and in the Western world generally, the problems confronting billions of people elsewhere seem remote and unfamiliar. In Europe, the memories of hunger that afflicted millions during the Second World War are fading rapidly. In North America, there still are substantial numbers of people (especially among the poor and the elderly) whose living standards, including daily nutrition, are inadequate. But population growth is not a key factor in the persistence of these circumstances. In the United States, population relocation rather than population growth produces troubles such as deteriorating urban living conditions, worse pollution, larger traffic jams, and longer waiting lines.

Nevertheless, our future is inextricably tied to those other parts of the world where population growth continues to be rapid, with all the consequences this entails. No country can exist in isolation, no matter how varied and rich its resources. Although the global food situation has dramatically improved over the past decade, the United States and other comparatively rich countries still export grains and other foods to countries that cannot adequately feed themselves. Such food exports (from the U.S. to Egypt, for example) are not just humanitarian gestures. They are good business as well as good politics. Food shortages lead to social disorder, and social disorder in distant countries can lead to costly involvement. In 1992, famine (caused by a combination of crop failures and clan conflict) afflicted Somalia, and televised reports on the suffering of millions contributed to the U.S. decision to intervene. This intervention, in cooperation with the United Nations, was intended to relieve the suffering of the Somalis—but it had disastrous consequences for the American and other U.N. forces. Thousands of Somalis were saved from starvation, but dozens of U.S. and other U.N. rescuers were killed by Somalis bent on political power.

Would Somalia have been better off with fewer inhabitants? In truth, Somalia's problems were only partially caused by food shortages; Somali clans were ruthless in denying food to rivals. But Somalia's population grows more than four times as fast as the U.S. population, and is among the fastest growing in the world. Curbing that growth rate,

Western countries argue, is a way to give food production a chance to catch up with the numbers to be fed.

The good news is that there are fewer cases such as Somali and Egypt than there were just 20 years ago. As we will see in more detail later, world food production has substantially caught up with population growth, and if distribution systems were better, no one on this planet would need die of starvation. Local or national conflicts, such as those experienced in recent years by Ethiopia, Sudan, Liberia, Rwanda, Afghanistan, and other strife-torn countries, have more to do with death by starvation than overall population numbers. Just three decades ago, population experts predicted mass starvation in India, Bangladesh, and other countries with large populations and high growth rates. Today, India is able to feed itself, and Bangladesh is very nearly able to do so—with populations nearly double those of 30 years past.

It always is possible, of course, that population growth will again outstrip the Earth's capacity to produce what is required. Those experts who saw disaster coming say that the current situation will not last, and they may be right. A serious environmental perturbation (for example, the failure of India's monsoon in several successive years) could create new crises. But at present, food supply is adequate, even if diets in many parts of the world should be better balanced. Where people are not fed, the causes often are political or strategic. Some African regimes have stopped food convoys from reaching refugees they regard as enemies. In the early 1990s, U.N. embargoes of Iraq and Haiti, designed to attain political ends, created malnutrition and hunger.

Even China has defeated hunger. Before the middle of this century,

China was a country of fewer than 350 million people, where famines were frequent and starvation was a constant threat. True, China had been ravaged by war for many years, but even during earlier periods of comparative stability, the specter of starvation always loomed. Today, China has more than 1.2 billion people, and widespread famines no longer occur. Certainly, there is local hunger in China, and diets generally are not as well balanced as would be desirable. However, the population has reasonable assurance that food will be available on a regular basis. This was accomplished by a sweeping reconstruction of China's rural economy, a reorganization that was part of the communist program after Mao Zedong took control in 1949. Many aspects of that reorganization were draconian and caused terrible hardships, often unnecessarily. The overall result of China's reconstruction, however, was the defeat of famine—even while the population more than doubled.

And yet China embarked on a strict population-control policy (see Chapter 8) even when its food battle was being won. Why? The answer lies in another arena altogether. While hunger and starvation no longer dominate population-growth concerns, other issues have come to the fore. One such issue is living standards. China's regime, along with the governments of more democratic countries, realized that material progress would be slowed, if not stopped, by unchecked population growth. To adequately house, educate, employ, and retire people, economies need to be able to catch up a bit every year, to make things better over the long run. But if population growth keeps outstripping economic growth, stagnation—or worse—results.

Another issue involves social stability, which is so important for

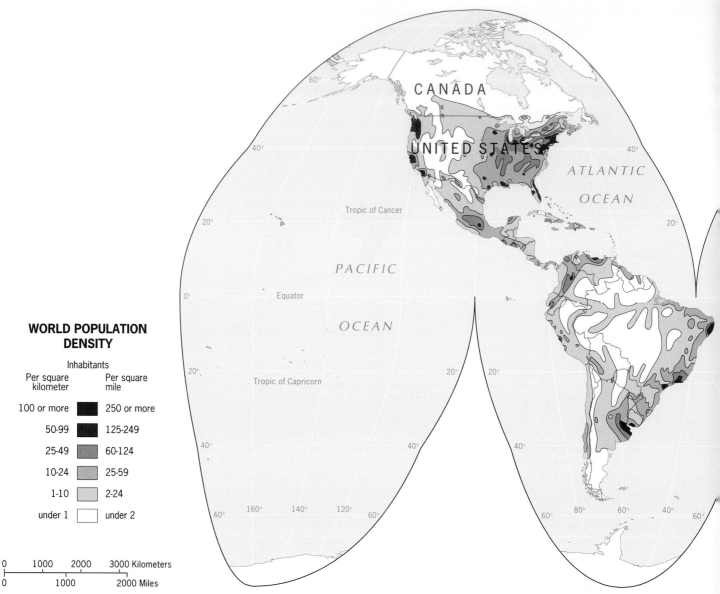

WORLD POPULATION DENSITY

Inhabitants

Per square kilometer		Per square mile
100 or more	███	250 or more
50-99	███	125-249
25-49	▓▓▓	60-124
10-24	▒▒▒	25-59
1-10	░░░	2-24
under 1	☐	under 2

| 0 | 1000 | 2000 | 3000 Kilometers |
| 0 | | 1000 | 2000 Miles |

FIGURE 6–1 World population density is mapped at six levels. Vast regions of the world, in all latitudes, remain sparsely inhabited or virtually empty.

security and economic progress. Rapid population growth creates large numbers of young people in a population compared to those of middle age and older. If jobs cannot be found for many of these younger people, unrest may result—disorder that can be severe enough to threaten the future of the state. In some Muslim countries today (Muslim populations are among the world's fastest growing), millions of young people, unable to find work and without a place in society, are blaming their governments and are turning to religious fundamentalists in their frustration. The consequences, as in the case of Algeria, can be disastrous.

The population question, therefore, has many sides, and food supply is only one of them. Most—though not all—scholars who study population issues agree that slow-ing the population spiral is essential for the future well-being of the world.

WHERE PEOPLE CLUSTER

For many and obvious reasons—history, terrain, climate, soil, water, accessibility, and so on—world

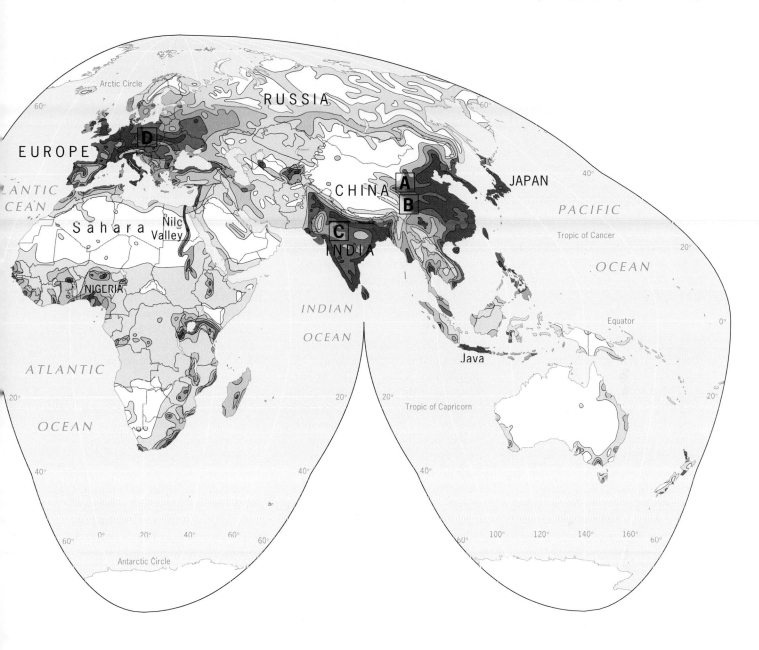

population is not distributed evenly over the continents. Even the most densely inhabited countries still have comparatively empty areas. As our map (Fig. 6-1) shows, parts of western China are as empty as the Sahara. In India, where crowding is such a serious problem, you can still travel through miles of sparsely peopled territory. The map depicts population distribution through levels of shading to indicate density per unit area: the darker the colors,

the larger the number of people clustered in an average unit area.

EAST ASIA

The most extensive area of such dark shading lies in **East Asia**, principally in China, but extending into Korea and Vietnam and "leapfrogging" to Japan. More than a quarter of the entire world's population is concentrated in this East Asian cluster, over 1.2 billion in China alone.

Observation of the dimensions of the East Asian population cluster reveals that it adjoins the Pacific Ocean from Korea to Vietnam, and that the number of people per unit area tends to decline from this coastal zone toward the interior. Also visible are several ribbon-like extensions of dense population, penetrating the interior (Fig. 6-1, A and B). A reference to a physical map of East Asia reveals that these extensions represent populations clustered in the basins and low-lands of China's major rivers. This serves to remind us that the great majority of people in East Asia are farmers, not city dwellers. True, there are great cities in China, and some of them, such as Shanghai and Beijing, rank among the largest in the world. However, the total population of these and other cities is far outnumbered by the farmers, who need the river valleys' soils, the life-giving rains, and the moderate temperatures to produce crops of wheat and rice to feed not only themselves, but also those in the cities and towns.

SOUTH ASIA

The second major concentration of world population also lies in Asia, and it displays many similarities to that of East Asia. At the heart of this South Asia cluster lies India, but the concentration extends also into Pakistan and Bangladesh and onto the island of Sri Lanka. Again, note the riverine and coastal orientation of the most densely inhabited zones, and the finger-like extension of dense population in northern India (Fig. 6–1, C). This is one of the great concentrations of people on earth, on the plain of the Ganges River.

The South Asia population cluster numbers as many as 1.4 billion people. Our map shows how sharply this region is marked off by physical barriers: the Himalaya Mountains rise to the north above the Ganges lowland, and the desert takes over west of the Indus River Valley in Pakistan. This is a confined region with a population that continues to grow rapidly. The capacity of the region to support this population under present sociopolitical circumstances has, by all estimates, already been exceeded. As in East Asia, the overwhelming majority of the people here are farmers, but in South Asia the pressure on the land is even greater. In

Bangladesh, more than 120 million people are crowded into an area about the size of Iowa. Nearly all of these people are farmers, and even fertile Bangladesh has areas that cannot sustain many people. Over large parts of Bangladesh the rural population density is between 3000 and 5000 people per square mile. To compare, the 1990 population of Iowa was about 3 million people, and less than 40 percent (according to the census) lived on the land, rather than in cities and towns. And the rural density of Iowa was 30 people per square mile.

EUROPE

Further inspection of Figure 6-1 reveals that the third-ranking population cluster also lies in Eurasia—and at the opposite end from China. An axis of dense population extends from the British Isles into Russia, and includes large parts of Germany, Poland, Ukraine, and Belarus; it also includes the Netherlands and Belgium, parts of France, and northern Italy. This European cluster contains about 700 million inhabitants, which puts it in a class with the South Asia concentration—but there the similarity ends. A comparison of the population and physical maps indicates that in **Europe**, terrain and environment appear to have less to do with population distribution than in the two Asian cases. See, for example, that lengthy extension marked D in Figure 6-1, which protrudes far into Russia. Unlike the Asian extensions, which reflect fertile river valleys, the European population axis relates to the orientation of Europe's coal-fields, the power resources that fired the Industrial Revolution. If you look more closely at the physical map, you will note that comparatively dense population occurs even in mountainous, rugged country, for example, along the boundary zone between Poland and its neighbors to the south. In

Asia, there is much more correspondence between coastal and river lowlands, and high population density than there generally is in Europe.

Another contrast lies in the number of Europeans who live in cities and towns. Far more than in Asia, the European population cluster is constituted by numerous cities and towns, many of them products of the Industrial Revolution. In Germany, 90 percent of the people live in such urban places; in the United Kingdom, also 90 percent; and in France, 73 percent. With so many people concentrated in the cities, the rural countryside is more open and sparsely populated than in East and South Asia, where about 30 percent of the people reside in cities and towns.

The three world population concentrations discussed (East Asia, South Asia, and Europe) account for over 4 billion of the world's approximately 6 billion people. Nowhere else on the globe is there a population cluster with dimensions that are even half of any of these. Look at the dimensions of the landmasses in Figure 6-1 and consider that the populations of South America, Africa, and Australia, combined, barely exceed that of India alone.

NORTH AMERICA

The next-ranking cluster, comprising the east-central United States and southeastern Canada, is only about one-quarter the size of the smallest of the Eurasian concentrations. As Figure 6-1 shows, the **North American region** does not have the large, contiguous high-density zones of Europe or East and South Asia.

The North American population cluster displays European characteristics and even outdoes Europe in some respects. Like the European region, much of the population is concentrated in several major cities, while the rural areas remain relatively sparsely populated. The major focus of the North America cluster lies in the urban complex along the eastern seaboard, from Boston to Washington, which includes New York, Philadelphia, and Baltimore. This great urban agglomeration is called **Megalopolis** by urban geographers, who predict that it is only a matter of time before the whole area coalesces into an enormous megacity. However, there are other urban foci in this region: Chicago lies at the heart of one, and Detroit and Cleveland anchor a second. If you study Figure 6-1 carefully, you will note other prominent North American cities standing out as small areas of high-density population, including Pittsburgh, St. Louis, and Minneapolis–St. Paul.

ELSEWHERE

Further examination of Figure 6-1 leads us to recognize substantial population clusters in Southeast Asia. It is appropriate to describe these as discrete clusters, for the map confirms that they are actually a set of nuclei, rather than a contiguous population concentration. Largest among these nuclei is the Indonesian island of Djawa (Java), with more than 120 million inhabitants. Elsewhere in the region, populations cluster in the lowlands of major rivers, for example, the Mekong. Neither these river valleys nor the rural surroundings of the cities have population concentrations comparable to those of either China to the north or India to the west, and under normal circumstances Southeast Asia is able to export rice to its hungrier neighbors. Decades of strife, however, have disrupted the region to such a degree that its productive potential has not been attained.

South America, Africa, and Australia do not sustain population concentrations comparable to those

we have considered. Subsaharan Africa's 600 million inhabitants cluster in above-average densities in West Africa (where Nigeria has a population of some 100 million) and in a zone in the east, extending from Ethiopia to South Africa. Only in North Africa is there an agglomeration comparable to the crowded riverine plains of Asia: the Nile Valley and Delta, which has over 60 million residents. Importantly, it is the pattern of the Nile agglomeration—not the dimensions—that resembles Asia. As in East and South Asia, the Nile Valley and Delta teem with farmers who cultivate every foot of the rich and fertile soil. However, the Nile's gift is minuscule compared to its Asian equivalents. The Ganges, Chang Jiang (Yangtze) and Huang He (Yellow) Rivers' lowlands contain many times the number of inhabitants than those who manage to eke out a living along the Nile.

The large light-shaded spaces in South America and Australia, and the peripheral distribution of the modest populations of these continents, suggest that here remains space for the world's huge numbers. And indeed, South America could probably sustain more than its present 330 million, if reforms in land ownership and use could take place. At present, while South America as a whole is not one of the world's hungry regions, there are, nevertheless, areas where poverty and malnutrition occur. Northeast Brazil is especially troubled economically, and certainly South America's capacity will be increasingly tested.

This raises an issue that is crucial in any study of population density and the capacity of a country to support its people: the level of technology that country has reached. You will note that Japan, a comparatively small island country (small compared to Australia, at least) has a population in excess of 125 million. Its population density

is at least as great as that of parts of China and India, but its farmlands are quite limited, not only by the size of the country but also by its mountainous character. What makes so large a population cluster in Japan possible—and indeed, well-fed and prosperous—is Japan's technological prowess, its industrial capacity, and its money-producing exports. Japan imports raw materials from all over the world, converts these materials into finished products in its factories, and exports the products to most parts of the globe. With the income from these exports, Japan can buy the food from the world markets that it cannot produce at home. Thus it is not enough to say that a country cannot support a certain population. We should qualify this by saying that under the present conditions of technology and political economy, it can or cannot support a given population depending on its status in the world market. True, Australia could not find a place for tens of millions of Chinese farmers. However, if tens of millions of Japanese came to Australia with their skills, technologies, factories, and international connections, Australia would be quite capable of accommodating them—and many more.

DISTRIBUTION AND DENSITY

In our discussion of world population distribution, we have used **population density** figures as the measure. On the face of it, this is a good index to use when comparing world areas. From each country's national census we obtain the total population. The country's area is a matter of record, and all that is required is to calculate the number of people per unit area (per square mile or kilometer) in the world's countries.

However, we already are aware—and Figure 6-1 reminds us—that the people of any country are not evenly distributed over the national territory. Thus the result of any calculation may be misleading. The United States, with 3,787,425 square miles (9,809,430 square kilometers) had a 1995 population of 263 million, and its average population density would, therefore, be figured as 69 per square mile or 27 per square kilometer.* This is the **arithmetic density** of the United States, and this is the figure that appears alongside those enormously high averages for Asian countries, such as Bangladesh (2,144 per square mile; 828 per square kilometer), Japan (859/331), India (752/290), and others. These averages do not, however, take account of the internal clustering of people within these countries. In the case of the United States, the average fails to reflect the emptiness of Alaska, the sparseness of population in much of the West, or the concentration of people in the eastern cities. As an even clearer example of the misleading nature of average density figures, consider the case of Egypt, with over 61 million inhabitants. As noted earlier, nearly all these people live in the Nile Valley and Delta. However, Egypt's total area is 386,660 square miles (about 1 million square kilometers), so the average density is about 160 per square mile or 61 per square kilometer. Obviously, the figure is rather meaningless when all those

TABLE 6–1	Population Densities for Selected Countries, 1995			
Country	1995 Population (millions)	Area (thousand sq mi/km)	Arithmetic Density (sq mi/km)	Physiologic Density (sq mi/km)
Egypt	61.9	386.7/1001.6	160/61	7973/3070
Japan	125.2	145.7/377.4	859/331	6770/2613
Netherlands	15.5	15.9/41.2	974/376	4425/1708
Bangladesh	119.2	55.6/144.0	2144/828	3601/1391
Colombia	37.7	439.7/1138.8	85/33	1687/651
India	930.6	1237.1/3204.1	752/290	1455/562
Nigeria	101.2	356.7/923.9	285/110	856/331
Argentina	34.6	1068.3/2766.9	32/13	673/260
United States	263.2	3787.4/9809.4	69/27	348/134

Sources: Calculated from World Population Data Sheet published by the Population Reference Bureau, Inc., from data on agriculture in the Encyclopaedia Britannica *Book of the Year* 1995, and from the United Nations Food and Agriculture Organization (FAO) *Production Yearbook* 1988. Note that population data in this table may not correspond with statistics drawn from other sources. (See box, "How Reliable Are Population Data?")

people are crowded onto the Nile's irrigable land and cultivable soils and the rest of the country is desert! It has been estimated that 98 percent of Egypt's population occupies just 3 percent of the country's total area.

ARITHMETIC AND PHYSIOLOGIC DENSITIES

Can we arrive at a more meaningful index of population density in individual countries? Yes—by relating the total population to the amount of cultivated land in the country, rather than to its whole area (see Table 6-1). In those overpopulated Asian countries, after all, it is the arable (farmable) land that matters, not the dry areas or the inhospitable mountains. Instead of the arithmetic density, we calculate the **physiologic density**, the number of people per unit area of agriculturally productive land. in the case of Egypt, while the arithmetic density is 160 per square mile (61 per square kilometer), the physiologic density is nearly *8000* people per cultivable square mile (3070 per

square kilometer). In Japan, the physiologic density also is very high: 6770 per square mile (2613 per square kilometer). In Europe, the country with the highest physiologic density is the Netherlands, reporting 4425 people per square mile (1708 per square kilometer).

Even these calculations are subject to error, however. In every country there are farmlands of different productivity. Some lands produce high crop yields (more than once a year in many Asian countries), while others are marginal or can sustain only livestock. All these variable levels of production are treated equally in our calculation of physiologic density. Still, the measure is much more useful than the arithmetic density index. Table 6-1 provides an indication of the usefulness of the concept of physiologic density. Note, for example, that the United States and Colombia have almost the same arithmetic density, but Colombia has a physiologic density more than four times that of the United States. Egypt's arithmetic density does not look especially high, but its physiologic density

---

*In 1991, the U.S. Census Bureau changed its definition of what constitutes the area of each of the 50 states by including the water areas of ponds, streams, and the territorial sea up to the 3-mile limit. This increases the total area of the United States by 168,655 square miles (436,816 square kilometers), thus creating a total of 3,787,425 square miles (9,809,430 square kilometers). See *New York Times*, Sunday, December 15, 1991, p. 26.

tells us what the real situation is in terms of cultivable land and the growing pressure on it. Argentina is the only country on the list with both relatively low arithmetic and physiologic densities. Also note that India's physiologic density, while high, is still moderate compared to those of its neighbor Bangladesh, or Japan.

AGRICULTURAL AND SETTLEMENT DENSITIES

Arithmetic and physiologic density measures are only two indexes used by population geographers to interpret patterns of population distribution. Another measure is the **agricultural density**. This measure differs from the physiologic density in that the calculations exclude all urban residents, making possible a more nearly accurate estimate of the pressure of people on the rural areas. In a country where a few large cities or towns exist (e.g., in Bangladesh), the agricultural density will be nearly as high as the overall physiologic density. Where large numbers of the population are crowded into major cities, there will be fewer people on the land, and the difference between agricultural and physiologic density will be greater.

Another population index is the **settlement density**, in which the measurement represents the amount of area in a country for each city with 100,000 people or more. In the United Kingdom, there are about 13,000 square miles (33,670 square kilometers) for each city. In the United States, there are 175,000 square miles (453,250 square kilometers), and the figure for China is 350,000 square miles (906,500 square kilometers).

Before returning to the issues associated with the growth of the world's population, we should remind ourselves of a reality that affects all our calculations and figures: the varying reliability of the information that we are compelled to use. When calculating the arithmetic density of a country, we must depend on population counts that may very well be inaccurate (but at least we can be fairly sure of the country's total area). When it comes to figuring physiologic density, we divide population data and "cultivable area" data, of which we are often uncertain. Since population problems are so vital to the world's nations and their future, there has been a major effort in the United Nations to help countries organize their census and to increase the effectiveness of data-gathering

systems. However, taking a census is an expensive business, and countries that cannot even afford enough food cannot be expected to place a very high priority on census accuracy, which is viewed as a costly luxury. Therefore, we should keep in mind that the statistics and data we have just used, and those we will use later, may be subject to considerable error.

Having examined the distribution of global and regional population, we now come to the crucial issue: population growth, its history, dimensions, spatial expression, and future. The next chapter links the map of distribution with the dynamics of demographic change.

KEY TERMS

Agricultural Density
Arithmetic Density
Census
Distribution
East Asia
Europe
Megalopolis
North American Region
Physiologic Density
Population Concentration
Population Data
Population Density
Settlement Density

7

PROCESSES AND CYCLES OF POPULATION CHANGE

If there are reasons to doubt the accuracy of some published population statistics, there is no uncertainty about another dimension of world population: its accelerating growth. Never before in human history have so many people filled the Earth's living space as today, and never has world population grown as rapidly as it has during the past 100 years. In 1975, world population reached 4 billion; it passed 5 billion in 1987, and will reach 6 billion in 1998. It took from the dawn of history to the year 1820 for the Earth's population to reach 1 billion. It required just 12 years to add the same number in the 1970s, and now it is taking only a decade to add the next billion. Even if the global rate of growth stabilizes or declines somewhat in years to come, there still may be 10 billion human inhabitants on this planet before the middle of the twenty-first century.

At present, about 188 million babies are born every year, and approximately 89 million people die. This means that we are adding nearly 100 million inhabitants to the

Geographica

- **The population explosion over the past 200 years has increased world population from under 1 billion to approximately 6 billion.**

- **Although hundreds of millions of people (many of them refugees or otherwise displaced) remain inadequately nourished today, the specter of global hunger has receded—perhaps temporarily.**

- **Rapid population growth appears to be a cyclic phenomenon that afflicts regions in turn. Europe's rapid growth occurred during the nineteenth century; over the past 30 years, South American growth rates have declined, whereas Africa's have increased.**

- **Access to education for women, and securing their rights in society, are keys to the reduction of population growth rates.**

- **The demographic transition model offers hope that world population will stabilize in the twenty-first century, but the model may not have universal applicability.**

world's population every year. Most of this increase occurs in those areas least able to support the new arrivals, and many millions among the year's deaths are young children who succumb to disease or starvation.

Can this go on indefinitely? Obvi-

ously not. Occasionally, there are signs that explosive population growth will be followed by a marked slowdown in the rate of increase and that world population will actually stabilize during the twenty-first century (see box, "A Stabilizing Population?"). This has already happened in some parts of the world; for example, in the United Kingdom, France, and several other developed countries, where population growth, after an explosive period of rapid increase, slowed to a trickle. But the population of France is less than one-twelfth that of India. What is really needed is a decrease in the rate of growth in countries with large populations and high rates of expansion—not only India, but also Indonesia, Bangladesh, Nigeria, Brazil, Mexico, and others.

Sometimes there are signs that a slowdown may be coming. In 1980, the Census Bureau of the United States reported that its research indicated that the world's overall growth rate had declined from approximately 2.1 percent per year during the years 1965 to 1969 to 1.8 percent during the period from 1975 to 1979. But when the growth rate was 2.1 percent, the world's population was approaching 4 billion, resulting in 80 million additional inhabitants each year. By the time the rate was down to 1.8 percent per year (possibly a low estimate), the population base was already between 4 and 4.6 billion. Calculate it for yourself: a 1.8 percent increase, on a base of 4.5 billion, *still* produces over 80 million additions.

Even while the global population growth rate has continued to decline, that reduction is offset by the ever-larger total on which it is based. The consensus is that world population in 1995 grew at just over 1.6 percent; this figure is encouraging—until we calculate that growth rate based on a population of 6 billion. The outcome: at the lower growth rate, world population is now growing by 100 million annually—20 million *more* than during the 1970s.

The world map of population growth rates by country (Fig. 7-1) also reveals the wide range of growth rates by region. That has

A STABILIZING POPULATION?

From time to time, agencies monitoring global population growth publish new projections of individual countries' futures. Occasionally, such projections suggest that most (if not all) of the world's national populations will stop growing at some time during the twenty-first century, reaching a so-called **stationary population level (SPL)**—as some Western European countries already have. This would mean, of course, that global population would stabilize, that the population explosion would be over, and that problems of numerous aged, not numerous youngsters, would challenge the world.

But such predictions require frequent revision, and the dates of anticipated stabilization are often moved back. In the late 1980s, the World Bank predicted that the United States would reach SPL in the year 2035 with 276 million inhabitants. Brazil would stabilize at 353 million in 2070, Mexico at 254 million in 2075, China at 1.4 billion in 2090, and India (destined to become and remain the world's most populous country) at 1.6 billion in 2150.

In the mid-1990s, those figures seem unrealistic. China passed the 1.2 billion mark in 1994; India reached 920 million in the same year. If we were to project an optimistic decline in growth rates for both countries, China would "stabilize" at 1.7 billion in 2070 and India in the same year at 2.0 billion. But population increase is a cyclic phenomenon, and overall declines mask lags and spurts (not to mention regional disparities). It is too early for the kind of optimism the notion of SPL stimulates.

been the case ever since records were kept: countries and regions go through stages of expansion (and in some cases even decline). Thirty years ago, population geographers worried about India and its high growth rate, certain that mass starvation lay ahead. In those days, India grew more rapidly than Africa. But today India's growth rate is down from 2.6 percent to 1.9 percent, whereas Africa's has grown from 2.4 percent to 2.8 percent.

Figure 7-1 reflects not only the rapid population growth of countries in Africa south of the Sahara (Kenya's for some time ranked as the fastest growing population in the world), but also the increased growth rates in Muslim countries of North Africa and Southwest Asia. Iran today is one of the world's most rapidly growing countries, followed closely by Saudi Arabia, Yemen, and Libya. Many of the Muslim countries' growth rates are

higher today than they were 30 years ago. In Subsaharan Africa, the end of colonialism and the failure of national economies often are cited as reasons for the upward population curve. In Africa as in the Muslim realm, tradition-bound society, slow modernization, and the lowly status of women are held responsible for what the map shows.

Population growth in the two largest human agglomerations, East Asia and South Asia, continues to be rapid. India's population approaches 1 billion as its growth rate slowly declines, but at 1.9 percent India still grows faster than the world as a whole. And China, which imposed severely restrictive population policies (see Chapter 8) to bring down its growth rate to 1.2 percent in the 1980s, has seen this rate creep up again to 1.3 percent (with more than 1.2 billion inhabitants, one-tenth of 1 percent means a great deal: specifically, 1.2 million

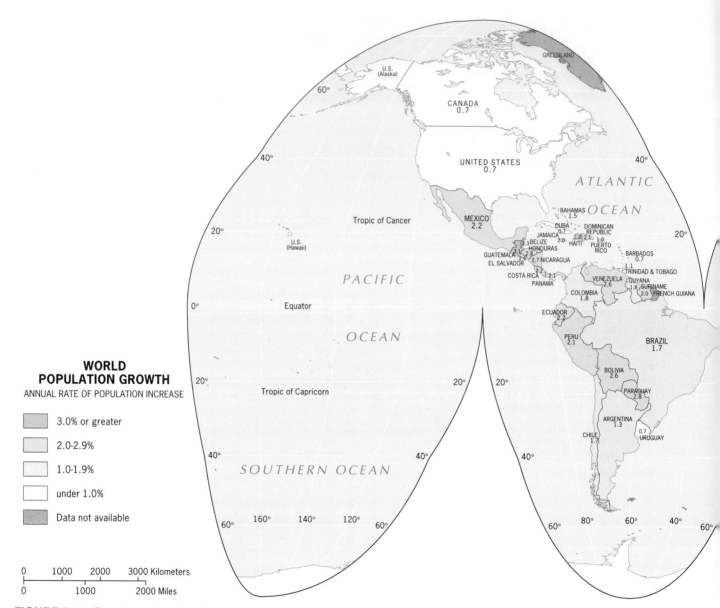

WORLD POPULATION GROWTH

ANNUAL RATE OF POPULATION INCREASE

- 3.0% or greater
- 2.0-2.9%
- 1.0-1.9%
- under 1.0%
- Data not available

FIGURE 7–1   Based on data from Population Reference Bureau, *Population Data Sheet 1995.* (Washington, D.C.: 1995).

additions annually, or 12 million in just one decade).

Today the geographic realm with marked declines in population growth rates is South America. Although most South American countries still are growing faster than the world average, the realm as a whole has seen a decline from over 3.0 to under 2.0 percent. Populous Brazil, for example, has gone from 2.9 percent in the mid-1960s to 1.7 percent today. Brazil's neigh-

bors, from Venezuela to the north and Peru to the west to Paraguay to the south, all have recorded significant declines; 30 years ago several of them were growing at 3.2 to 3.4 percent. And the three countries of the southern cone (Argentina, Chile, and Uruguay) are growing at well below the world rate.

As Figure 7-1 shows, the slowest growing countries lie in the economically wealthier zone extending from the United States and Canada

across Western Europe to Japan. In fact, not all the slow-growth countries (under 1 percent annual increase) are rich; those in the post–Soviet orbit, for example, are not well off at all. There, political and social conditions are inhibiting growth, as is the case in Russia itself. (Russia, by some accounts, is experiencing negative population growth, which means that deaths in a given year outnumber births).

DIMENSIONS OF GROWTH

As the figures quoted previously indicate, the expansion of human population has not proceeded in a *linear* manner, whereby something that grows increases by a uniform amount during a series of equal time periods. If you have $100 and add $10 to it the first year and each successive year, your $100 will become $200 after 10 years, $300 after 20 years, and so on. This is **linear** growth (Fig. 7-2A). However, if you invested your initial $100 at a rate of interest of 10 percent and it was compounded continuously, each increment would be based on the original amount, plus previously added interest. After 10 years, your $100 would have increased to $259; after 20 years it would have increased to $673. The difference between linear and **exponential growth** is obvious, and the world's human population has been growing at exponential rates (Fig. 7-2B).

DOUBLING TIME

Another way of looking at exponential growth is by comparing the rate of growth to the **doubling time** involved. Every rate of growth has a doubling time; for example, our $100 invested at 10 percent took about 7 years to double to $200, and then another 7 years to become $400, and then another 7 years to become $800. When the growth rate is 10 percent, therefore, the doubling time is around 7 years. During the middle of this century,

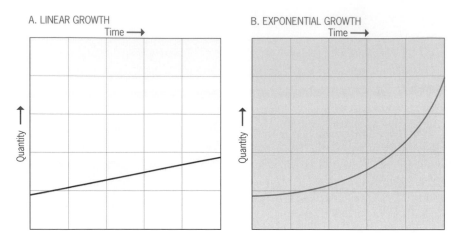

FIGURE 7–2 Population growth: (A) linear; (B) exponential; (C) doubling time.

when the world's human population was increasing at an average rate of 2 percent, its doubling time was 35 years (Fig. 7-2C).

During the mid-1980s, when the declining rate reached 1.8 percent, the doubling time rose to 39 years.

It is interesting to read the data on Figure 7-1 in the context of Table 7-1, because this reveals where individual countries are on the doubling-time curve. In 1995, the United States population was growing at 0.7 percent, yielding a doubling time of nearly a century: 98 years. Kenya and several other African countries, with growth rates in the 3.0 to 4.0 percent range, are doubling in as little as 20 years. Always, however, remember the base—the total on which the doubling takes place. Doubling the populations of the three largest East African countries (Kenya, Tanzania, and Uganda) would lead to growth from about 75 to 150 million in little more than 20 years. Doubling India's population of 930 million (1995) may take longer (40 years) but will add nearly 1 billion over that period.

Such staggering data underscore the magnitude of the challenge. A population that doubles in little

more than a generation presents insurmountable obstacles to programs of development and betterment.

A POPULATION EXPLOSION

This historical perspective suggests why the term **population explosion** has come into use. It is estimated that the world's population at the time of the birth of Christ was about 250 million. More than 16 centuries passed before this total had doubled to 500 million, the estimated population of 1650. Just 170

years later, in 1820, the population had doubled again, to 1 billion (Fig. 7-3). And barely more than a century after this, in 1930, it reached 2 billion. Now the doubling time was down to 100 years and dropping fast; the population explosion was in full gear. Only 45 years elapsed during the next doubling, to 4 billion (1975). In that decade, the rate of growth was approximately 2 percent per year, and the doubling time (Fig. 7-2) had declined to 35 years. The history of humanity has been not only one of increasing numbers but also one of increasing rates of increase.

TABLE 7–1   Rates of Growth and Doubling Times

Rate of Increase (as percentage)	Doubling Time (years)	Current (1995) Example
0.50	141	Netherlands
0.75	94	Australia
1.00	70	Taiwan
1.50	46	Indonesia
2.00	35	Peru
2.50	28	Malaysia
3.00	24	Pakistan
3.50	20	Côte d'Ivoire
4.00	17	Gaza

EARLY WARNINGS

Concern over the population spiral arose even before the full impact of the population explosion was felt. As long ago as 1798, a British economist named Thomas **Malthus** published a long essay entitled *An Essay on the Principle of Population as It Affects the Future Improvement of Society,* in which he sounded the alarm: population was increasing faster than the means of subsistence. Malthus recognized the nature of exponential growth and pointed out that population increases at what he called a geometric rate. The means of subsistence, he argued, grow only at an arithmetic (linear) rate. Malthus issued revised editions of his essay from 1803 to 1826, and he responded vigorously to a barrage of criticism (he had, in fact, condemned the social order in England). He suggested that the population growth in Britain might be checked by hunger within 50 years from the first appearance of his warning.

Malthus could not have foreseen the multiple impacts of colonization and migration, and, undoubtedly, he would not have believed that the United Kingdom could sustain between 50 and 60 million people, as it does today. Nor was he correct about the linear increase of food production. It, too, has grown exponentially as the acreage being cultivated has expanded, improved strains of seed have been developed, and fertilizers have been applied. However, the rate of increase of food production (and especially distribution) has not kept up with the rate of population growth, and although Malthus was wrong in terms of timing and detail, the essence of his argument still appears to have merit.

Karl Marx, the nineteenth-century socialist, suggested that the poverty of the masses foreseen by Malthus had less to do with their numbers than with the capitalist system governing them. Far from proposing a reduction in the rate of population growth, Marx wanted to alter the control and use of natural resources by taking them from the hands of the few and distributing them among the many. Others have criticized the Malthusian doctrine on the grounds that the Earth has proved capable of ever-expanding food production. There are still untapped resources, both on land (the Amazon and Congo (Zaïre) Basins could be made productive, for example) and in the sea (where globally organized fish harvests could be secured in perpetuity if international planning succeeded). Only technological and political progress needs to be made, these critics argue, to achieve these and other advances.

Those who feel the weight of Malthus's concerns (even if not every detail of his argument) are sometimes called the neo-Malthusians, and their number is growing. They point out that human suffering on a scale unimagined even by Malthus is now occurring, and they argue that it is not enough simply to assert that this planet must inevitably go through a period such as this—even if population stability were to be achieved in the twenty-first century. The time to attack the problem, they say, is now, with vigorous programs of population control and other strategies (of which more will be said later).

POPULATION STRUCTURE

Maps showing the regional distribution and density of population tell us about the numbers of people in countries or regions, but they cannot reveal two other important aspects of those populations: the

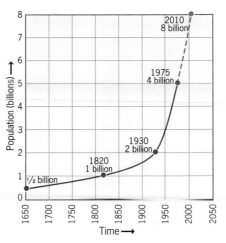

FIGURE 7–3 Population growth, 1650 to (estimated) 2010.

number of men and women, and their ages. This is very important, because a populous country where half the population is very young (say under 15 years of age) has very different problems from a country where a large proportion of the population is elderly. When geographers study populations, therefore, they are concerned not only with spatial distribution, but also with **population structure**.

The structure of a population is created by the number of people in its various age groups. It is visually represented by an **age-sex pyramid**. These pyramids display the percentages of the total population in age groups (normally 5-year groups). The sexes are divided to the left (males) and right (females) of the pyramid's center line.

Populations with high fertility as well as high mortality have broad-based pyramids, with large percentages in the youngest age groups. Populations with lower fertility and mortality have pyramids with narrower bases and a more rectangular shape. Figure 7-4 shows the 1990 population pyramids for countries with high growth rates: Kenya, Nigeria, India, and Brazil. Note that the percentages of people in the three youngest age groups

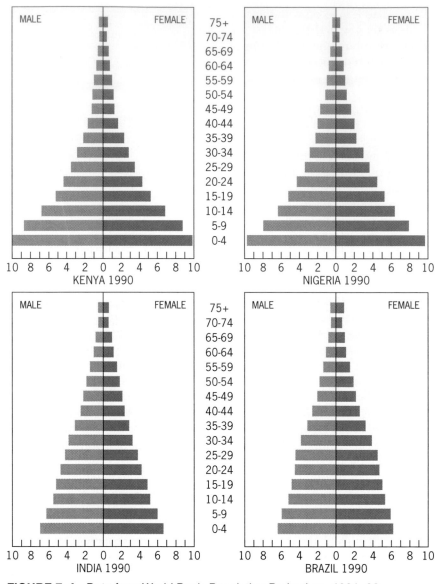

FIGURE 7–4 Data from World Bank *Population Projections,* 1991–92.

are much larger in Kenya and in Nigeria than in India or Brazil, indicating that a lowering of the rate of natural increase is in progress in the latter two populations. The data bear this out: in 1991, Kenya still had a birth rate of 46 per thousand and a death rate of 7, while India's birth rate had declined to under 31 per thousand with a mortality rate of just over 10. In Nigeria the comparable figures were 44 and 17, but in Brazil they were 27 and 8.

Figure 7-5 shows quite effec-

tively what happens to the population pyramid when both birth and death rates decline, narrowing the gap and thus lowering the rate of increase. Mexico still shows a broad-based pyramid, but less so than India and much less so than Nigeria. China's population pyramid reveals vividly the impact of Beijing's restrictive population policies: note that the percentages of children in the three lowest age groups is actually smaller than those in the next three groups. As we will note later, China's rulers im-

posed severe limitations on family size, and the results are evident in Figure 7-5.

Other factors led to the nearly rectangular age-sex pyramids for France and Japan. Economic development, urbanization, and general modernization brought with them smaller families—not by government edict, but through family planning and economic realities. As the pyramids show, there are nearly as many people in the upper age groups as in the lower ones. But the incomes of those in the middle groups must pay for the children to be raised as well as the elders to be pensioned. The transformation from the Kenya model to the Japan model is desirable, but the Japan model brings with it its own problems, including a shortage of young workers. In France, this has led to the immigration of foreign laborers from North Africa, who are changing the country's social mosaic.

DEMOGRAPHIC CYCLES

The study of population is the discipline of demography, and its spatial component is the field of population geography. We now turn to the demographic factors that underlie the patterns exhibited in Figure 7-1, in order to better understand the regional contrasts revealed therein. So far, we have viewed *global* population growth. But as we will see, while some countries and regions are growing faster than the world average, others are growing much slower. And some countries actually have declining populations, that is, "negative" population growth.

Populations go through stages of growth that are parts of their *demographic cycles.* Populations in different areas of the world, and sometimes even in different parts of the same country, are at different stages in their demographic cycles—which can have serious economic and political consequences.

NATURAL INCREASE

The natural growth of a population is recorded as the difference between the number of births and the number of deaths during a specific period. These two measures, the birth rate and death rate, are commonly expressed in terms of the number of individuals per thousand. In statistical tables, these are reported as the **crude birth rate (CBR)**, the number of live births per year per thousand people in the population, and the **crude death rate (CDR)**, the number of deaths per thousand.

THE BIRTH RATE

As Figure 7-6 shows, birth rates vary widely across the world. The highest birth rates today are recorded in Africa and Southwest Asia. For many years, countries in East Africa (most notably Kenya) have had birth rates ranking among the highest in the world; during the 1980s, Kenya, Tanzania, and Uganda all reported 50 or more births per thousand per year. Demographers describe birth rates higher than 30 as high, which puts most tropical American, African, and Asian countries in that category.

The lowest birth rates, the map shows, occur now in Europe, where several countries have CBRs of less than 15. Other areas with low rates are North America (the United States and Canada), Australia, New Zealand, Japan, and China. From what we know about the state of development around the world, it is clear that low birth rates are associated with modernization—with industrialization and urbanization—

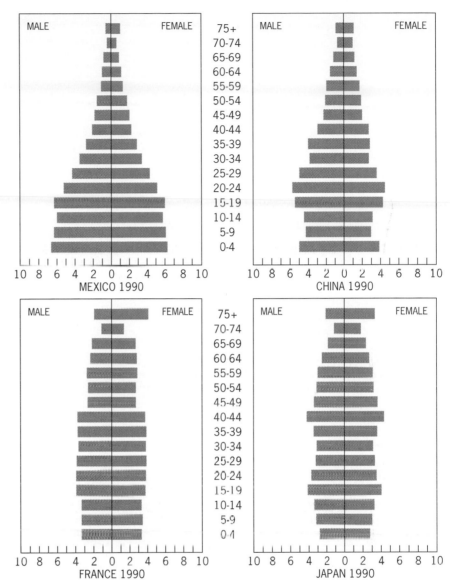

FIGURE 7–5 Data from World Bank *Population Projections,* 1991–92.

a generalization that holds for all except China. Just one generation ago, China still had high birth rates, although it is not yet an industrialized, urbanized nation. China achieved its low birth rate by imposing stringent population controls, about which more will be said later.

Looking closer at Figure 7-6, it would appear that a number of countries that are somewhere between underdeveloped and developed, such as Argentina, Colombia, and Thailand, also have

intermediate (or transitional) birth rates. This would suggest that birth rates are related to stage of economic development. That correlation is countered, of course, by what China has accomplished. Economic development is crucial, but there are other factors (including cultural traditions opposing birth control) that affect the patterns shown on Figure 7-6.

Another measure of the reproductive status of a population is the **total fertility rate (TFR)**. This is a measure of the number of children

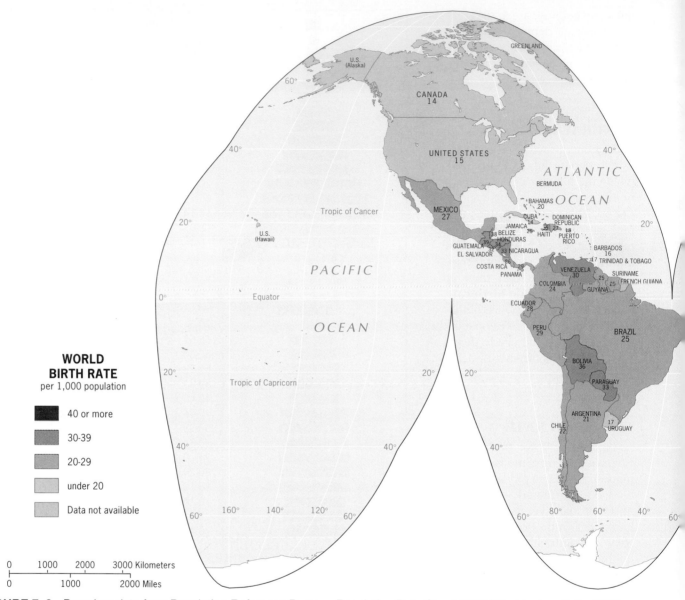

WORLD BIRTH RATE
per 1,000 population

- 40 or more
- 30-39
- 20-29
- under 20
- Data not available

FIGURE 7–6 Based on data from Population Reference Bureau, *Population Data Sheet 1995* (Washington, D.C.: 1995).

that are being born to women of childbearing age in the population. The TFR is usually reported as the number of children per woman, and it is a revealing statistic. For example, when Kenya was at the height of its population explosion in the 1980s, the number of children per childbearing-age women was 8.1! In China just 30 years ago, the TFR was 6.0; today it is 1.9).

Many countries have shown declining TFRs in recent years, which is a major reason for the optimism of some demographers about the long-term future of the world's human population. Not only China, but also India, Egypt, Brazil, and Mexico have lower TFRs today than one generation ago. India's TFR has declined from 5.8 to 3.4, Egypt's from 7.2 to 3.9, Brazil's from 6.3 to 2.9 and Mexico's from 6.7 to 3.1. On the other hand, Nigeria's TFR

still exceeds 6.0 (as does all of Africa's combined), and Pakistani women still bear an average of nearly 6 children.

Both birth rates and fertility rates show much spatial variation, but an overall decline has been in progress for several decades now, which is why world population growth has declined from over 2.1 percent to 1.5 percent over the past 25 years. As we noted earlier, however, the

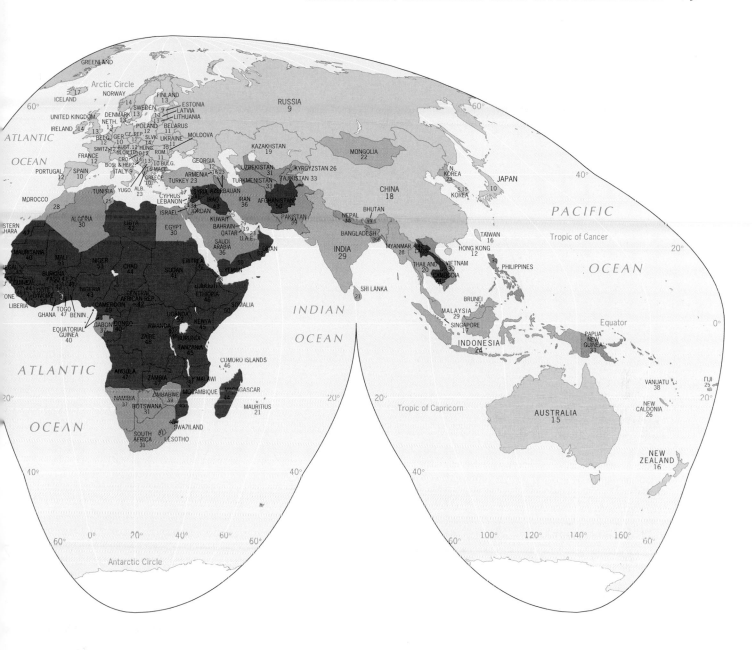

lower rate of natural increase still yields a higher increment than before, because of the expanded numbers of humanity.

THE DEATH RATE

The crude death rate (CDR) reports the number of deaths per thousand people. Also called the *mortality rate*, this figure has declined more dramatically than birth and fertility rates (Fig. 7-7). During the global population explosion, the widening gap between still-high birth rates and falling death rates signaled the rapid expansion of human numbers.

As Figure 7-7 shows, death rates are highest in tropical Africa, where a number of countries record more than 20 deaths per thousand in the population, and lowest in North America and most of South America, parts of Europe, Japan, China, and Australia. Also noteworthy are the low CDRs of several Southeast Asian countries. Here the correlation between economic development and low or declining death rates is less evident than appeared to be the case with birth rates—or we would not find Sri Lanka, Vietnam, or Paraguay among the lower rates. Figure 7-7 testifies not only to the role of economic

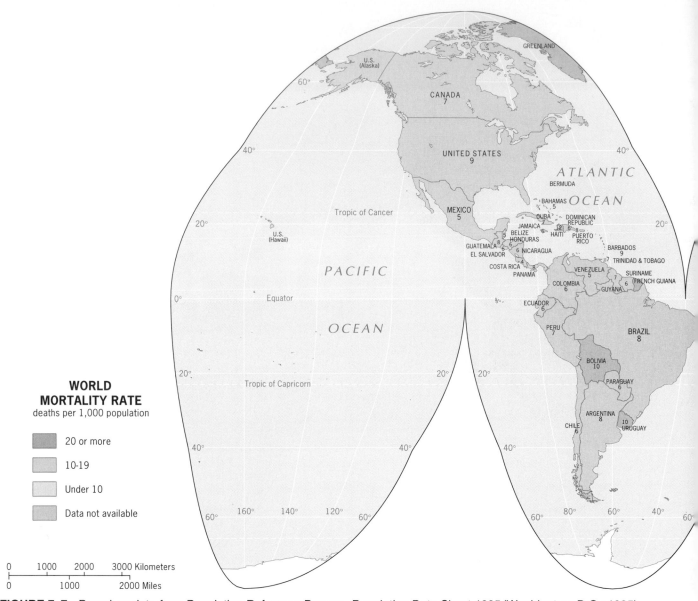

FIGURE 7–7 Based on data from Population Reference Bureau, *Population Data Sheet 1995* (Washington, D.C.: 1995).

development, but also to the diffusion of health facilities and medicines, hygienic practices, pesticide use, and improved nutrition to countries still in an underdeveloped stage.

Crude death rates should be seen, however, in the context of **infant mortality**. We will discuss this topic in detail in Part 4, where we study medical geography, health,

and nutrition. For the moment, we should realize that many children (more than 1 in 10 in many countries) die within the first year of their lives, so that high CDRs tend to reflect high infant mortality. This is only one reason why population data should be viewed in combination with population structure, as revealed by pyramids such as those in Figures 7–4 and 7-5.

PAST POPULATION CHANGE

We have become accustomed to thinking of population change as population growth, so pervasive is the phenomenon of human expansion during the twentieth century. But population change has not always been a matter of positive

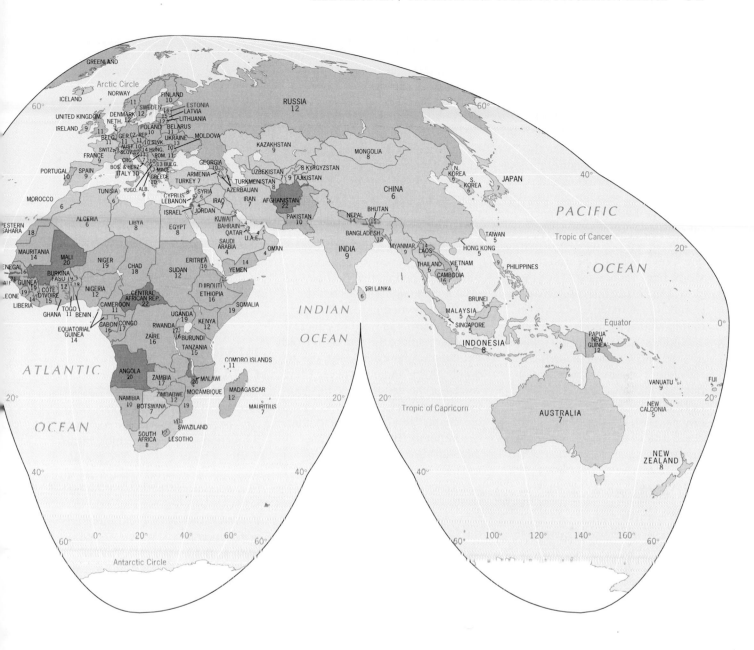

growth. There have been times when populations decline, sometimes precipitously, and the number of deaths per thousand has far exceeded the number of births in certain regions.

Previously, we noted that population increased slowly until the early nineteenth century; what we did not report was what kept historic growth so slow. Contributing significantly to this were epidemics and plagues, to which people often succumbed by the hundreds of thousands. Europe between 1348 and 1350 was ravaged by the bubonic plague, and fully one-quarter of the realm's entire population is estimated to have died. In this epidemic and its aftermath, many cities and towns were left with fewer than half their inhabitants. It is believed that the population of England, which was nearly 4 million when the plague began, was just over 2 million when it was over. A student of population change in the second half of the fourteenth century would have been more likely to talk of annual population decrease than of growth!

If there was not an epidemic,

then famine could reverse a period of population growth. There are records of famines in India and China during the eighteenth and nineteenth centuries in which millions of people perished; Europe was not safe from such disasters either. From Britain to Russia, the ravages of unusual weather periodically caused crops to fail and people to die from hunger (the Little Ice Age had a major impact). At other times, population gains were largely wiped out by destructive wars, of which Europe and the world have seen many. Thus the slow and steady increase of world population sometimes shown on graphs depicting its growth from 250 million at A.D. 0 to 500 million in 1650 and 1 billion in 1820 is something of a misrepresentation because it shows an average of countless unrevealed ups and downs. Birth rates were high, but death rates were high also, and there were times when there were many more deaths than live births.

Eventually, things began to change. In Europe (we know much less about Asia, Africa, and the Americas), there was a marked increase in the growth rate during the eighteenth century, and this time there was no major setback to erase the gains. This was the time of the Second Agricultural Revolution, when farming methods improved, yields increased, storage capacities were expanded, and distribution systems were improved. The Industrial Revolution began to wipe out the old problems in Europe as well: sanitation facilities made the towns and cities safer from epidemics, and modern medical practices began to have widespread effect. Disease prevention through vaccination introduced a new era in public health. Death rates declined markedly. Before 1750, they probably averaged 35 per 1000 (births averaged under 40), but by 1850 the death rate was about 16 per thousand. Consider what this means in

terms of natural growth rate: if in 1750 the birth rate was 39 per thousand, and the death rate 35 per thousand, then the rate of natural increase was 4 per thousand, or 0.4 percent. In 1850, birth rates were still high, perhaps 36 per thousand, but the death rate was 16 per thousand. Now the rate of natural increase was 2.0 percent. The change is especially spectacular in the context of doubling time. In 1750, it was of the order of 150 years; in 1850, it was only 35 years.

What happened to the large number of people that Europe was now generating? Millions left the squalid, crowded industrial cities (and the farms as well) to emigrate to other parts of the world, to North and South America, to Australia, to South Africa, and elsewhere. They were not the first to make this journey. Adventurers, explorers, merchants, and colonists had gone before them. Those early immigrants had decimated the indigenous population in many areas, by conquest, by forced exodus as slaves, and through the introduction of their diseases, against which the local people had no natural immunity. However, when the European colonization started in earnest during the nineteenth century, the Europeans brought with them their newfound methods of sanitation and medical techniques, and the effect was the opposite of what it had previously been. In Africa, in India, and in South America, death rates began to decline as they had in Europe, and populations that had long been caught in cycles of gains and losses commenced new, permanent growth—at increasing rates.

We can speak in only the most general terms about the indigenous populations of the Americas, Africa, Asia, and Australia before this phase of Europeanization. It is speculated that about the time of the first European contact, there were probably fewer than 25 mil-

lion people in all of North and South America; in Africa, south of the Sahara, there may have been 70 million. (Some recent estimates place these totals somewhat higher.) In China in the mid-seventeenth century, the population may have been less than 200 million; India probably had fewer than 100 million inhabitants. However, there is no doubt about the consequences of European involvement. It reduced the impact of periodic natural checks on the growth of numbers and swept these areas up in the explosive increase prevailing today.

DEMOGRAPHIC CHANGE

The population of a country (or a city, or any other specific region) is a function of three variables: births, deaths, and migration. The population number changes as a result of four conditions: births and inmigration (immigration), which add to the total; and deaths and outmigration (emigration), which subtract from it. Births (fertility), deaths (mortality), and migration are called the three demographic *variables*.

To calculate the demographic change affecting a country or region, we use the simple formula

$$TP = OP + B - D + I - E$$

where *TP* (Total Population) equals *OP* (Original Population) plus *B* (Births) minus *D* (Deaths) plus *I* (Immigration) minus *E* (Emigration). A population's **natural increase** is calculated by using only births and deaths. This can be done with available data in this chapter, by subtracting figures on the map of world mortality (Fig. 7-7) from those of births (Fig. 7-6). The demographic change formula explains why calculations based only on births and deaths do not

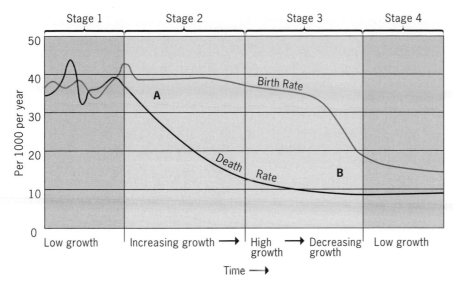

FIGURE 7–8 Four stages of the demographic cycle.

correspond to the figures in Figure 7-1 (World Population Growth). Population change, as recorded in Figure 7-1, also takes emigration and immigration into account. (Obviously, the world figures referred to previously in this chapter represent the natural increase for the globe as a whole, because our planet does not [yet] experience immigration or emigration!)

STAGES IN THE CYCLE: THE DEMOGRAPHIC TRANSITION

Demographers who have studied population growth in various parts of the world have argued that the high rates of increase now occurring in much of the underdeveloped world are not necessarily permanent. Today in Europe, for example, the situation is very different from what it was a century ago. In the United Kingdom in 1995 the crude birth rate was 13 and the crude death rate was 11, producing a rate of natural increase of just 0.2 percent. The last figure is reminiscent of the preindustrial period, when there also was a small difference between birth and death rates, but both were high; now both are

low. It is in the intervening stage, when birth rates remained high but death rates were lowered rapidly, that Britain's population explosion took place. It is not difficult, then, to discern four prominent stages in the United Kingdom's demographic cycle, marked by (1) high birth rates and high death rates and a small rate of growth; (2) continuing high birth rates, but declining and low death rates and a high rate of growth; (3) declining and low death rates but a still-substantial growth rate; and (4) low birth and low death rates, and, thus, a low rate of growth.

This sequence of stages has been observed in the population records of several European countries, and on this basis demographers have defined what they call the **demographic cycle** or **demographic transition**. Its four stages (Fig. 7-8) are

1. **High stationary stage,** with high fertility (births) and high mortality (deaths) and variable population, but little long-term growth.

2. **Early expanding stage,** with high fertility and declining mortality.

3. **Late expanding stage,** with declining fertility but, as a result of already-low mortality, continuing significant growth.

4. **Low stationary stage,** with low fertility and low mortality, and a very low rate of growth.

The *demographic transition* is represented by stages two and three, when high birth, high death rates decline to low birth, low death rates. During the transition, the initially rapid drop in death rates is not matched by lowered birth rates, so that a period of high natural increase results. The dimensions of expansion depend on the size of the base population and the curves of decline.

This is what happened in the United Kingdom and in much of Europe. Europe, as a continent, currently has a population growth rate of under 1.0 percent, after generating its own population explosion during which the United Kingdom's population grew from about 6.5 million in 1750 to 35 million just after 1900. If this is the rule, then we have reason to be optimistic. It would appear that the population "bomb" will eventually fizzle out, and that in due course, the European model of low birth and death rates and a nearly stable population, will prevail everywhere—or will it?

In Europe, the birth rate declined in large part because of the effects of industrialization, urbanization, and general modernization. In much of the developing world, the majority of the people have not been seriously affected by such changes, and if the world is to wait for them to occur, the population crisis will intensify. Furthermore, there are quantitative differences between the situation in Europe during the nineteenth century and that which is prevailing now in certain other parts of the world. When Europe's population revolution began (as such it was), the starting numbers were not great. Britain had between 6 and 7 million residents; Germany had 7; France, Belgium, and the Netherlands, combined (including some of Europe's most densely populated lands), had 18. Asia's major population clusters were already much larger when the population revolution commenced there. China may have had over 200 million inhabitants, and India over 100 million. Superimpose the growth rates of the second and third stages upon such numbers and the increments take on astronomical proportions.

Therefore, it may be unwise to assume that all countries' demographic cycles will follow the sequence of events that prevailed in urbanizing and industrializing Europe, or to assume that the explosive growth now prevailing in Bangladesh, Mexico, and numerous other countries will simply subside.

Optimistic projections (see page 71) suggest that a leveling off will occur when an "ultimate" population is reached, but there is little or no evidence for this. Occasionally, there are hopeful signs, and Sri Lanka has been cited as a case in point: the birth rate is declining, and so is the overall growth rate—*without* the kind of economic development usually considered a prerequisite for such a decline. A similar, noteworthy reduction in the population growth rate has been recorded in the Indian state of Kerala, where it now stands at 1.1 percent, compared to 1.9 percent for India as a whole. One interesting aspect of Kerala is its literacy rate, which, in this education-conscious southwest Indian state, is about 90 percent of the population, compared to just over 50 percent for all of India.

These remain isolated instances, however, and there is no proof as yet of a permanent, worldwide reversal in population expansion. There may be vague, long-range grounds for optimism, but at present no effective machinery has been found to defuse the population "bomb."

KEY TERMS

Age-Sex Pyramid
Crude Birth Rate (CBR)
Crude Death Rate (CDR)
Demographic Transition (Cycle)
Doubling Time
Exponential Growth
Infant Mortality
Linear Growth
Malthus
Natural Increase
Population Explosion
Population Structure
Stationary Population Level (SPL)
Total Fertility Rate (TFR)

8

DEMOGRAPHIES AND POLICIES

Population growth, we have noted, varies from realm to realm, region to region, and even from province to province within individual countries. Over time, too, population growth has been inconsistent. In the past, not much more than 30 years ago, South Asia and South and Middle America experienced the world's highest rates of natural increase, but during the late 1970s tropical Africa took the lead, its overall growth rate approaching 3 percent (representing a doubling time of 24 years). Still further back in history, it was Europe that witnessed its demographic transition, a population explosion that was mitigated by emigration and that populated the colonies and, later, the Americas and other regions culturally tied to industrializing Europe.

How things change. Today, European countries, in combination, have the lowest growth rate, as a realm, in the world. Individually, two dozen European countries have fertility rates that stand below the replacement level. (The total fertility rate, TFR, should be above 2.1 children per childbearing-age woman to sustain a population without

Geographica

- **For practical purposes, population data are reported by country. But demographic spatial variation *within* countries can be very large, for example, in India.**

- **During the twentieth century, national governments have pursued three kinds of population policy: expansive, eugenic, and restrictive.**

- **International agreements on population policies are difficult to reach, in part because religious doctrines and governmental goals may be incompatible.**

- **The most dramatic population-policy reversal in recent decades was performed by communist China.**

loss). Europe faces a decline in population in years to come, but more importantly, it confronts difficult social problems. A population that is not replacing itself also becomes a population of older people, who require state retirement pensions, social services, and other forms of support. But that support must be paid for from a dwindling tax base. Because not enough younger people are available to take jobs (and those who are in the job market tend to take

skilled positions), immigrant workers are needed, but this, too, can lead to social problems. In Germany, hundreds of thousands of Turkish immigrant laborers and their families have filled jobs but fueled animosities. When the Berlin Wall came down and the two Germanies were reunited, thousands of former East German workers went westward in search of jobs, but the presence of foreign labor caused tensions and violence.

Population decline is a two-edged sword. In this chapter, the focus is on the practical: How do governments and their agencies react to demographic problems, and what have been the results of past policies and actions? In 1995, France, among Western European countries, still was the only country to encourage its citizens, through subsidies and services, to have larger families. But France is not the only government in the world to look for ways to cope with the consequences of negative population growth. As we will see, Japan is in similar straits, but Japanese policy prevents the immigration of foreign workers. Singapore, too, saw an earlier population-control campaign (in which sterilization was encouraged, abortion was legalized, and larger families were punished) succeed to such a degree that the population stopped growing and started aging. Now Singapore's government urges families to have three or even four children. Balanced population growth is not easily achieved.

among all of Canada's provinces. (Figure 8-1 reveals the effects of natural increase *and* migration, and thus reflects the outflow from the Maritime Provinces as well as the immigration into the Pacific area.) In 1990, the Quebec provincial government introduced a budget that offered women a subsidy of $6000 (Canadian) for every child born after the first two. Canada already is a low-growth country, with only 27 million people in an area even larger than the United States (but less advantaged environmentally) and a rate of natural increase of 0.7 percent. Canada's overall growth rate, taking immigration and emigration into account, is about 1.4 percent, still well below the world average. For Quebec, the rate of natural increase is below Canada's, and the overall growth rate is near that of the country as a whole. Quebec's leaders want to encourage the rate of natural increase for political as well as economic reasons, because the great majority of

those born in the province are of French-Canadian parentage.

The Canadian example reminds us of the spatial variations within countries, especially larger countries, hidden by national statistics. It also indicates that national population policies may not be appropriate, or even acceptable, in particular regions of a country. It was the Quebec provincial government, not Canada's federal government, that offered a subsidy for family enlargement. As in all federations, the objectives of one region may diverge from those of the state as a whole. Quebec, where population (and politics) are concerned, is on its own track.

Another relevant case is India, where any data on overall population increase should be viewed against a regional background (Fig. 8-2). Demographically, there is not just one, but rather several Indias. Population growth is most rapid (and still truly explosive) in Assam and neighboring northeastern states

GEOGRAPHY OF DEMOGRAPHY

Just as world averages, and averages for the world's major geographic realms, conceal growth-rate variations in smaller regions or individual countries, so the national data we show on such maps as Figures 7-6 and 7-7 cannot convey internal contrasts *within* countries. These internal spatial differences can be large and consequential, as we noted in the case of the Indian state of Kerala.

An interesting example is the situation in Canada, in the context of the off-again, on-again campaign for independence in the province of Quebec (Fig. 8-1). Despite being overwhelmingly Catholic, Quebec has long had the lowest birth rate

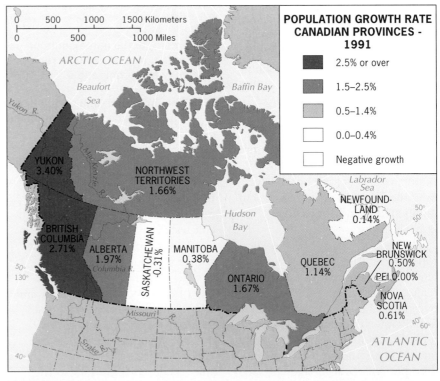

FIGURE 8–1

adjacent to Bangladesh, which are still caught in the unchecked spiral. In Nagaland and Mizoram, the rate of natural increase during the 1970s actually exceeded 4.5 percent, one of the world's highest. It has been about 2.5 percent in India's great eastern population cluster in the lower Ganges-Brahmaputra basin. As Figure 8-2 shows, the growth rate in the southern peninsula has been below the national average. An Indian average for population growth, therefore, reveals only part of the situation and none of its internal spatial variation. When the food situation was less secure than it has been in recent years, hunger often afflicted the crowded east at a time when food was adequate in the west.

The map of world population growth confronts us with an inescapable reality: the countries with high growth rates tend to be those variously identified as the "have-not" countries, the "underdeveloped" countries, or, more optimistically, the "developing" countries. These are the world's poorest countries, least able to afford to feed and house additional millions of people. The economic gains made by these countries under existing domestic political and economic structures are all but wiped out by the demands of their mushrooming populations, and reduced growth rates are an essential ingredient in any formula for improvement. As we will see later, high population growth rates form only one element in the overall condition of underdevelopment—but it is a critical one.

POPULATION POLICIES

From time to time, international concerns over global population trends lead to multinational discussions to seek ways to defuse the

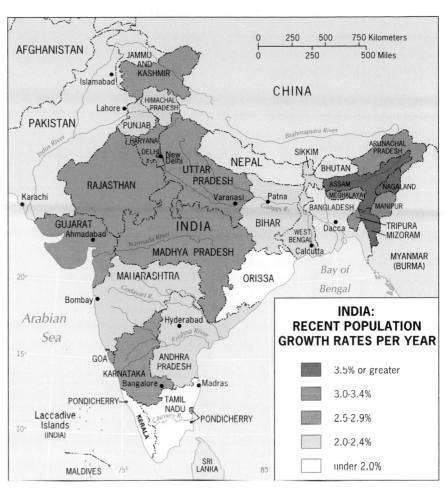

FIGURE 8–2 Data from Census of India since 1970, and from demographic reports of individual state agencies.

population explosion. In 1974, a full-scale gathering of the world's states for this purpose took place in Bucharest, Romania. The population spiral was in full force, global hunger and dislocation were looming (according to experts in attendance), and controlling population growth seemed to be a matter of overriding, worldwide priority.

But the minutes of the 1974 meeting paint quite another picture, and they remind us of the cost of the Cold War and of the difficulty in reaching international agreement on anything as sensitive as population issues. China, still in the aftershocks of its costly "cultural revolution," put the Marxist view bluntly: population control was a capitalist plot designed to inhibit the growth and

power of communist societies, and the Chinese would not agree to any multinational plan to limit growth. On the contrary, the Chinese applauded the (then) Soviet policy of giving special recognition and awards to women who had borne ten children or more.

The 1974 Bucharest Conference was the first in a series of United Nations-sponsored conferences on population issues, and while it was marred by ideological disputes, the great majority of the world's governments agreed on the urgency of overpopulation. China and the Soviet Union took similar, minority positions for different reasons: China saw family planning as a capitalist plot while the Soviet Union promoted births because its population structure still showed the impact of its enormous losses during World War II. Moscow encouraged large families because it saw its huge domain as underpopulated (a situation to which Soviet tyrants had contributed through the extermination of more than 30 million farmers, political opponents, and other dissidents during the 1930s). But the problems of overpopulation and spiraling growth were evident to most, communists and noncommunists alike.

U.N. population conferences are held every ten years, and the next meeting occurred in Mexico City in 1984. The contrast between 1974 and 1984 in terms of urgency and ideology is striking. By 1984, the Green Revolution had narrowed the food gap, and communist China, in its post–Mao era, had totally reversed its position on population growth. Now China was embarked on a severely restrictive population policy, and its growth rate had declined dramatically—so much so that the Beijing regime had been awarded a United Nations medal for achieving a rapid reduction in the national birth rate. In addition, the United States during the Reagan (Republican) era did not take an active role in support of family planning. At the conference, the U.S. kept a relatively low profile, and no major confrontations such as those at Bucharest occurred.

THE 1994 CAIRO CONFERENCE

A very different situation arose prior to and during the 1994 conference, which was called the U.N. Conference on Population and Development. A new and potentially crucial schism appeared, based on religious issues rather than political or ideological differences. Even before the conference convened in September 1994, full-page advertisements appeared in newspapers around the world criti-

cizing its objectives and warning of obstruction. These announcements were published by the Roman Catholic Church, which objected to the prospect that the conference would endorse **abortion** and artificial means of birth control.

Author's Video Link
↓
6
World Population
Conference

The Vatican was not alone in this position. A number of Islamic countries asserted that population-control measures were inconsistent with Muslim precepts, and Saudi Arabia and Sudan refused to participate at all. Fundamentalists on both sides of the world's major religious chasm—the Christian-Islamic one—found common ground in this area. The Vatican went so far as to censure the leader of the U.S. delegation (the vice president of the United States) and to seek the support of some of the most radical Muslim regimes.

The abortion issue dominated the debate during the first half of the week-long conference, delaying and restricting discussion of other matters. Ironically, the conference's consensus document is not binding on any of the 170 participant countries, but merely charts a course for the world to follow to achieve reduced population growth rates. Still, the Vatican sought to minimize references to abortion, including its availability as a "universal right" or its use as a means of family planning.

The Cairo Conference confirmed the growing strength of a worldwide phenomenon: religious fundamentalism (see Chapter 26). Not only Islamic and Christian faiths, but other religions as well are affected by this phenomenon, and its appeal was evident throughout the meeting as delegations

proclaimed their aversion to secularism and its indulgence, sexual permissiveness, and homosexuality. This pushed into the background a real key to the reduction of population growth: the education of women and the strengthening of their rights in all societies (see Chapter 17). When women have access to education and to paid employment, birth rates decline and development (the corollary theme of the conference) accelerates. Data from the World Bank indicate that when women do not reach high school, they have an average of seven children; but if just two of five women get a secondary education, that average drops to three. And because this smaller number of babies is better spaced (a mother's health improves when the time gap between children exceeds two years), the health of women and children also improves, saving the society medical costs.

But as underscored by Vatican stipulations on the role of women in the church, Islamic practices of polygamy, and Hindu traditions that disadvantage females, the rise of religious fundamentalism runs counter to the interests of women in societies ranging from the poorest to the richest. Some observers argue that the poverty that accompanies rapid population growth would be better combated by addressing the status of women in the world's societies than by attempting to enforce restrictive policies. On this matter, the conference made little progress.

POLICY OPTIONS

Although we tend to associate the notion of population policies with restriction control, such policies have not always been designed to limit population growth. As noted earlier, the former Soviet Union and China under Mao Zedong led other community societies in **expansive population policies**, policies that encourage large families and raise the rate of population growth. One of the countries that long pursued an ideologically based expansionist population policy was the host of the 1974 Bucharest Conference, communist Romania. After the revolution that toppled the communist regime, visitors found horrible conditions in Romania's orphanages: they were filled with children abandoned by parents who could not or would not care for them.

In the past, some governments engaged in pernicious practices generally referred to as **eugenic population policies**, designed to favor one racial sector of the population over others. The ultimate example of eugenics, of course, was Nazi Germany, but other countries also pursued such strategies, though in more subtle ways. Eugenic population policies could be implemented through discriminatory taxation, resource allocation, or other forms of racial favoritism. South Africa during its *apartheid* era constituted another example. Other countries accused of eugenic population policies during the twentieth century include Peru and Singapore.

At present, the majority of the world's countries seek to reduce the rate of natural increase through **restrictive population policies**. These policies range from the toleration of officially unapproved means of birth control in Catholic societies to outright prohibition against large families. In context of the Cairo Conference of 1994, it is important to realize how varied the situation is within Roman Catholic as well as Islamic societies. Demographic data indicate, for example, that Italians in the most Catholic country in the world are not adhering to the Vatican's rules, while Catholics in distant lands do obey them (see box, "Indonesia and the Philippines"). Again, although Islamic states in the Muslim heartland do little to reduce population growth, those far from Mecca do more.

Individual societies have experimented in different ways to achieve their demographic goals, as the following discussion of major national experiences indicates.

JAPAN

The Japanese experience remains a prime example of success—perhaps excessive success—in population control. During its nineteenth- and early twentieth-century era of modernization, expansion, and military victories, Japan's leadership encouraged families to have several children, and limiting families was actually opposed. However, Japan also had growing urban centers, which tended to somewhat reduce the birth rate. This combination of circumstances tended to stabilize the rate of growth.

At the end of World War II, Japan found itself with many hundreds of thousands of refugee nationals who had left the colonies. Soldiers came home and rejoined their families, and the American occupation was attended by the introduction of improved medical services and public health. The cumulative effect was an unprecedented increase in the birth rate and a simultaneous drop in death rates, and Japan's rate of growth, which over the decades had aver-

INDONESIA AND THE PHILIPPINES

Indonesia and the Philippines are island neighbors in Southeast Asia. Indonesia, its population approaching 200 million, is the world's fourth largest country and the largest Islamic nation. The Philippines is Asia's only Roman Catholic country, its population totaling about 70 million.

Religious fundamentalism affects both countries. In the Philippines, the powerful Roman Catholic church opposes the use of artificial contraceptives, and church and state have been locked in a battle over birth control. Abortion is prohibited by the country's constitution. Manila's cardinal demanded that the Philippine government boycott the Cairo U.N. Conference on Population and Development in 1994, and the issue roiled the nation. But the Philippines is a democracy, and while Manila did send a delegation to Cairo, the government could not afford to ignore the pronouncements or the power of the church. In the mid-1990s, population growth in the Philippines was one of Asia's highest at 2.4 percent and doubling in just 29 years.

Islamic Indonesia, on the other hand, has an authoritarian regime that does not tolerate the kind of opposition the Philippines must. In 1970, Indonesia's authorities began a nationwide family planning program, and when Muslim leaders objected, the government used a combination of coercion and inducement to counter their opposition. In Indonesia, too, the Cairo Conference was denounced by fundamentalist Muslims, but the government could afford to ignore them.

Indonesia's family planning program is generally regarded as the most successful in the Muslim world. In the 1970s, annual population growth was as high as 2.5 percent; in the mid-1990s, it was 1.5 percent, nearly a full percentage point below that of the Philippines. Doubling time had risen from 28 years to 43.

The contrast between these two neighbors, Christian and Muslim, reminds us that it is not possible to generalize about religion and family planning. It also underscores the authoritarian regime's advantages over a democratic government with regard to implementing desired policy.

aged about 1.3 percent, suddenly rose to 2.0 percent per year. That represents a doubling time of 35 years, and with Japan's population already about 70 million at the time, it represented a crisis.

In 1948, the Japanese government took action, and the results show clearly in the population pyramid (see Fig. 7-5). The **Eugenic Protection Act** legalized abortions for "social, medical, and economic reasons." Contraceptives were made available, and family planning clinics were set up throughout the country. Although contraception and female **sterilization** (also made available) helped reduce the birth rate, it was the enormous number of abortions that really brought it down. In fact, so many abortions were performed, perhaps 7 to 8 million in a decade, that the Japanese authorities began to worry about their effect on the well-being of the nation. They then began to encourage contraception by means of propaganda and educational programs.

In any case, the birth rate, which in 1947 had been over 34 per 1000, was down to 18 per thousand just one decade after the implementation of the Eugenic Protection Act. It was reduced to 13 per thousand by 1985; the death rate declined from 14.2 in 1948 to 7.5 in 1958 to 6.0 in 1985. Thus Japan's population, growing at less than 1 percent per year, in the early 1980s increased by about 1 million annually. Immigration always was very small and contributed little to population growth, and emigration, though slightly larger, has been similarly insignificant.

In the 1990s, however, Japan's demographic situation was a matter of growing concern for its leaders. The country's fertility rate had fallen to a new low of just over 1.5, far below the 2.1 needed to maintain the population without loss. This is still higher than the prevailing TFR in West Germany just before reuni-

fication, which was below 1.3. But Japan's rate showed no sign of leveling off. The effect of Japan's low fertility rate will be a decline of its population, which will reach a peak of approximately 127 million and then drop to 112 to 115 million by the year 2025.

The Japanese government in 1991 increased the benefits available to parents and began a public campaign to encourage larger families. But it will be difficult to reverse a trend so firmly established under the special conditions of Japanese life. Japan is a territorially small country, about the size of the state of Montana. It is among the world's most highly urbanized, industrialized, and regimented societies. Living space is at a premium; living costs are high. The financial and social burdens of raising a child are high, and parents are well aware that some child benefits will not be much help.

So Japan, like Germany, faces an aging population, dwindling work force, and shrinking tax base at a time when welfare and pension costs are rising.

What are Japan's alternatives? Labor immigration is not an option. The Japanese adamantly refuse to allow foreign workers in any numbers into their nearly homogeneous island nation. A Singapore-style campaign to reverse the downward population spiral is not likely in Japan, nor would it be likely to work. For the time being, Japan probably will turn to an old ally—technology—to stave off the inevitable. It still is possible to turn more work over to robots and other advanced technologies to keep the work force's productivity increasing. Some observers also have suggested that the demographic situation in the early twenty-first century will greatly expand the number of women who will enter the skilled work force.

None of this, however, will ultimately protect Japan from the

effects of less-than-zero population growth or **negative population growth**. With its borders effectively closed to immigration, its future problems will be substantially self-inflicted, proving again that in this age of interaction and interconnection, cultural isolation is no guarantee of a secure future.

INDIA

Demographers predict that some time during the first half of the twenty-first century, India will overtake China as the world's most populous country—if India's political framework holds together. In the mid-1990s, India's population still was growing at about 2 percent, adding 18 million per year to a population approaching 950 million.

The problems involved in formulating and executing a coordinated population policy in a country as culturally complex as India are enormous. India is a federation of 25 states and 7 so-called union territories, and the individual states have a great deal of cultural identity and political discreteness. As in all true federations, the will of the federal government cannot be forcibly imposed on the states. India's religious mosaic alone would make the imposition of a national population policy impractical.

Population planning began on a shoestring budget in the 1950s, not long after India became an independent country. Limited funds were made available for family planning clinics and programs, but in retrospect it seems that government leaders were not aware of the real dimensions of the population explosion at the time. But in the 1960s, India's official census left no doubt, and the government's investment in population planning increased. A national program was instituted, and the states were encouraged to join.

Despite this national effort, the

From the Field Notes

❝ Searing social contrasts abound in India's overcrowded cities. Even in Bombay, India's most prosperous large city, hundreds of thousands of people live like this, in the shadow of modern apartment buildings. Within seconds we were surrounded by a crowd of people asking for help of any kind, their ages ranging from the very young to the very old. Somehow this scene was more troubling here in well-off Bombay than in Calcutta or Madras, but it typified India's urban problems everywhere. ❞

population spiral continued, especially in India's populous eastern states. Also, social problems arose in some of the states where the campaign was pursued most vigorously. Maharashtra State instituted a plan that required sterilization of anyone with three children or more. Public opposition led to rioting and the program was modified, but not before 3.7 million persons had been sterilized. Other states also engaged in compulsory sterilization pro-

grams, but the social and political costs were heavy. Eventually, a total of 22.5 million persons were sterilized, but this form of population control could not be sustained.

Today, Indian states are using advertising, persuasion, and exhortation to urge families to have fewer children. Almost everywhere in the country one can see posters urging people to have small families, and a network of clinics has been established to aid women in even the

remotest villages. But the campaign has gone from compulsion to inducement, and a developing country such as India does not have the resources to make such a program effective.

As Figure 8-2 indicates, there are areas of progress in India, notably in the better educated areas of the south, but elsewhere as well. We should keep in mind the dimensions of India's population clusters, because several of India's states have 100 million inhabitants or more, which would put them among the world's larger countries. To make progress in any individual state in India is a significant achievement, but to achieve a coordinated decline in a democracy as large and diverse as India has proven impossible thus far.

CHINA

For nearly 30 years after the communist government took power, China's demography was as much a mystery to the outside world as China was as a whole. Estimates of China's population (and its rate of natural increase) varied widely. In 1978, the World Bank published its *World Development Report* with an estimated Chinese population of 826 million. Shortly thereafter, the Chinese government announced that the 1 billion mark had been passed. Guesses about China's population had been wrong by as much as 200 million!

If there were doubts about China's numbers, the political and social regime of Mao Zedong left no doubts about its views on family planning. At the 1974 Bucharest Conference, as noted, the Chinese representative denounced population policies as imperialist designs, aimed at sapping the strength of developing countries.

Following Mao's death, China's new leaders expressed very different views. If China was to modernize, they said, the population spiral would have to be brought under control. They wasted no time reversing the Maoist trend. In 1979, the Chinese government launched a policy to induce a married couple to have only one child. This would have stabilized China's population at about 1.2 billion by the end of the century.

The **one-child policy** was applied loosely at first, but when this had less effect than desired, enforcement was severely tightened in 1982. The result was dramatic. In 1970, population increase in China was at a rate of 2.4 percent (as estimated by China's own planners); by 1985, it was down to 1.1 percent. In 1983, when the growth rate had been reduced to 1.2 percent, the United Nations gave China (along with India) its first Family Planning Award.

These statistics are encouraging, but they conceal the hardships faced by families. After 1982, the government made it mandatory for women to use contraceptive devices after they had their one child. If a second child was born nevertheless, one member of the parental couple would have to be sterilized.

Such rules imposed severe hardships, especially on farming families. To do the work of farming, many hands are needed; and a large family is a rural tradition in many parts of the world. Therefore, many Chinese families defied the authorities: they kept pregnant women out of sight, did not register their babies, and prevented inspectors from visiting villages.

At this point, the Chinese government proved its power to rule without impediments from opposing politicians, judges, or human rights advocates. Offenders of the new policies were fired from their jobs, had their farmlands taken away, lost many benefits, and were otherwise disadvantaged in a society suddenly rushing to modernize. In some parts of China, it was much worse: pregnant women known to have one or two children were arrested at work, in the fields, or at home, and taken to abortion clinics to have their babies aborted—sometimes after more than 6 months of pregnancy. The national policies were imposed more harshly in some of China's provinces than in others. In southeast China, according to reports from visitors and Chinese reaching Hong Kong, the campaign was most severe.

China's Ministry of Public Health estimates that during the first six years of the population-control campaign, nearly 70 million abortions were performed in the country (where abortion was a crime, being regarded as murder, just a generation earlier). A sterilization program reached millions as well. During the 1980s, more than 20 million persons were being sterilized *annually* (three times as many women as men), according to government reports.

The effectiveness of the Chinese population policies was ensured, not only by government incentives and punishments, but also through the Communist Party, its officials, local chiefs, and members. Through their power, through promises of advancements and cash payments for local compliance, these party-member vigilantes had become the birth-control police. No village, neighborhood, factory, or collective had been without constant scrutiny.

But China is changing, and the student-led uprising that ended so tragically at Tienanmen Square in Beijing in 1989 is only one manifestation of it. In 1984, in response to rising complaints from rural areas, the government relaxed its one-child policy in the countryside. A couple with a daughter as a first-born were allowed to have a second child after a 4-year wait. Then the party-imposed system of controls began to break down as enforcement weakened, circumvention practices became more effective (sending an illegally pregnant woman to distant family members to await the birth, for example), and peasants with rising incomes could afford to pay the fine for unauthorized births. The results can already be seen in the vital statistics: fertility rates are rising, the downward trend of the growth rate has been reversed, and demographic goals for the 1990s are being exceeded. China's latest census reported a population of 1.21 billion, and the rate of natural increase has moved upward to 1.4 percent. Although this still is a low figure for developing countries, it means that China's goal for the end of the century—1.2 billion and a stable population—will be exceeded by at least 100 million.

Against these abstract figures should be seen the erosive impact of China's one-child-only policy in a society where sons carry on the family name. In the cities, still the abodes of a minority of Chinese, this was a feasible, enforceable objective. But in the tradition-bound countryside, where families have long been large and male children have represented security, succession, and farm labor, the notion of one (possibly female) child was not acceptable. Observers reported that the policy led to female infanticide, the killing of baby girls, and that hundreds of thousands of cases of this kind went unreported during the height of the one-child-only campaign. Demographers studying China's evolving population pyramid estimated that the number of surviving male children exceeded females by 300,000 annually (see Fig. 7-5). China's own population experts have expressed concern over this developing imbalance. In the China of the future, males will outnumber females quite substantially, with unpredictable social consequences.

Thus China's relentless drive for zero population growth tore the traditions of Chinese society and brought misery to millions, United Nations population awards notwithstanding. Chinese government and Communist Party officials acknowledge that the policy, when strictly applied, was severe. But they argue that in a China with 100 million excess births, many millions will be permanently mired in a cycle of stagnation and poverty. To get ahead, these officials argue, the country cannot allow its material gains to be negated by an ever-growing population. The end, they reason, will justify the means.

China's experience underscores the depth of the population dilemma. Even with an authoritarian government backed by party machinery, stringent policies could not be enforced over the long term. Significant short-term gains were quickly wiped out by subsequent reverses. The population spiral has once again become an obstacle to China's modernization. Given China's experience, India's regional progress is all the more remarkable, and Africa's challenge for the twenty-first century is ever more daunting.

KEY TERMS

Abortion
Eugenic Population Policy
Eugenic Protection Act
Expansive Population Policy
Negative Population Growth
One-Child Policy
Restrictive Population Policy
Sterilization

9

POPULATION EXPANSION AND ENVIRONMENTAL STRESS

In the first three chapters of Part 2, we have viewed demographic aspects of global and regional population change. Now the focus is on the impact of humanity's growing numbers on the natural environment inherited from planet Earth.

Biologists estimate that there may be as many as 25 million types of organisms on Earth, perhaps even more; most have not yet been identified, classified, or studied. *Homo sapiens* is only one of these, and in 10 millennia our species has developed a complex culture that is transmitted from generation to generation by learning, and is also to some degree encoded in our genes. We are not unique in possessing a culture: gorillas, chimpanzees, and dolphins have cultures, too. But ours is the only species with a vast and complex array of artifacts, technologies, laws, and belief systems.

No species, not even the powerful dinosaurs of epochs past, ever affected Earthly environments as strongly as humans do today. The

Geographica

- **While the populations of the affluent countries are often smaller than those of the poorer states, per capita consumption of resources in the rich countries is far greater.**

- **Water is a renewable resource, but water shortages threaten in many areas of the world. Conflict over water may come to rival recent conflicts over oil.**

- **Environmental stress is to a large extent attributable to the population explosion. Atmospheric pollution has increased as the Earth's human population has grown, notably since the Industrial Revolution.**

- **Deforestation, desertification, and soil erosion form a triple threat to the environmental future on this planet.**

- **The rapid accumulation of solid, toxic, and radioactive wastes in the technologically advanced countries is producing an increasingly serious disposal problem.**

dinosaurs (and many other species) were extinguished by what may have been an asteroid impact at the Cretaceous/Tertiary (K/T) boundary, as we saw in Part 1. Some biogeographers see an analogy and suggest that the next great extinction may be in the offing, caused not by asteroids but by humans, whose numbers and demands are destroying millions of species—and with them the inherited biodiversity of this planet.

This destructiveness is not just a matter of modern technology and its capacity to do unprecedented damage, whether by wartime forest defoliation, peacetime oil spills, or other means. As we noted in Part 1, human destructiveness manifested itself very early, when fires were set to kill entire herds of reindeer and bison, and entire species of large mammals were hunted to extinction by surprisingly few humans. The Maori, who arrived in New Zealand not much more than 1000 years ago, inflicted massive destruction on the native species of animals and plants in their island habitat—long before modern technology developed more efficient means of extinction. Elsewhere in the Pacific realm, Polynesians reduced the forest cover to brush and, with their penchant for wearing bird-feather robes, had exterminated more than 80 percent of the regional bird species by the time the first Europeans arrived. The Europeans proceeded to ravage species ranging from Galapagos turtles to Antarctic seals. European fashions had a disastrous impact on African species ranging from snakes to leopards. Traditional as well as modern societies have had devastating impacts on their ecologies and on the ecologies of areas into which they migrated.

Is wanton, excessive destruction of life a part of human nature, whatever a society's cultural roots? The question is as sensitive as questions about racism and sexism. Still, regional differences in attitude and behavior can be discerned. African traditional societies hunted for food or in a ceremonial context, but not for entertainment or amusement. The notion of killing for fun and fashion was introduced by Europeans. Hindu society and religious culture in India are more protective of the natural world than many others, as we note in Part 8 of this book. The extermination and near-extermination of many Indian species of animals was accomplished during (Muslim) Moghul and European colonial times.

Wanton destruction of the environment continues in various—indeed many—forms today, ranging from the deliberate spilling of oil and setting of oil fires by Iraqis during the 1991 conflict over Kuwait to the mercury poisoning of Amazonian streams by Brazilian gold miners. For the first time in human history, however, the combined impacts of humanity's destructive and exploitive actions is threatening the entire Earth's biodiversity. Most of that biodiversity has been concentrated in, and protected by, the great equatorial and tropical rainforests of South America, Africa, and Southeast Asia. Now the onslaught on this last biogeographical frontier is under way, and for the future of the planet, the consequences may be catastrophic.

PATTERNS OF CONSUMPTION

While it may be true that human societies are by nature destructive of the natural world of their environs, some surely are more so than others. Maps of world population tend to underscore the magnitude of populations in the poorer countries of the world, but they fail to convey another aspect of societies and their needs: the demands made, per person, on the resources of our planet.

The generally smaller number of people in the more affluent (developed) countries of the world make far greater demands on these resources than do the much larger numbers in the poorer countries. Just consider one category of consumption: energy. It has been estimated that a baby born in the United States during the 1990s will, at current rates, consume about 250 times as much energy over a lifetime as a baby born in Bangladesh over the same lifetime. In terms of food, housing and its components, metals, paper (and thus trees), and in many other ways, the consumption of the individual in already affluent countries far exceeds that of people in the poorer countries. To meet these demands, the developed societies have at their disposal a globe-girdling array of technologies that affect resources, ocean water, the atmosphere, and plant and animal life. Thus overpopulation in the poorer countries tends to be a local or regional matter, keeping villages and countryside mired in poverty. But a growing population in the richer countries also is a form of overpopulation, whose impact is not just local or regional, but global.

Therefore, when we think about the human impact on the physical environment, it is useful to do so geographically. People living in the less developed, poorer countries of the world tend to affect their immediate environments, putting pressure on soil, natural vegetation, and water supplies, and polluting the local air with the smoke of their fires. The burgeoning African population, for example, in many areas is causing peasants to farm slopes that are too steep and to cut down trees to make way for farmland. But the "reach" of affluent societies is much greater. The demand for low-cost meat for fast-food hamburgers in the United States led to the cutting down of trees in Central America, to make way for pastures and cattle herds. Thus the American (and European, Japanese, and Australian) consumer has influence over the fate of faraway environments.

Sometimes, it is difficult to separate the two. The destruction of the Amazonian rainforest involved, early on, attempts by foreign investors to harvest the forest selectively *and* to make the thinned-out forest productive by introducing compatible plants in the cleared patches. The experiment did not succeed, but it undoubtedly contributed to the "opening" of the Amazonian region. Now participants in the forest clearance range from local migrants to Japanese investors.

We should also remind ourselves that changes in the physical world are not always wrought by human intervention. As we noted in Part 1, nature has its own cycles of change. When climates warm and cool, even slightly, areas of the land surface become drier or wetter. In southern Forida, the struggle is on to save the Everglades—not just

from human encroachment, but also from drying up. But we do not know the fate of the Everglades in nature's own design, and by channeling water and protecting wildlife we may be countering it. When, during the 1970s, the Sahara's southern flank became even drier than usual, and the desert began to expand southward, climatologists reported that this happens periodically, in cycles of varying severity that are known to come every 17 to 22 years. While people and their livestock contributed to the destruction of desert-margin vegetation, they were not the cause of the crisis that affected the region for several years.

ENVIRONMENTAL STRESS

The natural environment is being modified and stressed by human action in many obvious and some less obvious ways. Among the more obvious actions causing **environmental stress** are the cutting of forests, the belching of pollutants into the atmosphere, and the spilling of oil into the oceans. Less obvious activities include the quiet burying of toxic wastes and consequent befouling of groundwater, the dumping of vast amounts of garbage into the oceans, and the use of pesticides in farming.

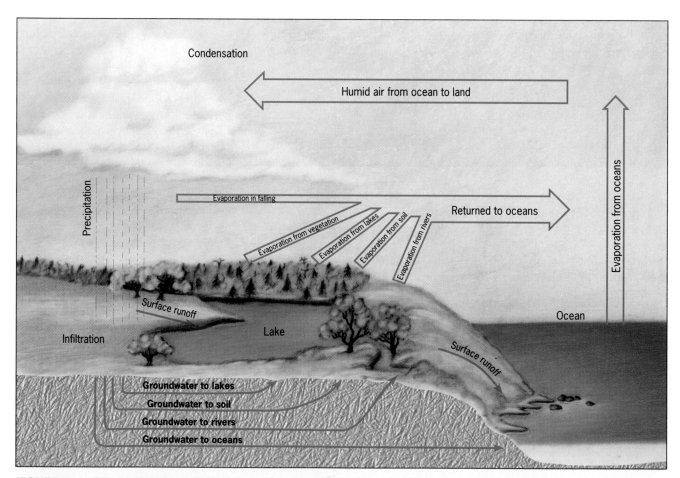

FIGURE 9–1   The hydrologic cycle carries moisture from the oceans and from other water bodies over the land, where precipitation, runoff, and evapotranspiration sustain the system.

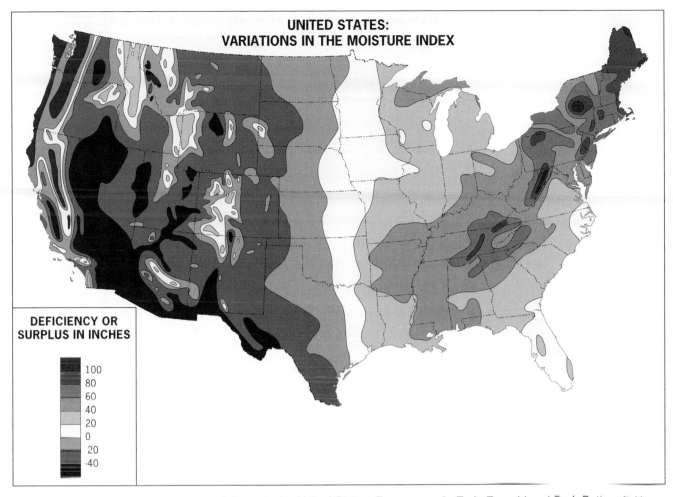

**UNITED STATES:
VARIATIONS IN THE MOISTURE INDEX**

**DEFICIENCY OR
SURPLUS IN INCHES**

100
80
60
40
20
0
20
-40

FIGURE 9–2 Moisture surplus and deficiency in the United States. From a map in E. A. Fernald and D. J. Patton, Editors, *Water Resources Atlas of Florida* (Tallahassee: Florida State University, 1984) p. 6.

We have built seawalls, terraced hillslopes, dammed rivers, cut canals, and modified our environment in many constructive, as well as destructive, ways. Key concerns about the global environment today focus on the following: the future of water supply, the state of the atmosphere (including problems ranging from acid rain to ozone depletion), desertification (in which nature and humanity are probably cooperating), deforestation, the prospects for the Earth's life-sustaining mantle of soil, and the disposal of the enormous quantities of waste generated by industry.

WATER

Water is part of that Earthly inheritance of resources that has developed over periods ranging from thousands of years (in the case of soils) to hundreds of millions of years (metallic ores). Humanity is now consuming these resources in periods ranging from centuries (ores) to decades (soils, species). As we note in more detail in Part 10, economic geographers differentiate between resources that are replenished even as they are used (*renewable* resources) and resources present in finite quantity and thus *nonrenewable*. Water, the

essence of life, is a renewable resource.

But the available supply of fresh water is not distributed evenly across the globe. Figure 1-5 (page 8) revealed the world distribution of precipitation, with the largest totals recorded in equatorial and tropical areas of Southeast Asia, South Asia, Central and coastal West Africa, and Middle and South America. That distribution is sustained through the **hydrologic cycle**, which brings rain and snow to the landmasses from the oceans (Fig. 9-1). The volume of precipitation the Earth provides is enormous; spread out evenly, it would each year cover the land area of the planet with about 33 inches (83 cm) of water. Much of that water is lost through runoff and evaporation, but enough of it seeps downward into porous, water-holding rocks called **aquifers** to provide millions of wells with steady flows. In the United States alone, there is an estimated 50 times as much water stored in such underground aquifers as falls on the land surface every year.

Despite such favorable data, the supply of water across the globe (and in the United States) is anything but plentiful (Fig. 9-2). Chronic water shortages afflict tens of millions of farmers in Africa and hundreds of thousands of city dwellers in southern California; water rationing has been imposed in rainy South Florida and in Spain, which faces the Mediterranean Sea.

In many areas of the world, people have congregated—as farmers, livestock herders, and urban settlers—where water supply is insufficient, undependable, or both. In California in the early 1990s, people were not allowed to wash their cars or refill their swimming pools, minor inconveniences compared to the fate faced by millions of Ethiopians trying, in the parched Sahara margins, to escape their country's civil war. In Florida, where a massive and growing urban population centered on Miami depends on the Biscayne Aquifer for most of its water, the long-term prospect is troubling: when seasonal rains fail to reach their projected averages, the Biscayne Aquifer is overused, and the threat of saltwater invasion from the nearby Atlantic Ocean looms. Such invasion can permanently destroy a freshwater aquifer.

For all humanity's technological progress, it is interesting to compare Figures 1-5 and 6-1, to note how hundreds of millions of people still cluster along several of the

From the Field Notes

66 We drove north on Route 89 from Tucson, Arizona, across the desert. Drought rules the countryside here, and dams conserve what water there is. Snaking through the landscape are lifelines such as this, linking Coolidge Dam to distant farms and towns. In the vast, arid landscape, this narrow ribbon of water seems little more than an artificial brook—but to hundreds of thousands of people, this is what makes life possible in the Southwest. 99

Earth's great rivers. Indeed, nearly three-quarters of all freshwater used annually by all humanity is used in farming, not in cities. In California, where about 80 percent of available water is used in irrigation, this has led to an intense debate over priorities: should the cities be provided with ample water at the expense of Central Valley farms, and should produce *not* harvested as a result be bought from farmers elsewhere—even overseas?

Industries use another 20 percent of water supply worldwide, in the process contributing heavily to pollution when the used water is returned to streams, lakes, and aquifers. When the iron curtain lifted from Eastern Europe, tests indicated that the region's rivers and groundwater were among the world's most severely polluted; inadequately regulated industries were to blame.

Just as humanity has expanded into climatically hostile environments, so population has moved

into inhospitably dry environs. One of the great ecological disasters of the twentieth century is occurring in Kazakhstan and Uzbekistan, whose common boundary runs through the **Aral Sea**. Streams that fed this large body of water were diverted to irrigate the surrounding desert (mainly for commercial cotton production). Heavy use of chemical pesticide ruined the groundwater below, causing a health crisis in the population described by some observers as an "ecological Chernobyl." In the meantime, the Aral Sea began to dry up, and by 1992 it had lost more than three-quarters of its total surface (Fig. 9-3).

Increasingly in our modern world, people have come to depend on water sources of uncertain future capacity. Rocky Mountain and Sierra Nevada snows feed the Colorado River ribbon of water and the aquifers that irrigate the California Central Valley. Lengthy aqueducts snake their way across the desert to thirsty urban communities. None of this slows the population's move to the Sunbelt (see Part 3), and the water situation there has just begun to unfold. So it is in coastal eastern Spain, where low water pressures in city pipes often deprive the upper floors of high-rise buildings of water flow, and in Southwest Asia and the Arabian Peninsula, where growing populations strain ancient supply systems and desalinization plants supplement nature. As oil already has done, water may well spark regional conflicts in the future.

THE ATMOSPHERE

The Earth, it is sometimes said, has six continents and seven seas—but it has only one **atmosphere**, a thin layer of air that lies directly above the lands and oceans. We depend on this atmosphere for our survival;

we breathe its oxygen, it shields us from the destructive rays of the sun, it moderates temperatures, and it carries moisture from the oceans over the land, sustaining crops and forests and replenishing soils and wells.

The atmosphere also has a truly amazing capacity to cleanse itself. In 1883, the Indonesian volcano Krakatau erupted catastrophically, throwing 2.5 cubic miles (10 cubic kilometers) of rock and ash into the atmosphere. Total darkness prevailed in the area for nearly three days; and dust from the explosion encircled the Earth and created vividly colored sunsets for years afterward. However, eventually the atmosphere cleared, and all trace of the event disappeared. In 1980, the eruption of Mount St. Helens in the northwestern United States caused a similar, though much smaller, globe-encircling streak of volcanic dust in the upper atmosphere. Again, the atmosphere purified itself.

Human pollution of the atmosphere, however, may result in longer lasting, possibly even permanent damage. True, the air disperses even the densest smoke and most acrid of chemical gases. But some of the waste pouring into the atmosphere may be producing irreversible change, not only in the **troposphere** (the lowest layer up to about 10 miles, or 16 km, high), but also in the upper-level **stratosphere**. The nature of the change is still being debated, but two centuries of industrial expansion have witnessed an enormous increase in the pollution of the troposphere. While there is global concern and considerable action to limit this pollution, the dimensions of the problem are beyond effective control. No one knew, for example, the true magnitude of pollution of the atmosphere (as well as surface and underground waters) in the former Soviet Union and Eastern Europe while these areas were under Soviet control. Then, when Western pol-

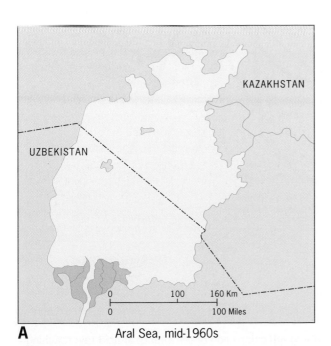

A   Aral Sea, mid-1960s

B   Aral Sea, mid-1990s

FIGURE 9–3   Affected by climatic cycles and afflicted by human interference, the Aral Sea in Turkestan (on the border of Kazakhstan and Uzbekistan) is dying. In a quarter of a century, it lost three-quarters of its surface area.

luters began to impose constraints on themselves, the explosive economic growth of Asian Pacific Rim countries produced another burst of industrial emanations and effluents.

Whether all this pollution is enough to cause long-term climate change remains an open question. Many scientists argue that tropospheric pollution enhances the Earth's heat retention (hence the "greenhouse" warming theories referred to in Part 1) and that its full effect will not be felt until well into the twenty-first century. While estimates of global warming have been lessened, supercomputer models in the mid-1990s still were predicting a global warming of 2°C to 3°C (about 3.5°F to 5.5°F) over the next 50 years. This might be enough to melt some glacial ice and raise sea levels as much as 6 inches (15 cm).

At least the frightening projections of the 1980s—triple the temperature rises, sea levels as much as 15 feet (4.5 m higher)—have been abandoned, and, as we noted earlier, the whole greenhouse notion is being reevaluated. It may well be that humanity's fouling of the atmosphere is taking place at a time when nature's cycle is moving toward a cooling of the planet, so that we have not felt the full effect of nature's design because it has been masked by human intervention. Some scientists suggest that the two opposite trends (human-induced warming, nature's cooling) may collide to produce a period of heightened climatic instability and extremes, the first indications of which already are evident.

Whatever the outcome, there is no question that growing human numbers and increased human activity, ranging from the burning of tropical forests to the industrial pollution of the atmosphere, are having an unprecedented impact on the atmosphere. The amount of a key "greenhouse" gas, carbon dioxide (CO_2), has been increasing as a component of the atmosphere at a rate of about 2 percent per decade; steel mills, refineries, and chemical plants account for a large part of this increase. Without doubt, there *will* be consequences; all that remains uncertain is *what* these consequences will be.

Acid Rain

A byproduct of the enormous volume of pollutants spewed into the atmosphere is **acid rain**. Acid rain forms when sulfur dioxide and nitrogen oxides are released into the atmosphere when fossil fuels (coal, oil, and natural gas) are burned. These pollutants combine with water vapor contained in the air to form dilute solutions of sulfuric and nitric acids, which are subsequently washed out of the atmosphere by rain or other types of precipitation, such as fog and snow.

Although acid rains usually consist of relatively mild acids, they are sufficiently caustic to do great harm over time to certain natural **ecosystems** (the mutual interactions between groups of plant and animal organisms and their environment). Already, there is much evidence that this deposition of acid is causing lakes and streams to acidify (with resultant fish kills), forests to become stunted in their growth, and acid-sensitive crops to die in affected areas; in cities, the corrosion of buildings and monuments is both worsened and

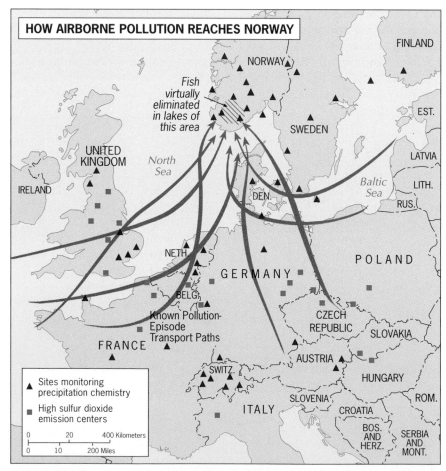

FIGURE 9–4 A vivid cartographic depiction of the impact of acid rain reaching Scandinavia from Western European sources. From *National Geographic,* Vol. 160, No. 5, November, 1981, p. 666.

accelerated. To some extent, acid rain has always been present in certain humid environments, originating from such natural events as volcanic eruptions, forest fires, and even the bacterial decomposition of dead organisms. During the past century, as the Industrial Revolution has spread ever more widely, the destructive capabilities of natural acid rain have been greatly increased by human actions.

The geography of acid rain occurrence is most closely associated with patterns of industrial concentration and middle- to long-distance wind flows. The highest densities of coal and oil burning are associated with large concentrations of heavy manufacturing, such as those in Western and Eastern Europe and the United States. As these industrial areas began to experience increasingly severe air pollution problems in the second half of the twentieth century, many countries (including the United States in 1970) enacted environmental legislation to establish minimal clean-air standards for the first time. For industry, the easiest solution has often been the construction of very high smokestacks (1000 feet [330 meters] or higher is now quite common) in order to disperse pollutants away from source areas through higher-level winds. These longer-distance winds have been effective as transporters, with the result, of course, that more distant areas have become the dumping grounds for sulfur and nitrogen oxide wastes. Regional wind-flows all too frequently steer these acid rain ingredients to wilderness areas, where livelihoods depend heavily on tourism, agriculture, fishing, and forestry. Where international borders are crossed by such airborne pollution, political problems develop (notably between the United States and Canada) and can be expected to intensify in the future.

The spatial distribution of acid rain within Europe offers a classical

From the Field Notes

❝ My first field experience in one of China's Autonomous Regions, the Guangxi-Zhuang A.R., designated for non-Han minorities, had mixed results. Land degradation here was more advanced than in any other part of China visited; desertification seemed to be in progress in many areas. The cause: overuse of the land, and the collapse of what appeared to have been sound terracing systems. My Chinese colleague told me that China's rules for population control *and* land use were relaxed in these Autonomous regions, often leading to ecological damage. ❞

demonstration of all of this. As Figure 9-4 shows, high sulfur-emission sources are located in the major manufacturing complexes of England, France, Belgium, Germany, Poland, and the former Czechoslovakia. The map also indicates that, unfortunately, prevailing windflows from these areas all converge northward to Scandinavia, with a particularly severe acid rain crisis occurring in southern Norway. Lake acidity there is already in the moderately caustic 4 to 5 range on the pH scale of 0 to 14 (7 is neutral), and most fish species, the phytoplankton they feed on, and numerous aquatic plants have been decimated.

New studies now reveal that countries of the former Soviet Union, especially Russia and Ukraine, suffer severely from acid rain. Antiquated, pollution-belching factories in the former Soviet Union's industrial heartlands continue to emanate the chemicals that make acid rain the threat it is. The first research studies on environmental degradation in the Asian Pacific Rim countries to report on acid rain suggests that the situation in East and Southeast Asia is worsening, with serious effects on the remaining natural vegetation.

If you have traveled along tree-lined roads in or near industrial areas, you may have seen brown-tinged or spotted leaves on trees that, overall, do not appear healthy. But if you were to stop and walk some distance from the road, the trees are likely to look better. Studies have shown that automobile-emitted smog, when exposed to bright sunlight, produces low-level concentrations of ozone that are damaging to plants. So even where acid rain is not a serious threat, trees can suffer from heavy

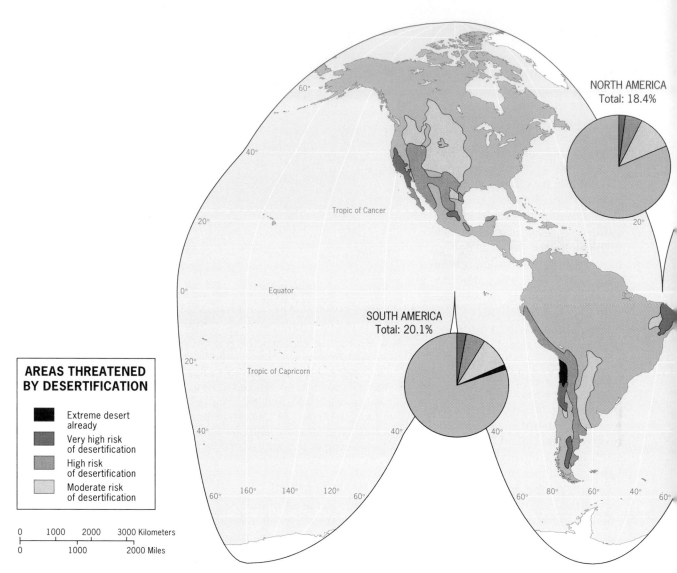

AREAS THREATENED BY DESERTIFICATION

- ⬛ Extreme desert already
- Very high risk of desertification
- High risk of desertification
- Moderate risk of desertification

```
0    1000   2000   3000 Kilometers
0        1000       2000 Miles
```

NORTH AMERICA
Total: 18.4%

SOUTH AMERICA
Total: 20.1%

FIGURE 9–5 Deserts expand and contract cyclically, but nature's cycles can be distorted by human intervention. This map shows areas threatened or affected. From several sources, including J. Turk et al., *Environmental Science* (Philadelphia: Saunders, 1984), p. 305.

vehicle use and exhibit symptoms comparable to those caused by acid rain.

DESERTIFICATION

Climatologists who monitor the changes that slowly modify the climatic map of the world (Fig. 2-3) have long known that the world's deserts are expanding, especially in areas where substantial human habitation flanks the arid zone.

This process has the same effect as the encroachment of glacial cold-

ness, because it increases the area of unlivable territory at the expense of habitable land. Desert margins that have supported some vegetation have been lost to the desert, and **desertification** now threatens desert peripheries from the United States to Africa, Asia, and Australia.

Desert expansion can result from natural causes, and some climatologists see in the southward march of the Sahara the kind of evidence of shifting climatic zones that may be related to an oncoming ice age. However, desertification is also the

result of human activity, a prime example of irreversible environmental modification. The southward march of the Sahara, which in the past 50 years has cost 270,000 square miles (700,000 square kilometers) of farming and grazing land, has been speeded by overgrazing, woodcutting, soil exhaustion, and other environmental misuse. Satellite photography has monitored the advancing edge of the Sahara, and over 20 years it has, on average, encroached southward at a rate of 4 miles (7 kilometers) annually. The

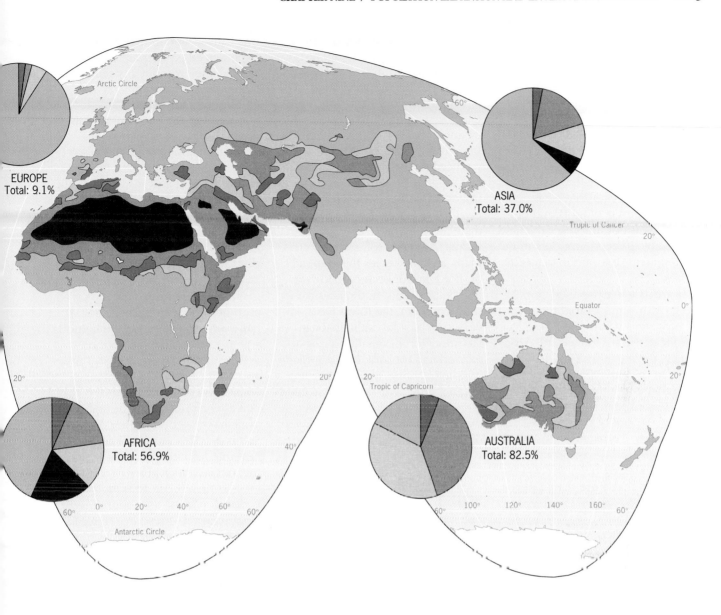

implications of this progression over an extended period of time are all too obvious.

Desertification became a matter of serious international concern during the great Sahel drought of the 1970s (which reappeared to the east in Ethiopia and Sudan in the mid-1980s). In 1977, it was the subject of the United Nations Conference on Desertification, held in Nairobi, Kenya. It became clear that desert encroachment was occurring in many areas of the world. Reports from East Africa, India, Argentina,

Australia, and North America all confirmed that fragile desert-margin ecosystems were being lost to desert encroachment (Fig. 9-5). In China and Algeria, cadres of workers were mobilized to plant vegetation that would anchor the shifting sands, but neither experiment was successful. As our maps indicate, rates of natural population increase are especially high in much of the desert-dominated Muslim realm. The southern margin of the Sahara lies on the edge of the fastest growing population zone on

Earth. The portents for future desertification are many.

DEFORESTATION

Just as the deserts are expanding at the cost of huge areas of habitable space, so are the world's forests yielding to the pressure of human numbers. From the equatorial rainforests of the Amazon Basin to the high-latitude forests of North America and Eurasia, the trees are felled and woodlands shrink.

The world's forests, especially

those of lower and middle latitudes, play a critical role in what biogeographers call the oxygen cycle. Atmospheric oxygen is consumed by natural processes, as well as by human activities. The great forests redress this loss through photosynthesis and its related processes, whereby oxygen is released into the atmosphere. The continued destruction of vast tracts of forest has begun to alarm ecologists and others, who warn of unforeseeable and incalculable effects—not only in the affected areas, but on the planet as a whole.

As we saw in Chapter 6, population growth is most rapid today in the very areas where the forests with the greatest biomass still exist, namely, the equatorial and tropical zones. In the early 1980s, the Food and Agriculture Organization (FAO) of the United Nations undertook a study of the rate of depletion of these forests. This analysis showed that 44 percent of the tropical rainforest had already been affected by cutting, and that more than 1 percent was being logged every year. If this rate of cutting were to continue, the entire equatorial rainforest would be gone in less than 90 years from now. Actually, the situation may be even more critical. Other studies have suggested that the FAO estimate was low, and that the rate of logging and cutting will destroy these forests within just 45 years.

This is what is happening in the great forested areas that still survive in South America, Africa, and Southeast Asia. The smaller surviving stands—in such places as Central America and West Africa—will be gone even earlier. The destruction of forest habitats results in a continuous loss of species of plants and animals which, by the thousands, are becoming extinct. In the Hawaiian Islands, for example, fully half of all its known plant species are today either extinct or endangered.

Again, the effects of **deforesta-** tion are not always obvious or clearly understood. The reforestation (and harvesting) of deforested areas is not the whole answer, even if it could be done on a large scale. Our forests in the United States, for example, consist mainly of *second-growth* trees, the forest that replaced the original forest after it was logged. However, the controlled second-growth forest does not (as the natural forest did) have many trees dying of old age, their trunks and limbs soft from rot. Thus many animal species that depend on holes in trunks and hollows in tree limbs cannot find places to nest. For them, the forest has ceased to be a favorable habitat. Deforestation has many causes— expanding farmland, logging, road-building, mining, and encroaching human settlement—and it has been going on for centuries. However, the threat to the last great reserves of undisturbed natural forest is recent and increasingly disquieting.

SOIL EROSION

The loss of potentially productive soil to erosion has been described as a "quiet crisis" of global proportions by ecologists Lester Brown and Edward Wolf. They point out that the increasing rate of this loss

over the past generation is not the result of a decline in the skills of farmers but rather of the pressures on farmers to produce more. In an integrated world food economy the pressures on land resources are not confined to particular countries; they permeate the entire world. Many traditional agricultural systems that were ecologically stable as recently as midcentury, when there were 2.5 billion people in the world, are breaking down as world population moves toward 5 billion. (p. 9)

Why has **soil erosion** increased so much? The cultivation of ever-steeper slopes, with hastily and carelessly constructed terraces, is one cause—and in many places inexperienced farmers are cultivating steep slopes without any terraces at all. As the pressure on land increases, farmers are less able to leave part of their soil fallow (unused) to allow it to recover its nutrients. Shifting cultivators (see Part 9) must shorten their field rotation cycle, and as a result their soil, too, is less at rest. As agricultural land use intensifies, water and wind erosion increase. Livestock are allowed to graze in areas where they destroy the fragile natural vegetation; lands too dry to be opened up for farming are nonetheless plowed, and soon the wind takes its toll. It has been estimated that the loss of soil to erosion amounts to more than 25 billion tons per year. Brown and Wolf calculate that this may constitute a depletion rate of 0.7 percent per year of all the soil now available, or 7 percent per decade. Soil is properly classified as a renewable resource, because it can regenerate under proper care. However, as these ecologists indicate, it is being "mined" as though it were a nonrenewable resource. International cooperation on food distribution, education of farmers and governments alike, and a worldwide dissemination of soil-conservation methods are urgent steps needed to solve this "quiet crisis."

Desertification and deforestation have been going on for a very long time, and it is always possible to point to old examples to argue that the so-called crises of today are really nothing new. The ancient Greeks deforested their habitat. The Spanish invaders of Mexico cut down the forests for building materials and firewood. Even without human intervention, deserts expand and contract as part of nature's own environmental fluctuations. However, there *is* a difference, and that difference was the topic of Chapter 2. The impact of human numbers on the Earthly environment is greater today than it has ever been.

Thus experts fear the damage is much more likely to be *irreversible* than has been the case in the past.

The lasting effects of intensified environmental exploitation can be seen in the landscapes of countries that have shared in the twentieth-century population explosion. In China, which under the rule of Mao Zedong (1949–1976) was officially opposed to restrictive population policies, the denudation of the countryside became so great that Chairman Mao ordered every Chinese citizen to plant at least one tree. That campaign yielded an estimated 500 million trees, but China's contemporary landscape remains pocked with erosion scars. Whole countrysides have been laid to waste, the topsoil gone soon after crops replaced natural vegetation. Now China is trying to undo the damage, but recovery is not always possible. In tropical Africa, where population is growing faster today than anywhere else on Earth, the environment is under unprecedented stress, frequently with tragic consequences. And in Brazil, the penetration of Amazonia's rainforest refuges marks a dreadful turning point in the biogeography of that critical region.

If all this is so clear, and the future of the global environment is at stake, why can the world not seem to take concerted action to protect it? In part, the problem lies with history. Long before the Amazonian forests were threatened, Europeans and Americans cut their forests down (and disputes over further cutting still continue). Most of the pollution befouling the global atmosphere was put there by the developed, industrialized countries. Now these countries are in the awkward position of leading the campaign to reverse the damage— by advising Brazil, China, India, and other developing countries what to do. But Brazil wants to mine the wealth of its Amazonian interior, and China does not want to constrain its industrial growth with

From the Field Notes

❝ Urban environmental deterioration results from rapidly growing human numbers and inadequate facilities to dispose of their trash and waste. In Bangkok, the burgeoning capital of Thailand, the problem seems to worsen by the year. People throw their garbage out of their doors and windows; tons of trash are dumped into the waterways. The health risks are huge; by some measures Bangkok is the world's most severely polluted city. ❞

environmental rules made by outsiders. Humanity's divisions are costly to the world at large, at a time when concerted action is needed.

DISPOSING OF WASTE

It is a sign of the times that the topic of waste disposal must be included in a discussion of

environmental stress as it relates to the population spiral. But if anything has grown faster still than population itself, it is the waste generated by households, communities, and industries—much of it a matter of bulk, some of it a source of danger.

The United States, the most prodigious consumer of resources, also is the most prolific producer of

solid waste. According to current estimates, the U.S. produces about 1.7 kilograms (3.7 pounds) of solid waste per person per day, which adds up to well over 160 million metric tons (just under 180 million tons) per year. But the U.S. is not alone. Other high-technology economies with a high ratio of disposables (containers, packaging, etc.) face the same problems.

One of the key problems, with geographic implications, involves disposal. The growing volume of waste must be put somewhere, but space for it is no longer easy to find. In the world's poorer countries, waste still is thrown onto open dumps, where vermin multiply, decomposition sends methane gas into the air, rain and waste liquids carry contaminants into the groundwater below, and fires pollute the atmosphere around. In countries that can afford it, such open dumps have been replaced by **sanitary landfills**. Here the waste is put in a hole that has been dug and prepared for the purpose, including floor materials to treat seeping liquids and soil to cover each load as it is compacted and deposited.

The number of suitable sites for sanitary landfills is declining, however, and designating new sites is increasingly difficult. Within the United States, landfill capacity has been reached or will soon be reached in about a dozen States, most of them in the Northeast and Midatlantic regions, and so it becomes necessary for those States to buy space from other states for this purpose. Trucking or sending garbage by rail to distant landfills is a very expensive practice, but alternatives are decreasing (see box, "The Sagas of the *Mobro* and the *Khian Sea*").

On a global scale, similar problems arise. The United States, the European Union, and Japan export solid (including hazardous) wastes to countries in Africa, Middle and South America, and East Asia. While the recipient countries are paid for accepting the waste, they do not have the capacity to treat it properly. So the waste often is dumped in open landfills, where it creates the very hazards the exporters want to avoid. In the late 1980s, the richer countries' practice of "managing" waste by exporting it became a contentious United Nations issue, and in 1989 a treaty was drawn up to control it. The treaty did not (as many poorer countries wished) prohibit the exporting of hazardous waste, although it did require the recipient country's prior consent before the waste could be transported.

The most hazardous waste of all is radioactive waste. It is useful to differentiate between **toxic wastes**, in which the danger is caused by chemicals, infectious materials, and the like, and **radioactive wastes**, which consist of low-level radioactive wastes that give off small amounts of radiation (produced by industry, hospitals, research facilities, and nuclear power plants) and high-level radioactive wastes, which emit strong radiation and are produced solely by nuclear power plants and nuclear weapons factories. In the United States, low-level radioactive wastes have for many years been disposed of in steel drums, placed in six special government-run landfills of which three are now closed.

High-level radioactive waste is extremely dangerous and difficult to get rid of. Fuel rods from nuclear reactors will remain radioactive for thousands of years to come and must be stored in remote locales where there is no possibility that they will contaminate water, air, or any other part of the environment. In fact, no satisfactory means or

THE SAGAS OF THE *MOBRO* AND THE *KHIAN SEA*

Disposing of waste can be a difficult challenge. In 1987, a barge named *Mobro*, loaded with garbage, was refused permission to unload its cargo at an Islip, New York landfill. Towed by the tugboat *Break of Dawn*, the *Mobro* set to sea in the hope of finding an alternative site for disposal. Arriving in North Carolina, the *Mobro* was again refused, and the tugboat towed it out to sea again. After a journey of 6000 miles (9600 km), during which it called at six states and three countries, the *Mobro* limped back into New York waters—where state officials finally allowed the garbage to be burned in a Brooklyn incinerator.

The story of the *Khian Sea* is an even less auspicious adventure. This was a ship under the Bahamian flag, hired by the city of Philadelphia to take a load of incinerated ash to Panama, where it was to be used as roadbuilding material. Incinerated ash contains toxic chemicals, and when the Panamanians realized that these materials would endanger the wetlands through which the road in question was being built, they refused to accept the cargo. This refusal started the *Khian Sea* on a two-year, five-continent journey in the hope of finding a country that would accept the toxic ash, but no buyer could be located. Then, one day, the ship appeared off the port of Singapore, its holds empty. To this day, only the crew members know what happened—whether the ash was dumped at sea or on some remote shore.

place for the disposal of high-level radioactive waste has been found. Among many suggestions there are those favoring deep shafts in the bedrock, chambers dug in salt deposits (salt effectively blocks radiation), ice chambers in Antarctica, burial beneath the ocean floor, and deposition in volcanically active midocean trenches. Meanwhile, spent fuel rods (which last only about three years in the reactor) are put in specially designed drums and stored in one of about 100 sites, all of them potentially dangerous. In the mid-1990s, the U.S. government was developing two major disposal sites, one for waste from commercial nuclear power plants at Yucca Mountain in southern Nevada, and the other near Carlsbad in southern New Mexico, for military waste.

There is an associated problem. Even if secure and safe storage can be found for high-level radioactive waste, the waste has to be transported from its source to the disposal site. Such transportation presents an additional hazard; a truck or train accident could have calamitous consequences.

The dimensions of the waste-disposal problem are growing and are becoming global. The emerging threat to the planet's environment is not just over the short term but can exist for centuries, indeed millennia, to come.

KEY TERMS

Acid Rain
Aquifer
Aral Sea
Atmosphere
Deforestation
Desertification
Ecosystem
Environmental Stress
Hydrologic Cycle
Radioactive Waste
Sanitary Landfill
Soil Erosion
Solid Waste
Stratosphere
Toxic Waste
Troposphere
Water

China's Great Wall was built to control movement and migration.

PART THREE

STREAMS OF HUMAN MOBILITY

At Issue

An estimated 4.8 million "undocumented" immigrants are living and working in the United States in the late 1990s. More than half—perhaps as many as two-thirds—of this number have crossed the porous border between the United States and Mexico. During the 1994 Gubernatorial and Congressional political campaigns in California, illegal immigration became a key issue. Placed before the voters was a measure whose intent was to deny immigrants without documents the opportunity to use educational, medical, and other social services and facilities. Proposition 187, as this measure was known, was endorsed by the Republican governor and approved by a substantial majority of the voters. Polls showed that among Californians who cast ballots, Proposition 187 was supported by all sectors (African Americans, whites, Asians) except Hispanics. The measure was immediately challenged in the State's courts, but by early 1995 similar measures were already being prepared in Florida and Texas. At issue: if the federal government cannot control the country's borders, should the States be required to pay the bills for the social services illegal immigrants require? Or should the federal government use tax revenues to subsidize the States where most undocumented immigrants live, thus spreading the burden to all? The United States is a nation of immigrants, but now it is divided on the issue of immigration itself.

10

WHY PEOPLE MOVE

What impelled our ancient East African ancestors to leave their familiar abode, to walk toward the unknown, to cross into Arabia, eventually into India, and ultimately into Australia? What could have persuaded early *Homo sapiens* to venture into the cold of Pleistocene Europe? To cross the Bering land bridge from Asia to America? To risk survival on the open sea in flimsy boats?

The question obviously goes to the heart of one of the basics of human behavior. To this day, and as long as humanity survives, people will seek new frontiers—new islands and continents in the past, and new planets and galaxies in the future. Risks will be taken and lives will be lost, but just as horizons receded in the past, so will the void still surrounding us. Our quest for the moon resulted from the same urge that dispersed *H. sapiens* in the first place.

Americans should know the answer to the question. The population of the United States is the most mobile in the world. More than 5 million people move from one state to another every year, and nearly seven times as many—an average of 35 million—move within

Geographica

- Many factors, including conflict, economic conditions, political strife, cultural circumstances, environmental change, and technological aspects, stimulate the migration process.

- Migrants move on the basis of their perceptions of destinations; distance tends to affect the accuracy of these perceptions.

- Migration usually takes place in stages. Rural-to-urban movement occurs in steps, often from smaller to larger centers; migrants tend to relocate repeatedly in the land of their destination.

- Voluntary migrations, such as the movement toward the Sunbelt in North America, are stimulated by pull as well as push factors.

- Forced migrations result from the imposition of power by stronger forces over weaker peoples; the modern manifestation of this condition is the repatriation of illegal migrants by governments unwilling to accept them.

their states, within their counties, or within their communities. On average, an American citizen moves approximately every 6 years. And this actually represents a slight *decline* in mobility: less than one generation ago, the average American moved every 5.5 years.

Human mobility is of central interest in human geography, because it is an inherently spatial process.

Human movement creates routes, streams of change. It speeds the diffusion of ideas and innovations. It intensifies spatial interaction and transforms regions. And as we will see, environmental circumstances often play a role in generating it. The whole breadth of human geography lies before us as we study our compulsion to move and to travel.

111

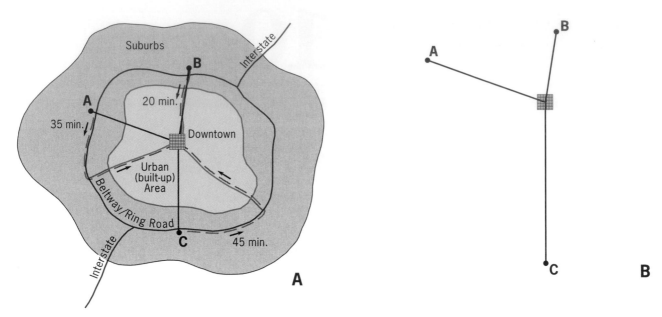

FIGURE 10–1   The absolute distance of three homes just outside an urban beltway (A) and their relative distance, once the travel times to the central city are measured (B).

SOME GEOGRAPHIC BACKGROUND

Human movement often results from a perception that conditions are better, safer, easier, or in some other way superior (or at least different from) in some distant place. We took note of the role of perception in human geography in Chapter 1, and now is the time to consider some aspects of it.

When people move, either permanently to a new abode or temporarily (for example, for a long vacation), they think in terms of the *direction* their travel should take. In geography, direction (like location) is viewed in two ways: *absolute* and *relative.* Just as absolute location refers to the global grid system, so **absolute direction** refers to astronomical determinants. Absolute north and south point, from any given location, to the north and south poles, respectively. Absolute east and west are directions exactly parallel to latitude lines. Intervening directions are given by measured degree; for example SE is south 45° east. Absolute direction thus is *compass* direction.

Relative direction, on the other hand, is more perceptual and less mathematical. During a cold winter, a Michigan family may contemplate a vacation (or perhaps a relocation) to the so-called Sunbelt. Exactly where is this Sunbelt? It lies to the south, obviously, but people's perceptions of it vary. Almost everyone would agree that Florida is part of the Sunbelt, but other areas (Arkansas and Utah, for example) are viewed differently. So it is with such directional images as the "Middle East," which implies that there is a "Near East" and a "Far East." Those perceptions derive from older British usage: the "Near East," viewed from London, consisted of Turkey, Egypt, Libya, and the coastal countries of the eastern Mediterranean. The "Middle East" was centered on Iraq and the Persion Gulf, and the "Far East" was the East Asian realm. That usage has been adopted, rather unfortunately, in the United States; the "Far East" across the Pacific ought to be called the "Far West!"

A second perception affecting human mobility is *distance*. Again, distance can be measured in *abso-lute* terms. Such distances can be read on maps, using the scales discussed in Resource A at the back of this book. But distance "as the crow flies" more often than not is irrelevant when it comes to people's travel or other movement. The U.S. system of interstate highways did not change the **absolute distance** between places that it connects, but it did alter the time it takes to travel by automobile between those places. Commuters are always looking for alternate routes between their homes and places of work, not because the absolute distance between these points changes, but because what we may call the *relevant*, **relative distance** is shortened by a quicker route (Fig. 10-1).

Research has shown that people's perceptions of both distance and direction are often greatly distorted, and this means that many travel decisions are made on the basis of inadequate information. Add to this the incomplete geographic picture people all too frequently have of areas to which they relocate, and it is understandable that a sometimes sizeable

MIGRATION AND DEMOGRAPHIC STRUCTURE

The age-sex pyramids of individual countries (see Figs. 7–4 and 7–5) summarize the structure of the population as a whole, but they conceal internal differences. Age compositions of cities often differ markedly from those of rural areas. Families in cities tend to be smaller, and there are fewer children, proportionally, than in the countryside. Even within cities contrasts occur, for the population pyramid of the white sector may differ substantially from that of the black sector. Obviously, the migration process that brings people to the cities from the countryside has an impact on their respective population structures, because many of the migrants are young adults in search of work. This age-selective migration can be discerned on the charts.

Migration can also be sex-selective, whether forced or voluntary. Far more male than female Africans were taken to the New World as slaves. In modern times, the number of male emigrants from European countries to America was much larger than the female total. At the beginning of the century, there were about 107 males in the United States for every 100 females, but time has eliminated that disparity, and now the statistics show women to be in a slight majority. Greater male wartime losses and the longer life expectancy of women have contributed to the reversal. In cities of India and Africa, males continue to outnumber females, sometimes overwhelmingly—in part a result of sex-selective migration and the cause of serious problems of social adjustment.

---

percentage of movers soon returns home.

MIGRATION

In Chapter 7, we saw that the total population growth or decline of a country is not only a matter of natural increase or decrease, but also involves the movement of people into or out of that country. In the case of the United States, the natural increase of population is substantially lower than the overall growth, because in-migration from other countries exceeds out-migration by several hundred thousand people every year. The low growth rates recorded in several European countries, on the other hand, reflect the permanent departure of citizens, as well as declining fertility rates.

Emigration (out-migration) and immigration (in-migration) are man-ifestations of the phenomenon of **migration**, the long term relocation of an individual, household, or group to a new location outside the community of origin. Long term, in this context, accounts for the reality that many migrants, after having moved, may move again, while others, following their departure, are unable to adjust or establish themselves and return home.

Migration has external as well as internal components. When migrants move from country to country, they become part of the vital statistics of the countries they leave and enter (see box, "Migration and Demographic Structure.") But as we note later, countries also experience *internal* migration—not in helter-skelter fashion but in often well-defined streams that change over time. In the United States during the 1980s and 1990, internal migration streams were moving people from east to west and from north to south. The older industrial states of the north and east were losing people to the Sunbelt; the U.S. Census Bureau reported that New York alone, between 1981 and 1988, had lost 330,000 persons to Florida and nearly 70,000 to California. But these are recent movements. During the first decades of the twentieth century, especially after World War I, a major internal migration stream carried tens of thousands of black families from the South to the industrializing cities of the very "rustbelt" from which people are moving away today.

CATALYSTS OF MIGRATION

What impels people to pull up stakes and leave the familiar for the uncertain? Research has shown that it usually is not just one factor, but a combination of factors that leads to an often fateful decision. The key factors are:

ECONOMIC CONDITIONS

Poverty has driven countless millions from their homelands and continues to do so. Perceived opportunities in destinations such as Western Europe and North America impel numerous migrants, legal and illegal, to cross the Mediterranean, the Caribbean, and the Rio Grande in search of better lives.

POLITICAL CIRCUMSTANCES

Oppressive regimes have engendered migration streams throughout history. More than 125,000 Cubans left their country in 1980 on the "Mariel Boatlift" to escape communist dictatorship. Vietnam's desperate "boat people" fled by the hundreds of thousands after Hanoi's communists took control of their country. In 1972, Uganda's dictator Idi Amin expelled 50,000 Asians from his African country. Both escape and expulsion mark migrations driven by politics.

ARMED CONFLICT

The dreadful conflict that engulfed the former Yugoslavia during the 1990s drove as many as three million people from their homes, and many (in 1995 the number still was uncertain) became permanent emigrants, unable to return to what remained of their abodes. During the 1980s, the bitter war in Afghanistan sent as many as six million people across the country's borders. In 1995, with their country still in disarray, most of these migrants seemed to be compelled to remain in Iran and Afghanistan.

ENVIRONMENTAL CONDITIONS

One of historical geography's major examples of environment-induced migration involved the movement of hundreds of thousands of Irish citizens from Ireland to the New World during the 1840s. Prolonged excessive rains rotted the country's potato crops, which created a famine; as a result, the demographics of both Ireland (the source) and the U.S. Northeast (the chief destination) were permanently altered. Environmental crises such as major earthquakes and volcanic eruptions also stimulate migrations. For example, every major earthquake in California is followed by a surge in emigration. But many of the emigrants return, so that the net outflow generated by such crises is comparatively small.

CULTURE AND TRADITION

People who are uncertain that their cultures and traditions will survive a major political or governmental transition, and who are able to mi-

THEORIES CONCERNING MIGRATION

The question, "What leads people to their decision to migrate?" has intrigued researchers for more than a century. Studies of the "migration decision" indicate that the intensity of a migration flow varies with such factors as the degree of difference between source and destination, the effectiveness of the information flow from destination back to source, and the physical distance between source and (ultimate) destination.

As long ago as 1885, the British demographer Ernst Ravenstein studied internal migration in England, and from his data derived several "laws" of migration. These formulations still retain their relevance today:

1. *Net migration amounts to a fraction of the gross migration between two places.*   Every migration flow generates a "return" or "counter" migration, so the actual migration is the volume of the original flow minus the return flow.
2. *The majority of migrants move a short distance.*   Since Ravenstein's time, average migration distance undoubtedly has increased, but step migration still prevails today.
3. *Migrants who move longer distances tend to choose big-city destinations.*   London was the great magnet in Ravenstein's time, and other British cities were mushrooming.
4. *Urban residents are less migratory than inhabitants of rural areas.*   In the England of Ravenstein's time, urbanization was drawing people toward towns and cities. The same phenomenon can be observed today in the developing countries.
5. *Families are less likely to make international moves than young adults.*   From Southeast Asia to Middle America to Africa, the evidence is that young adults are indeed the most mobile population group.

Among other conclusions, Ravenstein also suggested that there is an inverse relationship between the volume of migration and the distance between source and destination; that is, the number of migrants declines as the distance they know they must travel increases. This anticipates the formulation of geography's **gravity model**, a measure of the interaction of places. The gravity model predicts this interaction on the basis of the population sizes of the respective places, and the distance between them. It states that spatial interaction (such as migration) is directly related to the populations and inversely related to the distance between them. Expressed mathematically, the model holds that interaction is proportional to the multiplication of the two populations divided by the distance between them. Variants of this notion are applicable in many areas of human geography, especially economic geography.

grate to perceived safer havens, will often do so. When British India was partitioned into a mainly Hindu India and an almost exclusively Muslim Pakistan, millions of Muslim residents of India migrated across the border to the Islamic state.

Given the opportunity after decades of Soviet obstruction, more than two million Jews left the former U.S.S.R. for Israel and other destinations, unsure of their futures in the new Russia. South Africa's turbulent political transition during the mid-

1990s impelled many whites to emigrate to Australia, Europe, and North America.

TECHNOLOGICAL FACTORS

For many migrants, emigration is no longer the difficult and hazardous journey it used to be. While many migrants still move by simple and even difficult means, millions more now use options provided by modern transportation, more secure initial relocation, and more comfortable habitation. Researchers suggest that the growing availability of air conditioning greatly reduced the return migration from the Sunbelt back to the north, resulting in a larger net flow of regional migrants in the United States.

INFORMATION FLOW

News today travels faster than ever, including news of job opportunities and ways to reach desired destinations. Gone is the time when would-be emigrants waited months, even years, for information about distant places that might beckon them. Television, radio, and telephone have stimulated millions to make the "migration decision" by relaying information about relatives, opportunities, and communities already established in destination lands. Turks quickly heard about Germany's need for labor. Algerians knew where to go in France. Haitians knew that a "Little Haiti" had sprung up in the Miami area, an outpost in constant touch with the source of migrants.

PUSH AND PULL FACTORS

Geographers who study human migration have found it useful to identify conditions and perceptions

that tend to induce people to leave their abodes **(push factors)**, and have perceived circumstances that effectively attract people to certain locales from other places **(pull factors)** (see box, "Theories Concerning Migration").

From our preceding discussion of migration catalysts, we can deduce a number of push and pull factors. Usually, the decision to migrate results from a combination of the two, plus perceived obstacles (or lack thereof) that have nothing to do directly with place of origin or destination. Because a migrant is likely to be more familiar with his or her place of residence (source) than with the locale to which he or she is moving (destination), push factors are likely to be more accurately perceived, in general, than pull factors. Push factors will include individual and personal considerations such as work or retirement conditions, cost of living, personal safety and security, and, for many, weather and climate. Pull factors are likely to be more vague and to depend, perhaps, on several visits, at best. Many migrants move on the basis of excessively positive images and expectations regarding their destinations.

The geographic principle of **distance decay** comes into play here (Fig. 10-2). Prospective migrants are likely to have more complete and accurate perceptions of nearer places than of farther ones, which confirms the notion that the intensity of human activity, process, or function declines as distance from its source increases. Since interaction with faraway places decreases as distance increases, prospective migrants are likely to feel much less certain about distant destinations than about nearer ones. This leads many migrants to move less far than they originally contemplated. Indeed, many migration streams that appear on maps as long, unbroken routes in fact consist of a series of stages in **step migration**. A peasant family in Brazil, for example, is

likely to move first to a village, then to a nearby town, later to a city, and finally to a metropolis such as São Paulo or Rio de Janeiro. At each stage, a new set of pull factors comes into play.

But not all migrants complete all the steps. When 1000 people in a given year leave a village and migrate to a town, most if not all of them are likely to harbor notions about making it to—and in—the "big city." But eventually, only about 500 may in fact move from town to city, and of these, only 200 eventually see the skyline of the metropolis that impelled them to move in the first place. Along the way, **intervening opportunity** captured the majority. This is what happened when African Americans, after the First World War, migrated northward to seek work in such growing cities as Chicago and Cleveland. Many found employment in St. Louis and Cincinnati, intervening opportunities on their northbound course. Like distance decay, intervening opportunity is another geographic principle that has relevance in the study of migration, as well as in other aspects of human activity. A special kind of temporary migrants—tourists—also respond to intervening opportunities. Cost-conscious vacationers will choose a nearer, and thus cheaper, resort over a more distant one made costlier by a longer plane trip,

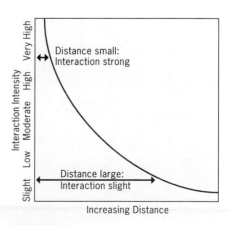

FIGURE 10–2

other things being approximately equal. Intervening opportunity is the constant worry of every resort locale that depends on long-range patrons.

VOLUNTARY AND FORCED MIGRATIONS

Our final look at the reasons people move focuses on two opposites: the luxury of choice and the terror of compulsion. The properties of two great modern migration flows—of Europeans to overseas settlements and Africans to the Americas—indicates that there are different *types* of migratory movements. The most obvious classification to be derived distinguishes between **voluntary** and **forced migrations**. However, within each of these categories there are different cases. African slaves were captured and transported in bondage like prisoners, then sold and placed in servitude. Other migrants who were forced to move faced quite different circumstances. To use a modern case: during the early 1970s, the African regime ruling Uganda decided to

oust nearly all the Asians in that country, many of whom were shopkeepers, traders, or otherwise engaged in commerce. They had no choice and were given very little time to get out of a country in which many of them had been born. As approximately 50,000 Asians were transported out of Uganda with only the belongings that they could carry, this was obviously a forced migration—but still a very different type of forced migration than that of the African slaves to America. We should, therefore, focus more closely on our two classes of migratory movements and examine their contents.

VOLUNTARY MIGRATION

Among the millions of Europeans who came to the Americas, most arrived with the hope of material improvement, greater opportunity, and better living standards. These same motives carried others from Europe to the African and Asian colonies—Portuguese and British to new farmlands in Angola and Kenya, Belgians and Dutch to the riches of the (then) Congo and Netherlands East Indies. Some of the emigrants, among them many

Irish families, left for the New World in the face of declining harvests and the specter of hunger, so that an element of force *does* enter the picture. The prevailing force, however, was the "pull" of opportunity beckoning elsewhere. Today, as we noted previously, this is the force that leads people to abandon their rural abodes and head for the cities.

Another kind of voluntary migration involves people's search for places where they can be with their own kind. The world is a mosaic of languages, religions, and ways of life, and there are minorities everywhere. Most of these minorities have become adjusted to life under their particular circumstances, but times do change. When independence came to Africa's European colonies, some of the white settlers were able to adjust to the new situation; they remained through the transition. Others could not confront it, so they departed, some to South Africa, others to Europe. Unlike the Asians forced out of Uganda, these Europeans were not ousted. If there was a "push" factor, it was often more in what they perceived might happen than in what actually did occur. Theirs was a voluntary emigration. Similarly, communities may decide to seek new abodes where they will enjoy more religious freedom, as many Muslims did when India and Pakistan were partitioned. People move for linguistic reasons, as well as for reasons of social and psychological adjustment. It is all a matter of perception and choice.

In the United States, we see another considerable migration flow in the movement of people who reach retirement age, and who leave their long-time homes for Florida, Arizona, or another Sunbelt locale where the weather may be milder and where costs may be lower (some move to Mexico). Again, this is mainly a voluntary migration, often planned for many years before the move is actually

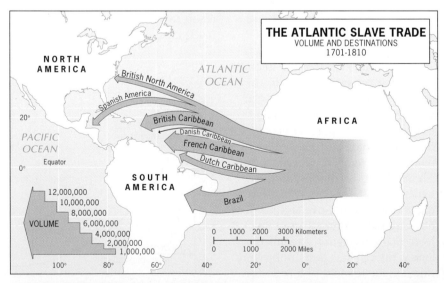

FIGURE 10–3 Dimensions of the Atlantic slave trade. After a map in P. Curtin, *The Atlantic Slave Trade* (Madison: University of Wisconsin Press, 1969), p. 57.

made. There are elements of cultural migration here, similar to those discussed in the preceding paragraph. Older people perceive that they will find themselves living in places where other retirees also reside, so that they may share that group's interests and activities. The impact of this migration flow can be seen in Florida's myriad high-rise condominiums and Arizona's sprawling retirement communities.

FORCED MIGRATION

Several of the world's largest migration streams have been forced migrations. The Transatlantic **Slave Trade**, which carried tens of millions of Africans from their homes to the Americas, with huge loss of life, was by far the most consequential. How many Africans were taken in bondage will probably never be known (estimates range from 12 to over 30 million), and Figure 10-3 is a guide only to the destinations and their proportions. By far the largest number of Africans were brought to plantations in the Caribbean and eastern South America. Today, the descendants of these people form the overwhelming majority in several Caribbean countries' total population. Actually, despite the substantial black population of the United States at present, the number of enslaved Africans who were taken to this country was quite small compared to the many who went as forced immigrants to the Caribbean and South America. By 1800, the black population of the United States was just 1 million (Fig. 10-3).

It is appropriate to reflect on the consequences that the quest for slaves had in Africa itself. Europe's emigrants were, for the most part, able to leave by their own choice (some did go as exiled prisoners or as indentured laborers), and by their departure they relieved, to some extent, the very pressures that forced them to go. In Africa, on the other hand, there was no such freedom of choice, and, far from improving the situation, the forced emigration greatly damaged the societies that were affected. From Europe, whole families left and joined communities in America that could, to some degree, cushion the effects of migration shock. In Africa, families were destroyed, children were orphaned, and communities were disrupted—and in America the African slaves faced not only terror, but loneliness as well. In Africa, the communities subjected to slave raiding, if they survived at all, found themselves without most of their younger men; in America, there was a shortage of women for a long time, even after freedom came. It took generations before the demographic effects of the slave trade were overcome and population structures in Africa and the Americas regained their long-term balance.

Nothing in human history compares to the North Atlantic Slave Trade, but other forced migrations also changed the world's demographic map. Tens of thousands of convicts were shipped from Britain to Australia, where they had a lasting impact on the continent's population geography, during the half century beginning in 1788. During Stalin's ruthless rule in the then-Soviet Union, many millions of non-Russians were forcibly moved from their homes to remote reaches of Central Asia and Siberia for reasons ranging from alleged treason to obstruction of the communist grand design. Nor is the ugly phenomenon of forced migration extinct today. It continues to exist in the form of **counter migration**, when governments send back migrants caught entering their countries illegally. In the 1990s, the repatriation of Haitian arrivals from Florida and of Vietnamese escapees from Hong Kong has captured the headlines.

By comparison, other migration streams—however desperate and whatever their causes—are benign.

Whenever we observe migrations, historic or current, we should realize that the flow of migrants represents only a small fraction of the population at the source; the migrants have made a choice that is not available to those moved forcibly. Another contrast lies in the "return" migration. All voluntary migration flows generate a return, or counter, migration. Some Soviet-Jewish emigrants have actually returned to Russia. Some winter-wary Canadians find that they cannot adjust to life in Florida and return home. So any voluntary migration flow represents the numbers going from source to destination *minus* those returning from destination to source. This cannot be said of forced migrations.

Today, newspaper headlines and television newscasts are dominated by reports of a type of migration that is rapidly growing: the often desperate migration of refugees escaping conflict and violence in their countries. This phenomenon constitutes a distinct kind of forced migration and is given special attention in a later chapter. Having examined the factors that stimulate migration, we turn next to the routes people follow when they migrate.

KEY TERMS

Absolute Direction
Absolute Distance
Counter Migration
Distance Decay
Forced Migration
Gravity Model
Intervening Opportunity
Migration
Pull Factors
Push Factors
Relative Direction
Relative Distance
Slave Trade
Step Migration
Voluntary Migration

11

WHERE PEOPLE MOVE

Having noted the factors and forces that cause people to move, we now turn to the geographic question: where are the major migration routes that help globalize and internationalize the world, past and present? Every day, millions of people are on the move, some across oceans and seas, others from village to town. Migration, we will find, occurs in surges, sometimes overwhelming the authorities who try to control it. At other times the surge may be encouraged: when Western Europe experienced a postwar economic boom, Europeans spurned jobs willingly done by Turkish and North African immigrants, and the migrants arrived by the millions.

We turn to these large-dimension migrations later, but first we should consider the many different forms manifested by human mobility. The great majority of people (that is, people not confined to a hospital bed, prison, or other facility) have a daily routine that takes them through an oft-repeated sequence of short moves. These moves create what geographers call **activity** (or **action**) **space**.

The magnitude of such activity space varies by society. North Americans' activity space, on average, is very large compared to that

Geographica

- Mobility is among the qualities that define the character of a culture, and American society today is the world's most mobile.

- A society's mobility is measured as the sum of cyclic, periodic, and migratory movements by its population.

- The voluntary migration of Europeans to the New World, the forced migration of Africans to the Americas, and the migration of Europeans to their overseas colonial empires are among migration streams that have transformed the world.

- Internal migrations, involving major population shifts, have occurred in the former Soviet Union, the United States, China, and other large countries.

- In the United States, the Northeast and the Midwest have been losing population for decades, while the South and West have been gaining.

- Physical as well as legal barriers are placed in the way of migrants, but few countries have succeeded in controlling immigration effectively.

of, say, Africans or Southwest Asians. Millions of American commuters travel greater daily distances than many Chinese village dwellers do in a year. Technology has vastly expanded daily activity spaces, as reflected by continuous shuttle flights between major cities such as Washington, D.C. and New York City.

TYPES OF MOVEMENTS

Migration, involving permanent relocation, is not the only form of movement that affects populations and communities. Mobility of all kinds is one of the defining characteristics of a culture.

Consider your own lifestyle in this context. You may go to classes every weekday, and perhaps to a job as well. This is a form of **cyclic movement**, and it defines your activity space. However, you may also have come from another town, perhaps even another state, to study at the college or university you now attend. Your arrival for the fall semester and your return trip after the spring is a different form of movement, **periodic movement**, involving a lengthy period of residence following your trip. After graduation, you may decide to take a position in a foreign country, perhaps as an employee of a business with international connections. That may lead to long-term residence in that foreign country, and your move becomes a case of **migratory movement**.

We already have noted that migration takes many forms. Cyclic and periodic movements, too, occur in numerous ways. We are creatures of habit, and our habits, from commuting to vacationing, define our activity spaces.

CYCLIC MOVEMENT

Cyclic movement involves journeys that begin at and bring us back to our home base. In farming villages around the world, the farmers walk or ride to the fields each morning, spend the day at work on the land, and return to the village at night. This *daily* cyclic movement has its equivalent in our urbanized society in the daily journey to work, commuting, a trip that sometimes involves hours of travel in automobiles, buses, trains, or subways. People working in the central business districts of large cities, such as New York and Chicago, are prepared to travel an hour or more each way every working day. Thus, despite the recent suburbanization of economic activity (to be discussed in Chapter 36), these central cities still have substantial drawing power over the surrounding labor force. Thousands of people, for example, travel from New Jersey into

and out of New York every day for work purposes.

Your trip to classes each day may be shorter, but it is nevertheless a form of cyclic movement. So, too, are shopping trips; if you would keep a record of those journeys, you would find yourself returning time and again to the same store or gasoline station. Again, visits to friends and other trips for social purposes are usually done during the same day and with approximately the same frequency during the week or month.

More time-consuming and less frequent are cyclic movements termed **seasonal movements**. Many of us take our vacations and holidays during the same period each year. We undertake a trip that may cover thousands of miles and extend over several weeks. Every spring, thousands of college students find their way to the beach towns of Florida on the warm Atlantic coast. Every winter, skiers from all over the country try the slopes of Colorado. Many people, of course, cannot afford the luxury of vacation travel. Still the flood of tourists in search of winter warmth or the challenge of ski slopes has the magnitude of a small-scale migration!

Not all seasonal travel is for fun and recreation, however. The herring fleets of Western Europe wait in port until the fish run, and then fan out into the North Sea and adjacent waters to pursue their catches. Again, such fishing trips may take one or more days, but the boats return to the port that is their home base, thus engaging in cyclic movement.

The cyclic movements discussed so far occur on given days (working days) or during given seasons (the Christmas and New Year's holidays, for example). Some cyclic movements, by contrast, are irregular in their timing. A common form of movement in this category is the business trip. People involved in sales and marketing take numerous

long-distance trips every year, but not normally according to regular and recurrent schedules. This form of movement is of an intensity that is surely a hallmark of our particular society. Every day tens of thousands of salespersons are in transit by air and automobile, traveling from one prospective buyer to another, before returning to the home base for recordkeeping and re-stocking.

Quite another form of irregular, yet cyclic, movement is **nomadism**. We may envisage nomadic groups of people as wandering aimlessly across steppe or desert, but in fact, most nomadic movement takes place according to travel patterns that are repeated time and again. Often, the climate and its seasonal changes influence the nomads' decisions to break camp and move, and, in that sense, this is to some degree a seasonal form of cyclic movement.

However, in those arid areas where nomadic peoples trek, year-to-year climatic patterns can vary enormously. Furthermore, nomadic people frequently do have a base to which they return for a period each year. The Maasai of East Africa, for example, establish a village where they remain while the rains permit a sedentary life. They even try to grow some crops nearby. When the rains begin to fail and drought encroaches, everyone packs their belongings on the backs of donkeys, and the cattle and goats are driven in pursuit of the essential ingredient of life: water. Eventually, the group will return to the village and, if the rains permit, will remain at the site for some months. In some years, there is hardly any rain, and the stay at the village base is brief.

PERIODIC MOVEMENT

Some forms of movement involve a longer period(s) of residence away from the home base than normal cyclic movements. When you leave home to go to college, you are likely to be away for 9 months of the year, except, perhaps, for a few brief vacations. Furthermore, whereas you may have gone off to college intending to return eventually to your home town, that may never happen. With a possible employment opportunity elsewhere, or graduate school, the chances are numerous that you will go on to still another location, rather than return. In the United States alone, over 2 million students are attending colleges and universities, the majority of them away from home. For them, a new residential location is established for a substantial period of time.

Other hundreds of thousands of people are relocated through their *military service*. This also is periodic movement—to military bases, training schools, and, of course, to combat zones. At the height of the Persian Gulf War, the United States had a half-million people in Southwest Asia, truly a mass movement involving a force numbering more than twice the whole population of Iceland. In a given year in the United States, perhaps as many as 10 million persons, including people in service and their families, are, in one way or another, moved because of their association in some capacity with the military. Many of them become familiar with the area to which they are moved, and remain there after their period of duty has expired.

The movement of *migrant laborers* and their families is also periodic, although it is more cyclic than that of college students or military personnel. The migrant labor force moves from place to place as crops ripen in different areas, and a temporary demand for labor arises there. This happens according to recurrent cycles, but the climate in various parts of the country is inconsistent and sometimes there is less work in certain areas during a particular year. If the crops are late, the migrants may arrive too early

and then must wait until they are needed. If the crops fail, or if the harvest is poor, there may not be enough demand for labor to put everyone to work. It is a precarious and difficult existence, and poverty is the rule among migrant farm workers. Unlike the college graduate and the discharged military personnel, migrant laborers do not have the opportunity of choice of residential location when they work temporarily in an area. They are trapped in a system of transience, from which escape is very difficult.

Another form of periodic movement is one we identify as **transhumance**. The term is used to denote a system of pastoral farming whereby livestock and their keepers adjust their abodes to the seasonal availability of pastures. Switzerland's mountainous areas are best known for this practice, but it occurs elsewhere as well. In the summer, the herd is driven up the slopes to high, fresh pastures in zones cleared of winter snow. Sometimes, the whole farm family takes up residence in cottages built especially for this purpose near the summer snow line. With the arrival of the colder weather in the fall, the cattle and goats and their keepers abandon the high pastures and summer cottages and descend to the lower valleys to await the winter. In some respects, this is a seasonal cyclic movement, but there is a far longer period of residence at the two bases, with very brief actual movement. This resembles the college-bound and military-dictated movement patterns, rather than seasonal movements such as tourism.

PERMANENT RELOCATION

Migratory movement is the most consequential of all the forms of movement we will discuss here. It

involves permanent relocation, a leaving behind of the old, and a new beginning. It has numerous causes and many manifestations, so many that, as we have noted, it is often impossible to discern the exact reasons underlying people's decisions to seek new abodes. Obviously, there are factors that *push* people away from their homes, and other forces that *pull* them to new, promising locations. Determining or measuring these forces is a difficult proposition. Oppression, discrimination, and the threat of war or natural catastrophe can drive people away; the attraction of better economic opportunity, greater freedom, or security can pull them to new homelands. Always, however, some of the people will move and others will stay behind.

MAJOR MIGRATIONS

The past five centuries have witnessed human migration on an unprecedented scale, much of it generated by events occurring in Europe. Major modern migration flows include (Fig. 11-1) from Europe to North America ①; from Southern Europe to South and Middle America ②; from Britain and Ireland to Africa and Australia ③; from Africa to the Americas during the period of slavery ④; from India to eastern Africa, Southeast Asia, and Caribbean America ⑤; from China to Southeast Asia ⑥; from the eastern United States westward ⑦; and from western Russia eastward ⑧. These last two migrations are internal to the United States and Russia, and our map does not show some other significant internal migrations, for example, the south-to-north movement of black Americans during the present century. We return to these great population shifts later in this chapter.

Among the greatest human migrations in recent centuries has been the human flow from Europe to the Americas. When, in Chapter

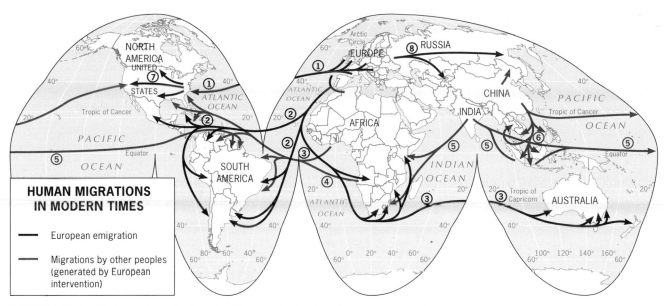

HUMAN MIGRATIONS IN MODERN TIMES

— European emigration

— Migrations by other peoples (generated by European intervention)

FIGURE 11–1   Major routes of migrants. From author's sketch.

7, we discussed the period of explosive population growth in nineteenth-century Europe, we did not fully account for this process, which kept the total increase far below what it might have been. The great emigration from Europe (① and ② on Fig. 11-1) began slowly. Over the several centuries prior to the 1830s, perhaps 2.75 million Europeans left to settle overseas in the newly acquired sphere of influence. Then the rate of emigration increased sharply, and between 1835 and 1935 perhaps as many as 75 million departed for the New World and other overseas territories. The British went to North America, Australia, New Zealand, and South Africa. From Spain and Portugal, many hundreds of thousands emigrated to Middle and South America. Early European colonial settlements grew to substantial size, even in such places as Angola, Kenya, and Java. True, millions of Europeans eventually returned to their homelands but the net outflow from Europe was enormous.

This European emigration has had no counterpart in modern world history in terms of size and numbers, but it is not the only ma-

jor migration flow to have occurred in recent centuries. The Americas were the destination of another mass of immigrants: Africans, transported in bondage—but migrants nevertheless. This forced migration began during the sixteenth century, when Africans were first brought to the Caribbean. In the early decades of the seventeenth century, they arrived in small numbers on the plantations that were developing in coastal eastern North America, and were among the very first settlers in this country.

Figure 11-2 indicates the extent to which the terror and destruction of slave raiding afflicted Africa. West Africa was exploited very nearly throughout, from Liberia to Nigeria and from the coast to the Sahara margins. So many Africans were taken from an area centered on present-day Benin to the Brazilian State of Bahia that significant elements of local culture remained intact. Today, strong ties exist between Bahia and Benin, and cultural exchanges are growing continuously. The entire Equatorial African coastal region was victimized as well, and Portuguese slave traders raided freely in the Portu-

guese domains of Angola and Moçambique. Arab slave raiders were active in East Africa and the Horn, often cooperating with the Europeans. Zanzibar, off the coast of mainland Tanzania, long was a major slave market.

In combination, the forced migrations from these **African migrant sources** inflicted dreadful damage on African societies and communities, and by their dimensions they changed the cultural and ethnic geography of Brazil, Middle America, and the United States. The route numbered ④ in Figure 11-1 is just one among many migrations, but its impact on both sides of the Atlantic sets it apart from all the others.

EXTERNAL AND INTERNAL MIGRATIONS

When our ancient ancestors began their momentous dispersal from Africa to Eurasia, Australia, and the Americas, the only boundaries they crossed were nature's. Rivers,

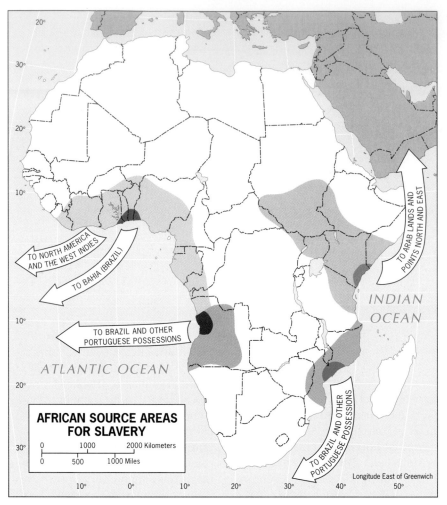

FIGURE 11–2 Areas most severely affected by slave raiding. Modified from D. K. Fellows, *Geography* (New York: John Wiley, 1967) p. 121.

temporary status) of many external migrants. Turks who are long-term residents of Germany are able to acquire German citizenship; Algerians and other North Africans in France also have been able to attain French citizenship. But the rules of admission *and* nationalization have recently been tightened in response to political pressures in the destination countries. In all countries that have accepted large influxes of foreign worker-immigrants (the United States included), there is a substantial gray area of immigrants with uncertain status. Keeping these caveats in mind, let us examine some major past and present migration streams, external as well as internal.

EXTERNAL MIGRATIONS

External migrations, we have noted, took Europeans to America and to other parts of the world; the Europeans in America, Africa, and Asia in turn generated the migration of other peoples. We have already considered the movement of Africans to the Americas, but other peoples were induced to move as well. Indentured Indian labor was brought to Natal, South Africa, and to areas of East Africa by the British. This intercontinental migration (⑤ on Fig. 11-1) substantially changed the ethnic mosaic of eastern Africa from Kenya to the Cape. Free Asian entrepreneurs followed the stream of indentured laborers, and eventually much of the local trade and commerce along the East African coast was in the hands of Asians.

The British were also instrumental in relocating Asians, mainly from India, to such Caribbean countries as Trinidad and Tobago and Guyana (the trans-Pacific stream marked ⑤ in Fig. 11-1). The Dutch brought many Javanese from what is today Indonesia to their former dependency of Suriname along the same route. Meanwhile, the colonial occupation of Southeast Asia presented opportunities for the

mountain ranges, and forest margins must have evoked a sense of barrier and obstruction, but none stopped the inexorable march of human migration.

Today's migrants face a very different situation. Political boundaries, not natural barriers, form the most difficult obstacles for people on the move. Agencies that monitor the annual stream of human migration use the globe's political framework to keep track of the numbers of migrants. Collecting information from embassies and consulates (where visas for legal immigrants are issued), border stations, refugee camps, and other formal as well as informal sources,

these agencies try to identify the world's migration flows, record the number of people involved, and gauge the net population changes resulting therefrom. To facilitate this work, they differentiate between migrants who cross international borders (*external* migrants) and those who move but relocate within their national boundaries (*internal* migrants). In any given year, internal migrants greatly outnumber external migrants. But it is the external migrants who change countries' vital statistics, affect economies, and often influence politics.

A complicating factor is the impermanence (and uncertain,

Chinese to function as middlemen, and a considerable immigration of Chinese to this region occurred (⑥ in Fig. 11-1). Chinese minorities in Southeast Asian countries (Fig. 11-3) represent substantial sectors of national populations: 14 percent in Thailand, 32 percent in Malaysia, and no less than 76 percent in bustling Singapore. The Chinese minority in Indonesia accounts for only about 2 percent of the total population, but Indonesia has nearly 200 million people, so that its Chinese minority is one of Southeast Asia's largest clusters. Several twentieth-century governments in Southeast Asia have discouraged and restricted Chinese immigration. Like the Asians in East Africa, the Chinese minorities are urban-based and disproportionately influential in trade, commerce, and finance in the Southeast Asian states.

A modern external migration, albeit on a smaller scale, is the flow of Jewish immigrants to Israel. This has been mainly a twentieth-century development. At the turn of the century, there were probably fewer than 50,000 Jewish residents in what was then Palestine. From 1919 to 1948, the United Kingdom held a mandate over Palestine, originally under the auspices of the League of Nations, and Britain encouraged the immigration of Jews from Europe. By 1948, there were perhaps 750,000 Jewish residents in Palestine, and an independent state of Israel was established through United Nations intervention and the partition of the area (Fig. 11-4). This in turn led to another migration stream: the displacement of 600,000 Palestinian Arabs who sought refuge in neighboring Jordan, Egypt, Syria, and elsewhere.

Author's Video Link
↓
3
Soviet Jewish Emigration

Jewish immigration continued, and Jewish migrants came from Europe, America, South Africa, and even from the former Soviet Union, despite obstacles created by the Soviets against Jewish departures. Since 1989, the number of Russian Jews arriving in Israel has increased sharply as a result of changed emigration policies. Israel's total population is approaching 5 million, and it is a nation generated by a still-continuing migration stream.

Postwar Movements

External migrations (authorized movements and organized resettlements, as well as refugee movements) usually follow wars, as happened with the Kurds of northern Iraq following the end of the Gulf War in 1991. One of the century's major resettlements occurred after the end of World War II, when as many as 15 million Germans migrated westward from their homes in Eastern Europe, either voluntarily or under expulsion. Before the Berlin Wall went up and the Iron Curtain was lowered, several million Germans fled Soviet-controlled East Germany into (then) West Germany. And millions of people left Europe altogether, to go to the

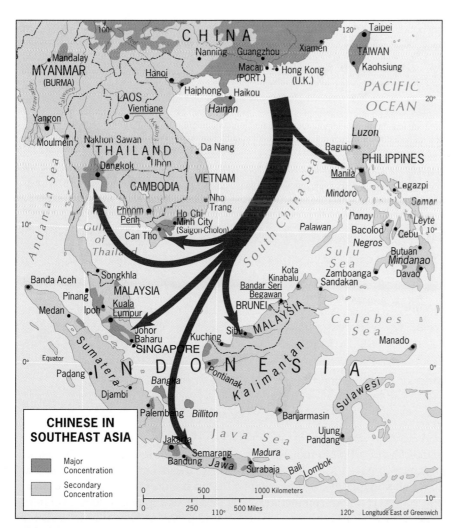

FIGURE 11–3 The great majority of Chinese emigrants left from southeast China.

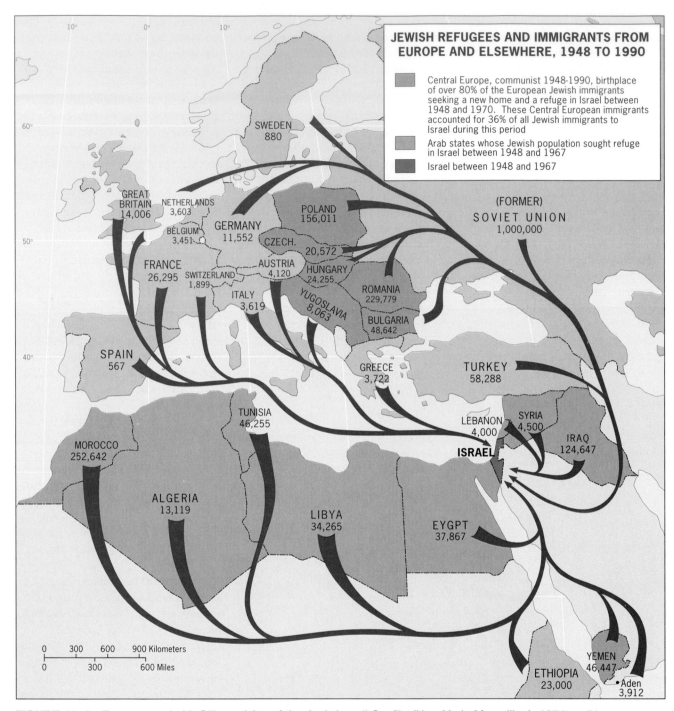

JEWISH REFUGEES AND IMMIGRANTS FROM EUROPE AND ELSEWHERE, 1948 TO 1990

Central Europe, communist 1948-1990, birthplace of over 80% of the European Jewish immigrants seeking a new home and a refuge in Israel between 1948 and 1970. These Central European immigrants accounted for 36% of all Jewish immigrants to Israel during this period

Arab states whose Jewish population sought refuge in Israel between 1948 and 1967

Israel between 1948 and 1967

SWEDEN 880
GREAT BRITAIN 14,006
NETHERLANDS 3,603
BELGIUM 3,451
GERMANY 11,552
CZECH. 20,572
POLAND 156,011
(FORMER) SOVIET UNION 1,000,000
FRANCE 26,295
SWITZERLAND 1,899
AUSTRIA 4,120
HUNGARY 24,255
ITALY 3,619
YUGOSLAVIA 8,063
ROMANIA 229,779
BULGARIA 48,642
SPAIN 567
GREECE 3,722
TURKEY 58,288
TUNISIA 46,255
LEBANON 4,000
SYRIA 4,500
IRAQ 124,647
MOROCCO 252,642
ISRAEL
ALGERIA 13,119
LIBYA 34,265
EYGPT 37,867
YEMEN 46,447
ETHIOPIA 23,000
Aden 3,912

0 300 600 900 Kilometers
0 300 600 Miles

FIGURE 11–4 From a map in M. Gilbert, *Atlas of the Arab-Israeli Conflict* (New York: Macmillan), 1974, p. 51.

United States (1.8 million), Canada (1.1 million), Australia (1 million), Israel (750,000), Argentina (750,000), Brazil (500,000), Venezuela (500,000), and to other countries in smaller numbers. As many as 8 million Europeans emi-grated from Europe in this postwar stream.

As often happens, this out-migration played a role in stimulating a counter-migration. European countries, rebuilding in the postwar period, now found themselves in need of labor. Not only did millions of workers move from one European country to another (notably from Italy, Spain, Greece, and Ireland to the industrial heartland) but additional millions of foreign workers migrated from North Africa (mainly to France) and from Turkey (mostly to Germany).

In 1992, European unification created even greater opportunities for intra-European (but still international) migration and job-seeking. Among the countries of the European Union, circulation is virtually as free as it is among states of the United States; and foreign workers also will find new doors opened. An example of the impact of migration on the European demographic makeup comes from Italy. Before European Union, Italy was the natural stepping stone from North Africa into Europe, but it was not yet easy for North African workers, once in Italy, to cross into France or Germany. As more immigrants arrived, southern Italy, the region known as the Mezzogiorno, became strongly North-Africanized. Muslim workers and families arrived, but found their

migration obstructed. As Italy struggled to accommodate the influx, the already-poor Mezzogiorno became an area of even higher unemployment, social unrest, and cultural animosity.

In early 1992, a significant development occurred in Algeria that could lead to further emigration from that country to Europe. In elections for the Algerian parliament, a party called the Islamic Salvation Front triumphed on a platform of Islamic fundamentalism. For three decades, Algeria had been a secular state in which religion and the state were separate. But Algeria's economy, based on oil and natural gas exports, deteriorated, and social conditions worsened. This led to frustration and unrest, and the Islamic Salvation Front seemed to offer an alternative. Its leaders proposed the institution of

an "Islamic Republic" in the Muslim tradition, as was already in place in Iran, Pakistan, and Sudan. But in Algeria, a large urbanized and considerably Westernized segment of the population would find itself at odds with an Islamic regime in which the *sharia* law would prevail. The situation had the potential to magnify once again the emigration of Algerians to Europe at a time when the immigrant communities already in Europe were facing difficult times both economically and socially.

By mid-1995, the situation had deteriorated seriously. Extremists on both sides appeared determined to preclude any negotiated settlement of the crisis: Muslim militants threatened all foreigners still present in Algeria and murdered many, while the military campaign against the militants led to the repression and

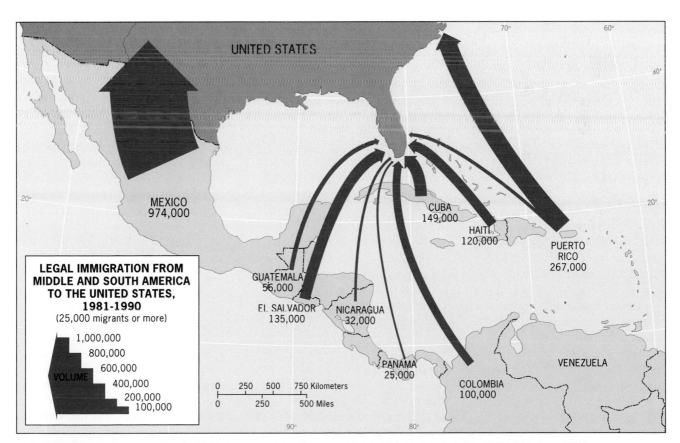

FIGURE 11–5 Based on data in U.S. Bureau of the Census, *Statistical Abstract of the United States: 1991* (111th edition). Washington, D.C., 1991, p. 10.

killing of Muslims, not all of them extremists. The turmoil in Algeria had repercussions in neighboring Morocco and Tunisia, where the actions of the Islamic Salvation Front resonated among the poor and the politically frustrated. European Union countries across the Mediterranean from North Africa, facing the brunt of a mass emigration from the region, met to coordinate their response.

The Americas

External migration in the Americas has focused on the United States and Canada. Even before Cuba's socialist course was set, thousands of Cuban citizens applied for residency in the United States. During the 1960s, this migration stream intensified and was formalized as the "Cuban Airlift," an authorized movement of persons desiring to escape communist government. The great majority of the Cuban immigrants first landed near, and then remained in, the greater Miami area. In southern Florida they developed a core of Hispanic culture, and in due course Dade County declared itself bicultural and bilingual (Fig. 11-5). Throughout the 1960s and 1970s, Cubans continued to arrive in the United States as refugees (see Chapter 12) until, in 1980, another massive, organized exodus occurred during the "Mariel Boatlift," which brought more than 100,000 Cubans to U.S. shores. The Cuban influx persisted throughout the 1980s. At the end of the decade, the official number of Cuban arrivals was 488,770.

An even larger, although less precisely enumerated, immigration stream was reaching the southwestern United States from Mexico (Table 11-1). So much of this movement has been unauthorized that demographers are unable to estimate even within hundreds of thousands what its magnitude may be. During the 1980s, legal immigration from Mexico was nearly 1 million; since 1961, it has exceeded 2 million. This migration stream has transformed the southwestern borderland of the United States.

As Table 11-1 shows, immigration from Asia during the decade of the 1980s exceeded even that from Middle America. Nearly 2.5 million Asians entered the United States legally. The Philippines was the leading source country, followed closely by Vietnam and three East Asian countries. Europe, on the other hand, once the primary U.S. source area, contributed only 9.8 percent of the immigrants (about 0.59 million) in the period from 1960 to 1990.

Prospects

The 1990s have witnessed sweeping changes. Major strides were taken toward European unification. The Soviet Union underwent irreversible politico-geographical dissolution. Eastern European countries, freed from Soviet domination and swept by political winds of change, strained and buckled under regional and social pressures. The Horn of Africa was in turmoil. South Africa was entering a new and uncertain post-Apartheid era. And from Canada to Sri Lanka, divisive forces were straining the fabric of the state.

Which of these developments are likely to generate major, external migration streams? When several thousand desperate Albanians crossed the Adriatic Sea to become refugees in Italy, the potential for European dislocation was underscored. When civil war broke out in Rwanda and about half that country's population of over 8 million became victims or refugees (see Chapter 12), the potential in Africa

TABLE 11–1 Sources of Legal Immigrants into the United States, 1981–1989 (thousands)

Realm		Leading Countries	
Africa	156.4		
Asia	2,478.8		
		Philippines	431.5
		Vietnam	352.6
		China and Taiwan	341.8
		South Korea	306.5
Europe	593.2		
		United Kingdom	126.2
		Poland	76.9
Middle America	2,065.0		
		Mexico	974.2
		Dominican Republic	209.6
		Jamaica	188.8
		Cuba	148.6
		El Salvador	134.4
		Haiti	119.9
North America	102.4		
		Canada	102.4
South America	370.1		
		Colombia	100.2
		Guyana	84.0
Other realms	35.6		

Source: United States Department of Commerce, Bureau of the Census, *Statistical Abstract of the United States, 1991*. 111th Edition. Washington, D.C., 1991, p. 10.

for mass dislocation was again emphasized. But the greatest potential for large-scale migration is tied to the future of the former Soviet Union. The failure of the political system in the wake of an economic breakdown could generate not only a world-endangering civil war, but also a vast westward migration of Russians and others into Europe.

INTERNAL MIGRATIONS

Internal migration involves population relocation within a country. Such movements can also involve significant population shifts, even though no international border or ocean is crossed by the migrants. During the last decades of the tsarist period in Russia, the great Siberian expanses east of the Urals were invaded by growing numbers of peasant farmers in search of new lands and new opportunities. This flow was strengthened by the construction of the Trans-Siberian Railroad to Vladivostok, started in 1892. Eventually, World War I and, subsequently, the Russian Revolution, stemmed the tide of eastward migration, but, after the reorganization of the 1920s it became Soviet policy to stimulate the development of Siberia once again. Natural resources were opened up, industrialization was supported, and various incentives were used to induce people to move eastward to places such as Novosibirsk and Krasnoyarsk. The German invasion from the west during World War II further strengthened Soviet resolve to develop eastern regions of the realm, and more than 2 million people were resettled east of the Ural Mountains. Until the collapse of the Soviet Union, relatively rapid growth in the east continued, spurred on by official policy. Also contributing to the realm's population shift was the comparatively fast rate of natural increase in the Muslim republics of Central Asia—never

reliably enumerated in Soviet censuses, but unquestionably a major factor. Today, long-term trends and developments in the former Soviet sphere are interrupted by the breakdown of order, but the map still bears the mark of one of the great long-term internal migrations anywhere in the world. It is identified as flow ⑧ in Figure 11-1.

Other major internal migrations have changed the population map of China. When China's communist planners embarked on their industrialization program, China's Northeast (formerly called Manchuria) became a principal focus because of its raw materials and existing infrastructure. (The Japanese had previously held Manchuria as a colony, and they established facilities for its exploitation). Huge state industrial complexes were built, and workers were encouraged to move to the new heartland. Millions did so, and China's Northeast grew rapidly, a product of officially sanctioned migration.

Today, China embraces new economic policies, and the Northeast has become something of a rustbelt, its inefficient state enterprises running far below capacity. China's new economic focus lies on its eastern and southern Pacific coast, and now workers are moving in large numbers to this part of the country. When the authorities in Shanghai

announced the establishment of a new development area, the Pudong District, as many as three million job-seekers descended on the city. Labor migration to the more southerly growth zones has been larger still. In China, with its huge population numbers, economic reorientation leads to massive human movement.

The United States

Americans, as we noted previously, are the world's most mobile people. The effects of two historic internal migrations are etched permanently on the population map: the westward movement of the population as a whole, and the northward migration of black Americans from the rural South to the urban North.

The West continues as a major migration destination, as is reflected by the sustained westward shift of the center of gravity of U.S. population (Fig. 11-6). Note that this map also reflects the southward movement of recent decades; after 1960, the center of U.S. population moved not only westward but also southward.

The northward migration of African Americans from the South was a small stream until the years of World War I, when the in-migrations from Europe were cut off. Industries continued to expand and the labor market grew rapidly, re-

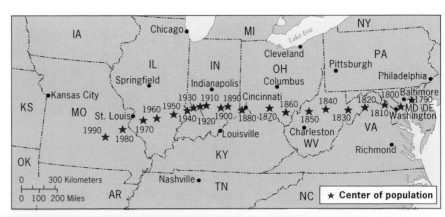

FIGURE 11–6 From U.S. Bureau of the Census, *Statistical Abstract, 1991*, p. 8.

quiring more employees. Now a campaign began to recruit black workers from the South, and blacks responded by leaving the South by the hundreds of thousands. Most moved to the cities of the Northeast and Midwest. The flow continued after the end of the war and, indeed, accelerated during the 1920s after newly legislated quotas sharply curtailed European immigration; following a decline during the depression years of the 1930s, it resumed its upward climb. At the turn of the century, only 10 percent of the black population lived outside the South; in 1990 it was about 50 percent. This means that the black population of the United States became urbanized even more rapidly than the white population did, for the vast majority of those who went to the industrialized North came from rural areas in the South. Today, about 80 percent of African-Americans living in rural areas remain in the South; of those in the North, over 90 percent reside in metropolitan areas. This helps explain the apparent Southern concentration of African-American population shown in Figure 11-7: the Southeastern core area is extensive, but substantially rural. The urban concentrations of the North show less spatial extent, but they represent much larger numbers of people.

During the 1970s, the long-term pattern of African-American migration to northern and western cities from the South changed, quite surprisingly. Survey data began to reveal a new situation: more African Americans were leaving the North and returning to the South than were leaving the South for northern destinations. This reversal of a trend of many decades appeared to have several causes. Undoubtedly, it resulted in part from changed civil rights conditions in the South. Disillusionment with living conditions in the urban North and West was also a factor. Perceived economic opportunities in the growing cities of the South played a role as well. One effect of this new situation could be observed in the growth figures of Southern cities. Black residents of Northern cities migrate to Southern cities, not to rural areas. Thus, the rural black southerner became urbanized in the North and then relocated to a Southern city. On the map, this adds up to a rural-to-urban flow in the South, now experiencing one of its most dramatic growth periods.

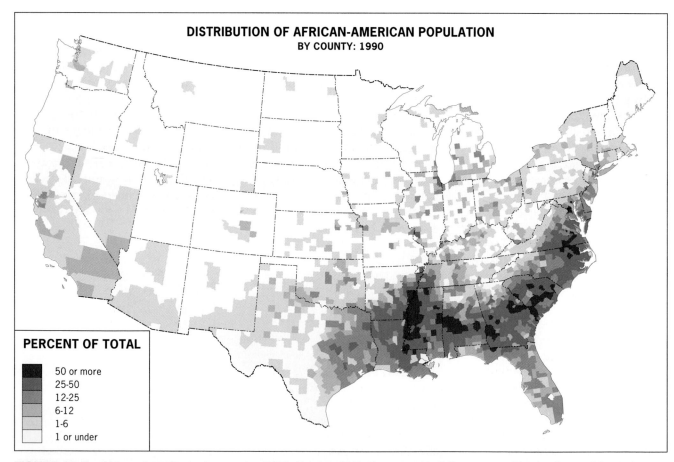

DISTRIBUTION OF AFRICAN-AMERICAN POPULATION
BY COUNTY: 1990

PERCENT OF TOTAL

- 50 or more
- 25-50
- 12-25
- 6-12
- 1-6
- 1 or under

FIGURE 11–7 African-Americans, by county, 1990. Source: U.S. Department of Commerce, Economics and Statistics Administration; Bureau of the Census.

Regional Migration in America

A migration stream is never a one-way flow of migrants. It is the *net* movement of people: the total of the flow from origin to destination minus the return flow from destination back to source. Even some Jewish migrants who left Russia for Israel in the late 1980s and early 1990s decided to return, or to move elsewhere, because they were unable to settle down in the land of their original destination.

Internal population movement in the United States, too, involves multiple streams. The U.S. Bureau of the Census divides the United States into four regions: the Northeast (including New York, Pennsylvania, New Jersey and the New England states); the Midwest (from Ohio westward to the Dakotas, Nebraska, and Kansas); the South (from Maryland and Delaware to Texas, and including West Virginia and Kentucky); and the West, from the mountain states to California (and including Hawaii and Alaska).

The Northeast and Midwest have lost population to the South and West for more than three decades now. Table 11-2 reports the percentage of the U.S. population living in each region: note that the Northeast declined from nearly 25 percent to just over 20 percent, and the Midwest from nearly 30 percent to 24 percent during the period from 1960 to 1990. The South, on the other hand, rose from under 31 percent to over 34 percent, and the West from under 16 percent to over 21 percent.

When we look at the actual numbers of migrants, however, we can see that these are not one-way movements. Take the year 1987 to 1988, for example (the latest year for which detailed data were available at the time of writing). In that year, some 679,000 people left the Northeast, and about 444,000 of them moved to the South. But 448,000 people moved *into* the

TABLE 11–2	U.S. Population Percentage by Region, 1960–1990			
	1960	**1970**	**1980**	**1990**
Northeast	24.9	24.1	21.7	20.4
Midwest	28.8	27.8	26.0	24.0
South	30.7	30.9	33.3	34.4
West	15.6	17.1	19.1	21.2

Source: U.S. Department of Commerce, Bureau of the Census, *Statistical Abstract of the United States: 1991.* 111th edition. Washington, D.C., 1991, p. 19.

Northeast, so that the outmigration for that year amount to only 231,000—the *net* difference between emigration and immigration. For the Midwest, this net difference was even less: 829,000 emigrants, but 741,000 immigrants, for a loss of just 88,000. Again, the South and West may be gaining population, but not everyone who moves there stays there. In 1987-1988, 1.36 million people entered the South, but 946,000 moved away. And in that year, the West actually had a slight loss, after many years of continuous gains.

Over the long term, the southward and westward shift in U.S. population has continued, the southward component becoming stronger. Add to this the arrival of external immigrants, a great majority of whom arrive on southern and western shores or cross southern land borders, and we can see that a new population map of the United States is in the making.

CONTROLLING MIGRATION

Migration control and its attendant problems have become hot issues around the world. In Europe, right-wing political parties whip up anti-immigrant sentiment. In East Asia, Hong Kong authorities are criticized for sending Vietnamese "boat people" home. In California,

the State government demands federal help to provide services for hundreds of thousands of illegal immigrants; if the federal government cannot control its borders, so the argument goes, the States should not have to foot the bill. In Cuba, the Castro regime actually uses migration as a menace: in August 1994 Castro threatened to open Cuba's doors to a flood of emigrants that "will make the Mariel boatlift look like child's play." And in the United States, the government faces reproach for preventing tens of thousands of Haitians from entering Florida.

Efforts to restrict migrations are nothing new, however. Media coverage, democratic debate, and political wrangling only make it seem so. China's Great Wall was built in part as a defensive measure, but also as a barrier to emigration (by Chinese beyond the sphere of their authorities) and immigration (mainly by Mongol "barbarians" from the plains to the north). The Berlin Wall, the Korean DMZ (demilitarized zone), the fences along the Rio Grande—all evince an old desire by governments to control the movement of people across their borders.

LEGAL RESTRICTIONS

Usually, however, the obstacles placed in the way of potential immigrants are legal, not physical. Restrictive legislation made its appearance in the United States in

1882, when Congress approved the Oriental Exclusion Acts (1882 to 1907). These **immigration laws** were designed to restrict the immigration of Chinese people to California. In 1901, Australia's government approved the Immigration Restriction Act, an instrument that terminated all nonwhite immigration into the newly united Commonwealth. This act, too, was aimed primarily at Japanese and Chinese (but included South Asians as well). It also had the effect of prohibiting immigrations by South Pacific islanders who had entered Australia to work on the large sugar plantations. These workers, the Kanakas, were the target of a specific provision that facilitated their deportation by the end of 1906. The White Australia Policy was one of the issues on which the Australian colonies were united prior to the establishment of the Common-wealth, and it remained in effect until it was modified in 1972, and again in 1979.

In the United States, restrictive legislation affecting European immigrants was passed in 1921. The balance of European immigrants had been shifting from Western Europe to Southern and Eastern Europe, and numerous immigrants had no training and no resources—at a time when industry's need for skilled labor was declining. The 1921 legislation was a quota law, allowing each European country to annually permit the emigration to the United States of 3 percent of the number of its nationals living in America in 1910. This had the effect of limiting annual immigration to about 357,000 Europeans, most of them from western Europe. In 1924, the Immigration Act lowered the quota to 2 percent and made 1890 the base year, which further reduced the annual total to 150,000 immigrants.

The National Origins Law took effect in 1929. It sustained the limit of 150,000 immigrants per year, but it also tied immigration quotas to national origins in the population of the United States in 1920. This law had the effect of preventing the immigration of Asians: immigration slowed to a trickle during the 1930s, and, in some years, emigration actually exceeded immigration.

After 1940, the restrictions on immigration to the United States were modified. In 1943, China was given equal status with European countries to send emigrants to the United States, and, in 1952, Japan received similar privileges. A new Immigration and Nationality Act (1952) was designed to incorporate all preceding legislation, establishing quotas for all countries and limiting total immigration to under 160,000. However, far more immigrants entered the country as displaced persons (refugees), and by doing so filled quotas for years ahead. Estimates vary, but more than 7 million immigrants may thus have entered the United States between 1945 (the end of World War II in Europe) and 1970. It was recognized that the 1952 law was a failure, and in 1965 the quota system was abolished. New limits were set: 170,000 immigrants per year from countries outside the Western Hemisphere, and 120,000 from countries in the Americas (this was the first official restriction on immigration from Western Hemisphere countries). The number of Cuban, Haitian, and Mexican arrivals far exceeded these limitations in the 1970s and 1980, however.

The United States and Australia are not the only countries to restrict immigration. Selective immigration, whereby persons with certain backgrounds (criminal records, poor medical histories, subversives) are barred from entering, is practiced by many countries. Other countries

From the Field Notes

❝❝ A truly ugly sight, this spiked, barbed-wire fence along the waterfront of (still-Portuguese) Macau. To the right, the beach belongs to China; the road to the left lies in Macau. To stop the Chinese from leaving the communist state and entering the colony, barriers like this were constructed (the border between Hong Kong and China was reinforced in a similar way). As the transfer of these last European colonies approaches, these barriers to migration are losing their relevance. But illegal emigration from China continues, and barriers to migration are being built in many other areas of the world—including the U.S.-Mexican border. ❞❞

have specific requirements: South Africa long demanded "pure" European descent; New Zealand favored persons of British birth and parentage; Brazil preferred people with a farming background; and Singapore now courts financially secure persons of Chinese ancestry. Various limits are placed on the number of immigrants by South American countries, and quota systems are being instituted. Thailand has restricted Chinese immigration, and Myanmar (Burma) limits immigration from neighboring India. In France, problems associated with

the large and growing Arab population from North Africa have resulted in calls for the repatriation of those without residency permits and for the restriction of further immigration from the former French North African dependencies (Algeria, Morocco, and Tunisia).

As world population mushrooms, the volume of migrants will likewise expand. In an increasingly open and interconnected world, neither physical barriers nor politically motivated legislation will stem tides that are as old as human history.

KEY TERMS

Activity Space
African Migrant Sources
Commuting
Cyclic Movement
External Migration
Immigration Laws
Internal Migration
Migration Control
Migratory Movement
Nomadism
Periodic Movement
Seasonal Movement
Transhumance

12

GEOGRAPHY OF DISLOCATION: THE REFUGEE CRISIS

On April 6, 1994, the presidents of two neighboring African countries, Rwanda and Burundi, were killed when their plane, approaching the Kigali Airport for a landing, suddenly disintegrated. News reports that evening described the crash as unexplained and without warning. No one knew that it would mark the beginning of one of the largest refugee crises the world had ever witnessed.

Rwanda and Burundi are small, densely populated, landlocked countries in a region of large, sprawling states. On the map they seem to lie in the northwest corner of Tanzania, as though they were carved out for some purpose. And indeed they were. Whereas Zaïre (then the Congo) to the west was owned by Belgium, Rwanda and Burundi were part of German East Africa. When the First World War broke out, Belgian forces from the Congo pushed into the northwestern corner of German East Africa. When the war ended, the Belgians argued that they should get a share of the spoils. While most of German

East Africa was placed under British control, Rwanda and Burundi were given boundaries and awarded to Belgium.

What Belgium got was an old meeting ground for two African peoples and a reservoir of labor for its Congo copper mines. The two

132

peoples were the Hutu, a Bantu nation of farmers, and the Tutsi, a Nilotic people who moved with their cattle into the hilly countryside between Lake Victoria and Lake Tanganyika. The Hutu always were much more numerous than the Tutsi (who used to be known as the Watusi and who, on average, were rather taller than the Hutu). But the minority Tutsi fared well under Belgian rule. They moved to the towns, were given influential jobs, and staffed the police and administrative services. Tutsi owned large tracts of land and made serfs of the Hutu so that, when independence came in 1962, Rwanda and Burundi were essentially feudal states.

The withdrawal of the Belgian colonists was the signal for the beginning of score-settling in Rwanda and Burundi. Before CNN and other media brought the carnage into the world's living rooms, hundreds of thousands were killed in an endless series of reprisals. Tutsi domination soon was ended in Rwanda, but in Burundi the Tutsi minority held on to power longer. In four months in 1972, the Tutsi in Burundi killed an estimated 100,000 Hutu.

In Rwanda, the Hutu majority (comprising about 84 percent of a population numbering about 8.3 million at the beginning of 1994) carried out massive retribution against the Tutsi. About 100,000 of the Tutsi fled during the 1970s and early 1980s to Uganda, Tanzania, and Zaïre. In Uganda, the Tutsi organized themselves into militias and trained for combat, hoping to return to power through the force of arms. Several times, Tutsi forces entered Rwanda, only to be beaten back by the Hutu army and its European (Belgian) supporters.

The crash of the presidential plane on April 6, 1994 may have been part of a plot. Whatever the cause, the incident was followed almost immediately by a wave of Hutu militia action in Rwanda, not only against Tutsi but also against "moderate" Hutu, that is, Hutu who had supported cooperation and coalition with the Tutsi. In an almost unimaginable campaign of extermination, the Hutu killed hundreds of thousands of Tutsi and tens of thousands of "suspect" Hutu. People were slain in church, in their school rooms, in hospitals. Not since the "killing fields" of Cambodia had the world witnessed such horror.

The killing produced a wave of refugees. As thousands of bodies washed downstream in rivers leading from Rwanda into Tanzania, a half million desperate Rwandans, Hutu and Tutsi alike, invaded their neighbor on foot. Almost overnight, a camp city the size of Denver, Colorado, arose on the Tanzanian side of the border. But worse was to come. As Tutsi forces from exile in Uganda saw their kinspeople murdered, they invaded from the north and pushed toward the capital, Kigali. This split the country in half, and the next wave of refugees, numbering more than 2 million, fled westward into Zaïre. By early August 1994, about half the population of Rwanda was dead, dying of cholera or starvation in the camps, or in precarious exile. It was, by most accounts, the worst refugee crisis in modern times.

A GLOBAL CRISIS

The Rwanda tragedy was the largest, but only the latest in a growing crisis of human **dislocation**. While it is true that the word "crisis" is overused these days, there can be no question that it is appropriate in this context. In 1970, there were officially about 2.8 million people of refugee status in the world. In 1980, the number was 8 million. In 1995, the **United Nations High Commission for Refugees (UNHCR)** accounted for some 25 million refu-gees, not counting an additional 27 million people displaced within their own countries. By the end of the century, at present rates of change, one in 100 people on Earth will be displaced. A refugee crisis is no misnomer (see box, "Dimensions of the Problem").

An important aspect of the crisis, which touches virtually every region in the world, is the determination of refugee status. The term **refugee** has specific implications, and many countries, in concert with the United Nations, given refugees special help. This means that other migrants, seeing advantages in refugee status, claim an asylum to which they are not entitled. Governments are compelled to make difficult distinctions between "genuine" refugees and migrants who may be just as poor and desperate—but who were not driven from their homes by the conditions stipulated in the United Nations definition of refugee status.

The international community is becoming increasingly aware of the growing number of people who are displaced and in fear but who do not leave their countries. Because cross-border refugee flows create enormous problems for the host countries, the U.N. and other agencies are now addressing this issue more vigorously, reasoning that an **intranational refugee** is more likely to return home than one who has crossed a border into another country. As we noted earlier, there probably are more intranational refugees in such countries as the former Yugoslavia, Cyprus, Sri Lanka, Cambodia, Angola, Liberia, and Somalia (among many others) than there are **international refugees** who have left their countries altogether. The case of Rwanda emphasizes this point. After the deathly exodus by more than two million Rwandans into Zaïre, relief agencies had great difficulty persuading the encamped refugees to return to Rwanda. Those refugees who had stayed in Rwanda itself (the intranational refugees) returned to their villages much more quickly. Once refugees become international refugees, their repatriation tends to be slower and more problematic.

Author's Video Link
↓
6
Refugees

This leads to another way to classify refugees, based on the duration of their exile. Many Palestinians who moved into countries neighboring Israel, principally Jordan, have become **permanent refugees**, people who still hold the status of a displaced person but who have become established in the host society. Other Palestinian refugees still live in refugee camps and await the opportunity to return to their perceived home; they retain the status of **temporary refugees**, awaiting repatriation.

CAUSES OF REFUGEE MOVEMENTS

In Chapter 10 we noted a number of catalysts of migration, ranging from war to technological factors. Pull factors were cited as the cause of many major migration streams—attractions of destinations ranging from superior business opportunities to better weather. When it comes to refugee flows, on the other hand, push factors dominate. Refugees are driven from their homes by conditions beyond their control.

Three principal causes of refugee movement prevail:

1. **War**
   International conflict as well as civil war generates refugees. The war between Soviet forces and Afghan resisters during the 1980s created one of the largest refu-

gee movements ever seen. The civil war in Rwanda in 1994 pushed the largest stream of refugees in modern times out of that country in a matter of weeks. The conflict in the former Yugoslavia forced Europe to confront the largest refugee problem it has experienced since the Second World War.

2. **Political Oppression**
   Compared to the horrors of ethnic warfare or other armed conflict, political persecution seems but a mild reason to escape as a refugee. But naziism, fascism, and communism oppressed countless dissidents and exiled millions as genuine refugees in fear of their lives. Today, harsh dictatorial regimes from Myanmar (Burma) to Sudan continue such practices. But in a world of true, partial, and non-democracies, it is sometimes difficult to distinguish harassed dissidents from endangered objectors.

3. **Environmental Crises**
   Floods, earthquakes, storms, volcanic eruptions, and other sudden and destructive natural phenomena can generate large refugee flows, international as well as intranational. Such events tend to produce more temporary and fewer permanent refugees, because people desire to return to familiar environs even when this entails taking considerable risk. Floodprone lowlands and lava-threatened hillslopes soon are repopulated, and earthquake risk does not deter people from returning to hazardous areas.

In addition to these principal catalysts of refugee movement, economic circumstances often are cited as a cause of refugee flows. But here the distinction between genuine refugees, facing starvation and death and migrating as a last resort, and those seeking a better life elsewhere, becomes blurred.

DIMENSIONS OF THE PROBLEM

When you investigate the refugee problem in geographic context, a problem that immediately presents itself involves numbers. The official United Nations agency that monitors refugee concerns (UNHCR) is only one office that seeks information on refugees and their needs, and UNHCR data often are contradicted by other sources.

Why is this so? Several reasons exist. First, there are different definitions of what constitutes a refugee. The United Nations defines a refugee as "a person who has a well-founded fear of being persecuted for reasons of race, religion, nationality, membership of a particular social group, or political opinion." Some countries interpret this definition variously; the words "well-founded" leave much room for judgment. Second, refugees often flee into remote areas of the world where counting them, let alone providing help, is difficult. And third, governments manipulate refugee numbers to suit their political objectives, so that reporting is unreliable.

The biggest problem has to do with internal refugees, that is, people displaced within their own countries, who do not cross international borders. Their numbers have been growing even more rapidly than international refugees, but estimates vary widely.

Whatever their numbers, refugees tend to be the most powerless, deprived, threatened people on Earth, often facing death while governments and relief agencies quarrel over rescue plans.

With the exception of certain economic changes, which may be (but not always are) gradual, the causes of refugee movement tend to be sudden, driving people away from their homes with little warning and no time to contemplate options. Thus while the *perception* of danger or social change creates migratory movement, the *experience* of disaster produces refugee flows. A good example comes from Moçambique, the former Portuguese dependency in southern Africa. When the first signs of the coming revolution appeared, a substantial number of the Portuguese settlers who had made that country their home decided to emigrate. Many moved to neighboring South Africa; others went to Europe. Later, the country was engulfed in revolutionary war, and those Portuguese who had stayed behind streamed toward the border, leaving virtually all of their belongings behind and losing, in some cases, their lives. The migration flow had become a refugee stream.

While it is not always easy to distinguish between a refugee and a voluntary (if desperate) migrant, refugees can be identified by at least three characteristics, individual or aggregate:

1. Most refugees move without any more tangible property than they can carry or transport with them. When the Gulf War's aftermath generated a vast refugee flow among Iraq's Kurds, these people walked in a giant column across the Turkish and Iranian borders. A minority were able to load possessions on trucks, cars, or animals.

2. Most refugees make their first "step" on foot, by bicycle, wagon, or open boat. In other words, the technological factor that facilitates modern migration (see Chapter 11) is inoperative here. Refugees are suddenly dis-

placed, limiting their options, and the great majority have few resources to invest in their journey.

3. Refugees move without the official documents that accompany channeled migration. External refugees almost without exception migrate without authorization and often carry little or no identifying paper.

As recent events in Africa underscore, refugee movements often happen suddenly and can involve millions in a matter of weeks, if not days. This means that the refugee map changes frequently. Usually, it is difficult to predict where the next crisis will occur (and impossible where natural calamities are concerned), so that preparing for a refugee exodus yet to come is mainly a fruitless exercise. In a recent study, the International Red Cross identified nearly 2000 locales in Africa where conflict and/or natural catastrophes might precipitate refugee movements at some future time. Other parts of the world may be less threatened today but no place on Earth is immune to the forces of dislocation.

In 1995, the UNHCR reported the following refugee numbers for the world's major realms:

Africa	7,450,100
Europe	6,056,600
Asia (excluding the former USSR)	5,773,500
Former Soviet Union	2,280,700
North America	1,290,800
South America	130,900
Pacific	50,400
Total	23,033,000

The total of more than 23 million does not include an estimated 26 million intranational refugees, who were displaced within their own

countries and are difficult to enumerate. We turn next to the world's major refugee regions (Fig. 12-1).

REGIONS OF DISLOCATION

Although the refugee situation changes frequently as some refugees return home as conditions allow while other, new streams suddenly form, the overall geography of refugees has a certain continuity. In the mid-1990s, Africa south of the Sahara had the largest number of refugees as well as the greatest potential for new refugee flows. While Europe ranked second, Europe's numbers were inflated by a relatively liberal definition of refugee status, although the war in the former Yugoslavia produced more than two million refugees by any measure. Most of the refugees reported by the UNHCR as living in Asia were in fact concentrated in Southwest and South Asia, with far smaller numbers in Southeast and East Asia.

AFRICA

The burgeoning population of Subsaharan Africa is severely affected by dislocation—and not only in terms of the 7.5 million "official" refugees accounted for by international agencies. Many more are intranational refugees, and their numbers also are in the millions. The brutal civil war in Angola has produced international refugees who entered Zaïre and Zambia, but uncounted millions have been displaced within the country by the seemingly endless struggles for power there. Large numbers of people are similarly displaced in Sudan and in Moçambique, although in 1995 the situation in Moçambique appeared to be improving.

Four of the world's largest refu-

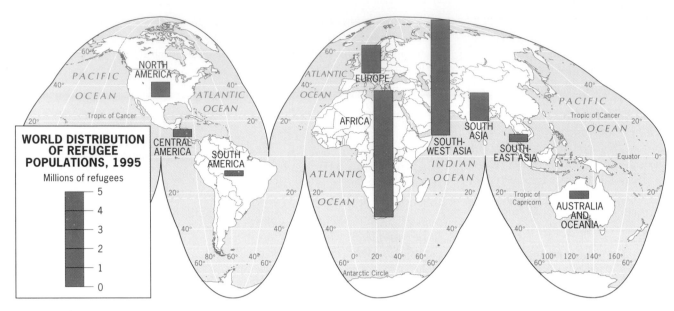

FIGURE 12–1 Based on press reports as of mid-1995.

gee crises afflicted Africa during the 1990s alone: the collapse of order in Somalia, the civil war in Liberia, the ongoing conflict in Sudan, and the disaster in Rwanda and its neighbors. Among the causes are those endemic to Africa: undemocratic, weak, and corrupt governments, historic ethnic rivalries, an excess of weapons (mostly supplied by the superpowers during the Cold War), and a lack of national cohesion. When things improve in one part of Africa, they seem to fall apart in another. In 1995, most of the nearly 1 million Moçambican refugees who had fled into neighboring Malawi were repatriated or on their way back home. But concern was growing for the future of Africa's most populous (and ethnically and culturally divided) state, Nigeria. A breakdown of order in Nigeria would generate human dislocation on a scale not seen in Africa.

In 1995, some two dozen African countries harbored significant refugee populations (Fig. 12-2). As the map shows, the Horn of Africa and neighboring Sudan remain regions of severe dislocation. Over the past five years, Somalia, Ethiopia, and

Sudan each have generated about 1 million refugees plus millions of displaced people within their borders. It was the hunger arising from

such dislocation that impelled then-President George Bush to intervene in Somalia with a U.S.-led United Nations campaign of relief.

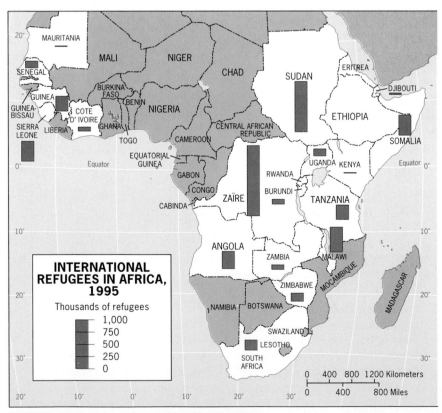

FIGURE 12–2 The refugee tide ebbs and flows.

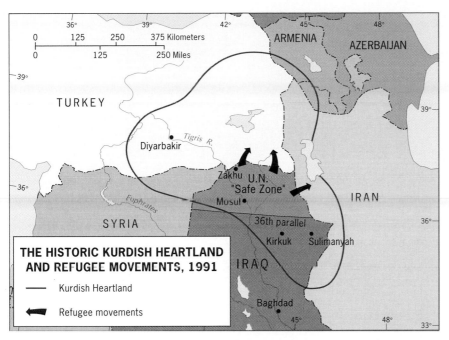

FIGURE 12–3 Historic homeland of the Kurds in Turkey, Iran, Iraq, Syria, and Transcaucasia.

Asia took place in 1991, when, in the aftermath of the Gulf War, the Kurdish population of northern Iraq, threatened by the surviving military apparatus under Baghdad's control, abandoned their villages and towns and streamed toward and across the Turkish and Iranian borders.

The refugee movement of Iraq's Kurds involved as many as 2.5 million people and riveted world attention on the plight of people who are condemned to such status by the actions of others (Fig. 12-3). It led the United States and its allies to create a secure zone for Kurds in extreme northern Iraq to persuade Kurds in Turkey and Iran to return to their country. But as Figure 12-3 shows, this zone was much smaller than the Kurdish domain in northern Iraq, and the effort was only partially successful. The Kurdish people of Iraq were severely dislocated by the events during and following the Gulf War.

The Palestinian Arabs

The Kurds are among these stateless nations of the world that are especially susceptible to such dislocation at the will (and hands) of others. Ever since the creation of the state of Israel in what was formerly the British Mandate of Palestine, hundreds of thousands of Arabs who called Palestine their homeland have lived as refugees in neighboring countries. Over time—now five decades—many of the Palestinians have been assimilated into the societies of Israel's neighbors, but a still larger number live in makeshift refugee camps. The Palestinians also call themselves a nation without a state (much as the Jews were before Israel was founded), and they have kept the issue of a national homeland alive in the political forums of the world.

The Palestinian problem has its roots in the geopolitical arrangements made after the end of World War I, when the area of Palestine (including both sides of the crucial

But even as this effort was under way, a less visible struggle in Sudan continued to create a huge refugee crisis. Sudan is regionally divided between an Islamic, Arabized northern region and a non-Islamic, African south. The Islamic northerners have been trying to subdue the rebellious south for decades, and this civil war has caused one of the world's longest and costliest refugee problems. Southern Sudan is one of the world's remotest places, and no one knows how many people are displaced; the Sudanese regime has been accused of preventing relief supplies from reaching the refugee camps because such supplies would also be consumed by political opponents. The refugees have no recourse, and so the number of victims of war continues to grow.

In West Africa, the three-way civil war in Liberia that began in 1990 produced 1.25 million refugees in a matter of months and destroyed the country's infrastructure. Tens of thousands died, and many hundreds of thousands saw their homes and villages burned in one of the most brutal civil conflicts to erupt in Africa. By 1995, an inter-African military force had stabilized the situation to some extent, and refugees were returning. But the damage done to Liberia will take more than a generation to repair, and a generation of sustained stability may not be in the offing.

Political conflicts, environmental conditions, and ideological changes have dislocated millions of Africans over the past generation. Mushrooming population, deteriorating environments, and latent civil strife will unfortunately ensure that the refugee cycle in Africa will not soon be broken.

SOUTHWEST ASIA

The two geographic realms of Southwest Asia and South Asia each have major refugee concentrations *and* exhibit qualities that are likely to generate additional refugee flows in the future. One of the most recent refugee crises in Southwest

Jordan River) was awarded to the United Kingdom to be administered as a League of Nations Mandate. It was official British policy to create a Jewish homeland in the region, but the Arabs were in the majority in Palestine, and the British moved cautiously, severely limiting Jewish immigration. After World War II, British administration in Palestine faced rising opposition from both Arab and Jewish residents. The Arabs feared that plans for a British-sponsored Jewish homeland would be implemented; Jewish residents and Jewish refugees from the Nazi holocaust resented British refusals to permit large-scale migration to the Holy Land. The British placed the problem before the United Nations, where a plan for a Jewish state was approved. The boundaries of the state of Israel confined the new country to the west of the Jordan River (Fig 12-4), but Arabs actually outnumbered Jews by about two to one within its territory. As soon as the British withdrew and the state of Israel was proclaimed (1948), the surrounding Arab countries attacked it, supporting the Arabs now under Israeli rule. This campaign failed, and it made refugees out of hundreds of thousands of Arabs who emigrated from Israel and settled in refugee camps around the country's periphery, from the Gaza Strip in the west, to Jordan in the east, Syria in the northeast, and Lebanon in the north (Fig. 12-4). There for nearly 50 years, they have remained as reservoirs for Palestinian militancy and as frequent victims of Israeli retaliation for Palestinian attacks.

As Figure 12-4 shows, not all the land west of the Jordan River was originally awarded to Israel. The United Nations partition plan awarded a compact area west of the Jordan River to the Palestinian Arabs, but in the conflict that followed Israel's creation, this area was invaded by the country then called Transjordan. This made the Jordan

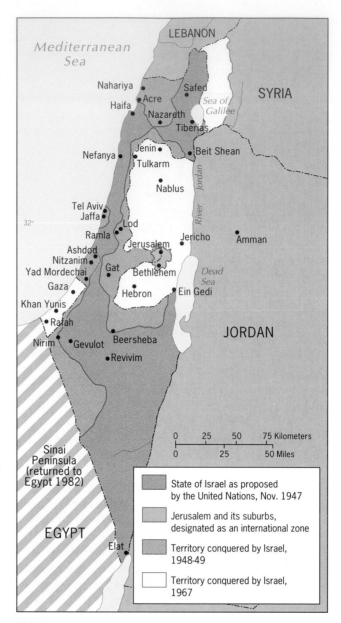

FIGURE 12–4 From a map in M. Gilbert, *Atlas of the Arab-Israeli Conflict* (New York: Macmillan, 1974), p. 38.

River, for part of its course, an internal river to Transjordan, and the country was renamed, simply, Jordan.

In 1967, a fateful conflict, the Six-Day War, erupted, and Israel repaid Arab aggression by occupying the Jordanian area west of the Jordan River, the "West Bank." In the same war, Israel occupied Syria's Golan Heights, a strategic corner in the northeast, and with the Gaza Strip Israel now controlled three consequential parts of former Palestine not originally awarded to it. (In this war, Israel also took Egypt's Sinai Peninsula, but yielded it during a later peace settlement with Egypt).

The 1967 Six-Day War extended Israeli rule over perhaps as many as 700,000 additional Palestinian Arabs, again worsening the refugee situation. Over time, a complicating factor arose: while many thousands of Palestinians were absorbed into the societies of the neighboring Arab countries to which they first fled as refugees, others remained refugees under the United Nations definition. As a result, published estimates of actual Palestinian refugee concentrations (as opposed to total numbers of Palestinians in the region) vary widely. In 1991, Palestinians living in Israel itself (820,000), or in the West Bank (925,000), were not classified as refugees, but those in the Gaza Strip (560,000) were. Estimates of Palestinian refugees in Jordan's population ranged from 900,000 to 1.7 million (*not* counting the new influx of many of Kuwait's 400,000 Palestinians forced out of that country after the Gulf War). Other estimates of Palestinian refugees are those in Lebanon (295,000 to 360,000), Syria (225,000 to 275,000), Iraq (70,000 to 90,000), Egypt (60,000), and Libya (25,000).

The Palestinian nation, that is, Arabs with Palestinian roots, may number 6 million; again, definitions vary. Whatever their status, Palestinians clearly constitute a major portion of the Jordanian population, and clearly the Palestinian desire for a national homeland cannot be met without the involvement not only of Israel, but also of Jordan, among other Arab neighbors of the state of Israel.

In 1994, significant developments occurred. Self-government came to Gaza and to the town of Jericho on the West Bank, and a peace accord was signed between Israel and Jordan. Despite this progress (and some signs that Syria might be drawn into the "peace process"), the Palestinian problem remains deep-rooted and difficult. Arab states often have been criticized for slowing the assimilation of Palestinians. They respond by arguing that such assimilation would signal Arab acquiescence to the status quo and the eventual abandonment of aspi-

rations toward a Palestinian state. In the meantime, hundreds of thousands of Palestinian refugees are caught in a geopolitical vise. Many have been born, lived their lives, and died as refugees—wards of the United Nations and other relief agencies—pawns in a power struggle that has yet to change the map of the region in their favor.

Afghanistan and Its Neighbors

Afghanistan during the 1980s was caught in the last campaign of Soviet imperialism and paid an enormous price for it. The Soviet invasion, in support of a puppet regime, and Afghan resistance generated a double migration stream that carried millions westward into Iran and eastward into Pakistan. At the height of the exodus, 2.5 million Afghans were estimated to be living in camps in Iran, and some 3.7 million gathered in tent camps in Pakistan's northwestern province and in southern Baluchistan. The Soviet invasion of 1979 seemed destined to succeed quickly, but the Russian generals underestimated the strength of Afghan opposition. United States support for the Muslim forces in the form of weapons supplies helped produce a stalemate and eventual Soviet withdrawal, but this was followed by a power struggle among Afghan factions. As a result, most of the more than 6 million refugees in Iran and Pakistan—about one-quarter of the country's population—stayed where they were.

By late 1994, an accommodation had been reached in the capital, Kabul, and refugees had begun to return to Afghanistan in considerable numbers. The UNHCR reported that nearly 750,000 Afghan refugees had been repatriated from Pakistan, and about 480,000 from Iran.

Afghanistan, however, lies in a contentious part of the world, and it

may not have seen the last of the aftershocks from the Soviet-Afghan conflict. Tajikistan, its neighbor to the northeast, has been in turmoil almost continuously since the Soviet collapse, and 25 percent of Afghanistan's population is ethnically Tajik. Another neighbor is Uzbekistan, and 10 percent of the Afghan population is Uzbek. The refugees are returning, but stability may not be assured.

SOUTHEAST ASIA

Since 1975, Southeast Asia has been the scene of some of the world's most tragic refugee movements. Even 30 years of war in Indochina did not produce so desperate an exodus as that of Vietnam's "boat people," or so severe a crisis as that which engulfed Cambodia. In terms of absolute numbers, these were perhaps not the world's largest refugee streams. But in terms of human suffering, they had no equal.

After the victory of communist forces in Vietnam and the departure of the last American military personnel and many South Vietnamese allies, the new regime commenced a program of restructuring Vietnamese society. Although not as extreme as what was done in Cambodia, this was a far-reaching project. Many Vietnamese found themselves assigned for relocation to new economic zones where a difficult subsistence awaited them; others faced "reorientation" camps. Virtually from the day of Saigon's defeat (April 1975), Vietnamese began to crowd into boats, many of them small and unseaworthy, and sailed and floated into the open ocean in hope of rescue and relocation. It is almost inconceivable that social conditions in any country could be such that hundreds of thousands would choose to face death rather than remain, and refuse, under any circumstances, to return to their homeland after facing starvation and exposure on the open sea.

When the exodus of the boat people began, it was a spontaneous movement generated almost entirely by "push" factors in Vietnam. However, there is evidence that the communist government made use of the refugees' desperation by encouraging, rather than arresting, their departure—not just implicitly, but by actually providing boats, towing people out to sea, and pressuring certain persons to board the boats. In the first half-year of the exodus, the great majority of the boat people were ethnic Vietnamese who could not adjust to the new order. Later, tens of thousands of Chinese people living in Vietnam, facing growing hostility by the new regime, boarded the boats and set out to sea.

As Figure 12-5 indicates, the Vietnamese boats entered the wide South China Sea. Those people fortunate enough to have boarded motorized vessels could head for refugee centers in Hong Kong or Macao, but most simply sailed and floated on the ocean currents and approached Malaysia and Thailand. How many people attempted this escape will never be known. It is estimated that between 40 and 70 percent of them were killed by storms, pirates, exposure, starvation, and the disintegration of their inadequate wooden boats. By the beginning of 1980, more than 400,000 Vietnamese, the overwhelming majority of them rescued boat people, had been counted in refugee camps and resettlement programs. This means that as many as 1 million Vietnamese may have been on the South China Sea.

The refugees in some instances were rescued at sea and taken to refugee centers in Japan, Hong Kong, Macao, or the Philippines. Those who drifted onto the beaches of Malaysia and Thailand, however, often were not so fortunate. Many were simply towed back out to sea again and abandoned. Others were taken to deserted islands and left to their own devices. Still others were moved into camps that were among the world's least adequate for refugee lodging. Insufficient food, inadequate facilities, disease, and other discomforts took a further toll on the boat people. Only after a United Nations Conference on Refugees in July 1979 did the plight of the Vietnamese emigrants ease somewhat. Repatriation to new homelands began. By 1990, the United States had accepted nearly 900,000 Vietnamese refugees. France and Canada (both 100,000+), Australia (50,000+), and (former West) Germany (40,000+) were the other leading destinations for relocated Vietnamese refugees.

The exodus of the boat people from Southeast Asia and the movement of Haitians in the Caribbean are similar in some ways, although the "push" factors impelling their voyages differ significantly. These two migration flows, however, may well be recognized in the future as vanguards of a new era in migration and refugee movement. When the Vietnamese government eventually agreed to inhibit the outflow of boat people, the volume of emigration by these means decreased— but it did not end. The governments of other countries may not be able to stem a tide of coastal emigration, either. Political, economic, and environmental crises will generate future armadas of seaborne refugees.

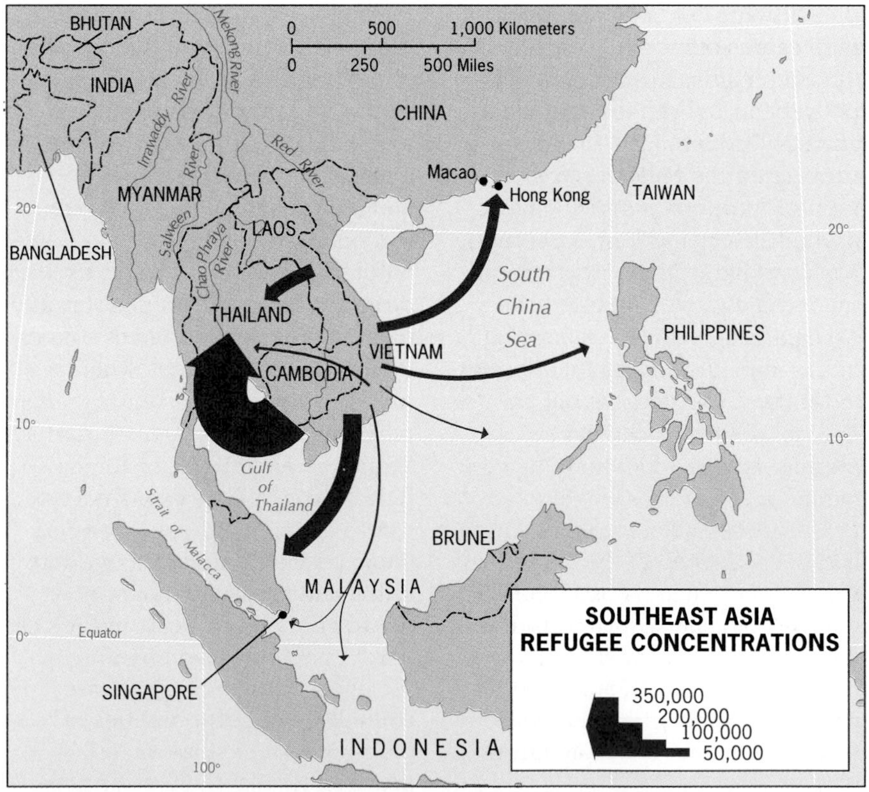

Cambodia

As the boat people left Vietnam by sea, Cambodians, when they could, walked westward, hoping to cross the boundary between Cambodia and Thailand. By mid-1991, more than 320,000 Cambodians were liv-

FIGURE 12–5 The major movement of refugees within Southeast Asia has been from Cambodia to Thailand.

ing in squalid refugee camps near the border, frequent victims of warfare, as the conflict that had engulfed their country spilled over its boundaries.

The Cambodian exodus had its roots in the period after the end of the Indochina War, when a communist regime took control of the country and forced the population from cities and towns into the countryside at enormous cost in human suffering. The capital city, Phnom Penh, was a ghost town; the rural areas were littered with death. In 1978, Vietnamese forces launched their initial attacks against the Pol Pot regime, and, in 1979 this government, one of the world's most repressive, fell—its remnants pushed into the country's northwestern corner. However, the Vietnamese are old enemies of Cambodia's Khmer nation, and conflict continued. As the number of refugees mounted, both sides interfered with relief efforts. The Vietnamese refused landing rights for aircraft carrying supplies, and the remnant of the Cambodian power group tried to intercept overland traffic. Desperation drove large numbers of Cambodian "land people" to walk westward; many died along the way or were killed by the forces of both sides. Those who did reach Thailand found themselves within reach of some food and medical help, but Thai cooperation in the relief effort was not unqualified. Again, the refugees—especially the numerous children—were the real victims of the region's geopolitical instability.

In the early 1990s, a wrenching refugee drama played itself out in Hong Kong. Nearly 60,000 Vietnamese refugees who had arrived there against the wishes of the Hong Kong administration, and who had no outward destination, were imprisoned under dire circumstances while repatriation plans progressed. When small groups were identified for repatriation to Vietnam, there

was resistance and violence; the Vietnamese in their internment camp also were reduced to fighting among themselves. Hong Kong, itself substantially the product of illegal immigration (but from China), was in turmoil over the issue; but the greater worry was the approach of China's takeover of Hong Kong from Great Britain in 1997. The plight of the Vietnamese refugees remained in the background.

MIDDLE AND NORTH AMERICA

In few areas of the world are economic circumstances so strongly contrasted, ideological opposites as intense, and distances as short as they are in the midsection of the Americas. These combinations—Caribbean poverty and U.S. wealth, Cuban communism and U.S. capitalism, and proximity—have generated an outflow of legal emigrants and refugees of enormous proportions. Certainly, the world map carries other areas of contrast between comparatively rich and poor, but most frequently there are transition zones, natural barriers, or great distances to deter mass migration. Asian and black immigration to the United Kingdom, for example, has been limited in part by the friction of distance from the source areas, and a major refugee problem has not arisen (except briefly, during the Asian exodus from Uganda). It is not difficult to imagine what the proportions of a refugee influx would have been if Britain lay just a few miles removed from coastal West Africa. Indeed, the world map suggests that there is only one combination of material contrasts and relative location comparable to the United States and the Caribbean, and that is Australia and its island neighbors to the north and northwest.

So large is the outflow of refugees from political, economic, and

environmental conditions in the Caribbean that U.S. estimates of the numbers are vague and inaccurate. Undoubtedly, the largest stream of migrants, as well as refugees, has come from Cuba, where the "push" factor was the new socialist order dating from 1960. In the more than 30 years since then, more than 1 million persons have left Cuba, the overwhelming majority of them for the United States. As noted previously, Cuban immigrants have transformed the cultural geography of southern Florida, and the huge resident Spanish-speaking population has come to constitute a "pull" factor in the continuing exodus. The prospect of reuniting families was a major impetus for the Mariel Boatlift of 1980, which eventually brought 125,000 new Cuban residents to the United States, many of them fitting all the qualifications of refugees.

However, the Cuban stream is only one of several other flows of migrants and refugees. Among Haitians who came to the United States during the Duvalier and Cedras regimes a far greater percentage of migrants were genuine refugees than among Cubans. Again, estimates vary, but by 1995 about 500,000 Haitians had come to the United States.

Unlike the Cuban emigrants, the Haitian movement has been mainly by sailboats, rafts, and some motor-driven vessels, and almost no one in this 25-year influx came with any tangible property or money. Many (the number will never be known) died at sea. In the true sense of the term, the Haitians are the Americas' "boat people," often setting out to sea without assurance of survival.

Cubans and Haitians have recently been the most prominent island refugees to come to the United States, but other, less publicized streams continue. It is estimated that more Jamaicans live outside Jamaica than remain in their own country. The United Kingdom has shared in the Jamaican immigration; over 300,000 now reside in New York City (about 12 percent of Jamaica's total population). Perhaps as many as 550,000 people from the Dominican Republic also live in New York—about 200,000 of them without authorization—a total equal to about 9 percent of that country's population. The Dominican population is not technically a refugee population, but it is substantially an unauthorized migration. Also contributing to the Caribbean population movement are smaller currents from Grenada, St. Kitts, Antigua, St. Lucia, and literally dozens of the Lesser Antilles. These migrations consist of combinations of legitimate emigrants and those who enter or remain in the United States illegally.

The question of legitimacy complicates the migration process from Middle America to the United States. It is a reflection of the growing seriousness of the immigration problem generally that the U.S., the country that once welcomed the world's "huddled masses," decided to reinforce its boundary with Mexico by erecting steel-mesh fences, nearly 12 feet (4 m) high, along lengthy stretches where illegal Mexican migrants were crossing in large numbers. Mexican job-seekers, the U.S. government argued, were not legitimate refugees by any standards, and illegal migrants must be stopped at the border or repatriated when identified. While the "Tortilla Curtain" with its fences and border patrols caused resentment in Mexico, substantial numbers of migrants managed to enter the U.S. anyway; in recent years, the flow has been estimated at as high as 1 million annually.

The refugee issue has become a divisive one in government circles. The Congressional Black Caucus criticizes the apparent discrimination between Cuban immigrants, who are readily admitted to the U.S. on the basis of their escape from a communist dictatorship, and Haitian immigrants, who must prove their "well-founded fear" before they are admitted and many of whom have been returned to Haiti. The United States Department of State, the agency responsible for processing immigrants of all kinds, points to the fact that the U.S. has been admitting people still fleeing communism not only from Cuba but also from Vietnam (about 50,000 Vietnamese still reach the U.S. annually); Jews from the former Soviet Union also are admitted freely. When it comes to other forms of oppression, the United States uses a quota system for admissions and will not allow unlimited immigration.

It is clear that the policy is inconsistent, or inconsistently applied. Recent news reports of the forced repatriation of boatloads of Chinese migrants, presumably escaping from communism as well, suggest that offending an important trading partner has something to do with the way the "escape from communist oppression" clause is applied.

EUROPE

If the UNHCR Report on Refugees for 1995 contains one surprise, it is not the growing total number of world refugees but the large total reported for Europe; more than 6 million in early 1995, the second largest number, by geographic realm, in the world. While the war in the former Yugoslavia has produced more than one-third of Europe's refugees (plus millions of displaced persons within the area of conflict), the remaining aggregate is unexpected. Except for the conflict in the former Yugoslavia, Europe has not experienced an Afghanistan or a Rwanda. Why are the numbers so large?

The answer lies in the same arena as it does in the United States: the designation of refugee status. And as in the United States, a some- times acrimonious debate is raging over the matter. In Europe, a group of 13 countries long recognized political oppression in poor countries as a legitimate reason to assign refugee status to an applicant and to award "asylum." In the early 1990s, European countries were processing about 700,000 such applications per year. But the **asylum seekers** generally were not stopped at the border: they were allowed to enter and wait, at public expense, for their case to come up. In 1994, Germany alone had about a half million asylum seekers on its soil.

Many of these **displaced persons** come not from distant lands but from poorer East European countries and from countries farther east, including the former Soviet Union. While Caribbean Islanders, North and Subsaharan Africans, and South Asians also continue to arrive, the majority of the asylum seekers now on the list are other Europeans. And indications are that Europe, like the United States, is seeking to limit the influx. Germany, for example, has proclaimed that all of its immediate neighbors are "safe" countries, where no political oppression occurs; hence any claim of political asylum involving these countries is void. But the changing policies also affected genuine refugees: those who managed to leave war-torn Bosnia, for example, found their path to relief much more troubled than was the case previously.

The reported number of refugees in Europe, therefore, may decline in future enumerations. Indeed, there is nothing in Europe (or North America) to match the misery of the refugee camps of Africa or Southwest Asia. Nevertheless, the potential for dislocation in Europe will not end with the cessation of the Yugoslavia War. Until economic and political stability are achieved in Russia and its neighbors, Europe faces the possibility of renewed influx.

RUSSIA AND ITS NEIGHBORS

Given the magnitude of the changes that have occurred in the former Soviet Union over the past decade, it is remarkable that the mid-1995 refugee total for this area remained as low as it was (between two and three million). Indeed, one of the largest refugee problems to arise here was caused by natural, not economic or political, circumstances: a massive earthquake in Armenia that displaced tens of thousands of people.

The reorganization and stabilization of Russia and its "Near-Abroad" (as the Russians call the countries of the former Soviet empire) have not yet been achieved, however, and this is one part of the world where the potential for dislocation is high. Already, the Transcaucasus region has witnessed devastating conflict involving Armenia and Azerbaijan in a war over territory and ethnicity and Georgia in a civil war. More than half of the reported refugee numbers come from this zone, and the situation in the Russian "republics" on the north slope of the Caucasus has been deteriorating.

In Turkestan (the former Soviet Central Asia), armed conflict also has generated refugee flows, notably in Tajikistan. This entire region is a mosaic of nationalities and its post-Soviet transformation is unleashing old animosities.

But the major risk is in Russia itself. Stability and continuity in Russia are crucial for the future not only of the "Near-Abroad" but also of Eastern Europe and the West. The breakdown of order in Russia could generate dislocation on a scale not seen since World War II.

PERSPECTIVE

This chapter has focused on the world's current major refugee problems. The price of a mushrooming global population, political and ethnic strife, and environmental deterioration, is human dislocation. While we discussed salient refugee streams, we could not account for many other refugee populations: the *de facto* partition of Cyprus, which dislocated tens of thousands of Greeks and Turks; the Guatemalans in Mexico; the Vietnamese in Malaysia; the New Guineans under Indonesian rule who have crossed into Papua New Guinea; and hundreds of thousands more. Inevitably, the decade of the 1990s will experience refugee crises unforeseen today.

Several circumstances point to a further increase in the global numbers of refugees as well. Twenty years ago, when the globe-girdling droughts of the 1970s developed, the Earth's population was nearly 2 billion people less than it is today. An ever larger number of people are at risk. Concurrently, the pace of environmental degradation increases as well. And the "New World Order" about which we hear so much these days is a misnomer for widespread political disorder. Virtually everywhere on the globe, political systems are under stress, incapable of accommodating the pressures of modern times. It is a combination destined to dislocate peoples the world over.

People who abandon their familiar surroundings because these have become unlivable commit an act of ultimate desperation. In the process, the habits of civilization vanish as survival becomes the sole imperative. The Earth's refugee population is a barometer of the world's future.

KEY TERMS

Asylum Seekers
Dislocation
Displaced Persons
Environmental Crises
International Refugees
Intranational Refugees
Permanent Refugees
Political Oppression
Refugee
Temporary Refugees
United Nations High Commission for Refugees (UNHCR)
War

Health care in urban areas often is limited to small, poorly-equipped clinics. Goa, India.

PART FOUR

PATTERNS
OF NUTRITION
AND HEALTH

At Issue

Among the wealthiest and economically most advanced countries of the world, the United States in the 1990s was alone in not having a national health program covering all citizens of all ages. This became a major issue during the 1992 presidential campaign, when all contenders—including the incumbent—proposed comprehensive health programs. Immediately after taking office, the new President embarked on an ultimately unsuccessful effort to establish such a program. His failure notwithstanding, medical statistics underscored the urgency of the matter: conditions in the poorer communities resembled those prevailing in the world's least-developed countries. Geography has much to do with this. In the world at large, there is enough food to ensure the survival of all; but transporting the food to those who are most in need remains an insurmountable obstacle. So it is with health services: the U.S. has the capacity, but many poor areas are not adequately served by hospitals and physicians.

At issue is the nature of the system that will bring affordable medical services to all: should it be a government agency, or should the private sector bear the bulk of the responsibility?

13

A GEOGRAPHY OF NUTRITION

Geographica

- **Daily calorie consumption varies regionally from high levels in the richer countries such as the United States and Canada, European states, Japan, and Australia to very low levels in poorer countries in Africa; the general situation has improved markedly over the past two decades.**

- **The Green Revolution, which resulted in the development of higher-yielding, faster-growing types of rice, wheat, and some other cereals, has had far greater effect in Asia and in the Americas than in Africa, where lesser grains, not yet affected, form the regional staples.**

- **Malnutrition affects locales even within many of the best- and adequately-fed countries of the world, where pockets of poverty are marked by low calorie supply.**

- **Although global food production today is sufficient to safeguard the entire world's population from hunger, concerns are rising that a future food emergency may develop as population growth, climate change, and energy costs pose risks for the twenty-first century.**

- **The mitigation of a future food crisis depends on policies and practices ranging from family planning and female rights to the improvement of distribution systems and the expansion of farmlands.**

Although continued rapid growth is racing world population beyond the 6 billion mark, newspaper headlines no longer warn of any threat to the global food supply. Just two decades ago, dire predictions of regional famines in countries with large populations and high growth rates regularly made the headlines and the evening news. And the neo-Malthusians' warnings seemed to have a sound basis: population growth was outpacing the Earth's capacity to provide enough food, let alone distribute it where it was most needed. Only a miracle could save the planet.

Then the miracle happened—in the form of **miracle rice** and other high-yielding grains, developed by technicians working in agricultural research stations. Crop yields per unit area rose dramatically, especially in Asia's paddies but also on the world's wheat fields. Fast as the world's population grew, food production grew faster, and the gap between demand and supply narrowed. India, long dependent on food imports, managed to feed itself. In China the threat of famine receded. Even Bangladesh came close to self-sufficiency. Hunger lost its power as a critical issue. Even concern over population growth receded from the front pages.

But is the threat really over? Not according to some of those who raised the alarm many years ago. In their book *Full House* (1994), au-

147

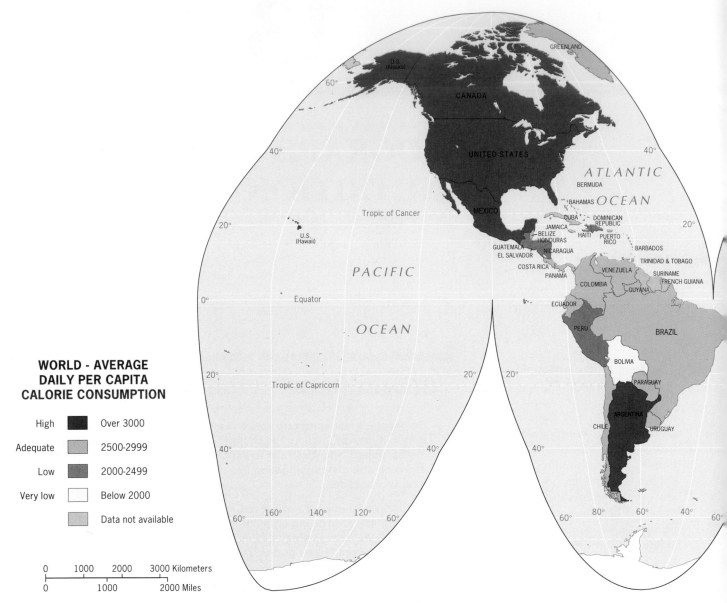

**WORLD - AVERAGE
DAILY PER CAPITA
CALORIE CONSUMPTION**

High		Over 3000
Adequate		2500-2999
Low		2000-2499
Very low		Below 2000
		Data not available

0   1000   2000   3000 Kilometers
0   1000   2000 Miles

FIGURE 13–1   Based on data from the World Bank *World Development Report, 1993*
(Oxford: Oxford University Press, 1994), pp. 258–259.

thors Lester Brown and Hal Kane argue that while population growth will continue to add more than 90 million mouths to be fed annually, and while the world will have nearly 9 billion inhabitants by 2030, world grain output will not keep pace. They predict that grain production will increase by only about 370 million tons over the next four decades, far below the rate of increase that accompanied the "miracle" of the 1980s. This will mean that population will once again outstrip food availability, leading to crises in such realms as Subsaharan Africa, South Asia, and China. Brown and Kane suggest that the recent narrowing of the food gap, followed by the renewed widening they predict, form part of a cycle that will periodically threaten humanity.

Grain production will not expand as rapidly as in the recent past, say the authors, because there are signs that the **"Green Revolution"** (the introduction of the new, more productive strains of grain and the resulting harvest increases) has run its course. In Japan, for example, production of rice rose rapidly to 4.7 tons per hectare (1.9 tons per acre) by 1984, but has not increased at all since then. In India, there is evidence that the fertilizers needed to grow the more productive types of grain are losing their effectiveness. Another concern is

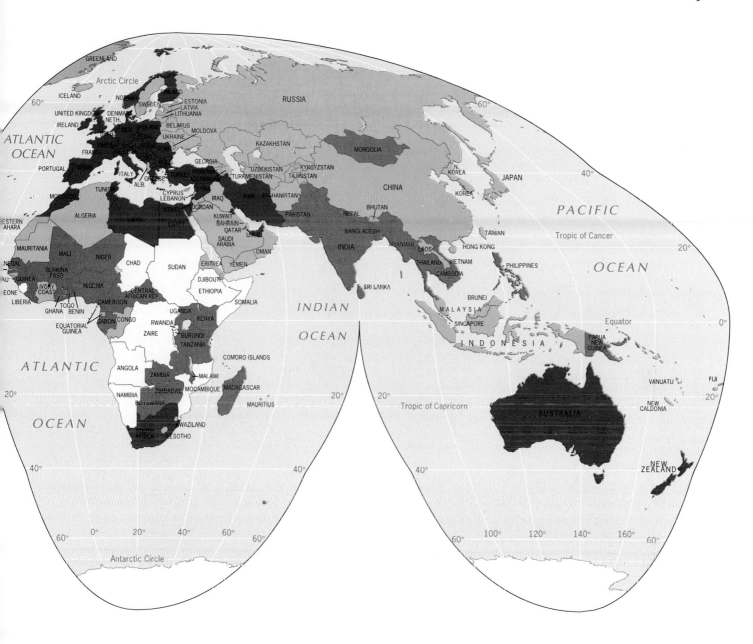

water: future shortages will lead to smaller harvests. And then there is the loss of farmland to ever-larger, sprawling urbanization. All this will lead to a substantial decline in the amount of grain supply for each person in the world, reviving the specter of widespread malnutrition or worse.

Not all observers see the situation this bleakly. Experts at the United Nations and at the World Bank, all of whom monitor world food production in detail, say that global grain production continues to increase at a healthy pace and shows no signs of slowing down. Japan's experience, they suggest, is due to special circumstances and does not represent the worldwide picture.

There is more to the issue than supply alone. Food availability also is a matter of geography. Whether there was inadequate supply or sufficient food (as measured in global terms), there always have been— and still are—people who are de-

prived of it. To a considerable extent this has to do with inadequate transport systems; the world has not achieved transport networks that can reach all people in need within reasonable time. It also relates to deliberate deprivation as policy; we noted earlier that some regimes still use food as a weapon, depriving civilian populations in war zones from their means of survival as a matter of strategy. So the provision of food is a matter of production as well as dissemination.

THE GEOGRAPHY OF NUTRITION

In this chapter we examine spatial aspects of food and nutrition. There is more to nutrition than quantity; it also is a matter of quality, that is, of dietary balance. In large areas of the world, even in this time of comparative food sufficiency, that balance still is lacking. A balanced diet includes carbohydrates (derived from staples such as rice, corn, wheat, and potatoes), proteins (from meat, poultry, fish, eggs, and dairy products), vitamins (from fruits and vegetables, as well as other sources), fats, and minerals. Proteins, a critical element in the diet, also may be derived from plant sources, including soybeans, peas, peanuts, and wheat. The amount of food intake is measured in terms of calories, which are units of "fuel" for energy production in the body.

No generalizations can be made concerning the calories need of individuals *or* nations. Males need more calories, on average, than females. Young adults need more calories than children or old persons. People of large stature require more calories than smaller people. Nations where average body size is considerably smaller than that of other nations do better with fewer calories than the larger-statured nations do.

Figure 13-1 reveals the wide range of **calorie intake** in today's world. The World Bank, one of the agencies that monitor global food consumption, groups countries according to calorie intake into four levels, ranging from high (over 3000 calories) to very low (below 2000). Note that the World Bank regards 2500 calories and over as "adequate," whereas the United Nations suggests that 2360 calories is adequate.

Based on the World Bank assessment as reflected by Figure 13-1, there still are countries in the dangerous "very low" category, all of them except Bolivia, in Africa. As the map shows, additional countries in the Americas, Africa, and Asia report inadequate calorie intake (2000 to 2499).

What Figure 13-1 does *not* show is the dietary balance in these countries. With few exceptions, the countries where there is a low calorie intake are also the countries where protein is in short supply. Recent studies have indicated that the first six months of life are critical in this respect: inadequate protein intake can damage brain and body for life. Furthermore, the food sources that are richest in proteins—meat, fish, and dairy

THE FOOD WEB

Plants, cultivated and wild, form the basic source of food for all the animal populations of the world, including humans. We acquire nutrients and energy by eating plant foods (vegetables, fruits, and grains) and by consuming meat from animals that have eaten plant foods (cattle, hogs, chickens, etc.). Human beings, therefore, are part of a **food chain**, a sequence of consumption that starts with the Earth's green plants. Plants derive their capacity for growth through the process of *photosynthesis*, the interception of some of the energy that reaches the Earth from the sun and its use in the conversion of carbon dioxide, water, and soil nutrients into living tissue.

Plants, the producers, are the first link in the food chain. The *primary consumers* are the animals that eat plants, the *herbivores*. They form the second link in the food chain. The third link is constituted by the animals that eat herbivores, the *carnivores*. These are the *secondary consumers*. There are carnivores that eat other carnivores, and they are the next link, the *tertiary consumers*. Thus the chain goes on.

Human beings are both herbivores and carnivores, eating plants as well as meat. We are *omnivores* and function as primary as well as secondary consumers. When we eat fish, we are tertiary consumers. The living world consists of an intricate network of food chains called the **food web**.

Consumption at each level of a food chain involves a large loss of energy. It may take 12,000 pounds of grain to feed a cow until it weighs 1000 pounds. Slaughtered and eaten by human beings, that cow's 1000 pounds may produce barely 100 pounds of human weight. However, had the humans eaten the grain directly, they—and not the cow—would have gained that 1000 pounds. Much more usable energy, therefore, it available to consumers lower on the food chain. (Primary consumers, thus, are in the best position).

Cattle are especially "expensive" in the food chain. The conversion ratio (the quantity of food required to raise the weight of a consumer at the next link in the food chain by one pound) is 23:1 for cattle, 11:1 for hogs, and only 3:1 for chickens (although calculations vary). One element of an eventual solution to future world food supply problems, thus, will involve more human consumers at lower levels of the food chain, and the resulting consumption of fewer meat products, especially beef. During the mid-1990s, more than 35 percent of food consumed in the United States, Canada, Australia, the United Kingdom, (former West) Germany, and France was of animal origin. It was less than 10 percent in such countries as Indonesia, India, Algeria, and Ethiopia. A narrowing of that gap would signal expanded food production and improved diets.

products—are all too often in short supply where they are most needed. It takes food to raise the animals that produce meat, and that food cannot be spared as animal feed where it is needed to keep people alive (see box, "The Food Web"); fish is not readily available either, in distant, interior areas, and canned or dried, it may be an expensive luxury. People's **diets** are determined by three principal factors: what the soil and climate can produce, what the economic circumstances are, and what the people's traditions are. There are places in the world where certain taboos limit people's access to the meat products that might improve their dietary imbalance, but, most of all, it is a shortage of surplus feed that creates the barrier. The result is that even persons whose caloric intake is marginally adequate are actually malnourished. There is "hidden hunger" even in the areas identified as having "adequate calories" (Fig. 13-1).

TABLE 13–1	Daily Calorie Supply per Capita in Selected Countries		
Large Supply		**Low Supply**	
United States	3666	Panama	2568
Spain	3543	El Salvador	2415
Germany	3514	Yemen	2322
New Zealand	3459	Thailand	2287
Australia	3322	Peru	2269
United Kingdom	3252	Philippines	2255
Syria	3168	Pakistan	2200
Mexico	3135	India	2104
Turkey	3080	Nigeria	2039
		Zaïre	2034
Adequate Supply		**Very Low Supply**	
Tunisia	2964	Sudan	1996
Jordan	2907	Kenya	1973
Hong Kong	2899	Bangladesh	1925
South Korea	2878	Haiti	1911
Japan	2848	Chad	1852
Morocco	2820	Somalia	1736
Brazil	2709	Ethiopia	1658
Indonesia	2670	Moçambique	1632
China	2632		
Chile	2584		
Colombia	2561		

Source: World Bank, *World Development Report 1991.* (Oxford: Oxford University Press, 1991), pp. 258–259.

DISTRIBUTION OF DIETARY PATTERNS

The map of average daily calorie consumption in the world's countries (Fig. 13-1) is based on data that are not always reliable, so it should be taken as a general impression of the global situation. Published statistical information about caloric intake, especially for the underdeveloped countries, is often based on rough estimates rather than accurate counts. Nevertheless, the map reveals rather clearly the world distribution of hunger and **malnutrition**. In the Americas, the northern- and southernmost countries are best fed (by this measure), notably Canada, the United States, Argentina, and Uruguay. Mexico's calorie availability has risen markedly since 1965, from 2570 to 3135 per capita. Brazil has

been in the "adequate" category for many years; the lowest food availability still plagues chronically underfed Haiti.

In Europe, calorie availability and intake are high virtually everywhere. If data from the former Soviet Union can be believed, that realm, too, was in the high-consumption category—despite frequent harvest failures and massive grain imports. The situation in the aftermath of the USSR's disintegration may not be so favorable.

In Africa, the situation remains bleak. Many countries are in the "low" or "very low" categories, and several actually have lower calorie availability today than in 1965. In 1993 not a single African country had a high calorie intake, and many had an intake of 2000 or lower (Table 13-1). Figure 13-1 reflects the economic, political, and environmental dislocations the African

realm has suffered over the past 25 years.

In Asia, a tier of countries containing huge populations also have low or very low calorie availability. Again, political and social disarray have contributed to this: the long war in Afghanistan made refugees of millions of people, and Iraq also suffered from the aftermath of conflict. India still has low availability, but Indonesia's situation has improved quite substantially (2670 calories as against 1796 in 1965).

Table 13-1 reveals how wide the range of available calories is in different parts of the world. In New Zealand and the United States, people consume nearly twice the calories available to people in Haiti and Moçambique. Again, the table should be read with caution. All the countries in the "large supply" category have a combined population of the same magnitude of that of India (low calories) alone. It is worth comparing Figure 13-1 and Table 13-1 to the map of world population distribution in Figure 6-1. Malnutrition still afflicts and shortens the lives of hundreds of millions in this world.

It is especially tragic that undernutrition and malnutrition affect so many of the world's children. When food supply in a village dwindles, the social order frequently falls apart and children (and women next) are the first and most serious victims.

Even when food is available in reasonable quantity, a dietary balance is never more crucial than it is during early childhood. A child's brain grows to about 80 percent of its adult size in the first three years of life, and an adequate supply of protein to the body is vital in this development. If there is not enough protein, brain growth is inhibited and mental capacities can be permanently impaired. There can be no subsequent recovery from the loss. Both mental capacity and physical growth are adversely affected by inadequate nutrition, so the unfortunate youngster born into an environment of deprivation faces a lifelong handicap.

Protein availability, of course, is only one (although perhaps the single most important) requirement for youthful good health. Other deficiencies also have a devastating impact on young bodies. For example, vitamin-A deficiency occurs in many poor countries (and in poverty-stricken regions of less poor countries as well). Vitamin A is ingested with eggs, dairy products, and animal liver; it also is contained in fruits and vegetables. These luxuries are not part of the diets of millions of children (and the decline in breast feeding has further reduced protein and vitamin intake), with the result that many suffer from skin diseases, low resistance to respiratory diseases, and gum and eye disorders. **World Health Organization (WHO)**

experts report that vitamin-A deficiency is a principal cause of blindness in India, Indonesia, Bangladesh, northeastern Brazil, and El Salvador. In eastern Asia alone, about 100,000 children become blind every year.

When we consider the nutritional data for Asian and African countries, therefore, we should remember that it is the children who are most severely affected by malnutrition—the children who cannot yet fend for themselves, and the aged who often no longer can. Young children, as we noted in Chapter 7, make up a disproportionate percentage of the populations of the world's poorer countries, where the population explosion still exacts a heavy toll on society.

REGIONAL ASPECTS OF NUTRITION

If you were to compare Figure 13-1 in this edition of *Human Geography* with Figure 3-1 in the first edition published nearly 20 years ago, you would be encouraged by the changes. Many countries in South America, Africa, and Asia show increases in their per capita calorie consumption. Far fewer countries are now in the lowest category (very low calories) than there were in the mid-1970s. Countries in the low category have moved up to adequate, and high consumption appears in regions previously untouched by such luxury, notably in North Africa and Southwest Asia.

As we noted earlier, some specialists would tell us that any optimism engendered by this comparison is likely to be dashed by future developments that will once again reduce the food supply. They may or may not be correct in this prediction, but meanwhile there is much to be concerned about in Figure 13-1, no matter how favorable the trends. While many countries

are better fed than they were two decades ago, too many countries still have too little to eat and suffer from poorly balanced diets as well. Africa south of the Sahara is the worst off. In the early 1990s, countries in Subsaharan Africa and in the transition zone between this realm and North Africa were among the world's hungriest and most dependent on food imports. Political and social dislocation has much to do with this: the worst-fed countries, such as Ethiopia, Moçambique, Chad, Angola, Rwanda, and others in Africa are going through, or have recently gone through, civil war and mass human displacement. But this is not the only reason why many African countries are poorly nourished. Even countries comparatively unaffected by conflict are not doing as well as the rest of the world.

In part, this situation is attributable to Africa's rapid population growth, which must be matched by increased food availability. But there is another major cause: Africa has been barely touched by the Green Revolution that gave new, higher-yielding strains of grain to the farmers of Asia. Some geographers describe what has happened to the genetic "engineering" of food crops as a new agricultural revolution, as important as the one ten thousand years ago and more significant than that which occurred prior to the Industrial Revolution. An agricultural revolution it may be, but it affected Africa far less than other realms of the world. In the first place, the peoples of Asia depend mainly on two crops, rice and wheat, grown mainly under irrigation. Africa's variety of crops is much greater (corn, millet, sorghum, wheat, some rice, and others). The Green Revolution has not yet affected all of these, although a new strain of sorghum has been developed which yields three times as large a crop as the standard variety, and has raised harvests in the Sudan. More problematic is the soil situation. In Asia, most rice and wheat is planted in fertile, deep soil. Africa's soils are not irrigated for the most part, and are thin, fragile, and easily damaged. Over-cropping of such soils can easily occur.

Although it may seem unlikely, in populous Africa there are also labor problems. Africa's population is growing rapidly, but the labor force in the farming areas is not always large enough to handle the farming chores when they must be done to ensure the best yields. Add to these conditions the poorly developed state of African agriculture generally—from equipment to farming methods to education to transportation—and the slowness of the Green Revolution to have an impact in Africa is understandable.

In the late 1980s, a development occurred that (again) raised hopes for Africa's farmers. Scientists announced that a new "miracle maize," a strain of corn first developed during the early 1980s and subsequently modified, was ready for distribution. This new maize, also called QPM (Quality-Protein Maize), is rich in the very protein that is so severely lacking in many African diets. Some researchers are predicting that this new corn, by the end of the 1990s, will significantly improve the nutritional balance for as many as 200 million people now primarily dependent on this grain.

Not everyone, however, is so optimistic. In his book, *The Changing World Food Prospect* (1988), author Lester Brown points out that the decline of grain production in Africa is not the only instance of reduced yields, and "miracle strains" may not be enough to reverse the trend. In Part 2 of our book, we considered the possibility that climatic amplitudes will increase, including droughts, floods, heat waves, and cold spells. Against this background, consider the drop in grain production in the United States in the middle and late 1980s: from 345

million tons in 1985, to 277 million tons in 1987, to 190 million tons in 1988. And corn harvests declined even more, from 212 million tons in 1985 to 116 million tons in 1988. In subsequent years production rose again, but such enormous swings in the harvest volume underscore that even the highly mechanized, modern U.S. grain-farming industry is not immune to wide fluctuations. In Africa, such variability spells disaster for subsistence farmers.

Another plan to reverse Africa's agricultural fortunes was announced by the **Food and Agriculture Organization (FAO)** in 1990: a program of massive fertilizer provision that would slow land degradation and soil erosion, prolong the productivity of fields, and thus stabilize peasants and farmers who would otherwise abandon overused land. To put this plan in perspective, we should note that the average African farmer uses—and can afford—very little fertilizer. A European farmer is likely to use more than 50 times as much fertilizer as an African farmer; thus African soils are being mined, become exhausted, and are lost. Supplying fertilizer directly to African farmers of up to 10 times that used previously, the FAO reasoned, would result in enhanced yields and reduced soil loss. And the direct supply of fertilizers, rather than cash to purchase them, coupled with an educational program, might achieve what similar schemes did not.

Will a combination of improved maize strains and more fertilizers reverse the downward slide of African farm production, and initiate a Green Revolution there? The magnitude and complexity of the food problem in Africa would suggest a negative answer, as long as populations double in little more than 20 years.

The improving situation in South and Middle America, by contrast, is directly related to the widespread decline in population growth rate

noted in Chapter 7. In South America, Bolivia long has been the poorest nourished country, but even there, per capita consumption in 1994 was about to cross the 2000-calorie line. In Middle America, only Haiti remains poorly fed, a result in large measure of its political troubles.

Undoubtedly, the most dramatic improvements (whether or not they prove to be permanent) revealed by Figure 13-1 have occurred in the tier of countries extending from North Africa through Southwest and South Asia into Southeast and East Asia. Here the Green Revolution had its fullest impact, lifting numerous countries from the very low and low categories into the adequate category—and some into the high-consumption category. In a comparatively stable Southeast Asia, Thailand and Vietnam are major rice exporters; India is in a position to claim food (if not yet nutritional) self-sufficiency; and even Bangladesh is closing the gap between demand and domestic production.

A word of warning in regard to Figure 13-1: the situation in Russia and its former empire, especially in Central Asia (Turkestan), is uncertain. For some years, no dependable figures have been published for many of the countries of the former Soviet empire, but there can be no doubt that the realm's economic troubles are translating into food and nutritional problems as well. In late 1994, a sample study of Russian population indicated that male life expectancy had dropped below 60 years. (Women still outlived men, on average, by several years, so that the national mean still stood above 60). The stunning decline indicated for Russian men suggested to scholars the possibility that overall health, including that related to food provision, was deteriorating. When more accurate data become available, the former Soviet Union may emerge as a realm vulnerable to the kind of food crisis some experts say lies ahead.

ENLARGING THE SCALE

Just as a world map of population growth, examined in Chapter 7, cannot convey demographic contrasts *within* individual countries, so Figure 13-1, also based on national statistics, conceals regional variations. India's northwest, for example, is better fed than its northeast. Brazil's northeastern region has a history of malnutrition and even famine.

Nor is regional hunger a monopoly of the poorest, underdeveloped countries. Even in the United States there is malnutrition. Hundreds of thousands of families in low-income urban areas and in poverty-stricken rural areas cannot afford to spend on food what would be required to balance diets adequately. People surviving on food stamp allocations often run out of food before the next allotment. In the United States, regional contrasts defined by hunger are not as sharp as they are in India or Brazil, but such regional contrasts exist nevertheless.

People in North America are quite accustomed to shopping in supermarkets where there are potatoes from Idaho, cereals from the Midwest, oranges from Florida, and many products from foreign countries—fruits and wines from Chile, coffee from Colombia, cheeses from Holland. Indeed, our preferences can affect land use in distant parts of the world, for example, through the conversion of forest to pastureland and by the use of grains to feed meat-providing animals rather than people (see box, "Feed Grains and Food Grains"). Such luxury sometimes makes it difficult to understand the factors that maintain the regional concentrations of food scarcity in the world. If Southeast Brazil is better fed than the Northeast, why not distribute the food differently so that the Northeast is better fed? How can one part of In-

dia be reasonably well-fed while people beg for food in the streets in another area of the same country? One huge problem is exactly that: getting the food to the people who need it immediately and most urgently. The world got a searing lesson in this during the 1970s, when a severe drought cycle struck West Africa's Sahara margins, the region known as the Sahel. When hunger and starvation overtook the people of the Sahel, there simply was not the necessary distribution system to get relief supplies to the people. Airplanes were used to drop bags of grain to people far removed from highways, roads, and trucks—but *no* armada of planes could bring enough food to the people. The cost was enormous, the loss factor high, and many people simply found themselves too far from where the planes brought the supplies and, thus, never saw the food.

But that was a crisis situation, and the Sahel effort was neither the first nor the last of its kind to fail. It always takes time to organize a massive relief program and to get it under way; the 1994 refugee crisis in and around Rwanda proved this again. Lives are lost while the operation gets started, and sometimes (as we noted earlier) regimes actually interfere with the supply lines. No such obstacles ought to exist, however, in countries where the situation is not critical, but where improved distribution systems could disseminate food more equitably.

In reality, regional malnutrition is only partly a function of the remoteness of the people afflicted by it. Northeastern Brazil, which periodically faces food shortages, *is* adequately connected to the better-provided parts of the country. But poverty reigns there, and unless food is brought in as part of a relief program, people could not afford to

FEED GRAINS AND FOOD GRAINS

Various grains—rice, wheat, corn, and others—produce about 53 percent of the world's food supply by direct consumption. Additional amounts of grains are fed to livestock and thus indirectly consumed. (Thus a distinction is drawn between the **food grains** and **feed grains**). In the United States and Canada, we consume as much as 1 ton of grains per person per year, but only 150 pounds of this comes to the table in the form of bread or cereal; the rest is consumed indirectly, in the form of meat and dairy products. In the food-poor countries, on the other hand, only about 400 pounds of grains, less than one-fifth the U.S. supply, is available for each person. Obviously, little of this meager amount can be spared for raising livestock. As a result, dairy products and meat are in short supply in the food-poor countries, and protein deficiencies compound poor nourishment.

Comparing the situation in another way, it takes five times as much soil, water, and fertilizer to sustain a person in the United States as it does to feed someone in India, Ghana, or Peru. The wealthier a nation becomes, the greater its demands on the food market. In the United States, people were eating an average of 55 pounds of beef in 1940. In 1995, Americans consumed about three times as many pounds. The consumption of poultry nearly tripled over the same period. Consider the increased investment in livestock in terms of feed grains to meet this demand—feed grains that could have been food grains available for export to hungry regions of the world!

buy what they really need in any case. So the poorer, hungrier parts of otherwise adequately fed countries are left to survive as best they can—until a crisis requires intervention. Once the crisis is over, normalcy returns in the form of insufficient calories and inadequate dietary balance.

A larger-scale map than Figure 13-1, therefore, would reveal pockets of food poverty even in the higher categories of consumption, evincing the need for continued improvement of the global system of provision and its national subsystems. These locales of persistent shortage and malnutrition impel the pessimists among scholars to warn that if the world of the plentiful present still suffers such failures, then a world with a foreboding future must prepare for worse—now.

A FUTURE GLOBAL FOOD EMERGENCY?

In this concluding segment of Chapter 13, we consider the circumstances that might lead to renewed food shortages on a regional scale, and we identify ways to address this potential world problem before it arises. When enhanced global warming became an international concern during the 1980s, concerted action was taken to reduce the contributions humanity was making to the heating of the "greenhouse." A comparable effort in the food-supply arena could soften the impact of a future emergency.

What might precipitate such a food crisis? We already have taken note of *population growth* as a major factor. In Africa today, the food problem is worsened by the high rate of population increase. While the global rate of population growth is slowing, and population is not growing as fast today in im-

portant countries (China, India) than was the case during the crises of the 1960s and 1970s, the world continues to add nearly 100 million people per year. Even if that rate declines, to an anticipated 70 to 90 million during the 2020s, the world will have to produce ever more food just to keep pace—a capacity it may not have.

We also noted *climate change* as a risk factor. If the prediction of some physical geographers comes true, the environmental problem of the first quarter of the twenty-first century may not be drought (always the enemy of farm productivity) but, rather, wide fluctuations in weather conditions that may bring storms, floods, freezes, heat waves, and other extremes capable of destroying crops and farmlands. These extremes may be related somehow to the warming trend that originally led climatologists to believe that human intervention was raising global temperatures. There are signs that nature itself is getting ready for one of its cyclic changes. If that is indeed the case, sustaining food production may become more difficult—let alone increasing it as required.

Pessimists among scholars studying this topic also point to *crop yields* as a concern. The Green Revolution, they say, has run its course, having narrowed the gap between demand and supply, but will no longer be able to continue its success. Paddies and wheat fields cannot be expected to produce ever more harvest tonnage, and as production levels off, the food gap will widen again. The failure of the Green Revolution in Africa is seen as a harbinger for the world of the future.

Concern also is rising over the possibility that the *cost of energy* will rise again, as it did (and contributed) during the last major food crisis. When energy costs rise, so does the cost of fertilizers, without which the Green Revolution loses

its clout. Farmers also need to be able to afford fuel to run irrigation pumps and other equipment. The impact of the last energy crisis has faded from memory; it is remembered in the U.S. mainly as a shortage at the gasoline pump. But for farmers living on the fiscal margin, a renewed rise in energy prices would be disastrous, as would be the impact on world food production.

Still another worry for the future lies in the apparent failure of *alternative sources* as dependable providers of calories *and* dietary balance. As the demand for food has grown and technologies of exploitation have become more efficient, one of the planet's last bounties—the oceans' fish fauna, source of valuable proteins—is being decimated. From midcentury to the late 1980s, the fish harvest from oceans and seas increased fivefold, and there seemed to be no limit to it. Fishing nations quarreled over fishing rights, poor nations leased fishing grounds to richer ones, and fleets of trawlers plied the oceans far and wide. International attempts to regulate these industries failed as governments flouted the rules. Meanwhile, there were early signals that overfishing was destroying fish stocks. Several regional fishing industries collapsed, for example, the cod fisheries on Canada's Grand Banks off Newfoundland. In 1975, biologists estimated the Atlantic bluefin tuna population at 250,000; today, there may be about 20,000 left, and the species is under consideration for placement on the endangered species list. From ocean perch and king crabs off Alaska to rock lobsters and roughies off New Zealand, depletion and overexploitation prevail. And the annual total catch is declining. We already may be beyond the point of recovery.

It is amazing but true that, in a time of food scarcity and dietary imbalance, **food taboos** still

From the Field Notes

❝ We watched the small fleet of fishing boats return from the North Sea to the port of Oslo, and talked to the crews. Every one of them complained that catches "these days" were small, a fraction of those of a decade ago. Prices are higher now, but this would not compensate for the loss of volume, said this fisherman. I had heard the same refrain in Scotland, Portugal, Canada, Sri Lanka, and elsewhere. Time after time on the high seas, I saw huge fleets of high-tech fishing boats complete with "factory ships" where catches are processed and prepared for canning. Marine food webs are disrupted by overfishing, and a critical food resource is endangered. ❞

deprive whole societies of opportunities to improve (if not balance) their diets. All the world's major religions have prohibited the eating of certain foods, either on particular days or permanently. Fast days of Christian faiths prohibit the consumption of fish, meat, or animal products (the Greek Orthodox religion has the most stringent rules). Judaism classifies a substantial number of animals, including the pig, camel, and certain species of fish, as unclean. Islam also prohibits the eating of pork. Hindu society, depending on caste, proscribes the eating of meat and even eggs, although meat other than beef is consumed by those of lower rank. Buddhism discourages the taking of animal life for purposes of routine nutrition. Various societies do not eat fish, eggs, or other potentially

nourishing foods, hunger and malnutrition notwithstanding. Social attitudes about food are deeply entrenched.

Yet another concern lies in the persistence of *colonial systems* in countries that attained political independence from imperial powers, but cannot change their economic geographies accordingly. Trapped in a world economic order they cannot change, and needing foreign exchange, decolonized countries have maintained the cash-crop estates and plantations of the colonial period. There, often on the country's best soils, the crops to be sold on foreign markets are produced. Senegal's peanuts, Angola's coffee, Zimbabwe's tobacco, Kenya's tea, and Sudan's cotton still flow from Africa, even while food production in the realm is grossly inadequate.

In any future global food crisis, the failure to restructure production in areas such as this will have serious consequences.

Concern is rising over the *loss of farmland* to urban growth—not only in the prosperous countries but also in the poorer areas of the world, where urbanization is speeding up. Although, in the totality of cultivable and grazable land, this loss seems statistically small, much of the lost acreage consists of the best, most fertile soils. Many cities were originally founded because they lay amid productive farmlands that could supply their needs. Now they sprawl across those farmlands. The American Farmland Trust, for example, reported in 1993 that twelve U.S. areas are severely affected, including California's Central Valley, South Florida, California's coastal zone, North Carolina's Piedmont, and the Chicago-Milwaukee-Madison triangle in Illinois-Wisconsin. These 12 areas represent only 5 percent of U.S. farmland, but they produce 17 percent of total agricultural sales, 67 percent of all fruit production, 55 percent of vegetables, and one-quarter of dairy products. Figures for other countries in the richer world (Japan) as well as the poorer (Egypt) prove that this is a global problem with serious implications for the future.

Author Video Link
↓
❻
American Farmlands

Finally, but possibly most ominously of all, are developments on the East Asian *Pacific Rim*. The combination of continued population growth (China alone adds 14 million people annually) and rising incomes is producing a change in the foods East Asians eat. The demand for pork, chicken, and beef is growing as diets change, and more and more grain is being used to feed livestock, not people. Add the loss of farmland referred to above (Japan has lost more than half of its farmland since 1950, Taiwan more than a third), and China could precipitate a world food crisis. Its demand will grow more rapidly than the world's exporters can supply, and its capacity to pay will limit availability for other needy regions and countries ranging from tropical Africa to South Asia. Thus the fruits of the Green Revolution may last only decades, not the generations it seemed to promise just twenty years ago.

Is the world facing a food emergency comparable to that of the 1950s and 1960s? The uncertainties are many, and the portents are troubling. The fundamental causes this time may *not* be alleviated by another (or a revived) Green Revolution. The structure of consumption is changing, and that will be a bigger problem to solve.

A MORE SECURE FUTURE

What can be done to prevent another food crisis from developing, or at least to reduce its severity? The ten arenas for action enumerated here can of course be supplemented by others, but in combination they would go a long way toward achieving a crucial global goal. It is clear that only effective international action can produce results in several of these arenas, such as the regulation of **ocean fishing**, and such international cooperation is difficult to achieve in our fractious world. International agreement is especially difficult to attain in some of the most critical fields listed. Here are ten key arenas for action.

1. **Formulate Population Policies.**
   As has been noted earlier, perhaps the most direct way to mitigate food crises is to reduce the rate of growth of the number of mouths to be fed. Family planning requires education and effective dissemination of supplies, a considerable challenge for poorer countries. It also requires various kinds of consensus that are difficult to achieve, as shown by the 1994 Cairo Conference on Population.

2. **Sustain the Green Revolution.**
   And expand it! "Miracle rice" allowed the Philippines to end five decades of dependence on food imports, and Mexico tripled its production of wheat in a few years. But higher-yielding grains need to be supplemented by strains that are drought-resistant and can withstand the weather extremes predicted by some environmentalists. Lesser grains such as millet and sorghum also must be improved through genetic engineering.

3. **Expand Farmlands.**
   Some experts believe that the world's cultivated area could be substantially expanded, perhaps more than doubled, if massive investments in irrigation and "soil reconstruction" were made. Divert billions of dollars from military to agricultural investment, they argue, and infertile soils could be reconstituted with organic and inorganic fertilizers and farmed with crops especially developed to grow there. The Amazon and Congo (Zaïre) Basins are identified as regions with agricultural potential, despite what is known about the infertility of soils under rainforest conditions.

4. **Stimulate Local Production.**
   A surprisingly large percentage of food is produced in small gardens and on small plots cultivated with great care by people who use household waste and compost to improve their patch of soil and who know just what to plant on it. In the former Soviet Union, people who worked on collective farms were allowed to cultivate a small plot for themselves (and to sell what they raised there). Production from those small gardens far outweighed what was grown on the collective farms. Agricultural development projects too often aim at the large scheme rather than the small-plot farmer, whose productivity could be crucial in a future food emergency.

5. **Encourage Land Reform.**
   The lesson above is that farmers who own their land tend to cultivate it more carefully and productively than those who work on someone else's soil. Yet much of the world's farm land remains in the hands of a comparatively small number of landowners (or under the control of inefficient communal groups). Land reform introduced by the United States in Japan expropriated absentee landlords and put small farms in the hands of the former tenants; the result was a tripling of output. Other countries have made progress in land reform, including Mexico and Egypt, where production also rose as a result. The process is slow and contentious, but it must be pursued worldwide.

6. **Improve Food Distribution Systems.**
   Should a food crisis develop during the first decades of the next century, geographers know where it will have strongest impact. During the 1960s and 1970s, inefficiencies in the then-existing distribution systems led to enormous waste and loss of food in transit.

Challenges arising from the continuing refugee problem presage the difficulties ahead, should a more massive emergency arise. Road, rail, and bridge building should be geared to anticipate regional needs based on precedents and population patterns.

7. **Develop Alternative Food Sources.**

There still are opportunities to develop new food sources, and a prominent one is **aquaculture**. While the oceans' fish fauna may not survive the current wave of overfishing, the raising of fish in ponds (even paddies!) and in controlled saltwater hatcheries is a growing industry. Compared to what the oceans have been producing (even in these years of declining production), aquaculture is but a small industry. But its possibilities are substantial and should be developed as rapidly as possible. Food scientists also are trying to achieve a "Food Revolution" in the laboratory, seeking to make food from grass, leaves, algae, even from oil.

8. **Strengthen Controls over Ocean Fishing.**

It may well be too late, but the international community should nevertheless organize to combat violations of regulations concerning ocean fishing. Japan and Norway are among countries that have violated international agreements; little is done to force them to do otherwise. This is a matter of life and death, and if countries such as Haiti and North Korea can be threatened with sanctions over various offenses against the international community, then already-rich countries depleting the oceans should face no less.

9. **Reduce Meat Consumption.**

The point was made earlier (see box, "Feed Grains and Food Grains"), but it is an important arena of action: meat consumption by people in the wealthier countries puts an enormous strain on economies and ecologies elsewhere. Quite apart from the fact that reducing one's red-meat consumption is good for health and well-being, such reduction has good effect in a wider sphere by lessening the use of grains to feed livestock and by limiting the conversion of forest to pasture in poorer countries where beef cattle are raised cheaply to serve wealthier markets.

10. **Promote Social Change.**

In many parts of the world, notably in Subsaharan Africa and South and East Asia, food emergencies afflict women more severely than men. In traditional societies, the male predominates to such a degree that he demands and takes a disproportionate share of the family's food supply. Thus the women are the most severely malnourished among the adults, and among the children, too, the male tends to be favored in the allocation of or competition for food. In traditional societies of Africa, it is not uncommon for women not only to be more severely malnourished than men, but to be responsible for hoeing the croplands, making the family's clothing, walking endless miles for water and firewood, cooking the meals, and numerous other tasks, in addition to bearing the children. Men do not perform nearly the share of work they could; not infrequently, they abandon the family and go to the city. It is obviously impractical to expect rapid change in traditions that are nearly as old as those societies themselves. However, it *is* possible to direct remedial programs to the women and children primarily, and to begin an attack on the maldistribution of responsibilities.

In the 1990s, we stand at the threshold of a new era in the world food situation, requiring action on a broad range of fronts and demanding global cooperation in several prominent areas of concern. The crisis of the early 1970s generated the first steps toward international action, but, when the emergency receded, the lessons learned seemed soon to be forgotten. Yet we may predict that the events of the 1970s were harbingers of the future. In time, a rising tide of world hunger may threaten world order. Even the most selfish interests in the well-fed countries have a stake in the war on malnutrition.

KEY TERMS

Aquaculture
Calorie Intake
Diets
Feed Grains
Food and Agriculture Organization (FAO)
Food Chain
Food Grains
Food Taboos
Food Web
Green Revolution
Malnutrition
Miracle Rice
Ocean Fishing
World Health Organization (WHO)

14

THE DISTRIBUTION OF HEALTH

Good health, like good and ade quate food, is unevenly distributed across the world. Sufficient calories and balanced diets help the body develop fully and well. People who are inadequately fed are susceptible to many debilitating diseases. Women who are healthy tend to bear healthy babies. Women who suffer from malnutrition and its related maladies are not so fortunate. It is estimated that 16 percent of babies born into the world of the 1990s—nearly one in six—are born underweight, and thus at a disadvantage in their struggle for survival. The vast majority of these births occur in the world's poorer countries, and millions of babies there do not survive their first year of life.

The world presents stark regional differences in terms of the distribution of food, but patterns of health show even greater contrasts. In North America, where food is generally adequate and inspected for quality, where drinking water is purified and treated, and where the diseases of hunger and malnutrition rarely occur, the general condition of the population is reflected more by obesity than anything else; America has been described as a

Geographica

- **Protein deficiencies still afflict populations, notably children, despite the general adequacy of available calories; dietary deficiencies continue to inhibit the development of the young in tropical areas.**

- **Infant mortality and child mortality reflect the general health of societies, and together form a gauge for the human condition.**

- **Average life expectancy maps conceal the far greater life expectancies of women virtually everywhere in the world, but they do underscore the aging of many of the world's populations.**

- **Location is a significant factor in a population's susceptibility to diseases of various kinds, protecting some and exposing others to carriers of various maladies.**

nation of overeaters. But an air trip of just a few hours can transport us to places where people, especially youngsters, visibly show the evidence of their malnutrition and dietary shortcomings. The disadvantages with which many children in the underdeveloped countries start their lives will be with them for life—if they survive their childhood.

Those crowded, unsanitary shantytowns that have arisen on the outskirts of cities from Mexico City to Madras, and from Lima to Lagos,

are reservoirs of risk where people are exposed to diseases long ago eradicated in the wealthier world. In 1990, an outbreak of cholera in Peru led to an epidemic reminiscent of another century, when such diseases killed millions in Europe. That a disease whose cause is known, whose transmission is understood, and whose cure is possible should kill more than 10,000 people and infect a million more is a sad reflection on the overall state of health in the poorer areas of the world. And the fact that by mid-1991, cholera cases, arising from the South American epidemic, had already been recorded in the United States reminds us how interconnected our world is. The health contrasts we will study in this chapter form a prediction of risk for the future.

MEDICAL GEOGRAPHY

The study of health in a geographic context is the field of **medical geography**. Many diseases afflicting human populations have their origin in the environment. They have source (core) areas, spread (diffuse) through populations along identifiable routes, and affect clusters of populations (regions) when at their widest distribution. Mapping disease patterns can produce insights into relationships between diseases and environmental, as well as cultural, phenomena. Associations between natural environments and **contagious diseases** (diseases capable of being transmitted) are of special interest to medical geographers, since geography deals with natural (physical) as well as human problems. Medical geographers also concern themselves with the location of health-care facilities for people who need them. If an underdeveloped country receives funding to establish 25 clinics, where should those clinics be located so as to be within the shortest possible aggregate distance from the maximum number of potential patients?

DISEASE AND NUTRITION

When examining disease, it is appropriate to return to the topic of the previous chapters, nutrition, because world regions where mal-

nutrition prevails are also areas of poverty, inadequate medical services, inadequate sanitation, and substandard housing. It is difficult, therefore, to identify the specific effects of malnutrition on people's susceptibility to disease, because so many other factors are present at once. However, there is little doubt about the effects of malnutrition on the growth and development of the body. The impact on children, especially, is devastating.

KWASHIORKOR AND MARASMUS

In the protein-poor tropical and subtropical countries, **kwashiorkor** ravages the children. With this ailment, the child's belly grows disproportionately large in a grotesque irony, while the skin loses its tone and discolors. The hair develops a reddish tinge and begins to fall out. Later, liquids collect in swelling limbs, the digestive system fails, and total apathy overcomes the child. Death may not be far away.

Many children die young, and in these countries the **child mortality rate** (the number of children who die between ages 1 and 5) is related directly to the incidence of kwashiorkor, the greatest killer of small children there. Importantly, a child can develop kwashiorkor even when enough total calories are available. Kwashiorkor is a result of *mal*nutrition, not necessarily *under*nutrition. Often it develops when a mother stops breast feeding her child (perhaps because of the birth of a new baby), and the child is put on a starchy diet.

An example from Africa indicates what may happen. In a region in Zaïre, the staple diet is the tropical banana. This fruit is filling enough, but it contains only about 1 percent protein by weight, so a child would have to eat about 20 pounds (10 kilograms) of bananas each day to satisfy its protein requirements! When the adults eat the banana,

they dip it into a sauce made of meat, vegetables, and spices, and this sauce contains enough protein to make up for the banana's deficiency. The small child, however, is unable to do as well as the adults, and cannot dip the banana and then turn it while putting it in its mouth, to avoid spillage. All too often the banana winds up in the child's mouth without any sauce at all. In this way the child eats enough not to feel hungry, but is still seriously malnourished, and the symptoms of kwashiorkor appear.

Where both deficiencies—lack of protein *and* insufficient calories—prevail, a child is likely to develop **marasmus**. With this disease, the body is thin and bony, the skin shrivels, and the eyes appear huge in the tiny, drawn face. Staple foods do exist with lower protein contents than even the banana, notably the cassava, a root crop grown in the tropics. The sweet potato, another staple in tropical areas, also has a very low protein content. Marasmus and kwashiorkor occur in these areas, and as many as half the children never reach their fifth birthday as a result.

Kwashiorkor and marasmus are among a host of other threats facing the malnourished. Calorie inadequacy and protein deficiency usually go hand in hand with vitamin insufficiency, and vitamin shortages are directly related to diseases of various kinds. Low vitamin-A intake is related to diseases affecting the eyes, and these also take a heavy toll on children. Beri-beri, which affects the nervous and digestive systems, as well as the heart, is related to vitamin-B deficiency, and it prevails in South and East Asia. Insufficiency in vitamin C contributes to the development of scurvy, and vitamin D is needed to ward off rickets.

This depressing (and far from complete) list of diseases directly related to hunger and malnutrition does not include the many other infectious and chronic diseases that prey on the ill-protected, malnourished body. Cholera, yellow fever, hookworm, malaria, and numerous other maladies ravage people already weakened by their imbalanced diets, and they take a heavy toll, if not of life, then of energy and longevity. Later in this chapter we will investigate some of these diseases and their diffusion. In the meantime, let us take note of the well-fed tourists and travelers from the comfortable world of plenty, who see people sleeping on sidewalks, resting on their jobs, or working at a snail's pace, in Guatemala, in Chad, in India, and in the Philippines, and who conclude that those people are not better off because they are lazy. And let us be better informed.

INFANT MORTALITY

A key gauge of the human condition is the **infant mortality rate (IMR)**. Infant mortality is recorded as a baby's death during the first year following its birth (unlike *child mortality*, which records death between ages 1 and 5). As in the case of other population statistics, infant mortality normally is given statistically as number of cases per thousand, that is, per thousand live births.

Infant mortality and child mortality reflect the overall health of a society. High infant mortality has a combination of causes among which the physical health of the mother is key: in societies where women bear a large number of babies, those women also tend to be inadequately nourished, exhausted from overwork, suffering from disease, and poorly educated. Many infants die because they are improperly weaned; demographers report that more children die because their parents do not know how to cope with the routine child-

hood problem of diarrhea than because of epidemics. This, plus malnutrition, is the leading killer of children in the world. Poor sanitation is still another threat to infants and children. More than one-fifth of the world's population, it is estimated, have no ready access to clean drinking water or to hygienic human waste-disposal facilities.

The map showing the world distribution of infant mortality (Fig. 14-1) reveals its high incidence in many of the world's poorer countries. The map shows infant mortality patterns at five levels ranging from 125 or more (one death for every eight live births) to fewer than 15. Compare this map to that of overall crude death rate (CDR) on pages 80 and 81, and the role of infant mortality in societies with high death rates is immediately evident.

In 1995, Afghanistan still had the world's highest infant mortality rate, an unenviable position it had held for more than a decade. Afghanistan's misfortune arose from its involvement in the war against the Soviets during the 1980s; its infant and child mortality rates always were among the world's highest, but the dislocation caused by the war worsened an already serious situation. After the withdrawal of the Soviets, Afghanistan continued to suffer from internal conflict, and the picture never improved. The lesson is that dislocation and refugee movements contribute significantly to the pattern shown by the map. We can readily identify other countries with high infant mortality rates that are, or recently have been, embroiled in conflict and forced migration, for example, Angola, Liberia, Somalia, Ethiopia, and Rwanda.

The lowest infant mortality rate among larger populations has long been reported by Japan, with under 5 deaths per 1000 live births. (Liechtenstein and Iceland, with comparatively minuscule popula-

tions, in some years report even lower rates). Japan's achievement is related not only to its stability, strong social fabric, and prosperity, but also to its cultural homogeneity. As is so often the case, a map based on national statistics conceals internal regional, ethnic, or other variation; but not in the case of Japan. In the United States, on the other hand, infant mortality rates among some sectors of the heterogeneous population are higher than among others, and its IMR of 8.0 represents an average. To take a more extreme case, the IMR of South Africa is an average of those of several nations within that country's borders. The IMR for South African whites is near the European average; for black Africans it is nearer the African average; and for the Coloured and Asian population sectors it lies between these two figures. The reported average of 46 per thousand, therefore, does not tell the "national" story as Japan's does.

In the mid-1990s, as many as 26 countries of the world still reported an IMR of 100 or more, and of these, 10 had rates of 125 or higher—one death or more among every eight newborns. But these numbers nevertheless represent a considerable improvement over the situation 20 or even ten years ago. Globally, infant mortality has been declining, even in the worst-afflicted regions. Still, the situation in many African and Asian countries remains grim.

Particularly jarring is the sharp contrast between tropical African and some Asian countries and the higher-latitude countries in both hemispheres. Although Japan regularly reports the lowest IMR among larger countries, Europe as a realm has very low rates as well, ranging from 5.1 in the Scandinavian countries to 11.0 in Mediterranean states; the rate rises somewhat toward the east. In Eastern Europe, Romania long has had the worst record,

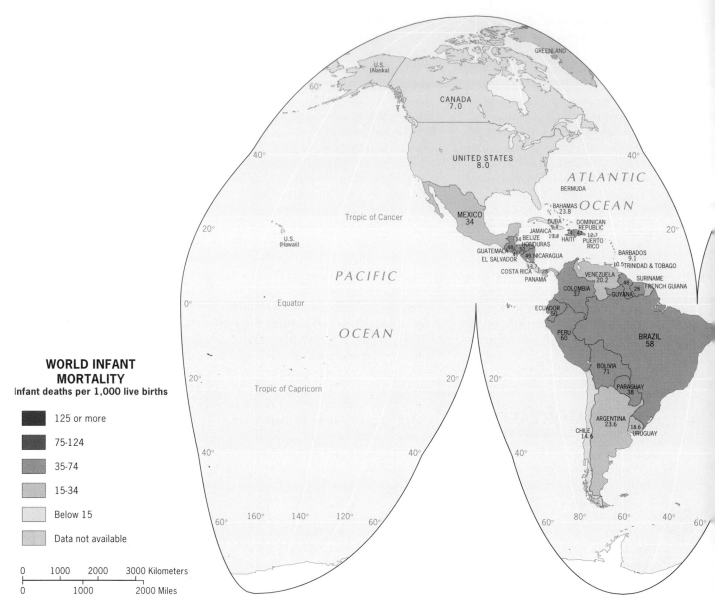

WORLD INFANT MORTALITY
Infant deaths per 1,000 live births

- 125 or more
- 75-124
- 35-74
- 15-34
- Below 15
- Data not available

| 0 | 1000 | 2000 | 3000 Kilometers |
| 0 | 1000 | 2000 Miles |

FIGURE 14–1   Based on data from Population Reference Bureau, *World Population Data Sheet 1995*. Washington, D.C., 1995.

resulting in part from harsh population policies imposed by the former communist regime. The contrast between Greece (8.3) and its neighbor Turkey (53.0) is noteworthy. Geographically, Turkey is part of the Southwest Asian–North African realm, not Europe; and unlike Greece, Turkey's IMR is a composite of a heterogeneous society that includes a Kurdish minority numbering over 12 million. Turkey, however, is seeking membership in Europe's still-developing union, and social conditions will have to improve if this is to happen. Turkey's IMR reflects circumstances that are not commensurate with European norms.

In the Americas, the map reveals some unexpected patterns. It is not surprising, given the material well-being of the United States and Canada with their superior medical facilities, that these two countries should have the hemisphere's lowest infant mortality rates (8.0 and 7.0, respectively, in the mid-1990s). It should also be expected that Haiti, poorest among the countries of the Americas and beset by conflict and disruption, would have the highest rate, comparable to those prevailing in parts of tropical Africa. But given the demographic transition in progress in Middle and South America (see Chapter 7), some IMRs in the hemisphere remain remarkably high. In South

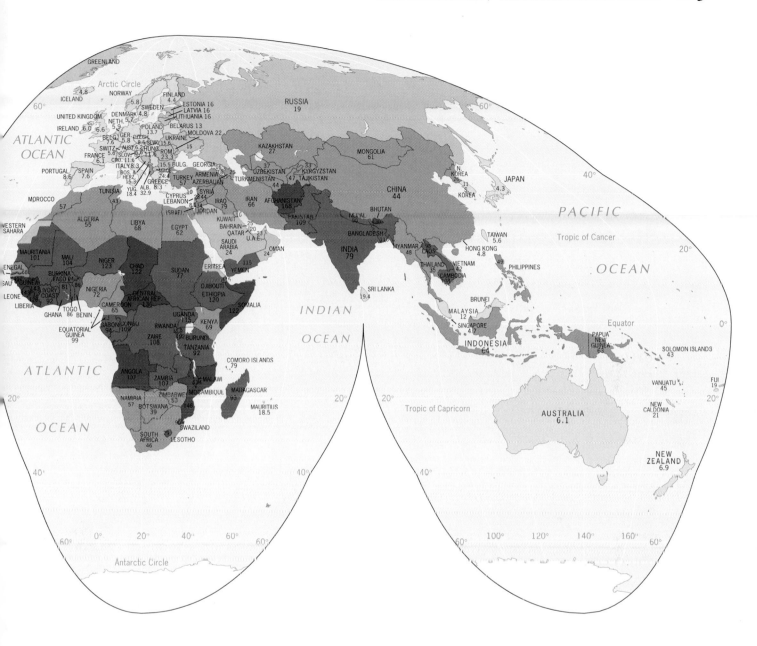

America, Peru still records 60 infant deaths per 1000 live births, and between 1991 and 1993 its IMR actually rose from 76 to 81 before declining somewhat. Bolivia still records 71, Brazil 58, Ecuador 50, and Paraguay 38. These are very high IMRs when compared to the overall CDRs for the same South American countries. In Middle America, too, infant mortality reveals how much progress still needs to be made. The contrast between the United States and Mexico (34) is of the order of that between Greece and Turkey, and other countries with comparatively high IMRs include Nicaragua (49), Guatemala (48), and Honduras (50). And in the Caribbean, the two countries on the island of Hispaniola—Haiti and the Dominican Republic—have the highest IMRs, explained by Haiti's poverty and dislocation and the Dominican Republic's economic circumstances (it is one of the region's poorest countries as well). But other Caribbean countries do better, for example, Cuba despite its isolation (9.4), Jamaica (13.2), and Puerto Rico (12.7).

The situation in Asia is a mixture of progress and stagnation. The concerted population-policy program begun by China during the 1970s continues to bring the IMR down. In 1990 it still was 33, far lower even than that of most South American countries; today it is 44. In India, the IMR has declined even more during the same period, but it was and remains high (74). As Fig-

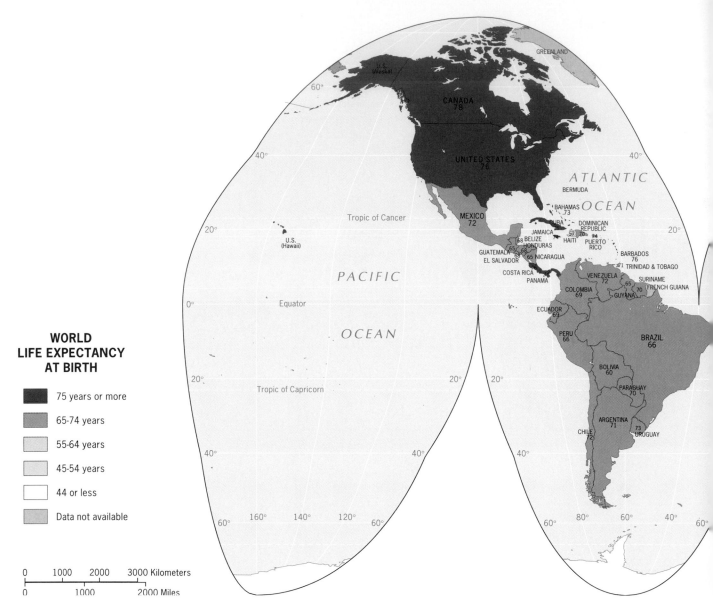

**WORLD
LIFE EXPECTANCY
AT BIRTH**

- 75 years or more
- 65-74 years
- 55-64 years
- 45-54 years
- 44 or less
- Data not available

0   1000   2000   3000 Kilometers

0   1000   2000 Miles

FIGURE 14–2 Based on data from Population Reference Bureau, *World Population Data Sheet 1995*. Washington, D.C., 1995.

ure 14-1 shows, a tier of countries extending from Yemen to Cambodia, and including such large populations as Pakistan and Bangladesh, continue to display IMRs as high as many African countries. Note, once again, the contrast between near-neighbors Indonesia (64) and Australia (6.1).

Numerous conditions play a role in creating the distribution revealed by Figure 14-1, and nutrition is one of them. Exposure to infectious and parasitic diseases, social conditions, and access to medical help also influence the pattern, and we will examine these and related issues in a later chapter. Figure 14-1 reflects, in some ways more realistically than any of our other maps, the sharp contrasts and variations in the well-being of societies in this world. In a sense, it is an index of sanitary conditions, medical services, the state of health of the mothers—in short, of the general welfare.

LIFE EXPECTANCY

In August 1994, newspapers around the world carried a brief report with important implications. The report stated that the **life expectancy** of Russian men had dropped below 60 and might be as low as 58, certainly no higher than 59 years. There was no evidence, the report stated, of a significant decline in the life expectancy of women, which held steady at 74. Just five years earlier, Russian

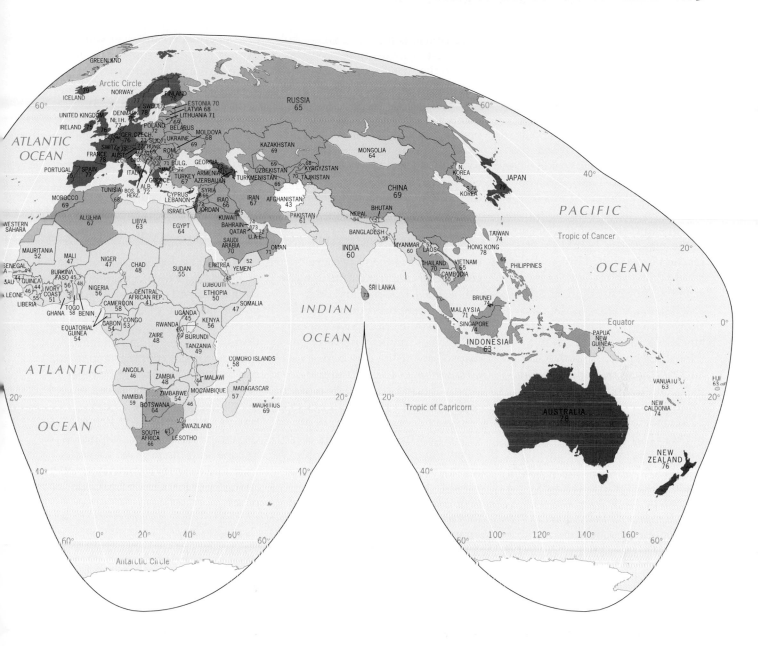

men could expect to live to the age of 62. A rapid drop of several years over a short period revealed serious trouble in Russian society.

Russian census taking never has been very reliable, and the report may have exaggerated the lowering of male life expectancy in the vast country. But it served as a reminder that life expectancy, which is rising almost everywhere in the world, can take a downturn even when a nation is not at war or in the grip of an environmental crisis, and that

women tend to be more resilient—and longer-lived—than men when the going gets rough. Virtually everywhere in the world, women's life expectancy is significantly greater than men's.

Life expectancy is another revealing measure of the well-being of a population. And again, the range in this index is enormous. A girl born in the United States in the mid-1990s can expect to live to the age of 79; in Canada, female life expectancy is even greater (81). But

a boy born in Uganda has a life expectancy of just 44 years, and a girl 46 years. Such low figures are reminiscent of the Europe of two centuries ago, when life expectancies there were in the 40s.

Figure 14-2 maps the *average* life expectancies in the world's countries as of the mid-1990s, but remember that female life expectancies are substantially longer than men's almost everywhere. Taking the geographic realm as a whole, women outlive men by about 9 years in Europe, 4 years in East Asia, 3 years in Subsaharan Africa, 6 years in South America, and 7 years in North America. In Russia the difference may be as much as 13 years, possibly even more. So the map should be seen in this context.

Given this variation by sex, the map also reveals huge regional contrasts. In the mid-1990s, the world average life expectancy was 68 for women and 64 for men. Most tropical African countries fell well short of these averages, but they were reached or exceeded by the majority of Middle and South American states. Southwest, South, and Southeast Asian countries, as the map shows, range from high life expectancies (Jordan, Sri Lanka) to low (Nepal, Cambodia). South Asia's giant, India, reported a female life expectancy of 60 years and 60 years for males.

Remarkable progress has been made in East Asia. Not only is Japan's average life expectancy among the highest in the world, but South Korea and Taiwan rank among the longest-lived as well. Most important of all, China in 1994 reached the 70-year plateau with a female life expectancy of 72 and 69 for males.

These life expectancy figures do not mean, of course, that everyone in those countries lives to that age. The figure is an average that takes account of the children who die young and the people who survive well beyond that average. Thus, the dramatically lower figures for the underdeveloped countries primarily reflect the high rate of infant mortality. A person who has survived beyond the childhood years is likely to survive well beyond the recorded expectancy. Those low figures for the food-short countries remind us again how hard hit are the children in the underdeveloped world.

Life expectancies, the many low figures on the map notwithstanding, have increased significantly over the past half century. Death control has certainly made more progress around the world than birth control, and life expectancies are slowly rising—even in the developed countries where they are already high. It has been predicted that life expectancies in the developed world may reach 85 years by the early twenty-first century, but that they will then level off because of natural aging of vital organs in the body. In the meantime, we should expect a continued increase in life expectancies in the underdeveloped countries as improvements in medical facilities, hygiene, and drug availability suppress death rates. Even now, the effects of these circumstances can be observed from maps showing life expectancies at advanced ages (e.g., 20 and 40 years). If maps can be drawn of life expectancy at birth, then it is also possible to construct maps of life expectancy (remaining years of life) at any other age. Such maps show much less contrast between the developed and underdeveloped countries. As we will note later, although infant mortality has been dramatically reduced in developed societies, much less progress has been made in the suppression of the diseases of middle and advanced age. The great contrast between advantaged and disadvantaged countries lies at the base of the population pyramid.

It is natural that increases in life expectancy should be seen as evidence of progress; they represent the defeat of scourges that afflict humanity in all parts of the world. But the implications of longer life expectancies must also be contemplated: there will be an ever-larger number of old people in the population, and these people will require ever more support. According to World Bank data, 500 million people worldwide were aged 60 or above, accounting for about 9 percent of the population. By 2030, demographers calculate, the number of people 60 and over will exceed 1.5 billion, and they will make up some 16 percent of the world's population. This figure— 16 percent—already has been exceeded in Western Europe, where more than 18 percent of the population in 1995 was 60-plus. By 2030, as much as *one-third* of Western Europeans are likely to be in this age bracket, and, if life-expectancy and growth figures can be trusted, one-quarter of Chinese!

Earlier we took note of the problems faced by societies where large percentages of the population are young. Figure 14-2 reminds us that quite a different set of challenges faces countries with **aging populations**, challenges already felt in some European countries and in Japan. In order to support the older people, younger workers will have to be more productive, and be taxed more heavily, than before. Governments will be hard-pressed to cope with the demand for services and the political dynamite of tax-raising for social security purposes.

AGE, LOCATION, AND DISEASE

In Chapter 7 we examined population pyramids of youthful as well as aging populations. The age structure of a population has important implications for people's health. Certain diseases affect specific age groups more severely than others. When a child gets the measles, it is usually a much less severe case than when an adult has this disease. On the other hand, an adult can normally cope better with diarrhea than a child, and many of the children in the world's malnourished countries die of diarrheic diseases.

Obviously, when the age structure of a population is such that a large proportion is young, as in many of the underdeveloped countries, that population has many more susceptible individuals than an older population. The threat of epidemics grows as the population numbers rise. For example, children who spent their early years in the countryside may not have been exposed to the tubercle bacillus, as city-dwelling children mostly are. In childhood, the effects are usually mild, but the impact is much more severe when the individual is older. Thus many of the teenage and young adult immigrants have no resistance. The cities are real markets for disease.

Age and location, therefore, are significant factors in a population's susceptibility to diseases of various kinds. Children in Sierra Leone, Senegal, and other West African countries face infectious and parasitic diseases that present a low risk to children in Sweden, Norway, and other European countries. On the other hand, adults and older people in industrialized countries suffer more from chronic diseases, such as heart disease and cancer, than do their counterparts in the underdeveloped countries. Maps of disease distributions, when compared to maps of population distribution, underscore the regional concentration of particular diseases and the exposure of certain population clusters to them. For example, a disease known as onchocerciasis, or "river blindness," prevails especially in the African savanna zone that extends, south of the Sahara, from Senegal in the west to Kenya in the east. It exists with lesser intensity elsewhere, notably in areas of Middle and northern South America. Another disease, a debilitating malady called schistosomiasis (or bilharzia), affects the liver, intestines, and bladder. It poses a high risk to inhabitants of Africa between the Sahara and the Kalahari, and in the Nile Valley as well, and it also prevails in north and northeast South America and East Asia.

At different scales or levels of generalization, location also plays its critical role. In areas where onchocerciasis occurs, people who are born in river valleys (the breeding sites of the flies that transmit the disease), or who migrate into these areas, run a much greater risk than those living in upland areas away from streams. In Puerto Rico, schistosomiasis is three times as prevalent in the moist eastern part of the island (where the snail that transmits it thrives) as in the west. In Chicago, cancer deaths occur with much greater frequency in the densely populated downtown and near north side areas than they do in the northern and western suburbs. Whether global, regional, or local, maps reveal patterns that can be crucial in the analysis and defeat of disease.

In this chapter we have examined two key indices of well-being: infant mortality and life expectancy. We turn next to the relationships between geography and disease.

KEY TERMS

Aging Population
Child Mortality Rate
Contagious Diseases
Infant Mortality Rate (IMR)
Kwashiorkor
Life Expectancy
Marasmus
Medical Geography

15

SPATIAL PATTERNS OF DISEASE

Many of the maps we have examined in Parts 3 and 4 reflect an underlying reality: destructive diseases afflict certain regions of the world more severely than others. Regional disparities in death rates, infant mortality, life expectancy, and other health indicators are in large measure attributable to spatial variations in the general well-being of the population.

The maps make it clear that tropical areas, with their warmth and humidity (and thus intense biological activity) are the cauldrons of sickness. Malaria, for example, is the most devastating parasitic disease in the world today, and it is concentrated in tropical Africa, where about 10 percent of the world's population suffers more than 90 percent of all infections, contributing directly to high incidences of infant and child mortality there. Other tropical diseases, such as yellow fever and sleeping sickness, burden these same populations. For reasons to be discussed below, many tropical ailments remain confined to their environmental limits. But others spread far and wide. AIDS, the feared plague of the late twentieth century, probably had tropical or-

Geographica

- **Tropical and especially equatorial areas, with their warmth and humidity, are zones of intense biological activity and hence the sources of many disease-transmitting viruses and parasites.**

- **Certain major diseases remain contained within tropical or near-tropical latitudes, but others, originating in the tropics, spread into all parts of the world; AIDS originated in tropical Africa and is now a global pandemic.**

- **Overpopulated urban shantytowns with inadequate sanitation and contaminated water supplies are highly susceptible to outbreaks of old as well as new diseases; the South American cholera epidemic of the 1990s began in the slums of Lima, Peru.**

- **Despite the worldwide attention focused on AIDS, the leading killers in the Western world are the chronic diseases including heart diseases, cancer, and strokes; maps on the incidence of these afflictions suggest certain environmental links.**

- **From the inoculation of children in remote rural areas of Africa to the location of hospitals and clinics in inner cities of America, the distribution of treatment facilities poses a major challenge to medical geographers and other planners in the health field.**

igins but has become a worldwide malady.

Medical geographers, therefore, are interested not only in the regional distribution of diseases, but also in the processes and paths whereby diseases spread or diffuse. The diffusion process also can be represented and analyzed by cartographic methods, and maps can enable geographers to make important predictions. For example, a map showing the location and extent of an outbreak of diarrheal diseases can serve as an early alert for the development of kwashiorkor, often a successor to such an epidemic. Maps showing the distribution of unvaccinated, and thus susceptible, populations in urban areas can assist in preparation for crisis situations.

DISEASE CLASSIFICATION

In this chapter, we investigate the geographic distribution of major diseases as well as their routes of diffusion. For our purposes, diseases may be classified into three categories:

1. **Infectious Diseases**
   About 65 percent of all human illnesses are of the infectious type, resulting from an invasion of parasites and their multiplication in the body. Malaria is a prominent example.

2. **Chronic or Degenerative Diseases**
   These are diseases of longevity, of old age. They do not kill instantly, but cause long-term deterioration of the body. Cancer and heart disease are common chronic diseases in our society.

3. **Genetic or Inherited Diseases**
   Certain diseases can be traced directly to one's parentage and to the chromosomes and genes that define one's makeup. Hemophilia, sickle-cell anemia, and lactose intolerance are among these inherited maladies.

Some diseases occur in confined regions; others spread worldwide. When a sudden outbreak in some locale leads to a high percentage of afflictions and a substantial number of deaths in a region, the phenomenon is called an **epidemic**. Peru's

recent cholera outbreak had epidemic proportions. When the outbreak spreads worldwide, as various forms of influenza have done since the beginning of the present century, a **pandemic** develops. Many diseases, however, have a limited range, because the organisms that transmit them are restricted by environmental conditions.

Certain diseases become established in a population without a spectacular epidemic or pandemic. Even today, many people in the United States have venereal disease of some kind, and some of these people may not be aware that they harbor such a disease. Such a situation, in which a disease is carried by many people (or **hosts**) in a condition of near equilibrium and without leading to a rapid and widespread death toll, means that this disease is **endemic** to that population. This is not to suggest that an endemic disease has no effect on the well-being of the people who have it. General health *does* deteriorate, and energy levels are lowered; susceptibility to other diseases may rise. On college campuses, a malady called mononucleosis often is described as endemic to the population (and again, some people have it without being aware of it).

HOW DISEASES SPREAD

Infectious diseases are spread by disease-causing organisms that range from microscopic, one-celled protozoa to parasitic worms and insects. The list of **agents**, as these organisms are called, is almost endless and includes viruses, bacteria, and other microorganisms that can invade the body or contaminate elements of the environment: worms, such as hookworms, and tapeworms; insects that burrow under the skin; and many more.

The viruses are a unique group of infectious agents, smaller than bacteria, composed of a core of nucleic acid and layers of protein, and, in some instances, fatty substances. These viruses can infect animal cells and cause diseases such as measles, influenza, polio, and probably certain forms of cancer.

When we are afflicted by an infectious disease, we are hosts to that disease organism. When a population contains a large number of hosts, a **reservoir** has been formed from which the disease may expand or diffuse to additional susceptible people. These then become additional hosts, strengthening the disease reservoir.

The spreading of a disease occurs in several ways. Some agents are transmitted from one person directly to another by contact. In this case, the disease is carried from one host to the next without any intermediate host. A handshake, a kiss, or some other form of touching can transmit the agents. Even standing close enough to a person so that tiny moisture particles from exhaled air reach you can have the same effect. Diseases that are transmitted this way are grouped together as *nonvectored* diseases, because they do not need an intermediate host or vector for their propagation. The common cold, measles, venereal diseases, and mononucleosis are among the nonvectored diseases.

When a disease is carried from one host to the next by an intermediate host, the disease is considered *vectored*. In such instances, an intermediate host plays a critical role in the transmission process, because the parasite (the agent) undergoes change in its body. For example, no one can contract malaria by touching another person who already has the disease. A mosquito is essential to the transmission process. Furthermore, it is not just a case of the mosquito biting the infected person and then the susceptible host. Rather, a para-

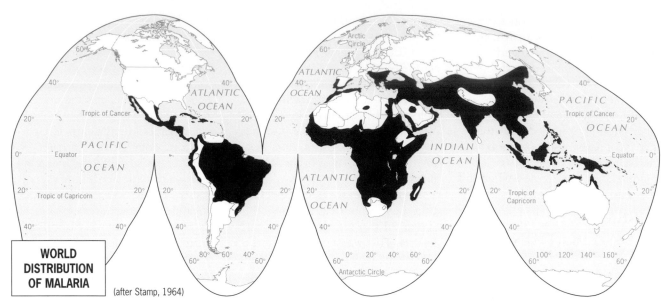

FIGURE 15–1 Thirty years ago, malaria's global distribution was similar to today's; the battle against it is a stalemate. From L. D. Stamp, *The Geography of Life and Death* (Ithaca: Cornell University Press, 1964), p. 132

site must go through a significant change as part of its life cycle while it inhabits the mosquito and before it is injected into the susceptible person. Insects (including various kinds of mosquitoes, flies, and ticks) are the most common vectors, but worms, snails, and larger animals, such as house pets, can also function as vectors.

Disease organisms are also transmitted by water, soil, food, and feces. These are nonbiological **vectors**, sometimes called mechanical vectors, or **vehicles**. In this case, the agent does not necessarily undergo a biological change between infected host and susceptible potential host, but the vehicle sustains it between hosts.

Infectious diseases can thus be grouped according to whether they are vectored or nonvectored. These categories are not absolutely exclusive, of course. Some diseases can be transmitted directly, by contact, or via some vector or vehicle. Humans themselves can function as vectors. Also, there is uncertainty about the way some diseases are transmitted, such as cancer, which is classified as a chronic disease but, in some forms, possibly a viral

disease. Still, the differentiation between nonvectored and vectored diseases is useful, because there are associated geographic contrasts as well. Cholera, a vehicle-vectored disease, spread worldwide during several successive nineteenth-century pandemics (for the story of its defeat, see box, "Cholera and the Map"). Malaria, on the other hand, is a vectored disease regionally restricted by the environmental limits of the mosquito that transmits it.

Hundreds of millions of people, especially in the world's equatorial and tropical regions, face a combination of undernourishment, malnutrition, and prevalent disease. When we examine data on population numbers, growth rates, and demographic structures, we do not adequately know the condition or degree of well-being of the people these data represent.

VECTORED INFECTIOUS DISEASES

As noted above, tropical (and especially equatorial) environments enhance biological activity. Here,

vectors and agents abound, and infectious diseases spread rapidly and comprehensively through host populations.

MALARIA

As Figure 15-1 shows, **malaria** has worldwide distribution and is absent only from higher latitudes and drier environments. Although Africa's tropics suffer most from this disease, malaria also prevails in India, Southeast Asia, China, and the tropical Americas.

Several different types of malaria exist, some more severe than others; not only human beings but also various species of monkeys, rats, birds, and even snakes can be affected by it. Malaria's virulence results from the effectiveness of its vectors, three African mosquitoes (*Anopheles gambiae*, *A. arabiensis*, and *A. funestus*), although the role of these mosquitoes in the diffusion of the disease was not determined until late in the eighteenth century. The sequence is now well known: the mosquito stings an infected host and sucks up some of the disease agents. In the mosquito's stomach, the parasites reproduce and multiply, eventually reaching its saliva. When the mosquito stings the next person, some of the parasites are injected into that person's blood stream. Now the person who has been stung develops malaria and becomes a host.

Malaria has killed or incapacitated countless millions of people. The efficiency of one of its vectors, *A. gambiae*, was revealed when this mosquito was accidentally introduced into Brazil in 1938. In a matter of months, Brazil faced the most serious malaria epidemic it had ever experienced, with more than 14,000 deaths in less than a year. A quick eradication campaign wiped out *A. gambiae* before it could spread far from its Brazilian base; had the mosquito diffused into the Amazon Basin, South America might today suffer as severely from malaria as Africa does.

Compared to the death toll in Africa and Asia, however, Brazil's epidemic was but a minor incident. During the 1950s, health authorities estimated that malaria was responsible for 1 million deaths *per year* in India alone, and in Africa the toll was substantially higher. Most of the victims are children five years of age or younger, and malaria is a major factor in the infant and child mortality rates discussed in Chapter 14. If they survive, they develop a certain degree of immunity, although someone infected by malaria is likely to be debilitated and lacking energy. Whole populations are so afflicted, and entire regions have been abandoned by peoples who simply could not withstand the ravages of the disease. The historic abandonment of extensive irrigation systems and apparently fertile lands, sometimes ascribed to climatic change, was in some instances probably due to the advance of malaria.

Malaria manifests itself as a recurrent fever and chills, with associated symptoms, such as the enlargement of the spleen, and,

practically always, anemia. The victim is not only deprived of energy, there is also an increased risk of other diseases taking hold in the weakened body. Antimalarial drugs exist, but to defeat malaria it is necessary to eliminate the vector, the mosquito. In 1955, a massive worldwide program against malaria was launched by the World Health Organization following a remarkably successful campaign in Sri Lanka (then Ceylon). As Figure 15-1 shows, Sri Lanka has been freed of malaria. This was not so until the mid-1940s, when a massive, islandwide attack on the mosquito was launched with the aid of a pesticide called *dichloro diphenyl trichloroethane* (DDT). The results were dramatic; the mosquito was practically wiped out, and so was the high death rate attributable to malaria.

In 1945, the death rate had been 22 per 1000; in 1947 it was down to 15 per thousand, and by 1954 it was an unprecedented 10 per 1000. In 1972, Sri Lanka reported a death rate of only 8 per 1000, a figure further reduced to 6 per 1000 by 1985. Malaria had been defeated. Of course, the conquest of malaria produced some other problems. The birth rate in Sri Lanka, 32 per 1000 in 1945, showed no signs of declining proportionally, and in 1972 it was still 30 per 1000 (abating to 21 by 1995). Thus, while malaria was eradicated, the population growth rate rose to double what it had been. There is no solution yet to the problems arising from that new situation.

The campaign against malaria in Sri Lanka may have been exemplary, but it may not have been the final battle. Success in campaigns against major diseases often is only temporary. Following the Sri Lanka experiment, a massive assault was launched against the malaria mosquito in India, and the number of new cases of the disease declined dramatically. But ten years later, In-

dia reported 60 million people infected with malaria, more than half as many as had the disease before the antimalaria campaign began. What the effort proved was the mosquito's capacity for fast population rebound after even the most intensive application of insecticides. Today the war against malaria is going in a different direction: genetic interference with the mosquito so that its capacity to transmit the malaria parasite, *Plasmodium*, is destroyed. By introducing "engineered" mosquitoes into the general population, it is anticipated that those incapable of transmitting malaria will eventually replace *A. gambiae* and its cohorts.

But all this will take many years, and in the meantime malaria remains a worldwide scourge, with the mosquito surviving pesticide campaigns and the effectiveness of antimalaria drugs declining. The misery caused by this disease remains incalculable.

YELLOW FEVER

The distribution of **yellow fever** (Fig. 15-2) indicates that this disease is confined to tropical and neartropical areas, but in past centuries it extended far beyond these confines. The disease is caused by a virus that is transmitted by various kinds of mosquitoes, and it has been one of the great killers of world population. In the Americas, there were devastating epidemics and serious outbreaks in the Caribbean islands, in tropical Middle and South America, and serious outbreaks as far from the tropics as Boston. The southern United States was repeatedly invaded by yellow fever, always a dreaded disease; the last major outbreak struck coastal cities, especially New Orleans, as recently as 1905. Europe, too, experienced severe attacks of yellow fever; not even England and France were spared.

Today, the disease has been

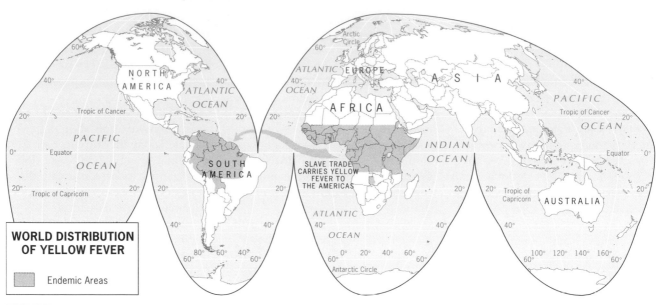

FIGURE 15–2   Approximate areas in Africa and South America where yellow fever has long been endemic.

driven back to the areas where it has been endemic, and there is a vaccine available, which can provide long-term immunity. Eradicating it is a difficult proposition, however, since yellow fever also affects monkeys and several species of small forest animals. In the tropics, therefore, immunization of humans is the only solution.

It was yellow fever that contributed importantly to the failure of Ferdinand de Lesseps, builder of the Suez Canal, in his attempt to cut a canal across Panama's mosquito-infested swamps in 1876. Not until a massive campaign of eradication had been waged could a second attempt at the Panama Canal be made in 1905.

As the name of the disease suggests, its onset, some days after the bite of the vector mosquito, is marked by high temperatures. Headaches and backaches accompany the fever, as does vomiting. Sometimes, unchecked vomiting leads to death. In less acute cases, and since the virus attacks the liver, jaundice occurs, and the deposition of bile pigment colors the eyes and skin quite yellow. Once the disease has been contracted, there is no

treatment, and it has to run its course. Where the disease is endemic, the local population has developed a degree of immunity. Still, there is always a sufficient reservoir of susceptible people to sustain a high-intensity outbreak, and the threat of yellow fever still prevails for millions of people.

SLEEPING SICKNESS

The diffusion of African **sleeping sickness** is thought to have begun about A.D. 1400, from a source area in West Africa (Fig. 15-3). The tsetse fly, of which Africa has many species, is the vector; its distribution indicates the extent of occurrence of the disease (Fig. 15-3). The fly sucks blood from an infected animal or person, and, in doing so, ingests the single-celled agents or trypanosomes. In the fly's body, these trypanosomes undergo reproduction, and eventually they reach the insect's salivary glands. When the fly next bites a person or an animal, it spreads the infection to new hosts.

Africa's wildlife population forms a veritable reservoir for sleeping sickness, because many of its great

herds of antelope are carriers of the disease (Fig. 15-4). The fly infects not only people, but also their livestock, and its effect on Africa's human population has been incalculable. It has inhibited the development of livestock herds where meat and milk would provide crucial elements in seriously imbalanced diets. It prevented the adoption of the animal-drawn plow and cart in Africa before the Europeans arrived there. It channeled the diffusion of cattle into Eastern and Southern Africa through tsetse-free corridors, destroying the herds that moved into nearby infested zones. Most of all, it ravaged the population, depriving it not only of potential livelihoods but also of its health.

In humans, sleeping sickness begins with a fever, followed by a swelling of the lymph nodes. Next the inflammation spreads to the brain and the spinal cord, producing the lethargy and listlessness that give the disease its name. Death may follow. When livestock get the disease, called nagana, the consequences are similarly severe, as the sick animal withers away to die within a year of infection. In some

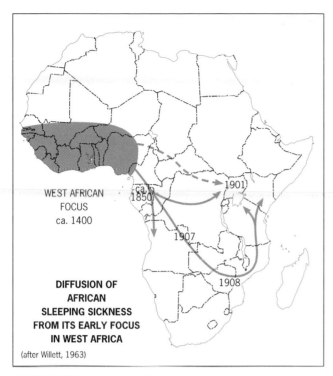

FIGURE 15–3   From K. C. Willett, "Trypanosomiasis and the Tsetse Fly Problem in Africa," *Annual Review of Entomology*, Vol. 8 (1963), p. 197.

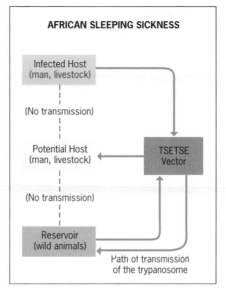

FIGURE 15–4   Transmission of African Sleeping Sickness

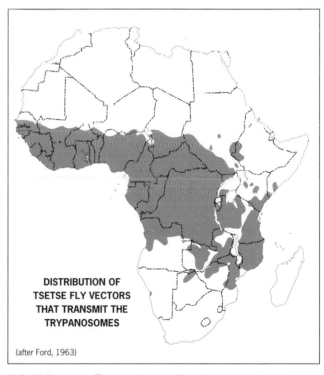

FIGURE 15–5   From J. Ford, "The Distribution of the Vectors of African Pathogenic Trypanosomes," *Bulletin of the WHO*, Vol. 28 (1963), p. 655.

areas, the disease is accompanied by a grotesque swelling of the limbs, control of which is lost before long. The animal stumbles helplessly about, is eventually crazed, and then dies.

Sleeping sickness is one of the tropics' real scourges, and while progress has been made in combating this dreaded disease, much of Africa is still affected by it (Fig. 15-5). The most promising line of attack is at the vector—killing the flies in massive eradication campaigns. Sometimes whole villages have been moved from infested to tsetse-free zones. The killing of infected wildlife, destruction of the bush that the tsetse fly needs as its habitat, and other methods have been attempted. Africa is large, however—some 11.7 million square miles (over 30 million square kilometers)—and over much of the continent, the tsetse fly still rules.

These are just three of dozens of vectored infectious diseases that continue to ravage populations in tropical regions. *Schistosomiasis*, also known as **bilharzia**, is a debilitating disease transmitted by freshwater snails. The vector sends infected larva into still- or slow-moving water, and when these penetrate the human skin they develop into mature, egg-laying

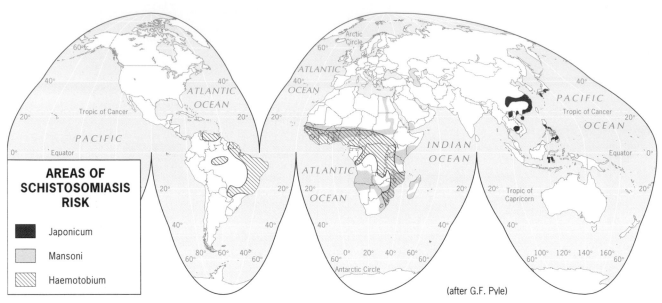

FIGURE 15–6   Areas where people are at risk from three types of Schistosomiasis (bilharzia). From G. Pyle, *Applied Medical Geography* (Silver Spring: Winston/Halsted, 1979), p. 47.

worms. In the host's liver and other organs, the eggs wreak havoc. When fast-moving streams in tropical areas were dammed for electricity-generating or agricultural-development purposes, the dams became ideal environments for the snails that transmit schistosomiasis, and local people paid the price for progress. Figure 15-6 shows world areas at risk from three types of this disease. Another vectored disease is *onchocerciasis* or **river blindness**, so named because it afflicts ribbons of population living in river valleys in West Africa and elsewhere. The vector is a fly; the parasite eventually reaches the eyes, depriving the victim of sight. In the tropics, the risks are everywhere, and the threats to good health are numerous.

NONVECTORED INFECTIOUS DISEASES

Infectious diseases, as we noted earlier, can be transmitted by vectors such as flies and mosquitoes, or they can be transmitted directly

from person to person, normally (but not always) without an intermediate live carrier. Such vehicles as contaminated water or food may transmit the disease. When direct transmission takes place, several possibilities exist: (1) close bodily contact, through which such maladies as venereal diseases and mononucleosis are transmitted; (2) the contamination of water and food by fecal material, which spreads cholera and infectious hepatitis, for example; and (3) the contamination of air when tiny droplets of saliva are expelled by infected persons and then inhaled by others, as in the case of tuberculosis, influenza, and the common cold.

CHOLERA

Perhaps the most frightening disease in this group is **cholera**, also called Asiatic cholera, a term used to denote a set of diseases in which diarrhea and dehydration are chief symptoms. Cholera is an ancient disease, with its focus in India, and it remained confined there until the beginning of the nineteenth century. Then in 1816, it spread to

China and Japan and to East Africa and Mediterranean Europe in the first of several devastating pandemics. This initial wave abated by 1823, but by then the very name cholera struck fear in people worldwide. People in communities everywhere had died by the hundreds, even thousands. Death was horribly convulsive and would come in a matter of days, perhaps a week, and no one knew what caused the disease or how to avoid it when it invaded.

It was not long before a second pandemic struck, from 1826 to 1837, when cholera crossed the Atlantic and attacked North America. During the next pandemic, from 1842 to 1862, England was severely hit, and cholera again spread into North America (Fig. 15-7). During this period, the vehicle for cholera was discovered (see box "Cholera and the Map") and for the first time, it was possible to take evasive if not yet preventive action. As Figure 15-7 shows, cholera during the 1842 to 1862 pandemic spread southward along the East African coast and reached what is today northern Moçambique and Madagascar. It then spread through the Middle

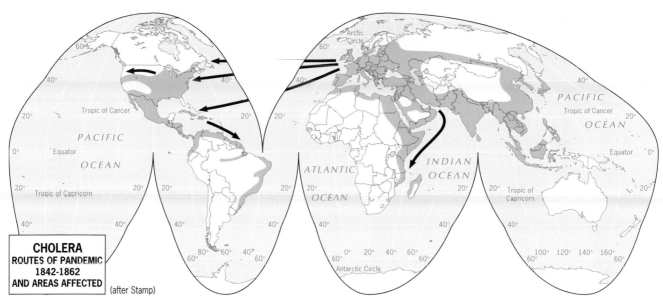

FIGURE 15–7 From L. D. Stamp, *The Geography of Life and Death* (1964).

East to Europe and was carried across the Atlantic to North America. The disease diffused across the United States in patterns displayed in Figure 15-8. It arrived in December 1848 in New York and New Orleans, and soon spread into the interior, mainly northward along the Mississippi Valley. It reached Chicago on April 29, 1850, about the same time it was traveling westward to San Francisco, where it struck late in the same year.

There was only a brief respite before the last great world cholera pandemic began in 1865. Now, however, people knew to take precautions against contaminated water, and although the advance was worldwide, this was to be the last of the great cholera waves. In the United States, cholera reached the East Coast in May 1866 and spread rapidly into the interior, reaching Detroit on May 29 and Chicago on July 21. This time it moved southward through the Mississippi Valley, meeting a northward attack which had originated in New Orleans in July as well. However, the disease failed to reach the West Coast during the 1865 to 1875 pandemic.

Although there were later ad-

vances of cholera, it has for decades been confined to its South Asian endemic zone. Nevertheless, predictions that it had been defeated everywhere except in Asia proved premature. Europe, after being free from cholera for 50 years, had an outbreak in 1972 in Naples, Italy, causing deaths. Also in the

1970s, parts of Africa not recently affected reported cholera cases, in a pandemic that invaded 29 countries in two years and had not totally receded by the mid-1990s.

The refugee crisis that sent more than 1 million people from Rwanda to Zaïre's makeshift camps in mid-1994 was worsened by still an-

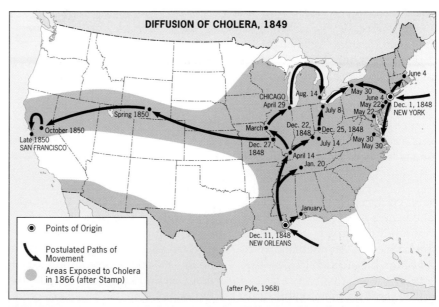

FIGURE 15–8 From L. D. Stamp (see Figure 15-7), 1964, and G. F. Pyle, "The Diffusion of Cholera in the United States in the 19th Century," *Geographical Analysis*, 1 (1969), p. 59.

CHOLERA AND THE MAP

The map below (Fig. 15-9) was drawn by Dr. John Snow in 1854. It represents the streets and squares of Soho, a district of London. In those days, people still drew their water at municipal pumps and carried it home. Each *P* symbol on the map represents the location of such a pump.

Dr. Snow had been working on the problem of cholera for many years, and he had become convinced that contaminated water was to blame for carrying the disease to its victims. When the pandemic that began in 1842 reached England, the Soho district was severely hit. On the street map, Dr. Snow located every cholera death in Soho by marking the place of residence of each victim with a dot. Approximately 500 deaths occurred in Soho and, as Dr. Snow's map took shape, it became evident that an especially large number of those deaths were clustered around the pump on Broad Street. At the doctor's request, city authorities removed the handle from that pump, making it impossible to draw water there. The result was dramatic: the number of reported new cases declined almost immediately to near zero. Dr. Snow's theory about the role of water in the spread of cholera was confirmed.

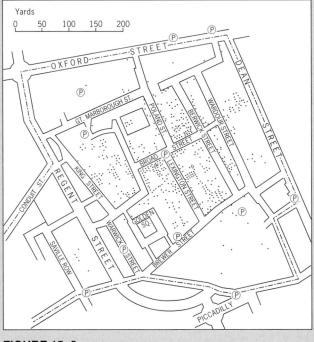

FIGURE 15–9

in the hemisphere was affected. In early 1995, more than 1 million cases had been reported and about 10,000 people had succumbed.

The epidemic that originated in Peru apparently came from fecal contamination of the municipal water supply in one of Lima's shantytowns, but cholera's diffusion through Ecuador and Chile was blamed on contaminated shellfish and raw vegetables irrigated with sewage-contaminated water. Cholera is defeated by high standards of sanitation, but burgeoning urban populations form ready reservoirs when hygiene breaks down—as continues to happen in tropical Asia. Vaccines exist, but unfortunately the cholera vaccine remains effective (and decreasingly so) for a period of only six months. If it is difficult to vaccinate an entire population even once, you can imagine the chances of doing so twice every year.

The symptoms of cholera are well known. Within a half day of infection, the host's small intestine is invaded and its functions blocked; diarrhea and vomiting follow, and the body becomes rapidly dehydrated. Unless countermeasures are taken, the skin shrivels, blood pressure falls, and muscular cramps and coma follow. The sequence of events can be over in two days, but may last for seven. The countermeasures include the replacement of the body's fluids and salt, and antibiotics to combat the infection. However, these luxuries are not available in the slums of Asia's crowded cities, where cholera always lurks.

INFLUENZA

Every year, tens of thousands of people succumb to the "flu," a malady that strikes millions worldwide, although the great majority recover. Older people, and those who are weak, are especially susceptible. In the United States in a typical year,

other cholera outbreak. River and lake waters were contaminated by thousands of corpses, and cholera spread rapidly. An international relief effort was needed to stem the tide.

The most alarming outbreak of cholera in this century, however, was the epidemic that began in

Peru in December 1990. The Americas had been free from cholera for more than a hundred years, but the fast-spreading epidemic infected nearly 400,000 people during its first year and killed almost 4000. By the end of 1991, only four countries in the Americas remained untouched, and in 1992 every country

influenza is the cause of death for some 20,000 persons.

In some years it is much worse. In 1918, a worldwide pandemic killed between 20 and 30 million people as an especially virulent strain of the virus diffused worldwide. Influenza, once a new strain has begun to spread, diffuses when people inhale the airborne virus; and it spreads rapidly. A single infected person in an airplane or bus can transmit it to dozens of others.

Why do new epidemics and pandemics of influenza occur? The answer apparently lies in the life cycle of the influenza A virus, which comes from China (hence the names given to recent pandemics, such as "Chinese flu" and "Hong Kong flu"). There the virus resides in birds, especially in waterfowl. The virus cannot be transmitted directly from birds to people, however. But the virus *is* transmitted from birds to pigs and from pigs to humans.

Chinese farming practices put ducks (major carriers of the influenza A virus) in close proximity to pigs and in turn to people. People ill with the flu can transmit the virus to pigs. So, medical geographers believe, the pig is host to strains of influenza A virus from both birds and humans, and this means that new strains of the virus can form in the host. Next the new strain is transmitted from pigs to people, and the latest epidemic (and possibly pandemic) and is under way (Fig. 15-10).

Influenza, therefore, has a vector at its source, but once it spreads away from its core area, it is spread by contact. As we noted previously, the distinction between vectored and nonvectored infectious diseases is not always hard and fast.

AIDS

The last two decades of the twentieth century witnessed a medical catastrophe: the global spread of a disease called **AIDS** (Acquired Immune Deficiency Syndrome). Firm evidence of its existence was recorded in 1981, and before the end of the decade a pandemic was in progress. Despite a massive research effort on several continents, AIDS defied treatment. To be diagnosed with AIDS meant death, if not sooner, then later. Prominent persons—sports figures, actors, scholars, artists—were infected. The virus that causes AIDS got into the blood supply, and people in need of blood transfusions risked exposure. Writers compared the fear of AIDS to the fear of cholera during the 1800s.

The dimensions of the AIDS pandemic still are uncertain. Persons infected by the HIV (Human Immunodeficiency Virus) do not immediately, or even soon, display visible symptoms of the disease. In the early stages, only a blood test will reveal infection, and then only by indicating that the body is mobilizing antibodies to fight the HIV. People can carry the virus for years without being aware of it. During that period, they can unwittingly transmit the virus to others. Official reports of actual cases of AIDS, therefore, lag far behind the reservoir of those infected. In early 1994 the Centers for Disease Control in

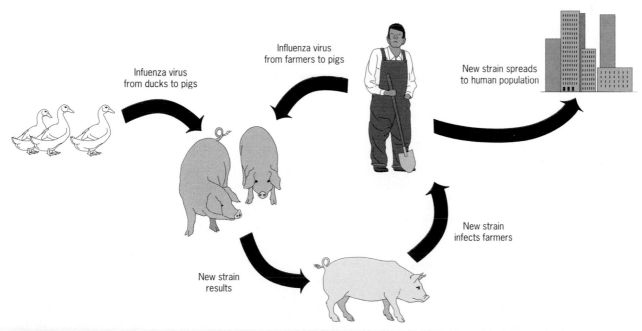

FIGURE 15–10 The life cycle of an influenza (new strain) virus.

Atlanta had recorded 412,000 AIDS cases in this country, and estimates of the number infected surpassed one million.

These data for the United States, however, pale before those from Africa. Official statistics for African countries still give no indication of the magnitude of the AIDS epidemic there, and for obvious reasons. The medical system, already overwhelmed by the long-prevailing maladies of tropical Africa, cannot cope with this new onslaught. Many of those ill with AIDS live in remote villages or in the vast shantytowns of Nairobi, Kinshasa, or other large cities, and do not see a doctor. But staggering evidence of the impact of AIDS is everywhere, and WHO surveys have begun to unveil the real magnitude of the disease in Africa: over 10.7 million HIV cases in 1995.

Most disconcerting are the trends. Since AIDS is a blood-borne disease, and it is transmitted most efficiently through (often undetected) blood contact, sexual practices in a society can presage routes of diffusion. Patronage of prostitutes along the Kampala (Uganda)—Nairobi (Kenya)—Mombasa highway in East Africa, for example, is known to be one such diffusion route. In their book, *The Geography of AIDS* (1991), medical geographers G. Shannon, G. Pyle, and R. Bashshur report on a series of tests on female prostitutes in Nairobi: in 1981, 4 percent tested positive for the virus; in 1984, 61 percent; and in 1986, 85 percent. In Blantyre, the largest city of Malawi, pregnant women in 1984 showed an infection rate of 2 percent; in 1990, the rate was 22 percent. About one-third of babies born to infected women are themselves infected with the AIDS virus.

Infection rates in East and Central Africa's cities are high, ranging from 8 percent of adults in the Zaïre capital of Kinshasa, to 30 percent in Kigali, capital of Rwanda. These levels have been reached relatively recently, so that the real devastation of the epidemic in Africa has not yet begun. The cities were the large reservoirs, but the rural areas have not escaped the ravages of AIDS. Surveys in rural areas of Uganda and Zaïre indicate that between 8 and 12 percent of the adult populations in those places is infected. The present state of medical knowledge holds out no long-term hope for those infected, and AIDS, before the end of the century, will alter the population-growth rates of much of tropical Africa.

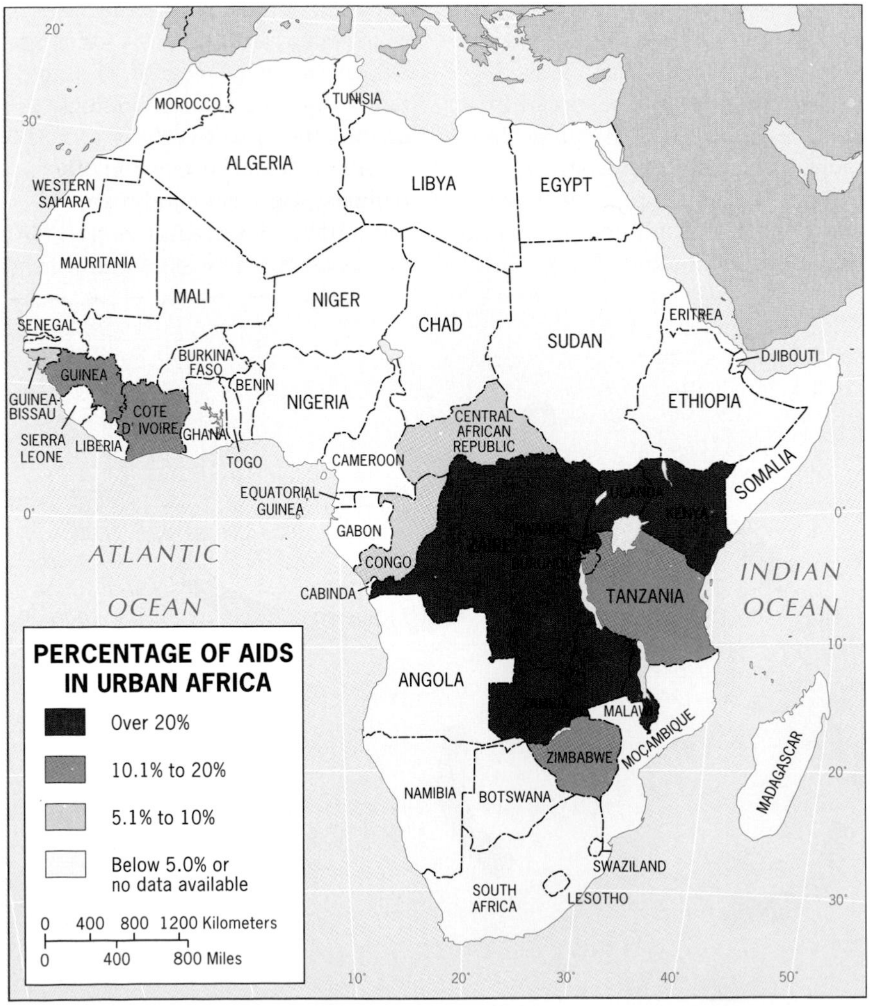

SOURCES AND PATTERNS

Medical geographers have joined the worldwide effort to learn more about, and thus to combat, AIDS. The disease displays puzzling regional properties, and its source and global diffusion routes still are matters for debate. To begin with, there are at least two viruses, HIV-1, the virus responsible for the East and Central African epidemic and, apparently, the ensuing pandemic, and a more recently discovered HIV-2, active in West Africa. It is now believed that the HIV-2, identified only in 1986, has been active in West Africa since the 1960s. This virus is strongest in the far west of the region, infecting about 10 percent of adults in Guinea-Bissau. But

PERCENTAGE OF AIDS IN URBAN AFRICA

- Over 20%
- 10.1% to 20%
- 5.1% to 10%
- Below 5.0% or no data available

FIGURE 15–11 Based on medical and press reports as of June, 1995.

HIV-1, which may have arrived in West Africa as late as the early 1980s, appears to be a more virulent strain. In the capital of Côte D'Ivoire (Ivory Coast), Abidjan, more than 7 percent of adults are reported to carry the HIV-1, and nearly 4 percent carry the HIV-2 or both viruses.

Do HIV-1 and HIV-2 have different sources of origin, or is one a mutation of the other? The discovery of HIV-2 complicated an already difficult problem: where and how AIDS first infected human hosts. When the first AIDS cases were diagnosed in the United States and Europe, male-to-female ratios of carriers were of the order of 17 to 1. An apparently similar disease in Central and East Africa had a male-to-female ratio of close to 1 to 1, but for a time it was thought that these contrasts indicated different diseases. When it became clear that the same virus (HIV-1) was the cause, and a pandemic was obviously developing, the search for its source intensified.

To know the geographic source of a disease such as AIDS is important, because the virus that causes it must be a mutation of an earlier one and may in turn give rise to new mutants. At present, all the evidence points to an African origin for AIDS. Not only is Africa's cross-continental "AIDS Belt" the largest and oldest concentration of cases, but also an obvious link—to animals, frequently the sources of viruses that afflict humans—exists here (Fig. 15-11). Research indicates that nonhuman primates, such as Central Africa's Green Monkey and West Africa's Mangabey Monkey, carry Simian Immunodeficiency Viruses (SIVs) that are similar, but not identical, to the HIVs. The possibility that a mutation in some intermediate host created HIV, or that some other nonhuman primate may yet prove to carry HIV, is being pursued. African monkeys are eaten as a matter of local tradition;

their blood is directly absorbed during ritual. Thus the possibility exists that AIDS found a first foothold in East-Central Africa, and perhaps independently in West Africa. (Some researchers believe that West Africa's HIV-2 may in fact be the older). From tropical Africa, the virus was carried to all parts of the world on airplanes and boats.

Today, HIV continues to defy all efforts to contain it. In Southeast Asia, Thailand has become, in the words of geographer P. R. Gould, "[an AIDS] catastrophe in the making . . . in its eventual magnitude it may well exceed the terror of the killing fields of civil war in neighboring Cambodia." Professor Gould's book *The Slow Plague* (1993) alerts us not only to the geographic dimensions of AIDS but also to the prospect that this disease may be just one of several poised to assail our populous, vulnerable world.

THE CHRONIC DISEASES

Dramatic as the AIDS pandemic is, the number of AIDS cases worldwide pales against those stricken by heart diseases, cancers, strokes, and lung ailments. The chronic diseases always have been leading causes of death; in the United States a century ago, tuberculosis, pneumonia, diarrheal diseases, and heart diseases (in that order) were the chief killers. Today, heart disease and cancer head the list, with cerebral hemorrhage (stroke) next and accidents high on the list as well (Table 15-1). At the turn of the century, tuberculosis and pneumonia caused 20 percent of all deaths; today, they cause less than 5 percent. The diarrheal diseases, which were so high on the old list, are now primarily children's maladies, and infant mortality in the United States was still quite high in 1900. Today, these diseases are not even on the new list of the 10 leading causes of death in this country. The modern list of deadly diseases is a list of the afflictions of middle and old age, reflecting our increased life expectancy.

Table 15-1 reflects some other realities, some not so positive. Although the diseases of infancy have been defeated to a large extent, and such infectious diseases as tuberculosis and pneumonia are lesser threats than they were, the battles against cancer and heart disease are

TABLE 15–1 Leading Causes of Death in the United States, 1989 (thousands)

Cause	Number	Rate per 100,000
1. Heart diseases	934.3	376.4
2. Cancers	497.2	200.3
3. Strokes	147.5	59.4
4. Accidents	94.8	38.2
5. Influenza, pneumonia	75.2	30.3
6. Diabetes	46.6	18.8
7. Suicide	31.2	12.6
8. Cirrhosis of the liver	26.4	10.6
9. Homicide, legal action	23.0	9.3
10. Arteriosclerosis	19.1	7.7

Source: U.S. Department of Commerce, Bureau of the Census, *Statistical Abstract of the United States: 1991* (111th Edition). Washington, D.C., 1991, p. 79.

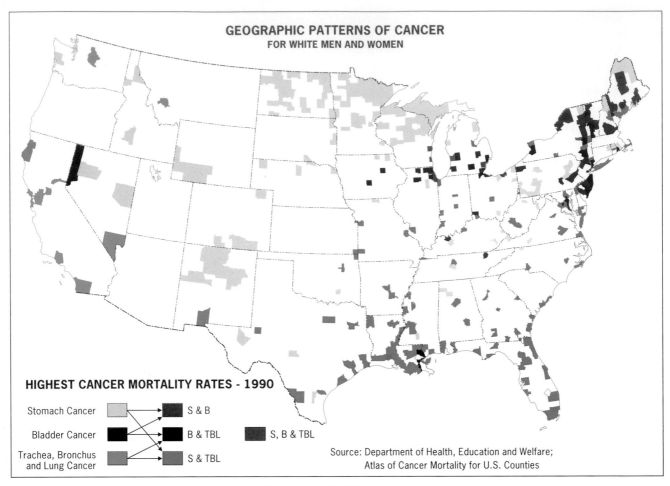

GEOGRAPHIC PATTERNS OF CANCER
FOR WHITE MEN AND WOMEN

HIGHEST CANCER MORTALITY RATES - 1990

Stomach Cancer → S & B

Bladder Cancer → B & TBL   S, B & TBL

Trachea, Bronchus and Lung Cancer → S & TBL

Source: Department of Health, Education and Welfare;
Atlas of Cancer Mortality for U.S. Counties

FIGURE 15–12   Regional aspects of cancer incidence as of 1990.

far from won. Modernization has brought with it new lifestyles, new pressures, and new consumption patterns, and we do not know how these circumstances affect our health. People often smoke cigarettes because they find it relaxing, but lung cancer—a major modern killer— has been linked to smoking. In order to distribute adequate food supplies to populations concentrated in huge urban areas, we add various kinds of preservatives to foods, without being sure of just how, in the long run, these preservatives will affect our health. In our overfed society, we substitute artificial flavoring for sugar and other calorie-rich substances, but some of those substitutes have been

proven dangerous. The map of cancer and heart disease shows as heavy a concentration of these problems in our modernized part of the world as some of the major infectious diseases do in the underdeveloped regions (Fig. 15-12).

The chronic diseases also are known as the degenerative diseases, maladies obviously associated with old age. Arteriosclerosis involves the narrowing and sometimes the blocking of arteries carrying blood to vital organs, including the heart, brain, and kidneys. This appears to be the result of long-term accumulation of fatty material and calcium on the interior walls of arteries, and the risk

increases with age. High-cholesterol diets contribute, over long periods of time, to the buildup of the blockages, as, apparently, do the sedentary habits of urban life.

At the opposite end of the life cycle, new dangers also confront children. As everyone knows, children will chew on almost anything—toys, utensils, and whatever else is in reach. In the poorer areas of the cities and towns, where many families live in substandard housing, the paint peels off the walls and the children pull at the slivers and chew on them. The paint contains lead, and it is now known that many children sustain lead poisoning this way. Lead poisoning has several negative effects on the body, and one of them is brain damage.

In addition, there are rising fears that the water of many areas in the United States contains substances conducive to the development of various forms of cancer. Chlorine and fluoride are added to water to reduce the risk of contamination, and other chemicals are used to treat water pollution of various kinds. We are not sure of the long-term effect when we consume water over the years, however, and we may be substituting one risk for another. It is one thing to start using treated water at middle age, but it is another to begin consuming it virtually at birth. When something is consumed from birth, any damaging substances have a long time to build up. Water treatment, on the scale at which it occurs today, is a relatively new phenomenon, and only the most recent generation has been using chemically modified water all along. The results in terms of disease and mortality are yet to be ascertained.

GENETIC DISEASES

The genetic or inherited diseases are disorders with origins that lie in chromosomes and genes, and that can be transferred from one generation to the next. Genetic diseases are not always well understood, although some, such as sickle-cell anemia, have been studied intensively. Hemophilia is another such disease.

Genetic diseases result from gene mutations or accidents to the chromosomes. In some cases, a mutation may occur in the fetus while a child is still unborn, an accident that affects the child in spite of the fact that both parents are completely normal (mongolism is such an instance). Radiation and viruses may also damage a parent's chro-

mosomes; the role of drugs in gene mutations is still uncertain. In a geographic context, however, other forms of inherited disease are of greater interest. Certain genetic diseases are concentrated in specific populations, and others appear to be associated with particular natural environments. Phenylketonuria, for example, occurs mostly in the European (Caucasoid) geographical race (see Chapter 16). People who have this disorder cannot convert one kind of amino acid into another, and unless it is diagnosed and treated early, mental retardation results.

Metabolic problems—the body's inability to process all elements of the diet—are among noteworthy genetic diseases. Enzymes facilitate critical reactions within the body, and a chromosomal failure to produce an adequate quantity of a particular enzyme (or perhaps to produce any amount of this enzyme at all) leads to metabolic malfunction. Such a disorder can be inherited. A prominent example is the malady called primary adult lactose intolerance. People who suffer from this disorder do not possess an adequate supply of one of a set of enzymes needed to break down the milk sugar lactose. This "milk allergy," or galactosemia, when severe, leads to damage of the liver and spleen; young children display a swelling of the abdomen, face, hands, and feet because fluid accumulates. Mental retardation can occur among children, but this is comparatively rare. The symptoms are more likely to be mild, including stomach and intestinal pain after milk is consumed or foods that contain lactose are eaten.

People who experience such discomforts will reduce or eliminate their intake of milk. This does not happen randomly. (For example, the disorder is much more prevalent among African Americans than among whites). In India, primary

adult lactose intolerance is the rule, rather than the exception. (About 80 percent of India's population probably has some intolerance, and in China the figure may be even higher.) In Africa, the peoples of the forest zone, who do not have cattle or milk livestock, have high intolerance to lactose; but the savanna dwellers, who are also pastoralists, have a much lower intolerance.

People who cannot comfortably consume milk and other foods containing lactose may, as a result, suffer from deficiencies in the nutrients that these foods contribute to the body, especially calcium. This has led to some unusual supplementing of diets, including the ancient custom of earth-eating, *geophagy*. In West Africa, this time-honored practice involves the eating of clay for medicinal and dietary reasons.

Thus inherited diseases of metabolic origin have regional expression, and they can be studied geographically in the context of historic migration routes, acculturation (see Chapter 18), natural environments, ethnic distributions, and other spatial phenomena. The geography of inherited disorders still holds many unexplored learning opportunities.

DISTRIBUTION OF TREATMENT

Most of us, when the need arises, have access to a physician or hospital. We may find the treatment to be very expensive and insurance costs to be high, but treatment and expertise are available to almost everyone. During the twentieth century, the United States and several other countries developed extensive and complex health care systems, with facilities ranging from small private physicians' offices to huge medical schools complete with research laboratories and hospitals. The richer, developer countries could afford such luxuries: Sweden, the Netherlands, the United Kingdom, Canada, and Australia are among countries with well-developed health care systems.

As we noted previously, many people in the poorer countries do not receive essential vaccinations and never or only rarely see a medical facility of any sort. The contrast between the "have" and the "have-not" countries in this context is vividly illustrated by a single statistic: the number of people per doctor. In the United States in the early 1990s, there was one doctor for every 460 persons and one hospital bed per 192 people. Compare these figures to those of India, where there is one doctor for every 2522 people and more than 1300 people per hospital bed. In Egypt, the situation is somewhat better: 767 persons per doctor and about 480 people per hospital bed. In Nigeria, however, there are approximately 7900 persons for every doctor and nearly 1140 per hospital bed. Such figures make a strong case for the position that the underdeveloped countries need highly trained, specialized doctors less than they need medical technicians capable of coping with the more urgent and widespread health problems—technicians who can be trained more rapidly and far more cheaply than physicians.

TRADITIONAL MEDICINE

Statistics of this kind also explain the continuing role of **traditional medicine** in the societies of underdeveloped countries. The term *barefoot doctor* has come to denote these practitioners of "bush medicine," who function from China to Indonesia to Africa. Often, they are more welcome and better trusted by villagers needing medical help than modern physicians are. In a traditional society, illnesses are still thought to be of mystical origin and caused by a devil, a spell, or some other supernatural force. For such ailments, many people believe modern medicine to be useless—indeed, inappropriate. Western doctors in African villages, for example, faced opposition to their treatment of people stricken by delirium which, it was believed, is caused by the devil. The will of god was being manifested; to interfere would be improper. In such instances, the traditional doctor, as physician, magician, and priest, performs functions for the victim and community far beyond what a modern "medicine man" can do.

The "barefoot doctor" in Asia and Africa does, in many instances, mix some modern medicine with traditional practices. The availability of drugs and other medical materials has expanded the capacities of the local practitioner, and many of them skillfully combine their traditional talents with a dose of modern medicine. In Indonesia, these *dukuns* often are the sole contact between rural people and medicine of any kind. On the large island of Kalimantan, for example, there is one modern physician for every 50,000 inhabitants. (In the Netherlands, Indonesia's former colonial ruler, the figure is 396.)

Such comparisons suggest that the developed countries have achieved satisfactory health care delivery systems, but when we examine these modern systems in some detail, we discover that even in the United States and in certain other Western countries, those elaborate medical systems are not doing the job as well as they could.

Some of the major problems involved are geographical in nature. Even with our favorable doctor/people ratio, there is a shortage of physicians in the United States. Perhaps even more importantly, those doctors now available are not distributed as well as they could be; there are too many doctors in some areas and too few in others. Furthermore, what is true of doctors' offices is true of hospitals as well: hospitals are frequently located in places that make them inaccessible to many potential patients.

Studies have shown that distance is an important factor in the use made by sample populations of hospital facilities. An important criterion in the locational planning for hospitals, therefore, should be their closeness to the largest possible number of people they are intended to serve. However, there has not been enough cooperation between planners of cities and regions and planners of the nation's health facilities.

Another major shortcoming of our health delivery system lies in its unequal availability to the various population groups that constitute our nation. Whereas some of us can go to a doctor's office and be treated within an hour, others wait for half a day or longer in understaffed clinics. As with nutrition, it is the poor people who are least adequately served by the system, and the statistics tell the results.

In a study of the health situation in Chicago in the 1960s, the contrasts between the poor and the well-off were revealed by some dramatic figures. In the poor areas, infant mortality was 100 percent greater than in the wealthier areas; syphilis-related deaths were 300 percent higher; gonorrhea-connected mortality was over 1600 percent higher. More than four times as many children died from pneumonia; diarrheal diseases afflicted 60 percent more children than in the wealthier areas.

Some of the details in this study would seem to apply to distant underdeveloped countries, rather than to sections of our own society. So again, where the need is greatest, the system frequently fails to deliver. Those favorable statistics on doctors and hospital beds conceal some serious inequities here at home.

This chapter has focused on only a few of the topics related to the state of health of the world's population. The problems of medical geography should not be viewed in isolation from the other issues raised regarding population. Improved medical systems in underdeveloped countries may prevent diseases from claiming as many lives as in the past—only to add to the numbers later dying of starvation. Even the developed countries have still not achieved satisfactory health delivery systems, but the underdeveloped countries need something very different: integrated programs that combine planning efforts in areas of nutrition, sanitation, health services, and family planning. The tasks ahead are numerous and enormous, and the future of the world depends on those who will tackle them.

KEY TERMS

Agent	Influenza
AIDS	Malaria
Bilharzia	Pandemic
Cholera	Reservoir
Chronic Diseases	River Blindness
Endemic	Sleeping Sickness
Epidemic	Traditional Medicine
Genetic Diseases	Vectors
Hosts	Vehicles
Infectious Diseases	Yellow Fever

She worked ten hours a day, six days a week, moving sun-dried bricks. Bali, Indonesia.

PART FIVE

GEOGRAPHY AND INEQUALITY

At Issue

Ours is a world divided not only by race, but also by sex. We are all too familiar with the consequences of our racial fragmentation and the disunity and disadvantage that underlie it. We tend, however, to be less aware of the effects of our gender division. Many studies document the gender-based inequalities that still afflict our own society, but in other areas of the world gender is not merely a matter of variable opportunity or differential pay; it is a matter of life or death. Female infanticide, the deliberate neglect of female children, and the merciless exploitation of girls creates demographic contrasts on the two sides of the population pyramid that make averages meaningless. On large parts of our globe, women live—almost literally—in a different world from that of men. The geography of gender is as consequential as that of race, and it needs our urgent attention.

16

THE SPATIAL MIRAGE
OF RACE

When you, as an international traveler, enter a country for a visit, you may be asked to fill out a questionnaire to be presented, with your passport, to the immigration office. As often as not, one of the questions will be "What is your race?" The appropriate answer, of course, is "human." All the people of this world belong to the same *species*.

However, the answer "human" on the questionnaire is not the one that is wanted. (In fact, it may get you into trouble). What the questionnaire is asking is what *kind* of human being you are, that is, to what recognizable group you belong. The term "race" has become synonymous with something other than the human species. It focuses on our differences rather than on our similarities.

This is as frustrating to biologists and anthropologists (though far more consequential) as the misuse of geographic terms such as state, nation, or frontier is to human geographers. Indeed, many anthropologists have proposed that the whole concept of human "races" be abandoned. And yet there is the inescapable truth that we humans do not in some ways look alike and that our differences have regional expression.

Geographica

- **All humanity constitutes one race, but human groups differ physically from each other, and these differences, not our much greater similarities, have become synonymous with race.**

- **Current research is producing new evidence of the early arrival (or evolution) of our distant ancestors in Asia, notably Southeast Asia; the map of *Homo*'s dispersal from Africa into Eurasia may have to be redrawn.**

- **According to the multiregional evolution theory, human-origin stocks evolved in four geographic realms following the emigration of *Homo erectus* (or a predecessor) from its African source area.**

- **Nine geographical populations are commonly identified, among which the European (Caucasoid) is today the most widely dispersed, the East Asian (Mongoloid) is numerically the largest, and the African (Negroid) the oldest.**

RACE AND REALITY

Let us remind ourselves of the positive side first. Of the biological unity of our human species there is no doubt: no matter where we live on this planet and whatever our physical attributes, we have the capacity to interbreed and produce offspring. We are the human species.

We may think that we look quite dissimilar (enough so to contribute to conflict among us), but some other species display a much wider variation. Take dogs, for example. All dogs belong to the same species, but a Saint Bernard, on appearance alone, does not seem to have much in common with a fox terrier, or a wolf with a Pekingese. But it is not appearance that is the key. Rather, it is the *genetic* makeup of the individuals. Within a species, the chromosomes of reproducing organisms are identical in number and size, and they carry very similar groups of *genes*.

Nevertheless, groups of individuals *within* a species do display certain physical characteristics that tend to set them apart from others. In the human species, these groups (sometimes called *subspecies* or *populations*) exhibit regional clustering. This regional variation results *not* from differences in the fundamental genetic makeup of each group, but from differences in *gene frequencies* among populations. For example, some people are blue-eyed, others brown-eyed; the former dominate in the population of northern Europe while the latter prevail in southern Europe. Another variation related to gene frequencies has to do with blood type. As we will see below, the O type dominates in Native American populations, while the A type prevails in Western Europe. We are all too well aware of other differences among human populations. All of them occur within the human race, not between races.

What has caused the regional variation in the appearance of humans in clustered populations, the variation that bedevils human relationships so strongly? What is often called a race is in fact a combination of physical attributes in a population, the product of a particular genetic inheritance that dominates in that population (such as Australia's Aborigines, North Africa's Berbers, or Asia's Mongols). This inheritance varies from population to population, and it most probably results from a long history of adaptation to different environments. For this reason, the use of the term *race* for such populations is in error. This is no simple, technical misuse: the implications are critical. It denies the essential commonalities of our species whose

recognition is key to a world in which all may live in peace.

Unfortunately, our understanding of the biological concept of race does not mitigate the differences that mark the original populations that make up our human species. This is the negative side: after tens of thousands of years of movement and migration, mixing, and intermarriage in our increasingly mobile world, human populations marked by distinct physical attributes still are clustered in particular areas of our planet. The cultures they forged span the full range of human capacity—and often give rise to conflict when they collide. Understanding the geographic background to such discord can help defuse it.

Let us keep one other reality in mind as we approach this sensitive topic. What is often called "racial" conflict is nothing of the sort. The recent and disastrous breakdown of order in Rwanda is a case in point. The Western press implied that there is a palpable difference between the Tutsi and the Hutu "races" who killed each other by the hundreds of thousands. While Tutsi and Hutu did meet here and in areas around Rwanda long ago, and fought over land and primacy, those distinctions had largely faded when the most recent civil war broke out. No one can discern a Tutsi from a Hutu just by physical appearance. The war was over status, advantage, opportunity. The conflict was cultural, not "racial." Culture transcends "racial" stereotype: many of Rwanda's Hutu, through social success and/or intermarriage, had "become" Tutsi, the more advantaged of the Rwandans. And many paid the price at the hands of other Hutu.

So it is culture, not the misused notion of race, that often fires conflict among human groups. In the former Yugoslavia, both the Bosnian Muslims and the Serbs, as well as the Croats, are Slavs. In Northern Ireland, no one can tell an un-

adorned Catholic from a Protestant, but the thousands who have died in that now-dormant conflict were almost all of Irish or distant Scottish ancestry. In Israel, nothing of any constancy distinguishes Jew from Palestinian—except culture.

In this chapter, we consider the possible origins and salient consequences of the regional variations of populations of the human race. Over the past century, views of this topic have changed numerous times, and this chapter can only be a progress report. We still are learning about our geographic sources, and the data, as we will see, can be interpreted in various ways.

CAUSES OF HUMAN VARIATION

Our biological properties and differences, as noted earlier, are encoded in our genes. Any change in the chemistry of a gene, a **mutation**, manifests itself in some physical way. Many mutations are accidental and harmful; for example, they may interfere with reproductive capacity, or they may increase susceptibility to certain diseases. But other mutations are beneficial, conferring on individuals in a population an advantage that may contribute to survival under particular environmental conditions.

Imagine a population of olive-colored insects inhabiting a leafy forest. Birds prey on these insects, spotting them against the green background. Mutations in some of the insects will cause color variation: some will be greener than others, and some will carry a heavier shade of brown. The greener insects will be more difficult to see, and they will survive—and reproduce—in greater numbers. **Natural selection**, thus, will favor this variety. When our hominid ancestors faced widely different environments, natural selection probably played a role in the emergence of variation in such properties as skin color and physique.

When our **Homo sapiens** predecessors migrated in groups into distant, often isolated habitats, they developed **gene pools** that encoded certain biological properties throughout these communities. This is not to suggest that genetic change could not take place in isolation; on the contrary, **genetic drift**, a process that affects gene frequencies, undoubtedly did take place, imprinting certain characteristics on such populations. (See box, "Genetics.").

Mutation, natural selection, and genetic drift, therefore, create differences between populations. But in our world, few population groups are isolated any longer. Gene pools can still be recognized, but **gene flow** now prevails. Gene flow involves the movement of genes from one gene pool to another through reproduction. Such gene flow reduces differences between populations and thus has the opposite effect. If a population with tall average stature mixes with a population dominated by short stature, the number of both tall and short people will decline in favor of a growing population of medium height.

HUMAN BIOLOGICAL VARIATION

It is an inescapable reality that human populations still vary and that their differences are, in part, matters of physical appearance. Populations also differ in other ways, for example, in terms of their vulnerability to particular diseases (see Chapter 15). But the most consequential contrasts geographically lie in such characteristics as skin color, physique, facial shape and expression, hair quality, and other visible features.

GENETICS

When Charles Darwin published his *Origin of Species* in 1859 (complete title: *The Origin of Species by Means of Natural Selection or the Preservation of Favoured Races in the Struggle for Life*), his critics seized upon a major weakness: how traits were inherited from generation to generation. But before the end of the nineteenth century, the broad principles of **genetics** were understood, and this field was given its name by the English biologist William Bateson. The term **gene** was introduced to signify the physical basis of an inherited quality. The genes were defined as units of inheritance for certain traits (say, eye color or body size), together forming a **genotype**. The expression of those traits (say, brown eyes or tall build) forms the **phenotype**.

A century ago it was believed that groups of people of similar appearance (phenotype) would share, and therefore repeat, a single genotype. But today it is known that all individuals (except identical twins) are genetically unique, and each has his or her own "genetic fingerprint." Groups of people (Australian aborigines, East African Maasai, Japanese) each have similar genotypes, but individuals within those groups have unique genetic makeups. This uniqueness makes possible the identification of a person through his or her DNA, which can be derived from even a small sample of blood, hair, or saliva.

Skin Color

The cloak of color we all wear is the most pervasive of biological-physical traits, and our differentiation by color has bedeviled human relationships for uncounted centuries.

Human geographers and anthropologists have been challenged by one of the most obvious of spatial correlations: the prevalence of dark skins in low latitudes of the Old World, from tropical Africa through southern India to Australia. This generalization applies, of course, to peoples who have occupied such equatorial and near-equatorial regions for millennia. Only the first, aboriginal Australians are dark-skinned; later immigrants are not.

A complicating factor involved here also serves as a useful object lesson: as obvious and evident as it may be, skin color is not a reliable indicator of racial relationship. The peoples of southern India, New Guinea, and Australia are as dark-skinned as Africans are, but black

Africans, southern Indians, and aboriginal Australians are not closely related genetically. Thus there must be something else they share that has endowed long-term inhabitants of low latitudes with dark skins.

Skin color is a matter of pigmentation, a protective element against strong radiation from the sun. The more *melanin* pigment, the darker the skin. However, there are internal variations within groups: there are dark-skinned northern Europeans, and light-skinned Africans. These variations notwithstanding, the first image in the perception by one people or culture of another still is likely to be one of skin color. This is true despite the fact that the color of human skins varies from nearly white to nearly black, through all the intermediates (Fig. 16-1).

Various theories have been advanced to account for the spatial distribution of skin pigmentation shown in Figure 16-1, which reveals that tropical populations in South

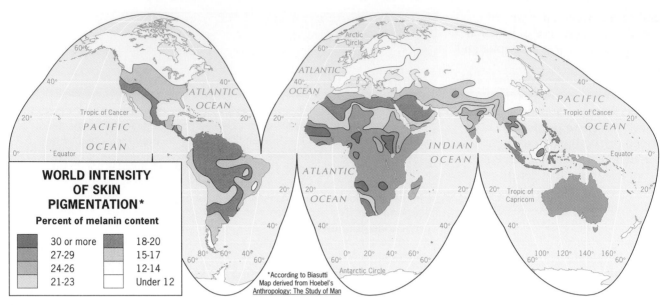

FIGURE 16–1 From a map in E.A. Hoebel, *Anthropology: The Study of Man* (New York: McGraw-Hill, 4th Rev. Ed., 1972), p. 67.

America have lighter skins than peoples of the African and Australasian tropics. This aspect of the map should be related to what we saw in Part 2 regarding the diffusion of humanity. Whatever the outcome of the current debate concerning the timing of the arrival of the first Americans (whether 13,000 years ago or more than 30,000 years ago), it is evident that the first human inhabitants of tropical America arrived quite recently compared to those of tropical Africa and Asia. If selective and adaptive processes resulted in the high concentrations of melanin over time, those processes have not had sufficient time to run their course in the Americas.

This leads to the question of why Australia's Aboriginal peoples, who may have arrived there between 40,000 and 50,000 years ago, display such intense pigmentation. This does not, in the context of millennia, seem to be an arrival time sufficiently different from the Americas to explain the pattern in Figure 16-1. The answer is geographic: the diffusion route of Australia's predecessors was tropical, so that even before their migration into Australia,

these peoples had inhabited low latitudes for a very long time. The first Americans, however, appear to have taken the Bering route from Asia into North America, and their source area lay in the high latitudes. Even after entering North America, these earliest American peoples probably did not reach tropical latitudes for some thousands of years. So the difference in terms of tropical habitation (between Australia and the Americas) is far greater than the actual entry dates suggest.

If long-term exposure to equatorial and tropical environments generated dark skin, what was the advantage promoted by natural selection? Melanin protects inner layers of the skin from damaging, cancer-causing ultraviolet rays from the sun. Dark-skinned people living under the intense tropical sun are protected much more effectively than lighter-skinned people from sunburn and cancer.

An additional factor involves the body's production of vitamin D, the vitamin that fights rickets in the body. The same ultraviolet radiation intercepted by darkly pigmented skin also stimulates the body's pro-

duction of vitamin D. Excessive sunlight, however, causes softening and calcification of bones in people who cannot withstand the high intensity of ultraviolet radiation. Thus a modern theory holds that people living for long periods in higher latitudes, where sunlight is weaker, have acquired light-colored skin through natural selection, in part because this allows maximum penetration by ultraviolet radiation, the production of vitamin D, and the development of a strong skeleton. But in the lower latitudes, dark skins protect against excessive penetration by the sun's damaging rays, and the risks of excess vitamin D in the body.

These notions do not explain all of the distributions shown in Figure 16-1, but they do suggest some of the factors behind the global pattern of skin pigmentation. Other intriguing geographic questions remain unanswered, however. There are peoples with reddish and yellowish skins, whose physical appearance cannot yet be readily explained. The human cloak of color still conceals some of its secrets.

Physique and Size

When it comes to the body build and size of populations, our perceptions may again be at variance with reality. We may think of East Africa's Tutsi (Watusi) people as unusually tall, but the data show otherwise; many Tutsi appear tall because they are, in fact, lean. We perceive certain peoples as short, others as short- or long-limbed. Few of these generalizations hold up against the measurements.

There is, nevertheless, a general relationship between the mean body weight in a population and the mean annual temperature of the areas in which that population is located. According to **Bergmann's Rule**, people are naturally more slender in warmer areas and heavier in cooler zones. Put another way, Bergmann's Rule holds that the lower the mean annual temperature is, the higher the population's mean body weight will be. But while Bergmann's Rule can be confirmed statistically, there remains the question whether this environmentally related variation is due solely, or primarily, to natural selection. We have noted previously that nutrition in warmer areas of the world tends to be less adequate than it is in the cooler zones. On the other hand, Bergmann's Rule also applies to many mammals and even birds, which develop larger bulk in cooler, higher latitudes than in warmer, lower latitudes. So while proof for human populations is not available, given differences in diets and food availability, the tendency does appear to exist, and Bergmann's Rule may explain observed regional variations.

Returning to variations in the mean height of populations, it has become clear that stress, diet, and other conditions prevailing in a society can be determining factors, and again the genetic role is uncertain. Average heights can change remarkably quickly. When you have the opportunity to visit Euro-pean museums, note how small the suits of armor were in which European warriors fought. The average European today may be 10 inches (25 centimeters) taller. More recent evidence of rapid height increase comes from the United States. Anthropologist W. A. Stini, in his book, *Ecology and Human Adaptation* (1975), reported that the average height of males in the United States increased by 2 inches (5 centimeters) between the First and Second World War. Since the end of World War II, the Japanese have been growing markedly taller as well. Again, there are no totally satisfactory explanations for these variations in humanity's physical appearance.

Other Physical Traits

Populations also differ in terms of the form of their skulls, the structure of their faces, and the properties of their head hair. For a long time, anthropologists believed that the *cephalic index* (the ratio of the breadth and length of the skull) might yield substantial insight into the evolution of discrete population groups, just as archeologists use skull analyses to chart the evolution of humanity. However, while it was possible to record a clustering of prevalent head shapes (Japanese have round heads; western Europeans have long heads), it did not prove possible to derive credible conclusions from such data.

We noted previously that environment may influence body stature and weight; the same may be true for facial features. It has long been known that populations living for long periods in the warm, moist tropics tend to have short, wide, flat noses. People living under arid conditions, including low-latitude deserts and high-latitude dry zones, are likely to have long, narrow noses. Such long, thin noses may cool and warm air more effectively than broad, short noses, and may help soften the effect of dry air on the lungs.

Regional differences in head hair also exist; it may be straight or woolly, fine-textured or thick. Asians tend to have straight hair, Europeans often have curly hair, and Africans have woolly hair.

One of the most characteristic facial properties is the **epicanthic fold**, a small piece of overlapping skin that gives the eyelid a particular appearance. This physical trait prevails in East Asia and is associated specifically with the Mongoloid (Asian) population group. But the epicanthic fold is not a unique Mongoloid feature. It also appears in Southern Africa's San (the people formerly called the Bushmen), and among Native Americans.

None of these physical features (nor others not discussed, such as the form of the lips and the degree of protrusion of the lower jaw) has provided cultural geographers with a satisfactory racial-regional differentiation of humanity. Anthropologists could do little more than classify peoples according to individual traits and map their distribution; meaningful covariances were difficult to find. More recently, however, another physical feature has been studied with more success. This is one we cannot normally see at all: people's blood, and the types into which it is grouped.

BLOOD FACTORS

We all know that various **blood groups** exist. The classification is based on the presence or absence of agglutinative (clotting) agents, which cause a clotting of red blood cells when mixed with alien blood that does not contain them. There are four blood types: A, B, AB, and O. The letters A and B denote blood carrying those types of agents, respectively; AB carries both, and type O does not have ei-

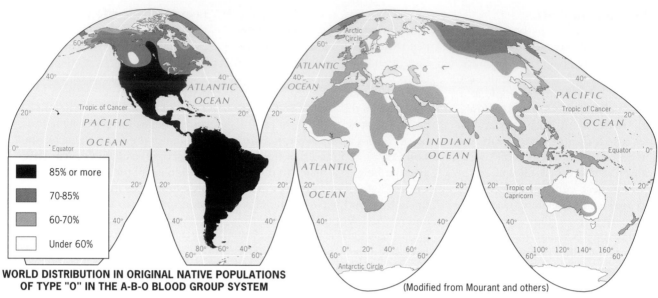

WORLD DISTRIBUTION IN ORIGINAL NATIVE POPULATIONS OF TYPE "O" IN THE A-B-O BLOOD GROUP SYSTEM

(Modified from Mourant and others)

FIGURE 16–2   From a map in E.A. Hoebel, *Anthropology: The Study of Man* (New York: McGraw-Hill, 4th Rev. Ed., 1972), p. 75, modified with additional data.

ther. When the existence of blood types was discovered, data soon began to accumulate from all over the world on this newly recognized trait. Since a person has only one blood type, the resulting statistics were a great deal less hazy than skin color or height. A population might vary from 5 feet, 1 inch (155 centimeters) to 6 feet, 4 inches (193 centimeters) in stature, with 5 feet, 9 inches (175 centimeters) the average; the skin color might average "brown," but there might be variation from very light to very dark. The blood type, however, would be reported in hard figures: 70 percent O, 20 percent B, 10 percent A (AB is quite rare).

The world distribution of blood types holds much interest, although it remains subject to different interpretations. The O type is strong, for example, among Native Americans (over 70 percent, and often 90 percent); in Northeast Asia, it is still over 70 percent, and among Mongoloid peoples in East Asia it is 30 to 40 percent (Fig. 16-2). Does this mean that the affinity between Native Americans and Asians is biologically confirmed? Some

researchers think so: they feel that the O type was diluted in Asia by contact with other genes, but that the Native Americans, by migrating into the Americas, retained their O type almost unchanged. This view holds that the "original" blood type was O, and that first A, then B, and later, AB types evolved and began to supplant the O type. Indeed, the O type remains strong in comparatively isolated areas of the world, such as central Africa and (Aboriginal) northen Australia. It might also explain the prevalence of the A type in Western Europe and the B type farther to the east, a later intrusion (Figs. 16-3 and 16-4). However, the same theory raises questions. Although the O type dominates in large areas of Africa, the B type occurs there as well. Where did that B gene come from?

How did it also get to islands of the Pacific Ocean and even into the Americas? Many scholars now believe that hominids ranged far more widely over this Earth in ancient times than was long believed, and that very early migrations are the answer. More recent research on other aspects of blood relationships

has provided new evidence, but has also raised new questions regarding the conclusions drawn so far. Red-cell and white-cell counts, enzyme relationships, and immunological data have generated new maps and posed additional problems in the search for humanity's distant origins. Whatever the eventual answers, the analysis of blood types has added enormously to the arsenal of evidence in the search for the origins and early dispersals of humanity.

Perhaps the single most significant result of this research on human blood groups relates to the old concept of race. It demonstrates that no one race has a monopoly on a particular blood group, and that all the blood groups can be found in all human groups. What varies is their frequency. This confirms that humanity is not an aggregate of separate races but really a continuous series of genetically intertwined populations. Such spatial variations as we observe result from historic migrations, temporary isolation, and other factors such as massive invasions, deathly famines, and epidemics.

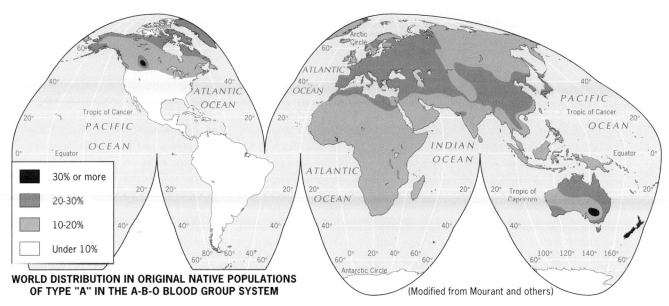

WORLD DISTRIBUTION IN ORIGINAL NATIVE POPULATIONS OF TYPE "A" IN THE A-B-O BLOOD GROUP SYSTEM

(Modified from Mourant and others)

FIGURE 16–3 After Hoebel (1972), Mourant (1969) and others.

PERSISTING HUMAN REALMS

At the beginning of this chapter, it was predicated that all people are members of one race—the human race. In Chapter 4 we learned that the "Eve Theory" postulates that we are all Africans, descended from a common ancestor who emerged, most likely in East Africa, perhaps more than 200,00 years ago. *Homo sapiens* rapidly dispersed into (and beyond) Eurasia, according to this theory, overcoming hominid predecessors and establishing hegemony from Finland to Tierra del Fuego.

The Eve Theory leaves no doubt regarding humanity's common ground, but it fails to answer an obvious question: How did humanity come to be divided by inherited biological characteristics revealed by different, even contrasting phenotypes? As much as we would like it to be otherwise, the reality is that humanity is fragmented into regionally expressed groups, for which the wrongly applied term *race* has unfortunately come into use.

Because of the pejorative associations of the term, and because many social scientists dismiss the concept altogether, the question concerning the causes of our re-

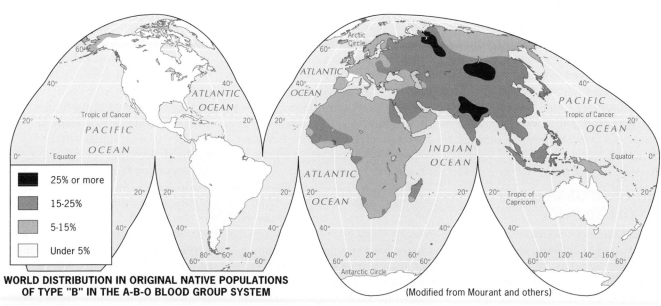

WORLD DISTRIBUTION IN ORIGINAL NATIVE POPULATIONS OF TYPE "B" IN THE A-B-O BLOOD GROUP SYSTEM

(Modified from Mourant and others)

FIGURE 16–4 After Hoebel (1972), Mourant (1969) and others.

gionally different phenotypes has received less attention than perhaps it should have. The United Nations even grappled with the terminology, substituting "ethnic group" for race in its official statements, but this was merely a substitute, not a solution. In some ways, the problem is akin to geographers' efforts to define geographic realms and regions; we know they exist, but defining them with general acceptability is sometimes difficult and often contentious. But remember what was said about the region: it extends as far as the arbitrary criteria on which it is based extends. So it is with the realms of human population: there is nothing absolute about them. One could use any criterion or set of criteria (height, blood type, eye color) and, on such bases, distinguish 3, or 9, or 30, or some other number of human population groups.

Is it possible to generalize about humanity's realms? The common thread lies in the biological basis for any and all spatial groupings we identify, whether the group is as small as the San of Southern Africa or as large as the Caucasians of Eurasia. In this context, regional populations are expressions of varying gene frequencies, not cultural groups. Humans can learn and acquire any of the countless cultures that have emerged over time; there is no barrier, in intelligence or otherwise, to such transculturation. Indeed, by some measures the globalization of culture is well ahead of the gene flow that would erase our biological differences.

MULTIREGIONAL EVOLUTION?

While the Out of Africa ("Eve") theory seems to confirm the essential unity of humanity, not all scholars are persuaded by the evidence (or the methodology by which that theory was formulated). Paleo-

anthropologists argue that the mitochondrial DNA studies (see Chapter 4) are unreliable, but that skulls, bones, and teeth provide incontrovertible evidence. The fossil remains do appear to contradict the Out of Africa theory, at the very least in terms of timing. If modern *H. sapiens* spread from Africa in just the past 200,000 years *and* suffered a major evolutionary setback about 70,000 years ago—resulting from climate change in the wake of the gigantic Toba eruption—how could so few replace so many ancestors in such widespread areas in so short a time? Furthermore, even if that process did take place, perhaps over a longer period than the DNA evidence suggests, why are our regional-racial differences so pronounced?

In the 1990s, the long-held theory that human phenotypes differ because human societies and cultures evolved regionally, and initially separately, was regaining ground. The debate has ebbed and flowed for many years; in the 1960s, a book by the anthropologist Carleton Coon, *The Origin of Races* (1962), set off a storm. Thirty years later, Milford Wolpoff and his colleagues were reformulating the idea that evolutionary patterns in Africa, western Eurasia (Europe), eastern Eurasia (China), and New Guinea-Australia show uninterrupted lineages lasting as long as two million years or more, leading directly to the present populations still concentrated in those realms. In the fossil record, they say, there is no evidence of a sudden replacement of local people by African *H. sapiens.*

How does this fit in with what is theorized about earlier Hominid emigrations from Africa? At the very least, it suggests that the timing of the earliest outmigrations from our common source area has been miscalculated. And now, evidence is forthcoming to complicate matters still more. In February 1994, scien-

tists reported that **_Homo erectus_** fossils from the Indonesian island of Java yielded dates of 1.8 million and 1.6 million years ago—long before the species was believed to have migrated from Africa. Those dates are as old as the oldest *H. erectus* dates from Africa. Does this mean that *H. erectus* started walking away from Africa a million years earlier than has been thought? Does it mean that the African and Southeast Asian versions of *H. erectus* are two distinct species, evolving independently? Or might it mean that *Australopithecus, Homo's* forerunner, is the one who migrated out of Africa, giving rise to successors in both realms?

While the fossil evidence from Java was being debated, Russian scientist announced that they had tentatively dated *H. erectus* bones from a site at Dmanisi (north of the Caucasus between the Black and Caspian Seas) at 1.5 million years old. It is clear that the story of humanity will have to be rewritten.

Does all this mean that the Eve hypothesis is no longer tenable? Not yet, because the link between *H. erectus* and *H. sapiens* (African *or* Asian) remains unclear. Ultimately, the genetic evidence may provide the answer, and measurements of skulls and bones may go the way of the manual typewriter. But for the moment, the **multiregional evolution theory** has regained ground. Its implications are that the changing skull forms we see (with increasing brain capacity) and modifying skeletal features (lighter limbs, smaller teeth) all form part of an evolutionary sequence that happened in four world realms, yielding similar, but not identical, humans. In Europe, to answer an old question, intermediate forms such as Neanderthals and Cro-Magnons are *part* of the transition toward *H. sapiens*. Whatever the answer, the multiregional hypothesis implies that there are four concentrations of human stock,

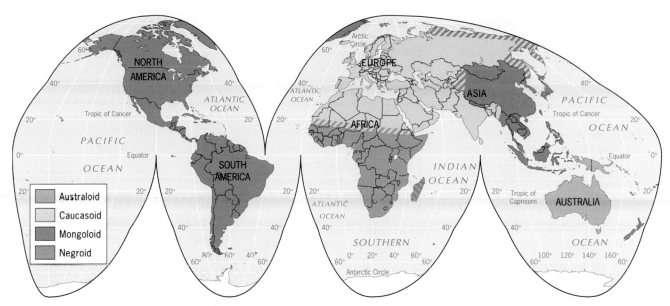

FIGURE 16–5 The source areas of the world's four main human stocks based on the multiregional evolutionary hypothesis. From author's sketch.

each with ancient evolutionary roots:

1. The *Negroid* Stock
2. The *Australoid* Stock
3. The *Mongoloid* Stock
4. The *Caucasoid* Stock

As Figure 16-5 shows, these human stocks could not have lived in total isolation, and there must have been gene flow among them for a very long time. The map also reminds us that the Americas were entered from northeast Asia from Mongoloid stock. The Pacific, too, was initially peopled from East Asia, but as in the Americas, the migrant populations developed distinct phenotypes over time.

Some geographers suggest that the Australoid stock may not rank with the other three in terms of age or origins. There is no record of aboriginal ancestry beyond about 60,000 years ago, the estimated time they first entered northern Australia. If the fossils found in Java are ancestral to a Mongoloid stock that spread northward into East Asia, then another lineage may be

needed to explain the presence of the Australoid population. The search for evidence, we should note, has concentrated on Indonesia, not New Guinea, where other fossils may await discovery.

GEOGRAPHIC EXPRESSIONS

Despite millennia of movement and contact, human subspecies continue to cluster in geographic realms such as Africa south of the Sahara, South Asia, or Middle America. Within each of the four human stocks enumerated above, there are smaller populations marked by particular gene frequencies and phenotypes.

In the past, anthropologists referred to these populations as **geographical races**. Their classifications distinguished, for example, between East Asians of Mongoloid stock and Native Americans also (originally) of Mongoloid stock. The anthropologist Stanley Garn, in his book *The Human Races* (1971), proposed a framework of nine such populations based on phenotypes. Note that both Carleton Coon and Stanley Garn still used the term *race*

freely to mean something other than its biological definition; both were severely criticized for doing so.

Garn and others argued that, while it may be possible to recognize fewer human stocks and more individual populations, there are nine "geographical races" on a global scale. These are identified as follows.

1. **African**
   The population of Africa south of the Sahara and, by late migrations, also of North, Middle, and eastern South America. Although dark skin is commonly associated with this population, there is much variation in this phenotype. This applies also to the very curly head and body hair. Africans display a considerable range in stature, but many are relatively tall and long-limbed.

2. **Asian (Mongoloid)**
   Occupies Eastern and Southeastern Asia, and also occurs in Madagascar. Numerically the largest geographic population today. One frequent common trait is the epicanthic or inner-

eye fold. Stature tends to be short and skin color dark, with mainly brown eyes, but regional variations abound, from comparatively tall Tibetans to relatively light-skinned Mongolians.

3. **European (Caucasian)**
Today the most widely dispersed population on the planet. Europeans, North Africans (Moroccans, Egyptians), Southwest Asians (Turks, Iranians) all form part of this geographic population. Skin color ranges from very light to quite dark. Hair is thin and tends to turn gray with age, noses tend to be high-bridged, and body hair is substantial.

4. **Indian**
Occupies the realm extending from Pakistan to Bangladesh and south to Sri Lanka. Long confined to this well-defined realm. Notable similarities exist between European and Indian phenotypes; while Indian skins tend to be darker, the face, high-bridged nose, head hair, and patterns of graying and balding all resemble European features, suggesting a mutual Caucasoid origin.

5. **Native American**
Prevails today in only a few, comparatively small regions of the Americas, where once they were the sole inhabitants. Connection to northeast Asian population suspected but not yet proven. Lengthy isolation after comparatively late arrival in the Americas. Epicanthic fold occurs commonly, especially in women. Eye color tends to be dark, head hair coarse and straight, body hair sparse. Stature varies but is frequently stocky. Skin color is medium.

6. **Australian**
Arrived in Australia about 50,000 years ago but numbered perhaps 300,000 when the Europeans reached the landmass. Skin color

is characteristically dark. Hair is sometimes reddish, even blond among children. Lower as well as upper jaw protrusion is common, and brow ridges are often pronounced, so that eyes appear to be deep-seated. Teeth often are unusually large, a characteristic feature.

7. **Papuan (Melanesian)**
Inhabits the island of New Guinea and smaller islands to the east. Among the world's most dark-skinned populations. Hair is long and woolly, stature comparatively tall. Other features resemble those of the Australian population; research is yet to prove the historic linkage the map suggests.

8. **Micronesian**
Perhaps the most poorly justified of Garn's geographical populations. Believed to have arisen from mixture of East Asian and Melanesian stocks. Skins are dark, eyes are dominantly brown, hair is mainly black and frizzy. Stature resembles that of Melanesians.

9. **Polynesian**
Inhabits the islands of the Pacific from Hawaii to New Zealand and from Fiji in the west to Easter Island in the east. Probably the most recent arrivals in their current realm. Known for excellent physique, strong and relatively tall body build, medium-colored skin, and dark hair and eyes.

These nine geographical populations were defined on the basis of phenotypes, blood chemistry, dental analysis, and spatial proximity. But of course this regionalization does not account for smaller, local subspecies embedded within these regional majorities. Further analysis may modify this scheme in other ways: the Australian, Papuan, and Micronesian populations may well

be a single population, and there may not be sufficient genetic evidence to separate Polynesians and Micronesians from the Asian stock. In that case, the number of subspecies may lie somewhere between the four of the multiregional hypothesis and the nine of Garn and his followers.

GROUP, CULTURE, AND STATUS

In 1994, the appearance of a series of books in the United States focused renewed attention on an old and tendentious question: the relationships between race (as used to identify human populations such as those just enumerated, as well as smaller groups), capacity, and intelligence. To what extent do the genes that encode physical attributes, such as those described above, also transmit these unseen traits?

This is a key question because it goes to the core of culture and the way it is perpetuated and evolves. Anthropologists long argued that culture is learned; that is, it is acquired through nurture. But sociobiologists made a case for the notion that at least part of the transmission of culture takes place genetically. This would mean that certain traits marking particular cultures have become instinctive. By extension, it would suggest that some of these traits would therefore be difficult to learn for people who are not part of those cultures. In *The Bell Curve: Intelligence and Class Structure in American Life* (1994), R. J. Herrnstein and C. Murray argue that what they call "cognitive ability" (that is, intelligence) is not only declining in American society as a whole, but that its distribution is becoming such that society will eventually be divided into a small caste of ruling intelligentsia and a much larger, incapable and powerless underclass. The widening gap, they suggest, is directly attributable to innate ability, which is concentrated and perpetuated more strongly in certain sectors of the population than in others. In a multicultural society such as the United States, this spells trouble for the future, because intelligence—which in the authors' view can be quantitatively measured—will vary by population group. It will mean, they say, that the powerful intelligentsia will be drawn almost exclusively from one or two groups, and not from others.

The proof of this assertion, Herrnstein and Murray report, lies in the results of the intelligence tests (tests of Intelligence Quotient, or IQ) taken by thousands of people over a period of half a century. Of all population groups tested, Ashkenazi Jews of European origin test higher than any other group; in the United States, Asians score highest, followed closely by whites. A larger gap separates whites from African Americans. These relative positions have not changed, although the combined test scores have gone slightly up (and now down) over the years. The authors interpret the results as meaning that intelligence is powerfully affected by the genes of one's ancestors.

The assertion that race (meaning population group) and intelligence can be correlated is nothing new. Even a century ago, the advance of European societies over African cultures was interpreted through studies of skull shapes and cranial (brain) capacities. None of this proved anything of the sort, of course, but then came the intelligence testing that led to IQ examinations. For a long time, the cultural biases of the test instruments made many of the data suspect, and not until comparatively recently were tests improved to counter this distortion. It also is

clear that IQ scores improve when those tested experience an improved learning environment, indicating that nurture *is* a factor in the flowering of individual intelligence.

What was missing from the ensuing debate was the geographic perspective. Earlier, we encountered the notion of environmental determinism, whose proponents argued that the natural environment, chiefly climate, controls human capacities and predetermines their fate in this world. But environments change, and peoples (carrying their cultural baggage) migrate. While it is true that the current world map puts the most advanced technological cultures in the realm dominated by the European (Caucasian) population group, and that culture of technology may well be perpetuated, in part, by heredity, the pendulum has swung in other directions in the past. Civilizations in Asia and Africa had developed sophisticated cultures long before most European societies had managed to rise above simple tribal organization. For thousands of years, the greatest achievements in administration, legislation, education, agriculture, construction, writing, and other fields were made in China, in Southwest Asia, and in North Africa—not in Europe. People of those civilizations would have looked upon European societies much as some whites now look upon others.

If we happen to live at a time when Europeans are at the summit of modern technological culture, there are indications that change already is in the offing. The very IQ results that put Asians at the top may be an indication of this change, but the map provides more powerful evidence. Developments in East Asia are not limited to industrial production and general modernization. Innovation and invention are part of it. Whatever

makes the pendulum swing, the time for East Asia may be arriving. And the time for South Asia and Subsaharan Africa will come again.

ADVANTAGE AND OPPORTUNITY

Physical attributes can have a significant effect on people's status *within* societies as well. When the United States became embroiled in Haiti's affairs during the 1990s, American observers described how the small population of privileged in that poorest of Western Hemisphere countries happened to be the five percent of generally lighter complexion—a mulatto minority in a black society. This minority, descended from the French colonists and their African spouses, retained the advantage they had two centuries ago. It had nothing to do with greater ability or capacity. It was a matter of historic privilege, defended, sometimes bloodily, over the years.

This is not an isolated instance. In India, lighter-skinned families have for centuries enjoyed advantage and privilege. Here, this dates from the Moghul (Mongol) invasions and from Caucasoid penetrations of Indian society, combined with the hierarchical system of social caste in traditional Hindu society. At the opposite end of the social ladder, the lowest castes are populated by those with the darkest skins.

No matter where one goes in this world, physical appearance, notably skin color, remains a critical factor in people's relationships and in the advantages and opportunities (or lack thereof) they have. If the elites do better in IQ tests than the disadvantaged, better learning environments undoubtedly contribute; it will take longer than a few hundred years for heredity to come into play.

Undoubtedly, the uniform of color we all wear is the first and most pervasive attribute in the first perception others have of us. How many millions of conflicts, individual and collective, small and large, have begun because of this attribute? The "racial" stereotype remains a huge obstacle to the true, voluntary integration of societies.

But it is not the only one. Just as certainly, the next attribute to make its mark is a person's sex. In many (perhaps nearly all) societies, females do not have the same opportunities, responsibilities, incomes, comforts, or influence over personal affairs as males do. There are cultures in which being born female means moving through life in a corridor of society so unlike that of males that much of that society would be unrecognizable to the woman if she were to break out of her confining role. Before we focus on the geography of culture, therefore, we turn first to the geography of gender.

KEY TERMS

Bergmann's Rule	Genotype
Blood Groups	Geographical Race
Epicanthic Fold	*Homo erectus*
Gene	*Homo sapiens*
Gene Flow	Multiregional Evolution Theory
Gene Pool	Mutation
Genetic Drift	Natural Selection
Genetics	Phenotype

17

A GEOGRAPHY
OF GENDER

Ours is a world of racial diversity, cultural variety, and economic disparity. We view these variations spatially, and study ethnic homelands, culture hearths, and regional economic contrasts. In doing so, we must generalize, as we learned when the delimitation of regions was discussed. We often remind ourselves that ethnic homelands contain minorities and that developed regions contain pockets of underdevelopment. There is, however, another kind of inequality of which we remind ourselves less frequently: the inequality of the sexes, of **gender**. The purpose of this chapter is to raise our awareness of the variability of gender relationships across the human world.

When topics such as population growth or migration or food production arise in human geography, these tend to be discussed in the aggregate. When a country's high population growth rate is cited as a threat to its future stability or its development potential, we may not put the data in the current social context: what of the women in that society who bear the children and raise them, who are confined, probably for life, to a village, as their

Geographica

- Demographic statistics for individual countries (or divisions within countries) tend to conceal gender gaps, differences between females and males ranging from life expectancies to literacy rates.

- In all but six countries of the world (five of these in South Asia), women outlive men for periods ranging from less than one year to ten years or more; in this context, the gender gap is widest in the richer countries and smallest in the poorer.

- Female infanticide and the abortion of female fetuses are practices occurring widely in India, China, and other countries where tradition and economics combine to threaten girls and women; population-control policies have contributed to this human disaster of massive proportions.

- Work performed by women as unpaid labor in households and on the land would, if measured in monetary value, increase the world's total paid production by about one-third; in the poorer countries women produce more than half the food, transport water and firewood, build dwellings, and perform numerous other tasks.

mothers and grandmothers were? Their husbands and brothers suffer no such constraints; their way to the beckoning city lies open. The men and women born and raised in that village live, in reality, in different worlds.

So it is with migration. We read the total numbers: a half-million Ethiopians dislocated by war, a million Soviet Jews leaving their homes for Israel or the United States. Behind those numbers lie vastly different, gender-related experi-

199

ences. In the African refugee camps, the women and female children always are the worst off in the struggle for survival. In voluntary migrations, males tend to dominate the decision-making process and, in their new destinations, quickly widen their activity spaces and social networks. Females find themselves in a very different situation, especially if there are young children in the migrating family. Again, the man's and the woman's perspectives on the experience differ strongly. "It's a man's world," goes the old saying, and male dominance remains the rule rather than the exception in the world today.

Modernization and economic development, to be sure, reduce inequalities between men and women. But even in Western Europe and in the United States, equality has not been achieved. There still are wage differentials, that is, women and men are not always paid the same amount for the same work. In corporate, political, and many other settings, maps of inequality can still be drawn. In a recent study, geographers Susan Hanson and Geraldine Pratt found that men surveyed in Worcester, Massachusetts, had an average wage per hour (1987) of $15.45, compared to $9.34 per hour for women. Women took jobs closer to their homes than men, and they worked hours that made it easier for them to handle their domestic burdens, mainly the care of children. This put the women at a disadvantage when it came to advancement in their jobs. Asked whether convenience to the man's job location is more important than a household's proximity to the woman's job, more than twice as many people asked—men *and* women—said that they would move nearer the man's job rather than nearer the woman's job. From such data, Professors Hanson and Pratt derived a pattern of occupational segregation that results when

women take lower-paying jobs, in more restricted locations, with less hope of advancement. Patterns of this kind may not be as obvious in the cultural landscape as those of racial segregation or ethnic concentration, but they prove the continuing existence of gender inequality, even in our modern society.

Nevertheless, women in Western (and other modernizing) societies have made enormous progress during the twentieth century, progress that stands in stark contrast against their sometimes deteriorating position in traditional societies. Proof that wealth and economic prosperity do not automatically improve the rights and opportunities of women came vividly from Saudi Arabia in 1990. In this oil-rich, high-income country, women are not, by law, permitted to drive automobiles. During the commotion created by the Gulf War, foreign troops, including vehicle-driving female soldiers, entered Saudi Arabia. Perhaps emboldened by their presence, several dozen Saudi women, many educated abroad, got into their families' cars and drove through the streets in defiance of the law. But their campaign was short-lived: they were arrested, and the ban on driving by women in Saudi Arabia was reaffirmed. At the threshold of the twenty-first century in a major country with many international connections, this is an almost unimaginable discrimination, but it reveals in a meaningful way a host of other restrictions that afflict the status of women in one geographic realm of the world.

In this chapter, we assess the circumstances under which women live and work in five geographic contexts: demography and health; family and social conditions; education and opportunity; economy and productivity; and politics and public life. At times we will depend on anecdotal and subjective information, because data on the conditions,

roles, and contributions of women often are inadequate or incomplete. This in itself is a reflection on gender inequality in the overwhelming majority of the world's cultures and countries.

DEMOGRAPHY AND HEALTH

In Chapter 7, we noted that population pyramids for certain countries show that women, notably in the higher age categories, outnumber men. On average, women today live about 4 years longer than men, but this differential varies spatially. In the developed countries, the **longevity gap** widened between 1950 and 1990 from 5 to 7 years. The author Ruth Leger Sivard, in her book, *Women: A World Survey* (1985), noted that this widening gap resulted not only from medical and other advantages associated with socioeconomic progress; also, "women seem to have been less inclined to adopt some of the unhealthy habits often associated with affluence: cigaret smoking in particular, but also the excessive consumption of food and alcohol, fast driving (and high accident rates), high levels of stress." However, writes Dr. Sivard, the increased stresses on women trying to deal with the competing demands of the home and workplace, plus lifestyle changes associated with modern times, may in time erode the gender-longevity gap.

In the mid-1990s, women outlived men everywhere except in just six of the world's approximately 200 countries and territories (Fig. 17-1). In three of these six (India, Nepal, and Malawi), men and women have equal life expectancies. In the other three (Bangladesh, Bhutan, and the Maldives), men live one to three years longer. According to data from the United Nations, the Population Reference Bureau, and the World Bank, women live 3 years longer than men in Africa, 6 years longer in South America, and 8 years longer in Europe. Note that five of the six countries in which men live as long or longer than women are located in a single geographic realm, South Asia. Here life is especially difficult for women, and the closing of the longevity gap reflects this hardship.

In virtually all cultures, men tend to marry women who are younger, so that married women can expect to outlive their husbands, sometimes by as much as ten years. This seems to favor women in this man's world, until we note that widowed women often face a life of inadequate support. Hundreds of millions of women who have spent lifetimes sustaining families die alone, in poverty, without sufficient support from a deceased husband's residual pension, from the state, from children, or from savings.

QUALITY OF LIFE

Life-expectancy figures say nothing about the quality of life. During their lifetimes, women's health problems and concerns differ from those of men. Pregnancy and childbirth, especially in the poorer realms of the world, confront women with high health risks. According to the United Nations study entitled *The World's Women 1970–1990*, published in 1991, women who become pregnant in the poorer, underdeveloped realms of the world face a risk due to pregnancy that is 80 to 600 times higher than that faced by women in the developed, richer countries. In this respect, South Asian women suffer the highest **maternal mortality rate**, with approximately 650 maternal deaths per 100,000 births. The risk for African women is nearly as high. In the developed countries of the Western world, these deaths may number as few as 5 per 100,000. Inadequate medical services, an excessive number of pregnancies, and malnutrition are among the leading causes of maternal death in the world's poorer countries (Fig. 17-2). Add to this the fact that an estimated 250,000 women die each year from illegal abortions, and we are reminded that men face nothing comparable during the equivalent years of their lives.

In Chapter 13, we discussed nutritional patterns in the world, using average calorie consumption as the key measure. Again, such averages conceal gender differences: in underdeveloped realms of the world, women are less well nourished than men, and female children are even worse off. The World Health Organization (WHO) reports indicate that anemia, a consequence of malnutrition, affects the majority of women in these regions, as well as two-thirds of all pregnant women in Africa and South and Southwest Asia. During their reproductive years, women need nearly three times as much iron in their daily diets as men. But in many traditional societies, it is customary for the men to eat first and eat most of the available food, leaving what remains (often the less nutritious food) to the women and children. Mothers, as a matter of custom, favor boys over girls when their turn for eating comes, so that the girls are at a double disadvantage.

Under all these circumstances, it is all the more remarkable that womens' life expectancies—even in the underdeveloped world—exceed those of men, a situation that results, in the words of Dr. Sivard, from their being genetically programmed to have lower mortality than men, thus from being intrinsically stronger. But as we have noted, the differential is not uniform and is affected by spatial variations in the cultural-economic environment under which women work and give birth.

FEMALE INFANTICIDE

Women may live longer than men, and in the upper age categories women may outnumber men, but in early life it is another story. In October 1990, UNICEF published a disturbing report entitled *The Lesser Child: The Girl in India*. It revealed that 300,000 more girls than boys die in India each year, and many more are never born—aborted after gender-detection tests.

As a result, the ratio of women to men in India continues to widen in favor of men. During the twentieth century, the gap has grown from over 970 women per thousand men to under 930. In Haryana, the State that surrounds the capital of New Delhi, the figure in 1992 was 873 females for every 1000 males, a disproportion so extreme that it has been known to occur only in societies where war had ravaged the population. In 1994, the United Nations reported that India as a whole had 133 single men for every 100 single women.

Many thousands of female infants, the 1990 UNICEF report indicated, continue to be killed. It is done by feeding them poisonous oleander berries, by smothering them immediately after birth, by denying them food, and by other "traditional" means. But modern techniques of prenatal gender detection—ultrasound and amniocentesis—contributed far more to the imbalance now seen in India. Women's groups in several of India's States began to agitate for a federal law that would outlaw such tests, but in India it is difficult to counter virtually anything that contributes to population control. Still, the Indian Parliament in July 1994 passed a law prohibiting prenatal tests solely to determine the sex of a fetus. But a provision in the law punishes women for taking the test—when such tests are most commonly forced on women by male heads of families who want male heirs. Fathers want to see the

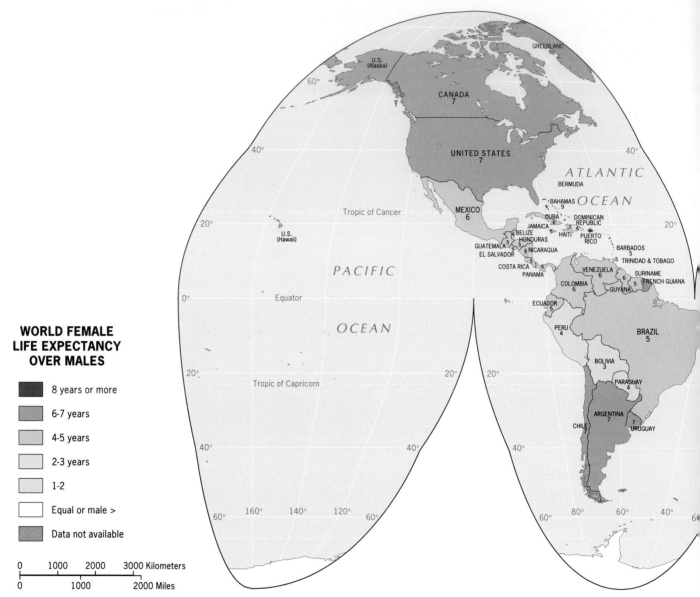

WORLD FEMALE LIFE EXPECTANCY OVER MALES

- 8 years or more
- 6-7 years
- 4-5 years
- 2-3 years
- 1-2
- Equal or male >
- Data not available

FIGURE 17–1 Female life expectancy over male (years).

family lineage preserved through males; the oldest son (there must be one) in Hindu society lights the funeral pyre of the father. And the supposedly outlawed, but widely practiced, tradition of dowry, by which families with sons receive payments from the brides' parents, makes male offspring valuable commodities in the marriage business, but daughters liabilities.

Under such social conditions, will a law against prenatal testing work? Earlier, when the debate on the issue gained momentum, three

States (Maharashtra, Rajasthan, and Haryana) imposed a testing ban in advance of the federal law. Its effect was minimal; the clinics went underground, and since the required equipment can be moved easily, a thriving black market developed. What is needed, research indicated, is change in cultural traditions regarding the status of women in Indian society. Laws against infanticide and dowry payments already are on the books. If those laws are enforced (as is rarely the case), the result will exceed anything a law

against prenatal testing can achieve. Indeed, the ban may have the unintended effect of increasing the level of **female infanticide**: fathers who must wait for the birth to know the gender of their offspring may be tempted to do what an abortion could not.

Although the situation in India is dreadful, India is not alone in its traditional preference for male offspring. When China implemented its one-child-only policy (see Chapter 7), the one child the overwhelming number of couples

wanted was a male. While the policy brought the overall population growth rate down in short order, it also imbalanced the female-male ratio to an even greater extent than was already the case. In 1995, the Chinese government published figures indicating that, while the great majority of Chinese are married by age 30, nearly 10 million people in their thirties still remained single—and in this age group, men outnumbered women by more than 10 to 1. The number of abortions following gender-detection tests (which are

legal in China) skyrocketed. And again, millions of Chinese babies and infants do not survive because of food deprivation, denial of medical care, abandonment, and murder. Now, China's unbalanced population pyramid is exacting its revenge on society. The number of males unable to find wives will double, even triple, during the first decade of the twenty-first century. Chinese scholars warn that this may lead to social disorders ranging from increased prostitution to higher suicide rates among males, as well

as other problems that could have a major impact on Chinese society in the next century.

There *is* a spatial-economic difference between the developing problems in India and China. In India, female infanticide appears to be most prevalent among the poorest sectors of society, notably in remote rural areas (although it is by no means absent elsewhere). In China, female infanticide has long occurred in poor and remote areas, but the one-child policy was most effectively policed in the urban and

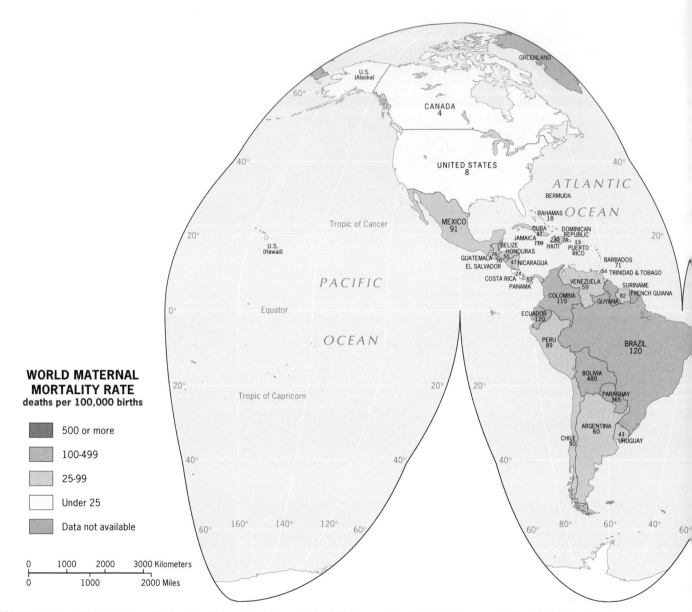

FIGURE 17–2   World Maternal Mortality Rate. Data from United Nations, *The World's Women 1970–1990* (New York, 1991), p. 67.

near-urban areas. This led to a substantial increase in female infanticide in China's more developed areas, where the scarcity of female marriage partners has now become acute.

Will the lot of women in such countries as India, China, South Korea (where male births exceed female births by nearly 15 percent), and elsewhere improve as lopsided population pyramids reflect the growing need for women? Governments would have to be persuaded to offer incentives such as educational opportunities and tax relief to couples who have girls. Governments would also have to enforce laws against cultural traditions that sustain societal biases against girls and women. But governments are dominated by men, and habits work against such interventions.

As we have noted repeatedly in this book, family planning is an important component of material progress. But without legal constraints and balanced incentives, its impact on women can be devastating.

FAMILY AND SOCIAL CONDITIONS

As noted previously, data on life expectancy and maternal mortality tell us nothing about the quality of

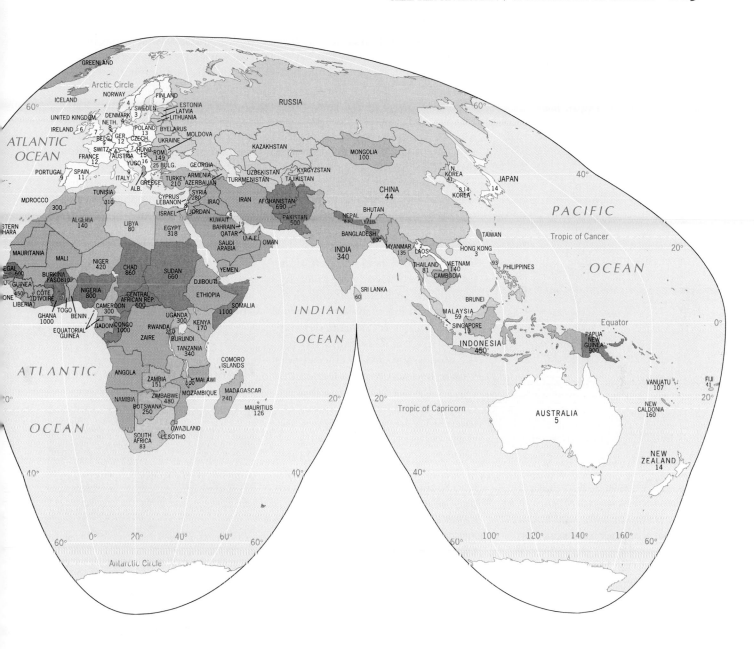

life of women. We can discern some aspects of this issue from more detailed statistics, for example, from child mortality figures that indicate a higher mortality for girls aged 2 to 5 years than for boys (Table 17-1). Note that the rate for Pakistani boys during the late 1980s was less than 37 per thousand, but for girls, over 54. In Haiti, the rate stood below 48 for boys, but over 61 for girls. In Bangladesh, the **gender gap** was nearly 11. Such discrepancies reflect a dreadful contrast in treatment of girls and boys,

a discrimination that, even if the girls survive these early years, puts females at a lifelong physical and emotional disadvantage. As the table shows, this pattern is not confined to South Asia or the Caribbean region. It occurs in East and Southeast Asia, and in South America as well.

The infant mortality data reflect the lower status of girls and women in many societies. As the United Nations report on women (1991) states: "Although girls contribute much to the family—in Africa and

Asia they often work seven or more hours a day—many societies consider them a burden. They are discriminated against as children and married off early. In addition, some societies expect women to start having children at a very young age . . . in Mauritania, 39 percent of girls are married by age 15 and fifteen percent have given birth. In Bangladesh, 73 percent of girls are married by age 15, and 21 percent have had at least one child."

Other information about wom-

TABLE 17–1	Mortality Rates Among Girls and Boys Aged 2 to 5 for Selected Countries

	Deaths per 1000	
Country	**Girls**	**Boys**
Pakistan	54.4	36.9
Bangladesh	68.6	57.7
Haiti	61.2	47.8
Thailand	26.8	17.3
Colombia	24.8	20.5
Costa Rica	8.1	4.8
Philippines	21.9	19.1
Turkey	19.5	18.4
South Korea	12.7	11.8
Venezuela	8.4	7.6

Source: United Nations, *The World's Women 1970–1990,* New York, 1991, p. 60.

en's lives in traditional societies can be found in various sources, ranging from death certificates to hospital records, and from local studies to newspaper reports. We know comparatively little about this, because much of what happens in rural areas is simply not known. Geographers Bonnie S. Lloyd, Janice J. Monk, and Arlene C. Rengert, in an essay entitled *Landscapes of the Home* (1982), point out that men are traditionally associated with the outdoors. The cultural landscape, they argue, is essentially a male-created and -dominated landscape. The indoor home is the female space, which is, by implication, less studied and less well known. So our knowledge of the quality of life of women in rural as well as urban settings is fragmentary.

What we do know is often dismaying. Domestic violence, of which women, being generally less physically strong, are overwhelmingly the victims, is a global, cross-cultural phenomenon. It happens among the rich as well as the poor and in modern as well as traditional societies. When surveys are conducted, the results indicate an astonishingly high incidence of such violence. A recent U.N. study investigated 1500 divorce cases in Austria: violence against the wife was cited in nearly 60 percent of these cases. In another study from Thailand, more than 50 percent of women from a Bangkok slum area reported regular beatings by their husbands. A study from Brazil reported two dozen unpunished domestic murders in one state alone: the murdered wives were killed by "justifiably" jealous husbands.

Scattered information of this kind does not allow us to make dependable maps, but it does underscore the contrasting circumstances under which men and women live. In India, where Hinduism prescribes a reverence for life, girls still are forced into arranged marriages. Disputes between families over the bride price to be paid by the bride's family to the groom's father often lead to the death of the bride, who may be punished fatally for her father's failure to fulfill the marriage agreement. In modern times, such **"dowry deaths"** should not occur at all, or at least should be declining sharply. But official figures indicate otherwise: in 1985, the number was 999, in 1987, 1786 women in India died at the hands of vengeful husbands or in-laws, and in 1989, the latest year for which data are available, 2436 perished. And these figures report only confirmed dowry deaths; many more are believed to occur but are reported as kitchen accidents or other fatal domestic incidents.

Indian governments (federal as well as State) have set up legal aid offices to help those women who seek assistance, and in 1984 the Family Courts Act was passed in New Delhi, creating a network of "family courts" to hear domestic cases, including dowry disputes. But the judges tend to be older males, and their chief objective, women's support groups allege, is to hold the family together, that is, to force the threatened or battered woman back into the family fold. Hindu culture attaches great importance to the family structure, and the family courts tend to operate on this principle.

India is a multicultural country, and powerful communities sometimes seek to institute their own laws in place of those promulgated in New Delhi. With the resurgence of Muslim fundamentalism came a controversy over the rights of divorced Muslim women in India. The (national) Indian Civil Code

From the Field Notes

❝She and her daughter came walking along the path to the village near Kanye, Botswana, carrying huge, burlap-wrapped bundles on their heads. I had seen them go earlier to fetch pails of water; in the early afternoon they were working in the field, weeding the maize (corn). Later I saw them with batches of firewood that must have weighed 60 pounds or more. In the evening, they would cook the meal. From the village I could hear men arguing, laughing.❞

gives some rights and protections to women who have succeeded in obtaining a legal divorce, including child support. Representatives of the Muslim communities in India argued that this contravenes Islamic law, and they proposed a separate Muslim Woman's Bill that would deny maintenance to divorced Muslim women in India. This discriminatory legislation was sought in order to deny Muslim women even the limited rights they could secure under the Indian Civil Code.

Indeed, the circumstances of women in the great majority of Muslim societies are even more restrictive than in India, where legal help and aggressive women's movements have given support as well as visibility to the women's plight. Our story about those Saudi women who were arrested upon driving the family car is but a sidelight to a far more serious situation: many women in Muslim society live a medieval existence of isolation and servitude. It is a situation many modern Muslim political and social leaders deplore, and there are Muslim women who have succeeded in breaking their societal handcuffs, and who have become doctors, lawyers, and other professionals. But Islamic laws and rules restrict even their lives; they may wear modern, even Western dress in the privacy of their homes and compounds, but in public they must appear cloaked and veiled.

The resurgence of Islamic fundamentalism, and the accompanying reappearance of the severe *Sharia* laws, have an especially strong impact on women in Muslim society. When the last Shah of Iran sought to modernize his country, he gave women unprecedented freedoms, including the right to wear, in public, clothes of their choice. This was one of the Shah's actions that galvanized fundamentalist opposition to his (in other ways ruthless) rule. After his downfall and the assumption of power by the late Ayatollah Kho-

meini, women were ordered to resume wearing the long cloaks of traditional Islamic society, as well as veils over their faces. Muslim men policed the streets to enforce this order, and many women were arrested; some, it is alleged, were even executed for flouting the fundamentalist dress code. Again, the rules were made by men and imposed by men. To a house-confined, village-based, traditional-bound woman, the Islamic realm looks very different than it does to a traveling, politicking, coffee-house-plying man.

As we will note later in this chapter, the circumstances under which African women live vary widely. In parts of West Africa, women control markets and commerce, and have a powerful position in society. But in most of the realm, men live more freely (and often comfortably), eat better, do lighter work, and do less to support the children. As we noted previously, gender inequality around the world differs only in degree, not in kind.

EDUCATION AND OPPORTUNITY

Education is the beacon of opportunity, the chance to escape from poverty and stagnation, to improve one's circumstances, and to fulfill one's potential. Where educational levels are higher, women's circumstances are better. It is no accident that most of what has been said about India does not apply to the southern Indian state of Kerala, where women are better educated than elsewhere. In Kerala, the gender gap actually favors women; women's health is better and women have fewer children. Education is the key.

To us in North America, it is normal for all girls and boys to attend school; in fact, it is the law. Imagine

a situation in which, at age five or six, the boys go off to elementary school but the girls stay home, doing chores—it is simply inconceivable! But in much of the less-developed world, this is exactly what happened. Women's education was a lower priority, and women's access to education was inferior to men's. That produced an educational gap that still exists today. In India, for example, the overall adult literacy rate is estimated to be 55 percent. But the United Nations and UNICEF estimate that between 65 and 75 percent of all Indian women are illiterate. It is a legacy of the gender gap in educational opportunity.

And yet, the situation is improving. Long-term data for education are available, and they prove that worldwide, the educational gender gap is narrowing, that girls now go to school, at least at the elementary-school level, where previously they did not (or did in far smaller numbers), and that a growing number of women reach levels of higher education. Experts predict that it will take several generations for the legacy of educational discrepancy to disappear, but progress is being made.

This progress, however, varies spatially. In the mid-1990s, there still were nearly 600 million illiterate females and more than 350 million illiterate males (the great majority of them adults) in the world. Girls are going to school in the same numbers as boys in many countries now, not only in Europe, North America, and developed East Asia, but also in Middle and South America. But progress lags in South Asia and in Africa south of the Sahara. Also, sharp contrasts remain between rural and urban areas. United Nations studies show that these may be strongest of all in Middle and South America, where 1 in 4 rural women aged 15 to 24 is illiterate, compared to only 1 in 20 in urban areas. (In black Africa, the

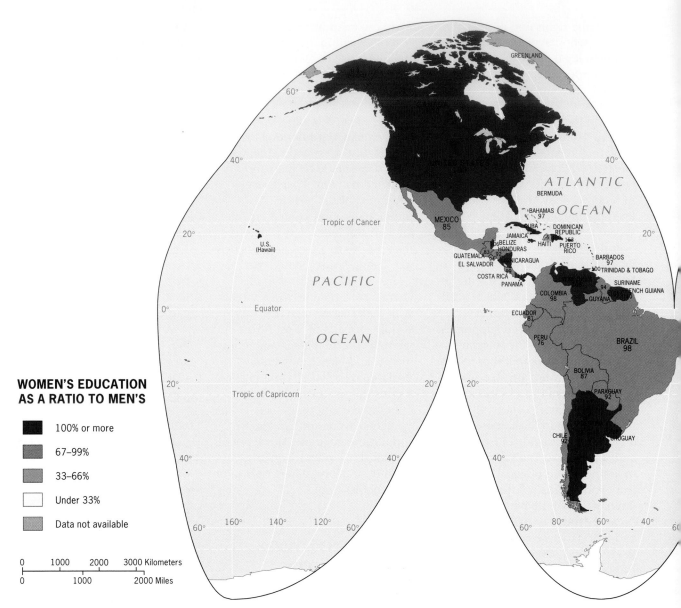

WOMEN'S EDUCATION AS A RATIO TO MEN'S

■ 100% or more

▨ 67–99%

▨ 33–66%

☐ Under 33%

▨ Data not available

FIGURE 17–3 This map represents the average of data for all three levels of education during 1985–1987. Data from United Nations, *The World's Women 1970–1990* (New York, 1991), p. 50. Later informal data suggest that the situation has been deteriorating since the late 1980s.

figures are more than 7 in 10 for rural areas and more than 4 in 10 for urban areas).

Every relevant study shows that although progress over the past four decades has been substantial, major obstacles remain. Women still are denied access to training in such practical fields as forestry, fishing, and agriculture; they still have difficulty breaking into male-

dominated professions. Some societies still will not allow women to teach boys (although the teaching profession is generally open to women). In the developed realms, women have become physicians, lawyers, and other professionals, although, as the Hanson-Pratt study showed, educated women in our literate society still face special job-related difficulties.

Figure 17-3 summarizes the global situation in a very general but revealing way. A similar map was made by Dr. Ruth Leger Sivard a decade ago in her study, *Women: A World Survey*: it was based on the question, "If male education equals 100, where does female education stand on a scale of 1 to 100?" Our map is based on the ratio of female to male enrollment at all three lev-

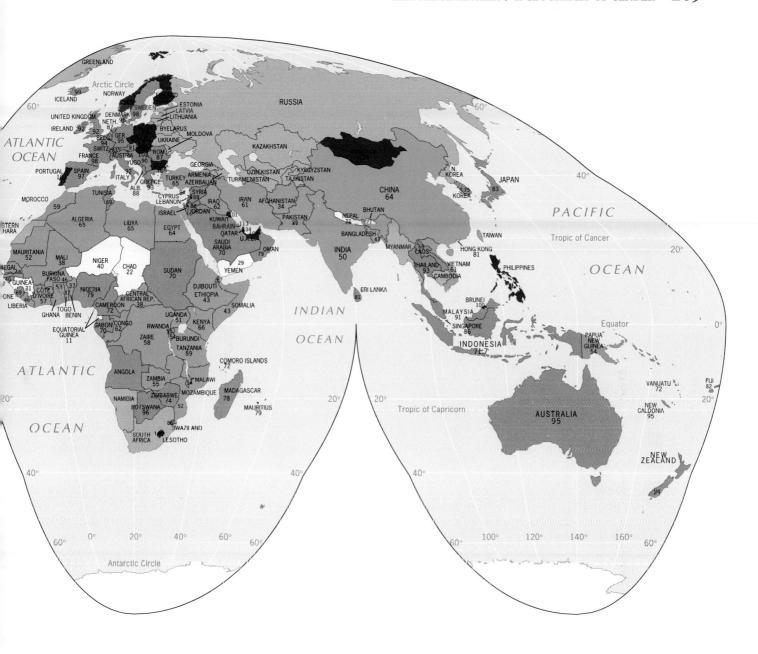

els of schooling and is thus a very general average for each country. Nevertheless, the spatial pattern tells us much about the regional status of **women's education**. Note that the gender gap is narrowing in Middle and South America, but remains very wide in tropical Africa and South Asia, as well as parts of Southwest Asia and North Africa. Rapid population growth, limited budgets, government priorities, and cultural impediments combine to cause the disparities shown in Figure 17-3.

When we read maps such as Figure 17-3, it is important to keep in mind the doubtful validity of data. United Nations and World Bank data, for example, vary widely in their reportage both of the current situation and the progress women have made in the education arena. Recent reports from Africa and Asia suggest that this progress has in fact been halted or even reversed. Especially in Africa, economic setbacks and armed conflicts have combined to erode education systems, and women's education suffers most under such conditions. While women's education has advanced in some Muslim countries, it has declined in others, notably where the power of fundamentalists has risen. Women are taking the brunt of events in Algeria, for example. Women's education also suffered in Iran following the revolution.

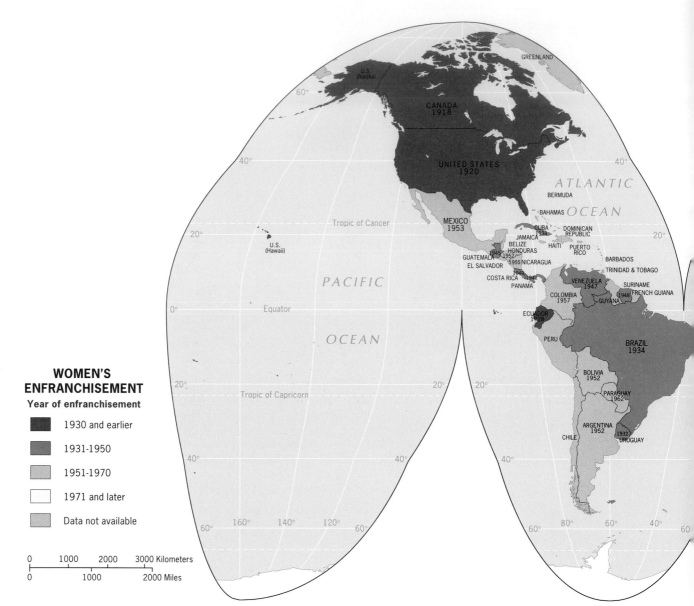

FIGURE 17–4   Based on data from United Nations, *The World's Women 1970–1990* (1991, p. 39) and from other sources including R.L. Sivard, *Women: A World Survey* (Washington, D.C.: World Priorities, 1985).

ECONOMY AND PRODUCTIVITY

If evidence of women's long-term progress and work in education is a matter of record, the opposite is true where their economic contributions are concerned. When economists calculate the total annual production of goods and services in a country, they do not include the unpaid labor of women in the household, nor, usually, the work done by rural women in the less developed realms of the world. Scholars estimate that if **women's productivity** in the household alone were given a dollar value (for example, by calculating what it would cost to hire people to perform these tasks), the world's total annual GNP (that is, the gross national product for all countries combined; see Part 11) would grow by about one-third. In the less developed world, women produce more than half of all the food; they also build homes, dig wells, plant and harvest crops, make clothes, and do many other things that are not recorded as economically productive.

Although the circumstances of rural women in the less developed areas are generally difficult if not desperate, the situation of African women today probably is the worst. Apart from those areas in West Af-

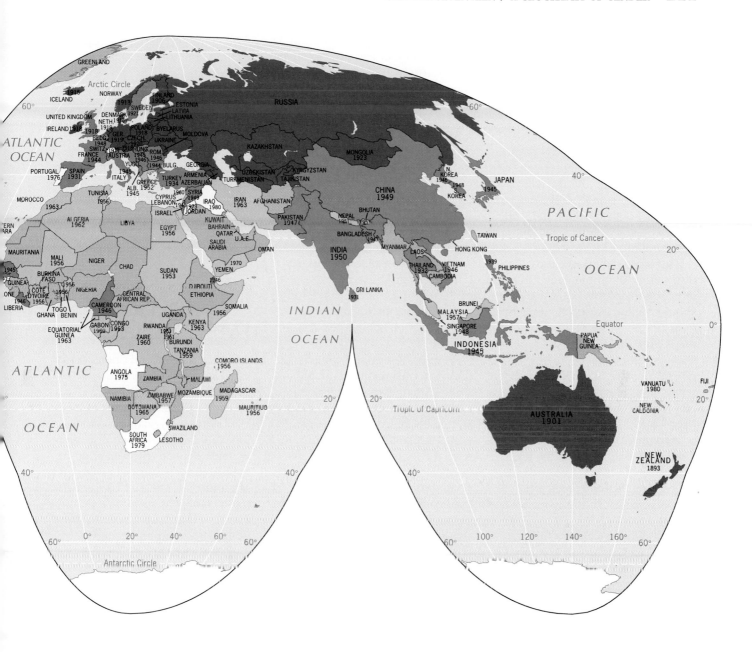

rica where women have come to dominate commerce, women in Africa south of the Sahara have few rights and daunting responsibilities. They produce an estimated 70 percent of the realm's food, almost all of it without any modern equipment. Their back-breaking hand-cultivation of corn and other staples is an endless task made worse by ecological deterioration. Water availability is declining, and the exhausting walk to the nearest pump gets longer. Firewood is be-

ing cut down in ever-larger circles from the village, and the task of hauling it home worsens every year. As the men leave for the attractions of faraway towns, perhaps to marry other wives and have other children, the villages strain for survival.

If the home-building, head-of-the-household woman goes to the bank for a loan, however, she is likely to be refused: banks in Africa generally do not lend money to rural women. Not having heard

from her husband for years and having reared her children, she might wish to apply for a title to the land she has occupied and farmed for decades, but land titles are usually not awarded to women. Only a small number of African women have the legal right to own property.

Meanwhile, girls in the village are inducted early into the cycle of female poverty and overwork that has trapped their mothers and previous generations. Money for school fees is often short; what is available first goes to pay for the boys. As soon as she can carry anything at all, the girl goes with her mother, to weed the fields, to bring back firewood, or to fetch water. She will do so an average of perhaps 12 hours a day, seven days a week, for the years she remains capable of working. But the national statistics, at the end of the year or at the end of her punishing life, will say nothing about her contribution to the country.

Therefore, when we study the distribution of farming and of crops in later parts of this book, we should remind ourselves of distributions not revealed by available maps. In East Africa, cash crops such as tea are called "men's crops," because the men trade in what the women produce. (In the commercial sector, too, women play a major role). But when the government of Kenya tried to stimulate the productivity of the tea plantations, it handed out bonuses—not to the women who did the harvesting, but to the men who own the land.

Although the quality of life for women may be lowest in rural Africa today, circumstances are not much better in many other regions. For women, village life in South Asia or Middle and South America has similar prospects. But their productivity also is prodigious: an estimated 40 percent of all the food consumed in Middle and South America is produced by women bent to the soil.

IN THE LABOR FORCE

Despite these conditions, the number of women in the "official" labor force is rising. The United Nations estimate of women in the labor force in 1990 was 828 million. All but one geographic realm showed increases between 1970 and 1990: in the developed realms, from 35 to 39 percent of the labor force; in Middle and South America, from 24 to 29 percent; in East and Southeast Asia, it rose very slightly to 40 and 35 percent, respectively. In black Africa, the percentage of women in the labor force actually declined, from 39 percent in 1970 to 37 percent in 1990. As the report, *The World's Women 1970–1990,* states, women "generally continue to be the last to benefit from job expansion and the first to suffer from job contraction—particularly in the stagnant or declining economies of Africa and Latin America and the Caribbean. In Africa, due to especially severe economic conditions, the growth in the female labor force has fallen well behind population growth."

In most of Asia and virtually all of Africa, the great majority of wage-earning women still work in agriculture. In black Africa, nearly 80 percent of wage-earning women work on plantations and farms; in Asia, the figure probably still exceeds 50 percent. Although the number of women working in industries in these areas still is comparatively small, it *is* rising. That rise was slowed by the global economic downturn of the late 1980s and early 1990s, and by mechanization, which is one of those job-contraction phenomena that first affects women in the labor force.

Economic geographers have noted that many women, in all parts of the world, engage in what is called "informal" economic activity, that is, private, often home-based activity such as tailoring, beer brewing, food preparation, soap making, and so on. Women who seek to escape their rural-subsistence environment but who cannot enter the formal sector often turn to such work, and in the migrant slums that encircle so many urban areas today, informal economic activity is the mainstay of the community. As with subsistence farming, however, it is difficult to assess the number of women involved, their productivity, or their contribution to the overall economy.

Wherever they work and at whatever job, women still face job discrimination, occupational segregation, and wage inequities, in developed as well as less-developed societies. The world of economic gain and decision making still is a male-dominated world in which women's contributions and perspectives remain undervalued.

POLITICS AND PUBLIC LIFE

America is a free and open society in which anyone can seek elected office. Approximately half the voters in the United States are women. Yet only 8 of the nation's 100 Senators and 2 of its 50 governors were women. Female representation in the Congress is somewhat stronger, but it does not begin to approach parity. How has such male domination developed, and more to the point, why is it perpetuated?

The answer lies in the past as well as the present. To us, the universal franchise is normal and routine, but women in the United States did not achieve full **enfranchisement**—specifically, the right to vote—until 1920 (Canada instituted women's suffrage in the same year). This came a half-century after the U.S. government approved the 15th constitutional amendment giving the vote to all *male* citizens "without regard to race, color, or previous condition of servitude." By the time women became voters (and could become office-seekers), the male domination of political institutions and networks was well established and deeply entrenched. The current pattern is a legacy of recent history, well protected by incumbents, and reflective of a gender gap of still another kind.

TABLE 17–2	Percentage of Seats in National Parliaments Occupied by Women, 1987 and 1994	
	1987	**1994**
United States	5.3	10.9
Canada	9.6	17.3
Australia	6.1	12.6
New Zealand	14.4	21.2
Sweden	28.5	33.5
Norway	34.4	39.4
Finland	31.5	39.0
Denmark	29.1	33.0
Netherlands	20.0	29.3
France	6.4	5.7
United Kingdom	6.3	7.4
Japan	1.4	6.7
Algeria	2.4	6.7
Morocco	0.0	0.6
Egypt	3.9	2.2
Côte d'Ivoire	5.7	4.6
Kenya	1.7	3.0
Zaïre	3.5	4.2
Zimbabwe	9.0	12.0
Brazil	5.3	5.5
Argentina	4.7	14.2
Mexico	10.8	7.0
India	8.3	7.3
China	21.2	21.0
Vietnam	17.7	18.5

Source: United Nations, *The World's Women 1970–1990,* New York, 1991, pp. 32–34; and Interparliamentary Union, *Report* (Geneva, 1995), pp. 16–26.

Although the United States was not the first country to respond to women's demand for the vote (New Zealand did so in 1893, and Australia in 1902), it was in the vanguard of this movement. As Figure 17-4 shows, some Western countries unconditionally enfranchised women as recently as 1971 (Switzerland) and 1976 (Portugal). In Muslim Southwest Asia, there still is no universal suffrage in certain countries. Other countries, for which the United Nations cannot provide data, have not formally enfranchised women. The map underscores the recency of women's right to vote: it is, essentially, a twentieth-century phenomenon.

But the legal right to vote does not translate immediately into political power or political representation. As Table 17-2 shows, the political participation by women in parliamentary bodies remains limited. It is strongest in the developed countries of the world, and weakest, in general, in the less-developed realms. Yet even where it is strongest, it does not reach 40 percent; in most developed countries, it fails to reach 15 percent. Note that the cluster of Northern European countries has the world's highest representation, averaging more than one-third of all representatives, whereas the United States, Canada, the United Kingdom, and France have much lower representation. Economic development and prosperity obviously do not automatically enhance women's participation in government: Japan's figure of 6.7 percent is among the world's lowest.

As we noted previously, existing, male-dominated power structures make the entry of women into the political arena difficult. But the overall situation is improving, despite the figures given in Table 17-2. When the 1994 data (the latest available) are compared to those for 1987, a general increase in women's representation can be discerned. For example, women's parliamentary representation more than doubled in the U.S. during these 7 years, and it increased substantially in all the Northern European countries. It also doubled in Australia and increased in New Zealand, Canada, the Netherlands, the United Kingdom, and France. And as we know, women have become national leaders in a few countries in recent decades: Thatcher (United Kingdom), Aquino (Philippines), Chamorro (Nicaragua), Gandhi (India), Bhutto (Pakistan), Ciller (Turkey), and several others have not only attained their countries' highest office, but have also gained international prominence and respect.

During the coming century, women will, in many countries, achieve representative equality in government, and their role as national leaders will become less unusual. What effect will this have on national and international political interaction? Dr. Ruth Leger Sivard reminds us that "the few women who have attained the highest positions in male-dominated governments have not avoided confrontational politics. Yet in broad opinion surveys women have revealed attitudes significantly different from men's. When women have had a chance to use power in settings where there is a deep feminist consciousness and social commitment to justice—as in the Nordic countries—government policies are noteworthy for their emphasis on equality, development, and peace."

In Part 5 we have dealt with sensitive geographic topics of race and gender. What we have learned here will help us understand contrasting views of the same world, conflicting impressions of the same experience, and divergent reactions to the same social environment. We should keep these realities in mind when we turn to the regional imprint of culture, the cultural landscape.

KEY TERMS

Dowry Deaths
Enfranchisement
Female Infanticide
Gender
Gender Gap
Longevity Gap
Maternal Mortality Rate
Women's Education
Women's Productivity

The cultural landscape of urban Portugal exemplified in Porto.

PART SIX

LANDSCAPE AND THE GEOGRAPHY OF CULTURE

At Issue

What is culture? How is it transmitted from generation to generation? These are far more tendentious questions than might at first appear. Hundreds of cultural geographers and anthropologists have given different definitions of the concept of culture; whereas those of geographers tend to focus on landscapes and environments, those of anthropologists center on institutions and systems. But the burning issue has been (and remains) that of cultural transmission. Is all culture the result of nurture, of learning ways of doing things? Or is part of our cultural heritage what that term implies, *inherited?* If the latter can be supported by evidence, then how much of our cultural "baggage" is biological? One-third? Half? The debate rages on.

18

CULTURE ON THE LAND

Ours is a time of unfathomable contradictions. On the one hand, we witness the globalization of human behavior in modernizing societies: high-rise living, Western dress, usage of the English language, fast-food habits, demands for democracy and minority rights, better education, declining family size. On the other, we watch in horror when the habits of civilization vanish in Eastern Europe, tropical Africa, the Middle East, and Southeast Asia as countless thousands fall victim to group conflict. At the root of both phenomena lies **culture**—human expression at its strongest and weakest, at its best and worst.

Culture has spatial expression, which is one reason why so many geographers study it. Many of the world's current conflicts are cultural struggles, waged to secure or expand the territorial base of a culture. Culture also expresses the relationship between human society and the natural environment. Small wonder that cultural geography holds a central position in the discipline.

Geographica

- **Culture has spatial expression and reflects the relationships between human society and natural as well as social environments.**

- **A culture is a complex system, expressed on the Earth's surface as a culture region with boundaries defined on the basis of cultural criteria.**

- **A cultural landscape expresses the tangible and intangible properties of a culture; its spatial extent defines the limits of that particular culture complex.**

- **Culture hearths are the crucibles of innovation and the sources of technology; from these hearths the influences of change radiate outward.**

- **Diffusion processes disseminate inventions as well as philosophies and beliefs; these processes can be analyzed to reconstruct past propagations and to predict future ones.**

THE CULTURE CONCEPT

Earlier in this book we encountered a key geographic concept, the regional concept, and found that this idea continues to be the subject of debate. So it is with the concept of culture. In fact, the term *culture* is not even used with consistent meaning in the English language! When we speak of a "cultured" individual, we tend to mean someone with refined tastes in music and the arts, a highly educated, well-read person who knows and appreciates the "best" attributes of society. However, as a scientific term, culture refers not only to the music, literature, and arts of a society, but also to all other features of its way of life: prevailing modes of dress; routine living habits; food preferences; the architecture of houses and public buildings; the layout of fields and farms; and systems of education, government, and law. Thus culture is an all-encompassing term that identifies not only the whole tangible lifestyle of a people, but also the prevailing values and beliefs.

Author's Video Link
↓
1
Geographically Speaking: Cultural Geography

The concept of culture is closely identified with the discipline of anthropology, and over the course of more than a century anthropologists have written many different definitions of it. The noted scholar M.J. Herskovits defined culture tersely as "the man-made part of the environment." Another anthropologist, M. Harris, called it "the learned patterns of thought and behavior characteristic of a population or society." Another anthropologist, E. Adamson Hoebel, in his book *Anthropology: The Study of Man* (1972), defined culture as

[T]he integrated system of learned behavior patterns which are characteristic of the members of a society and which are not the result of biological inheritance . . . culture is not genetically predetermined; it is noninstinctive . . . [culture] is wholly the result of social invention and is transmitted and maintained solely through communication and learning.

This definition touches on a current hotly debated issue: the transmission of culture from one generation to the next. Older definitions such as Hoebel's routinely say that culture can only be transmitted through learning, but recent advances in sociobiology and related fields suggest that certain behaviors may have genetic lineages, so that culture has an "instinctive" component as well as a "learned" one. This larger question is the concern of fields other than cultural geography, although some related matters, such as human **territoriality** (an allegedly human instinct for territorial possessiveness that varies across societies) and **proxemics** (individual and collective preferences for nearness or distance as displayed by different cultures) have spatial, and therefore geographic, dimensions that may lie at the root of some of the serious group conflicts continuing today.

COMPONENTS OF CULTURE

A culture is a complex system, so complicated that it is necessary to unravel its interconnected parts. A **culture region** (the area within which a particular culture system prevails) is marked by all the attributes of a culture, including modes of dress, building styles, farms and fields, and other material manifestations. Cultural geographers identify a single element of normal practice in a culture as a **culture trait**. For example, the wearing of a turban is a culture trait of Muslim society; for centuries, it was obligatory for men to wear this headgear. Although it is no longer required, the turban continues to be a distinctive trait of Muslim culture. Males in Sikh society still routinely wear a characteristic turban. The use of simple tools also constitutes a culture trait, and eating with certain utensils (knife and fork or chopsticks) is a culture trait.

Culture traits are not necessarily confined to a single culture. More than one culture may exhibit a particular culture trait, but each will consist of a discrete *combination* of traits. Such a combination is referred to as a **culture complex**. In many cultures, the herding of cattle is a trait. However, cattle are regarded and used in different ways by different cultures. The Maasai of East Africa follow their herds along seasonal migration paths, consuming blood and milk as important ingredients of a unique diet. Cattle occupy a central place in Maasai existence; they are the essence of survival, security, and prestige. Although the Maasai culture complex is only one of many cattle-keeping complexes, no other culture complex exhibits exactly the same combination of traits. In Europe, cattle are milked and dairy products, such as butter, yogurt, and cheese, are consumed as part of a diet very different from that of the Maasai. The European diet also includes beef (under normal circumstances, the Maasai would never slaughter one of their cattle for its meat).

Thus culture complexes have traits in common, and so it is possible to group certain complexes together as **culture systems**. Ethnicity, language, religion, and other cultural elements enter into the definition of a culture system; for example, China may be so designated. China's culture system consists of a number of quite distinct culture complexes, united by strong cultural bonds. Northern Chinese people may eat wheat and those in the south may eat rice as their staple, and the Chinese language as spoken in the north may not be quite the same as that spoken in the south, but history, philosophy, environmental adaptation and modification, and numerous cultural traditions and attitudes give coherence to the Chinese culture systems.

An entire culture system, on the map, is represented by a culture region. West Africa, Polynesia, and Central America may be designated as culture regions, each constituted by a combination of culture complexes as considerable diversity but still substantial uniformity. Note the convergence here between the regional concept and the culture concept: problems of scale and criteria make consistent generalization difficult. Many geographers prefer to refer to regions such as Han China, West Africa, and Polynesia as **geographic regions** rather than as culture regions, because their def-inition is based not only on cultural properties but on locational and environmental circumstances as well.

An assemblage of culture (or geographic) regions forms a **culture realm**, the most highly generalized regionalization of culture and geography on the world map. Together, the culture regions of West, East, equatorial, and Southern Africa constitute the African culture realm. Once again, there are good reasons for calling these **geographic realms** of the human world: the criteria on which they are based, al-though dominated by cultural characteristics, extend beyond culture.

CULTURAL GEOGRAPHIES PAST AND PRESENT

The colonization and Europeanization of the world have obliterated much of the cultural geography of earlier times. Very little is left of the map we might have constructed of indigenous North American cultures (Fig. 18-1); a map of aboriginal Australian cultures, too, would differ

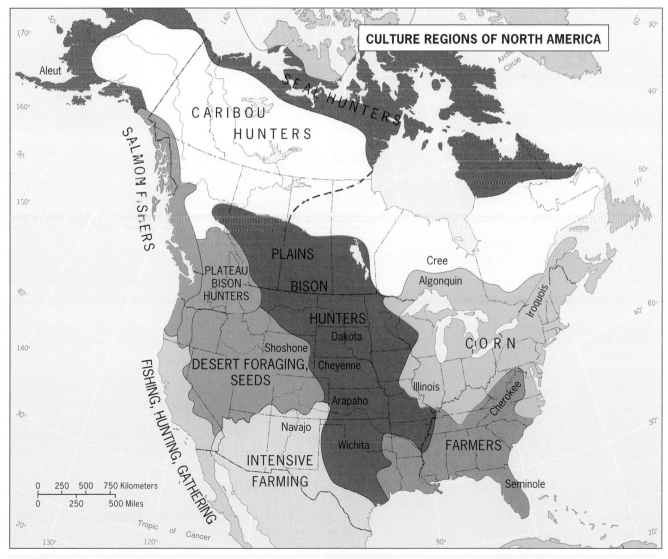

FIGURE 18–1 A consensus regionalization of indigenous American cultures. Modern boundary lines for spatial reference.

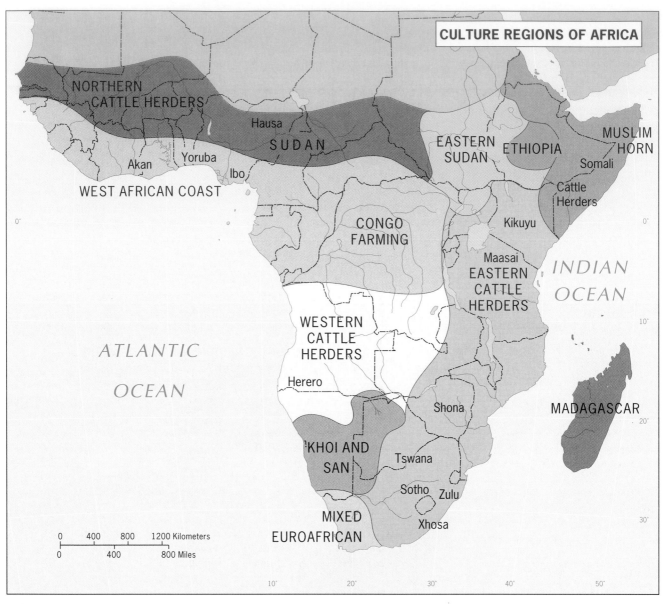

FIGURE 18–2   Generalized regionalization of cultures in Africa south of the Sahara.

radically from that of today. It is important, therefore, to view any map showing culture regions or geographic realms in temporal perspective. Maps of indigenous or "traditional" culture complexes do not show the regional patterns resulting from the world's Europeanization and its associated migrations, for example a map of indigenous African culture regions (Fig. 18-2). On such maps, New Zealand would be shown as a part

of Polynesia because its indigenous Maori population has Polynesian affinities. Maps of "modern" culture regions and geographic realms do not reflect historical patterns, but represent dominant present-day realities. In a modern context, New Zealand would constitute a segment of a geographic realm shared with Australia and dominated by European cultural norms. The world's cultural mosaic is a jigsaw of traditional and modern regions.

CULTURAL GEOGRAPHY

The field of cultural geography is wide-ranging and comprehensive. To organize it, we focus on six prominent topics of study and research.

1. **Cultural Landscape**
   The imprint of cultures on the land creates distinct and characteristic cultural landscapes.

2. **Culture Hearths**

Several sources, crucibles, of cultural growth and achievement developed in Eurasia, Africa, and America.

3. **Cultural Diffusion**

From their sources, cultural innovations and ideas spread to other areas. The process of cultural diffusion continues to this day.

4. **Cultural Ecology**

The relationships between the natural environment and human society must be understood to better comprehend the nature of culture.

5. **Cultural Perception and Ethnicity**

Larger cultures divide into trait-based ethnic groups, minorities whose self-perception helps perpetuate their strength and identity.

6. **Culture regions**

The definition, delimitation, and analysis of culture regions create a spatial summation of culture.

In this chapter, we focus on the first three of these rubrics.

THE CULTURAL LANDSCAPE

A culture gives character to an area. Often, a single scene, a photograph or picture, can reveal the cultural milieu in which it was made. The architecture, the mode of dress of the people, the means of transportation, and perhaps the goods being carried—all reveal a distinctive cultural environment.

The people of any particular culture transform their living space by building structures on it, creating lines of contact and communication, tilling the land, and channeling the water (see box, "Sequent Occupance"). There are a few exceptions: nomadic peoples may

---

SEQUENT OCCUPANCE

The concept of cultural landscape can assume practical qualities when an area has been inhabited—and transformed—by a succession of residents, each of whom leaves a lasting cultural imprint. A place and its resources are perceived differently by peoples of different technological and other cultural traditions. These contrasting perceptions are reflected in their respective cultural landscapes. Therefore, the cultural landscape today is a collage of these contributions, and the challenge is to reconstruct the contributions made by each community. In 1929, Professor Derwent Whittlesey proposed the term **sequent occupance** to identify such cultural succession and its lasting imprints.

Obviously, the most productive studies of sequent occupance are performed where the cultural succession has involved societies with fairly elaborate and distinctive material cultures, as was the case in several areas of Africa. Sequent occupance has left its marks in both rural and urban settings. Thus the ancient San used the hillsides and valleys of Swaziland to hunt and gather roots, berries, and other edibles. Then the cattle-herding Bantu found those slopes to be good for grazing, and they planted corn and other food crops in the valleys. Next came the Europeans to lay out sugar plantations in the lowlands, but after using the higher slopes for grazing, they planted extensive forests, and lumbering became the major industry.

The Tanzanian city of Dar es Salaam provides an interesting urban example. Its site was first chosen for settlement by Arabs from Zanzibar, to serve as a mainland retreat. Next it was selected by the German colonizers as a capital for their East African domain, and it was given a German layout and architectural imprint. When the Germans were ousted, following their defeat in World War I, a British administration took over Dar es Salaam, and the city began still another period of transformation; a large Asian population left it with a zone of three- and four-story apartment houses, which seem to be transplanted from Bombay. Then in the early 1960s, Dar es Salaam became the capital of newly independent Tanzania, under African control for the first time. Thus Dar es Salaam experienced four quite distinct stages of cultural dominance in less than one century, and each stage of the sequence remains imprinted in the cultural landscape.

---

leave a minimum of permanent evidence on the land, and some peoples living in desert margins (such as the few remaining San clans) and in tropical forest zones (Pygmy groups) alter their natural environment little. However, most of the time, there is change: asphalt roadways, irrigation canals, terraced hillslopes.

This composite of artificial features is conceptualized as the **cultural landscape**, a term that came into general use in geography in the 1920s. The geographer

whose name is still most closely identified with this concept is University of California Professor Carl Sauer. In 1927, he wrote an article entitled "Recent Developments in Cultural Geography," in which he produced a deceptively simple definition. The cultural landscape, he said, constitutes "the forms superimposed on the physical landscape by the activities of man." However, when human activities cause change in the actual physical or natural landscape, does the physical landscape then become a cultural

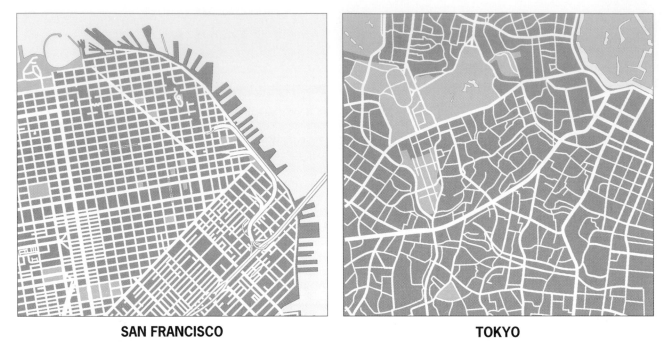

SAN FRANCISCO

TOKYO

FIGURE 18–3 Both San Francisco and Tokyo are laid out on comparatively high-relief urban topography. But their functional structures differ markedly.

landscape? For example, when a dam is built in the upper course of a river, that dam can affect the whole character of that river downstream, even hundreds of miles away. It can alter the strength of the river's flow and the rate of deposition of sediments in a delta. Does that mean that the river is no longer part of the natural landscape and, therefore, has become a cultural landscape feature? Similar issues are raised by human-induced erosion of untilled soil and by regenerated, formerly cutover forests. Anyone who is interested can trace the debate in the geographic literature. For our purposes perhaps the best definition is the broadest: that the cultural landscape includes all identifiably human-induced changes in the natural landscape, involving the surface as well as the biosphere.

Thus a cultural landscape consists of buildings and roads and fields and more, but it also has an intangible quality, and "atmosphere," which is often so easy to perceive and yet so difficult to define. The smells and sights and sounds of a traditional African market are unmistakable, but try to record those qualities on maps or in some other way for comparative study! Geographers have long grappled with this problem of recording the less-tangible characteristics of the cultural landscape that are often so significant in producing the regional personality.

The more concrete properties of a cultural landscape are a bit easier to observe and record. Take, for example, the urban "townscape" (a prominent element of the overall cultural landscape), and compare a major U.S. city with, say, a leading Japanese city. Visual representations would quickly reveal the differences, of course, but so would maps of the two urban places. The U.S. central city, with its rectangular layout of the central business district (CBD) and its far-flung, sprawling suburbs, contrasts sharply with the clustered, space-conserving Japanese city (Fig. 18-3). Again, the subdivision and ownership of American farmland, represented on a map, looks unmistakably different from that of a traditional African rural area, with its irregular, often tiny patches of land surrounding a village. Still, the whole of a cultural landscape can never be represented on a map. The personality of a region involves not only its prevailing spatial organization, but also its visual appearance, its noises and odors, and even its pace of life.

CULTURE HEARTHS

As long as human communities have existed on this Earth, there have been places where people have done well, where they have succeeded, where invention and effort have been rewarded by an increase in numbers, growing strength, comparative stability, and general progress. Conversely, there have been areas where communities have not done well at all. The areas where success and progress prevailed were the places where the first large clusters of human population developed, both because of sustained natural increase and because other people were attracted there. The increasing numbers brought about new ways to exploit locally available resources and also generated power over resources located farther away. Progress was made in farming techniques and, consequently, in yields. Settlements could expand. Society grew more complex, and there were people who could afford to spend time not in subsisting, but in politics and the arts. The circulation of goods and ideas intensified. Traditions developed, along with ways of life that became the example for other places, far and near. These areas were humanity's early **culture hearths**, the sources of civilization, and outward from here radiated the ideas, innovations, and ideologies that would change the world beyond.

Culture hearths should be viewed in the context of time as well as space. Long before human communities began to depend on cultivated crops or domesticated animals, culture hearths developed based on the discovery and development of a tool or weapon that

made subsistence easier or more efficient. Fishing techniques improved and waterside communities prospered and grew long before the momentous changes of the first Agricultural Revolution began. Thus the Inuit people, with their early and inventive adaptation to their frigid, watery environment, developed a culture hearth, just as the ancient Mesopotamians did. The nomadic Maasai and their remarkable cattle-based culture still inhabit the region in which they achieved their culture hearth.

Some culture hearths, therefore, remain comparatively isolated and self-contained, but others have an impact far beyond their bounds. When the innovation of agriculture was added to the culture complexes that already existed in the zone of the Fertile Crescent, it soon diffused to areas where it was not yet practiced and affected culture complexes far and wide. In the culture hearth itself, the practice of cultivation led to an explosion of culture, the evolution of an infinitely more elaborate civilization, where one innovation followed another.

Thus it is appropriate to distin-

guish between culture hearths, thousands of which have evolved across the Earth from the Inuit Arctic to Maori New Zealand, and the source areas of early as well as modern **civilizations**. These latter also began as culture hearths, but their growth and development had wider, sometimes global impact. Early culture hearths (Fig. 18-4) developed in Southwest Asia and North Africa, South and Southeast Asia, and East Asia in the valleys and basins of the great river systems. The Middle and South American culture hearths evolved thousands of years later, not in river valleys, but in highlands. The West African culture hearth emerged later still, strongly influenced by Nile Valley and Southwest Asian innovations.

It is important to note that all the ancient culture hearths shown in Figure 18-4 achieved breakthroughs in *agriculture*. Irrigation techniques, crop domestication, planting, seeding and weeding methods, harvesting, storage, and distribution systems all progressed, and individual cultures achieved remarkable adaptations to maximize environmental opportunities.

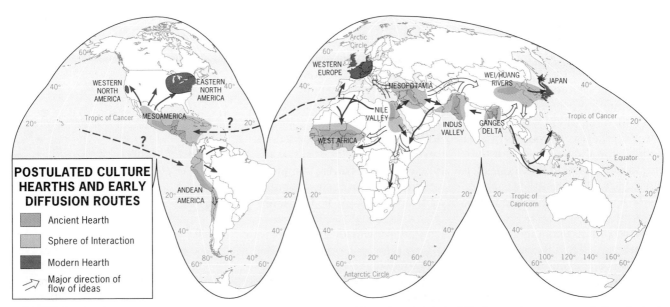

FIGURE 18–4 Ancient and modern culture hearths. The ancient hearths and their diffusion routes are speculative; today's industrial and technological culture hearths are superimposed. SOURCE: Author's sketch.

FROM ANCIENT TO MODERN CULTURE HEARTHS

The locations and the nature of the cultural innovations of recent centuries are both very different. With the onset of the Industrial Revolution, the world was transformed from new hearths, new sources of invention and diffusion. The ancient Agricultural-Urban Revolutions were followed, millennia later, by equally consequential Industrial-Technological Revolutions that created totally new cultural landscapes. These revolutions were (and are) centered in Europe, North America, and East Asia (Fig. 18-4). Think of the ways our daily lives have been changed by the inventions made in these hearths of innovation and how effective modern dissemination systems are. Also note that Western Europe was the dominant industrial hearth in the nineteenth century, a position that was taken over by the United States during the twentieth century. Now Japan has eroded the North American lead, and other East Asian industrial-technological giants are rising. Will the next century witness yet another shift?

CULTURAL DIFFUSION

The ancient culture hearths were foci of cultural maturation and strengthening, of innovation and invention. They were sources of ideas and stimuli. From these source areas, newly invented techniques, tools, instruments, and ideas about ways of doing things radiated outward, carried by caravan and army, by merchant mariner, and by teacher and clergy. Some of the innovations that eventually reached distant peoples were quickly adopted, often to be modified or refined; others fell on barren ground. The process of dissemination, the spreading of an idea or an innovation from its source area to other cultures, is known as the process of **cultural diffusion**. Today the great majority of the world's cultures are the products of innumerable ideas and innovations that arrived in an endless, centuries-long stream. Often it is possible to isolate and trace the origin, route, and timing of the adoption of a particular innovation, so that the phenomenon of **diffusion** is a valuable element in the study of cultural geography.

The appearance of a particular technique or device in widely separated areas does not necessarily prove that diffusion did occur. Various cultures in parts of Asia, Africa, and the Americas developed methods of irrigation, learned to domesticate animals and plants, and reached other achievements by **independent invention**. Furthermore, a major invention did not guarantee rapid diffusion and adoption everywhere. The wheel, surely a momentous invention, was not adopted in Egypt until 20 centuries after its introduction in nearby Mesopotamia.

Diffusion occurs through the movement of people, goods, or ideas. Sauer focused attention on this process. He summarized his views cogently in *Agricultural Origins and Dispersals* (1952), a book that appeared at about the same time that the pioneering diffusion research by the Swedish geographer Torsten Hägerstrand began to appear in print. This fascinating research attracted many geographers to study how diffusion processes operate.

Geographers today identify several different processes whereby diffusion takes place. The differences have to do with various conditions: whatever it is that is diffusing through a population, the distribution and character of that population, the distances involved, and much more. Consider two examples: the diffusion of a disease (such as the Asian "flu") through a population and the diffusion of the use of FAX machines. Involuntary exposure is involved in the first case, and voluntary adoption in the second. Both are, however, manifestations of diffusion processes.

EXPANSION DIFFUSION

Geographers today classify diffusion processes into two broadly defined categories: expansion diffusion and relocation diffusion. In the case of expansion diffusion, an innovation or idea (or a disease!) develops in a core or source area and remains strong there while also spreading outward. Later, we study the spread of Islam from its hearth on the Arabian Peninsula to Egypt and North Africa, through Southwest Asia, and into West Africa.

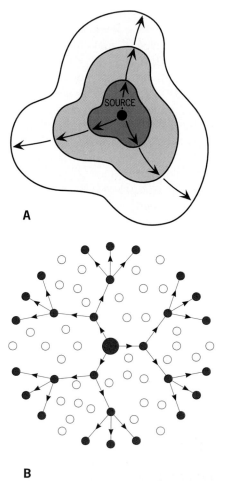

FIGURE 18–5 Expansion diffusion (A) and hierarchical diffusion (B).

This is a case of expansion diffusion. If we had the data from which to draw a series of maps of the Islamic faithful at 50-year intervals beginning in A.D. 620, the area of adoption of the Muslim religion would be larger in every successive period. Expansion diffusion is thus a very appropriate term (Fig. 18-5).

Expansion diffusion takes several forms. The spread of Islam is a form of **contagious diffusion**, a form of expansion diffusion in which nearly all adjacent individuals are affected. A disease can spread this way, infecting almost everyone in a population (but not everyone may show symptoms).

However, an idea (or a disease, for that matter) may not always spread throughout a fixed population as just described. For example, the spread of AIDS in the United States over the past decade has not affected everyone in the total population, but (here in North America) it has affected particularly vulnerable persons, thus leapfrogging over wide areas and appearing as mapped clusters in distantly separated cities. This represents another kind of expansion diffusion called **hierarchical diffusion**, in which the main channel of diffusion lies through some segment of those susceptible to (or adopting) what is being diffused. In the case of AIDS diffusion, the hierarchy is the urban structure in the United States; the sizes of cities, towns, and villages will be reflected by the sizes of the clusters of those infected.

Hierarchical diffusion also is illustrated by the spread of the use of FAX machines. Here the hierarchy is determined by the equipment's affordability and the potential users' perception of need. Again, the pattern is likely to show an urban-based order. But not all innovations are adopted in cities and towns. An improved piece of farm machinery will show quite a different diffusion pattern.

A third form of expansion diffusion is **stimulus diffusion**. Not all

ACCULTURATION AND TRANSCULTURATION

When cultures of different strengths make contact, the stronger culture prevails. The culture of the weaker society may be somewhat changed, considerably modified, or even completely transformed, but, in every case, the stronger culture will contribute certain of its qualities to the weaker one. This process, whereby a culture is substantially changed through interaction with another culture, is called **acculturation**. It is obviously a correlative of cultural diffusion.

Actually, the process of acculturation is not the one-way street our definition might suggest. Stronger cultures do impose many of their attributes on weaker ones, but they also may well adopt some of the weaker culture's properties.

After the Spanish invaders overthrew the Aztec kingdom, Spanish culture began to prevail: towns were transformed, a new religious order was introduced, new crops were planted. Acculturation proceeded, but Spanish culture also absorbed some influences. Aztec motifs pervaded Spanish architecture. Aztec crops were transplanted to Iberia. Spaniards began to wear clothing that revealed Aztec color and cut. In Mexico, there is a saying that citizens who do not have Aztec blood in their veins nevertheless have the Aztec spirit in their minds.

Some small, isolated culture groups in remote locales have experienced little acculturation, while others have been strongly affected. Until the recent penetration and destruction of the rainforest reached them, Brazil's Yanomami people remained beyond acculturation's reach. At the other end of the continuum are societies that have been radically changed, notably Japan, which intentionally adopted European technology. Japan's voluntary Westernization stands in strong contrast to the acculturation imposed by European colonial powers on their overseas domains.

Although acculturation is not exclusively a one-way process, the flow of innovations, ideas, and practices (voluntary or forced) is dominantly in one direction, far overshadowing any "reverse" movement. Occasionally, there is contact between culture complexes more nearly equal in strength and complexity, and then a genuine exchange follows, in which both cultures function as sources and adopters. This process is referred to as **transculturation**. It usually happens within the realms of the major geographic races: for example, during contact between English and French, German and Italian, or Korean and Japanese culture complexes.

ideas can be readily adopted by a receiving population; some are simply too vague, too unattainable, or otherwise impractical for immediate adoption. But this does not mean that such ideas have no impact at all. They may result in local experimentation and eventual changes in ways of doing things. At first, the idea of industrialization was not transmitted to pre- or nonindustrial societies through any particular artifact, but it did stimulate attempts to mechanize local handicraft manu-

facturing and thus had an indirect impact.

RELOCATION DIFFUSION

Expansion diffusion, we noted, takes place through populations that are stable and fixed (theoretically, at least; we know that all societies are to some extent mobile). It is the innovation, the idea, or the disease that does the moving. Relocation diffusion involves the actual movement of individuals who have already adopted the idea or innovation, and who carry it to a new, perhaps distant, locale, where they proceed to disseminate it (see box, "Acculturation and Transculturation").

Another form of relocation diffusion is **migrant diffusion**. There are times when an innovation originates somewhere and enjoys strong—but brief—adoption there. By the time it reaches distant places of adoption, it has already lost its position where it started. The diffusion map thus would show a continuous outward shift to new adopters, but there would be no stable core area. Some diseases display this process as well, including milder influenza pandemics. By the time these reach North America and Europe, they already have faded away in China, so that the diffusion pattern is one of migrant, rather than contagious, diffusion.

These are some of the leading processes of diffusion and the factors favoring it. However, there are also forces that work against diffusion and the adoption of ideas and innovations. One of these is distance, and another is time. The farther it is from its source, the less likely an innovation is to be adopted, and the "innovation waves" become weaker. Again, the acceptance of an innovation becomes less likely the longer it takes to reach its potential adopters. In combination, time and distance cause *time-distance decay* in the diffusion process.

Another force working against diffusion processes is the cultural barrier. Certain innovations, ideas, or practices are not acceptable or adoptable in particular cultures because of prevailing attitudes or even taboos. We have already noted the food preferences and strong taboos of various cultures. Prohibitions against alcoholic beverages, as well as certain forms of meat, fish, and other foods, have restricted their consumption. Cultural barriers against other practices (modern medicine and hygiene, the use of contraceptives, and so on) also have inhibited diffusion processes. Cultural barriers can be powerful obstacles against the spread of ideas as well as artifacts.

In this chapter we have viewed some significant aspects of the geography of culture: its contents, imprints, and dissemination. We now turn to the challenging issues of environmental influences and locational identities.

KEY TERMS

Acculturation
Civilization
Contagious Diffusion
Cultural Diffusion
Cultural Landscape
Culture
Culture Complex
Culture Hearth
Culture Realm
Culture Region
Culture System
Culture Trait
Diffusion
Geographic Realm
Geographic Region
Hierarchical Diffusion
Independent Invention
Migrant Diffusion
Proxemics
Sequent Occupance
Stimulus Diffusion
Territoriality
Transculturation

19

CULTURES, ENVIRONMENTS, AND REGIONS

In Chapter 18, we examined three geographic aspects of culture: how it is imprinted on the landscape, where it arose, and why it diffused. In the chapters that follow, the concepts of cultural landscape, culture hearths ancient and modern, and diffusion processes and routes will prove to be useful as we investigate its environmental and locational dimensions.

In the present chapter, we explore some of the more challenging aspects of cultural geography: the relationships between culture and environment (natural as well as artificial), the role of place and location, and the ingredients that give regionally expressed cultural landscapes their special qualities.

As we have noted, the cultural landscape reflects more than a society's technological achievements, its modernization (or absence thereof), its organizational capacities, and its pace of daily life. It also reveals much about a society's relationship with the natural environment it affects, and by which it is influenced. Pollution-belching smokestacks, contaminant-oozing

Geographica

- In the transmission of culture traits from generation to generation, two kinds of environment play their respective roles: the physical (natural) environment and the cumulative cultural (social) environment.

- The relationships between natural environment and human society are complex and not yet well understood; early theories suggesting that natural environments dictate or determine the course of human development have been discarded.

- Culture has spatial expression, and culture regions exhibit clear spatial differentiation; a cultural heartland or core area gives way to a domain within which the core culture dominates.

- Culture is proving to be a powerful force threatening the survival of multicultural countries in the post–Cold War world; some subnational cultural groups already have achieved political independence by secession.

- Architecture, both domestic and monumental, is the leading influence in shaping cultural landscapes; its forms reflect responses to both natural and social environments and become integral parts of regional cultures.

landfills, and sludge-clogged streams also form part of some cultural landscapes. Monuments, billboards, statues, and graffiti contribute as well, as do skyscrapers and slums, suburbs and soybean fields. The cultural landscape thus also mirrors the values held by a

227

culture, its priorities and principles. The late President Balewa of the African state of Nigeria, on a visit to the United States, was asked what impressed him most about the American cultural landscape. Was it the tall buildings of New York, where he was attending a United Nations conference? Was it the noisy, busy traffic in the city's streets? No, he said. Nothing impressed him so much as what he called the voluntary adherence to the law, a public obedience that made people, individually and collectively, stop for red traffic lights, wait in line at bus stops, and merge in order when traffic lanes compelled it. That, said President Balewa, was his most memorable image: no tangible element of the cultural landscape impressed him as much as this intangible one. It revealed, he said, what must be an integral part of American culture: to obey the law.

Many Americans would be surprised by that observation; the New York of today is not the New York President Balewa saw. But compared to many other world cities, New York does remain relatively orderly. And Lagos, the largest city of Nigeria, still provides a basis for comparison.

ENVIRONMENT AND CULTURE

The term *environment*, in the context of culture, has a double meaning. What the former President of Nigeria saw in New York was part of an overall social environment, the kind of environment in which culture is transmitted and learned. Language, religion, dress modes, food habits, musical preferences—all these are part of this social environment, in addition to many other customs. Among the many definitions anthropologists have used to explain the culture concept, virtually all refer in one way or another to the "learning" or "acquisition" of behaviors, beliefs, values, techniques, and lifeways that prevail in a particular society or population.

But there is another side to environment, and that is the physical stage, the natural environment that forms the setting for a culture. Human cultures have evolved under widely varying natural environments, and have adapted to their environmental conditions in many different ways. Such adaptations can be discerned in the cultural landscape: the higher the pitch of roofs, for example, the higher the average annual precipitation. Houses in flood-prone areas are likely to be built on stilts or on mounds. Houses in high-latitude Scandinavia tend to face southward, turning their back walls to frigid Arctic winds and maximizing the sunlight of summer.

There are deeper issues, however. Chinese beliefs that revered and ancestral spirits reside in mountains and trees and other components of the natural landscape are ancient and durable. **Geomancy**, the adjustment by the living to the perceived wishes of the spirits of the dead, still plays a significant role in traditional China. Elsewhere, too, concepts of godly power in rivers and volcanoes persist. Because the Buddha liked to sit and preach under large, shady Banyan trees, those trees have taken on a holy aura that has protected them from destruction in thousands of South and Southeast Asian villages. In Hawaii, Native Hawaiians objected vigorously when power companies decided to drill into the hot subsurface of the Big Island to harness thermal power, fearing the wrath of their god-queen, Pele. When the project nevertheless proceeded and Mauna Kea erupted shortly thereafter, destroying an entire suburb, locals were not surprised. For tens of thousands of years, the awesome powers of nature have dominated human perceptions of the natural world.

Against this background, the geographic questions under the rubric of **cultural ecology** seem more complicated still. Human cultures exist in long-term accommodation with their physical environments, seizing the opportunities those environments present and suffering from the extremes they sometimes impose. No culture, no matter how technologically sophisticated, can escape from nature's destructive force, as the annual list of tornado-caused casualties in the United States attests. But some cultures have overcome the apparent limitations of their natural environments more than others. The widespread diffusion of the air conditioner, for example, undoubtedly contributed to the strength of the Sunbelt migration discussed in Chapter 11. We begin by recounting some geographic speculation about the relationships between culture and nature.

ENVIRONMENTAL DETERMINISM

Looking again at the map of ancient culture hearths (Fig. 18-4), we note that these crucibles of cultural achievement and expansion lie in apparently unfavorable climatic zones (see Fig. 2-3). Did these cultures have enormous adaptive capacity, or have climates changed so much that the present map is no longer relevant as a guide to Figure 18-4? In any case, what are the optimum environmental conditions for the well-being of civilizations? Can we, in fact, generalize about the "best" environmental conditions for the human success story?

Twenty-three centuries ago, Aristotle answered this last question affirmatively when he generalized about the peoples of cold, distant Europe as being "full of spirit . . . but incapable of ruling others," and those of Asia as "intelligent and inventive . . . [but] always in a state of subjection and slavery." Many geographers after Aristotle have held similar views. How easy it is to view people living in cold climates as "hardy, but not very intelligent," those of the warm tropics as "lazy and passive," and those in the intermediate zones as productive and progressive. Aristotle's views on this topic were nothing if not durable. As recently as the first half of the twentieth century, there still was strong support for similar notions.

Here is how Ellsworth Huntington (1876–1947), a twentieth-century geographer, stated it in *Principles of Human Geography*, published in 1940:

The well-known contrast between the energetic people of the most progressive parts of the temperate zone and the inert inhabitants of the tropics and even of intermediate regions, such as Persia, is largely due to climate . . . the people of the cyclonic regions rank so far above those of other parts of the world that they are the natural leaders.

The doctrine expressed by these statements is referred to as environmentalism or, more precisely, **environmental determinism**. It holds that human behavior, individually and collectively, is strongly affected by, and even controlled or determined by, the environment that prevails. It suggests that the climate is the critical factor in this determination: for progress and productiveness in culture, politics, and technology, the "ideal" climate would be, say, that of Western Europe or the northeastern United States. The people of hot, tropical areas or cold, near-polar zones might as well abandon hope. Their habitat decrees that they will never achieve anything even approaching the accomplishments of their mid-latitude counterparts. Huntington's map of "level of civilization" (Fig.

19-1) summarized this position effectively.

So for a time, geographers set about their attempts to explain the distribution of present and past centers of culture in terms of the "dictating environment." In the early part of this century, this remained a major theme in the discipline, the manner in which the natural environment conditions human activities. Quite soon, though, there were geographers who doubted whether these sweeping generalizations about climate and character, and environment and productiveness, were really valid. They recognized exceptions to the environmentalists' postulations (e.g., the Maya civilizations in Mesoamerica arose under tropical conditions) and argued that humanity was capable of much more than merely adapting to the natural environment. As for the supposed "efficiency" of the climate of Western Europe, this was an interesting idea, but not scientifically proved. Surely, it was best not to base "laws" of determinism on inadequate data in the face of apparently contradictory evidence.

The arguments helped guide the search for answers to questions about the relationships between human society and the natural environment in different directions, but the unqualified environmentalist position was still held by a dwindling few for several decades. For a more penetrating approach, it is interesting to read S.F. Markham's *Climate and the Energy of Nations* (1947), still an environmentalist statement but based on more substantive information. Markham had the advantage that Huntington's works were available alongside the criticisms these had evoked. Other scholars, in geography and in cognate disciplines, had grappled with the problem as well.

Markham thought that he could detect, in the migration of the center of power in the Mediterranean

(from Egypt to Greece to Rome and onward), the changing climates of that part of Europe during the most recent several thousand years of glacial retreat. He argued that Egypt was much cooler in its prime than it is now. When the Greeks rose to prominence, Greece's climate also was more conducive to the generation of "energetic" people. Rome was so cool that public hot baths were part of daily life. In all of this, Markham saw the northward movement of isotherms—lines connecting points of equal temperature values. Like his predecessors, he tried to determine the "optimum" temperature for physical and mental activity, and he was sure that these temperatures prevailed, in turn, in Egypt, Greece, Rome, and later in Western Europe.

However, geographers grew increasingly cautious about such speculative writings, and they began to ask their questions about societal-environmental relationships in new ways. There is still the old interest in how humanity is affected by its natural environment, but if generalizations are to be made, they ought to come from detailed, carefully designed research. Everyone agrees that human activity is in certain ways affected by the natural environment, but people are the decision makers and the modifiers, not the total subordinates the environmental determinists believe them to be.

Reactions to the school of environmentalism produced counterarguments. A school of **possibilism** emerged, made up of geographers who argued that the natural environment's role amounts to no more than to limit the range of choices available to a culture. Thus the natural environment is viewed as affording opportunities rather than imposing limitations. The choices that a society makes depend on the people's requirements and the technology available to them to satisfy these.

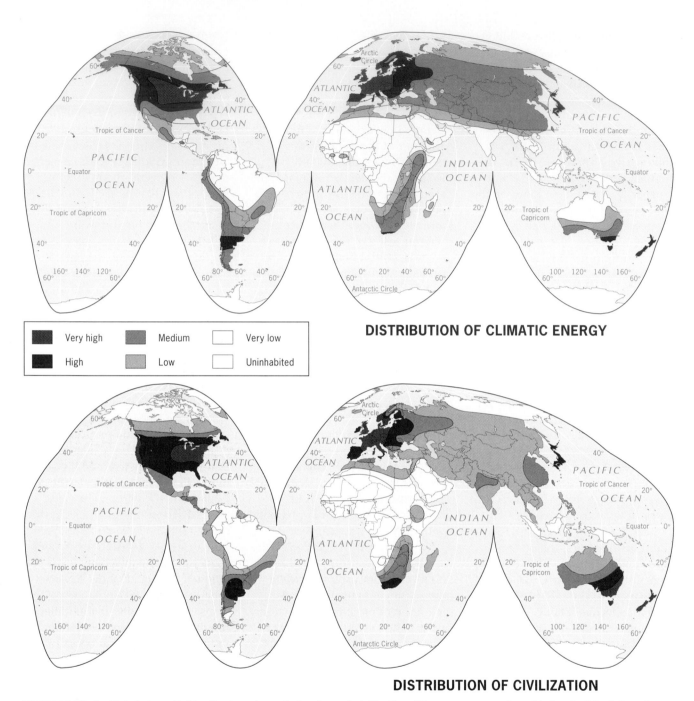

DISTRIBUTION OF CLIMATIC ENERGY

Very high   Medium   Very low

High   Low   Uninhabited

DISTRIBUTION OF CIVILIZATION

FIGURE 19–1 This is how E. Huntington viewed climate and civilization. These maps are from his book *Principles of Human Geography* (New York: John Wiley, 1940), p. 352. Below these maps, the author states that they are "based on the opinion of fifty experts in many countries."

One obvious conclusion is that the degree of influence of the natural environment declines with increasing modernization and technological sophistication. Those of us who spend the majority of our time in "artificial" heated and air-conditioned environments are much more independent of the natural environment than people who live more traditional, generally more rural lives. In that sense, humans have the capacity to modify, indeed to transform, their natural environments. Yet this leaves some unanswered questions. Geographers have studied all kinds of human behavior in our modern communities and have found that no matter how insulated from the natural environment, some influences seem to persist. Changeable weather, heat and cold waves, and humidity in the air seem to influence significant numbers of people in their physical and mental activities, even when these people spend most of their time indoors within controlled environments. Even the stage of the moon's cycle seems to have some effect: certain crime rates have been correlated with lunar periods.

No wonder that cultural ecology has stimulated some intense debates. To participate, one must have a strong grounding in both physical and cultural geography, because this field lies at the interface between the two.

CULTURE REGIONS

In Chapter 18, we saw two maps of early **culture regions**, revealing distributions that prevailed at some time in the evolving culture history of North America and Africa. Those patterns have been modified, even erased (to a greater degree in North America than in Africa) by the Europeanization of America and the colonization of Africa. Reconstructing them, nevertheless, provides insight into the world's historical geography.

The regional concept also is useful when we seek to improve our understanding of contemporary cultures. In Chapter 1 we noted that **regions** are defined on the basis of certain specific criteria and that the choice of criteria depends on the goals of the research. Two kinds of regions were identified: *formal* regions, marked by a certain homogeneity or internal uniformity, and *functional* regions that are held to-

gether by systems of interaction. We used the example of the Amazon Basin as an instance of the former and a city with its hinterland connections as an instance of the latter.

In cultural geography, the notion of the formal region is the most productive. Formal regions can be identified by the prevalence of a single culture trait or a combination of culture traits. In Figure 19-2, three formal regions are represented: one defined on the basis of a particular culture trait (A), a second one based on a second culture trait (B), and a third in which a combination of these two traits is recorded. Were we to add more culture traits, one multitrait culture complex would emerge as the core of the culture in which these traits are represented.

THE AMERICAN WEST

This is what was done by Professor Donald Meinig in an article entitled "American Wests: Preface to a Geographical Introduction" (1972). Using the regional method, Professor Meinig identified six discrete cultural cores (he called them nuclei) in the U.S. West, each the focus of larger cultural regions (Fig. 19-3). As the map shows, several secondary nuclei were less clearly defined by maps of culture traits.

Meinig suggested that culture regions such as those he mapped as formal regions in the American West evolve through four coincident stages of development. First, *population* increases, and an original settlement grows by expansion. Second, *circulation* patterns change as internal communications intensify and external connections become more effective. Third, *political* organizations, rudimentary at first, grows more complex and involves a greater number of spheres. Fourth, *regional culture* emerges, and then begins to become submerged in a developing national culture. It is important to keep in

mind that these are not successive but parallel developments. Thus population influx continues as circulation patterns intensify, while political organization grows more complex and cultural identity strengthens. Of course, it is possible for a regional culture *not* to be submerged in a national culture, through isolation by distance or inaccessibility, through racial or linguistic separateness, or perhaps through religious distinctiveness. The Mormon culture region outlined in Figure 19-3 retains some sharp landscape identities. Although it is indeed an "American" landscape, the Mormon region is distinct from other American "Wests." The dominant, impressive, sometimes towering, (always meticulously maintained) temple rises above a townscape marked by compactness and closeness; houses, nearly always neatly kept and relatively modest, are spaced closely together in the Mormon tradition of communal association. Absent are taverns and bars; comparative quietness is part of the Mormon nonmaterial landscape.

But culture regions normally are not sharply bounded; rather, they merge into neighboring, different culture regions. Professor Meinig's map, at the scale shown, cannot reveal this, but the multiple-trait region that defines the **core area** or nucleus of a culture region always is smaller than the whole. This core area is the essence of the culture and its landscape; it is its focus, its heartland. Here lies what is hallowed and revered by those whose culture is represented. Here, too, lies the culture's most important, most representative urban center, where religious shrines, museums, schools, and other institutions ensure its perpetuation.

Inevitably, in our multicultural world, such a core area gives way to a surrounding zone in which elements (traits) of the culture continue to exist, but in which other influences also can be observed. In

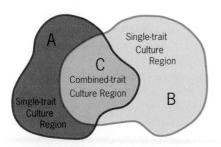

FIGURE 19–2 Single-trait and Combined-trait Culture Regions

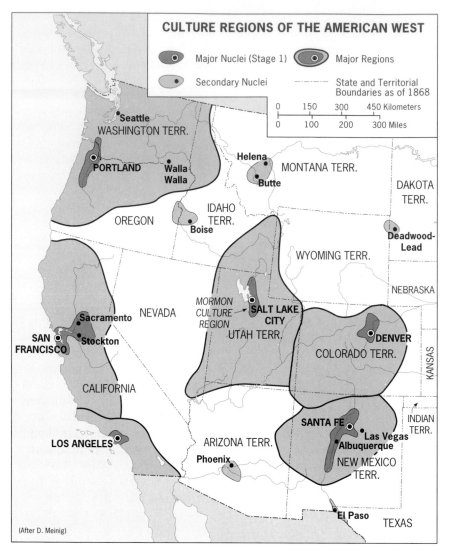

FIGURE 19–3 From D. Meinig, *Annals* of the AAG, 62 (1972), p. 159.

a more detailed study of the Mormon culture region, Professor Meinig defined the Mormon culture region's core area and found it to be quite small (Fig. 19-4), but encircling it was a much larger cultural **domain** in which Mormon traits dominated, though not to the exclusion of all else. As the map shows, this domain prevails over virtually all of the State of Utah and extends into neighboring Idaho and Wyoming as well as extreme eastern Nevada and northern Arizona. Within this domain, the core culture dominates, but this domination (as measured by combinations of traits) also has its limits. Beyond its cultural domain, Mormon culture has a

sphere, a sphere of influence but not a dominant presence. As Figure 19-4 shows, this sphere is quite extensive, stretching from the Mexican border to the state of Washington, with outliers even farther north as well as east.

The Mormon culture region represents a **subnational culture**, that is, a regionally expressed culture that forms part of a larger culture. Language, for example, is not a defining trait of Mormon culture; Mormons, like the overwhelming majority of U.S. residents, speak English. The Mormon core area, domain, and sphere are not defined primarily by language, as some culture regions are. Some of the

world's major cultures are also **national cultures**, their domains coinciding with the political boundaries of countries and their spheres extending into other countries. The French culture region often is cited as an example of a national culture, with its core area centered on Paris, its domain coinciding with the nation's borders, and its sphere extending into neighboring Belgium and Switzerland.

CULTURE AND AUTONOMY

The attributes of culture can evoke strong emotions. One might assume, given the internationalization of our globe, that regional cultures would be on their way toward amalgamation in national cultures and that national cultures would also lose their distinctiveness in an interconnected, integrating world. While it would be possible to cite instances where this is indeed happening, there are many areas of the world where cultural regionalism is strengthening, not weakening. As we will note in a later chapter, numerous countries today face divisive forces, some so strong that they have already ripped the state apart. Those forces, more often than not, are unleashed by cultural urges. In multicultural countries, individual cultural groups no longer feel that the state treats them fairly or equitably. Such groups, driven by a desire for self-determination, may opt to seek independence—or at least a loosening of the bonds that tie them to the state. The case of Cyprus illustrates what happens when mutual distrust overtakes a multicultural society. On this island in the eastern Mediterranean, a Greek majority and a Turkish minority lived in an uneasy—but functioning—state, spatially integrated so that Greeks and Turks shared most parts of the territory. But the system collapsed, and today Turks occupy the northern part of Cyprus and Greeks the south, each autonomous in their own domain.

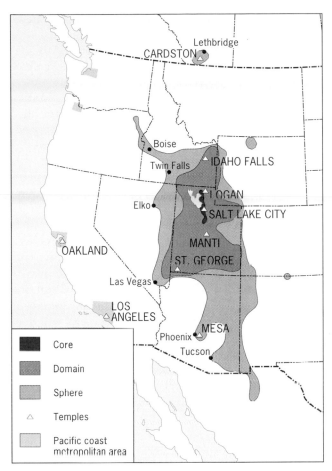

FIGURE 19–4 The Mormon Culture Region. From D. Meinig, *Annals of the AAG*, 55 (1965), p. 191.

as the Serbs or the Croats. Their dominant culture trait is their adherence to a local version of Islam. Note that the Bosnian non-Muslims are not referred to as Orthodox Christians or Catholics, but as Serbs or Croats. As a result, the Muslims in former Yugoslavia are perceived as ethnic holdovers from the time when the Ottoman Turks ruled there. But they are not. They are the descendants of Slavic converts, and their struggle underscores the power of culture.

From Native Hawaiians to Flemings, from Quebecers to Zulus, images of cultural autonomy and political self-determination infuse cultures around the globe. What makes culture such a powerful motivator? Part of the answer lies in geography, in the comfort of the cultural landscape, the familiarity of routine activity space, the solace of security in a traditional social environment forged over centuries of continuity. That social environment, of course, is tangibly represented by the cultural landscape. We focus next on prominent features in the cultural landscape that contribute to the strength of regional culture.

Author's Video Link
↓
3
Historical Geography
of Cyprus

The collapse of the former Yugoslavia illustrates the strength of cultural imperatives as well. Look closely at a cultural-geographic map of Yugoslavia, and you will see that the country's cultural geography was at odds with its political geography—its internal boundaries created divisions within which there were numerous cultural minorities. One such internal division, however, was also a culture region: Slovenia. The Slovenes' domain coincided almost exactly with their political territory. When the notion of independence diffused through the former Yugoslavia, the Slovenes were the first to achieve it; their quest was unimpeded by cultural minorities in their midst, because there was none. Later, when other cultural groups inside the former Yugoslavia also sought independence, minority cultures feared that they would fare badly under majority regimes. And soon the war was on, a war of cultures.

The war in Yugoslavia is sometimes referred to as an "ethnic" conflict, but it is not and has not been such for a very long time. All the people of the former Yugoslavia were and are Slavs (the name of the country meant "Land of the South Slavs"). What divides the South Slavs is culture: religion, language, tradition, not ethnicity. The Bosnian Muslims always were just as Slavic

Author's Video Link
↓
4
Yugoslavia

ARCHITECTURAL FORMS

It goes without saying that structures—buildings, bridges, towers—form the dominant components of a cultural landscape. But these are not the only elements of it. Structures create an assemblage of visible attributes, a composite of shapes that defines the regional culture. The landscape of culture, however, is in the mind as well as in the eye. Intangible qualities also contribute to its formation, qualities that would not appear on a photograph or an ordinary map. Enter an African or an Arab town, and you may be greeted by sounds of music and smells of cooking, the shouts of traders and the bustle of people—all of which will remain essential ingredients of your perception of these cultures.

It is therefore useful to differentiate between what cultural geographers call **material culture** and its manifestations, represented in the cultural landscape by buildings, roads, cultivated land, and other tangible evidence of human activity, and **nonmaterial culture**, including the sounds and smells of a place, the intangibles that often give it special character.

The distinction might appear obvious, but it actually is not so simple. For example, consider music, clearly an aspect of nonmaterial

culture. Certainly, music and musical expression are nonmaterial elements of culture. However, only unaccompanied song would truly represent nonmaterial culture; other music is made with instruments, and these represent material culture. Thus the cultural geography of musical styles and forms, and their diffusion, would indeed be a study in nonmaterial culture. The study of the development, use, diffusion, and distribution of musical instruments, however, would venture into material culture. *Nonmaterial* culture is usually taken to include (in addition to music), theater and dance, plays and literature, art (painting), food habits and preferences, law and legal systems, language, and religion.

The landscape of material culture is dominated by buildings ranging from the simplest dwelling to the

most magnificent monuments. In the monumental buildings lies much of a culture's heritage; their forms attest to the triumphs, aspirations, aesthetics, values, and priorities of a society. But even the most modest dwellings can reveal much about a culture and its norms. Careful examination of a photograph of an urban scene can tell you much about the cultural region it represents. Even people's clothing functions as an indicator of culture.

Architectural achievements rank among a culture's proudest expressions of identity and capability. The ancient Egyptians built huge pyramids to commemorate, in death, the greatness of their leaders, and to this day those architectural wonders remain hallmarks of Egyptian culture, attracting an unending stream of visitors from virtually all parts of the world. The ancient Greeks and

From the Field Notes

❝ In 1982, when I first saw the old center of the city of San Salvador in the State of Bahia, Brazil, the historic buildings were losing their centuries–old battle against the elements. Things were even worse in 1986, but by then the United Nations had begun to take an interest in this, one of the officially designated 'Historic Treasures' of the world. In 1994 reconstruction was in full swing, as hundreds of churches, public buildings, and villas were being renovated. A cultural landscape of the 1700's was revived. ❞

Romans built great public buildings supported by tall stone columns, and their designs are still copied 20 centuries later by governments wanting to create impressive and imposing administrative headquarters. Islam's greatest material achievements were in the architecture of its great mosques, its arabesque motifs diffused around the world under various names (such as "Mediterranean" and "Spanish" styles). The technological prowess of modern Western cultures is displayed in steel-and-glass skyscrapers, enormous domed stadiums, and huge vaulted structures (such as those of modern airports) enclosing large spaces. Thus architecture is a reflection of a culture's assertion of identity and values, priorities and aspirations, and technology and economy.

TYPES

Architecture represents a culture system in several ways. In many cultures, *religious* architecture is especially expressive, and other buildings include religious motifs, adopted from churches, mosques, and pagodas. In the next section, the dominance of religious architecture in various cultures, past and present, will be illustrated. The architecture of *governmental* buildings is a second type. Governmental architecture is often imposing, designed to symbolize authority and power. Governments give their capital cities a special atmosphere, sometimes through the construction of ultramodern buildings, or by recreating the great columned structures of ancient Greece and Rome. Industrial and *commercial* architecture symbolizes the modern manufacturing age, the age of trade, transportation, and money. The great skyscrapers of America's cities represent this form of architecture, creating skylines that dwarf the tallest towers of Medieval Europe's cathedrals. Among

PUBLIC ARCHITECTURE

Public architecture is revealed in the style and form of buildings such as museums, universities, hospitals, and recreational centers. Unlike *commercial* architecture, which tends to dominate central-city townscapes, and *governmental* architecture, which clusters at the heart of capitals, public architecture is more dispersed throughout the urban area. This has meant, in many instances, that there is ample space for architects to exploit, and many magnificent public buildings have been designed. Frank Lloyd Wright, regarded by many as the greatest among many distinguished U.S. architects, counted among his achievements the designs of a golf club in Chicago, a college in Florida, a museum in Los Angeles, and one of his most famous creations, the Guggenheim Museum in New York.

structures of *public* architecture are the buildings of universities, libraries, hospitals, and sports arenas (see box, "Public Architecture"). Recreational structures are a subgroup of public architecture and include the modern sports arenas that mark the edges of major cities. Finally, *domestic* architecture, the architecture of people's houses, constitutes a key element in any region's cultural landscape. Ordinary people's homes are not normally designed individually by an architect, but standard layouts do result from architectural experimentation and engineering. At one time, the incorporation of interior running water, electricity, and other utilities, and the inclusion of specialized rooms (bathrooms and kitchens) was a challenge that required an architect's planning. In the modern Western city, the suburban "model" home now routinely includes such amenities.

STYLES AND REGIONAL SOURCES

Architecture is a science (especially an engineering science) as well as an art, and architects represent a culture in a very special way. Architectural style may be viewed at four spatial levels. First, there is the *individual* style of a particular architect, whose work may become famous or remain comparatively unnoticed because it is similar to that of many other architects. At first, the work of such an architect may be so advanced or innovative that his or her work stands alone, apart from prevailing styles. However, as time goes on, these innovations become incorporated in the work of other architects. A cluster of architects, all representing a particular style (e.g., the distinctive form of the U.S. West), exemplifies a *regional* style that characterizes a culture system and thus a culture region. At the third level, certain countries exhibit a prevailing architectural style. Some governments have fostered and encouraged the development of domestic architecture as an element of nation building. Brazil, for example, has a distinctively *national* architectural style. Fourth, it is possible to recognize a certain unity in the architecture of still larger geographic units. The architecture of South Asia, China, Europe, or North America is the architecture of a geographic *realm*, including all of the national cultures forming a part of it.

Architecture may also be reviewed in a spatial-temporal perspective, relating style to a particular civilization and its environment (such as the ancient Mayas

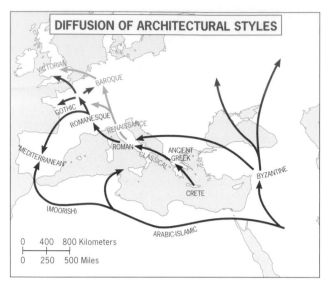

FIGURE 19–5 Old (red) and more recent (green) diffusion routes of architectural styles.

    We entered the Pantheon in Rome on an overcast day, but the great vaulted roof and its circular opening at the top of the dome did its job: the interior was well lit. To think that this was by no means the largest of these domed structures that stood in ancient Rome!

or the Incas), to a period of time and its locus (the Renaissance in Italy; Rococo expressions in France), or to a religious source (Buddhism and its pagodas; Islam and its mosques).

As noted previously, architectural concepts and ideas have diffused from one culture to others (Fig. 19-5), and architectural styles have changed significantly over time within culture regions as well. Ancient Egypt's architects designed and planned the construction of columned temples and rock-hewn tombs, as well as massive pyramids, all as much as 5000 years ago. In Babylonia and Assyria, also about 5 millennia ago, architects and builders copied with a scarcity of building materials (little wood or stone was available) by learning to make sun-dried bricks from heavy, clay-like soil. They built walls and discovered how to construct arches, a major innovation. Egyptian and Mesopotamian architectural accomplishments diffused to Crete in the Mediterranean Sea, where stone was available and where stone-working progressed considerably during the second millennium B.C.

Greek and Roman Innovations

Techniques in stone architecture diffused to Greece centuries later, and in the great Greek temples and Roman buildings of later years, *classical* architecture reached its zenith. The ancient Greeks created beautifully designed temples consisting of large interior spaces containing the sculpture of a god or goddess, surrounded by exterior rows of great tapered columns, which supported a set of massive stone lintels and an expansive roof. Most of these structures were built between 700 B.C. and the Roman conquest in the middle of the second century B.C. Part of one of the period's finest achievements, the Parthenon, still stands on the Acropolis amid modern Athens. Within the Parthenon stood a huge gold and ivory statue of Athena, and the whole temple was painted in bright colors, the city's dominant landmark.

Greek architectural techniques diffused to Rome, but later Roman innovations themselves constituted a major advance. The Roman architect-engineers built great

arches and vaults, and they were able to create huge domed roofs, such as that of the great Pantheon, thus enclosing more space than had previously been possible. Although the Pantheon in the city of Rome is the best preserved of the ancient Romans' classical architectural achievements, it was by no means the most impressive structure to grace ancient Rome. Great vault-roofed halls, or *basilicas*, served as public facilities; Rome's massive buildings were created for its emperors, the nobility, and the public—not for gods or goddesses. The Pantheon *does* reveal Greece's influence, especially in the impressive doorway, but the great dome, with its circular opening at the top, is a Roman invention, its light flooding the entire interior. Again,

From the Field Notes

❝ The Roman Colosseum inspires awe and revulsion. Awe at the capacities of the Roman architect–engineers, whose structure, built to accommodate 45,000 spectators, still stands 19 centuries later. Revulsion at what happened here—as the photograph at right reminds us. Exposed here are cells and hallways where people and exotic animals to be sacrificed in savage spectacles awaited their fate. ❞

although the Greeks had built impressively designed and executed outdoor theaters and stadiums, nothing rivaled the great Roman Colosseum, completed in A.D. 80 and capable of seating 45,000 spectators.

Classical architecture in the Roman Empire produced thousands of structures distributed across that realm from North Africa to Britain, built between approximately 100 B.C. and A.D. 300. Three historic events influenced the spatial development of architecture after this period. Early during the fourth century A.D., the Emperor Constantine the Great initiated the process that was to make the Roman Empire a Christian state by granting religious freedom to the empire's Christians. Next Constantine laid the basis for the eventual regionalization of the empire by relocating his capital from Rome to the city of Byzantium (renamed Constantinople, and later, Istanbul). Furthermore, the rise of Islam, with its distinctive architec-

tural traditions and achievements, brought Roman and Islamic architecture into fruitful contact.

Constantine's conversion to

Christianity and the religious freedom of Christians in Rome led to a wave of church building on the basilica pattern, and the stage was set

THE TAJ MAHAL

The Taj Mahal, one of the world's most admired buildings, was ordered built by Shah Jehan in memory of his beloved wife, Mumtaz Mahal, who died in childbirth in 1631. The mausoleum was designed by a group of Islamic architects from many parts of the Muslim world, including India, Persia, Turkey, Central Asia, and probably elsewhere as well. The ultimate design is attributed to one of these masters, Ustad Isa. Engineers, master builders, tile makers and layers, calligraphers, and other experts were assembled from all over the Islamic realm. More than 20,000 workers labored on the project, which was started in 1632 and continued until its completion in 1654.

The mausoleum, the central building, was finished in 1643, but work continued for more than a decade on the two flanking mosques, the four minarets, the walls, and the grounds. It stands on a marble base 23 feet (7 meters) high, and rises in a massive dome above the tombs of Shah Jehan and his wife. The mausoleum is also made of white marble, but the flanking mosques are made of reddish sandstone. Exquisite decorations and painstaking detail mark every surface of the Taj Mahal, a monument also to the capacities of Muslim architecture and creative engineering.

From the Field Notes

" From every direction, every angle, the great Notre Dame Cathedral impresses and amazes. For seven hundred years it has stood here, through revolution and war. The interior hall is breathtaking, its stained glass casting is a soft hue. From the top of the north tower, the view of the *Île de la Cité* is commanding; imagine what such a perspective must have meant centuries ago. This must have been a beacon, a sentinel, a symbol of power and continuity in the Paris region's darkest years. "

for the faith's eventual domination of the Western empire. The emergence of Constantinople as a Roman headquarters produced a distinctive regional architecture (called *Byzantine*), which diffused into Eastern Europe and Russia. Among the greatest examples of this style are the church of Saint Sophia in Istanbul and Saint Basil's church in Moscow, the latter built during the sixteenth century.

Elements of Byzantine architecture can be discerned in the Islamic architecture that evolved during the rise of Muslim power. The Muslims and the Romans made contact along a broad Mediterranean front, and a good deal of transculturation took place. Undoubtedly, the Islamic architects were among the most accomplished of their time. Their magnificent mosques and palaces stood from Spain to India. The Taj Mahal, believed by many to be

the most beautiful building ever created, was built by the Indian Muslim ruler, Shah Jehan, at Agra in the mid-1600s (see box, "The Taj Mahal"). Muslim architectural innovations diffused into the Balkans and Russia, into Southern Europe, and, in modified forms and at a later time, around the world.

Post-Roman Stagnation

The breakup of the Roman Empire and Europe's descent into the disarray of the Middle Ages was reflected in its architecture as well. This was the period (beginning during the mid-eleventh century and continuing into the early sixteenth) when the church was the focus of a feudal and fragmented society, and fortified castles and powerful monasteries were the foci of authority. Building styles and techniques reflected their Roman origins, but also the lapse of time; walls were thick,

interior spaces small, rooms dark. *Romanesque* architecture had its focus in Southern Europe, where thick walls made for cool rooms, small window spaces provided sufficient interior lighting, and church congregations tended to be small. Romanesque churches were marked by characteristic round arches and barrel-shaped roofs, and many were comparatively crude and simple, although some surviving examples display considerable elegance (e.g., in Florence's San Miniato and Vezelay's *Basilique de la Madeleine*).

Revival

Gothic architecture emerged slightly later and with a more northerly focus. Real progress returned to Europe with the revival of commerce that began late in the twelfth century, producing the wealth required for experimentation and

ART IN THE CULTURAL LANDSCAPE

Thousands of years ago, the ancient Egyptians, Cretans, Greeks, and Romans sculpted great images of gods, heroes, kings, and natural scenes. Rows of stone sculptures flanked the approaches to Greek temples. Rome was a city of statues and monuments, including elaborately sculpted triumphal arches. In China, ceremonial avenues (such as the one leading to the Ming Tombs) were embellished by great stone sculptures of people, animals, and mythical beasts.

Ornamental art continues to form a significant element in the cultural landscape. "Embellish this city with statues, columns [and] other ornaments," urged the French urban planner, engineer, and architect Pierre Charles l'Enfant, when he submitted to George Washington his grand design for what was to become the capital of the United States. Today, more than 300 memorials, statues, and other monuments grace the open spaces of Washington, D.C.

When you study this "public" art in your own city or town, you will be able to discern several kinds. *Representative* sculptures depict presidents, war heroes, or other prominent personalities. In other cultures, animals (horses, oxen, lions) are often represented. *Commemorative* sculpture includes triumphal arches, such as the famed *Arc de Triomphe* in Paris. In the United States, a tapered column often commemorates wars. *Symbolic* or exhortative sculpture is seen less often in the United States (the Statue of Liberty is the prime example) than in many other countries, especially in the former Soviet Union and in recently decolonized countries to symbolize their liberation. *Decorative* sculpture is often found in association with prominent architectural structures in the form of columns, wall sculptures, and mosaics.

From the Field Notes

❝ The Arc de Triomphe is itself a work of art. Standing nearby, you can discern the exquisite detail of ornamentation; go to the second level of the Eiffel Tower, and the Arc de Triomphe can be seen rising above the townscape of old Paris. Built to commemorate a revolution, this structure has become the rallying place for French nationalism. Millions converge on it when anniversaries of wartime events are observed. ❞

---

innovation. On the old Romanesque plan, architects and engineers now constructed new designs with pointed arches and crossed roof supports that could enclose more space and provide more light. Gothic cathedrals and churches were built in and by hundreds of communities (in France alone, the 100 years after 1160 produced 80 cathedrals and nearly 500 large churches), among them the great Notre Dame of Paris. Begun in 1163, the Cathedral of Notre Dame's first phase was completed in 1240 (additions were made for another 100 years), with magnificent flying buttresses and, originally, superb glass work. Notre Dame's windows are 85 percent glass and only 15 percent frame—frame made not of steel, but of stone. In its time, the great cathedral was an unparalleled technological achievement, its great hall capable of containing nearly 10,000 persons. It still stands today, after centuries of shameful neglect, vandalism, incompetent restoration, and the ravages of age, a monument to Gothic architecture's style and workmanship.

Romanesque and Gothic cultural landscapes in Europe were characterized by dominant religious architecture and modest mass housing. During the late Middle Ages, the commercial age brought the beginnings of change as Gothic designs were also applied to some public buildings, universities (Oxford and Cambridge in England), and private homes. However, the Roman Catholic church continued to predominate, its cathedrals towering over the towns of the realm, and its authority supreme.

Change did not begin until the *Renaissance*, Europe's rebirth, when there was a renewed interest in Greek and Roman arts and sciences, and a search for classical principles. This happened during the fifteenth and sixteenth centuries, and it transformed the cultural landscape (see box, "Art in the Cultural Landscape"). Gothic technology and engineering were combined with classical forms and shapes, and thus was created Saint Peter's Church in Rome, first conceived by Bramante, its gigantic dome designed by Michelangelo, and its fabulous colonnade and Baroque-style *piazza* created later by Bernini. The Renaissance diffused from its Italian source area to Germany, France, Spain, and Britain, where St. Paul's is a fine example. It also affected nonreligious buildings to an unprecedented extent. Palaces, public buildings, and private homes were designed and built, and with an ever more elaborate Renaissance motif. Cities and towns were changing; townscapes were becoming more varied.

The seventeenth century witnessed the intensification of religious conflict in Europe. The Protestant challenge generated the Counter-Reformation, the Catholic revival. Its effects could be seen in the period's architecture, especially in Italy, where such elaborate designs were superimposed on Renaissance forms that a *Baroque* style was distinguished. Baroque ornamentation also diffused outward from Italy, but lost many of its excesses along the way. Baroque period architecture in France and England (including Paris' Louvre and Versailles' Louis XIV Palace) was rather less ornate, less showy than the Italian version. Eventually, the French Baroque gave rise to a special style of architecture and decoration known as the *Rococo*, characterized by smallness and intricate detail.

During the eighteenth century, the *Romantic* age began in Europe—in architecture, art, and music. However, events were about to overtake Europe's series of internal cross-fertilizations. The New World had been located, and the diffusion of architectural styles across the Atlantic had begun. The Industrial Revolution was gaining momentum, and the functionalism of industrial designs overtook the luxurious ornateness of the Romantic and Baroque designs. The Industrial Revolution also produced

the necessary wealth for revivals of old architectural styles, and so a new series of Gothic, Baroque, and Romantic buildings arose. Noteworthy among these are the Houses of Parliament in London, a Gothic design dating from the 1830s (construction was completed in 1867). The (old) Paris Opera, an elaborate Baroque design, was built in 1875. In the United Kingdom, the wealth of the British Empire was reflected by the mixed design, often Romantic style of *Victorian* architecture, which still characterizes much of the townscape of London today.

EASTWARD

The diffusion of architectural styles from Rome into Western Europe and eventually to America, and from Byzantium to Eastern Europe and Russia, was matched by an eastward expansion of Hindu, Buddhist, and Islamic architecture. Hindu religious architecture was marked by columned temples and extremely intricate carving and sculpting. It diffused eastward into Southeast Asia, where one of Hinduism's most magnificent relics is the great temple of Angkor Wat in Cambodia. Buddhism, with its distinctive temples, monasteries, and *stupas* gave Indian architecture a characteristic design that diffused throughout Southeast Asia. Elements of Buddhist religious design diffused to China, and ultimately, to Japan.

Whereas the builders of Roman Europe and those of Southeast Asia's monumental temples used stone (brick and mortar came into use in Europe later), the main building material in China and Japan was wood. Impressive structures were erected and embellished with delicate carvings, and the pagoda motif of slightly upward-curved lower roof lines was adopted for house building as well. With the colonial invasion and subsequent modernization, buildings of

From the Field Notes

❝ The urban landscape of Bangkok, Thailand displays some of the world's most wretched slums, but it also exhibits magnificent palaces, pagodas, and shrines. Among the most elaborate is the Grand Palace, whose three dominant buildings symbolize three stages in the country's historic evolution. As I quickly discovered, to visit the palace and its grounds is to leave one world and enter another. It also is a lesson in Thailand's geography and history. ❞

brick and mortar began to rise over the East Asian urban landscape, and modern Western architecture diffused to this realm as well, especially to Japan. China's commitment to modernization began to accelerate the change in townscapes from Beijing to Guangzhou, but Chinese cities—far more than Tokyo, British-administered Hong Kong, or Singapore—still retain the imprint of the earlier age.

SECULAR URBAN LANDSCAPES

In a sense, the secular architecture of modern America represents a return to pre-Christian times in Rome, and the diffusion process just described has come full circle. In

AMERICAN ARCHITECTURE: COLONIAL TO MODERN

In America, architecture during the late eighteenth century produced a *Colonial* style that mainly derived from British versions of the Renaissance. Perhaps the best example of this form is Carpenter's Hall in Philadelphia (built in 1770), but it is also reflected by thousands of more modest houses in the Northeast, representing the "New England" style. Before long, other adaptations appeared: first a transplanted Roman style, represented by the early nineteenth-century Rotunda at the University of Virginia (Charlottesville) and the Virginia State Capitol in Richmond, and later by a variety of Greek, Gothic, Renaissance, Romantic, and combined forms. Many homes in the East and Southeast were adorned with Greek-style columns, producing imposing facades. The original building of Washington's Smithsonian Institution, completed in 1847, is an excellent example of this *Revival* period in architecture, in this case a Gothic variation. The pointed arches of Princeton University's oldest buildings also evince this Gothic revival, and there were even some Romanesque adaptations. Eventually, various forms of Renaissance architecture became the centerpieces of nineteenth-century American architecture. Boston's Public Library remains a prominent representative landmark of this direction.

Not until the last quarter of the nineteenth century did an architectural style originate in America itself. The introduction of the steel "skeleton" made possible the construction of buildings of great height and enormous interior space. The first skyscraper, a 10-story building in Chicago, was completed in 1884. For a time, architects combined the use of ornamentation with their modern construction, covering the steel skeletons of their office buildings with columns and other Gothic and Baroque-style embellishments. However, soon a truly *Modern* architectural style evolved, and the ornate was abandoned in favor of clean, lean lines, wide expanses of glass, and efficient use of expensive urban space. The contemporary skyline of American cities was taking shape.

The use of steel and concrete made possible the creation of new and innovative architectural landmarks. Needle-thin towers with high-level platforms rose higher than even the tallest skyscrapers. Modern stadiums, architectural and engineering achievements in themselves, were now modified, and became "domed" interior sports arenas, enclosing the largest amount of space ever within a single undivided hall. Airport buildings dramatically displayed modern architectural capacities with soaring vaulted ceilings, huge unbroken expanses of glass, and unique designs. Some of these newest structures, in fact, are increasingly called *Postmodern*, and are found not only in big-city downtowns, but increasingly in the booming retail and office clusters that are emerging throughout suburban America in the 1990s.

Rome before Constantine, the great *forums* were clusters of public buildings (courts, theaters, libraries, baths). The Christian advent shifted the focus of architecture to the religious. Post-Roman and Medieval times witnessed the construction of great Romanesque and Gothic cathedrals and monasteries, and Europe's cultural landscape reflected the primacy of the church.

The importance of the church continued during the Renaissance, but public architecture was making inroads; the nobility and the merchant had wealth to match the church. The Baroque period was a time of royal splendor, and the revolutions that shook Europe during the eighteenth and nineteenth centuries confirmed the decline of the church's role. The Romantic and Victorian expressions were those of comfort, commercial success, and political security, and the centers of European towns and cities were embellished by the elaborate mansions and townhouses of the merchants and businessmen. Factories, warehouses, and auction rooms—the landscape of industry—now contained the largest buildings. When the Industrial Revolution took root in North America, the church had had very little time to establish an architectural dominance over urban places. Modern architecture accurately reflected the strength of industry and commerce in the New World (see box, "American Architecture: Colonial to Modern"). In Europe, as well as in America, the old ornamentations disappeared and practicality became the new objective. "Structure is the aesthetic" was the ruling dictum, and architects led by Le Corbusier and his followers transformed cityscapes. Europe's first truly modern skyscraper rose above Paris, designed by Perret and capped at nine stories in 1903. The Western city of the twentieth century was in the making. For some of the results, see Part 11.

Architecture is the leading influence in forging cultural landscapes, and architectural forms reflect society's reponses to both natural and social environments. Domestic architecture tells us much about regional conditions past and present: sail up the Nile River from Egypt to Uganda (you have to make a few detours past dams and rapids), and you will see the flat-roofed Arab house give way to the cone-shaped African housetop. Look at Figure 2-3, and you can predict where this happens: the virtually rainless Sahara gives way to the moisture of East Africa. As so often happens, this also marks a cultural transition. In the social sphere, the symbolism of the commercial skyscraper replacing the church spire as the dominant and tallest structure in town hardly needs emphasis. Architecture reflects social realities too.

But there is more to the cultural landscape than architecture. The character of a culture region also is defined by modes of dress, and these in turn form an important part of the image the culture presents to the world. We turn next to the forming of such images: how cultures and culture regions are perceived.

KEY TERMS

Architecture
Core Area
Cultural Ecology
Culture Region
Domain
Environmental Determinism
Geomancy
Material Culture
National Culture
Nonmaterial Culture
Possibilism
Public Architecture
Region
Sphere
Subnational Culture

20

CULTURAL PERCEPTIONS AND PROCESSES

Although architecture dominates in the cultural landscape (even simple dwellings in remote forests or mountains constitute architectural forms), other aspects of daily life also contribute. During the 1960s, when thousands of students from African countries came to study in the United States, a Geography professor conducted a survey of their early images of cultural landscapes in this country. Among the top five impressions was a variation of the following: "People and things move so fast here! Everyone seems to be running from one appointment to the next!"

The pace of life is not something that shows up on maps, but it is an aspect of cultural landscapes nevertheless. Courtesy is another. A similar survey in Britain produced many references to the British habit of "queueing," of lining up neatly to await one's turn boarding a bus or paying a bill. Again, this is an image-making tradition that does not have the permanence of an architectural style or a street grid.

Such intangibles in the cultural

Geographica

- People's traditional apparel plays an important part in the composition of the total cultural landscape; attire can make a cultural or even a political statement.

- Cultural regions can be mapped using criteria selected for that purpose, but such regions also exist as part of people's mental maps; perceptual U.S. regions such as the "South" or the "Bible Belt" form examples of these spatial constructs of the mind.

- Ethnic regions and ethnic neighborhoods form part of virtually all larger societies, and ethnicity often serves as a bond for smaller groups while functioning as a barrier to cultural integration in a wider context.

- Cultural revival and cultural linkage continue to reinvigorate ethnic communities.

landscape help define the personality and character of a region. Importantly, they also can contribute to cultural conflict. The violation of traditions by outsiders often leads to the kinds of irritations that produce strife. Personal and aggregate habits are sensitive matters.

LANDSCAPES OF APPAREL

The attire of people in the streets and on the roads is a significant image-maker in the cultural landscape. **Apparel** can make a cultural, even a political statement:

243

of defiance, of commitment, of tradition.

Our awareness of the implications of apparel contributes to our appreciation of cultural landscapes. For example, amid the French-influenced buildings of Dakar, the long, graceful, flowing robes of the Wolof people confirm that this is West Africa, not a Mediterranean coast. The traditional garb of indigenous Fijians—the *sulu*—is more than a garment. It establishes a cultural identity in a plural society. In India, Hindu men tend to wear short coats, and the women wear a long scarf or robe (*sari*). Muslim men, as well as women, wear a long white cotton shirt that hangs over trousers. Westerners in semi-formal attire are identified by shirt, trousers, and coat. The necktie has become a symbol of Westernization.

Clothing is an important aspect of material culture, and although it is not a fixed feature in the cultural landscape, it is a formative element of that landscape nevertheless. An Islamic society is immediately identified by a high incidence of long, widesleeved gowns and turbans. The kimono is as closely associated with traditional Japan as any other element of its culture. Headgear, footwear, hair fashions, jewelry, and even tattooing and cosmetics, typify regional cultures, all contributing to the world's many landscapes of adornment.

ORIGINS AND DIFFUSION

Humanity's expansion into uncomfortable environments (and changing environments where stable human communities existed) led to the need for clothing, but protection was only one of the motivations toward dress. A growing sense of modesty appears also to have played a role, as well as a desire for group and class distinction

as communities grew more complex. A yearning for adornment and beautification was expressed in clothing, as well as in accessories. A sense of power and affiliation is also expressed by uniforms and religious garb.

Thus clothing became a matter of beauty and status, as well as protection, and communities with different perceptions and needs developed different kinds of bodily cover. Probably the oldest form of clothing was the piece of animal skin, draped over the shoulders. Pieces of soft tree bark were similarly used. Cloaks, capes, and mantles became increasingly decorative in some societies (the Polynesian Hawaiians made magnificent, vividly colored capes using thousands of bird feathers), but remained merely functional elsewhere (as among the cattle-herding peoples of East Africa).

Draping a garment over the body is more effective when the garment is woven or knitted. The invention of forms of weaving and knitting probably occurred in different areas of the world, separate inventions about which relatively little is yet known. It is reasonable to assume that the technique of knitting was learned by peoples in regions where sheep were domesticated, probably in Central Asia, but there is a remarkable lack of correlation between apparent environmental imperatives and the use of cloth. Peoples in the coldest regions (such as Tasmania, where winters are frigid, and in Tierra del Fuego, in subantarctic South America), when first encountered by Europeans, wore very little clothing or none at all. Societies in warmer environments were better clothed.

It is possible to discern some early regional differentiation in the use of textiles. In East Asia, the Chinese developed the use of silk. South Asian societies employed jute. Forms of cotton were grown in

From the Field Notes

❝ Men wear the *sulu* in Fiji, a wraparound garment that evolved from Polynesian dress modes. It certainly is an element of the local cultural landscape. We all acquired a *sulu* and found it comfortable and very suitable to the tropical environment. In fact, we wore *sulus* during our entire stay in Suva, and soon forgot how unusual this dress mode had at first appeared to us. ❞

Southwest Asia, East and Northeast Africa, and in Middle America, where sisal and henequen also were in use. Not only cloaks and capes but also blankets and even headgear were made of woven or knitted textiles.

Tailoring appeared and diffused much later. For all their accomplishments, the Romans wore comparatively simple, loose tunics and long, sleeved togas, although these were decorated and colored to identify class and status. Tailored clothing appeared as a culture trait among peoples of the Siberian and American northlands, where envi-

From the Field Notes

" Over the years, the wearing of traditional dress has become less common in modernizing Japan, even in the smaller towns of the interior and the west coast. When I saw this mother and her daughter on the Ginza in Tokyo, it was unusual enough to record it. Except for ceremonial occasions, only the very old still wear traditional garb. "

ronment certainly must have been a factor; form-fitted clothing protects better than loosely draped mantles. Tailoring may have been invented independently in China, where it developed into a fine art. Among the Eurasian and American subarctic peoples, tailoring involved the sewing together of pre-cut pieces of cured reindeer or caribou skin to make coats, trousers, hats, gloves, and boots. The Inuit and Canada's Native peoples refined the technique considerably, created fur-lined collars and sleeves, and dyeing and decorating their garments.

Whether tailoring was invented by the ancient Chinese and diffused northward to the Arctic-fringe peoples of Northeast Asia, or whether the basic technique was invented there and spread into China to be refined, is still an unsolved geographic problem. The Chinese, using their exquisitely fine silks,

created the most exquisitely beautiful clothing, and their techniques diffused westward and into Europe during the Middle Ages. European clothing styles, like those of monumental architecture and serious music, went through periods of elaboration and embellishment, but eventually (following the Industrial Revolution), a more or less standard European style evolved. Suits and dresses came to symbolize not only European cultures, but also European power and conquest. Mass-produced cotton and woolen textiles made inroads among virtually all cultures, and wearing the European fashion became a personal statement of modernity and worldliness. Christian prescriptions imposed new standards of modesty on peoples for whom partial coverage of the body had always been a matter of sensible adjustment to the natural environment. So the drab cotton dress replaced the colorful

sarong, and the shirt and trousers took the place of the handsome cloaks and mantles of non-Western cultures.

REGIONAL CLOTHING

And yet the impress of clothing still marks the cultural landscapes of world regions. It was one of the major aims of the Iranian revolution of the late 1970s to return to Islamic dress codes (especially for women), but Islamic influence over dress remains strong in most Muslim societies. More than perhaps any other element, clothing styles in a picture of a Middle Eastern street scene reveal the cultural norms. The sari continues to be worn by millions of Indian women, and the dhoti by Indian men, as was the case before the Muslim invasion. Western-style dress has been widely adopted in Japan, but the kimono remains an item of national culture. In West Africa, traditional dress with bright colors and loose form continues to be worn, along with the business suit and fashionable European-style dress.

Regional variations can be observed within geographic realms as well. In India, Zoroastrian women wear their sari over the right shoulder and not, as others do, over the left, thus marking their area of concentration in and around Bombay. The stronger impact of Islam in northern India compared to the south is also reflected in dress codes. Although it is mainly a ceremonial attire now, the kilt is still routinely worn by men in Scotland.

FOOTWEAR

Hundreds of millions of people in this world do not normally wear a boot, shoe, sandal, or any other protection for the foot. Footwear is a necessity in harsh environments, but it is a luxury in warmer climes where other needs may be more pressing. Again, different kinds of footwear were invented or adopted in various areas of the world; the Inuit made heavy boots, Native Americans learned to make moccasins, and sandals developed in temperate climes from the Mediterranean to South Asia. The leather shoe, an accessory to modern European-style clothing, has diffused to virtually all parts of the world, but it remains a symbol of comparative wealth and, in black Africa, for example, chiefly an urban phenomenon.

Footwear also is sometimes associated with culture regions. *Klompen*, or wooden shoes, immediately evoke an image of the Netherlands, although their routine use there is mainly a thing of the past. Cowboy boots typify the American Southwest, especially Texas. Cleated wooden-soled sandals are traditional footwear in East Asia.

HEADGEAR

Only in the most frigid regions on Earth is the wearing of protective headgear an absolute necessity. Inuit and other far-northern peoples developed effective caps and fur hats, but peoples living under the searing tropical sun did not. Migrations into new and different environments did lead to protective adaptation, such as the straw "Panama" hat in tropical American environments and the cowboy hat of the sun-drenched, semiarid southwestern United States. However, most headgear is embellishment, beautification, or a mark of status or authority.

As such, headgear affords almost unlimited opportunities for adornment and the establishment of identity. When the Ottoman Turks expanded their empire in Asia, Africa, and Europe, they took to wearing a bright red fez, a flat-topped, rimless hat that became a symbol of their power. Its use was abolished by Turkey's modern leader, Kemal Ataturk, in 1925, but it continued to be in use in some Muslim countries afterward, including Indonesia, where its color is black. The English bowler hat also became a symbol of sorts, as it was diffused around the world with British colonial representatives. The religious use of headgear need hardly be emphasized, ranging from elaborate Sikh turbans to simple Jewish skullcaps. As a symbol of authority, headgear is used in numerous ways to establish rank in military forces and police units. The particular shape of the English policeman's helmet remains in use in many formerly British dependencies, establishing that identity at a glance.

ADORNMENT

Clothing, footwear, and headgear all form part of the overall material culture landscape, and so do styles and fashions of personal adornment. Hairstyles are among the more prominent types of personal adornment. In some cultures, the growing of a large beard is an indi-

FOLK CULTURE AND POPULAR CULTURE

Human geographers distinguish between material and nonmaterial culture. They also find it useful to differentiate between folk culture and popular culture.

Folk culture describes the dwellings, dress modes, tools, and other artifacts of material culture, and the institutions and traditions, as well as other achievements, of nonmaterial culture, all belonging to a usually small, often isolated, relatively changeless, tradition-bound community. Self-reliance, subsistence, and technological simplicity mark these fragile cultures, of which only remnants remain in the modernizing, developed world.

Popular culture, in contrast, identifies the changeable, urban-centered, media-drenched, fad-addicted society with which we in North America are well acquainted. While elements of folk culture survive even in this mobile, nontraditional, heterogeneous cultural environment, these have been overwhelmed by the mass-produced, disposable, innovative manufactures of the industrial age.

Popular culture is mass culture, regional culture, even national culture. Its landscapes have diffused far and wide, so that (natural environmental contrasts aside) the small-town commerical strip and motel row in South Carolina is visually very similar to that in, say, Oregon. But the diffusion of popular culture has not erased regional distinctions. The South today may be less distinctly Southern than it was two generations ago, but its cultural heritage (much of it modified from earlier folk traits) still exists. Perceptual regions, therefore, also are called **popular regions** and, at larger scales, **vernacular regions**.

As we note later in this chapter, folk-culture heritage may be strengthened, even resurrected, in the interest of ethnic identity and political separatism. This blend of folk culture and popular culture poses a challenge to the political order for many national cultures today.

cation of status, for example, among Sikhs and Shiite Muslims. Mustaches are popular in Western cultures as evidence of masculinity and as decoration.

Other forms of personal beautification include tattooing, which among Maori New Zealanders has developed into a veritable art form, and various kinds of scarification, declining in incidence but characteristic still of Africa and Australian/ Melanesian cultures. Ear piercing by women in Western cultures continues as well.

The wearing of jewelry and other kinds of ornaments is so universal a practice that it is difficult to establish regional identities. Nevertheless, certain regional cultures do display characteristic types. Indian traditions are rich and varied, and Indian women (and men as well) wear much jewelry, including large earrings and pendants, long and multichained necklaces, elaborate bracelets, and pins. Indian women have sometimes embedded a jewel in the center of the forehead and pierced the left nostril to carry a jewel there. In China, on the other hand, jewelry is designed to beautify the costume, rather than the body, and the "loud" necklaces and bracelets of other cultures are rare. In Africa, a long tradition of gold jewelry making served mainly the chiefs and others of high rank, especially in West Africa, but other kinds of adornment reached high standards. The beadwork of the Maasai, for example, symbolizes a person's position in the community (e.g., eligibility for marriage), as well as serving to beautify.

Regional cultural landscapes consist of these and many more components that together form what we may call the culture's total geographic inventory. This chapter reminds us how widely cultural innovations have diffused, and yet culture regions retain their spatial identities. These spatial identities

form the basis of regionalisms all over the world, and they are often carefully protected and nurtured by the people whose histories they represent. This leads us directly into the twin topics of the next step in our investigation of the geography of culture: the way cultural regions, landscapes, and their inhabitants are *perceived*, and how such perceptions sometimes contribute to strong ethnic identities in the mosaic of culture.

PERCEPTUAL REGIONS

How is the cultural landscape perceived? This is part of a larger question in human geography, a question that is relevant to every aspect of the field. In Part 1, we noted that people of all cultures have spatial memories, or *mental maps*, that form part of their equipment to function in their activity spaces. Our discussion of population geography referred to perceptions of population growth and its relationship to economic development: from *our* viewpoint, many countries are underdeveloped and poor. From the perspective of those countries, our society may seem overdeveloped and wasteful. In discussing migration, we compared "push" and "pull" factors, both matters of perception, one usually more accurate than the other. So it is with culture and the cultural landscape. Our perceptions of our own community and culture may differ quite sharply from others' perceptions thereof. Such perceptions, and misperceptions, are the topics of this chapter. As we will see, this topic ranges from the abstract—the mapping of **perceptual regions**—to the practical.

As diverse definitions of the regional concept, as well as the concept of culture, remind us, these

are intellectual constructs to help us understand the nature and distribution of phenomena in human geography. Even the scholars who use them do not agree entirely on their properties. But they do concur that we all carry impressions and images of regions and cultures. These perceptions are based on our accumulated knowledge about such regions and cultures (see box, "Folk Culture and Popular Culture"). The natural environment, too, is part of this inventory. Visualize Swiss culture, and the unifying image of a mountainous, Alpine environment may come to mind, when in fact Swiss culture is divided by language, religion, and tradition.

Although it is easy to explain in general terms how one perceives a **culture region**, the exercise becomes much more challenging when we are asked to put our impressions on a map. For example, consider a regional term often used in various contexts, the *Mid-Atlantic Region*. Weather forecasters on television can be seen to refer to the "Mid-Atlantic area" or the "Mid-Atlantic States" as they divide their maps into manageable pieces. But where *is* this Mid-Atlantic region? If Maryland and Delaware are part of it, then eastern Pennsylvania is, too. But where, across Pennsylvania, lies the boundary of this partly cultural, partly physical region, and on what basis can it be drawn? There is no single best answer (Fig. 20-1).

Again, we all have a mental map of the *South* as a culture region of the United States. But drive southward from, say, Pittsburgh or Detroit, and it will be impractical to try to discern a specific place where you enter this perceptual region. You will note features in the cultural landscape that you perceive to be associated with the South until, at some stage of the trip, they begin to dominate the area to such a degree that you will say to yourself, "I

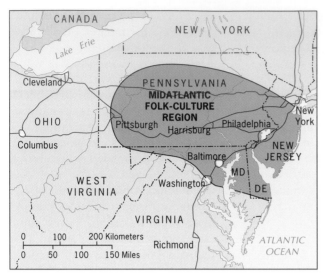

FIGURE 20–1 One delimitation of a Mid-Atlantic culture region. See H. Glassie, *Pattern in the Material Folk Culture of the Eastern United States* (Philadelphia: University of Pennsylvania Press, 1968), p. 39.

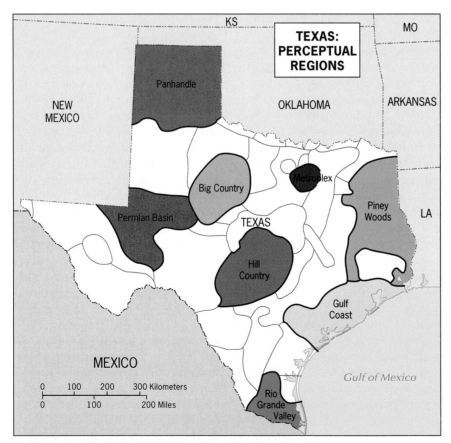

FIGURE 20–2 Prominent perceptual regions of Texas. From T.G. Jordan, "Perceptual Regions in Texas," *Geographical Review* 68 (1978), p. 295.

am really in the South now." This may result from a combination of features of material as well as non-material culture: the form of houses and their porches, items on a road-side restaurant menu (grits, for example), a local radio station's music, the sound of accents you perceive to be Southern, a succession of Baptist churches in a town along the way. These combined impressions now become part of your overall perception of the South as a region.

Perceptual regions can be studied at all levels. The dozen world geographic realms that form the basis of a course in world regional geography are perceptual units at the smallest of scales; at the opposite, largest end of the scale is (for example) a minute region defined by one of the remaining communities of Amish culture in the United States. Quite possibly, our perceptions are weakest and least accurate at each end of the scale: at the small scale because so much information must be synthesized that images become distorted, and at the large scale because most diminutive cultures within cultures are not well defined as part of our general spatial knowledge. An interesting example of regional definition at an intermediate scale occurs in an article by Professor Terry Jordan entitled, "Perceptual Regions in Texas" (1978). Like all of us, Texans use regional-cultural names for various parts of their state, and Professor Jordan, in this article, determines where such names as *Panhandle, Gulf Coast, Permiam Basin,* and *Metroplex* actually apply (Fig. 20-2).

UNITED STATES PERCEPTUAL REGIONS

The cultural geographer Wilbur Zelinsky tackled the enormous, complex task of defining and delimiting the perceptual regions of the United States and southern Canada. In an article entitled "North America's Vernacular Regions" (1980), Professor Zelinsky identified 12 major perceptual regions on a series of maps. Figure 20-3 summarizes these regions (it deletes two small and comparatively unfamiliar names), and, of necessity, it shows overlaps between certain units. For example, the more general term "the West" obviously incorporates more specific regions, such as the Pacific Region and part of the Northwest.

The problem of defining and delimiting perceptual regions can be approached in several ways. One of these involves an elaborate system of interviews in which people residing within, as well as outside of, the postulated region are asked to respond to questions about their home and cultural environment. Professor Zelinsky, in this 1980 study, used a different technique: he analyzed the contents of the telephone directories of 276 metro-

politan areas in the United States and Canada, noting the frequencies with which businesses and other enterprises list themselves with regional or locational terms (such as "*Southern* Printing Company"). The resulting maps, in several instances, show quite a close similarity between regions so defined and those of culture regions in North America as delimited by geographers, indicating that popular perceptions about regions are sometimes quite accurate.

CULTURE REGIONS AND REGIONALISM

Culture regions also can represent an emotional commitment on the part of those who identify themselves with them. Among the perceptual regions shown in Figure 20-3, one is unlike any of the others: the South. Even today, five generations after the Civil War, the Confederate flag still has a regional connotation, the "Bible belt" still

prevails, and in songs and dialects, the South's unique position among American regions is entrenched. Certainly, a "New South" has emerged over the past several decades, forged by Hispanic immigration, urbanization, Sunbelt movements, and other processes. But the South—especially the rural South—continues to carry imprints of a material culture long past. Its legacy of nonmaterial culture is equally strong, preserved in language, religion, music, food preferences, and other traditions and customs.

In the South, such cultural attributes give a certain social atmosphere to the region, an atmosphere that is appreciated by many of its residents and is sometimes advertised as an attraction for potential visitors. "Experience the South's warmth, courtesy, and pace of life," said one such commercial recently, illustrated by a sun-drenched, seaside landscape, a bowing host, and a couple strolling a palm-lined path. Such images may or may not represent the perceptions of most inhabitants of the region, but few Southerners would object to publicity of this kind.

The South has its vigorous supporters and defenders, and occasionally a politician uses its embattled history to rouse racial antagonism in search of votes. But today the South is so multifaceted, so diverse, so vigorous, and so interconnected with the rest of the United States that its regional identity is mainly a matter of academic interest. No group, or combination of groups, in the South today seeks to mobilize regional sentiment toward the region's secession from the United States. No one is proposing any form of autonomy for a state or group of states south of the Mason-Dixon line.

Elsewhere, however, discrete and strongly defined culture regions have become political (and even

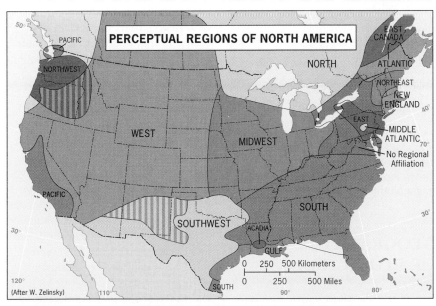

FIGURE 20–3 From W. Zelinsky, "North America's Vernacular Regions," *Annals* of the AAG 70 (1980), p. 14.

From the Field Notes

❝ This streetcorner seemed to symbolize changing perceptions of Singapore. Once a busy, congested town in which traditional Chinese houses and shops dominated the cultural landscape and street markets flourished, Singapore is in the final stages of a transformation to high–rise modernity. This is *not* a case of sequent occupance, but rather one of substitution through modernization. ❞

actual) battlegrounds. Emotional attachments to territory and tradition can run so strong that they supersede feelings of nationhood. This leads us to a complex and current topic in cultural geography: **ethnicity**.

GEOGRAPHY OF ETHNICITY

We all use the term *ethnic* routinely: to describe a city's neighborhood, to identify a certain restaurant's cuisine. In the American mosaic of cultures, ethnic enclaves are common and have names such as "Little Italy," "Chinatown," or "Little Havana." Such names signify clusters of people whose ancestries and cultures give them a common ground, a special identity in a city's social mix. Ethnic heritage lingers in the countryside, too, and sometimes place names form part of the evidence, for example, Holland (Michigan), Denmark (Wisconsin), and Stockholm (North Dakota).

Exactly what does the term *ethnic* mean? It comes from the ancient Greek word *ethnos*, meaning "people" or "nation." In Latin, the adjective became *ethnicus*, and hence ethnic, also an adjective. But look in any good English dictionary and note what happens when it is used in the combined form, for example *ethnology* and *ethnogeny*. Now the definitions begin to specify a crucial component: race. The adjective ethnic, therefore, refers to culture (traditions, customs, language, religion) and, in a general, often vague sense, to racial ancestry.

This racial identity is largely a matter of self-perception. When, in 1991, the Yugoslavian republic of Slovenia declared its independence, local newspapers carried reports justifying that decision on various grounds. Those reports frequently referred to the rights of the Slovenian "race" to control its own domain. But in the ethnic makeup of Slovenia, race is much less consequential than cultural and natural environments. Slovenian is a discrete Slavic language (see the discussion in Part 7), and Slovenia lies to the northwest of the religious transition zone that crosses Yugoslavia, between Roman Catholicism and Eastern Orthodox faith (see Part 8). As we noted previously, natural environment also plays its role in the forging of cultural identity. Slovenians refer to their country an an Alpine, not a Balkan, republic. Slovenian nationalists may have called upon race to bolster the people's nationalism, but the strength of Slovenian ethnicity is based on other cultural traditions and customs.

Ethnicity thus accrues from different combinations of cultural traditions, racial background, and even physical environments. In Northern Ireland, there is no racial distinction between two ethnic groups locked in a tragic struggle: the dominant ethnic glue is religion, Catholic for one community, Protestant for the other. In Belgium, that glue is principally linguistic. In Northern Belgium, the Flemings form an ethnic entity of more than 6 million people. Heirs to the rich culture history of Flanders, the Flemings speak a Dutch-derived language. Southern Belgium is the domain of nearly 4 million French-speaking Walloons. The capital, Brussels (Bruxelles), lies north of the ethnic chasm that splits Belgium, a divide so deep that each region has its own parliament. As in so many multiethnic countries, one ethnic group (in this case the Walloons) fears domination by a larger or more powerful ethnic group within the national boundaries.

Race can, of course, be a very strong force in ethnic gestation. A good modern example is the growing strength of the Maori (Polynesian) community in New Zealand, now numbering about 450,000 in a population of 3.5 million people. Growing ethnic awareness and identity have impelled the Maoris to launch a campaign not just to improve their position in New Zealand society, but also to regain about half of the national territory. Asserting that the British settlers of New Zealand have violated the Treaty of Waitanga, dated 1840, the Maoris have begun extended court battles to achieve this. In the process, the ethnic consciousness of Maori society is strengthening, and at the heart of it lies Maori ancestry.

Thus, like culture, ethnicity exists at many spatial dimensions. Ethnic communities in American cities and towns often are quite small, sometimes numbering no more than a few thousand people. On a national scale, ethnic groups, as in the case of Yugoslavia and Belgium, number in the millions. The underlying rationale is the same: there is comfort and security in the familiarity of one's own culture and cultural landscape. In the smaller urban communities, group identity and cohesiveness yield advantages for the individual: it constitutes a social network and, in case of personal difficulty, a safety net. Members of a particular ethnic community may be especially successful in certain businesses in the larger urban scene, and they will promote their "own" in such businesses. For new arrivals, an ethnic neighborhood will ease the transition because a familiar language is still in use, the

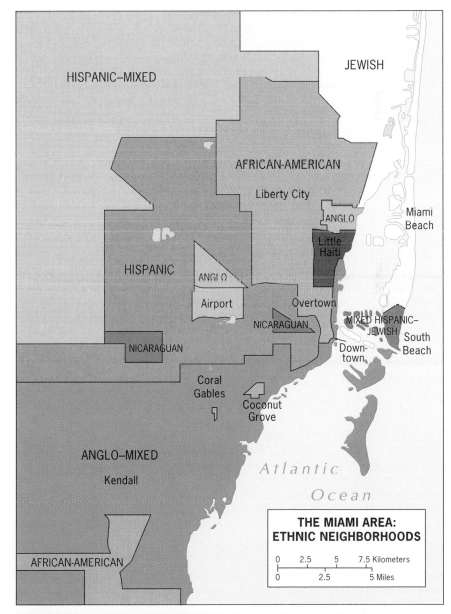

FIGURE 20–4 Ethnic majorities in Miami-area neighborhoods, 1992.

ETHNICITY AND ENVIRONMENT

The ethnic neighborhoods in American cities developed as immigrants clustered in particular areas of growing metropolitan areas. Having left the crowded cities and sweatshop industries of Europe, many of these immigrants were familiar with urban environs. Jobs, not climate or landscape, were the determinants of location.

Others, however, came with rural backgrounds and experience in farming. To them, something approaching a familiar natural environment was desirable. Thus it is no accident that rural ethnic groups in America often are associated with natural environs similar to those of their source areas: Scandinavians in Minnesota, Finns in northern Wisconsin, Germans in central and southern Wisconsin, Hollanders in western Michigan, and Italians in California.

These rural **ethnic islands** in the cultural mosaic of America reflect the perceptions of their inhabitants, both of the natural environment they left behind (which they knew quite well) and the environment they selected here (of which they knew much less). Similar relief and natural vegetation did not always mean similar climate and soils, and some communities could not adjust. But many more made the right choice, and from the German and English dairy farmers of Wisconsin to the Italian winegrowers of California, they brought prosperity to the lands they occupied.

Young Cuban-Americans, born in Florida, are adopting American cultural norms.

Does this mean that the Cuban ethnic neighborhood will disappear from Miami's urban scene? All ethnic communities go through transitions before stabilizing, and Miami's Cuban community is no exception. It is presently in transition, a process that will be further affected by the coming political changes in Cuba itself. Eventually, the Miami urban mosaic will contain stable Cuban-American ethnic neighborhoods in addition to its other ethnic clusters (Fig. 20-4).

Acculturation, even in the American "melting pot," is not quickly leading to the assimilation of ethnic cultures or neighborhoods (see box, "Ethnicity and Environment"). Two factors appear to be responsible: first, the process of cultural revival that continuously reinvigorates ethnic communities, and second, the growing awareness of cultural linkage that is infusing ethnic groups with new (and sometimes problematic) energy.

The process of **cultural revival** takes several forms. In both urban and rural settings, people of similar ethnic background at first clustered in particular areas, but later diffused outward, relocating some distance

common church marks the urban landscape, and stores carry products valued in the local culture. Thus there is advantage in the self-preservation of an ethnic neighborhood, where local group cohesiveness protects and preserves customs and traditions to mutual advantage.

of Miami's Little Havana was forged by a transplanted community now one generation older. The Spanish (only)-speaking, aged domino players in the neighborhood's parks now represent a dwindling minority. The old values (strong family ties, regular Catholic church attendance, strict schooling) still prevail, but acculturation is eroding them.

ACCULTURATION AND ETHNICITY

The persistence of the urban ethnic neighborhood (not only in America, but in cities throughout the world) seems to contradict what we noted previously about the pervasiveness of popular culture. Certainly, the diffusion of popular American culture traits affects ethnic neighborhoods and erodes their cohesiveness. This process is evident today in Miami's Cuban neighborhoods, in which the strength of ethnic identity is far greater among the old than among the young. The Cuban townscape

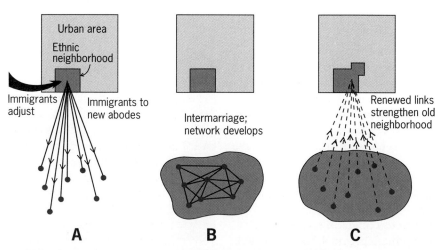

FIGURE 20–5 Immigration, intermarriage, and cultural revival.

(sometimes quite far) from the clustered community that once served as a stepping stone during the difficult days of immigration (Fig. 20-5A). In their new locale, over several generations, these dispersed migrants increase in numbers, intermarry, and form a loose network of often successful families still conscious of their shared ethnicity (Fig. 20-5B). As this dispersed population matures, its comparative prosperity generates funds with which to revive the old ties to the common cultural source. Now the old neighborhood is reinforced and reenergized by these renewed links (Fig. 20-5C). For example, the newspapers published in various languages for particular ethnic communities have seen both their total circulation and their regional dissemination grow as a result.

A renewed awareness of **cultural linkage** also tends to counter assimilation. Such awareness is strengthened these days by the enhanced flow of information through the modern media. In recent years we have witnessed this in the United States: during the breakdown of the Soviet empire, Lithuanian-Americans marched on the White House in support of Lithuania's struggle for independence and Ukrainian communities in the U.S. rallied for Ukrainian sovereignty. Serbian and Croatian neighborhoods, in North America as well as Europe, are galvanized by the struggle in the former Yugoslavia. African-Americans in the United States marched in solidarity with black South Africans during the struggle to end *Apartheid*. Such emotional involvement revives ethnic consciousness and culture.

CANADA AND QUEBEC

As the foregoing paragraphs suggest, cultural revival and cultural linkage are cyclic processes. Lith-

From the Field Notes

❝ Automobile license plates in Quebec send a cultural-political message: 'I remember.' What will not be forgotten is Quebec's Frenchness, its aspirations to be 'itself' in a greater Canada. But Anglophone Canadians living in Quebec may not *souvenir* anything of the sort. ❞

uania and Ukraine achieved independence; the common cause that stimulated and aroused ethnic consciousness in American-Lithuanian and American-Ukrainian communities lost its urgency. But a conflict between Russia and Ukraine, for example, over the Crimea Peninsula, could quickly revive it.

Cultural consciousness also seems to ebb and flow without such external stimuli. Economic circumstances in a community vary over time, and prosperity plays a role in cultural perception and sensitivity. As a result, ethnic communities that have long been stable and undergoing assimilation during good economic times may erupt in disharmony and even separatism when times get tough. Other causes may lie in perceived discrimination, political leadership (a powerful political figure can inspire cultural revival), and anticipated threats to cultural identity (the growing use of English words in local vocabularies, for instance).

All these forces affect Canada today. Like the United States, Canada is a **plural society** and, viewed in

a world perspective, one of the most stable and successful. Canada's population of more than 27 million people consists of more than one ethnic group and includes people with British, French, Native American, Asian, Eastern European, and other ancestries. Territorially, Canada is even larger than the United States. Despite its ethnic diversity, Canada's population is only slight more than one-tenth that of its southern neighbor.

Again, like the United States, multicultural Canada is governmentally organized as a federal state. But the two systems look and work quite differently. Canada is divided administratively into 10 provinces, two territories, and the specially designated territory of Nunavut, set aside for the indigenous peoples who rightfully call themselves the First Americans (Fig. 20-6). The two territories, Yukon and the Northwest Territories, together occupy an area larger than Alaska occupied by less than 100,000 people.

Canada's 10 provinces range in size from tiny, Delaware-sized Prince Edward Island to vast Que-

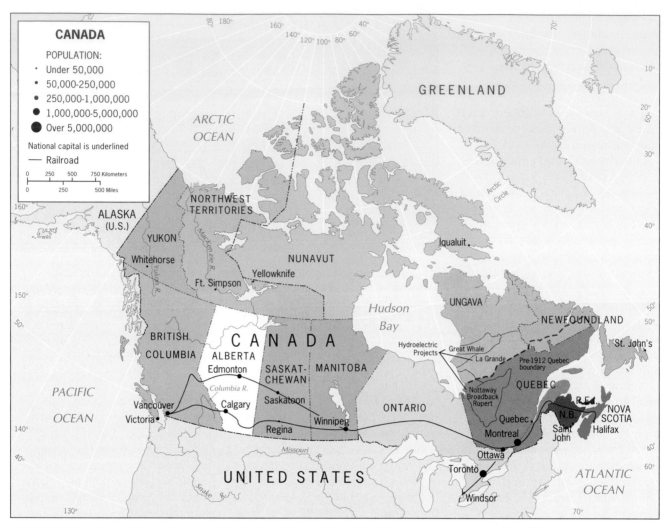

FIGURE 20–6 Canada's provinces and territories. The entity entitled Nunavut was proposed in 1992 to recognize the territorial rights of indigenous peoples in this area.

bec, more than twice as large as Texas. Each province has its own Legislative Assembly (Quebec calls this its *National* Assembly) and Premier. The country also is divided into 295 federal electoral districts, from which representatives to the House of Commons (Canada's Congress) are chosen.

Because of its vast regional geography, Canada faces diverse problems in its various provinces. The economies of the Atlantic Provinces have long stagnated. In the far west, British Columbia's economy grows more rapidly—but so does its immigrant population, posing a

social and cultural challenge. Such regional contrasts were anticipated when, in 1867, the British North America Act established the Canadian federation. At the time, not all of present-day Canada joined; much of the West had yet to be organized. But the last province to join the federation was not a western one; it was Newfoundland, a holdout until 1949.

Modern, prosperous Canada would seem to have everything: a vast territory with a wealth of resources, a small, slow-growing population, a modern economy with high incomes by world stan-

dards, and a system of government that can accommodate the regionalisms its huge area may bring. Canada's provinces are accustomed to a degree of autonomy of which other constituents of federal states can only dream; Canada truly has been a federation of consensus. And yet Canada has suffered from the tensions of its fundamental duality for over a century. Periodically acute crises have been sparked by changes in government policy, attempts to negotiate constitutional solutions to regional concerns and even terrorism. The fundamental cause: ethnicity and ethnic revival.

FRENCH CANADA

To understand how cultural stresses pushed Canada to this critical stage, we should take account of the historical geography of settlement and the federation's relative location. Contemporary eastern Canada was settled first by aboriginal people and later (c. 1000 A.D.) by the Norse in Newfoundland, and possibly by Basque fishermen between 1000 and 1500 A.D. The French, followed by the British, entered what is present-day Canada in the 1530s. *New France*, during the seventeenth century, grew to encompass the St. Lawrence basin, the Great Lakes region, and the Mississippi valley. (The names of the great French missionaries and explorers who led this advance are still on the map today: Marquette, La Salle, Duluth, and others). In the late 1680s, a series of wars between the English and the French began, ending with France's defeat and the cession of New France to Britain in 1763.

By the time Britain took control of New France, the French had made considerable progress in their American domain. French laws, the French land-tenure system, and the Roman Catholic church prevailed, and substantial settlements (including Montreal on the St. Lawrence) had been established. The British, anxious to avoid a war of suppression and preoccupied with problems in other American colonies, gave former New France (the region extending from the Great Lakes to the mouth of the St. Lawrence) the right to retain its legal and land-tenure systems, as well as freedom of religion.

After the American War of Independence, the British were left with a region they called British North America (the name Canada was not yet in use), but whose cultural imprint still was strongly French. The war drove many thousands of British refugees northward, and soon there were difficulties between the

French and the English in British North America. In 1791, heeding appeals by British settlers, the British Parliament divided Quebec into two provinces: Upper Canada, the region upstream from Montreal centered on Lake Ontario, and Lower Canada, the valley of the St. Lawrence. Upper and Lower Canada became, respectively, the provinces of Ontario and Quebec. By parliamentary plan, Ontario would become English-speaking and Quebec would remain French-speaking (Fig. 20-6).

This earliest cultural division did not work well, and in 1840, the British Parliament tried again, this time by reuniting the two provinces in the Act of Union. Upper and Lower Canada would have equal representation in the provincial legislature. This, too, was a failure, and efforts to find a better system led to the 1867 British North America Act, establishing the Canadian federation (initially of Upper and Lower Canada, New Brunswick, and Nova Scotia, later to be joined by the other provinces and territories). By this Act, Ontario and Quebec were once again separated, but this time Quebec was given important guarantees. The French civil code was left unchanged, and the French language was protected in parliament and in the courts.

One hundred years later, an event occurred that at the time seemed little more than a noteworthy incident, but which in fact was a portent. The President of France, Charles de Gaulle, while visiting Canada on the occasion of its centennial celebrations, made unconcealed appeals to French nationalism. In Montreal before a huge audience, he ended a speech by shouting *Vive le Quebec Libre!* The thunderous response from the crowd left no doubt that he had touched a sensitive nerve in Quebec society. Quebecers had not had a strong Canadian champion, let

alone an international one. Polls indicated that most Quebecers felt themselves to be second-class citizens in their own country; that bilingualism meant that French-speakers had to learn English, but not vice versa, and that Quebec was not getting its fair share of the wealth of Canada.

ETHNIC REVIVAL

Since the 1960s, the intensity of ethnic feeling Quebec has risen in surges, despite government efforts to satisfy Quebec's demands. In the 1970s, while a Quebecer was Prime Minister of Canada, it seemed that a new constitution might satisfy Quebec's demands. In 1976, a political party that espoused separatism in Quebec finally came to power in the province, but in 1980, Quebec's voters rejected sovereignty when given that option in a referendum. Yet the new constitution did *not* satisfy Quebec, and polls indicated that, given another chance, voters in Quebec would indeed support separation from Canada. To prevent a crisis, Quebec was asked to present its terms for continued membership in the Canadian federation. It did so, the key demand being its recognition as a "distinct society" within Canada. At a meeting at Meech Lake in 1987, the 10 prime ministers of all of Canada's provinces agreed to these terms, which were to be ratified by their parliaments. When the deadline for ratification came, in 1990, the parliaments of Newfoundland and Manitoba had failed to ratify, and Quebec had reason to feel rejected. Demands for a new referendum on secession arose immediately.

In the meantime, ethnic issues in Quebec, especially those involving language, reached unprecedented intensity. More than 85 percent of Quebec's more than 7 million people speak French at home, but that still leaves a substantial minority of non-French speakers. In 1977, the Quebec Parliament passed a law that compelled all businesses in the province to demonstrate that they functioned in French. This led to an exodus of businesses and individuals to Ontario. Canada's Supreme Court ruled against Quebec's language legislation, but this only emboldened the provincial lawmakers. In 1988, Quebec enacted a law that not only reinstated the legislation the Supreme Court had invalidated, but also added a regulation that made it illegal to exhibit any outdoor commercial sign in a language other than French within the entire province of Quebec.

Predictably, such actions caused counterreactions elsewhere in Canada. With fewer than 700,000 French-speaking Canadians living outside Quebec, other provinces reconsidered the costs of bilingualism. If English could be treated as it was within Quebec, should French be accorded its rightful equality under the law in, say, Alberta or Saskatchewan? And feelings of ethnicity rose further among Canada's native peoples as well. Canada counts more than 500,000 native inhabitants, members of nearly 600 distinct bands. Their leaders pointed out that the "distinct society" clause in the Meech Lake Accord, if it could apply to French-speaking Quebecers, it certainly should apply to them. But the Meech Lake Accord says nothing about "distinct societies" of Quebec's indigenous peoples.

The prospect of Quebec's separation from Canada undoubtedly would intensify Native Canadian activism. Canada's Native peoples want their rights protected by the Canadian federal government against the provinces. Quebec's Amerindian communities, when they do not use their own languages, tend to use English, a legacy of the time when they supported the British during their North American wars. Quebec's Mohawks, for example, do not wish to become part of a sovereign Quebec.

TERRITORIAL ADJUSTMENTS

Such ethnic assertion among Canada's Native peoples could have a considerable impact on the future map of the country, since land claims are many and extensive. More immediately, it will have an affect on the future map of Quebec. If at some future time Quebec does succeed in achieving separation from (or perhaps some new form of association with) Canada, other "distinct societies" in the country are likely to claim similar rights. Among these will be the peoples of Quebec's northern frontier, the Cree, whose historic domain extends over more than half of the province of Quebec as it appears on current maps. Administration of the Cree was assigned to Quebec's government in 1912, an assignment that may well be invalidated by a move toward independence. In any case, the Cree probably would be empowered to seek independence as well. This would leave the French-speaking remnant of Quebec with about 45 percent of its present area.

Author's Video Link
↓
2
Crisis in Canada
Quebec Secession

The territory of the Cree is no unproductive wilderness. It contains large parts of the enormous James Bay Hydroelectric Project, a vast scheme of dikes, dams, and artificial lakes that will transform a large area of northern Quebec and yield electric power for a vast market within and outside the province.

The stakes of independence are high, and the risks are great.

None of this, however, seems to lessen the fervor of ethnic consciousness in the French community of Quebec. The province today is a prime example of ethnic revival; it also exemplifies ethnic linkage. De Gaulle sought to stimulate Quebec's emotional linkages to France, and today those ties are stronger than ever. The Quebec government has established an official presence in Paris that is as strong as that of Canada itself. *Maison Quebec* is a powerful magnet in Paris.

And yet, Quebec's role in Canada, compared to the position of ethnic minorities in so many countries of the world, has been very favorable. On average, people in Quebec earn nearly as much as Canadians nationwide. Quebecers have served as federal prime ministers for 30 of the past 47 years. Few, if any, countries have been as diligent in the encouragement of bilingualism and provision of federal government services in two official languages.

Quebec's grievances have been heard and have been resolved, from unfair taxation to proportional representation. It has not been enough to ward off divisive forces that may yet fracture the federation. The forces of ethnicity can disrupt even the most stable governmental system, especially when ethnicity is coupled with spatial identity, as in the case of Canada's Quebec.

Language, we have noted, is a central issue in Canadian cultural life. Language helps sustain ethnicity; it is a crucial element of culture. When an ethnic community perceives itself as threatened, it tends to protect and nurture its language as an indispensable key to its identity. We turn now to the geography of language, the medium of cultural preservation.

KEY TERMS

Apparel
Cultural Linkage
Cultural Revival
Culture Region
Ethnic Island
Ethnicity
Folk Culture
Perceptual Regions
Plural Society
Popular Culture
Popular Regions
Vernacular Regions

Ireland's highway signs, in Gaelic and English, help sustain the relevance of the Irish language.

PART SEVEN

PATTERNS OF LANGUAGE

At Issue

Language is one of the cornerstones of national identity, of cultural unity, of community cohesion. Old languages with historic roots, and languages spoken by threatened minorities, are nurtured and fostered by their speakers. But language also can be a weapon in cultural conflict and in political strife. In the United States, the growth of the Hispanic population has led to demands for official recognition of Spanish; this, in turn, spawned national countermovements called "English Only" and "English First." In Quebec, a campaign for political independence from Canada was accompanied by the official demotion of English in favor of Quebec's distinctive version of French. Language is a powerful component of local nationalisms in many areas. It is English, however, that has become the world's first language, often the key to individual success in a multilingual world. The Esperanto experiment failed long ago, and the issue now is: should English be promoted worldwide as the universal language?

21

A GEOGRAPHY OF LANGUAGE

People tend to feel passionately about their language, especially when they sense that it is threatened. Language is the essence of culture, and culture is the glue of society; without language, culture could not be transmitted.

Such passion is not felt only by small groups whose languages are threatened by extinction (of which there are many). It also is exhibited by cultures whose languages are spoken by the tens, even hundreds of millions. The French, in particular, are fiercely, even aggressively protective of their language. A former French President, Georges Pompidou, once stated that "It is through our language that we exist in the world other than as just another country."

More than 20 years ago these words were given the force of law: in 1975, the French government banned the use of foreign words in advertisements, television and radio broadcasts, and official documents, unless no French equivalent for such words could be found. In 1992, France amended its constitution to make French the official language of the Republic. And in

Geographica

- Language is the essence of culture, and no culture exists without it; when a people's language is perceived to be threatened, the defensive response often is passionate and protective.

- Mature and complex cultures attempt to maintain a standard language perpetuated by official state examinations and sustained by national institutions (in France, for example, the *Academie Fran-çaise*); but in this interconnected world of diffusing innovations, standards are difficult to uphold.

- More people speak languages belonging to the Indo-European Language Family than any other language family, and Indo-European languages are more widely distributed around the world than any others.

- Chinese is the individual language spoken by more people than any other language, but another individual language, English, has become the first true world language.

- The present distribution of languages, as revealed on maps, is useful in the reconstruction of cultural development and change.

1994, still another law was passed to stop the use of foreign (in fact, mainly English) words in France, with a hefty fine for violators. The French, said the government, would have to get used to saying something other than *le meeting, le corner, le drugstore,* and *le hamburger.*

Such legislation is unlikely to stop the "pollution" of French. In our interconnected world of diffus-

261

ing innovations, words will be borrowed and languages will change. But French is in no danger of disappearing. Communities that perceive a real and immediate threat to their (and their culture's) survival will protect their linguistic legacy even more forcefully. **Preliterate societies** (peoples who speak but who do not write their language) are at a far greater disadvantage. Although they can transmit their culture from one generation to the next, they do not accrue a time-spanning literature to serve as a foundation for ethnic preservation. Like endangered species, there are languages today on the verge of extinction, and others are threatened. The language mosaic of the world is constantly changing.

Linguists estimate that between 5000 and 6000 languages are in use in the world today, some spoken by many millions, others by a few hundred individuals. As we note in Chapter 22, there are many unsolved questions concerning the origins and diffusion of all these languages; but clearly the same migrations that led to spatial isolation and genetic differentiation among early human communities also led to linguistic heterogeneity. Modern research now is reconstructing the paths of linguistic diversification. That research is doing more than this: it also is throwing new light on ancient migrations.

The term **language** has been defined in numerous ways. Webster's Dictionary defines it as "a systematic means of communicating ideas or feelings by the use of conventionalized signs, gestures, marks, or especially articulate vocal sounds." Actually, sound communication (**vocalization**) is the crucial part of the definition. And such communication is *symbolic*, that is, in each language the meaning of sounds, and combination of sounds, must be learned.

But the definition is correct in asserting that other means of communication also constitute "language." Nonhuman primates such as chimpanzees also are able to communicate through symbolic calls, for example, by combinations of gestures and sounds that alert members of a group to the danger of a predator or the availability of preferred food. We know that elephants and dolphins, too, have forms of sound communication. But only humans have developed complex vocal communication systems that change dynamically over time and in space. How these open dynamic systems first emerged remains an unanswered question. What is now known about the vocal systems of nonhuman primates is that these are so basic and static that they are unlikely to have been forerunners of human language.

This means that human languages, even those spoken in preliterate societies, are fundamentally different from those of nonhuman primates. The Khoisan-speaking peoples of southwestern Africa may not have a word for *helicopter* in their linguistic inventory, but they have the symbols with which to describe this piece of unfamiliar technology, nevertheless. So the potential vocabulary of any language is infinite, and a language is a language, whether spoken by industrial and culturally complex societies or by simpler, smaller, nonindustrial peoples such as the San or the Yanomami of the Amazonian rainforest. The languages of such people are *not* in any sense primitive or intermediate.

Languages are not static, but change continuously. A vital, fermenting culture requires a flexible, changeable language. Read a few pages from one of Shakespeare's plays, and you realize how much the "King's English" has changed over several centuries. We witness changes in American English today;

the drug culture of the past three decades has expanded the vocabulary of commonly used words quite substantially. The computer revolution also has had an impact on English usage.

While it is true that language undergoes unending change in response to society's vigorous transformations, language also can be debased and corrupted. Some scholars argue that the degree of accuracy and proper use of the "standard" language is a barometer of a society's well-being, and that misuse and error evince a general decline in the culture it represents.

In this chapter, we examine the distribution and other geographic aspects of the world's jigsaw of languages. This will prepare us for an introduction to the fascinating study of language origins and diffusion, the focus of the chapter that follows. In the final chapter of Part 7, we look at some topics of special interest, including the language of place names.

STANDARD LANGUAGE

A language has several levels of variation. In complex cultures, there is likely to be a **standard language**, the quality of which is a matter of cultural identity and national concern. The standard language may in fact be sustained by official state examinations to be passed by teachers, civil servants, and others whose responsibility it is to maintain standards. The "King's English" is a popular reference to the real thing: in the United Kingdom, the English spoken by well-educated people in London and its environs is regarded as *British Received Pronunciation* (BRP) English, the standard to uphold.

Who decides what the standard language will be? Not surprisingly, the answer lies in regional influence and power. In France, the French spoken in and around Paris was made the official, standard language during the sixteenth century. In China, standard Chinese is the Northern Mandarin Chinese heard in and around the capital, Beijing. Although this is China's official standard language, the linguistic term "Chinese" actually incorporates many variants. This distinction between the standard language and other versions of it is not unique to China; it happens in all but the smallest societies. The Italian of Sicily is very different from that spoken north of Venice, and both tongues differ from the standard Italian of Latium, the region of Rome.

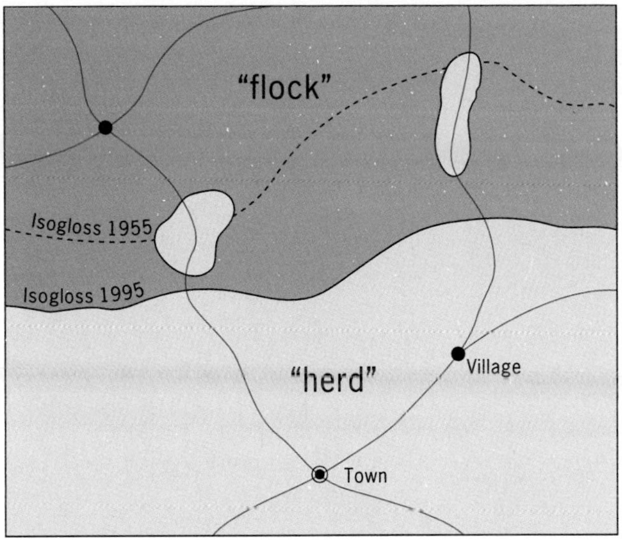

FIGURE 21–1 Isoglosses move over time. In this hypothetical case, the use of "herd" has receded in favor of "flock," but some outliers of "herd" remain.

DIALECTS

Such regional variants of the standard language are called **dialects**. Differences in vocabulary, syntax (the way words are put together to form phrases), pronunciation, cadence (the rhythm of speech), and even the pace of speech, all mark a speaker's dialect. Even if the written form of a statement adheres to the standard language, an *accent* can reveal the regional home of a person who reads the statement aloud. The words "horse" and "oil" are written the same in New England and in the South, but to the Southerner, the New Englander may be saying "hahse," and to the New Englander, the Southerner seems to be saying "all."

More often, however, actual vocabulary usage marks a language's regional differentiation, and a single word or group of words can reveal the source area of the dialect being used. Linguistic geographers map the areal extent of diagnostic words, marking their limits as **isoglosses** (Fig. 21-1). An isogloss, thus, is a geographic boundary within which a particular linguistic feature occurs, but such a boundary is rarely a simple line. Usually there are outliers of usage, as in Figure 21-1. This may signify either the growth and expansion of the dialect, or it may reflect its contraction, leaving the outliers as dwindling remnants. A series of large-scale maps over time will tell the story of that dialect's advance or retreat.

CLASSIFICATION AND DISTRIBUTION

In the context of cultural geography, we are interested in the way languages are distributed throughout the world, what processes created this distribution, and how the present pattern is changing.

Before we view maps of language distribution at various levels of scale, however, let us briefly consider the problem of language classification. This obviously relates to language definition: What is a language, and what is a dialect? That issue is a complex one. Some scholars have classified Quebecan French as a discrete language, whereas others insist that it remains a dialect of European French. In regions of Africa where Bantu languages are spoken, many of those languages are closely related to each other and share major portions of their vocabulary. The actual number of languages in use on Earth therefore remains a matter for debate. The most conservative calculation, which would recognize the maximum number of dialects, puts the number at about 3000. Most linguistic geographers today would recognize between 5000 and 6000 discrete languages, including more than 600 in India and over 1000 in Africa alone.

In the classification of languages, we use terms also employed in biology, and for the same reasons: certain languages are related to each other, and some are not. Languages grouped in **language families** are thought to have a shared, but fairly distant, origin; in the **language subfamily**, their commonality is more definite. These subfamilies are divided into **language groups**, which consist of sets of individual languages.

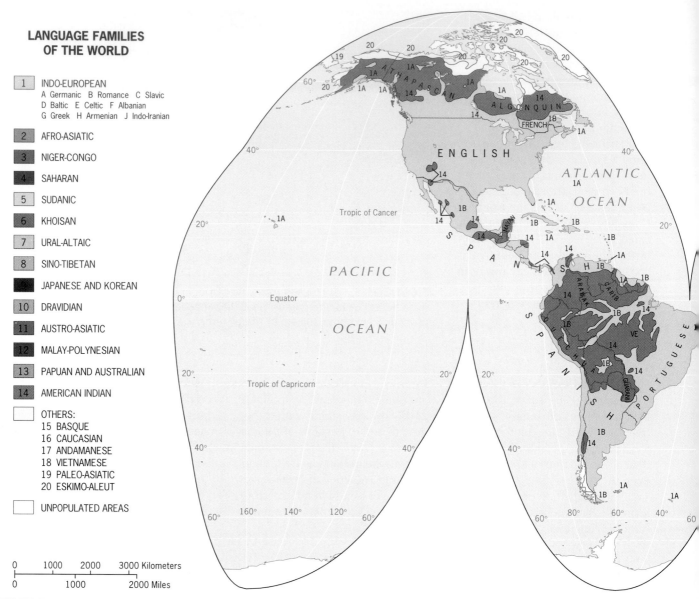

LANGUAGE FAMILIES OF THE WORLD

1 INDO-EUROPEAN
   A Germanic B Romance C Slavic
   D Baltic E Celtic F Albanian
   G Greek H Armenian J Indo-Iranian

2 AFRO-ASIATIC

3 NIGER-CONGO

4 SAHARAN

5 SUDANIC

6 KHOISAN

7 URAL-ALTAIC

8 SINO-TIBETAN

9 JAPANESE AND KOREAN

10 DRAVIDIAN

11 AUSTRO-ASIATIC

12 MALAY-POLYNESIAN

13 PAPUAN AND AUSTRALIAN

14 AMERICAN INDIAN

OTHERS:
   15 BASQUE
   16 CAUCASIAN
   17 ANDAMANESE
   18 VIETNAMESE
   19 PALEO-ASIATIC
   20 ESKIMO-ALEUT

UNPOPULATED AREAS

0   1000   2000   3000 Kilometers
0   1000   2000 Miles

FIGURE 21–2   Generalized map of the world distribution of language families, based on a map prepared for the first edition by Hammond, Inc. (1977).

Figure 21-2 shows the distribution of 20 principal language families of the world. On this map, only the Indo-European language family is broken down into subfamilies (greater detail is shown in Figure 21-3), a reminder of the level of generalization that must be employed at this scale. Spatially, the Indo-European language family (like the Caucasoid geographical race) is the world's most widely dispersed. As Figure 21-2 indicates, the

Indo-European language family dominates not only in Europe, but also in much of Asia (Russia and India, among other countries), North and South America, Australia, and in parts of Southern Africa. **Indo-European languages** are spoken by about half the world's peoples, and English is the most widely used Indo-European language today.

Linguists theorize that a lost language they call Proto-Indo-European existed somewhere in

east-central Europe or possibly eastward, in modern Turkey, and that the present languages of the Indo-European family evolved from this common heritage. In the process, as vocabularies grew and changed and peoples dispersed and migrated, differentiation took place. Latin arose out of this early period to be disseminated over much of Europe during the rise of the Roman Empire. Later, Latin died out and was supplanted by Italian,

French, and the other Romance languages.

As Figure 21-2 indicates, the Indo-European language family includes not only the major languages of Europe and the former Soviet Union, but also those of northern India and Bangladesh, Pakistan, Afghanistan, and Iran. This reflects the western source of the peopling of modern South Asia, and the probable route of ancient migration. More modern migrations carried Indo-European languages (principally English, Spanish, Portuguese, and French) to the Americas, Australia, and Africa.

THE MAJOR WORLD LANGUAGES

Although Indo-European languages are spoken by more of the world's peoples than any other language family, Chinese is the single largest language in terms of the number of speakers (Table 21-1), and English ranks second. The numbers in Table 21-1 should be viewed as only approximations for several reasons. English, for example, is not only spoken by 270 million North Americans, 60 million Britons and Irish, nearly 20 million Australians and New Zealanders, and by millions more in countries with smaller populations; it is also used as a second language by hundreds of millions of people in India, Africa, and else-

FIGURE 21–3 Generalized map of language–use regions in Europe, based on a map prepared for the first edition by Hammond, Inc. (1977).

TABLE 21–1 Numbers of Speakers of Major Languages of the World, 1994

Language Family	Major Language	Number of Speakers (Millions)
Indo-European	English	400
	Spanish	300
	Hindi	290
	Russian	225
	Bengali	200
	Portuguese	165
	German	100
	Panjabi	90
	French	80
	Italian	60
Sino-Tibetan	Chinese	1150
	Thai	50
	Burmese	35
Japanese-Korean	Japanese	125
	Korean	75
Afro-Asiatic	Arabic	165
Dravidian	Telugu	75
	Tamil	70
Malay-Polynesian	Indonesian	140

Estimates extrapolated from several sources.

where. French, too, is more widely used than its 80 million first-language speakers suggest. Furthermore, the numbers in Table 21-1 are based in some instances on population data that are not reliable. The regional languages of India (Indo-European as well as Dravidian) are among the world's largest, but exact data on the number of speakers are unobtainable.

It is noteworthy that Table 21-1 does not list any languages spoken in Africa south of the Sahara as major world languages. African languages are the topic of a later section of this chapter, but Figure 21-2 provides one of the reasons for the absence of African languages: the extreme fragmentation of the African language map. Africa south of the Sahara, as a geographic realm, still has a relatively modest population (about 600 million people in the mid-1990s), but more than 1000 languages remain in use there. Not including the Afro-Asiatic languages of North Africa, and also

excluding the Indo-European languages spoken by whites and Asians on the continent, black Africa's languages must still be grouped into four families (3, 4, 5, and 6 in Figure 21-2). In terms of the number of speakers, Hausa is estimated to be the largest African language, with perhaps as many as 50 million. Hundreds of African languages have fewer than 1 million users.

Other language families not included under the headings of Table 21-1 can be seen, in Figure 21-2, to constitute dwindling, often marginally located or isolated groups. Austro-Asiatic languages (11), spoken in interior locales of eastern India and in Cambodia (Khmer) and Laos, are thought to be survivors of ancient languages spoken in this realm before modern cultural development (and numerous external invasions) took place. Some scholars place Vietnamese in this family, but others do not. The Papuan and indigenous Australian languages (13), although numerous

and quite diverse, are spoken by fewer than 10 million people today. The languages of Native Americans (14) remain strong only in areas of Middle America, the high Andes, and northern Canada. Languages of the Eskimo-Aleut Family (20) continue to survive on the Arctic margins of Greenland, North America, and eastern Asia.

If you spend some time looking carefully at the map of world languages, some interesting questions arise. Consider, for example, the large island of Madagascar, off the East African coast. The predominant languages spoken on Madagascar are not of an African language family, but belong to the Malay-Polynesian family, the languages of Indonesia and its neighbors. How did this happen? Surely, Madagascar's closeness to Africa would suggest a very different situation. Actually, the map reveals a piece of ancient history still not well understood. Long ago, seafarers from the islands of Southeast Asia crossed the Indian Ocean. They may in fact have reached the East African coast first, and then sailed on to Madagascar. There they established settlements. Africans had not yet sailed across the strait between continent and island, so there was no threat to the Indonesian-Malayan presence. The settlements grew and prospered, and large states evolved on a Southeast Asian model. Later, Africans began to come to Madagascar, but by that time, the cultural landscape had been forged. Study an atlas map and compare the names of Madagascar's places to those across the water in Africa. The language map reveals a fascinating piece of historical geography.

Languages of Europe

The language map of Europe (Fig. 21-3) shows the Indo-European language family to prevail over this region, with pockets of the Ural-Altaic family occurring in Finland

and adjacent areas, Hungary (the Ugric subfamily), and Turkey, west of the Sea of Marmara. Subfamilies include the Germanic languages (English, German, Danish, Norwegian, and Swedish), the Romance languages (French, Spanish, Italian, Romanian, and Portuguese), the Slavic languages (Russian, Polish, Czech, Slovak, Ukrainian, Slovenian, Serbo-Croatian, and Bulgarian), and the Celtic languages (Breton, Welsh, and Gaelic). Language groups in Europe are represented by clusters, such as the Scandinavian languages, the Iberian languages, and the Slavic languages of Eastern Europe.

It is obvious from a comparison between Europe's linguistic and political maps that there is much coincidence between language and culture. The Romance languages, the subfamily of Romanic-Latin origin, dominate in five countries, including Romania. The eastern boundaries of Germany coincide almost exactly with the transition from Germanic to Slavic tongues. Even at the level of individual languages, boundaries on the political map can be discerned: between French and Spanish, between Norwegian and Swedish, and between Bulgarian and Greek.

Although Figure 21-3 shows a substantial coincidence between political and linguistic boundaries, significant exceptions do occur. The French linguistic region extends into Belgium, Switzerland, and Italy, but does not include (in France itself) the Bretagne (Brittany) Peninsula. The Celtic languages survive not only in Brittany (Breton), but also in Wales (Welsh), in western Ireland (Irish Gaelic), and in Scotland (Scots Gaelic), where they constitute remnants of an early period of European history before the wave of modern languages displaced them toward the realm's westernmost fringes. The use of Romanian extends well into Moldavia, signifying a loss of national terri-

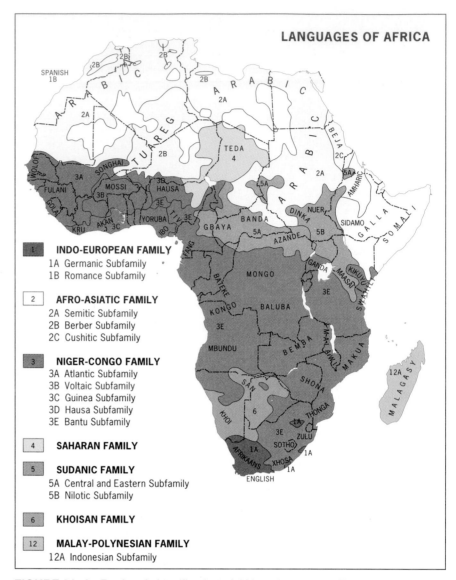

FIGURE 21–4 Regional classification of African languages. From a map prepared for the first edition by Hammond, Inc. (1977).

tory. Greek and Albanian are also Indo-European languages, with a regional distribution corresponding essentially (though not exactly) with national territories. Figure 21-3 underscores the complex cultural pattern of Eastern Europe: there are German speakers in Hungary, Hungarian speakers in Romania, Romanian speakers in Greece and Moldavia, and Turkish speakers in Bulgaria.

Although the overwhelming majority of Europeans and Russians speak Indo-European languages,

the Ural-Altaic language family is also represented in this realm. Finnish, Estonian, and Hungarian are major languages of this family, which, as Figure 21-2 shows, extends across Eurasia to the Pacific coast and includes Turkish, Kazakh, Uigur, Kirgiz, and Uzbek, among others. The Ural-Altaic languages are not viewed as a single family by all students of linguistic geography; some separate the more northerly *Uralic* from the southern *Altaic* families. However, there are reasons to group these languages together, and it is believed that they spread into Europe between 7000 and 10,000 years ago, to be overtaken by the Indo-European languages later. Their source area may have been a longitudinal zone along the Ural Mountains, from where migrations occurred both westward into Europe and eastward into Asia. Whatever their origins, the Ural-Altaic languages survive as the national languages of Finland and Hungary, remnants of an earlier linguistic map of western Eurasia.

Languages of Africa

The potential of the spatial study of languages and dialects in historical and cultural geography is especially evident in Africa. As we have noted, more than 1000 languages are spoken in black Africa, and linguists have been working to record many of these; most of them were unwritten. From the resulting data, it has been possible to gain some significant insights into Africa's cultural past.

The languages of Africa (Fig. 21-4) are grouped into four families, the largest of which is the Niger-Congo family, which extends from West Africa all the way to the south. This Niger–Congo family can be subdivided into five subfamilies. One of these is the Bantu subfamily, whose languages are spoken by most of the people near and south of the equator. In West Africa, the languages are of the Atlantic, Voltaic, Guinea, and Hausa subfamilies. The oldest languages of black Africa are the *Khoisan* languages, which share a "click" sound. These include the language of the San, still spoken by only a few thousand people in southwestern Africa. Perhaps the Khoisan languages were once the main languages over much of Africa, but they have been reduced to comparative insignificance by the Bantu invasion, just as Europe's Celtic languages were.

How can languages help us in reconstructing the cultural development of Africa? Consider what has happened in Europe, where the Romance languages' subfamily has differentiated into various languages, including French, Italian, Spanish, and Portuguese. Even within these individual languages, we can recognize differentiation, such as between Castilian Spanish and Catalan, and between Northern and Southern French and Walloon. Such differentiation develops over time, and it is reasonable to assume the more time that elapses, the greater will be the individuality of each language. Therefore, if the peoples of a large region speak languages that are somewhat different, but still closely related, it is reasonable to conclude that they have migrated into that region (or emerged there) relatively recently. On the other hand, languages that are of recognizably common roots, yet strongly different, must have undergone modification over a lengthy period of time.

Among the languages of the Niger-Congo family, those of the Bantu subfamily are much more closely related to each other than those of other subfamilies. It may be deduced, then, that the Bantu peoples and cultures of Central and Southern Africa are of more recent origins than West Africans. Even a little general knowledge of African names can suggest the affinities. Thus the word "Bantu" should actually be written *BaNtu* (people), with the *Ba* being a prefix. Sometimes the prefix is retained in common usage, sometimes not. The *Watusi*, for example, are sometimes called the Tusi or Tutsi. The people of southeastern Uganda are the BaGanda or Ganda. The Zulu of South Africa are actually the *Ama*-Zulu. In stories about Zimbabwe, you often read about the *Ma*Shona or Shona. Remember Basutoland, now called Lesotho? It was originally named after the Sotho, and BaSotholand was corrupted to Ba-

sutoland. The point is becoming clear: *Ba, Ma, Wa,* and *Ama* are not very far removed from each other linguistically, and they reveal close associations between languages and peoples spread far and wide across Africa from Uganda to Zululand.

It is not just a matter of prefixes, of course. In terms of vocabularies and in numerous other respects, Bantu languages reflect their close relationships as well. Linguists have traced the changes that occur over space in a single word, and thousands of miles away a word is often quite close to the way it started. Consider the familiar Swahili greeting, *jambo*, which you can use in coastal East Africa. In the eastern Transvaal of South Africa and Swaziland, people will recognize *jabo*!

The situation in West Africa is quite different. Certainly, there are languages that have close association, but the major languages of the West African subfamilies are much more discrete and individual. Of course, there are other pieces of evidence to support the conclusion that the peoples of Bantu Africa have a shorter history in that area than those of West Africa, but the linguistic evidence, and orally transmitted traditions, provide the basis.

Languages of India

The generalized mosaic of languages in India (Fig. 21-5) involves no less than four language families, but only two of these—the Indo-European family and the Dravidian family—have significant numbers of speakers among India's 930 million inhabitants. In the Karakoram Mountains of Jammu and Kashmir (the far northwest) live comparatively small numbers of Tibetan speakers, and along the border with Myanmar (Burma) in the east lies a cluster of Naga (Burmese) speakers. Also in the east of the country are small groups of Austro-Asiatic speakers, as noted previously. Otherwise, India speaks about 15 major

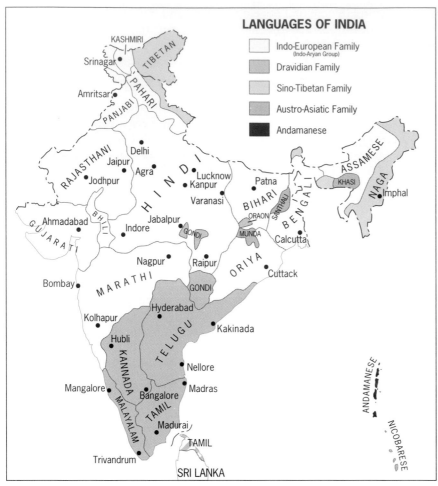

FIGURE 21–5 Major languages of the Indian subcontinent. From a map prepared for the first edition by Hammond, Inc. (1977).

languages, all but 4 of them Indo-European, and more than 1600 smaller ones, some spoken by only a few thousand persons.

As Figure 21-5 indicates, the four Dravidian languages are all spoken in a compact region in the south of the Indian peninsula. If the map suggests that these languages and the cultures they represent were "pushed" southward into the Indian cul-de-sac by the advancing Indo-European speakers, that impression is correct. The Dravidian languages are older, although there is as yet no certainty about their origins. Some scholars believe that Dravidian arose and developed in India and is in fact an indigenous Indian language family. Others suggest that Dravidian speakers first arrived thousands of years ago from central Asia, so that a connection with Ural-Altaic languages may exist. Still others link the Dravidians with the ancient Indus civilization which arose in what is today Pakistan. Indeed, a cluster of about 350,000 speakers of a form of Dravidian still exists in north-central Pakistan.

Today, the largest Dravidian language, with about 75 million speakers, is Telugu, the language of the Indian state of Andhra Pradesh. Tamil, with the richest literature, is spoken by approximately 70 million persons in Tamil Nadu. Kannada (also called Kanarese), the language of Karnataka, has approximately 35 million speakers, about the same number of Malayalam, spoken in the state of Kerala.

This close relationship between regional languages and political divisions in southern India also prevails in the north. Indeed, it is useful to compare Figure 21-5 with an atlas map of India's federal system, because this underscores the important role of languages in the development of this spatial structure. Hindi, the principal Indo-European language and India's largest, with nearly a quarter of a billion speakers, extends across several north-central Indian states. But east as well as west of India's Hindi speaking core lie states where other languages prevail: Orissa (Oriya is the principal language), Bihar (Bihari), West Bengal (Bengali), Punjab (Punjabi), Rajasthan (Rajasthani), Gujarat (Gujarati), and Maharashtra (Marathi). In the northeast, where India's linguistic map is especially complex, that situation is reflected by the existence of seven comparatively small states.

In addition to more than a dozen major languages, India also includes hundreds of lesser languages, both Indo-European and Dravidian, that cannot be shown on a map on the scale of Figure 21-5. Nevertheless, for so large a population, the Indian language mosaic (despite the presence of so many smaller languages) is not as intensely fragmented as is Africa's and is dominated, as in the case of Europe, by several major regional languages larger than many of the world's national tongues.

Chinese: Language or Languages?

The map of China's ethnolinguistic areas (Fig. 21-6) should be compared to the map of world population distribution (Fig. 6-1). That comparison will reveal that the

FIGURE 21–6 Languages in use in China. From a map prepared for the second edition of H. J. de Blij, *Geography: Regions and Concepts* (New York: Wiley, 1978) by Rand McNally & Co. (1978).

great majority of China's people, well over 90 percent, inhabit the area shown in orange in Figure 21-6. There the greatest contiguous population cluster on Earth speaks a single language—a language divided by dialects, but the same language nevertheless. Chinese is the world's largest language and one of its oldest.

The spoken dialects of Chinese are mutually unintelligible, and some scholars argue that Chinese is not one but several languages, among which Mandarin Chinese dominates with about 700 million speakers. Wu Chinese ranks next, with over 100 million, and Cantonese is third, with about 70 million. Various Chinese dialects differ about as much from each other as do the Indo-European Romance languages (Spanish, Italian, French, Portuguese), but these differences lie not in the grammar but in vocabulary and in the way words are pronounced. Thus people from the north, who speak Mandarin, have trouble conversing with Cantonese-speaking southerners. However, all would understand China's standard, "literary" language, written in characters and based on a national literature many centuries old.

Several efforts have been made during the twentieth century to create a truly national language in China. The latest of these is the so-called *pinyin* system, another attempt to establish a standard form of the Chinese language throughout China. The pinyin system is a phonetic-spelling system based on the pronunciation of Chinese characters in Northern Mandarin, China's standard language that is still the regional form of the capital and the north. But China is a country of many minorities, as Figure 21-6 reminds us, and the linguistic integration of its complex society will be a lengthy and difficult task.

One of the most interesting and challenging dimensions of the geography of language is the reconstruction of the routes whereby the distributions we have just examined have come about—the diffusion of peoples and their speech. While linguists attempt to establish the family tree of languages, geographers focus on the spatial implications of this effort: the routes of migration and linguistic diffusion. We turn next to this complicated topic, about which new information is constantly emerging.

KEY TERMS

Dialect
Indo-European Languages
Isogloss
Language
Language Family
Language Group
Language Subfamily
Linguistics
Preliterate Society
Standard Language
Vocalization

22

THE DIFFUSION OF LANGUAGES

The world today is a Babel of languages, a patchwork of tongues so intricate that it would seem to defy orderly interpretation. Certainly it is possible to identify languages related to each other, such as Spanish and Portuguese. Such are the similarities between these related languages that their common origin and recent divergence are beyond doubt. Furthermore, in the case of Spanish and Portuguese (and Danish and Swedish, and German and Dutch) there exists a historic record of the process. The Latin of Roman times gave rise to the Romance languages of today (Italian, Spanish, Portuguese, French, Romanian). In just a few centuries, a language that prevailed from Britain to the Bosporus was superseded by a quintet of derivatives.

Given the speed with which this happened, and the thoroughness of Latin's eclipse, can we hope to unlock the mysteries of earlier—much earlier—languages, and retrace the evolution of our modern Babel from what linguists call the Mother Tongue, the first language spoken by *Homo sapiens sapiens* perhaps as long as 200,000 years ago? That

Geographica

- **The search for the origins of languages goes back tens of thousands of years and yields information not only about language change but also about the ways of life and environments of the long-extinct speakers.**

- **Scientists do not yet agree on the dating of the origins of language; some believe that the use of language began with the rise of *Homo sapiens* perhaps 200,000 years ago or more; others argue that simple vocal communication began much earlier.**

- **Languages change through divergence, convergence, and replacement, making the spatial search for origins problematic; the location of the source of Proto-Indo-European still is being debated.**

- **The Pacific and American realms, where languages spread relatively recently, are providing useful information for the reconstruction of language-diffusion routes and processes.**

still is an elusive goal, but today, with the help of computers, remarkable progress is being made in the reconstruction of ancient, extinct languages and their paths of diffusion. This chapter focuses on the relevance of linguistic theory and discovery to historical geography.

FIRST NOTIONS

The diversification of languages has long been charted through the analysis of **sound shifts**. Take the Latin word for milk (*lacte*) and note that it becomes *latta* in Italian, *leche* in Spanish, and *lait* in French. Or the

273

Latin for the number eight (*octo*): *otto*, *ocho*, and *huit*, respectively. Even if the Latin roots for these words had never been known, linguists would have been able to deduce them.

This technique of backward reconstruction is crucial to linguistic research. If it is possible to deduce a substantial part of the vocabulary of an extinct language, then it may be feasible to go still farther back in history, and to recreate the words of the language that, in turn, preceded it. Called **deep reconstruction**, this still-controversial method has yielded some important and credible results. It takes the recreation of humanity's linguistic family tree back thousands of years, far beyond Latin.

More than two centuries ago, an Englishman named William Jones, living and working on behalf of the Crown in South Asia, undertook a study of Sanskrit. This language, in which ancient Indian religious and literary texts were written, proved a revelation to Jones: its vocabulary and grammatical forms bore a striking resemblance to the ancient Greek and Latin he had learned while in college. "No philologer [student of literature] could examine all three," Jones wrote, "without believing them to have sprung from some common source, which, perhaps, no longer exists." In the late eighteenth century, this was a revolutionary notion indeed.

During the nineteenth century, a scholar named Jacob Grimm (one of the fairy-tale-writing brothers) introduced the idea of sound shifts as a promising field for systematic study, which might prove the relationships between languages in a scientific manner. He pointed out that related languages have similar, but not identical, consonants (consonants are formed by the constriction of the sound channel, for example a **g** or a **v**). These consonants, he theorized, would change over time in a predictable way. Hard consonants, such as the **v** and the **t** in the German word *vater*, would soften into va**d**er (Dutch) and **f**ather (English). Looking backward, Grimm proposed, we should expect to record the opposite: a hardening of consonants.

From Jones's notions and Grimm's ideas came the first major linguistic hypothesis, the postulated existence of an ancestral **(Proto) Indo-European** language, the predecessor of Latin, Greek, and Sanskrit, among other ancient languages. This concept had major implications, because the proposed ancestral language would link not only the present and past Romance languages, but also other languages spoken from Britain to North Africa and South Asia.

The research tasks arising from these developments were several. First, the vocabulary of the postulated source language must be reconstructed. Second, the hearth or source where this language originated, and from which it spread, must be located. Third, the routes of diffusion by which this dispersal took place should be traced. And fourth, the ways of life of those who spoke and spread this language should be established.

THE LANGUAGE TREE

The Proto-Indo-European language gave rise to more than Latin, Greek, and Sanskrit, of course. As Figure 21-2 reminds us, the Indo-European language realm includes not only languages derived from Latin, but also the Slavonic (Slavic) languages (such as Russian, Ukrainian, Polish, Czech, Slovak, Bulgarian, and Slovenian) and the Germanic languages, including German, Swedish, Danish, and Norwegian. These, too, must have had common ancestors, all original branches of the Proto-Indo-European "tree."

The first scholar to liken the world's language families to branches of a tree was August Schleicher, a German linguist. He suggested in the mid-nineteenth century that the basic process of language formation is **language divergence**, that is, differentiation over time and space. Languages would branch into dialects; isolation then increased the differences between these dialects. Over time, those dialects would become discrete languages, as happened with Spanish and Portuguese and is now happening with Quebecan French. Although this idea was later challenged, it stood the test of time, and the language-tree model continues to be a central theme in language research (Fig. 22-1).

We should consider a complicating factor, however: the mobility of peoples of which we took note in Parts 1 and 3 of this book. While the divergence of languages went on, people migrated as well. Languages did not merely spread by contagious diffusion through static populations; they also were dispersed by relocation diffusion, of which the modern world offers numerous examples. Sometimes, such relocation diffusion caused long-isolated languages to make contact, creating **language convergence**. Such instances create special problems for researchers, because the rules of reconstruction (sound shifts, for example) may not apply or may be unreliable.

A further complication should be considered in view of modern cultural events. We know that the languages of traditional, numerically smaller and technologically less advanced peoples have been replaced, or severely modified, by the languages of stronger, dominant invaders. This process of **language replacement** goes on today, and there is every reason to believe that it has happened ever since humans began to use language, perhaps

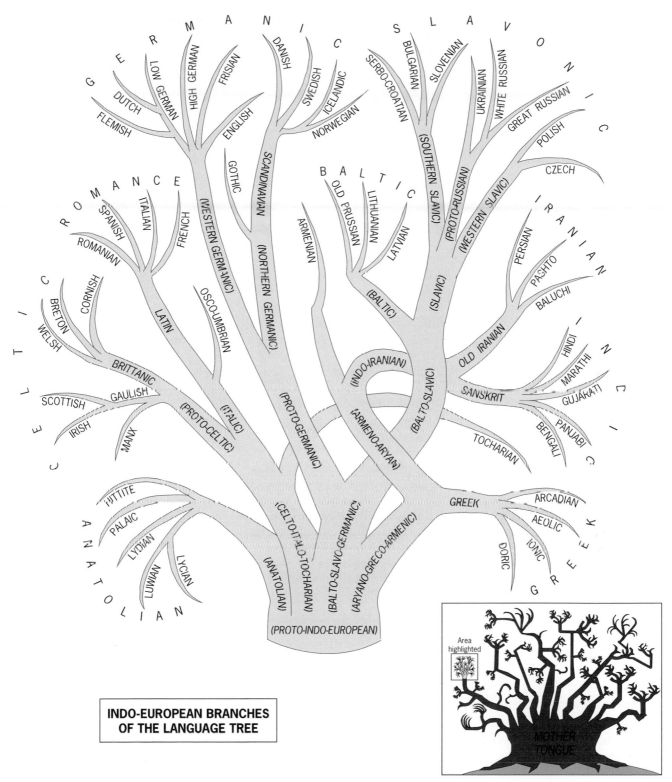

INDO-EUROPEAN BRANCHES OF THE LANGUAGE TREE

FIGURE 22–1 From T.V. Gamkrelidze and V.V. Ivanov, "The Early History of Indo-European Languages," *Scientific American*, March 1990, p. 111.

200,000 years ago. (In the next chapter we discuss the process of creolization, which is a form of language replacement now in progress in the Caribbean region and elsewhere).

Reconstructing even a small branch of the language tree, therefore, is a complicated proposition, with countless pitfalls to confront the analyst. Look again at the language map of Europe in Chapter 21 (Fig. 21-3). If only *all* the languages were members of the same family, the same branch of the tree! But things are not so simple. Hungarian, completely surrounded by Indo-European languages, is not of the same family as any of its neighbors. Finnish is another non-Indo-European language, apparently related distantly to Hungarian but mapped, nevertheless, as a member of a discrete subfamily. Estonian has a closer relationship to Finnish, as the map suggests. But a tantalizing enigma is presented by Basque, a distant family now isolated in a small region of northern Spain and southwestern France. What ancient proto-language gave rise to Basque? Similar questions arise in hundreds of locales elsewhere in the world, where linguistic islands survive, nearly engulfed by later waves of language diffusion. The human language tree is just beginning to become known.

ROOTS AND ROUTES

While linguistics built the inventory of Proto-Indo-European vocabulary, recreating an extinct language, human geographers and other scholars searched for the spatial solution: Where did it happen? Where lay the source of Proto-Indo-European? Knowledge of this hearth would enormously increase understanding of Eurasian historical geography.

The linguists' research produced many valuable clues. Reconstructions by scholars working independently often produced remarkably similar results. The proto-language had words for certain landforms, trees, and other features of the natural landscape, but it significantly lacked others. Such information helps indicate the environment where a language may have developed. For example, if a reconstructed language has no word for *snow*, this would suggest a tropical or equatorial source. If there were no word for *palm* tree, a cold-climate source may have witnessed the language's emergence. More specifically, if a certain diagnostic vegetation (an oak, pine tree, beech, birch, tall or short grass) is part of the vocabulary, the search for the environment where the language developed can narrow down. Again, many words for mountainous topography but few words for flat or plain land lead to the conclusion that high relief was the setting of the source area being sought.

Unfortunately, the search for the Proto-Indo-European source area became tinged during the first half of the twentieth century by **ethnocentrism**. German researchers, using archeological as well as linguistic data, argued that the Proto-Indo-European homeland lay somewhere in north-central Europe. They then used this inadequately based conclusion to promote master-race philosophies, and the notion became a part of Nazi self-justification. This episode coincided with the period when environmental determinism in geography (see Chapter 19) was a central theme in human geography, also corrupted to serve the purposes of Nazi master-race advocates. As in geography, this experience caused a scientific setback as many scholars shied away from this linguistic arena to avoid becoming tainted with the Nazi stigma.

Conquest Theory

More objective research did yield a different conclusion: that the Proto-Indo-European homeland lay somewhere north of the Black Sea, in the vast steppes of present-day Ukraine and Russia. The time, it was suggested, was more than 5000 years ago, and judging from the reconstructed vocabulary, the people used horses, knew of the wheel, and traded widely in many goods. The logical conclusion seemed to be that these early speakers of Proto-Indo-European spread westward on horseback, overpowering earlier inhabitants and initiating the diffusion and differentiation of Latin, Germanic, and Slavonic languages.

This **conquest theory** of language dispersal in Europe west of the Russian plains was long supported by a majority of archeologists, linguists, and human geographers. The sound shifts in the derivative languages (*vater* to *vader* to *father*, for example) seemed to represent a long period of westward divergence. The western-marginal location of older Indo-European languages (Breton in France, Scottish Gaelic and Welsh in Britain, and Irish Gaelic in Ireland) appeared to result from an engulfing later wave from the east.

Agriculture Theory

But not all scholars were convinced. As the archeological record in Europe became better known, alternative hypotheses made their appearance. Professors Luca Cavalli-Sforza and Robert Ammerman proposed the hypothesis that it was the spread of agriculture, not the thrust of conquest, that diffused the Proto-Indo-European language through Europe. This, of course, meant that the source area of the ancient language would have had to lie in an area of agricultural innovation, not in the Ukrainian-Russian grasslands where pastoralism, not farming, was the way of life. But where was this hearth? Was it in the Fertile Crescent we encountered in Chapter 19? Apparently not, because the still-emerging vocabulary of Proto-Indo-European has few words for plains but many different terms for high and low mountains, valleys, mountain streams, rapids, lakes, and other high-relief landforms. Soviet Professors Thomas Gamkrelidze and Victor Ivanov, who reconstructed much of the known vocabulary of the proto-language, published a book in 1984 on their work in which they reported that these terms were supplemented by words for such trees as mountain oak, pine, fir, willow, and ash. As to the zoogeography of the region, the language had names for such animals as lions, leopards, and monkeys—none of which lived in the plains north of the Black Sea.

Thus arose the **agriculture theory** (as opposed to the conquest theory) and its postulated source area: the hilly and mountainous, well-watered terrain of Anatolia in modern Turkey. The archeological record indicates that there, between 7000 and 9000 years ago, the horse had been domesticated, the wheel was in use, and the realm's leading hearth of agricultural innovation lay in nearby Mesopotamia.

In 1991, the agriculture theory received support from a modern methodology (see Chapter 16): the analysis of the protein (that is, gene) content of individuals from several thousand locations across Europe. This research proved the existence of distance decay in the geographic pattern: certain genes became steadily less common from southern Turkey across the Balkans and into western and northern Europe. This pattern was interpreted to mean that the farming peoples of Anatolia moved steadily westward and northward. As they did so, they mixed with the nonfarming peoples before them, diluting their genetic identity as the distance from their source area increased. Archeologists Robert Sokal, Neal Olden, and Chester Wilson argued that farming, learned by the earliest speakers of Proto-Indo-European, led to an unprecedented increase in population, to such an extent that out-migration was essential for communities to survive. Thus a slow but steady wave of farmers dispersed into Europe, a hypothesis very different from that involving conquering horseriders.

The agriculture theory can be invoked to explain a number of features of the language map of Europe. Professors Ammerman and Cavalli-Sforza proposed that, every generation (25 years), the agricultural frontier moved approximately 18 kilometers (11 miles) to enable the growing communities to survive. This would mean that the

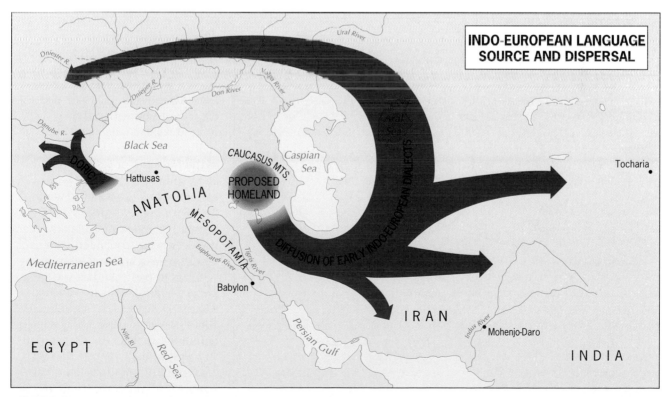

FIGURE 22–2 Postulated diffusion of an Indo-European protolanguage. From T.V. Gamkrelidze and V.V. Ivanov, *op. cit.*, 1990, p. 112.

European frontier would have been completely penetrated by farmers in about 1500 years, which is close to what the archeological record suggests. But some of the non-farming societies that existed in the path of this wave of transformation held out, and their languages, too, remained unchanged. Thus Etruscan did not become extinct until Roman times, and Basque survives to this day as a direct link to Europe's pre-farming era.

On the other hand, the agriculture theory also has its weaknesses. The high-relief Anatolian topography is no ideal environment for farming, and there is no strong archeological evidence for an agricultural culture hearth there. Also, despite the genetic gradient mapped in Europe, some language geographers continued to prefer the Soviet dispersal hypothesis, which

holds that the Indo-European languages that arose from the proto-language were first carried eastward into southwest Asia, then around the Caspian Sea, and then across the Russian-Ukranian plains and on into the Balkans (Fig. 22-2). As is so often the case when conflicting hypotheses exist, there may be truth in both options. If an Anatolian source did prevail, then the diffusion of Indo-European languages (then still dialects of Proto-Indo-European) could have spread both westward across southern Europe *and* in the broad arc shown in Figure 22-3. In any case, an eastward diffusion must have occurred to explain the relationships between Sanskrit and ancient Latin and Greek, first described by William Jones.

The geographic story of Proto-Indo-European is still developing,

but this has not deterred researchers from going back even further. What was the ancestral language for Proto-Indo-European? The answer is in the making.

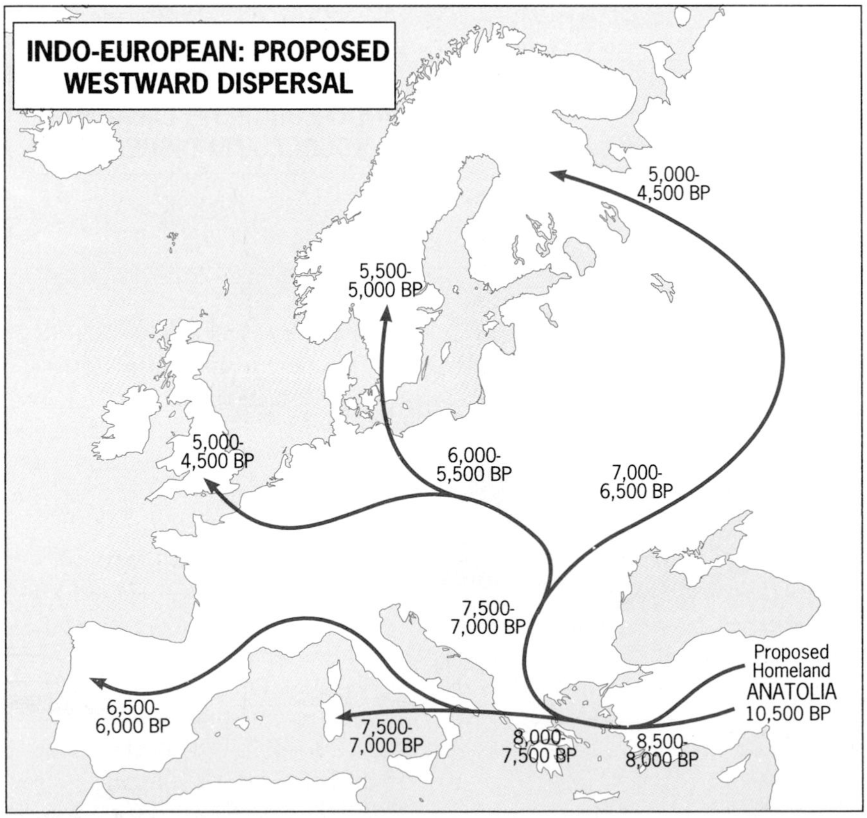

SUPERFAMILY

The evolution and diffusion of Proto-Indo-European that we have just discussed covers a period of, at most, 9000 years. But language development and divergence have been going on for ten times as long or more; we have just dissected a thin branch of an old, gnarled tree (Fig. 22-4).

This does not discourage modern linguists or language geographers, however. The British scholar Colin Renfrew carried the agriculture theory one step further by proposing that not just one, but three agricultural hearths gave rise to language families (Fig. 22-5). From the Anatolian source diffused Europe's Indo-European languages, from the western arc of the Fertile Crescent developed the languages of North Africa and Arabia, and from the Fertile Crescent's eastern arc spread ancient languages into present-day Iran, Afghanistan, Pakistan, and India, later to be replaced by Indo-European languages.

Russian scholars long have been in the forefront of research on ancient languages, but their work generally was not well known in the West; in fact, scholars within the former U.S.S.R. were for many years not even well acquainted with each other's research. The work of two scholars in particular has had great impact: Vladislav Illich-Svitych and Aharon Dolgopolsky. Starting in the 1960s, these two linguists tackled a daunting problem: the deep reconstruction of the language that was ancestral to Proto-Indo-European. Using words assumed to be the most stable and dependable parts of the vocabulary (such as those

FIGURE 22–3 The approximate timing of the westward dispersal of the Indo-European languages.

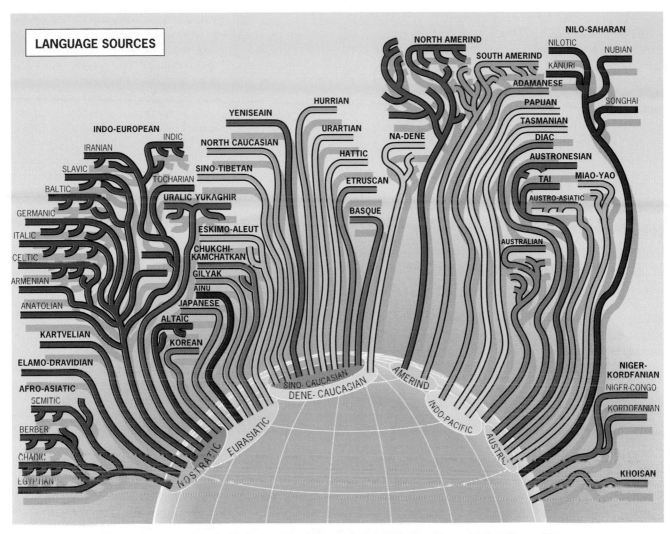

FIGURE 22–4 After a diagram in Philip E. Ross, "Hard Words," *Scientific American*, April 1991, p. 139.

identifying arms, legs, feet, hands and other body parts, and terms for the sun, moon, and other elements of the natural environment), they reconstructed an inventory of several hundred words. But what was most remarkable is that they did this independently, each unaware of the other's work for many years. When finally they met and compared, their conclusions were amazingly similar. They agreed that they had established the core of a pre-Proto-Indo-European language named **Nostratic**.

As with Proto-Indo-European, the evolving vocabulary of the Nostratic language revealed much

about the lives and environments of its speakers. There apparently were no names for domesticated plants or animals, so that Nostratic-speakers were hunter-gatherers, not farmers, as speakers of its successor language were. An especially interesting conclusion related to the words for *dog* and *wolf*, which turned out to be the same—suggesting that the dog may have been in the process of being domesticated. The oldest known bones of dogs excavated at archeological sites date from about 14,000 years ago, so Nostratic may have been in use about that time, well before the First Agricultural Revolution.

Nostratic is believed to be the ancestral language not only for Proto-Indo-European, and thus the Indo-European, language family as a whole, but also for the Kartvelian languages of the southern Caucasus region (16 on Figure 21-2), the Uralic-Altaic languages that include Hungarian and Finnish, Turkish and Mongolian, the Dravidian languages of India (Fig. 21-5), and the Afro-Asiatic language family in which Arabic is dominant. How long *before* 14,000 years B.P. it may have been in use, no one can yet establish. Neither is Nostratic's geography anywhere near solution. Where Nostratic was born, and

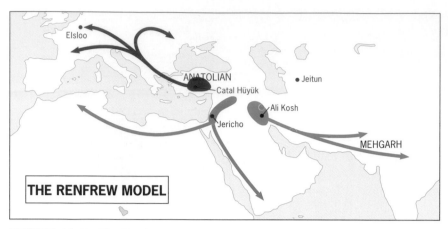

FIGURE 22–5   The Renfrew model: three source areas of agriculture each gave rise to a great language family. From "The Origins of Indo-European Languages," *Scientific American*, October 1989, p. 114.

what tongues gave rise to it, are unanswered questions. However, Nostratic links languages separated even more widely than the languages of the Indo-European family today. Some scholars have suggested that Nostratic (and its contemporaries, variously named Eurasiatic, Indo-Pacific, Amerind, and Austric, among others more or less fanciful) is a direct successor of a Proto-World Language that goes back to the dawn of human history, but this notion is very speculative indeed. The inset of Figure 22-1 reminds us how little of the human language tree we know with any certainty.

FINAL FRONTIERS

The final stages of the dispersal of the older languages—before the global diffusion of English and other Indo-European languages—occurred in the Pacific realm and in the Americas. One would assume that the historical geography of these events would be easier to reconstruct than the complex situation in western Eurasia; after all, the peoples who canoed across the

Pacific brought their languages to unpopulated islands, and the human penetration of the Americas also led to no linguistic convergence with preexisting tongues. Therefore, if we needed a testing ground for linguistic divergence without "noise," these would seem to be fine natural laboratories. But when we follow the debates that have resulted from research into Pacific and American native languages, we find that the problems involved are not simple at all.

PACIFIC DIFFUSION

In our discussion of human racial distributions, we noted how late people first arrived in Pacific islands; New Zealand was reached by Polynesians little more than 1000 years ago. On the other hand, Australia was reached between 50,000 and 60,000 years ago, and New Guinea's first human population must have predated this invasion because through it lay the route to the southern landmass. Papuans as well as Native Australians were hunter-gatherers, although there is archeological evidence that root-crop cultivation began in New Guinea as long as 6000 years ago, a development that appears to have

led to population growth and the expansion of Papuan populations eastward into the Solomon Islands and westward into present-day Indonesia. This expansion brought farmers in contact with foragers and, predictably, the language mosaic of New Guinea and adjoining islands is extremely complex.

But the diffusion of peoples and their languages into the Pacific realm north of Indonesia and New Guinea did not begin from these areas. This sequence had its origin in coastal China, where farming had been well established and had matured considerably. The languages of the Chinese and Southeast Asian realms had undergone several transitions, and the sequence probably was similar to that from the pre-farmers' Nostratic to the farmers' Proto-Indo-European, discussed previously. Here in Asia, an ancestral language gave rise to the Austro-Tai family of languages, and out of this family, in turn, arose **Austronesian**. Language geographers believe that speakers of this language reached Taiwan (with a vocabulary replete with words for rice, field, farm, water buffalo, plow, and canoe). This may have happened about 6000 years ago, and after several centuries, these earliest Austronesian speakers managed to reach the Philippines. This movement resulted in the division of Austronesian into two dialects that later developed into major subfamilies. One of these, **Malayo-Polynesian**, became the forerunner of a large number of languages, including those spoken by the first settlers of Madagascar, the islands of Melanesia and Micronesia, Fiji (where **Fijian** was a discrete Malayo-Polynesian offshoot), and New Zealand, whose Maori people speak **Polynesian**, another derivative of this branch.

Considering the water-fragmented nature of the Pacific realm, the speed with which this process of diffusion—and the simultaneous divergence of languages—took place is remarkable. We may wonder why it took so long for the population-generating Agricultural Revolution in East Asia to stimulate emigration onto the islands off Asia's coast; but then the migrants rapidly spread far and wide from Madagascar in the west to Easter Island in the east. The historian Peter Bellwood charted the process; note that the whole eastern region of Polynesia was settled in a matter of several centuries (Fig. 22-6).

Although the lineages of Austronesian languages are better understood today, much remains to be learned about the reasons behind the complexity of the Pacific language map. Did successive waves or pulses of invasion stimulate divergence among the Malayo-Polynesian languages? Or was differentiation due to isolation?

And on the Asian mainland, there remains the question of Austronesian ancestries. Linguists do not have a model similar to Nostratic, the pre-farming language postulated for western Eurasia. The Pacific language arena is anything but simple.

AMERICAN INVASIONS

As Figure 21-2 indicates, the current language map of the Americas is dominated by Indo-European languages. These have engulfed the languages spoken in America for thousands of years—the languages of Native Americans.

The Native American population never was very large by modern standards. Estimates of the size of the Precolumbian population of the Americas have increased over the past years as anthropologists have learned more about indigenous

peoples, but even the highest of these speculations have not gone beyond 40 million, the number just before the European invasion. As we noted previously, it has long been believed that the Native Americans arrived via the Bering land bridge from Asia, and that the earliest immigrations occurred just 12,000 to 13,000 years ago. Given the modest numbers of people and their recent arrival, one would assume that the linguistic situation should be fairly simple. There were no preexisting peoples to be absorbed and no lifeways to be transformed. At the very least, the pattern should be much simpler than that of Eurasia.

These conclusions may be wrong. While some 40 language families have been recognized in the Old World, linguists have identified as many as 200 Native

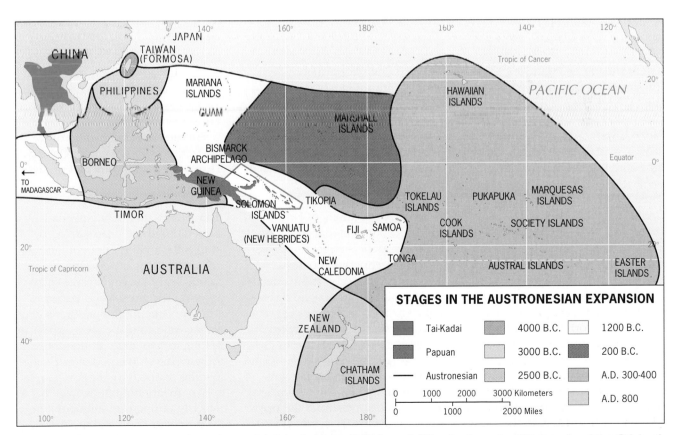

FIGURE 22–6 Bellwood's Pacific-realm model. Adapted from P. Bellwood, "The Austronesian Dispersal and the Origin of Languages," *Scientific American*, July 1991, p. 88.

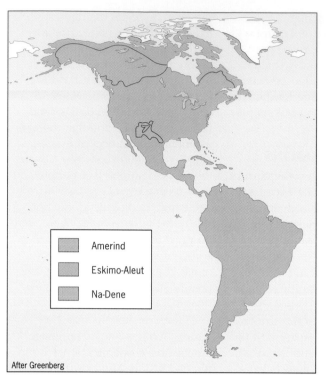

FIGURE 22–7 Greenberg's three indigenous language families. From R. Lewin, "American Indian Language Dispute," *Science* 242 (1988), p. 1633.

American language families, each (by some assessments) fundamentally different from the other. In a very brief period, the first American's languages diverged into the most intricately divided branch of the entire human language tree.

Or did they? Not all linguists agree. The American linguist Joseph Greenberg, in his book, *Language in the Americas* (1987), proposed that this mosaic of Native American languages is a mirage, and that, in fact, there are three families of indigenous American languages. Each of these language families, Greenberg asserts, corresponds to a major wave of migration from Asia into the New World (Fig. 22-7). The oldest and largest and most widely distributed family is the **Amerind** superfamily, which spread from the shores of Hudson Bay to the coast of Tierra del Fuego. The next old-est, next largest, but much less widely diffused family is the **Na-Dene**, whose languages are spoken by Native Americans of northwest Canada and part of Alaska, as well as the Apache and Navajo (the out-lier in the U.S. Southwest shown in Figure 22-7). Last to arrive in North America were speakers of the **Eskimo-Aleut** family of languages, still concentrated today along Arctic and near-Arctic shores.

The Greenberg hypothesis was strongly criticized by many linguists because, it was argued, he did not follow proper procedures of recon-struction. Rather than studying sound shifts and other details, Greenberg compared similar-sound-ing words across many known contemporary languages. Similar work in Africa produced the map shown in Figure 21-4, which also came under heavy fire when it was first published about 25 years ago; but today, that map enjoys wide acceptance.

The implications of the Green-berg hypothesis are far-reaching. If the Amerind languages are indeed members of the same family, then their divergence may have to be ex-plained on the basis of a longer period than the dating of the first immigration—12,000 to 13,000 years ago—would allow for. That would require a revision of a long-held view of the peopling of the Americas.

In the late 1980s and early 1990s, archeological data began to lend support to such a revision. A rock shelter in Pennsylvania produced artifacts dated at about 16,000 years B.P., and a site in Chile yielded ma-terial tentatively dated at 33,000 B.P. If this latter date can be confirmed, then the first wave across the Be-ring Strait may have come more than 40,000 years ago. (Some an-thropologists believe that there also were early transpacific migrations to coastal South America). The next several years should bring to light some crucial evidence, but at the moment, the archeological support for very early American immigration still is tentative.

Stronger support came from other directions. Professor Christy Turner for many years had studied dental variation among Native Americans, and based on dental data he had independently con-cluded that three waves of immigration peopled the Americas, and over a longer period than 12,000 years. Genetic studies also are producing results consistent with the Greenberg hypothesis: the Native American speakers appear to belong to one large group whose tongues have diverged over a lengthy period.

We should note, however, that a majority of linguists still doubt the three-wave notion and the three-family map of American language.

Such relationships, these scholars argue, should come from the careful reconstruction of individual languages, from which the ultimate family relationships will eventually become clear. To draw conclusions from the data Greenberg used, they say, is inappropriate and misleading.

Genetic research and archeological studies will ultimately resolve the issue, but in the meantime, we are reminded of the gaps still remaining in our knowledge—not just of the early development of humanity and its acquisition of language, but even of its most recent precolonial migrations. The modern map of languages conceals a complex and fascinating past, whose unraveling will help tell us not only where we were, but also why we are the way we are.

As interesting as the historical geography of language is, the problems of language in the modern world are many and urgent. Language, we noted previously, is a powerful component of ethnicity; it lies at the heart of many current conflicts. Language can be a barrier to advancement, a source of costly misunderstanding, or a divisive force. Governments manipulate language to bridge cultural and ethnic chasms; traders modify it to facilitate business. In the final chapter on geographic aspects of language, we consider mosaics of language at a larger scale.

KEY TERMS

Agriculture Theory
Amerind
Austronesian
Conquest Theory
Deep Reconstruction
Eskimo-Aleut
Ethnocentrism
Fijian
Language Convergence
Language Divergence
Language Replacement
Malayo-Polynesian
Na-Dene
Nostratic
Polynesian
Proto-Indo-European
Sound Shifts

23

LANGUAGE MOSAICS

In the United States of the 1990s, a language debate is raging. The recent immigration of Hispanic people is changing the country's cultural composition. In less than three decades, the ethnic balance of states from Florida to California has been transformed. In less than two decades more, Hispanics, not Americans of African ancestry, will constitute the largest minority in the country. The American melting pot is being stirred again.

But with the growing Hispanic presence has come a demand: the recognition of Spanish as the country's *de facto* second language, and in some areas, its elevation to equivalent status with English. This campaign quickly generated reactions, official as well as unofficial. State and local governments felt obliged to reaffirm the primacy of English. Organizations such as *English First* and *English Only* drew large memberships and used their financial power to spread their own message in the media. One of their oft-repeated arguments reminded Americans of the country's absorption of so many previously immigrant groups with foreign tongues: Germans, Italians, Swedes, and others, including most recently the hundreds of thousands of Asian arrivals from Vietnam and else-

Geographica

- **English, an Indo-European language that diffused worldwide during the era of colonialism, has become the globe's Esperanto, the language of elites, commerce, and business.**

- **No countries are truly monolingual (with only a single language in use) today; multilingual countries sometimes solve the need for a medium of intercultural communication by making a foreign tongue their official language.**

- **In several areas of the world, mostly (but not exclusively) in coastal zones, linguistic convergence necessitated by trade has produced mixed-origin tongues; some of these have developed into major regional languages.**

- **The study of place names (toponymy) can reveal a great deal about the contents and historical geography of a culture region; place names change as a result of ideological or political transitions.**

where. Why should Spanish be accorded an exception to a rule as old as the United States itself?

For an answer, Hispanics needed only to point to the map. Not only were their numbers growing faster than those of any other major ethnic community in the country, but the regional concentrations of Hispanics in several Southern, Southwestern, and Western states were unlike anything seen in the American melting pot before. In mobile, migrating America, where

ethnic Easterners have moved westward, black Southerners have moved northward, and white Midwesterners have moved southward, the Hispanic sector has begun to redefine the southern tier of the United States because it is anchored there. True, large Hispanic communities have grown in cities from New York to Denver. But the "Hispanicization" of America is a regional phenomenon, and from this comes the community's cultural strength in the national mosaic.

The issue involves more than ethnic pride. Those who oppose the assignment of any special status to Spanish point to the problems faced by bilingual (two-language) countries in which the linguistic division also has regional expression, as in Canada and Belgium. Those who support it proclaim that in those countries the cultures of the respective ethnic communities have been preserved, the weaker not submerged under the stronger. Nevertheless, the issue also has divided Hispanic communities internally. A national Hispanic policy organization in 1990 published the results of a study that showed that well over half of all Hispanic adults were functionally illiterate in English and that educational attainments of Hispanics were declining, compared to national averages. Hispanic educators blamed much of this on the apparent failure of Spanish speakers to make an effort to master the English language, sometimes encouraged in this posture by teachers unwilling to use English as a classroom medium. One such commentator wrote as follows in a national newspaper commentary:*

Is it not time we abandoned the false worship of cultural continuity? Bilingualism and biculturalism . . . are not providing a balance between the traditional and the mainstream that is a solid platform or springboard for advancement. Rather, they are means whereby we Hispanics maintain our own subordination and retard our ability to take advantage of the many opportunities available.

Debates of this kind are carried on in many countries. Note that the issue is not the preservation of the English language so much as its pri-

macy in the national culture. Command of English undoubtedly is an advantage not only in multicultural English-speaking countries, but also in the world at large. English has become the medium of international communication, especially in business, and the advantages inherent in its use outweigh cultural considerations. That, at least, is the position of several governments faced with the difficult choice of promoting their indigenous languages as opposed to English. In Malaysia, for example, the government for four decades after independence promoted the Malay language, Bahasa Melayu. (This was less a reversal of the norms introduced by the former colonizer, Britain, than a boosting of the Malay language as opposed to Chinese, spoken by about one-third of the country's population). But in 1994, the government of Malaysia announced that university courses in scientific and technical fields would henceforth be taught in English, not Bahasa Melayu. Malaysian nationalists were outraged, and a fierce debate erupted, but the government held its ground. Proficiency in English, it argued, was essential to the country's competitiveness in the world of economics. The lack of such proficiency was creating a bottleneck for foreign investors in Malaysia and for Malaysians involved in international trade. In truth, there was another problem. Malays learning English as a second language in the country's state schools were not doing nearly as well as Chinese citizens of the country, many of whom were going to private schools where English was taught rigorously. Greater command of English among educated Malays would improve their competitiveness at home too.

As we will see, some countries have made English (or another foreign language) an official language, relegating domestic languages to regional or secondary status. This,

too, provokes charges—of neocolonialism, of favoring the interest of educated elites. Again, we see that emotionalism and passion relating to languages is not just a matter of protecting threatened tongues. It also is a practical and current issue, and one that forms the focus of this chapter.

TRADE AND TONGUE

The position of traditional languages has changed substantially over the past several centuries—not for linguistic reasons, but for political ones. The European subfamily of the Indo-European languages rapidly spread over much of the globe, replacing and modifying local languages virtually everywhere. Then the world was bequeathed a boundary system that confined the speakers of many languages, for the first time, within bounded territories. These borders often separated people speaking the same language; more frequently, they threw together peoples with mutually unintelligible tongues. This created a host of difficulties both between and within states, problems that persist today.

Early in the twentieth century, a major effort was launched to create a world language, an artificial tongue that would eventually become the first or second language of all peoples everywhere. Called **Esperanto**, this invented language was based on Latin plus a combination of words from modern European languages. European schools introduced Esperanto, and Esperanto societies made their appearance in many countries during the interwar period. Even the League of Nations endorsed the idea—but Esperanto was no global tongue. It was and remained another Indo-European language, and its applicability was thus limited. Furthermore, Europeans were be-

---

*Phillip G. Vargas, "Without English Hispanics are Likely to Fail in America," in *The Miami Herald*, Sunday, April 7, 1991, p. C1. The quotation is from p. C4.

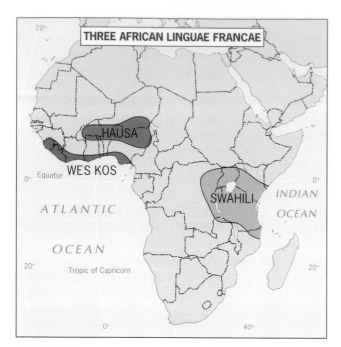

FIGURE 23-1

coming increasingly multilingual, and the need for Esperanto in a European context seemed to fade. The initiative failed.

LINGUA FRANCA

Where language planners failed, traders succeeded. Long before the Europeanization of the world, centuries before the global diffusion of English (which has in truth become the Esperanto of today), and before the invention of Esperanto, people of different tongues were forced to find ways to communicate as they traded, bargained, weighed, measured, and remunerated. Long-stable trade routes would create lengthy periods of such interaction, and this in turn resulted in the emergence of a **lingua franca**.

The term comes from the Mediterranean Sea and its numerous trading ports during the period following the Crusades. As the Mediterranean was opened to wider seaborne commerce, traders from the ports of southern France—the

Franks—followed the routes of the Crusaders, revitalizing ports of the eastern Mediterranean. But the locals did not speak the seafarers' language and thus began a process of convergence, in which the tongue of the Franks was mixed with the Italian, Greek, Spanish, and Arabic of the time. This mixture remained known as the *Frankish language*, the lingua franca, and it served for centuries as the common tongue of Mediterranean commerce.

Today, the term *lingua franca* continues to denote any common language spoken by peoples of diverse speech, as Arabic became during the expansion of Islam and English did during the colonial era. But the term is most appropriate for languages that, like the Mediterranean original, are products of linguistic convergence. One of the best modern examples is Swahili, the lingua franca of East Africa. Over centuries of contact and interaction, Swahili developed from African Bantu languages, from Arabic, and from Persian. Although not

a tone language as many other African languages are, Swahili has a complex vocabulary and intricate structure. It has become the Esperanto of a region that extends from southern Somalia to northern Moçambique, and from coastal Kenya and Tanzania to Uganda and the East African Great Lakes region; it is even in use in eastern Zaïre.

During the period when West Africa's interior kingdom thrived, and trade between the arid north and the moist, forested coast was intense, a lingua franca emerged in the cities and bustling markets of the Sudanic zone that extended from northern Nigeria westward to Senegal. That language, Hausa, still is a regional tongue used by speakers of other languages to communicate. Hausa is heard today not only in Nigeria but also in western Chad, in southern Niger, and even in Burkina Faso and eastern Mali (Fig. 23-1).

CREOLIZATION

When relocation diffusion sends speakers of a language far from their homeland, this language is likely to undergo change, if not grammatically, then in terms of pronunciation, rhythm, and speed. Australian English is distinguishable by few changes of vocabulary, but its cadence makes it unmistakable. English as spoken in India and South Africa also has distinguishing sounds.

In some instances, however, the mother tongue is changed much more radically. Through contact with other languages, it is simplified and modified to become what linguists call a **pidgin**. In the Caribbean region, English speakers met peoples speaking African languages, and before long a form of pidgin English developed. Ordinary people—not the colonialists or the elites—communicated across cultural barriers in this pidgin, which diffused throughout the islands. It even reached mainland South America, not only in English-speaking Guyana but also in Dutch-speaking Suriname.

Over time, a pidgin language may itself become the mother tongue as the home languages of its speakers are forgotten. African languages heard in the Caribbean in the early years following the first involuntary migration faded away, and were replaced by an ever more complex pidgin. This is an important form of language replacement, and the process is known as **creolization**. Now the original pidgin has become a form of lingua franca and is referred to as a **creole** language. A process similar to that just described occurred in the western Pacific region, where Melanesian pidgin is evolving into a regional creole language, based originally on English but now quite distinct. In coastal West Africa, a pidgin language called *Wes Kos* also continues to develop. Swahili, on the other hand, cannot be classified as a pidgin or successor to creole language; its complex structure and vocabulary ensure its place as a full-fledged Bantu language, although a distinct one. A former president of Tanzania, Julius Nyerere, proved the depth and capacity of Swahili by translating Shakespeare's plays into it.

Pidgin and creole languages are important unifying forces in a linguistically divided world. They tend to be simple and accessible, and thus rapidly disseminated. In Southeast Asia, a trade language called *Bazaar Malay* can be heard from Myanmar (Burma) to Indonesia and from the Philippines to Malaysia; it has become a veritable lingua franca. A simplified form of Chinese also serves as a language of commerce even beyond the borders of China.

Sometimes, the difference between a dialect and a pidgin or creole language becomes blurred. Quebecan French, we recall from the previous chapter, is regarded by some linguists as a dialect, but by others as a distinct language derived from French. It is not a creole language; neither is Afrikaans, originally a dialect of Dutch spoken at South Africa's Cape, but now a discrete language with Dutch, French, and even Malay components.

MULTILINGUALISM

At the beginning of this chapter, we touched upon the sensitive issue of language and status. Languages, including pidgin and creole forms, can promote understanding and interaction among disparate peoples; but language also can divide. In the opinion of many students of language issues, countries in which only one language is spoken are fortunate—and rather few. Such **monolingual states** include Japan in Asia, Uruguay and Venezuela in South America, Germany and Poland in Europe, and Lesotho in Africa. However, even in these countries there are small numbers of people using other tongues; more than a half-million Koreans in Japan, for example. In the modern world, there is no truly monolingual country left. English-speaking Australia has more than 180,000 speakers of aboriginal languages. Dominantly Portuguese-speaking Brazil has nearly 1.5 million speakers of Native American languages.

Countries in which more than one language is in use are called **multilingual states**. In some of these countries, the linguistic fragmentation reflects strong cultural pluralism and the existence of divisive forces. This is true in formerly colonial areas where peoples of diverse tongues were thrown together by the force of foreign interests, as happened in Africa and Asia. This also occurred in the Americas: as Figure 23-2 shows, Native American languages are spoken by more than half of the people in substantial areas of Guatemala and Mexico, although these countries tend to be viewed as Spanish speaking. Countries never colonized in comparable ways, but peopled from different cultural sources, may also display multilingualism. Canada's multilin-

FIGURE 23–2

gualism mirrors a cultural division of considerable intensity. In Belgium, a fairly sharp line divides the northern Flemish-speaking half of the country from the Walloon (French)-speaking south.

Multilingualism takes several forms. In effectively bilingual Canada and Belgium, it has regional expression; that is, the two major languages each dominate in particular, distinct areas of the country. In multilingual Switzerland, the linguistic map displays four such locales (Fig. 23-3). In Peru, centuries of acculturation have not erased the regional identities of the Native American tongues spoken in the Andean mountains and the Amazonian interior, and of Spanish as the language of the coast and the corridors of penetration. We noted previously the jigsaw of languages in the massive country of India, where entire states represent linguistic majorities.

But multilingualism has another dimension. In some countries (far fewer), multilingualism has less pervasive regional expression, and considerable interdigitation of speakers has developed. The white (European) community of South Africa is divided by two majority languages (Afrikaans and English) and several smaller tongues. Although Afrikaans remains the dominant language in part of South Africa's rural interior, there is no linguistic regionalism comparable to that of Canada or the former Czechoslovakia (where Czech was the language of the west and Slovak of the east). The European languages spoken in South Africa are set in a matrix of many more African languages, of course, but the phenomenon of their spatial interlocking is noteworthy. Natal and especially the city of Durban have English-speaking majorities; Cape Town and the Cape Province have a large Afrikaner presence. But neither excludes the other.

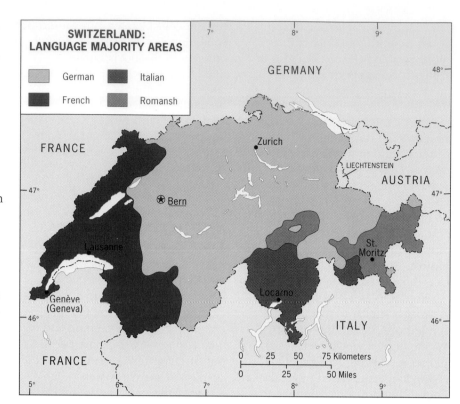

FIGURE 23–3 From a map in W.A.D. Jackson, *The Shaping of Our World* (New York: Wiley, 1985), p. 224.

This pattern is what Soviet planners had in mind when the former communist state was organized following the Russian Revolution: Russian would become the lingua franca of the U.S.S.R., and the diffusion of Russians and their language would create a state in which ethnolinguistic communities retained their identities and domains while "Russification" progressed around them. But 70 years later, the now-defunct Soviet Union is a patchwork of ethnolinguistic areas, in many of which the local language, far from receding, is being aggressively promoted and supported against the Russian wave.

Another country whose multiethnic and multilingual experiment failed was Cyprus, where Greeks and Turks shared a small but comparatively prosperous island. Although the Greek majority and Turkish minority often were at odds, there was remarkable interdigitation of the two during the first period after the country's independence (1960 to 1974), as Figure 23-4 shows. But a political crisis in 1974 led to Turkish armed intervention. Cyprus was partitioned, and both Turks and Greeks became refugees in their own country. Virtually all Turks moved north of the "Green Line" shown in Figure 23-4, and all Greeks were confined to the south of it. Another experiment in multiethnic and multilingual living had failed.

NIGERIA

Compared to Cyprus, and even to the former Soviet Union, Nigeria's multilingualism is more complicated still. Nigeria, with a population exceeding 100 million people, is more than twice as populous as the continent's next-ranking country. It is a

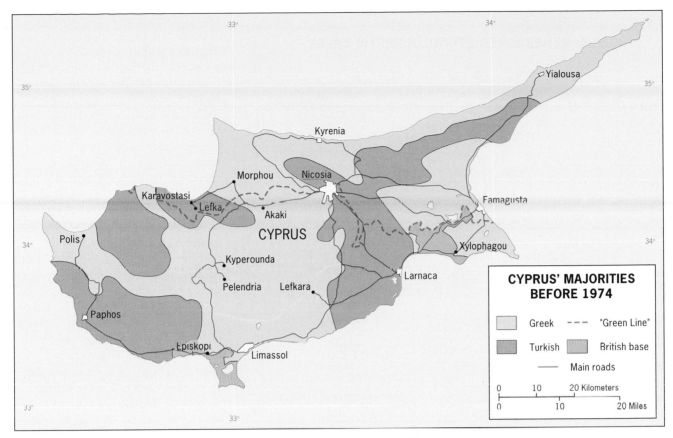

FIGURE 23–4 From a map in D. Downing, *An Atlas of Territorial Border Disputes* (London: New English Library, 1980), p. 30.

colonial creation of almost unimaginable linguistic diversity, with three major regional languages, more than a dozen major local languages spoken by 1 to 5 million people, and another 230 lesser but established tongues (Fig. 23-5). The three major regional languages, Hausa (the old lingua franca of the north, now spoken by some 35 million northerners), Yoruba (the leading language of the southwest, with 24 million speakers), and Ibo (the major language of the southeast, mother tongue of more than 20 million people), are strongly associated with regional cultures, and are thus unsuitable as national languages. Independent Nigeria decided to adopt English as its "official" language (see below), as India had done earlier. When Nigeria's 20 mil-

lion schoolchildren go to school, they first must learn English, the medium of all future instruction.

Certainly, the use of English has precluded major cultural conflict based on language, but Nigerian educators are having second thoughts about school policy. Children who during their first several years grow up speaking a local language suddenly are confronted, upon entering school, with a totally unfamiliar medium. The time and energy lost in learning the lingua franca, say these educators, doom millions of students to failure in other important areas. To them, knowledge of the language of success is irrelevant if they emerge from school (as many do after only six years) unable to function in local Nigerian society. So hearing the

echo of our own debate, we watch Nigeria reconsider its relationship with the lingua franca brought here by those who carved the multiethnic country out of the African realm in the first place.

OFFICIAL LANGUAGES

India and Nigeria are not the only countries seeking to solve multilingualism through the use of an "umbrella" language. Several dozen countries of the world have embraced the concept of an **official language** to serve this purpose. In theory, such an official language, already known by the educated and politically powerful elite, will enhance internal communication and interaction among peoples who speak diverse traditional languages.

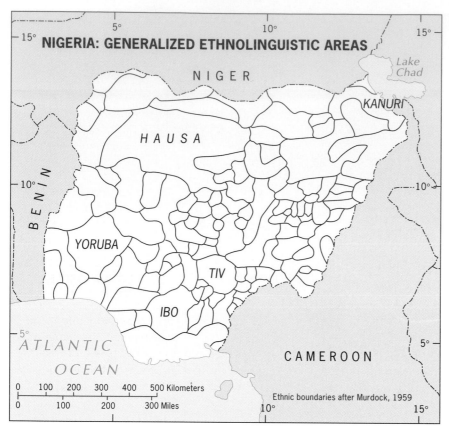

FIGURE 23–5 This map is actually a simplification of the ethnolinguistic mosaic of Nigeria. Detail from a map in G.P. Murdock, *Africa: Its Peoples and Their Culture History* (New York: McGraw-Hill, 1972).

official languages in the African country of Cameroon, because an English-speaking province was welded to the French-dominated colony shortly after independence. In Peru, Spanish and the Native American (Amerindian) language Quechuan have official status—and regional expression. In the Philippines, English and the country's creolized Spanish, Pilipino, are both official languages. Tiny Singapore, the city-state at the tip of the Malay Peninsula, has four official languages: English, Chinese, Malay, and the Indian tongue, Tamil. South Africa has the most official languages—eleven.

As would be expected, Canada recognizes both English and French not only as official languages, but also as equals in all governmental settings. The United States, on the other hand, never has proclaimed an official language—a decision many proponents of English now want the government to make.

TOPONYMY

We end our study of the geographic aspects of langauge by looking into one of its most interesting components: the origin and meaning of place names. Geography itself sometimes is wrongly assumed to be the study of place names for their own sake, but even if this were so, it would be a fascinating field. The systematic study of place names, or **toponymy**, leads to many valuable and useful insights. A seminal work that focused on this topic is George Stewart's *Names on the Land: A Historical Account of Place-Naming in the United States* (1958), a classic still worth reading. A number of subsequent studies have dealt with the significance of place names in individual States or regions.

Place names can reveal much

As Table 23-1 shows, many former African colonies have taken the language of their former colonial power as the official language, even though they may have thrown off the colonial yoke in violent revolution. Thus Portuguese is the official language of Angola, English is the language of Nigeria and Ghana, and French is the language of the Côte d'Ivoire.

Such policy is not without peril. As we noted in Nigeria, the long-term results of the imposition of a foreign language may not always be favorable. In some countries, including India, citizens objected to the primacy of a tongue they associated with subjugation and repression. In response, some former colonies chose not just one but two official languages: the Euro-

pean colonial language plus one of the country's own leading languages. As Table 23-1 shows, English *and* Hindi are official languages of India. In Tanzania, English and Swahili are official. In Mauritania, French and Arabic have this status. But this solution was not always enough. When Hindi was given official status in India, riots and disorder broke out in non-Hindi areas of that country. Kenya, which at first made English and Swahili official languages, decided to drop English after public opinion rose against what opponents called "archaic" rules, whereby candidates for public office must pass a test of their capacity to use English.

Further inspection of Table 23-1 reveals some noteworthy relationships. French and English are both

TABLE 23–1   Official Languages of Selected Countries of the World, 1995

Country	Language(s)
Angola	Portuguese
Benin	French
Botswana	English
Brunei	English, Malay
Burundi	French
Cameroon	French, English
Canada	English, French
Central African Republic	French
Chad	French
Congo	French
Djibouti	French, Arabic
Dominica	English
Equatorial Guinea	Spanish
Fiji	English, Fijian
Gabon	French
Ghana	English
Guinea	French
India	English, Hindi
Indonesia	Bahasa, Indonesian
Ivory Coast (Côte d'Ivoire)	French
Kenya	Swahili
Lesotho	English, Sesotho
Madagascar	French, Malagasy
Malawi	English, Chichewa
Mali	French
Mauritania	French, Arabic
Moçambique	Portuguese
Niger	French
Nigeria	English
Peru	Spanish, Quechuan
Philippines	English, Pilipino (Tagalog)
Rwanda	French, Kinyarwanda
Senegal	French
Seychelles	French, English
Sierra Leone	English
Singapore	English, Malay, Chinese, Tamil
Somalia	English, Somali
South Africa	English, Xhosa and 9 others
Suriname	Dutch
Swaziland	English, SiSwati
Tanzania	English, Swahili
Togo	French
Uganda	English
Zaïre	French
Zimbabwe	English

guese place names of Santa Catarina State, Brazil, lies the town named Blumenau. Check more closely, and you will discover that German immigrants played major roles in the development of this southern Brazilian state: the German fondness for flowers that appears in so many German place-names (Blumberg, Blumenhof, Blumenort, Blumenthal, and Blumenstein), is reflected by the map here in South America. The largest city of Tanzania, East Africa, has an Arabic name: Dar es Salaam (Haven of Peace). The map reveals an historical geography long past, and a place name alerts us to it.

Toponyms (place names) make reading a map a fruitful and sometimes revealing exercise. Of all the readily available atlases, the National Geographic Society's *Atlas of the World* (currently in its sixth edition) probably carries a greater number of place names than any other. A careful eye will spot Roman imprints on the map of Britain, German names on the map of France, and Dutch names in Australia. Sometimes, the links are harder to find. The Brazilian state of Bahia has a number of place names that seem to have West African origins, notably from Benin and Nigeria. And indeed, these two areas were linked by the forced migration of Africans in bondage. The map betrays this dreadful past.

Many place names consist of two parts, sometimes connected and sometimes separate. These are a *specific* (or given) part and a *generic* (or classifying) part. For example, the capital of the Netherlands, Amster/dam, refers to the city's major river (the Amstel) and the dam that was built on it that enabled settlement of the site. The name Battle Creek (Michigan) consists of a reference to an event (specific) and a landscape feature (generic). Countless such names mark the landscape: Johns/town,

about the contents of a culture area, even when time has erased other evidence. A cluster of Welsh place names in Pennsylvania, French place names in Louisiana, or Dutch place names in Michigan reveals not only national origins, but also may provide insight into language and dialect, routes of diffusion, even ways of life. Amid the Portu-

Pitts/burgh, Nash/ville, Chapel Hill, Little Rock, and so on.

Such generic names can sometimes be linked to each of the three source areas of Eastern dialects and their westward diffusion. It became a Northern habit to lay out towns and cities by compass directions. To this day, foreign visitors are impressed by the American use of these directions to show the way ("go four blocks east, then three blocks north"). This led to the naming of adjacent settlements by direction as well: *East* Lansing (Michigan), *West* Chester (Pennsylvania), *North* Chicago (Illinois), *South* St. Paul (Minnesota). This is a mainly (though not exclusively) Northern phenomenon on the map today.

The historian George Stewart classified place names into ten categories. These include *descriptive* names (Rocky Mountains), *associative* names (Mill Valley, California), *incident* names (Battle Creek, Michigan), *possessive* names (Johnson City, Texas), *commemorative* names (San Francisco), *commendatory* names (Paradise Valley, Arizona), *folk-etymology* names (Plains, Georgia, or Academia, Pennsylvania), *manufactured* names (Truth or Consequences, New Mexico), *mistake* names, involving historic errors in identification or translation (such as Lasker, North Carolina, named after the state of Alaska!) and so-called *shift* names (relocated names; double names for the same feature [Alpine Mountain]). Each of these categories contains cultural-geographic opportunities. For example, the capital of Russia has an associative place name. Moscow is actually spelled *Moskva* in Russian, but *kva* is Finnish for water. A check on other toponyms in the Moscow region confirms the ancient presence of Finnish peoples in what is now the Russian heartland. Another example is the southern tip of South America, Cape Horn, which can be categorized as a mistake name. The Dutch named this area Cape Hoorn, after a Dutch town. The English interpreted this as Cape Horn, which the Spanish, in turn, translated into *Cabo Hornos*—meaning Cape of Ovens!

CHANGING NAMES

Like language itself, the names of places can elicit strong passions. When African colonies became independent countries, one of the first acts of many of the new governments was to change the names of places that had been named after colonial figures. Not only the names of cities and towns were changed, but also countries themselves were renamed: Upper Volta to Burkina Faso, Congo to Zaïre, Nyasaland to Malawi, Northern and Southern Rhodesia to Zambia and Zimbabwe, respectively. New names such as Sri Lanka (Ceylon), Bangladesh (East Pakistan), and Indonesia (Netherlands East Indies) appeared on the map of Asia.

The **name changes** of cities and towns, however, seemed to evoke stronger reactions even than that of territories. Some governments carried this campaign further than others, changing not only European names but even indigenous names deemed to have a colonial tinge. Thus Leopoldville (named after a Belgian king) became Kinshasa, capital of Zaïre; Salisbury (Zimbabwe), named after a British leader, was renamed Harare; and Lourenço Marques, commemorating a Portuguese naval hero, became Maputo. On the other hand, Etoile (Zaïre), Colleen Bawn (Zimbabwe), and Cabo Delgado (Moçambique) stayed on the postcolonial map.

The next round of name-changing occurred during and after the collapse of the Soviet Union. Thousands of places, named after Soviet-era personalities or slogans, were renamed—sometimes to their Czarist-era appellations, to the chagrin of those who disapproved of the demise of the communist state. Reformers, nationalists, and unreformed communists argued bitterly over these changes, and many people continued to address their mail according to the older usage. Leningrad became St. Petersburg, Sverdlovsk went back to Yekaterinburg, its name under the Czars, and Andropov was renamed Rybinsk, which is how it was known before the communist ruler died.

Today, the still-new majority government of South Africa faces decisions of this kind. Again, the multicultural nation is divided: some black Africans want to rename their country Azania, a move strongly opposed by whites, Coloureds, and Asians. Cities and towns named after Afrikaner and British figures, such as Stellenbosch and Durban, Potgietersrus and Port Elizabeth, are likely to see their names replaced. Evidence of an era will be erased from the map, and the process will not serve to unite an already divided citizenry. The government, to be sure, has little choice: pressure from its supporters will force action it may prefer to defer.

Obviously, the whole sphere of language in cultural geography affords innumerable opportunities for research and study. Language is a vital element in the reconstruction of past cultures. The transmittal of oral literature and its interpretation opens up whole new possibilities. The professional storyteller in an African village is not just a picturesque figure of incidental interest: he holds in his tales the history and psyche of the people of whom he speaks. The study of dialects and the spatial character of word modification can tell us much about peoples' movements, their external contacts or isolation, former distribution, and more. Then there is the relevant issue brought up by so many when it comes to debates about the value of learning a foreign language: language can reveal much about the way a people view reality in their own culture as well as other cultures. In their structure and vocabulary and in their ability (or inability) to express certain concepts and ideas, languages reflect something of the way people think of and perceive their world. There are African languages that have no word, or term for the concept of a god. Others (in Asia) really have no system for the reporting of chronological events, no time scale, as it were. It would be difficult for us to understand those peoples' perception of the world about them, preoccupied as our culture is with the supernatural and dating and timing. Learning the language would be a first, timid step. However, the rewards could be enormous.

Language and religion are two cornerstones of culture. Ethnic consciousness is aroused as deeply by religious fervor as it is by issues of language. Like language, religion has ancient, still-veiled roots. From a cluster of sources, the world's great religions diffused widely—a process still going on today. We turn next to this vital dimension of human culture in a spatial context.

KEY TERMS

Creole
Creolization
Esperanto
Lingua Franca
Monolingual States
Multilingual States
Name Changes
Official Language
Pidgin
Toponymy

Religious revival: a Russian Orthodox Church gets a facelift in St. Petersburg.

PART EIGHT

GEOGRAPHY OF RELIGION

At Issue

Religious fundamentalism is resurgent throughout the world. From the pulpits of Alabama to the mosques of Algeria, the drive is toward the foundations of the faith. And from the villages of Northern Ireland to the contested lands of the Middle East, religion lies at the heart of nationalism. Religion stokes the fires of war in Bosnia, Kashmir, and the Transcaucasus. Some cultural geographers express the fear that the cold ideological war of the twentieth century may be followed by a hot religious war along the Islamic front of the twenty-first. Here is the key issue: can modern-secular and fundamentalist-religious countries coexist?

24

RELIGIOUS ORIGINS AND DISTRIBUTIONS

Religion and language lie at the foundation of culture, vital strands in the fabric of society. Like language but in a different way, religion confers identity. In many societies less dominated by modern technology than ours, religion is the great binding force, the dominant rule of daily life. From eating habits to dress codes, religion sets the standards for such communities.

Like languages, religions change continuously. Although religious leaders and their bureaucracies attempt to ensure conservatism as well as continuity, the faiths nevertheless change with the times. In the process, the great religions of the world have been adopted across cultural barriers and language boundaries. Persuasion will not lead people to change the language they speak, but it can induce them to profess adherence to a new faith. Conversion still goes on as missionaries, traditional and modern, spread their beliefs in receptive markets. The new freedoms being enjoyed in the independent republics of the former Soviet Union have led to such memorable spectacles as the proselytizing by American evangelists before mass audiences

Geographica

- Despite the modernization and secularization of urbanizing societies, religion still dominates the lives and behaviors of billions of people in areas ranging from food proscriptions to family planning.

- The several faiths of Christianity, having been diffused through European colonialism and aggressive proselytism, in combination constitute the largest and most widely dispersed religion today.

- Islam is today the world's fastest growing major religion, possibly a portent of a new (or revived) form of global ideological competition as Christian and Muslim interests clash.

- Christianity and Islam together hold the allegiance of nearly half the world's total population; no other faith comes close, and the third largest religion, Hinduism, is not a global but a cultural faith.

in Russia—where religious practice until a few years ago was carried on furtively and quietly in an officially atheistic state. Just as the map of languages continues to change, so does the pattern of religion.

Religion prominently marks the cultural landscape: churches and mosques, cemeteries and shrines, statues and symbols mark it. Religion is proclaimed even in codes of dress (veils, turbans) and personal habits (beards, scars). In modern

societies, such outward and overt displays of religious self-identification have declined, but in more traditional societies they continue. In the Islamic Republic of Pakistan, the government in 1991 proclaimed that possessing a beard would henceforth be a condition for a judge to be appointed to the country's Islamic courts. Such rules, reminiscent of medieval times, remind us that religions, like languages, are undergoing divergence.

297

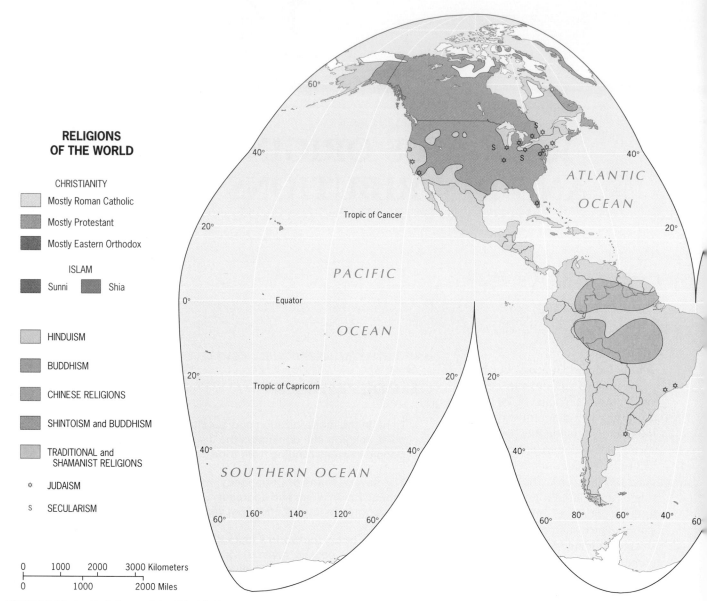

**RELIGIONS
OF THE WORLD**

CHRISTIANITY

Mostly Roman Catholic

Mostly Protestant

Mostly Eastern Orthodox

ISLAM

Sunni   Shia

HINDUISM

BUDDHISM

CHINESE RELIGIONS

SHINTOISM and BUDDHISM

TRADITIONAL and
SHAMANIST RELIGIONS

✡   JUDAISM

S   SECULARISM

0   1000   2000   3000 Kilometers

0   1000   2000 Miles

FIGURE 24–1   Religions of the World. From a map prepared for the first edition by Hammond, Inc. (1977).

In Part 8, we consider the sources, diffusion, and transformation of the world's great religions, their regional distribution and their cultural landscapes. Again like language, religion can be a strong unifying force, but it can also serve to divide and foster conflict. Such strife lies at the heart of several of the world's problem areas: Northern Ireland, Yugoslavia, India, Ethiopia, and others. The study of religion has many geographic dimensions.

GEOGRAPHY OF RELIGION

In many areas of the world, especially in non-Western areas, **religion** is so vital a part of culture that it practically constitutes culture. Thus it is not surprising that we should have difficulty defining exactly what a religion is. The phenomenon manifests itself in so many different ways: in the worship of the souls of ancestors living in

natural objects, such as mountains, animals, or trees; in the belief that a certain living person or persons possess particular capacities granted by a supernatural power; or in the belief in a deity or deities, as in the great world religions. In some societies, notably in the Western, industrialized, urbanized, commercialized world, religion has become a rather subordinate, ephemeral matter in the life of many people. However, in societies in Africa and

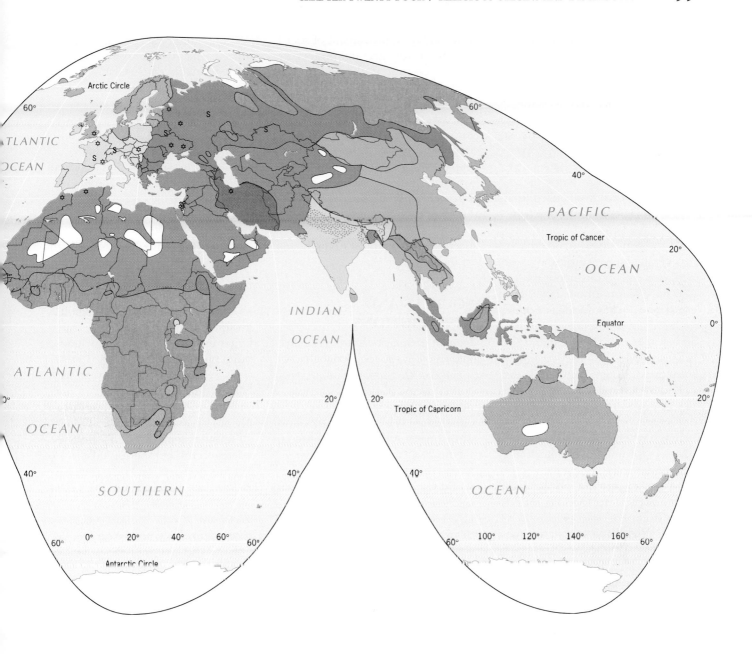

Asia, religious doctrine may exert tight control over behavior, during the daytime through ritual and practice, and even at night in prescribing the orientation of the sleeping body.

If we cannot precisely define religion, we can at least observe some of the properties of this element of human culture. There are, of course, sets of doctrines and beliefs relating to the god or gods central to the faiths. In each faith, there will also be a number of more or less complex rituals through which these beliefs are given expression. Such rituals may attend significant events in peoples' lives: birth and death, attainment of adulthood, and marriage. They are also expressed at regular intervals in a routine manner, as is done on Sundays in most of the Western world. Prayer at mealtime, at sunrise and sundown, at night when retiring, or in the morning when arising, commonly attends religious ritual. Such ritual is likely to involve the use of religion's literature, if such a literature exists. (We are most familiar with the Bible and the Koran.)

Religions, especially the major, world-scale faiths, such as Christianity and Islam, have produced vast and complex organizational structures. These bureaucracies have a hierarchy of officers and command a great deal of wealth. Rank and status are confirmed by costume and authority over people's lives. The religious officers police and maintain the approved set of standards and the code of ethics peculiar to each religion.

From this brief statement of properties, it is evident how strongly a culture may be dominated by the precepts of the prevailing faith. Some scholars have argued that the idea that people ultimately depend on some supernatural power over which they have no control has led to apathy, even laziness; but obviously, others have been inspired to compete and achieve. The idea that a "good" life has rewards and "bad" behavior risks punishment must also have an enormous cumulative effect on cultures. Modes of dress, the kinds of food people should and should not eat, commerical practices, and even the location and structure of houses may be determined by the rules of religion. It is hardly necessary to remind anyone of the daily influence of religious heritage when our calendar, our holidays, prominent architectural landmarks, many place names, even the slogan "In God We Trust" on the money we spend comes directly from that source. Even in societies that have sought to divest themselves of religion and religious influence, such as China, those very influences continued to affect living conditions and cultural landscapes as a whole. Imagine, then, the role of religion in an almost totally Roman Catholic society, such as Spain. In Islamic society also, it is religion that sustains and perpetuates the culture. Religious doctrine has determined that much of India is vegetarian (and overrun by holy animals), that the eating of pork is taboo in Muslin countries (eliminating the profitable pig from domestic economies), and that eating meat on Fridays was inappropriate for Roman Catholics.

If we may be subjective about such matters, organized religion has had powerful positive as well as deep negative effects on human societies. Religion has been a major force in the improvement of social ills, the sustenance and protection of the poor, the furtherance of the arts, the education of the deprived, and in medicine. However, religion has also thwarted scientific work, encouraged oppression of dissidents, supported colonialism and exploitation, and condemned women to inferior status in society. In common with other bureaucracies and establishments, large-scale organized religion has all too often been unable to adjust to the needs of the times.

SOURCES AND DISTRIBUTIONS

Human geographers are naturally interested in the locational characteristics of the major religions, their source areas, dispersals, distributions, and present patterns of adherence. The spatial distribution of the major religions is depicted in Figure 24-1, which necessarily shows the dominant religions in world regions, not the intricate mosaic that would be revealed by larger-scale maps. For example, India (except for the northwest) is shown as a Hindu region, but other religious faiths also continue to survive there (Islam remains strong in several parts of the country). Figure 24-1 should therefore be viewed as a generalization of a much more intricate set of distributions. With this caveat as background, the map does reveal the dominance of the Christian religions, the wide dispersal of Islam, the coincidence of Hinduism with one of the world's major population concentrations, and the survival of Buddhism.

Figure 24-1 should be viewed in conjunction with Table 24-1, which reports the latest available data on religious affiliation. Tables such as 24-1 should be used cautiously, however, because the information from which they are derived is not reliable. When you compare similar tabulations from other sources, you will encounter substantial discrepancies. This results not only from undependable census data, but also from definitional problems. Some census counts takes a much broader view of (for example) who is a Christian than others do. Consider, for instance, the annually published table in the *Encyclopedia Britannica Book of the Year 1995*, which reports the "religious population" of the world. It gives the number of Christians in North America (the United States and Canada) as 246,319,000. But the *1993 Yearbook of American and Canadian Churches* reports only 147,130,000 "members of religious groups" in the United States. The larger estimate, therefore, includes a huge number of "assumed" Christians, whose only contact with the faith is through the routines of our society, and many of whom probably are agnostics.

Another remarkable discrepancy relates to the number of Muslim adherents in North America. Here the *Britannica Yearbook* reports a total of below 3 million, whereas the *Yearbook of American and Canadian Churches* counts over 6 million (the latter number appears to be more nearly correct).

Table 24-1, therefore, is an approximation based on a number of sources, and it also should be viewed as a very rough estimate. But certain conclusions are beyond doubt: the Christian churches presently have the largest number of adherents and are geographically the most widely dispersed on Earth. More than 1.6 billion Christians include about 520 million in Europe and the former Soviet Union, a number that is growing with the resurrection of the Eastern Orthodox Churches in Russia and its neighbors; approximately 350 million in North and Middle America, a total that is also growing as a result of the rapid population increase in Mexico and other Middle American countries; approximately

300 million in South America, perhaps 250 million in Africa, and an estimated 165 million in Asia. Christians, therefore, account for nearly 40 percent of all the world's members of major religions. Islam, with more than one billion adherents, ranks second; there are about 165 million more Muslims than Roman Catholics today.

As we note in more detail later, the world's religions are themselves divided. Roman Catholicism is the largest constituency of **Christianity**. Figure 24-1 reveals the strength of Roman Catholicism in Europe, areas of North America, and Middle and South America. The Protestant churches prevail in Northern Europe and in much of North America, as well as in Australia and New Zealand, and also in South Africa. The Eastern Orthodox churches now count as many as 180 million adherents in Europe, Russia and its neighboring states, Africa (where a major cluster survives in Ethiopia), and North America.

The faiths of **Islam** (also a divided religion) dominate Northern Africa and Southwest Asia, extending into the former Soviet Union and China, and including outlying clusters in Indonesia, Bangladesh, and southern Mindanao in the Philippines. Islam is strongly represented along the East African coast, survives in Albania, has an outlier at South Africa's Cape of Good Hope, and has adherents in the United States (see box, "America's Black Muslims and Their Continuing Evolution"). Islam has approximately one billion faithful, more than half of them outside the culture realm often called the Islamic World. A substantial Islamic minority still resides in India, where 100 million Muslims adhere to the faiths. As Table 24-1 shows, approximately 170 million Muslims reside in Subsaharan Africa, mainly in interior West Africa, where Nigeria alone has about 55 million adherents. Islam, the fastest growing of the world religions, is spreading rapidly southward across Africa. Southwest Asia and Northern Africa, however, remain the Islamic heartland with about 400 million followers.

The salient division within Islam is between Sunni Muslims (who constitute the great majority, as reflected by Figure 24-1 and Table 24-1) and the Shiah or Shiite cluster, which is concentrated in Iran. A comparison between Figures 24-1 and 6-1 will prove that the largest Muslim country does not lie in the comparatively sparsely populated Southwest Asian/Northern African source area, but in Southeast Asia: Indonesia is the world's largest dominantly Islamic state, with about 165 million believers.

In terms of number of adherents, **Hinduism** ranks after Islam as a world religion, but there are significant structural differences between Hinduism, Christianity, and Islam. The Hindu religion is without a comparable ecclesiastical organization, lacking the kind of bureaucracy that is familiar to Christians and Muslims. Certainly, there are holy men, but they represent literally thousands of gods. Thus unlike Christianity, or Islam, Hinduism is polytheistic, fragmented by numerous cults, and without a prescriptive book, such as the Bible or the Koran. Again, unlike Christianity or Islam, Hinduism remains concen-

TABLE 24–1   Estimated Adherents to Principal World Religions, By Geographic Realm, 1996 (in millions)*

| Religion | Americas | | | Europe | Sub-saharan Africa | North Africa and Southwest Asia | Asia | | | Russia | Pacific | Totals |
	North	Middle	South				South	South-east	East			
Christianity	208.1	140.8	296.2	409.6	253.1	5.0	24.7	90.5	50.0	110.7	15.3	1,604.0
Roman Catholic	94.7	128.6	281.8	255.3	109.1	0.3	5.5	69.7	13.0**	4.9	6.9	969.8
Protestant	107.4	12.1	14.2	107.2	114.6	4.3	19.2	20.8	37.0**	9.1	7.9	453.8
Orthodox	6.0	0.1	0.2	47.1	29.4	0.4	—	—	—	96.7	0.5	180.4
Islam	6.1	0.2	0.3	13.9	171.9	401.3	327.1	182.6	29.3	3.2	0.2	1,136.1
Sunni	6.0	0.2	0.3	11.9	164.5	260.4	319.4	180.1	29.3	3.2	0.2	975.5
Shiite	0.1	—	—	2.0	7.4	140.9	8.7	2.5	—	—	—	160.6
Hinduism	1.0	0.3	0.4	0.7	1.7	2.3	741.3	5.9	0.3	—	0.4	754.3
Buddhism	0.6	0.1	0.4	0.3	—	0.1	22.5	168.7	151.2	0.9	—	343.9
Chinese Religions	0.1	—	0.1	0.1	—	—	0.1	9.1	253.0	—	—	262.5
Sikhism	0.3	—	—	0.2	—	—	20.1	—	—	—	—	20.6
Judaism	7.4	0.2	0.7	2.1	0.1	4.7	—	—	—	2.7	0.1	18.0

*Geographic realms in accordance with De Blij/Muller definition. **Official count is 7.7 million Christians in state-sanctioned churches, but counting unregistered Christian worshippers the actual total may be about 50 million. Data from various sources, including *The 1994 Encyclopaedia Britannica Book of the Year*, United Nations statistics, and official church bulletins. Published statistics vary widely, and these figures should be viewed as rough approximations. Data extrapolated to 1996.

trated in a single geographic realm, the region of its source (it is regarded as the world's oldest organized religion). The vast majority of the 750 million Hindus live in India, although the faith also extends into Bangladesh, Myanmar, Sri Lanka, and Nepal.

Buddhism, another religion that had its source in India, is now a minority faith in that country, but still remains strong in Southeast Asia, China, and Japan. Buddhism's various faiths are estimated to have about 340 million adherents, and again, this is a strongly regional religion, as Figure 24-1 shows. **Shintoism**, the Japanese ethnic religion closely related to Buddhism, has numerous followers in Japan—but just how many is uncertain. The reported figures depend on just who is a Shinto adherent; the number of registered worshippers is given as under 3.4 million, but Japanese publications refer to as many as 45 million "followers." It is generally agreed, however, that Japan's modernization is reducing the importance of Shintoism in Japanese culture.

The **Chinese religions** also have elements of Buddhism mixed with local Chinese belief systems. As we will note later, the traditional Chinese religions never involved concepts of supernatural omnipotence. Confucianism was mainly a philosophy of (Earthly) life, and Taoism held that human happiness lies in one's proper relationship with nature. Chinese Buddhism was a pragmatic version of what the Buddha had originally preached, and it related well to Chinese religious styles. The faiths survive in China today, but we do not know in what strength. The data given in Table 24-1 should be considered as rough estimates only.

Our map shows **Judaism** to be distributed throughout parts of the Middle East and North Africa, Russia, Ukraine, and Europe, and parts of North and South America. Juda-

ism is one of the world's great religions, but apart from the state of Israel, it is now scattered and dispersed across much of the world. Today, Judaism has about 18 million adherents.

Finally, Figure 24-1 shows large areas in Africa and several other parts of the world as "Traditional and Shamanist." **Shamanism** occurs in various forms in many parts of the world. It is a community faith in which people follow their *shaman*, a religious leader, teacher, healer, and visionary—but in the ancient Chinese tradition, a man of *this* world, not of another. Such a shaman appeared to various peo-

ples in many different parts of the world, in Africa, in Native America, in Southeast Asia, and in East Asia, where shamanism may first have taken form. Scholars of religion have noted the similar effects of such appearances on the cultures of peoples scattered far and wide across the world, and they employ the term *shamanism* to identify such faiths. We might guess that if these shamanist religions had developed elaborate bureaucracies (which they did not) and had sent representatives to international congresses (as do the Christian faiths), then they would have negotiated away their differences and created

AMERICA'S BLACK MUSLIMS AND THEIR CONTINUING EVOLUTION

The faith of Islam has a foothold in the United States on the strength of an Afro-American religious and erstwhile nationalist movement commonly called the Black Muslims (known officially as the **Nation of Islam**). The movement was born in the 1930s, although it traces its antecedents to Ali's Moorish Science Temple of America, established as early as 1913. In 1930, a split developed in the Temple movement, and one of the fragments was to become the Nation of Islam, under the initial leadership of W.D. Fard.

The Nation of Islam was founded on American blacks' desire to be delivered from white oppression. Believing themselves to be members of a lost Islamic tribe, the Black Muslims await messianic deliverance; they often compare themselves to the children of Israel in Egyptian bondage. W.D. Fard preached this message in the Nation's first temple in Detroit. In 1933, the Chicago Temple of Elijah Muhammad was founded, and upon Fard's sudden disappearance, Muhammad became the Nation's leader. Fard became a Mahdi, a savior to the Black Muslims, but it was Elijah Muhammad who brought the Nation of Islam unprecedented strength. In 1935, membership in the Nation was just a few hundred; by 1960, it was probably in excess of 10,000 and when Elijah died in 1975, there were perhaps a half-million members and active sympathizers. The largest temples (now called Mosques) are No. 7 in New York and No. 27 in Los Angeles.

The ideology of the Nation of Islam had been a mixture of nationalism (including a separate homeland as a primary objective) and much modified Islam (although the faith's "five pillars" were prescribed). Tight discipline, substantial contributions from members, business enterprises, educational programs, a newspaper (*Muhammad Speaks*), and an annual convention on February 26 and 27 all contributed to the Nation's cohesion and appeal. In the late 1950s and early 1960s, a young member named Malcolm X rose to prominence in the movement, bringing it unprecedented national visibility. A clash with orthodox leadership followed. Malcolm X was assassinated in February 1965—a low point for the Nation.

Elijah Muhammad's death in 1975 marked the end of an era, and his son, Wallace Muhammad, immediately began a modernization program. He ended the Black Muslim's aloofness from politics in America (Elijah had condemned participation as sinful), strengthened the movement's ties with African and Caribbean countries by creating mosques there, permitted the first white person to join the movement, and began to bring ritual and practice back toward orthodox Islam. Several of these reforms were first advocated by Malcolm X, and in recognition of Malcolm's efforts, the Harlem Mosque was renamed after him.

In the early 1980s, Wallace changed his name to Imam Warith Deen Muhammad, and the name of the organization to the American Muslim Mission. In 1985, this organization announced that it was disbanding, but encouraged its local member groups to move into the mainstream of the Islamic faith.

The Nation of Islam, however, survived this transition as well. During the late 1980s, it regained national attention in two arenas: through its role in black neighborhoods as a force against drug use, and through its espousal of Islamic causes internationally. Muslim leader Louis Farrakhan's anti-Semitic rhetoric thrust the Nation of Islam into the national spotlight.

In the early 1990s, the Nation of Islam was benefiting from its increased credibility in the black community, and from the growth of Islam in America generally. In 1992, there were more than 6 million practicing Muslims in the United States, most of them immigrants from Asia, North Africa, and Southwest Asia. These immigrants have stimulated the establishment of some 600 mosques nationwide, many of which have been joined by African-American faithful. Present estimates suggest that more than 1 million black Americans are Muslims. Islam is this country's fastest-growing faith.

The Nation of Islam still is associated with superiority, aloofness, and separatism. Only a small minority of black American Muslims are members. Recent hardening of anti-Semitic rhetoric on the part of some of the organization's leaders threatens a return to the divisiveness of earlier years. But the Nation remains a barometer of the African-American community, and should it move toward the mainstream of evolving American Islam, its importance would increase.

---

still another world religion. However, unlike Christianity or Islam, the shamanist faiths are small in scale and remain comparatively isolated.

Shamanism, therefore, is **traditional religion**, an intimate part of a local culture and society. However, not all traditional religions are shamanist. Traditional African religions involve beliefs in a god as creator and indivisible provider, in divinities both superhuman and human, in spirits, and in a life hereafter. Christianity and Islam made inroads into traditional religions, but as the map indicates, they have failed to convert the African

peoples, except in particular areas. Where Figure 24-1 shows that traditional religions do exist, they remain in the majority today.

SOURCE AREAS

The major religions originated in a remarkably small area of the world. Judaism and Christianity began in what is today the Israel-Jordan area. Islam arose through the teachings of Muhammad, a resident of Mecca in western Arabia. The Hindu religion, which has no central figure and is a complex, multifaceted faith, originated in the Indus region of what is today Pakistan, long before

Christianity or Islam. Buddhism emerged from the teachings of Prince Siddhartha, a man who renounced his claims to power and wealth in his kingdom, located in northeast India, to seek salvation and enlightenment in religious meditation.

These source areas coincide quite strongly with the culture hearths shown in Figure 18-5, and there can be no doubt that while developments in other spheres were occurring in these regions—urbanization, irrigated agriculture, political growth, increasingly complex social orders, and legal systems—religious systems also became more sophisticated. Like the technological innovations, the faiths diffused far and wide.

THE RISE OF SECULARISM

Figure 24-1 might mislead us into assuming that populations in those areas mapped as Christian or Buddhist do in fact adhere entirely to their faiths. This is not the case, as Table 24-1 should emphasize. Even the most careful analysis of worldwide church and religious membership produces a total of about 4 billion adherents—out of a world population approaching 6 billion. Hundreds of millions of peoples are not counted in Table 24-1, because they practice traditional religions. But even when they are taken into account, it is clear that additional hundreds of millions do not practice a religion at all. Furthermore, even church or religious membership figures do *not* accurately reflect the number of active members of the church, underscoring the rise of **secularism** (indifference to or rejection of religious ideas) in the modern world.

This, of course, should not surprise us in North America, where the church plays a declining role in culture and society. However, there are other countries where antireligious ideologies have contributed

From the Field Notes

66 In Bangkok, Thailand, stands this relatively modest Buddhist shrine called the Golden Temple. Inside is one of Thai Buddhism's icons: a solid–gold statue of the Buddha, found buried in alluvium on a farm and displayed here before an endless stream of worshippers and visitors. 99

to the decline of organized religion. Church membership in the former Soviet Union dropped drastically during the twentieth century under communist rule. Maoist China's drive against Confucianism was, in part, an antireligious effort as well. Elsewhere, communist regimes found it possible to accommodate powerful religious structures (as in Poland and Cuba), but the rise of Marxism contributed importantly to the decline in church membership.

The rise of secularism has accelerated during the twentieth century, but it is not a new phenomenon. After the collapse of the Roman Empire, Europe was controlled by the Catholic church: politics, science, farming, and all other spheres of life were dominated, if not directly managed, by the church. Following the Protestant challenge, the erosion of clerical power accelerated, and the fortunes of the monasteries crumbled. The state took over the functions that the church had held, and the separation

of church and state became a political cornerstone. Even in modern-day Rome, bastion of Roman Catholicism, church and state exist side by side, each with its bureaucracy and hierarchy.

With this separation came the freedom to choose—not only with whom to worship, but whether to worship at all. People abandoned organized religion in growing numbers, and even if they continued to profess an affiliation with a church, their participation in church activities declined. Traditions also weakened. For example, there was a time when shops and businesses were closed almost universally on Sundays, and the "seventh day" really was a day of sermons, rest, and introspection. But today, the shopping centers are mostly open as usual, and Sunday is increasingly a day to handle business and personal affairs, not to attend church.

Exceptions to such developments do exist. Traditions are stronger in some culture regions

than in others, and Sunday observance does continue, for example, in the Mormon culture area. However, in the Christian realms of the world, from Canada to Australia, and from the United States to Western Europe, the decline of organized religion as a cultural force is evident. This is so even in the still strongly Roman Catholic regions of Southern Europe and Latin America. In Europe, religious prescriptions relating to birth control serve to fuel disaffection. In Latin America, the church finds itself in a difficult position in the face of revolutionary movements.

Although the rise of secularism and the decline of church affiliation marks the Christian realms of the world, we should take note of other trends elsewhere. In the Muslim world, a new-found power based on oil revenues and a resurgence of revolutionary fervor have the effect of strenghtening Islam's position. Several governments have committed funds in support of the faith and its followers in areas where it is spreading or under pressure. Furthermore, although there may be overall decline in adherence to the major faiths, we should take note of the rise of several smaller religions of growing importance, such as Ba-ha'i, Cao Dai, Jainism, and the Spiritual Church of Brazil. The rise of secularism may in fact be primarily a condition of industrialization and urbanization, a failure of the church to adjust to modernizing society (the fate of Shintoism in Japan certainly seems to confirm this). In more conservative, more rural, and more tradition-bound societies, the strength of the faiths is sustained.

GLOBAL AND REGIONAL RELIGIONS

The world's many religions can be grouped or classified according to several different sets of criteria, each with its particular advantages

DIMENSIONS

One such typology is based on religions' "reach." The true **global religions** of today are Christianity, Islam, and the various forms of Buddhism. These faiths have found followers around the world, although Christianity and Islam more so than Buddhism. These global religions are sometimes called the *universal religions*. We may call the **cultural religions** those faiths that primarily dominate one national culture, as Hinduism does in India, Confucianism and Taoism in China, and Shintoism in Japan (see box, "Shintoism"). The cultural religions are sometimes referred to as *regional* or *ethnic* religions. Judaism is a special case because of its global dispersal. The **traditional religions** of Africa form the focus of a third group of religions, also represented in Native South America, in interior areas of Southeast

From the Field Notes

❝ In Saigon (Ho Chi Minh City), Vietnam stands this reminder of the universality of the Christian religion. It is a rather unremarkable Roman Catholic church (*cathedral*, my host corrected me), but its location in this Buddhist country, and its survival through war and oppression as a functioning place of worship, are noteworthy. ❞

Asia, and in New Guinea and northern Australia. The traditional religions also are referred to as *local* religions in recognition of their limited areal extent.

FOCUS

Religons can also be classified on the basis of their focus. **Monotheistic religions** worship a single deity, a God or Allah. **Polytheistic religions** worship more than one deity, even thousands, as in the case of Hinduism. **Animistic religions** involve the belief that inanimate objects, such as mountains, boulders, rivers, and trees, possess souls and should be revered.

The map of the distribution of the world's religions reveals the spatial contrasts. Christianity is not only the largest but also the most widespread religion, disseminated on the wings of conquest and colo-

nialism. Islam has also diffused widely, but mainly in Africa and Asia. At the scale of Figure 24-1, Islam's footholds in the United States, South Africa, and other outposts cannot be shown, but Islam is a universal faith nevertheless. Buddhism, its concentration in Southeast and East Asia notwithstanding, also transcends cultural and political boundaries.

Compared to these "universal" faiths, Hinduism, Confucianism, Taoism, and Shintoism are really regional, not global religions. The map once again shows a general picture, not the details. There are many local areas in India where beliefs other than Hinduism prevail, but Hinduism's virtual confinement to India (and its prevalence there) are accurately depicted. Confucianism and Taoism are appropriately called the Chinese religions (or rather, belief systems). Shintoism, again, is the particular faith of the

SHINTOISM

Emperor worship, a reverence for nature, and a strong feeling for land and nation are elements that forged the *Shinto* religion of Japan. Early Shintoism arose from ancient forms of shamanism and other traditional religious faiths, and developed into a national religion that unified state and faith; religion and government were indivisible. Then Buddhism made substantial inroads, and Shinto was much modified. However, the events of the nineteenth century in East Asia, and Japanese determination to reject external influences, brought Shinto back as a religious-political force. In the period following the 1868 Meiji Restoration, Buddhists were persecuted, Buddhism attacked, and Buddhist shrines removed. Later these campaigns became less intense, but Shinto remained the state religion. Following Japan's defeat in World War II, Shinto's role as the official state religion was terminated, and the doctrine relating to the emperor's divine descent was also rejected. This has led to a further decline of Shintoism in Japan, where Buddhism has experienced some revival. Shintoism is a prime example of the cultural religion, its rise and decline closely related to the vigor of the regional culture.

Japanese, virtually confined to a national state.

The traditional religions still prevail in areas of the world where the impact of external forces is weakest. For centuries, these local faiths have been repressed by missionaries who have tried to convert, and conquerors who have sought to impose, and still they survive. Again, the map cannot show a detailed pattern for several reasons. Even where Christianity and Islam have penetrated, as in much of Africa, the new faith is often adopted not in place of, but rather alongside, the old. Many a "Christian" African has not altogether abandoned a belief in old, traditional powers.

Having viewed the spatial distribution of the world's major religions and assessed their numerical strengths, we turn next to three geographic properties: their locational origins, their routes of diffusion, and their imprints on the cultural landscape.

KEY TERMS

Animistic Religion
Buddhism
Chinese Religions
Christianity
Cultural Religions
Global Religions
Hinduism
Islam
Judaism
Monotheistic Religions
Nation of Islam
Polytheistic Religions
Religion
Secularism
Shamanism
Shintoism
Traditional Religions

25

RELIGIONS: LOCATION, DIFFUSION AND LANDSCAPE

The major religions arose and dif fused much later than the great language families. Even the oldest, Hinduism, emerged long after the First Agricultural Revolution had transformed the cultural landscape of Southwest Asia. Christianity appeared while the Roman Empire was in full flower, and Islam was founded several centuries later. As a result, the historical geography of the dispersal of the global religions is better known than that of the earliest languages.

In this chapter, we trace the spread of the belief systems that have contributed so strongly to the formation of modern culture regions. It is remarkable that after tens of thousands of years of human development and migration, the great faiths all arose within a few thousand years and a few thousand kilometers of each other, all in Asia (Fig. 25-1).

Geographica

- **Hinduism is the oldest of the world's major religions, but the faith did not diffuse far beyond its homeland in South Asia; it remains a cultural religion today, strongly influencing Indian cultural landscapes.**

- **Buddhism, with fewer than half the number of adherents of Hinduism, arose as a reaction to Hinduism's negative characteristics and became a global religion; it continues to expand.**

- **The more liberal atmosphere in communist China is reviving both the Chinese religions of old *and* the Christian and Islamic faiths; Confucianism and Taoism continue to shape Chinese society.**

- **With only about 18 million adherents, Judaism has a global importance far greater than its numbers would suggest; this is the oldest religion to arise west of the Indus River.**

- **Christianity's three major branches (Roman Catholicism, Protestantism, Orthodoxy) diffused into virtually all parts of the world; the Orthodox churches are experiencing a revival in the postcommunist Russian sphere.**

- **Islam, youngest of the world religions, has two major sects, the majority Sunni and the minority Shiah; this division arose almost immediately after the prophet Muhammad's death and took on regional overtones when Shiism became the state religion of Persia (Iran).**

HINDUISM

Chronologically, the Hindu religion is the oldest of the major religions, and one of the oldest extant religions in the world. It emerged without a prophet or a book of scriptures, and without evolving a bureaucratic structure comparable to those of the Christian religions. Hinduism appears to have begun in the region of the Indus Valley, perhaps as long as 4000 years ago. The fundamental doctrine of the faith is

307

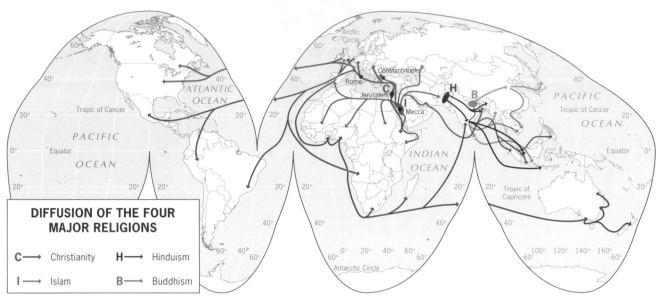

DIFFUSION OF THE FOUR MAJOR RELIGIONS

C ⟶ Christianity   H ⟶ Hinduism
I ⟶ Islam   B ⟶ Buddhism

FIGURE 25–1 Major routes of religious dispersal. This map does not show smaller diffusion streams; Islam, for example, is gaining strength in North America, although its numbers are still comparatively small.

the **karma**, which involves the concept of the transferability of the soul. All beings are in a hierarchy; all have souls. The ideal is to move upward in the hierarchy and then to escape from the eternal cycle through union with the **Brahman**, at the tope of the ladder. A soul moves upward or downward according to one's behavior in the present life. Good deeds and adherence to the faith lead to a higher level in the next life. Bad behavior leads to demotion. All souls, those of animals as well as humans, participate in this process, and the principle of **reincarnation** is a cornerstone of the faith: mistreat animals in this life, and chances are that you will *be* that animal in a future life.

Hinduism's doctrines are closely bound to Indian society's **caste system**, for castes themselves are steps on the universal ladder. However, the caste system locks people in social classes, reducing mobility—an undesirable feature manifested especially in the lowest of the castes, the **untouchables**. Until a generation ago, the untouchables could not enter temples, were excluded from certain schools, and were re-

stricted to performing the most unpleasant tasks. The coming of other religions to India, the effects of modernization during the colonial period, and especially the work of Mahatma Gandhi, India's famous

leader, loosened the social barriers of the caste system and bettered somewhat the lot of the 80 million untouchables.

Hinduism, born on the Indian subcontinent's western flank,

From the Field Notes

❝ The various religions approach in different ways the disposition of the deceased. We in the dominantly Christian, Western world are familiar with large, sometimes elaborate cemeteries. The Hindu faith requires cremation of the body. Wherever large Hindu communities exist outside India itself you will see this equivalent of the funeral parlor, pictured here in Mombasa, Kenya. ❞

HINDU BALI

The Indonesian island of Bali became a refuge for Hindu holy men, nobles, and intellectual during the sixteenth century, when Islam engulfed neighboring Java. Since then, the Balinese have developed a unique faith, still based on Hindu principles but mixed with elements of Buddhism, animism, and ancestor worship. The caste system prevails, but the lower castes outnumber the higher castes by nearly ten to one, so that the system divides the society less than is the case in India. Holy men, military personnel, and merchants rank at the top of the hierarchy.

Religion is at the focus of life in Bali, and temples and shrines dominate the cultural landscape, which is further characterized by some of the world's most meticulously terraced hillslopes (rice is the staple). Religious festivals, feasts, and other ceremonies occur frequently, and streets and roads are colorfully decorated to mark each event. Participation is almost universal, and although Bali has about 3 million inhabitants, it has numerous orchestras, actors and actresses, dancers, and artists. The island's unique religion is at the heart of a culture that has been described as a celebration of life.

Java retains only architectural remnants of its Hindu age.

DIFFUSION

Hinduism has not spread by expansion **diffusion** in modern times, and has remained essentially a cultural religion of South Asia. During the colonial period, however, many hundreds of thousands of Indians were transported to other areas of the world, including East and South Africa, the Caribbean, northern South America, and the Pacific islands (notably Fiji). This relocation diffusion did not form the foci of growing Hindu regions, and few non-Indians were converted to the faith.

CULTURAL LANDSCAPE

Hinduism is more than a faith, it is a way of life. Meals are religious rites; prohibitions and commands multiply as the ladder of caste is ascended. Pilgrimages follow prescribed routes, and rituals are

spread eastward across India and soon, before the advent of Christianity, into Southeast Asia. It would penetrate by first attaching itself to prevailing traditional faiths and then slowly supplanting them. Later, when Islam and Christianity appeared and were vigorously promulgated in Hindu areas, Hindu thinkers sought to assimilate certain of the new teachings into their own religion. For example, elements of the Sermon on the Mount now form part of Hindu preaching, and Christian beliefs led in some measure to the softening of caste barriers. In other instances, the confrontation between Hinduism and other faiths led to the formulation of a compromise religion. Thus the monotheism of Islam stimulated the rise of the **Sikhs**, who disapproved of the worship of all sorts of idols and who disliked the caste system, but who nevertheless retained concepts of reincarnation and the karma.

As Figure 25-1 shows, the Hindu faith evolved in what is today Pakistan, reached its fullest development in India, and spread to some extent into Southeast Asia. Hinduism, however, has not been widely disseminated. In Southeast

Asia, Islam overtook Hinduism, and most of the results of its early diffusion have been erased. In overwhelmingly Muslim Indonesia, the island of Bali remains a Hindu outpost (see box, "Hindu Bali"), but

From the Field Notes

❝ Even where Hindu minorities are not large, their religious shrines are elaborate and reflective of the faith and its many special features. One of these, of course, is a reverence for all life and especially the holy cow. Not only do cows wander the streets of India, but they appear prominently in the religious art that adorns Hindu shrines. This pair sits atop a streetcorner temple in Singapore. ❞

attended by millions. Festivals and feasts are frequent, colorful, and noisy. Hindu doctrines include the belief that the erection of a temple, modest or elaborate, bestows merit on the builder and leads to heavenly reward. As a result, the Hindu cultural landscape—urban as well as rural—is characterized by countless shrines, ranging from small village temples to structures so large and elaborate that they are virtually holy cities. The location of shrines is important because there should be minimal disruption of the natural landscape. The temple should be in a "comfortable" position (for example, under a large, shady tree) and near water whenever possible, because many gods will not venture far from water, and because water has a holy function in Hinduism. A village temple should face the village from a prominent position, and offerings must be made frequently. Small offerings of fruit and flowers lie before the sanctuary of the deity honored by the shrine.

Thus the cultural landscape of Hinduism is the cultural landscape of India, the cultural region. Temples and shrines, holy animals by the tens of millions, distinctively garbed holy men, and the sights and sounds of endless processions and rituals all contribute to an atmosphere without parallel. The faith is a visual as well as an emotional experience.

BUDDHISM

Buddhism appeared in India during the sixth century B.C. as a reaction to the less desirable features of Hinduism. It was by no means the only protest of its kind (**Jainism** was another), but it was the strongest and most effective. As previously mentioned, the faith was founded by Prince Siddhartha, known to his fol-

lowers as Gautama, heir to a wealthy kingdom in what is now Nepal. He was profoundly shaken by the misery he saw about him, which contrasted so sharply against the splendor and wealth that had been his own experience. The Buddha (enlightened one) was perhaps the first prominent Indian religious leader to speak out against Hinduism's caste system. Salvation, he preached, could be attained by anyone, no matter what his or her caste. Enlightenment would come to a person through knowledge, especially self-knowledge: the elimination of covetousness, craving, and desire, the principle of complete honesty, and the determination not to hurt another person or animal. Thus part of the tradition of the karma still prevailed.

Following the death of the Buddha in 489 B.C., at the age of 80, the faith grew rather slowly until, during the middle of the third century B.C., the Emperor Asoka became a convert. Asoka was the leader of a large and powerful state that covered India from the Punjab to Bengal, and from the Himalayan foothills to Mysore. Asoka not only set out to rule his country in accordance with the teachings of the Buddha, but he also sent missionaries to the outside world to carry the Buddha's teachings to distant peoples. Buddhism spread as far south as Sri Lanka, and later west toward the Mediterranean, north into Tibet, and east into China, Korea, Japan, Vietnam, and Indonesia, all over a span of some 10 centuries (Fig. 25-1). However, while Buddhism spread to distant lands, it began to decline in its region of origin. During Asoka's rule there may have been more Buddhists in India than Hindu adherents, but after that period of success the strength of Hinduism again began to assert itself. Today, Buddhism is practically extinct in India, although it still thrives in Sri Lanka, Southeast Asia, Nepal, Tibet, and Korea. Along with

other faiths, it also survives in Japan.

Buddhism is fragmented into numerous branches of which the leading are two sectarian groups, Mahayana Buddhism and Theravada Buddhism. Theravada Buddhism is the monastic faith of the source, Gautama's teachings, and it survives in Sri Lanka, Myanmar (Burma), Thailand, Laos, and Cambodia. It holds that salvation is a personal matter, achieved by worldly good behavior and religious activities, including periods of service as a monk or nun. Mahayana Buddhism, practiced mainly in Vietnam, Korea, Japan, and for centuries in China, holds that superhuman, holy sources of merit do exist, and that salvation can be aided by appeals to these sources. The Buddha is regarded as a divine savior. Mahayana Buddhists do not serve for periods as monks, as the Theravadans do, but spend much time in personal meditation and worship. Other branches of Buddhism include the Lamaism of Xizang (Tibet), which combines monastic Buddhism with the worship of local demons and deities, and Zen Buddhism, the contemplative form prevalent in Japan.

Buddhism is experiencing a period of revival that started two centuries ago and has recently intensified. It has become a global religion, unlike Hinduism, and has diffused to many areas of the world. However, the faith has suffered severely in its modern hearth in Southeast Asia. Militant communist regimes have attacked the faith and destroyed its institutions in Cambodia, Laos, and to a considerable extent, in Vietnam as well. In Thailand also, Buddhism has been under severe pressure, afflicted by rising political tensions from which the influential faith could not escape. Yet the appeal of Buddhism's principles has ensured its continued diffusion, notably in the Western world.

From the Field Notes

❝ Is all that glitters Buddhist gold? From the spires of pagodas to the countless likenesses of the Buddha, gold seems to be the preferred image in Buddhist society. These women lovingly restore a statue by applying gold leaf (the vessel in which the material is fired stands on the left) in a public park in Chiang Mai. ❞

CULTURAL LANDSCAPE

When the Buddha received enlightenment he sat under a large tree, the Bo tree at Bodh Gaya in India, now a place of pilgrimage for Buddhists of all branches and sects. (The Bo tree now growing on the site is believed to be a descendant of the original tree). The Bo tree has a thick, banyan-like trunk and a wide canopy of leafy branches. Because of its association with the Buddha, the tree is protected, revered, and the object of pilgrimages wherever it is believed that Buddha may have taught beneath its branches. It has also been diffused as far as China and Japan as a symbol of the faith, and marks the townscape of numerous villages and towns.

Buddhism's architecture includes some magnificent achievements, including the famed structures at Borobudur in central Java (Indonesia). The shrines of Buddhism include bell-shaped structures that protect relic mounds, temples that enshrine an image of the Buddha in his familiar cross legged pose, and large monasteries that tower over the local townscape. The pagoda is perhaps Buddhism's most familiar structure, its shape derived from the relic (often funeral) mounds of old. Every fragment of its construction is a meaningful representation of Buddhist philosophy.

CHINESE RELIGIONS

While the Buddha's teachings drew converts in India, and the issue of the transmigration of souls was debated there, a religious revolution of quite another kind was taking place in China. Confucius (551–479 B.C.) and his followers constructed a blueprint for Chinese civilization in almost every field—philosophy, government, education, and more. In religion, Confucius addressed the traditional Chinese cults that included beliefs in heaven and the existence of the soul, ancestor worship, sacrificial rites, and shamanism. He postulated that the real meaning of life lay in the present, not in some future abstract existence, and that service to one's fellows should supersede service to spirits.

Chinese philosophy was at the same time being influenced by another school. The beginnings of **Taoism** are unclear, but many scholars believe that an older contemporary of Confucius, Lao-Tsu, slightly preceded Confucius' teachings by publishing a volume entitled, *Tao-te-ching*, or "Way and Its Virtue." In his teachings, Lao-Tsu focused on the oneness of humanity and nature: people, he said, should learn to live in harmony with nature, viewing themselves as but an insignificant element in the great universal order (see box, "Feng Shui"). Taoist virtues were simplicity and spontaneity, tenderness, and tranquility. It advocated against competition, possession, even the pursuit of knowledge. Taoist transgressions were war, punishment, taxation, and ceremonial ostentation. The best government, according to Lao-Tsu, was the least government.

Taoism suffered much falsification as time went on, and it became a cult of the masses. Lao-Tsu himself was worshipped as a god (among many), something of which he would have disapproved. People, animals, even dragons became objects of worship as well, and a sort of Taoist witchcraft emerged. In the face of this aberration, Confucius' emphasis on the present, on good relationships between people (parents and children, rulers and subjects) proved its practicality.

Both Taoism and **Confucianism** had great and lasting impacts on Chinese life. Confucius was appalled at the suffering of ordinary people at the hands of feudal lords,

FENG SHUI

Chinese cultural traditions include a deep appreciation for nature. To exist in harmony with nature was a precept of both Taoism and Confucianism, and it was a principle to be adhered to in life—as well as in death.

In life, **Feng Shui** revealed itself through popular opposition to modernization. The ancient belief that the powerful spirits of ancestors, dragons, tigers, and other beings all occupy natural phenomena (mountains, hills, rivers, and trees) also held that to disturb nature would incur their wrath. Nothing should be done to nature without consulting the geomancers, men who knew the desires of the spirits. When, in 1876, engineers tried to lay the first railroad inland from the port of Shanghai without consulting the geomancers, local opposition was so strong that the project had to be abandoned. The geomancers had not approved.

The communist regime in the 1950s also confronted Feng Shui. China's geomancers had long identified suitable gravesites for the deceased, again to leave the dead in perfect harmony with their natural surroundings. Burial mounds were an important part of rural Chinese communities, taking up much land that could have been farmed. The pragmatic communities had little regard for such practices, and they proceeded to level burial mounds during their communization program in the rural areas. This led to strong opposition by tradition-bound villagers, and generated a reserve of deep resentment that was to explode much later, contributing to the revolutionary changes of the 1970s. Geomancy is still a powerful force in modernizing China.

and he urged the poor to assert themselves. He was not a prophet who dealt in promises of heaven and threats of hell. Confucius denied the divine ancestry of China's aristocratic rulers, educated the landless and the weak, disliked supernatural mysticism, and argued that human virtues and abilities, not heritage, should determine a person's position and responsibilities in society.

Notwithstanding his Earthly philosophies, Confucius took on the mantle of a spiritual leader after his death in 479 B.C. His teachings diffused widely throughout East and Southeast Asia. Temples were built in his honor all over China. From his writings and sayings emerged the *Confucian Classics*, a set of 13 texts that became the focus of education in China for 2000 years. In government, law, literature, religion, morality, and in every conceivable way, the Confucian Classics were the Chinese civilization's guide.

Elements of Buddhism, introduced into China during the Han Dynasty, also formed part of the society's belief system. Buddhism's reverence for the aged, the departed, and nature in general made it easily adaptable to Chinese philosophies.

Thus China developed a quite discrete religious posture, taking elements from several teachings to create, if not a distinct single faith, certainly a Chinese religious way of life. Over the centuries, Confucianism (with its Taoist and Buddhist ingredients) became China's state ethic, although time did modify Confucius' ideals. Worship of and obedience to the emperor became a part of Confucianism, for example. During the twentieth century, political upheavals in China led to reactions against Confucian philosophies, first, during the Republican period after 1912, and more seriously under the communist regimes after 1949. However, Confucianism has been China's beacon for a very long time. It will be difficult to eradicate two millennia of cultural conditioning in a few decades. The dying spirit of Confucius will haunt physical and mental landscapes in China for years to come.

JUDAISM

The oldest major religion to emerge west of the Indus Valley, Judaism grew from the belief system of the Jews, one of several Semitic, nomadic tribes that traversed Southwest Asia about 2000 B.C. The Jews led an existence filled with upheavals. Moses led them from Egypt, where they had suffered oppression, to Canaan, where an internal conflict arose and the nation split into two, Israel and Judah. Israel was subsequently wiped out by enemies, but Judah survived longer, only to be conquered by the Babylonians. Regrouping to rebuild their headquarters, Jerusalem, the Jews fell victim to a sequence of alien powers and saw the Romans destroy their holy city again in A.D. 70. Now the Jews were driven away and scattered all over the region, and eventually into Europe and much of the rest of the world. For many centuries, indeed, until the late eighteenth century, they were persecuted, denied citizenship, driven into ghettos, and massacred. As the twentieth century has proved, the world has not been a safe place for Jewish people, even in modern times.

In the face of such constant threats to their existence, it has been their faith that has sustained the Jews, the certainty that the Messiah would come to deliver them from their enemies. The roots of Jewish religious tradition lie in the teachings of Abraham, who united his people, and during whose time the faith began to take shape. Among the religions adhered to by the ancient Semitic tribes, that of the Jews was unique in that it involved the worship of only one god, who, the Jews believed, had selected them to bear witness to his existence and his works. However, the Jewish faith also evinced many contacts with other beliefs and other peoples. From **Zoroastrianism**, which arose in Persia during the sixth century B.C., Judaism acquired its concept of paradise and hell, angels and devils, judgment day, and resurrection.

Modern times have seen a division of Judaism into many branches. During the nineteenth century, when Jewish people began to enjoy greater freedom, a Reform Movement developed, with the objective of adjusting the faith and its practices to current times. However, there were many who feared that this would cause a loss of identity and cohesion, and the Orthodox movement sought to retain the old precepts as effectively as possible. Between those two extremes is a sector that is less strictly orthodox, but not as liberal as the reformers: the Conservative movement. We observe here the stresses of an acculturation process of Jewish society in America.

The objective of a homeland for the Jewish people, an idea that gained currency during the nineteenth century, produced the ideology of **Zionism**. Zionist ideals were rooted in a determination that Jews should not be absorbed into and assimilated by other societies. Zionism's goal of a Jewish state became a reality in 1948, when Israel was created under U.N. auspices on the shores of the eastern Mediterranean.

As Table 24-1 shows, the Jewish faith presently has about 18 million adherents, but the distribution of Jews proves that Judaism is indeed a universal religion. Seven million reside in North America, about 5 million in Europe and the former Soviet Union, and the total for Asia, over 4 million, includes the Jewish population of Israel itself.

CHRISTIANITY

The Christian religions had their beginnings in the Jews' search for deliverance from Roman oppression and the appearance of Jesus. Many saw in Jesus a manifestation of God, but probably even more hoped that he would be a temporal as well as spiritual leader, and secure freedom as well as salvation. Among the Apostles was Paul, a Jew who had a Greek education and who, after the crucifixion, began offering the teachings of Jesus to non-Jews. It was Paul who played a central role in organizing the Christian church and in disseminating Jesus' teachings to the European Mediterranean world.

After Paul's death, the church continued to grow, but at the cost of many lives, as Roman authority resisted its intrusion. A crucial event in the development of the Christian faith was the conversion of the Emperor Constantine, and from the fourth century A.D. onward, it was the Roman state religion. The Roman Empire was soon to decline and break up, and while the sector centered on Rome fell on hard times, the eastern half, with Constantinople (now Istanbul in Turkey) at its heart, became the focus. It was there, in the eastern realm, that Christianity thrived and from where it radiated into other areas, including the Balkan Peninsula. Today, the Eastern or Orthodox Church still forms one of the three major branches of the faith (Fig. 25-1), despite the blows it sustained when Constantinople fell to the Turks and Islam invaded Eastern Europe (in the fifteenth century), and again when the church was threatened in Russia by the rise of communism (in the twentieth century).

In Rome, the papacy was established and there came to life the center of the second branch of the faith, Roman Catholicism. In the Middle Ages, the power of the church was at its zenith, with all the excesses this involved; a reaction was inevitable. It came during the fifteenth and sixteenth centuries, with the teachings of Luther, Calvin, and others. Widespread friction and open warfare marked the deteriorating relationships among Christians of different views on the continent. However, the Protestant movement—the third major branch—could not be denied.

DIFFUSION

The dissemination of Christianity occurred as a combination of expansion and relocation diffusion. The worldwide dispersal of Christianity was accomplished by the era of colonial acquisition on which Europe embarked in the sixteenth century. Spain invaded Middle and South America, bringing the Catholic faith to those areas. Protestant refugees, tired of conflict and oppression and in search of new hope and freedom, came in large numbers to North America. A patchwork of missionary efforts produced mixed conversions in much of black Africa; Catholicism made inroads in Zaïre, Angola, and Moçambique. A very small percentage of the people in formerly British India were converted to Christianity; Catholicism scored heavily in the Philippines during the period of Spanish control.

Today, Christianity is the most widespread and largest of the global religions, and although the number of its adherents may be declining in some places, it is still gaining adherents in many areas.

From the Field Notes

❝ In the light of dawn I looked toward the city of Bordeaux and saw a sight that must be representative of a Christian Europe that once was: the tower and steeple of a cathedral rising tall over the townscape. Today, the commercial skyscraper, not the symbol of the faith, tends to dominate urban landscapes. ❞

The faith has always been characterized by the aggressive and persistent proselytism of its proponents, and Christian missionaries created an almost worldwide network of conversion during the colonial period (Fig. 25-1).

CULTURAL LANDSCAPE

The cultural landscapes of Christianity's various branches reflect the changes that the faith has undergone over the past centuries. In Medieval Europe, the cathedral, church, or monastery was the focus of life. In the towns, other buildings clustered around the tallest—the tower, steeple, and spire of the church, the beacon that could be seen (and whose bells could be heard) for miles in the surrounding countryside. In the square or plaza in front of the church the crowds would gather for ceremonies and festivals in which the faith played its role, whether or not the event was primarily religious. Good harvests, military victories, public announcements, and all else was done in the shadow of the symbol of religious authority.

The Reformation, the rise of secularism, and the decline of organized religion's power are all reflected in the cultural landscape as well. The towns in Europe, in which the cathedral still rises above the townscape, are reminders of the region's Roman Catholic-dominated history. Protestants tend to regard a house of worship differently; it need not be especially large, imposing, or ornate. In Protestant regions, therefore, churches tend to blend into the local architecture, and may be identifiable only by a sign that announces the name of the coming Sunday's speaker and the title of the sermon.

In most large cities, cathedral and church now stand in the shadow of another kind of structure: the multistory office building—the skyscraper—symbol of the power of commerce and money. Churches are likely to be built outside the central business district, where land costs less. Except for some large-scale projects (such as the great Washington Cathedral), most modern religious structures are not as impressive and elaborate as those of earlier times. Other kinds of symbolism are needed now to sustain the church, in this age of televised sermons and drive-in places of worship.

We should note that certain denominations, especially those that may be regarded as the more conservative, have more durable cultural landscapes in which older traditions of the authority and influence of the church remain visible. In the United States, the best example is undoubtedly the Mormon culture region; to a lesser extent the Northeast, with its history of Catholic power and particular combinations of denominations, is another.

The cultural landscape also carries the imprint of death. It is appropriate to relate this topic to the cultural landscape of Christianity, because no faith (other than perhaps those of China) uses land so liberally for the disposition of the departed. Hindus, Buddhists, and Shintoists cremate the dead, and it is noteworthy that this practice prevails in regions where living space and farmland are at a premium. However, Christian faiths bury their dead, often with elaborate rituals and in spacious cemeteries that are carefully tended and resemble parks in their layout. Class expresses itself even in death: some graves are marked by a simple tombstone, whereas others are elaborate, temple-like marble structures. Whatever the nature of the monuments to the dead, however, the more impressive aspect of this culture trait is the amount of space that is devoted to graveyards and cemeteries, even in severely crowded urban areas where land prices have risen enormously—a reflection of the tradition of the power of the church. This also re-

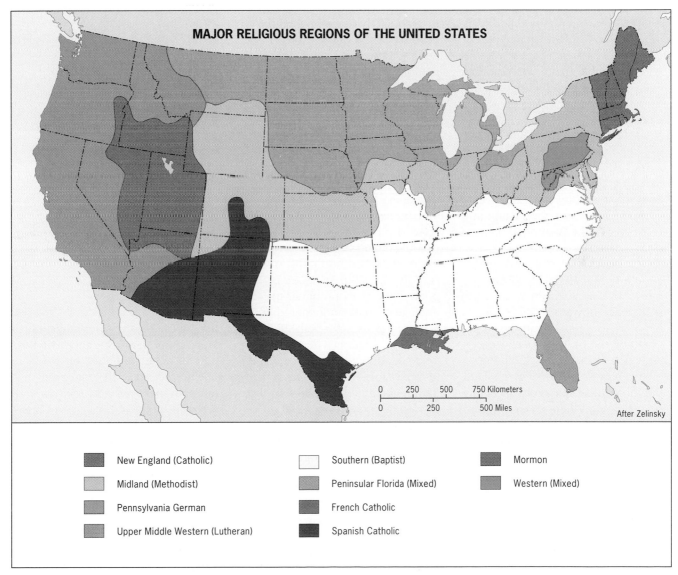

MAJOR RELIGIOUS REGIONS OF THE UNITED STATES

0   250   500   750 Kilometers
0   250   500 Miles

After Zelinsky

New England (Catholic)   Southern (Baptist)   Mormon

Midland (Methodist)   Peninsular Florida (Mixed)   Western (Mixed)

Pennsylvania German   French Catholic

Upper Middle Western (Lutheran)   Spanish Catholic

FIGURE 25–2   A generalized map of religious regions in the United States. Modified from W. Zelinsky, "An Approach to the Religious Geography of the United States." *Annals* of the AAG 51 (1961), p. 139.

veals the reality that cemeteries and funeral-related establishments represent a significant economic enterprise in Western cultures, further evidence of the secularization of formerly religious functions and responsibilities.

REGIONS

The Mormon culture region is only one of several regions in the United States in which religion forms a crucial cultural component. Professor Wilbur Zelinksy, in his article, "An Approach to the Religious Geography of the United States" (1961), constructed a map of religious regions later slightly modified, that identifies seven such spatial units (Fig. 25-2). Several of these regions will be familiar to anyone who has even the most general impression of the United States. The New England region, for example, is strongly Catholic; the South's leading denomination is Baptist; the Upper Middle West has large numbers of Lutheran affiliations; and the Southwest is dominantly Spanish Catholic. A broad region extending from the Middle Atlantic to the Mormon region has a mixture of denominations in which no single church dominates, which is also true of the West. As Professor Zelinsky's map shows, several of the major regions can in turn be subdivided on the basis of local clustering, such as the French Catholic area centered on New Orleans and the mixed denominations of Peninsular Florida, where a large Spanish Catholic cluster has recently emerged in metropolitan Miami.

The culture regions of Christian denominations in the United States are better known and understood than similar regions in other geographic realms. Data on religious affiliations are more nearly accurate and available for the United States, Canada, and Europe, but similar information for the former communist-controlled countries is

not provided, and the religious geography of Sub-Saharan Africa and the world of Islam is also less accessible. It is obvious that a great deal of research remains to be done in this interesting field.

ISLAM

The faith of the Muslims is the youngest of the major religions, having been born of the teachings of Muhammad, who was born in A.D. 571. According to Muslim belief, Muhammad received the truth directly from Allah in a series of revelations that began when the prophet was about 42 years of age. During these revelations, Muhammad involuntarily spoke the verses of the Koran (Qur-an) the Muslims' holy book. Muhammad, a student of religion even before this event, admired the monotheism of Christianity and Judaism; he believed that Allah had already manifested himself through other prophets (including Jesus). However, he, Muhammad, was the real and ultimate of prophets.

Muhammad became a towering figure in Arabia during the seventh century A.D. Born and soon orphaned, he grew up under the tutelage of his grandfather, then leader of Mecca (Makkah). Following his grandfather's death, an uncle continued his upbringing. After his visions, Muhammad at first had doubts that he could have been chosen to be a prophet, but once convinced by continued revelations, he committed his life to the fulfillment of the divine commands. In those days, the Arab world was in religious and social disarray, with various gods and goddesses admired by peoples whose political adjustments were, at best, feudal. Soon Muhammad's opponents sensed his strength and purpose, and they began to combat his efforts. The prophet was forced to

From the Field Notes

❝ The graceful minarets of the mosque in Male, capital of the Maldives, evince the attention Muslim communities lavish on their shrines. Whether at the heart of the world of Islam or on its margins, the mosque is the focus of life and its appearance in the townscape is a matter of pride and commitment. ❞

flee Mecca for the safer haven of Medina (al Madinah), and from this new base he continued his work.

The precepts of Islam constituted, in many ways, a revision and embellishment of Judaic and Christian beliefs and traditions: There is but one god, who occasionally reveals himself to prophets. Islam acknowledges that Jesus was such a prophet. According to Islamic belief, what is Earthly and worldly is profane; only Allah is pure. Allah's will is absolute; he is omnipotent and omniscient. All humans live in a world created for their use, but only to await a final judgment day.

Islam brought to the Arab world

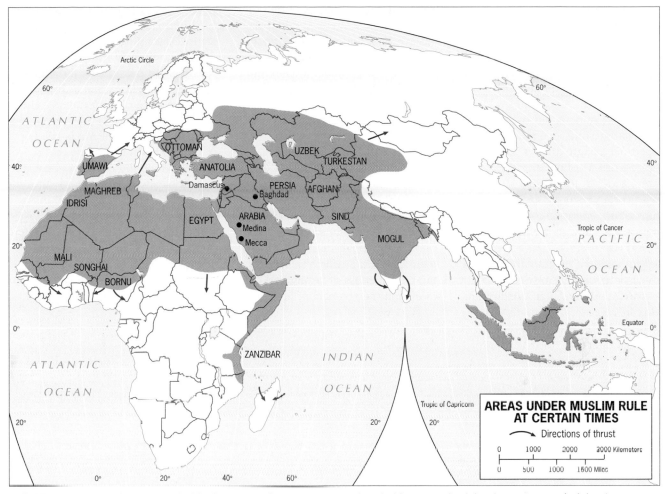

FIGURE 25–3 Muslim dogma holds that areas that were at any time in history under Islamic sway remain Islamic forever—even if Islam is temporarily ousted.

not only a unifying religious faith, but also a whole new set of values, a new way of life, and a new individual and collective dignity. Apart from dictating observance of the "five pillars" of Islam (repeated expressions of the basic creed, frequent prayer, a month of daytime fasting, almsgiving, and at least one pilgrimage to Mecca), the faith prescribed and proscribed in other spheres of life as well. Alcohol, smoking, and gambling were forbidden. Polygamy was tolerated, although the virtues of monogamy were acknowledged. Mosques made their appearance in Arab settlements, not only for the Friday prayer, but also to serve as social gathering places to bring communi-

ties closer together. Mecca became the spiritual center for a divided, far-flung people for whom a joint focus was something new.

The stimulus given by Muhammad, spiritual as well as political, was such that the Arab world was mobilized overnight. The prophet died in A.D. 632, but his faith and fame continued to spread like wildfire. Arab armies formed, they invaded and conquered, and Islam was carried throughout North Africa. By the early ninth century A.D., the Muslim world included emirates extending from Egypt to Morocco, a caliphate occupying most of Spain and Portugal, and a unified realm encompassing Arabia, the Middle East, Iran, and most of what is to-

day Pakistan (Fig. 25-3). Muslim influences had penetrated France, entered Italy, and invaded Turkestan in Central Asia as far as the Aral Sea. Ultimately, the Arab empire extended from Morocco to India and from Turkey to Ethiopia. The original capital was at Medina, in Arabia, but in response to these strategic successes it was moved, first to Damascus and then to Baghdad. In the fields of architecture, mathematics, and science, the Arabs far overshadowed their European contemporaries, and they established institutions of higher learning in many cities, including Baghdad, Cairo, and Toledo (Spain). The faith had spawned a culture, and it is still at the heart of that culture today.

REGIONS AND SECTS

As Figure 24-1 shows, Islam is a divided faith. The religion's principal division occurred early, almost immediately after the prophet's death, and it was caused by a conflict over his succession. A complicated conflict arose, punctuated by murder and warfare and, eventually, by doctrinal disagreements. The orthodox **Sunni** Muslims eventually prevailed, but the **Shiite** Muslims, who were masters at political manipulation, survived as small minorities through the Muslim world. Then early during the sixteenth century, an Iranian (Persian) dynasty made Shiism (or *Shiah*) the only legal faith of that Muslim em-

pire—an empire that extended into present-day southern Azerbaijan, eastern Iraq, and western Afghanistan and Pakistan. This gave the Shiite sect unprecedented strength, and created the foundations of its modern-day culture region centered on the state of Iran (Fig. 25-3). Approximately 13 percent of all Muslims (about 160 million persons) adhere to the beliefs of Shiah.

In a general way, the differences between the Sunnis and the Shiites may be viewed as a matter of practicality and Earthly knowledge, as opposed to idealism and the supernatural. Sunni Muslims believe in the effectiveness of family and community in the solution of life's

problems; Shiites follow the "infallible" *imam*, the sole source of true knowledge. Whereas Sunni Muslims are comparatively reserved, Shiite Muslims are passionate and emotional (as recent events in Iran and Lebanon have demonstrated). The death of their early leader's son, Husayn, the child of Ali, is celebrated with intense processions during which the marchers beat themselves with chains and cut themselves with sharp metal instruments.

Aggressive Shiah Islam has influenced Sunni Islam in several ways. The passion motive has been diffused eastward into Pakistan, Afghanistan, and India, where

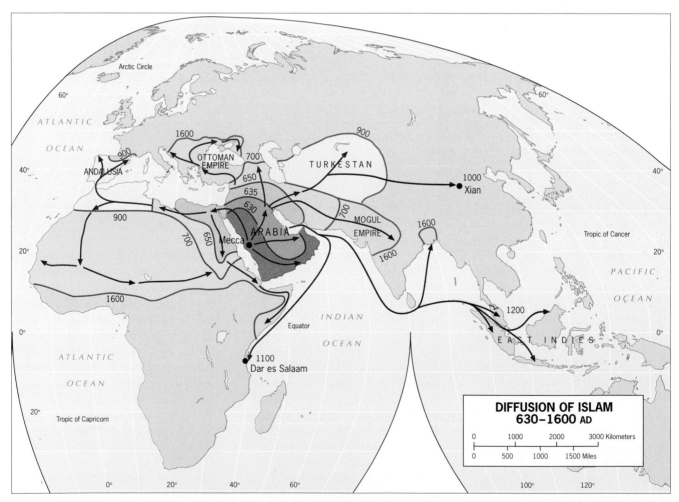

FIGURE 25–4

Sunni masses engage in similar rituals. The admiration and indeed veneration of the Shiite's early leader, Ali, has diffused throughout Sunni Islam, and is reflected in the respect shown to his family's descendants, the *sayyids* of East Africa and the *sharifs* of North Africa, by all Muslims. The revolutionary fervor of Iran during the late 1970s and 1980s stirred all of Islam, although it also produced violent conflict along the cultural boundary between Iran and its Sunni-dominated neighbor, Iraq.

DIFFUSION

The spread of Islam from its Arabian source area is a classic example of expansion diffusion, and its subsequent dispersal to Malaysia, Indonesia, South Africa, and the New World resulted from relocation diffusion Fig. 25-4. Unlike Hinduism, similarly diffused through the relocation process, Islam attracted converts wherever it took hold, and new core areas soon proved to be effective source areas for further dispersal. As Figure 25-3 shows, Islam's regions include not only North Africa and Southwest Asia, but also Bangladesh, Malaysia (to be a Malay *is* to be a Moslem), and Indonesia. As Table 24-1 indicates, although Islam's adherents are concentrated mostly in Asia (nearly 520 million), Africa south of the Sahara (about 170 million), and Southwest Asia/North Africa (400 million), there are also about 41 million Muslims in the independent states (once part of the Soviet Union) north of Iran and Afghanistan, and perhaps 14 million in Europe and 6 million in the Americas. Islam is experiencing a modern resurgence, and its expansion is likely to continue.

CULTURAL LANDSCAPE

Islamic cities, towns, and villages are dominated by the elaborate, ornate, sometimes magnificently designed and executed mosques, whose balconied minarets rise above the townscape. As in the Catholicism of old, the mosque often constitutes the town's most imposing, most carefully maintained building, the focus of life. From the towering minarets the faithful are called to prayer, filling the streets and paths as they converge on the holiest place, there to bend to the ground in disciplined worship.

At the height of Islam's expansion into eastern North Africa and Southern Europe, the Muslim architects combined their skills with the Roman blueprints of an earlier age, and from this coalescence came some of the world's greatest architectural masterpieces, including Spain's Alhambra Palace in Granada and the Great Mosque of Cordoba. During the eleventh century, the practice of glazing the tiles of domes and roofs developed, and to the beautiful arcades and arched courtyards were added the exquisite beauty of glass-like, perfectly symmetrical cupolas. Muslim architecture represents the unifying power of Islamic monotheism: the perfection, vastness—indeed endlessness—of the spirit of Allah.

In architecture, Islam achieved its greatest artistic expression, its most distinctive visible element. Even in the smallest town, the community contributes to build and maintain its mosque in tribute to Allah. As such, it symbolizes the power of the faith and its role in the community. Its primacy in the cultural landscape is a confirmation of the reality that in the Muslim world, religion and culture are one.

This chapter has focused on the world's major religions, but to hundreds of millions of people, local variants of the global or regional faiths are more immediately important. In the dominantly Christian United States alone, for example, there are more than 60 denominations, including such churches as the Christadelphians, the Evangelicals, the Moravians, the Schwenkfelders, and the Wesleyans. Some of these denominations, such as the Pentecostal Churches, encompass a dozen or more discrete groups with memberships ranging from under 5000 people to over a half-million.

It is often said that "all politics is local"; the same may be said of church and faith. So when outside forces threaten change to the comfort and familiarity of religious routine, people often respond violently. Memories of past conflict or repression, or fear of future uncertainties, can make religion a fuse for ethnic strife. We conclude our overview of the geography of religion with a discussion of the problems of coexistence.

KEY TERMS

Brahman
Caste System
Confucianism
Diffusion
Feng Shui
Jainism
Karma
Reincarnation
Shiite (Shiah)
Sikhs
Sunni
Taoism
Untouchables
Zionism
Zoroastrianism

26

RELIGION, CULTURE, AND CONFLICT

Language and religion are two of the most powerful forces shaping the geography of culture. In Part 7 we noted the role of language as a unifying and culture-conserving covenant; a threat to the language is perceived as a threat to the culture as a whole. Language, too, can create a gulf between peoples otherwise united by traits and traditions, and even by a political border. In many countries of the world, language disputes fuel the fires of division.

So it is with religion. Religious beliefs and histories can bitterly divide peoples who share virtually all else, people who speak the same language, have the same ethnic background, and make their living in similar ways. Such divisions arise not only between people adhering to different major religions (Muslims and Christians in the former Yugoslavia, for example), but also among adherents of the same world religion. Some of the most destructive conflict has pitted Christian against Christian and Muslim against Muslim. In this chapter, we examine the role of religion in perpetuating cultural strife, and use our geographic perspective to anticipate problems of the future.

Geographica

- When boundaries between major religions (interfaith boundaries) lie across countries, those countries confront powerful actual or latent divisive forces.

- Boundaries between branches of a major religion (intrafaith boundaries), though generally less divisive than interfaith boundaries, still are capable of producing cultural conflict.

- Religious fundamentalism is a worldwide phenomenon, affecting virtually all religions including Islam, Christianity, and Hinduism.

- The cultural cores of Christianity and Islam, with their respective conservative hierarchies, lie in close proximity in Europe and Southwest Asia/North Africa; the prospect of intensified disharmony and even conflict is growing.

RELIGION AND RELATIVE LOCATION

A comparison between Figure 24-1 and a map of the world's political framework proves that there are countries lying entirely within the realms of individual world religions, while other countries straddle the boundaries between the major faiths, the **interfaith boundaries**.

Countries that lie astride interfaith boundaries are subject to strong forces of cultural division. As Figure 24-1 shows, several countries in Africa are in this situation, including Africa's most populous state, Nigeria. With about 100 million inhabitants, Nigeria is Africa's giant; Nigeria also (as we noted earlier) is a multilingual country. Superimposed on its linguistic diversity is a religious regionalism that makes the north a Muslim zone and the south a domain where Christianity prevails, along with local domestic religions.

This north-south division puts the main ethnic group of the north, the Hausa-Fulani, in the Muslim camp, and the two main culture cores of the south, the Yoruba of the southwest and the Ibo of the southeast, in the Christian-animist sphere. These nations (for such they are) have considerable disdain for each other. Muslim Hausa sometimes say that Yoruba are godless and uncultured. Ibo at times characterize the Hausa as backward and uneducated. To northerners, the Ibo may appear as money-mad merchants who will do anything for a price. Nigeria as a country was born an uneasy federation with three States centered on these dominant, mistrustful nations. Today it is a framework of 30 States trying to make multicultural civilian government work (military regimes have ruled for most of the country's independence period).

When Nigeria conducted a census in 1991, Nigerians were not asked to state their religious preference. The numbers, however, are estimated as follows: Muslims, 50 million; Christians, 37 million; others (chiefly animists), 12 million. A substantial number of Yoruba, perhaps 2 million, are Muslims. Islam in Yorubaland long has had a moderate tone, however, and some geographers describe the Yoruba as "middlemen" between Christian easterners and more dogmatic Muslim northerners, defusing the tensions that might long ago have led to religious conflict. In 1993, a Muslim Yoruba was elected president of Nigeria, but the military regime then in power would not allow him to take office.

In the north, Islam predominates overwhelmingly, but Christian communities do exist—and coexistence has been the rule despite sporadic skirmishes. But during the 1990s, Nigeria's fundamental religious division has begun to threaten the future of the state. In the north, Muslim preachers are calling for an

"Islamic Republic" in Nigeria, emboldened by the decision of the country's president to allow Nigeria to join the Islamic Conference Organization (ICO), the global association of Islamic countries. In the south, Christian leaders were outraged by these developments and said so from their pulpits. Today, voices favoring secession are being heard in the south, notably in the southeast (where the Ibo tried to secede once before, with disastrous results).

Will Nigeria's location astride an interfaith boundary ultimately destroy the country? The potential for such a breakdown is growing. The domination of national affairs by Muslims is becoming an issue in the south, and the aggressive expansion of Islam among smaller Nigerian population groups adds to the problem. The potential for a fracture along religious lines is growing.

Any such development would be disastrous. Nigeria is an African cornerstone, a crucible of West African culture rich in literature and the arts. Nigeria in 1995 was OPEC's (Organization of Petroleum Exporting Countries) fourth largest oil producer (the United States has been Nigeria's chief customer). Nigeria's survival as a multicultural society is an achievement on a par with India's, and its Christian-Islamic coexistence has served as a model for countries where conflict has marked such relationships. The breakup of Nigeria would be a catastrophe, but the potential for it is growing.

Nigeria is not alone in its situation in Africa's transition zone between Islam and non-Islam. As Figure 24-1 shows, several other countries, including Chad, Sudan, and Ethiopia, straddle this interfaith boundary. In the case of Sudan, Muslim north and Christian-traditional south have waged war for nearly as long as the country has been independent. But in fact the

conflict is more complicated than that. Sudan's northern provinces contain about 60 percent of the total population, but while this region is overwhelmingly Muslim, only about two-thirds of the northerners speak Arabic as their native language. These Muslim but non-Arab northerners, including the Nubians, have been the targets of anti-Islamic propaganda from the south.

What intensified the struggle between the north (where the capital, Khartum, is located at the confluence of the White and the Blue Nile) and the south was the decision by the Muslim-dominated regime to impose Islam's **sharia religious laws** over the entire country, south as well as north. Sharia laws, especially the criminal code, are harsh (prescribing, for example, the amputation of hands or limbs for theft). In the south, where people are ethnically and culturally of African background and where Christianity has made inroads among traditional religions, that action canceled any prospect of a compromise.

The religion-stoked war in Sudan has cost incalculable casualties and damage. Millions have been dislocated, hundreds of thousands have starved; both sides, but especially the Khartum regime, have interfered with relief supplies provided by international agencies to help the refugees. In 1992, when the war seemed stalemated, Nigeria sought to broker a peace, and in the Nigerian capital of Abuja the northerners promised to rescind the sharia regulations and to allow freedom of belief and religious observance. But by 1994, when the north seemed to have victory in its grasp, these commitments were abrogated.

The lesson of Sudan is not lost on Nigeria: the cost of religious conflict there would be immeasurable. But both Nigeria and Sudan underscore the risks of a location that entails the constant threat of religious confrontation.

Developments in the so-called "Horn" of Africa in the mid-1990s have changed the map. As Figure 24-1 shows, Ethiopia's religious map is even more complicated than that of Nigeria or Sudan. At the heart of the former mountain kingdom lies the cultural core area of Amharic Christians who, from their nearly impregnable natural fortress, controlled the lowlands in all directions. The wave of Islam lapped at the base of the mountains, but the Christian rulers kept control. (Fig. 26-1). When the last of Ethiopia's emperors fell in 1974, the Amharic rulers still controlled the Muslim Eritreans in the north, the Muslim Somali pastoralists in the east, and a huge arc-shaped region of other African peoples to the west and south. But a revolution was brewing, and in 1991, the military dictatorship that had inherited the state from the imperial dynasty was overthrown.

In 1995, the future of Ethiopia remained uncertain. The revolution that destroyed the old order created a new state on the African map: Eritrea, dominantly Muslim and culturally distinct from the former empire of which it had been a part. But Eritrea's secession did not end Ethiopia's religious multiculturalism. Ethiopia still contains a large Muslim population of Somalis in its eastern zone; the south and west are non-Muslim; and Coptic Christians still cluster in their highland domain. The separation of Eritrea (which had the effect of landlocking Ethiopia) is likely to prove to be only one step in a series of changes that underscore the perils of straddling an interfaith border.

SOUTH ASIA

While Britain ruled its South Asian colonial empire, extending from Pakistan in the west to Bangladesh in the east and from Kashmir to Sri lanka, its giant domain lay astride a deep and divisive interfaith boundary. When independence approached, the British made that boundary a political border between Islamic Pakistan and multicultural India. The establishment of that political boundary was accompanied by one of the largest human migrations of modern times as millions of Muslims crossed into Pakistan and Hindus moved eastward into what would be India.

While Pakistan became an almost exclusively Islamic state, India proclaimed itself a secular federation, in which all faiths would be tolerated and freedom of religion would prevail. India, however, continued to face the problems of an interfaith-boundary-straddling location. Within India's borders, religious communities as large as many nations faced each other across deep cultural divides.

For more than 30 years following India's independence (1947), religious conflict in India was sporadic and, given the dimensions of the country and its populations, relatively minor. But during the 1980s, several developments occurred that shook the stability of the state. First came a campaign by Sikhs for greater (or outright) independence. India's Sikhs found themselves at a disadvantage in an India dominated by Hindus in which the Muslims, not the Sikhs, were the most powerful religious minority. The Sikhs demanded a separate State in the Punjab, and when this demand did not achieve results, militant Sikhs began a push that was accompanied by militancy and terrorism. In 1984, the Indian Army raided the Sikhs' holiest shrine, the Golden Temple in Amritsar, causing more than 1000 deaths. Four months later, India's prime minister, Indira Gandhi, was assassinated by Sikh members of her bodyguard.

The Sikh demand for a separate State (to be named Khalistan, if it ever comes about) is based in part on the concentration of Sikhs in the Panjab (Punjab) of northwestern India (Fig. 26-2). Sikhism, as we saw in Chapter 24, arose as a reaction to Hinduism and Islam. By world standards, it is not a large religion; there are about 20 million adherents, more than 90 percent of them in northwest India. Sikhism, like so many other prescriptively peaceful faiths, has become associated with violence and death; the objectives of Sikh political leaders and Sikh religious leaders are now inseparable. But as the map shows, although Sikhs are in the majority in most of the districts of Punjab, the state also includes significant Hindu minorities. The situation is somewhat

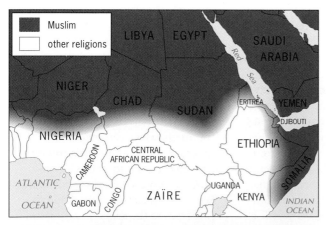

FIGURE 26–1 Religious and political geography across the African Transition Zone.

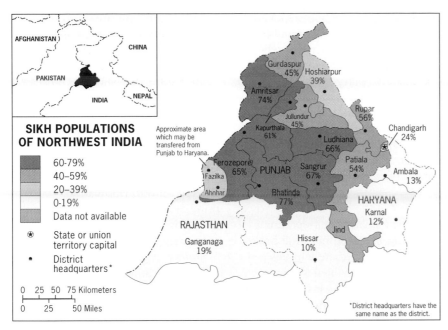

FIGURE 26–2 From a map in M.I. Glassner and H.J. de Blij, *Systematic Political Geography*, 4th ed. (New York: Wiley, 1989), p. 402.

reminiscent of Northern Ireland and is no closer to a solution.

The second development that threatened India's stability occurred during the late 1980s, when the site of a holy shrine claimed by both Muslims and Hindus became a battleground between the two groups. This struggle focused on a shrine at Ayodhya in the State of Uttar Pradesh. A building housing both a temple and a mosque sat atop a mount deemed holy by both Hindus and Muslims, but in 1986 a local judge ruled it to be a Hindu site. Hindu pilgrims came to the site by the thousands, and a militant Hindu group announced plans to tear down the mosque portion of the building and to expand the temple section. Muslims protested, but Hindus argued that the site was in fact the birthplace of the Hindu god Rama and that its original temple had been torn down by the Muslims during the Moghul period. In 1989, the issue aroused religious passions throughout India, and clashes killed nearly 400 people.

The third threat to India's conti-

nuity arose in part from the kinds of skirmishes just described. For the first time in memory, Hinduism began to exhibit the sort of militant radicalism long associated with other faiths. The beginnings of this Hindu "fundamentalism" can be traced to 1983, when reactions to Sikh and Muslim militancy led to "Save Hinduism" marches all across the country. Ten years later, Hindu fundamentalism had become a major force in Indian politics. It is strongest in the Indian heartland in the north-central region of the country, but it is spreading. To many observers, Hindu militancy, activism, and fundamentalism seem contradictory; it is not in the nature of the faith to be aggressive. But modern ideas have reached even this most ancient of the large religions. Hindu leaders see the results of activism and appeals to fundamentalism elsewhere, and they understand the rewards.

The rise of fundamentalism is a phenomenon that seems to affect virtually all religions today, and we will devote attention to this serious

development later in this chapter. Its appearance in India, where it is now embodied in a conservative Hindu political party, is evidence that a return to the basics of faith is a notion that has worldwide appeal.

REVIVAL IN THE FORMER SOVIET UNION

When the Soviet Union was forged from the tsar's empire inherited by communist revolutionaries, now nearly three generations ago, the socialist planners confronted a difficult task: to satisfy the territorial aspirations of dozens of diverse peoples. Most of these peoples had participated in the revolution, and many were rewarded with some form of areal identity as the territory was carved up into a multitiered political mosaic. At the top of this hierarchy were the original Soviet Union's 15 Soviet Republics; other territories were of lower rank. Russia, the largest and dominant Soviet Republic, itself was divided into 16 territories, each of which was awarded some degree of autonomy.

The Soviets not only inherited more than 100 "nationalities" or ethnic groups, their languages, beliefs, and lifeways: they also became heirs to parts of two great religious realms. Under the tsars' rule, the Russian branch of the Eastern Orthodox Church had thrived, marking unmistakably the Russian cultural landscape from Kiev to St. Petersburg (Leningrad). The tsars also had subjugated the vast steppes and deserts of Central Asia, where Islam was the prevailing faith. East of the Caspian Sea, the Soviet empire included the physical and cultural landscapes of Southwest Asia, the cities studded with magnificent mosques and the countryside dotted with oases.

Between the Caspian and Black Seas, the Soviets acquired two neighboring territories strongly infused with religion. The Armenians, mainly on the Black Sea side, were

Christians whose ethnic cohorts had fought for survival in the land of the Ottoman Turks. The Azerbaijani, on the Caspian Sea side, were Muslims of the Shiite faith, Persians (Iranians) in all but historic-geographic fate.

The Soviet communists determined to make an atheistic state out of their country, and they discouraged religious practice on both sides of the interfaith boundary that extended from the Black Sea to the Chinese border. In Russia, they carried off church bells and other religious paraphernalia and demolished many churches altogether, converting others to secular use. In the Soviet Muslim realm, they tolerated Islamic practice among the old, but obstructed it among the young. Time, they believed, would erase the diverse religious imprints on both Christian and Muslim societies.

In laying out the administrative framework of the future, however, the Soviet planners proved to be poor geographers. In the area of Armenia and Azerbaijan they attempted to delimit boundaries to separate the Christian and Muslim ethnic domains. The result (Fig. 26-3) was a layout that could be made to function while Soviet authority controlled both "republics," but that was a blueprint for religious conflict when that control diminished. A large **exclave** of Christian Armenia, called Nagorno-Karabakh, was created as an **enclave** within Muslim Azerbaijan. Azerbaijan also was divided through the creation of an exclave named Nakhichevan, which was established on the Iranian border.

When in the late 1980s the Soviet Republics attained self-determination, long-latent ethnic strife broke out almost immediately in this sensitive area. Azerbaijani Muslims, long cut off from their Iranian Shiite counterparts, broke through the southern border and acquired weapons in the process. Soon Muslims and Christians were locked in combat, with Armenian refugees streaming from Nagorno-Karabakh westward and even fleeing by boat across the Caspian Sea from the Muslim capital, Baku, where many had long worked as laborers. More than 70 years of Soviet domination had done little to soften Armenian-Christian memories of Islamic oppression, or to lessen the intensity of Azerbaijani-Muslim dis-

taste for Christian unbelievers. Today, the now-independent republics of Transcaucasia remain a place of tension and conflict.

As Figure 24-1 shows, Transcaucasia is not the only part of the former Soviet empire that is affected by an interfaith boundary. The Soviets also held sway over a vast region of central Asia, a region called Turkestan. There, they subjugated a Muslim population numbering between 40 and 50 million (Soviet census figures for this region always were suspect).

It was Soviet communist policy to promote atheism, and this policy applied to central Asian Muslims as well as Russian Christians. But centuries of Muslim history and ideology cannot be stamped out in short order, and when the Soviet Union collapsed, Islam quickly revived in the central Asian republics. Most of Turkestan's Muslims adhere to Sunni Islam, although there are pockets of Shiism in the region and Iranian clerics have been trying to rekindle the Shiah sect. Simultaneously, the Russian Orthodox (Christian) Church is experiencing a resurrection in Russia and among Russians outside Russia itself, and these events are creating the potential for friction.

Potentially the most serious spatial problem lies in Kazakhstan, territorially the largest state in former Soviet Central Asia. As Figure 24-1 shows, the Islamic-Christian interfaith boundary runs right across Kazakhstan, whose north is strongly Russified and whose south remains typical of Islamic Turkestan. An estimated 47 percent of the population of between 17 and 19 million adheres to Islam, while about 17 percent now belong to the Russian Orthodox Church. Virtually all the Christians live in the north, and almost all the Muslims in the south. Compared to Transcaucasia there is little spatial interdigitation between the Islamic and Christian communities, but neither do Christians and

FIGURE 26–3 Two exclaves in Transcaucasia.

Muslims have their own countries—unless the interfaith boundary becomes a political border at some future time. For Kazakhstan, the religious map suggests, the future holds a major challenge.

EUROPE

No discussion of interfaith boundaries and their impact on countries is complete without reference to Europe's tragedy, Yugoslavia. Ever since the Ottoman Turks converted Slavic communities in their Eastern European empire to Islam, the region has had residual Muslim pockets—and thus interfaith boundaries. In the former Yugoslavia, these clusters of Islam were quite large territorially and numerically, and lay centered on Bosnia and its capital, Sarajevo.

The scale of Figure 24-1 does not allow for sufficient detail to illustrate the complexity of the former Yugoslavia's cultural map, but the Muslim-Christian interfaith boundary there lay in an area where an intrafaith boundary also prevailed: a boundary between the Serbian Orthodox Church centered on the country's east and its Serbian population, and the Catholic Church whose religious domain includes Croatia. Caught in the middle were the Muslims, and when Yugoslavia's political system collapsed, the Muslims found themselves attacked by both Christian camps. The term **ethnic cleansing** came into use to describe the ouster of Muslim (and other) communities from their homes and lands—Serbs and Croats both ousted Muslims, but Serbs and Croats also "cleansed" each other's territories. Where they could, Muslims drove their Christian adversaries away, but it was the Muslim minority that suffered most. (As we noted earlier, there is nothing strictly "ethnic" about Yugoslavia's communities; they all are of Slavic ancestry and what divides them is culture, not race).

The lesson of Yugoslavia relates to the risk an interfaith boundary poses to any state, no matter how long peoples of different religions have cohabited. While Yugoslavia was a relatively young state, having been formed from the chaotic aftermath of World War I before 1920, its seven major and 17 smaller cultural groups had managed to live together for nearly three generations before disaster struck. During the Second World War, Nazi-supporting Croats fought anti-Nazi Serbs, but after 1945 Yugoslavia resumed its quest for nationhood under communist rules imposed by its strongman president, Tito. After Tito's death, and following an uneasy period of rule by committee, Yugoslavia was swept up in the post-Soviet disintegration process and latent religious differences became actual grounds for combat.

The result has been disastrous not just for Yugoslavia. After World War II, Europeans proclaimed that what had happened during the war would never happen again, a commitment often reiterated while European nations moved toward unification. In Yugoslavia, Europe had its chance to prove that its collective power and influence would indeed prevent outrages comparable to what happened during the Second World War. But Europe failed, casting doubt on the credibility of all those grand declarations and manifestos that underlie the framework of European Union.

OTHER INTERFAITH BOUNDARIES

The problems of religious militancy and its ethnic-regional expression plague several other countries at various degrees of intensity. In populous Bangladesh, where the southern lowland regions remain Muslim-dominated and the interior is Hindu, the level of interfaith conflict has been lower than in India. Hindu fundamentalism has not yet made inroads here, and the level of Muslim militancy has until recently been relatively low (in 1994, however, evidence of growing Muslim fundamentalism in Bangladesh came in the form of the arrest and forced exile of the author of a book allegedly blasphemous of Islam).

The future of the interfaith boundary in Bangladesh will depend directly on the religious situation in neighboring India. If India manages to accommodate its huge Muslim minority successfully, and if conflict with Islamic Pakistan can be avoided, Bangladesh is likely to remain calm. Should serious interfaith strife occur in South Asia's giant, Bangladesh will feel the ripple effects.

Another neighbor of India, the island country of Sri Lanka, has experienced an episode of conflict with religious overtones. About 70 percent of Sri Lanka's 18 million inhabitants are Buddhists, but in the north and northeast a Tamil-speaking, ethnically Dravidian, religiously Hindu minority has developed. This Tamil-Hindu minority has since 1984 fought a war of secession, in which religion became an ever stronger force. Buddhist shrines were targeted, and Hindu holy sites were attacked in retaliation. The Indian government tried to assist the Sri Lanka government to settle the issue, even through the armed intervention. In India, Hindu fundamentalists decried this support for Buddhists against Hindus, and this may have led to the assassination of Prime Minister Rajiv Gandhi, son of Indira and political candidate again in 1991.

By late 1994, the conflict was in a stalemate, but the mid-1994 elections in Sri Lanka brought a new, more leftist government into power. Hopes rose that Sri Lanka might yet survive its ethnic-religious conflict in one piece, but the reality of its interfaith boundary will not disappear.

In Southeast Asia, an interfaith

From the Field Notes

❝ A field trip in the area of Vienna, Austria included a reminder of the changing religious mosaic of Europe, and the evolving pattern of interfaith boundaries there. This thriving mosque stands near the banks of the Danube Canal. Turkish workers, refugee Bosnian Muslims, and other adherents of Islam came here to worship, to play (there were many children on the grounds), and to patronize the sizeable bazaar. Islam's presence in Europe is growing and changing. ❞

INTRAFAITH BOUNDARIES

Interfaith boundaries, we have just noted, can threaten the stability of entire countries. By comparison, countries that contain **intrafaith boundaries** would seem to be less troubled.

In general, that is indeed the case. Western European countries have Catholic as well as Protestant communities, and often these communities have regional expression, as in the case of Switzerland (Fig. 26-4). In the early 1990s, the great majority of these countries were not experiencing religious or ethnic conflict. In Eastern Europe, factors other than (or in addition to) religious ones lay at the root of strife.

The single most intractable problem in Western Europe continued to be that of Northern Ireland, where a Protestant majority and a Catholic minority were in conflict over their coexistence and their future. The issue stems from the period when Ireland, in its entirety, was a British dependency. A substantial Protestant British population immigrated into overwhelmingly Catholic Ireland during this time, many from Scotland. Most settled in the northeastern corner of the island, loyal representatives of the Protestant British Crown in a hostile religious environment.

When the Catholic Irish rose in revolt against British colonialism and won the day, Ireland was partitioned to protect this Protestant minority. But the Northern Ireland that was thus carved from the new Republic contained a substantial Catholic minority, who were left unprotected. In the 1920s, when the map of a future Ireland was being drawn, it was assumed that time and economic development would soften the religious animosities in "the North" (Fig. 26-5).

This was not to be the case. The Protestant majority in Northern Ire-

boundary between Islam and Christianity touches the southern Philippines. As Figure 24-1 shows, the southernmost islands of the Philippines have Muslim populations, comparatively small minorities in a Catholic-dominated country. Although Muslim adherents constitute only about 5 percent of the population of the Philippines, this small minority has campaigned vigorously, and sometimes violently, for improved status in the country.

One of the most consequential interfaith boundaries lies in Southwest Asia, in Israel and between Israel and its neighbors. The Jewish presence in Gaza always was small, but major Jewish settlement in the West Bank blurred what once had the makings of an interfaith bound-

ary between Israel and Jordan. Israel's control over Gaza, the West Bank, and the Golan Heights put many miles of interfaith boundaries within the sphere of Israeli jurisdiction.

Significant events in the early- and mid-1990s began to change this religious-political mosaic as self-government was awarded to Gaza and to small areas inside the West Bank. Palestinian Arabs were empowered to run their own affairs within these initially limited zones; stability and satisfactory coexistence may lead to further adjustments and, as seen from the Arab side, a legitimate Palestinian state. But Israel lies astride what may well be the world's most sensitive interfaith boundaries, and a successful transition is by no means assured.

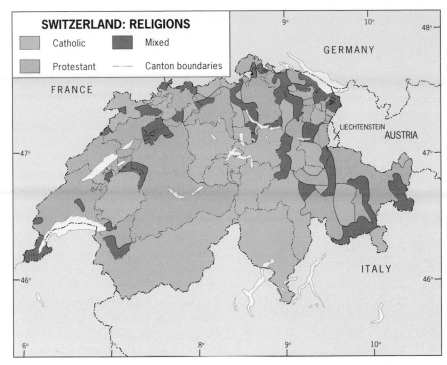

FIGURE 26–4 From M.I. Glassner and H.J. de Blij, *Systematic Political Geography*, 4th ed. (New York: Wiley, 1989), p. 535.

land's population constituting about two-thirds of the total (now about 1.6 million) held all the economic and political advantage. Charges by Catholics of discrimination and repression were given emphasis by a campaign of terrorism, which in turn brought British troops to the area. As time went on, the situation deteriorated, worsened by economic stagnation. Although the Republic of Ireland was sensitive to the plight of Catholics in the North, no official help was extended to those who were carrying on the violence.

In Northern Ireland, religion gave identity to the two communities locked in this tragic struggle. As many observers have noted, the conflict is not strictly religious; it is a conflict over access to opportunities, over civil rights, and over political influence. But religion, and religious history, are the banners beneath which the opposing sides march, and church and cathedral

become the symbols of strife, not peace.

IN THE ISLAMIC REALM

Within the Christian realm, no other intrafaith conflict currently has the same intensity. In the Muslim realm, however, conflicts between the majority Sunni and minority Shiite branches have pitted followers of Islam against each other. Undoubtedly the most destructive war of its kind in modern times, the Iran-Iraq conflict of the 1980s was a battle between Sunni-dominated Iraq and Shiite-ruled Iran. The war began over a territorial issue but was sustained by religious enmity. Although the Shiites constitute only about 12 percent of all Islamic people, they proclaim themselves the true followers of Muhammad and often resent the less dogmatic, more worldly Sunni.

The depth of this division was revealed in the aftermath of the

Gulf War, when the Sunni-controlled army of defeated Iraq moved immediately against the Shiite communities of the south (Figure 24-1 shows where these are located), to preclude any opposition or cooperation with neighboring Iran. Elsewhere in the realm, Shiite and Sunni factions have been in conflict in Lebanon, and factional conflict also has attended the annual pilgrimage to Mecca, claiming thousands of lives.

RELIGIOUS FUNDAMENTALISM

It is, today, a worldwide phenomenon: a drive by religious leaders and, spontaneously, by millions of their followers, to return to the basics of the faith, to the roots of religious beliefs. It is a force that is often born of frustration—frustration at what is seen as the breakdown of society's mores and values, at the loss of religious authority, at a failure to achieve economic goals, at the corruption of political systems.

People in one society often see **religious fundamentalism** in other societies and fear it, without recognizing it in their own. In the United States, religious fundamentalism often is taken to be synonymous with Islamic fundamentalism. Such incidents as the pronouncement of a death sentence over the author of an allegedly blasphemous book by a religious regime in Iran seem to confirm a medievalism that, surely, could not infect any branch of Christianity. But in other cultures the repeated killings of physicians willing to perform legal abortions by religious zealots in this country suggest something equally fearful. Fundamentalism and extremism are

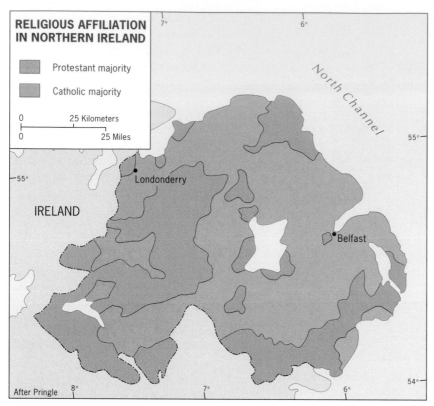

RELIGIOUS AFFILIATION IN NORTHERN IRELAND

Protestant majority

Catholic majority

0   25 Kilometers

0   25 Miles

North Channel

Londonderry

IRELAND

Belfast

After Pringle

FIGURE 26–5 From D.G. Pringle, *One Island, Two Nations*? (Letchworth: Research Studies Press/Wiley, 1985), p. 21.

closely related, and their appeal is global.

All religions are affected today by the modernization of the world. Education, radio, television, and travel have diffused notions of individual liberties, sexual equality, freedom of choice, questions about religious as well as secular authority, and other ideas that may clash with religious dogma. Some churches have managed to change with the times, allowing women to serve as priests and liberalizing their doctrines. But others have gone the opposite way, reaffirming fundamental dogma and obstructing the influences of modernization. In the process, battle lines are being drawn that suggest that, after the capitalism-communist ideological struggle of the past half century, we may be about to witness a religious contest. The drive toward fundamentalism is creating a climate of

mistrust that could lead to strife, possibly pitting Christians against Muslims, both dominated by fundamentalist philosophies.

Among Christian religions, the Roman Catholic Church in recent years has resisted innovations deemed incompatible with the fundamentals of the faith, notably involving issues of birth control and family planning but also relating to the role of women in the religious bureaucracy. Religions tend to be male-dominated, and few women have managed to enter the hierarchy. More consequential, from a global viewpoint, is the Roman Catholic Church's position on family planning. In a world of exploding populations, the church continues to militate against the use of artificial means of birth control as well as abortion. During the September 1994 United Nations Conference on Population and Development, the

Roman Catholic Church even sought an alliance with Islamic countries against those who would favor population control.

But the Roman Catholic Church is not the only Christian church to be buffeted by—or resist—the forces of change. All the Christian churches face influences of modernization and secularization, because they prevail in regions where the world's most rapidly modernizing societies lie (the exception is Japan, where Shintoism has also been affected). But the world's other major faiths also confront the pressures of change. Not all Muslim communities, for example, adhere with equal propriety to the rules of the Koran. The prohibition against alcohol, a Muslim tenet, is not observed with equal steadfastness. The laws of Islam, which are very strict and which call for severe punishment of offenders, are not equally applied throughout the Muslim religious realm.

Such inconsistency and dispute leads to reaction, not only in the religious bureaucracies but also among the masses of believers. In general, the clergy tend to be conservative, with some prominent liberalizers reflecting the forces of modernization. Church and mosque memberships are divided in response. The geographic dimension is not difficult to find: in the Catholic church, the modernizers are located far from the heartland, in the Netherlands and in the United States. In the Muslim realm, conservatism is strongest in a tier of countries that extends from Sudan to Pakistan, and weakens into Turkey to the northwest and into Malaysia and Indonesia to the east, where what is sometimes described as a "laissez-faire" Islam prevails.

Even in those "moderate" wings of Islam, however, fundamentalism is raising its head. In Malaysia, the prospect of the general application of sharia law raised fears among the Chinese and other minorities; the government talked of this possibility in response to demands by certain clerics. In Indonesia, a back-to-basics movement among Islamic preachers has found fertile soil, especially among those in rural areas who remain remote from the changes affecting Indonesian society elsewhere.

Countering religious fundamentalism entails political risks, as is evident from the care U.S. politicians take in not offending the "religious right." When the former Shah of Iran tried to limit the power of the **Imams** as he sought to modernize the state, he provoked a religious movement that eventually overthrew his throne. Imams are Shiite Muslim leaders whose appointment is regarded as sanctioned by Allah. They are without sin and infallible, and therefore a potent social as well as political force. In Iran during the revolution, they imposed the most basic of Shiite religious rules and practices upon their followers. After the Shah was replaced by an **Ayatollah**, a supreme religious leader, those rules and practices became state law. Women, whose position had advanced under the Shah's regime, suffered setbacks. Those who had adopted Western dress modes were arrested on the streets and forced to wear Muslim headgear, veils, and long robes. Many lost positions in commerce and administration.

What happened in Iran during the 1970s and 1980s was perhaps the most telling manifestation yet of the consequences of the current resurgence of fundamentalism in organized religion. The process took a violent course in Iran, but it was, and is, happening in other regions and countries as well. When religion becomes a political force, when the power position of religion in a country is threatened by secularization, when the revered shrines of a faith are imperiled or damaged, when the excesses of a modernizing society become repugnant to those who prefer established ways, or when ethnic conflict arises over other issues, people often turn to the most basic tenets of their faith. Thus religion becomes a binding force, a bulwark against adversity, and a proclamation of strength and unity.

Like religion generally, therefore, fundamentalism can constitute both a unifying and a divisive force. The role of fundamentalist "preachers" and their massive following in the United States has divided the Protestant churches of America, especially when the personal and financial excesses of certain of the evangelical sermonizers became public knowledge. The debate within the Catholic church has created a split between orthodox and liberal. In Muslim societies, fundmentalism has stimulated the formation of political movements whose aim is to reverse the move toward secularization and, if possible, to seize political power.

In Algeria during the 1990s, such a movement has come close to overthrowing the government. In 1991, a conservative Muslim political party was poised to win national elections, having appealed to voters eager to replace a corrupt secular administration with an Islamic regime. Rather than allowing the final round of voting to take place, the Algerian government cancelled the election; the Muslim movement then began a campaign of violent opposition. Some saw a parallel with Iran, and Muslim leaders called for an **Islamic Republic** in Algeria.

Foreigners were targeted and dozens were killed; but thousands of Algerians lost their lives in a continuing exchange of reprisals. In late 1994, France, Algeria's former colonizer, fearful of a mass exodus of Algerians to French shores, tried to mediate. But the Muslim fundamentalists appeared to have the upper hand, and the future of Algeria was in doubt.

The struggle in Algeria emboldened Muslim fundamentalists elsewhere to challenge government and authority. In Algeria's neighbor, Tunisia, Muslim clerics called for the end of secular government; in Egypt, Muslim radicals attacked foreign tourists and thus destroyed one of the country's major sources of income. Disorder would generate dissatisfaction, and out of dissatisfaction would arise the Muslim answer to the prevailing order.

It is often said that we live today in an age of religious tolerance. Compared to the Middle Ages, that certainly is true. But religious feelings can quickly translate to actions reminiscent of those times. Add the fundamentalist phenomenon to the interfaith and intrafaith divisions the world still faces, and religion can be seen to have the capacity to plunge societies into conflict.

KEY TERMS

Ayatollah
Enclave
Ethnic Cleansing
Exclave
Imam
Interfaith Boundary
Intrafaith Boundary
Islamic Republic
Religious Fundamentalism
Sharia Religious Law

Rice, the staple of billions, stands in the paddies of Indonesia.

PART NINE

CULTURAL LANDSCAPES OF FARMING

At Issue

Much of the world's farmland still is cultivated in old, traditional ways—but yields are much higher now than they were in ancient times. The Third Agricultural Revolution has narrowed the gap between global demand and world farm production. But the crucial issue remains: people still die of starvation, and many millions of others continue to suffer from malnutrition. The links between producers of plenty and consumers in crisis still are too weakly developed. Emergency grain supply to refugees in sudden and urgent need, for example, remains inadequate, and not only because warring factions often interfere with shipments. The remoteness and isolation of the displaced can also become factors. It can happen to anyone—to Bosnians, Liberians, Somali, Bangladeshi. At issue is the world's ability and willingness to ensure the most efficient possible dissemination of needed farm products.

PART NINE

27

LIVELIHOODS FROM LAND AND SEA

When we examined the problems arising from any attempt to define the concept of culture, it was obvious that this term represents and encompasses all human thought and activity, from belief systems to technological implements. In human geography, we are especially interested in the imprints made by human culture on the landscape. These include not only the marks of religion and language, but also the impress of economic and political activities.

It is not difficult to envisage cultural landscapes of farming. The drama of the urban landscape is concentrated in comparatively small areas, but agriculture transforms whole countrysides. The range of agricultural landscapes is enormous, from the vast, rolling wheatlands of the Great Plains in America to the meticulously terraced hillslopes of rice-farming Asia; from the vineyards of France to the pastures of New Zealand. In Part 9, we begin a discussion of economic activity that will carry us from farmlands to factories to urban complexes. Our journey through human geography will now reach the field of economic geography.

Economic geography is concerned with the various ways in which people earn a living, and how the goods and services they produce in order to earn that income are spatially expressed and organized. These activities range from the simple to the complex and from the ancient to the modern. Before we focus on farming, we should identify the entire range of activities that, together, constitute the **spatial economy**.

Geographica

- Humanity's economic activities can be classified into five categories ranging from rural-based primary (extractive) industries to urban-centered service and technological pursuits.

- Agriculture, the deliberate tending of crops and livestock in order to produce food and fiber, may be less than 12,000 years old and emerged sequentially in several world regions.

- The First Agricultural Revolution achieved plant domestication; the Second Agricultural Revolution involved improved methods of cultivation, production, and storage; and the Third Agricultural Revolution (now in progress) is based on research and technology in plant genetics.

- Subsistence agriculture, producing little or no surplus and miring hundreds of millions of people in a near-continuous struggle for survival, still prevails over large regions of tropical Africa, Asia, and the Americas.

- One of the earliest models of the spatial economy was developed by J.H. von Thünen in Germany and accounted for observed agricultural patterns around urban market centers.

333

FIVE CATEGORIES OF ECONOMIC ACTIVITY

One way to simplify and organize the wide range and huge variety of humanity's economic endeavors is to distinguish five types of such activity:

1. ***Primary Activities***
   Hunting and gathering (ancient ways of survival), farming of all kinds, livestock herding, fishing and aquaculture, forestry and lumbering, mining and quarrying are all primary activities. These are activities in the *extractive sector* in which workers and the natural environment come into direct contact; in the process, the environment sometimes suffers.

2. ***Secondary Activities***
   The manufacturing industries convert raw materials into finished products, an activity that began as soon as stones and bones were shaped into tools. We recognize major stages in human history in terms of such conversion (the Bronze Age and the Iron Age, for example), and today the secondary activities include an almost infinite range of *production* from simple to complex comodities. Toys, warships, pottery, steel, chemicals, buildings—all these are products under this category.

3. ***Tertiary Activities***
   Today, hundreds of millions of workers are employed in the so-called *service industries.* Visit the skyscrapered downtown of an American city, and the people in all those offices, banks, hospitals, and shops represent the tertiary sector. They connect producers to consumers, thus facilitating commerce and trade; as lawyers, doctors, dentists, teachers, and librarians, they provide crucial services in a complex society.

4. ***Quaternary Activities***
   In technologically advanced societies, a growing number of people are busy collecting, processing, manipulating, and providing *information.* This is a product of the computer age, the era of satellite data transmission, and the unprecedented volume and flow of intelligence. Geographers working with geographic information systems (GIS) participate in these activities.

5. ***Quinary Activities***
   Some economic geographers recognize a fifth level of activity, one we may collectively call the *decision-making* occupations. These are the managerial or control-function activities that guide the world's numerous major corporations; decisions are made largely on the basis of information flow from the quaternary sector. Although few individuals perform these functions, their impact on the world economy is enormous.

While it is convenient to identify categories of activity, it is also evident that these five categories represent a continuum: there are overlaps and interconnections. Take the case of farming. Most farm products are marketed as they are harvested (rice, oranges, potatoes), but some are cooked, dried, salted, or otherwise converted before distribution. These latter products

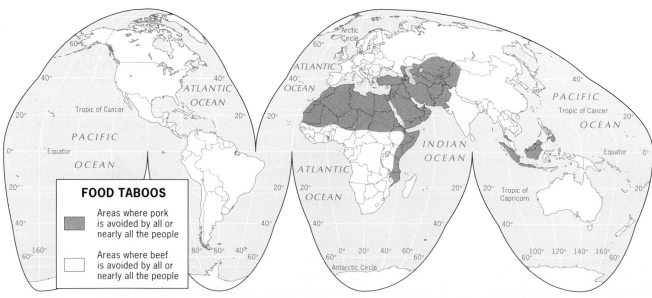

FIGURE 27–1 Prohibitions and bans against certain foods affect diets in many areas of the world. Mapped here are only the major taboos.

would qualify as secondary manufactures, since raw materials were converted into different commodities. Nevertheless, all farming industries, from subsistence rice growing on small plots to commercial wheat cultivation on huge estates, are regarded as primary activities. These primary activities form the focus of the present chapter.

AGRICULTURE'S PERSISTENCE

Our investigation will touch on the full range of the activities just enumerated, but Part 9 focuses on **agriculture**, the deliberate tending of crops and livestock in order to produce food and fiber.

In late 1994, the U.S. Bureau of the Census announced the passing of a noteworthy milestone: the number of farmers in the United States had fallen below 2 million. Not since the mid-nineteenth century, when the American population was barely over 20 million, had the Census counted so few farming families.

Does this statistic mean that farming is no longer an important component of the U.S. economy? Hardly. Total production is at an all-time high. But the nature of farming has changed: mechanization and farm consolidation have driven millions of small farmers off the land. The transformation of the U.S. economy from an agricultural to an industrial and technological one has altered the pattern of employment. Still, American farm output is enormous and remains one of the world's largest.

In the chapters that follow, we will move our focus from farming to industry and technology, but it is well to remember that, in the majority of the world's countries today, agriculture remains by far the leading employment sector. Indeed, in some societies people continue to live and work as they generally did thousands of years ago. The revolutionary changes so commonplace in our lives have barely touched the existence of hundreds of millions of our contemporaries in Asia and Africa. *We* may be witnessing the beginnings of a postindustrial age, but they have not. The first half of this chapter, therefore, focuses on the way these people made, and continue to make, their living.

ANCIENT LIVELIHOODS IN A MODERN WORLD

The processes whereby food is produced, distributed, and consumed form a fundamental part of every culture. The way in which land is allocated to individuals or families (or bought or sold), the manner in which it is used for food production, the functions of livestock, and the consumption of food from crops and animals are all aspects of culture. In the previous chapters, we noted that food consumption is often related in important ways to religious influence and dogma. Adherents of Islam and Judaism avoid pork; Hindu believers do not consume beef or other kinds of meat (Fig. 27-1). Various other forms of partial or total abstinence occur among human cultures, including periodic fasts. Such prescriptions, like the religions that generate them, tend to be old and persistent, and can change only slowly. Other food avoidance, we noted in Chapter 15, relates to certain people's intolerance to particular substances, such as dairy products, eggs, or fish.

BEFORE FARMING

Most of the food humanity consumes comes, directly or indirectly, from the soil, and **farming** has long been established as the basis of existence all over the world.

There was a time, however, before the invention of agriculture, when human communities were based on livelihoods other than farming. Viewed in the perspective of total human history, farming is actually a very recent innovation (its beginnings date back a mere 12,000 years). Even today, a few small societies survive much as they did before agriculture was developed: by hunting and gathering what food nature has to offer, and sometimes by fishing. Peoples who still subsist this way have been pushed into difficult environments by more powerful competitors (as the San of Southern Africa were by the Bantu and the white invaders), and their survival seems to involve the weathering of one crisis after another. Cyclical drought is the worst enemy. It withers the vegetation, kills or drives off the wildlife, and cuts off natural water supplies, such as springs.

Still the San of Southern Africa, the aboriginal black peoples of interior Australia, the Native Americans of Brazil, and several other groups in the Americas, Africa, and Asia manage to sustain themselves in the face of great odds. They do so by knowing and exploiting their environment exhaustively. Every seed, root, fruit, berry, and beetle is sought out and consumed. Hunting is accomplished with poisoned spears, bows and arrows, clubs, and sticks. When the people do not depend on a particular water hole for their own water supply, they may poison it and follow the animals that have drunk there. Thus the community must be on the move much of the time. The group cannot become too large, nor can settlements normally be permanent. However, without agriculture and the practice of storing food in preparation of future periods of shortage (very few hunting-gathering peoples do this), life is difficult. It was easier where the land was more productive, but most of the surviving hunting-gathering peoples have been driven from better-endowed areas into dry, cold, and otherwise less hospitable environments.

We should therefore not be misled into the assumption that the human groups that survive today as hunters and gatherers are entirely representative of the early human communities that lived by the same means. While Europe's plainlands opened up following the most recent glacial retreat, our distant ancestors hunted the mammoth and other plentiful wildlife. They set elaborate traps and cooperated in driving wildlife to areas where it would be vulnerable. Communities then were much larger than the present-day (San) clans. Very early on, there were peoples who subsisted on hunting and gathering and fishing who had learned to specialize to some extent in some area of production. The oak forests of parts of North America provided an abundant harvest of nuts, sometimes enough to last more than a full year, and so Native American communities collected and stored this food source. Others living near the Pacific Ocean coast became adept at salmon fishing. The buffalo herds of interior North America also provided sustenance for centuries before being virtually wiped out. In more northerly regions, people followed the migrations of the caribou herds. The Eskimo and the Ainu (now confined to northern Japan) developed specialized fishing techniques.

We can deduce to some extent the means by which our preagricultural ancestors survived. Undoubtedly, certain of the hunting-gathering communities found themselves in more favorable locations than others. For example, it may be that forest margins provided such advantages. There people could gather food in the forest when hunting yielded poor results,

to return to hunting when the opportunities improved again. Possibly those communities could become semisedentary and stay in one place for a length of time, perhaps to create a more or less permanent settlement. That is one of the contributions the eventual development of agriculture made: it permitted people to settle permanently in one location, with the assurance that food would be available in seasons to come.

TERRAIN AND TOOLS

The capacity of early human communities to sustain themselves was enhanced by their knowledge of the terrain and its exploitable resources, and also by their ability to improve tools, weapons, and other equipment. Such technological advances came slowly, but some of them had important effects, each time expanding the resource base. The first tools used in hunting were simple clubs, tree limbs that were handle-thin at one end and thick and heavy at the other. These were used not only to strike trapped or pursued animals, but also to throw at hunted wildlife. The use of bone and stone and the development of spears made hunting far more effective. The fashioning of stone into hand axes and, later, handle axes, was a crucial innovation that enabled hunters to skin their prey and cut the meat. It was now also possible to cut down trees and to create even more efficient shelters and tools.

The controlled use of fire was also an early and critical achievement of human communities. Fires caused by natural conditions (lightning, spontaneous combustion of surface-heated coal) provided the first opportunities for control. Excavations of ancient settlement sites suggest that attempts were made to keep a fire burning continuously once it was captured. Later, it was learned that fire could be generated

by manual means, by rapid hand rotation of a wooden stick in a small hole, surrounded by dry tinder. Fire became a focus for the settlement, and the campfire became a symbol of the community. It was a means of making otherwise unpalatable foods digestible. It was used in hunting as a way to drive animals into traps or over cliffs. This greatly enhanced ancient communities' capacity to modify the natural landscape.

In the meantime, tools and equipment were developed as well. Perhaps the first tool of transportation ever devised was a strong stick carried by two men, over which hung the limp body of a freshly killed gazelle. Simple baskets were fashioned to hold gathered berries, nuts, and roots. Various forms of racks, packing frames, and sleds were developed to facilitate the transport of logs, stones, firewood, and other heavy goods. Fishing became a more important means of survival for communities situated along rivers or on shorelines, and primitive rafts and canoes soon made their appearance (controlled use of fire made the dugout canoe possible).

Even before the momentous developments involving animal and plant domestication, rudimentary forms of metal-working had emerged, although true **metallurgy**, the technique of separating metals from their ores, came later. There is evidence that fragments of native copper, nuggets of gold, and pieces of iron from meteorites were hammered into arrowheads and other shapes by craftspeople in ancient communities. Equipment made of stone also went far beyond simple knives and axes. Stone pots and pounders, grinders, and simple mills were developed to treat seeds, grains, and other gathered edibles. Meat was roasted and other foods were cooked; dietary patterns and preferences began to develop. Therefore, long before the revolutionary changes in animal and plant domestication occurred, preagricultural human communities and settlements were characterized by considerable complexity not only in dwelling forms, but also in tools, utensils and weapons, food preferences and taboos, and related cultural traits.

FISHING

It is quite likely that our distant ancestors learned to fish and added dried fish to their diets during the warming period that accompanied the melting of the latest of the Pleistocene glaciers. Perhaps 12,000 to 15,000 years ago, these glaciers melted, sea levels began to rise, and coastal flatlands were inundated as the seawater encroached on what we today call the continental shelves. We may surmise that until this time, coastal waters over most of the Earth had been cold and rough, and that shorelines were marked by steeply dropping relief. Therefore, coastal areas were not the most hospitable parts of the human habitat, and marine life was not nearly as plentiful as it was to become.

When glacial melting began and water levels rose, the continental shelves became shallow seas, full of coastal lagoons and patches of standing water. The sun warmed these thin layers of water very quickly, and soon an abundance of marine fauna flourished. Coastal regions became warmer, more habitable places to establish settlements, and numerous communities moved to the water's edge. There people were able to harvest all kinds of shellfish, and they learned to cut small patches of standing water off from the open sea, thereby trapping fish. And equipment was invented to aid in catching fish: harpoons, with which larger fish could be speared, and

baskets, suspended in streams where fish were known to run.

In several areas of the world, human communities were able to achieve a degree of permanence by combining hunting and fishing with some gathering, and by making use of the migration cycles of fish and animal life established during the changing climatic regimes. Native American peoples along the Pacific coast and on Arctic shores, the Ainu of Japan and coastal East Asia, and communities in coastal western Europe, caught salmon as they swam up rivers and negotiated rapids and falls. (Huge accumulations of fish bones have been found at prehistoric sites near such locations).

When the salmon runs ended, people stalked deer during their annual spring and fall movements, trapping them where they would habitually cross rivers or in narrow valleys they would traverse each season, or in some other favorable place. The summer salmon runs and the wildlife migrations of fall and spring would leave only the winter to endanger the permanence of the settlement. It had been learned that dried meat could remain edible for months and, undoubtedly, the coldness of winter provided natural refrigeration that retarded spoilage. However, the early fishers and hunters had their bad years, too, and sometimes the months of winter brought hunger and death. Such winters forced the riverside dwellers to abandon their settlements in pursuit of the distant herds.

The development of **fishing** as a means of total or partial subsistence was attended by the invention of a wide range of tools and equipment. Among the earliest innovations for catching fish and other aquatic life was a simple stone trap used in tidal channels. Stones would be removed during the incoming tide, permitting fish to enter an inlet; they would then be replaced at high tide. When the next low tide

drained the closed-off pool, water could seep out between the stones, but the fish would be trapped. Crescent-shaped stone traps on a tidal flat had the same effect, but traps were eventually refined by the creation of basket-like, wicker devices that could be used in stream channels, and nets of rough twine that could be stretched across an inlet or placed off a shoreline.

The fishing spear was to fishing what the arrow was to hunting, and various kinds were invented, ranging from simple pointed sticks to more refined harpoon-like spears. The use of hooks and bait led to the invention of hooks made from wood, bone, horn, and seashells. Most importantly, however, the resources of rivers and seas induced people to construct the means to pursue them, and from the first simple rafts there developed more elaborate canoes and sailing boats. The role of these innovations in the eventual worldwide diffusion of humankind hardly needs emphasis.

AGRICULTURAL ORIGINS

The earliest domestication of plants and animals was discussed in Part 1, where we concluded that this process may have begun nearly simultaneously in several areas of the world. The first conscious cultivation of plants may have involved root crops, not seed plants, and South and Southeast Asia may have been regions of agricultural innovation. Not long thereafter, the momentous developments that transformed the Fertile Crescent began, and the **First Agricultural Revolution** was in progress at least 10,000—possibly as long as 12,000—years ago. As we noted during our examination of language patterns, this First Agricultural Revolution, wherever it took hold, was accompanied by a modest population explosion, the out-migration of farmers and their new techniques, and the absorption of foraging (hunting-gathering) peoples in their paths.

Events in the Americas, where independent agricultural techniques developed much later than in South and Southwest Asia, prove that the First Agricultural Revolution extended over thousands of years. Here, too, it appears that the first cultivation of roots and cuttings was followed later by more sophisticated seeding methods.

When all the proven and postulated source regions of **plant domestication** are mapped, irrespective of the timing of the event, a surprisingly global distribution results (Fig. 27-2). Cultural geographers Joseph Spencer and William Thomas, in their book, *Cultural Geography* (1969), where this map first appeared, emphasized that particular local groupings of plants constituted the basic ingredients for each regional agricultural development zone. In the Mesoamerican region, for example (Region

6 in Figure 27-2), maize (corn), squashes, and several kinds of beans were basic to farming. In Southeast Asia (Region 1) on the other hand, taro, yams, and bananas were the leading food plants. In Southwest Asia (Region 4), the domestication process centered on wheat, barley, and other less significant grains.

The **agricultural origins** in China (Region 7) recently have attracted greater attention because the timing may have been earlier than was long believed—so early, in fact, that Chinese farmers may have been among the world's first. The food surpluses and population increases that developed here produced the wave of emigration that peopled Taiwan, the Philippines, and the Pacific islands.

Another agricultural source region of much interest lies in West Africa (Region 9). This region was recognized quite late, and it is not certain that independent invention occurred there. As Table 27-1 indicates, however, secondary domestication clearly did take place in West Africa.

Although Table 27-1 is very detailed, it is worth careful attention, if only because it reveals the enormous range of crops that were selected early and cultivated around the world. At various times and in different locales, groups of crops became mainstays of life. Soon knowledge needed to farm such crops productively diffused outward from these agricultural hearths. It is thought that millet, a small-seed grain, was introduced to India from West Africa, and sorghum, another grain crop, from West Africa to China. The watermelon spread from West Africa, first to nearby regions but eventually all over the world. Corn (maize) spread from Middle America into North America. Later, after the Portuguese brought it across the Atlantic, it became a staple in much of Africa. The banana came from Southeast Asia, as did a variety of yams. The process of dispersal unfolded slowly for many thousands of years, but the worldwide communications network established with the expansion of Europe during the past 500 years greatly accelerated it.

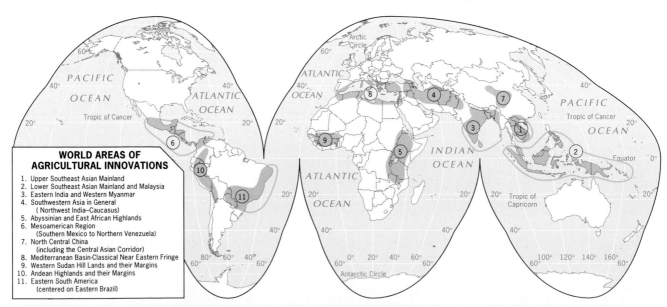

FIGURE 27–2 Cultural geographer Carl Sauer identified eleven areas where agricultural innovations occurred. From C.O. Sauer, *Agricultural Origins and Dispersals* (New York: American Geographical Society, 1952), p. 24.

ANIMAL DOMESTICATION

While our distant ancestors learned to plant crops, they also began to keep animals as livestock. As we saw in Chapter 22, the Nostratic proto-language contained the same word for *wolf* and *dog*, suggesting that domestication was in progress perhaps as long as 14,000 years go.

How did it happen? Perhaps **animal domestication** became possible when communities became more sedentary. Animals became part of the local scene and were kept as pets or for some other (e.g., ceremonial) purpose. Quite possibly, animals attached themselves to human settlements as scavengers, and even for protection against predators, thus reinforcing the idea that they might be tamed and kept. Any visitor to an African wildlife reserve can observe that when night falls, a permanent camp will be approached by certain species (gazelle, zebra, monkeys) that spend the night near and sometimes even within the camp's confines. With daybreak, the animals wander off, but the dangers of the next nightfall bring them back. Similar behavior probably brought animals to the settlements of the ancient forest farmers. Hunters might bring back the young offspring of an animal killed in the field and raise it. Such events probably contributed to the emergence of the concept of animal domestication.

Just when this happened is still a matter for debate. Some scholars believe that animal domestication came earlier than the conscious cultivation of the first plants, but others argue that animal domestication began as recently as 8000 years ago—well after the practice of crop agriculture had started. In any case, the goat, pig, and sheep became part of a rapidly growing array of domestic animals, and in captivity they changed considerably from their wild state. Archeological re-

search indicates that when such animals as wild cattle are penned in a corral, they develop types different from the original as time goes on. Protection from predators led to the survival of animals that would have been eliminated in the wild, and then inbreeding entrenched the modifications that nature would have wiped out. Our domestic versions of the pig, the cow, and the horse differ considerably from those first kept by our ancestors.

How did the ancient communities select their livestock, and for what purposes were livestock kept? It is thought that wild cattle may have been domesticated first for religious purposes, perhaps because the shape of their horns looked like the moon's crescent. Apparently, cattle were strongly associated with religious ritual from the earliest times and, as we have

noted, there remain societies today where cattle continue to hold a special position as holy animals. However, those religious functions may also have led to their use as draft animals and as suppliers of milk. If cattle could pull sled-like platforms used in religious ceremonies, they could also pull plows. If cattle whose calves were taken away continued to produce milk and needed to be milked to provide relief, cattle could be kept for that specific purpose.

As in plant domestication, it is possible to identify certain regions where the domestication of particular animals occurred. In Southeast Asia, the presence of several kinds of pigs led to their domestication, along with the water buffalo, chickens, and some other bird species (ducks, geese). In South Asia, cattle were domesticated and came to oc-

From the Field Notes

❝ Attempts to tame wildlife started in ancient times, and still continue. At Hunter's Lodge on the Nairobi-Mombasa road we met an agricultural officer who reported that an animal domestication experiment station was located not far into the bush, about 10 miles south. On his invitation, we spent the next day observing this work. In some herds, domestic animals (goats) were combined with wild gazelles, all penned together in a large enclosure. This was not working well; the gazelles continued all day to seek escape. By comparison, these eland were docile, manageable, and in good health. Importantly, they also were reproducing in captivity. Here, our host describes the program. ❞

TABLE 27–1 Chief Source Regions of Important Crop Plant Domestications
(after J.E. Spencer and W.L. Thomas)

A. PRIMARY REGIONS OF DOMESTICATIONS

1. The Upper Southeast Asian Mainland

Citrus fruits*	Yams*	Eugenias*	Teas
Bananas*	Cabbages*	Job's tears	Tung oils
Bamboos*	Rices*	Lichi	Ramie
Taros*	Beans*	Longan	Water chestnut

2. Lower Southeast Asian Mainland and Malaysia (including New Guinea)

Citrus fruits*	Yams*	Sugarcanes	Lanzones	Gingers*	Cardamom
Bananas*	Almonds*	Breadfruits	Durian	Brinjals*	Areca
Bamboos*	Pandanuses	Jackfruits	Rambutan	Nutmeg	Abaca
Taros*	Cucumbers*	Coconuts	Vine peppers*	Clove	

3. Eastern India and Western Burma

Bananas*	Rices*	Peas*	Vine peppers*	Kapok*	Sunn Hemp
Yams*	Amaranths*	Grams	Gingers*	Indigo	Lotus
Taros*	Millets*	Eggplants	Palms*	Safflower	Turmeric
Beans*	Sorghums*	Brinjals*	Mangoes	Jute	

4. Southwestern Asia in General (Northwest India-Caucasus)

Soft wheats*	Poppies*	Beets*	Apples	Plums*	Pistachio
Barleys*	Oats*	Spinach	Almonds*	Figs	Walnuts
Lentils*	Rye*	Sesames	Peaches*	Pomegranates	Melons
Beans*	Onions	Flax	Soft Pears*	Grapes*	Tamarind
Peas*	Carrots*	Hemp	Cherries*	Jujubes*	Alfalfa
Oil seeds*	Turnips				

5. Ethiopian and East African Highlands

Hard wheats*	Barleys*	Oil seeds*	Coffees
Millets*	Peas*	Cucumbers*	Castor beans
Sorghums*	Beans*	Melons*	Okras
Rices*	Vetches	Gourds*	Cottons*

6. Meso-American Region (Southern Mexico to Northern Venezuela)

Maizes	Sweet potatoes	Custard apples	Muskmelons	Cottons*
Amaranths*	Squashes	Avocados	Palms*	Agaves
Beans*	Tomatoes*	Sapotes	Manioc	Kapok
Taros*	Chilli peppers	Plums*		

---

cupy an important place in the regional culture. Later, the domestication of the Indian elephant was accomplished, although the use of the elephant as a ceremonial animal, as a beast of burden, and as a weapon of war never did involve successful breeding in captivity (and some scholars argue that the elephant never really became a domesticated animal). In Southwest Asia and adjacent areas of Northeast Africa, domesticated animals included the goat, sheep, and camel. In the expanses of Inner Asia, the yak, horse, species of goats and sheep, and reindeer were among domesticated animals. In the Mesoamerican region (including the Andes from Peru northward and Middle America to the latitude of central Mexico), the llama and alpaca were domesticated animals, along with a species of pig and the turkey.

Although regional associations such as these can be made, they should be regarded with caution. When animal domestication began, there were numerous species of a large variety of fauna, and these were domesticated simultaneously. The water buffalo, for example, was probably domesticated in Southeast and South Asia during the same period. Camels may have been domesticated in inner Asia as well as Southwest Asia. The pig was domesticated in numerous areas. Different species of cattle were domesticated in regions other than South Asia, where the Zebu emerged from early domestications. Dogs and cats attached themselves to human settlements very early

B. SECONDARY REGIONS OF DOMESTICATIONS

7. North-Central China (including the Central Asian corridor)

Millets*	Cabbages*	Rhubarb	Bush cherries*	Jujubes*
Barleys*	Radishes*	Mulberries	Hard pears*	
Buckwheats	Naked oat*	Persimmons	Apricots	
Soybeans	Mustards	Plums*	Peaches*	

8. Mediterranean Basin—Classical Near Eastern Fringe

Barleys*	Grapes*	Parsnips	Carrots*
Oats*	Olives	Asparagus	Garlic
Lentils*	Dates	Lettuces	Sugar beet
Peas*	Carobs	Celeries	Leek

9. Western Sudan Hill Lands and Their Margins

Sorghums*	Fonio	Peas*	Gourds*	Kola nut
Millets*	Yams*	Oil seeds*	Oil palms	
Rices*	Beans*	Melons*	Tamarind*	

10. Andean Highlands and Their Margins

White potatoes	Strawberries	Quinoa	Arrocacha
Pumpkins	Beans*	Oca	Ulluco
Tomatoes*	Papayas	Cubio	

11. Eastern South America (centered on Eastern Brazil)

Taros*	Pineapples	Cacao	Tobaccos
Beans*	Cashew nut	Passion fruits	
Peanuts	Brazil nut	Cottons*	

Source: J.E. Spencer and W.L. Thomas, *Introducing Cultural Geography*, 1978. Reproduced by permission from John Wiley & Sons.
*The asterisk indicates domestication of related species or hybridized development of new species during domestication in some other region or regions. Some of these secondary domestications were later than in the original region, but evidence of chronologic priority seldom is clear-cut.
The plural rendering of the crop name indicates that several different varieties/species either were involved in initial domestication or followed thereafter.
The term "oil seeds" indicates several varieties/species of small-seeded crop plants grown for the production of edible oils, without further breakdown
In regions 2 and 3 the brinjals refer to the spicy members of the eggplant group used in curries, whereas in region 3 the eggplants refer to the sweet vegetable members.
None of the regional lists attempts a complete listing of all crop plants/species domesticated within the region.
The table has been compiled from a wide variety of sources.

(they may have been the first animals to be domesticated) and in widely separated regions. Only a few animals have a comparatively specific source, including the llama and the alpaca, the yak, the turkey, and the reindeer.

DIFFUSION

Again, as in the case of crops, the dispersal of domesticated animals—first by regional expansion and later by worldwide diffusion—blurred the original spatial patterns of domestication. Chickens are now part of virtually every rural village scene, from Indonesia to Ecuador. Donkeys (probably first domesticated in Southwest Asia) now serve as beasts of burden the world over. Goats and sheep, cattle and horses, and dogs and cats are globally distributed. Even the elephant made its appearance not only in China, but also in ancient Europe as part of Hannibal's Carthaginian forces in combat against Rome.

Efforts at animal domestication still continue today. Among Africa's huge herds of antelope and other wildlife, there are species that may be capable of domestication as livestock, for example, the large eland, a potential source of meat in a region of imbalanced diets. Several rural experiment stations in Africa's savannalands are working to find ways to control and breed the region's wildlife. There has been some success with a species of eland, but less with various species of gazelles. Africa's powerful buffalo have not proven susceptible to domestication, however. Indeed, only about 40 species of higher animals have been domesticated worldwide.

Thus the process of animal domestication, set in motion more than 8000 (and perhaps as long as 12,000) years ago, still continues. Communities that were able to combine the cultivation of plants and the domestication of animals greatly lessened their dependence on single or limited food resources, and this achievement was critical in the evolution of human civilization.

SUBSISTENCE FARMING

We tend to think of agricultural geography in terms of cash cropping (i.e., farming for sale and profit), plantations, ranches, mechanization, irrigation, the movement of farm products, marketing exports and imports, and so on. When we associate certain crops and products with particular countries, these are usually cash commodities: Brazilian coffee, Colombian tobacco, Egyptian cotton, Australian wool, and Argentinian beef, for example. However, the fact is that a great number of the world's farmers are not involved in commercial agriculture at all. Hundreds of millions of farmers use their plots of land primarily to grow enough food to survive, sometimes with only marginal success. Their chief objective is subsistence, not profit. The shifting cultivators are **subsistence farmers**, as are nomadic pastoralists who follow their life-sustaining herds of livestock (see box, "Shifting Cultivation"). However, the subsistence farmers in many other areas of the world (Fig. 27-3) cannot migrate, nor do they practice slash-and-burn agriculture. They are confined to a small field of more fertile soil, from which they must intensively wrest the means to survive, year after year. And very

SHIFTING CULTIVATION

Ancient farmers learned to plant crops, but they knew little about soils, fertilizing, or irrigation. It is likely that they had to abandon areas in tropical and subtropical zones after the soils became infertile and the crops stopped growing. Then these farmers would move to another parcel of land, clear the natural vegetation, turn the soil, and try again. This practice of **shifting cultivation**, like hunting and gathering, still goes on today. In tropical areas, where the redness of the soil signifies heavy leaching of soil nutrients but where luxuriant natural vegetation thrives, a plot of cleared soil will carry a good crop at least one time, and perhaps two or three times. Then, however the area is best left alone, to regenerate its natural vegetative cover and to replenish the meager soil with nutrients lost during cultivation. Several years later, the plot may yield a good harvest once again.

Shifting cultivation is a way of life for many more people than hunting and gathering. Between 150 million and 200 million people sustain themselves this way in Africa, Middle America, tropical South America, and parts of Southeast Asia. At one time in human history, this was the chief form of agriculture in the inhabited world, just as hunting and gathering were previously the prevailing modes of existence. It goes by various names: *slash-and-burn* agriculture, *milpa* agriculture, *patch* agriculture, and others. As a system of cultivation, it has changed little over thousands of years of practice.

The controlled use of fire played a major role in the development of shifting agriculture as a technique of farming. Trees were cut down and all existing vegetation burned off. The resulting layer of ash contributed to the soil's residual fertility. The crops planted in these cleared patches were those found growing in their native regions: tubers in the humid, warm tropical areas, grains in the more humid subtropics, and vegetables and fruits of various kinds in cooler zones. Shifting cultivation gave ancient farmers their earliest opportunities to experiment with various plants, to learn the effect of weeding and crop care, to cope with environmental vagaries, and to discern the fading fertility of soil under sustained farming.

likely, they do not own the soil they till.

Scholars customarily classify agricultural societies into such types as "subsistence," "intermediate," and "developed" or, using different terms to express the same idea, "primitive," "traditional," and "modern." Actually, the world's many hundreds of societies lie along a continuum, and these divisions are for purposes of simplification and discussion and are not absolute. Neither is the definition of the term *subsistence* beyond debate. It is sometimes used in the strictest sense of the word, that is, to refer to farmers

who grow food only to sustain themselves and their families or communities, who use their natural habitat to find building materials and firewood, and who do not enter into the cash economy of their country at all. Those remaining societies where shifting agriculture is practiced, in remote areas of South and Middle America, Africa, and South and Southeast Asia, would qualify under this definition. On the other hand, farm families living at the subsistence level, but who sometimes sell a small quantity of produce (perhaps to pay taxes imposed by some authority), would not. Yet the term *subsistence* is

The process of shifting agriculture thus involves a kind of natural rotation system in which areas of forest are used without being permanently destroyed. It does not require a nomadic existence by the farmers, because usually there is a central village, with parcels of land in several directions, which are worked successively. When the village grows too large and the distances to workable areas become too great, a part of the village's population may move to establish a new settlement some distance away. This implies, of course, that population densities in areas of shifting agriculture cannot be very high; there has to be space. However, high population densities were rare in ancient times, and today shifting agriculture continues only in areas where population densities are far lower than, say, such crowded regions as the Nile Delta or Ganges Valley.

Shifting agriculture appears destructive, wasteful, and disorganized to people who are accustomed to more intensive types of farming. There are no neat rows of plants, carefully turned soil, or precisely laid-out fields. In fact, shifting agriculture conserves both forest and soil, its harvest yields are substantial given the environmental limitations, and it requires better organization than uninitiated observers might imagine. It also requires substantially less energy than more modern techniques of farming.

in times of scarcity, and that there is no point in expecting fertilizer to become cheaper and improved seed strains to solve age-old problems.

ALTERNATIVES

It is tempting to try to think of ways by which the subsistence agriculturalist might be helped to escape this situation, when the rewards might not only be higher productivity, but also better nutrition, healthier children, and longer lifer spans. European colonial powers put such thinking into practice in a variety of ways: by demanding taxes that compelled the farmers to raise some funds, by genuine assistance in the form of land consolidation schemes, soil surveys, crop research, and social incentives, and by initiating forced cropping schemes. The colonial powers were in the business of making a profit, and it was often frustrating to them that subsistence-farming areas could not be made to produce some gain. Forced cropping schemes were designed to solve this problem. If a

surely applicable to societies where small-plot farmers may sometimes be able to sell a few pounds of grain on the market, but where poor years threaten hunger, where poverty, indebtedness, stagnation, and (sometimes) tenancy are ways of life. The Native American peoples in the Amazon Basin, the

sedentary farmers of Africa's savanna areas, villagers in much of India, and peasants in Indonesia all share subsistence not only as a way of life, but also as a state of mind. Experience has taught the farmer and his father and grandfather before him that moments of comparative plenty will be paid for

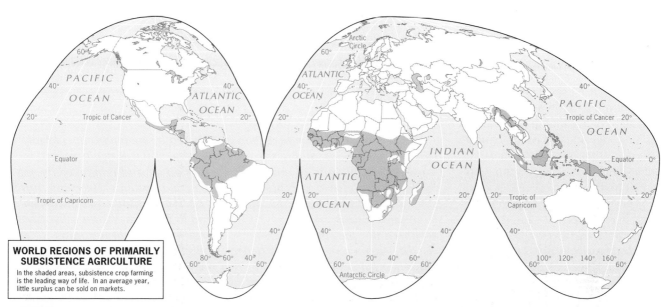

WORLD REGIONS OF PRIMARILY SUBSISTENCE AGRICULTURE

In the shaded areas, subsistence crop farming is the leading way of life. In an average year, little surplus can be sold on markets.

FIGURE 27–3 Definitions of subsistence farming vary. India and China are not shaded because farmers sell some produce on markets; in equatorial Africa and South America, subsistence allows little of this.

farming population in a subsistence area cultivated a certain acreage of, say, corn, it was compelled to grow a stipulated acreage of some cash crop—cotton, for example—as well. Whether this cotton would be grown on old land formerly used for grain, or on newly opened land, was the farmers' decision. If no new land was available, the subsistence farmers would simply have to give up food crops for the compulsory cash crops. In many instances, severe local famines resulted, and indigenous economies were disrupted and damaged. The colonial powers, however, enforced their cropping schemes regardless. Among the most notorious projects of this kind was the large-scale forced cropping project involving cotton in formerly Portuguese Moçambique.

If you read some of the literature relating to subsistence agriculture, you will find many scholars wondering, with less profit motive than the colonialists, how "to tempt [subsistence farmers] into wanting cash by the availability of suitable consumer goods," as agricultural specialists A.N. Duckham and G.B. Masefield said in their book, *Farming Systems of the World* (1970). We seem to have this compulsion to promote "progress" and "modernization," and one way to do so is to help subsistence farmers escape their cycle of stagnation. However, there are some aspects of subsistence farming that we should not lose sight of. Changing those farmers' attitudes could have destructive effects on their society's cohesion. Subsistence brings with it the communal holding of land, and society is of necessity quite equal: surpluses are shared by all in the community, the accumulation of personal wealth is restricted, and individual advancement at the cost of the group as a whole is limited. As economist A.H. Bunting wrote in *Change in Agriculture* (1970):

VON THÜNEN'S SPATIAL MODEL OF FARMING

One of the first economic geographers who tried to analyze the factors behind the location of agricultural activities was Johann Heinrich von Thünen (1783–1850), who experienced the Second Agricultural Revolution firsthand. Von Thünen farmed an estate not far from the town of Rostock in northeast Germany. Von Thünen studied the emerging spatial patterns of farming around towns such as Rostock, and he noted that one commodity or crop gave way to another in Rostock's hinterland—without any visible change in the soil or climate or terrain. When he mapped this pattern, he found that each town or market center was surrounded by a set of concentric rings within which the production of particular commodities or crops dominated.

Nearest the town, farmers produced commodities that were perishable and commanded high prices, such as dairy products and strawberries and similar specialized crops. In von Thünen's time, a belt of forest still stood around the town, used for firewood and building; but immediately beyond, the ring-like pattern of agriculture continued. In the next ring the crops were less perishable and bulkier, including wheat and other grains. Still farther out, livestock raising began to replace field crops.

Von Thünen used these observations to build a model of the spatial distribution of agricultural activities in his study area. As with all models, he had to make certain assumptions. (For example, he assumed that the terrain would be flat, that soils and other environmental conditions would be everywhere the same, and that no barriers to direct transportation to market would exist). Under such circumstances, von Thünen reasoned, transport costs would govern the use of land. The greater the distance to market, the higher the transport costs that had to be added to the cost of production of a crop or commodity. At a given distance to market, it would become unprofitable for a farmer to produce high-cost, perishable commodities—and market gardens would give way to field crops such as grains and potatoes. Still farther away, livestock raising would replace field agriculture.

Von Thünen's model (including the ring of forest) is often described as the first-ever effort to analyze the spatial character of economic activity (Fig. 27-4). He published it as part of a monumental series of works called *Der Isolierte Staat* (The Isolated State) which, in many ways, constitutes the foundation of a geographic field known today as *location theory*. To-

To allocate the land or manage the seasonal migrations, and to survive through hardship and calamity these societies have to be cohesive, communal and relatively little differentiated socially and economically: the chiefs, elders or elected headmen may be little richer than their fellows—to many of whom they are in addition linked by ties of relationship within the extended family. Mutual dependence, *imposed by the environment and the state of the agricultural art, is maintained and reinforced by genetic relationships. The community is enclosed socially and may even tend to be isolated culturally. Landlords and feudal rulers are unknown; the cultivators are poor but free.*

Perhaps this describes to some extent the ancient human commu-

day, his works still command geographers' attention, and **Thünian patterns** are discerned in many parts of the world. The hinterland of Chicago is one such place: take the train to Denver, and you cannot miss a certain concentric zonation that puts dairying and market gardening nearest the city, cash grains such as corn (plus soybeans) in the next "ring," more extensive grain farming and livestock raising beyond, and cattle ranching in the outermost zone. All this despite the fact that none of von Thünen's assumptions hold here: soil quality changes, as does the climate; other markets interfere; and transport faces constrictions. Around Chicago and in other areas, the logic of von Thünen's fundamental geographic notion is sustained by what we see in the field.

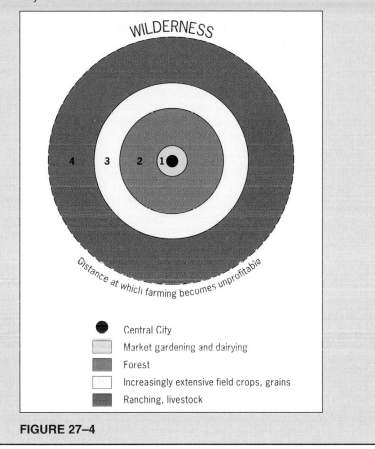

FIGURE 27–4

ble distribution of resources breaks down. The distribution of wealth becomes stratified, with poor and nearly destitute people at the bottom and rich landowners at the top. It is thought by some scholars that the innovation of irrigation may have contributed to the first differentiation of a subsistence society. There is also no doubt that the greatest number of societies that are today "intermediate" find themselves in their present situation as a result of the changes brought to their part of the world by expanding, modernizing Europe. In the aftermath, it is a bit ironic to call these the "traditional" societies, as is often done, for they are caught between traditions destroyed when the European invasion came and traditions found inadequate when the Europeans sought to introduce their own.

So in our modernizing world, there are still countless millions of farmers whose methods of cultivation, communities, and lifestyles relate quite directly to those prevailing thousands of years ago, when the blessings of agriculture first made life somewhat more secure.

SECOND AGRICULTURAL REVOLUTION

In our changing world, we sometimes tend to look on the Industrial Revolution as the beginning of a new era, the sole stimulus for development and modernization. In doing so, we lose sight of another revolution, which began even earlier and had enormous impact on Europe and other parts of the world: the **Second Agricultural Revolution**. This was perhaps a less dramatic development than the revolutionary changes that affected

nities that first developed agriculture as a way of life, and that have shown such amazing durability. Change the economic system and there will be unpredictable and incalculable modifications in the societal fabric, which indeed may break apart under the stresses of so-called "progress."

Of course, this *is* happening. Subsistence land use is changing to more intensive farming and cash cropping—even to the kind of mechanized, almost automated kind of farming in which huge pieces of equipment, not people, do the work and actually touch the soil. In the process, societies from South America to Southeast Asia are profoundly affected. Land once held communally is parceled out to individuals when cash cropping becomes a major element in life. The system that ensured an equita-

Europe's industries and cities, but it had far-reaching consequences nonetheless. It began slowly, and at first, took hold in a few widely scattered places. Unlike the Industrial Revolution, its origins and diffusion cannot be readily traced. However, after centuries of comparative stagnation and a lack of innovation, farming in seventeenth- and eighteenth-century Europe underwent significant changes. The tools and equipment of agriculture were modified to do their job better. Methods of soil preparation, fertilization, crop care, and harvesting improved. The general organization of agriculture, food storage, and distribution were made more efficient. Productivity increased to meet rising demands. Europe's cities were growing, and their growth produced new problems for the existing food supply systems. By the time the Industrial Revolution gathered momentum, progress in agriculture made possible the clustering of even larger urban populations than before. Had an agricultural revolution not been in progress, the course of the Industrial Revolution would undoubtedly have been very different.

The Industrial Revolution contributed importantly to sustain the Agricultural Revolution. The harnessing of power made mechanization possible, and tractors and other machines took over the work done for so long by animals and human hands. The cultural landscape of commercial agriculture in some regions changed as much as the urban landscape of industrializing cities, as fields of wheat and other grains, sown and harvested by machine, cloaked entire countrysides. Even where tradition continued to prevail—in the vineyards of France's Bordeaux and the ricefields of East Asia—the impact of modernization was felt, if not in harvesting methods, then in research leading to improved fertilizers and more productive crop strains.

Farming, as we are aware, is by no means possible everywhere on this Earth. Vast deserts, steep mountain slopes, frigid polar zones, and other environmental obstacles prevent agriculture over much of our globe. Where farming *is* possible, the land and soil are not put to the same use everywhere. The huge cattle ranches of Texas represent a very different sort of land use than the dairy farms of Wisconsin—or the paddies of Taiwan.

Within a few miles of the subsistence lifestyles of forested Middle America lie rich plantations whose products are shipped by sea to North American markets. We can observe the differences around our own cities: travel by car or train from Chicago, Cincinnati, or St. Louis into the countryside and you can see the land use change. Close to the city, the soil is used most intensively, perhaps for vegetable gardens of crops that can be sent quickly to the nearby markets. Farther away, the fields are larger and time becomes a lesser factor. The cornfields of Iowa are dotted by grain elevators for storage and shipment, and some of the grain may be consumed not in Chicago or St. Louis, but in India or Bangladesh.

Still more distant from the Midwestern cities, we enter the pasturelands of the Great Plains, almost an opposite extreme from those vegetable gardens: the land is allocated by the hundreds of square miles rather than by the acre.

UNDERSTANDING THE LAYOUT

What factors and forces have combined to produce the spatial distribution of farming systems existing today? (See box, "von Thünen's Spatial Model of Farm-

ing.") This is a very complicated question, to which no complete answer may be possible. It not only involves the effect of different conditions of climate and soil, variations in farming methods and technology, market distributions, and transportation costs, but also has to do with the domination of the world by an economic structure that favors the developed Western world: the United States, Canada, and Europe.

Decisions made by colonial powers in Europe led to the establishment of plantations, from Middle America to Malaya, the products of which were grown not for local markets, but for consumers in Europe; United States companies similarly founded huge plantations in the Americas. The European and Western impact transformed the map of world agriculture just as the pattern of European farming was changed by the Agricultural Revolution. The end of colonial rule did not simply signal the termination of the agricultural practices and systems that had been imposed on the formerly colonial areas. Even food-poor underdeveloped countries must continue to grow commerical crops for export on some of their best soils where their own food should be harvested. Agricultural systems and patterns long entrenched are not quickly or easily transformed.

THIRD AGRICULTURAL REVOLUTION

Earlier in this book, we discussed the "Green Revolution" which has pushed back the specter of hunger at a time when the population explosion seemed to threaten the kind of global famine Malthus predicted two centuries ago. This **Third Agricultural Revolution** still is in progress, based on new, higher-yielding strains of grains and other crops developed in laboratories by modern techniques of genetic engineering. Some scholars now suggest that this revolutionary development will spell the end of the threat of famine because ever-better strains will be invented. Others argue that there will be a limit to the capacities of the new strains, so that population expansion will again reach the limits of agricultural production. In 1994, a somber study by Lester Brown predicted that the benefits of the Third Agricultural Revolution would be used up by the third decade of the twenty-first century. Weeks after its appearance, researchers announced the development of a new strain of rice that would counter the threat Brown had described. The race between population and food production is not over—and should the planet undergo significant climate change, even the Third Agricultural Revolution may not be enough to overcome the challenge. More on this in the next chapter, when we investigate modern commercial farming.

KEY TERMS

Agricultural Origins
Agriculture
Animal Domestication
Farming
First Agricultural Revolution
Fishing
Metallurgy
Plant Domestication
Second Agricultural Revolution
Shifting Cultivation
Spatial Economy
Subsistence Farmers
Third Agricultural Revolution
Thünian Patterns

28

COMMERCIAL AGRICULTURE ON THE LAND

While von Thünen was studying his Isolated State as a closed system totally unaffected by outside influences, the Europe of von Thünen's time was in the process of mobilizing much of the world to support its own sustenance and comfort. Europe's cluster of colonizing powers functioned much like the central city in the Isolated State model, as a market for agricultural products from all around, but with an added dimension: Europe manufactured and sold in its colonies the finished products made from imported raw materials. Thus the cotton grown in Egypt, Sudan, India, and other countries colonized by Europe was bought cheaply, imported to European factories, and made into clothes, many of which were then exported and sold, often to the very colonies where the cotton had been grown in the first place.

Obviously, we should not view world agriculture in the kind of isolation assigned by von Thünen to his experimental model. The evolution of a worldwide transport network, of ever-growing capacity and efficiency, continually changed

Geographica

- Evidence of Thünian patterns, resulting from domination by the world's wealthier market clusters, can be discerned even on a small-scale world map of agriculture.

- Suitable natural environments plus plentiful labor led colonial powers to establish plantation- and luxury-crop agriculture that persists to this day, decades after decolonization, largely because poorer countries need the cash this continues to generate.

- In general, the world's two key grain crops represent different societies: wheat tends to be grown on large landholdings by mechanized means in the richer countries, whereas rice is grown labor-intensively on small plots in poorer societies. Exceptions: wheat is the staple in northern China and in northwest India.

- Mediterranean agriculture, a specialized form of farming under a dry-summer climatic regime, yields typical crops in five world areas where these conditions prevail.

the competitive position of various agricultural activities. The beef industry of Argentina, for example, secured a world market when the invention of refrigerated ships made long-distance transportation possible for what was previously a highly perishable commodity. Euro-

pean colonial powers did not simply permit farmers in their dependencies to decide on the crops they would grow for export to Europe: they frequently imposed the cultivation of specific crops on traditional farmers. American economic power made itself felt in

Middle and South America, creating an empire of plantations and orienting production to the U.S. market. Thus the forces tending to distort any world von Thünian zonation are many.

Yet we can observe in this global pattern of agriculture, represented by Figure 28-1, elements of the same sort of order that von Thünen recognized in his Isolated State. We have already noted that the Industrial Revolution had a major impact on agriculture, and when we attempt to describe the relationships between the urbanized core areas of the world and agricultural patterns, we should view those urban centers as urban-industrial cores, not merely as markets. To these urban-industrial cores, in Europe, North America, Japan, and Russia, flow agricultural (and industrial) raw materials and resources from virtually all parts of the inhabited world. Superimposed on the regional zones and the continental-scale zonation we saw in North America, therefore, is a world spatial system that also exhibits elements of concentric zonation.

EMERGING WORLD PATTERNS

It is important to recognize, as we examine world agriculture in the following pages, that the pattern we observe has come about only partly through the decision-making processes envisaged by von Thünen. In the poorer countries (many of them former dependencies) much of non-subsistence farming is a left-over from colonial times, and this cannot simply be abandoned. Such "cash" farming is needed because it continues to provide a source of revenue that is badly needed, even if the conditions of sale to the urban-industrial world are often not favorable. In the Caribbean region,

whole national economies depend on sugar exports (the sugar having been introduced by the European invaders centuries ago). Selling the harvest at the highest possible price is an annual concern for these island countries, but they are not in a good position to dictate: sugar is produced by many countries in various parts of the world, and also by farmers in the technologically developed countries themselves (Fig. 28-1). Thus it is the importing countries that fix tariffs and quotas, not the exporters. In the ideological conflict with Cuba, the United States cut off its imports of Cuban sugar. While the Cuban export trade was cushioned by alternative buyers in Canada and the Soviet sphere, this was a staggering blow. The wealthy, industralized importing countries can threaten the very survival of the economies of the producers—much like the farmers in von Thünen's Isolated State, who were at the mercy of decisions made by the buyers in the central-city marketplace.

There are occasional signs that the producing countries are seeking to unite, to present a common front to the rich, importing countries (as the OPEC states did in the oil production arena during the 1970s). As we know, the OPEC cartel eventually was defeated, and such collective action is even more difficult for countries with other products to sell. First, the wealthy importing countries can make deals with non-cartel countries to break any joint monopoly. Second, the withholding of produce in the exporting countries may stimulate domestic production among the importers. For example, although cane sugar accounts for more than 70 percent of the commercial world sugar crop each year, farmers in the United States, Europe, and Russia produce sugar from sugar beets. Already in Europe and Russia, these beets produce 25 percent of the annual world sugar harvest. Collective

action by countries producing sugarcane could therefore easily serve to drive up that percentage.

COTTON AND RUBBER

Farming in many former colonial countries, therefore, was stimulated and promoted by the colonial powers, representing their imperial interests. **Cotton** and **rubber**, two industrial crops, are good examples. Today, cotton is grown in the United States, in Northeast China, and in the Central Asian Republics of Turkestan. Another large producer, India, owes its cotton fields to colonial Britain. However, cotton cultivation was promoted on a smaller scale in numerous other countries: in Egypt's Nile Delta, in the Punjab region shared by Pakistan and India, in Sudan, Uganda, Mexico, and Brazil.

Cotton cultivation expanded greatly during the nineteenth century, when the Industrial Revolution produced machines for cotton ginning, spinning, and weaving that multiplied productive capacity, brought prices down, and put cotton goods within the reach of mass buyers. As they did with sugar, the colonial powers laid out large-scale cotton plantations, sometimes under irrigation (e.g., the famed Jezira Scheme, in the triangle between the White Nile and Blue Nile Rivers in Sudan). The colonial producers would receive low prices for their cotton. The European industries prospered as cheap raw materials were converted into large quantities of items for sale at home and abroad. Today, many of the former colonial countries have established their own factories producing goods for the domestic market, and synthetics, such as nylon and rayon, are giving cotton industries increasing competition. Still the developed countries have not stopped buying cotton, and for some developing countries, cotton sales remain important in the external economy.

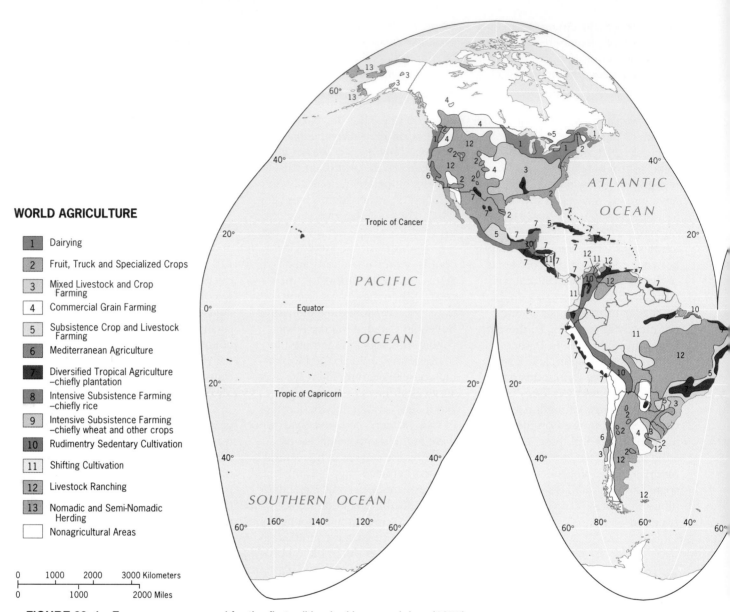

WORLD AGRICULTURE

1	Dairying
2	Fruit, Truck and Specialized Crops
3	Mixed Livestock and Crop Farming
4	Commercial Grain Farming
5	Subsistence Crop and Livestock Farming
6	Mediterranean Agriculture
7	Diversified Tropical Agriculture –chiefly plantation
8	Intensive Subsistence Farming –chiefly rice
9	Intensive Subsistence Farming –chiefly wheat and other crops
10	Rudimentry Sedentary Cultivation
11	Shifting Cultivation
12	Livestock Ranching
13	Nomadic and Semi-Nomadic Herding
	Nonagricultural Areas

FIGURE 28–1 From a map prepared for the first edition by Hammond, Inc. (1977).

Japan, the United Kingdom, and Western European countries continue to import cotton fiber, but the developing countries have a formidable competitor for those markets from cotton growers in the United States, whose cotton exports also go there.

The case of rubber is more complicated. Initially, rubber was a substance not cultivated but gathered, collected from rubber-producing trees that stood (among many other tree species) in equatorial rainforests, mainly those of the Amazon Basin in northern South America. Those were the days, around 1900, when the town of Manaus on the Amazon River experienced a veritable rubber boom. A similar, if less spectacular, period of prosperity was experienced by the rubber companies exploiting the Congo (Zaïre) Basin in Africa.

The boom in wild rubber was short-lived, however. Ways were sought to create rubber-tree plantations, where every tree—not just some among many—would produce rubber, where the trees could be given attention, and where collecting the rubber would be more efficient and easier. Seedlings of Brazilian rubber trees were planted elsewhere, and they did especially well in Southeast Asia. Within two

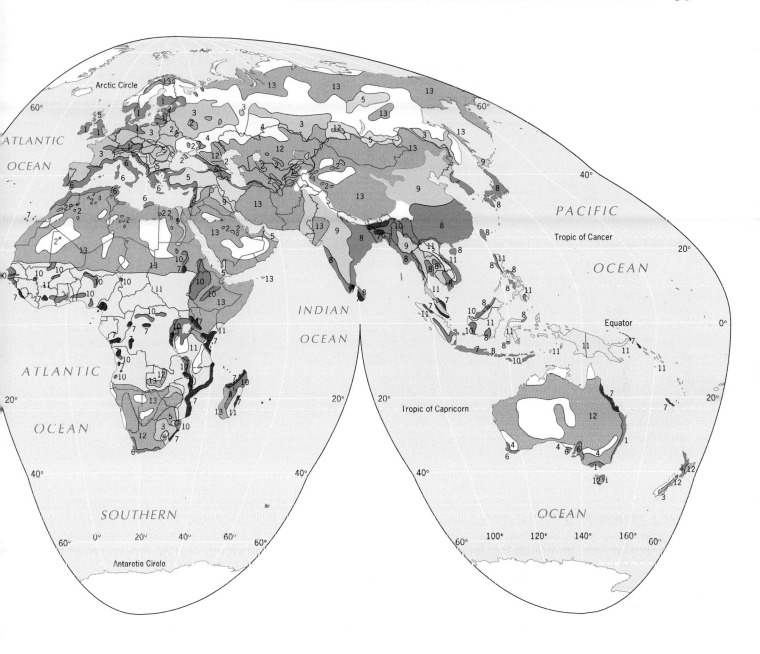

decades after the Amazonian rubber boom, nearly 90 percent of the world's rubber production came from new plantations in colonial territories in Malaya, the Netherlands East Indies (now Indonesia), and their neighbors.

As time went on, more and more uses for rubber were found, and consumer demand grew continuously. The advent of the automobile was an enormous boost for the industry, and most of the rubber now produced is still used to manufacture vehicle tires. Then World War II forcefully brought the need for alternative sources for rubber to U.S. attention, since Japan had occupied much of Southeast Asia. This stimulated the production of synthetic rubber, and although plantation-produced rubber came back to some extent after the war, synthetic rubber has remained in the lead. In 1994, world production was approximately 15 million tons, 10+

million of it synthetic; of the remaining 4.8 million tons, 78 percent continued to be produced on the plantations of Southeast Asia.

The expanded development of rubber plantations in Southeast Asia, rather than in sections of the Amazon Basin or the Congo (Zaïre) Basin, relates less to environment than to the availability of labor. The colonial powers were aware that Southeast Asia combined conditions of tropical environment and labor availability that neither Amazon South America nor equatorial Africa could match. Eventually, a large-scale African rubber industry developed in Liberia (West Africa), an industry destroyed during the country's disastrous civil war of the 1990s. Lately, efforts have been made to introduce the plantation system along the Amazon River in the heart of northern Brazil.

LUXURY CROPS

Similar considerations—a combination of suitable environment and available labor—led the European colonial powers to establish huge plantations for the cultivation of such **luxury crops** as tea, cacao, coffee, and tobacco. **Coffee** was first domesticated in Northeast Africa (in the region of present-day Ethiopia), but today it thrives in Middle and South America, where approximatley 70 percent of the world's annual production is harvested. The United States buys more than half of all the coffee sold on world markets annually, and Western Europe imports most of the remainder.

Compared to coffee, **tea** is consumed in greater amounts in the areas where it is grown: India, China, Sri Lanka, and Japan. Whereas coffee is the beverage cultivated and consumed dominantly in the Americas, tea is the Eurasian equivalent: it goes from the Asian producing areas to the United Kingdom and the rest of Europe. Tea is a rather recent addition to Western diets. It was grown in China perhaps 2000 years ago, but became popular in Europe only during the nineteenth century. The colonial powers (mainly the British) established enormous tea plantations in Asia, and thus began the full-scale flow into European markets, which persists strongly today.

From the Field Notes

❝ In Durban, South Africa, I was reminded of an old field lesson: if you cannot do an excursion and want to know what the city's rural environs yield, go to the farmers' market. On Grey Street near the port city's downtown is just such a market. Citrus fruits were the bargain of the day, grown on the sunny slopes of the Province of Natal. ❞

GLOBAL DISTRIBUTION OF COMMERCIAL AGRICULTURE

The total area occupied by such crops as rubber, coffee, and tea constitutes but a tiny fraction of the cultivated land on our planet. So small are these patches of high-value luxury crops that they appear as mere dots on maps such as Figure 28-1. The larger regions depicted on the world map of agriculture represent the crops of sustenance: rice, wheat, and other grain farming.

Figure 28-1 emphasizes that virtually all countries have more than one kind of agricultural economy. Even at the small scale imposed by the global view our map represents, it is clear that numerous countries are regionally divided into subsistence-farming areas and commercial-crop production zones. Later, when we investigate the secondary and tertiary economic activities, we will see that this regionalism also prevails in these sectors. In China, for example, the eastern provinces along the Pacific coast are strongly commercial economies, while much of the interior remains dominantly subsistence-based.

Commercial agriculture is the hallmark of modern, highly developed economies, although one version of it, **plantation agriculture**, persists in underdeveloped countries side by side with subsistence. In Figure 28-1, plantation agriculture (7 in the legend) can be seen to continue in countries in tropical Middle and South America, Africa, and South Asia. Laid out to produce bananas and sugar, coffee and cocoa in Middle and South America, rubber, cocoa, and tea in West and East Africa, tea in South Asia, and rubber in Southeast Asia (among other specialized and luxury crops), these plantations have survived the period of decolonization and continue to serve the rich markets of the world. Many plantations in the underdeveloped world still are owned by European or American individuals or corporations, but even when they were taken over by governments of newly independent countries, they were kept operating—because they were an important source of needed income from foreign sources.

On the map, it can be seen that by far the largest areas of commercial agriculture (1 through 4 in the legend) lie in more developed countries outside the tropics. **Dairying** (1) is widespread in the northeastern United States and in northwestern Europe. Fruit, truck, and specialized crops (2), including the market gardens von Thünen saw around Rostock, can be found in the eastern and southeastern United States and in widely dispersed small areas where environments are favorable (note that major oases show up on the map in Africa's Sahara and in Central Asia). Mixed livestock and crop farming (3) extends over much of the eastern United States, Western Europe, western Russia, and over smaller areas in Uruguay, Brazil, and South Africa. Commercial grain farming (4) prevails over the southern prairie provinces of Canada, the Dakotas and Montana in the United States, as well as Kansas and adjacent areas. Spring **wheat** (sown in the spring and harvested in the summer) grows in the northern zone, and winter wheat (sown in the autumn and harvested in the spring of the following year) is used in the southern area. An even larger belt of wheat farming extends from Ukraine through Russia into Kazakhstan. By comparison, the Argentinian and Australian wheat zones are areally smaller, but their exports figure importantly in world trade.

Note that commercial **rice** growing does not appear as a separate item in the map legend, although we know that it exists: the United States is the world's leading exporter, followed by Thailand and Vietnam. The reason has to do with the nature of production. The wheat farming just described is carried out on huge landholdings with large machines that sow and har-

THE THIRD AGRICULTURAL REVOLUTION

Twelve thousand years ago, momentous developments were taking place in a few small areas of Southwest Asia: the practice of sowing seed and harvesting grain heralded the First Agricultural Revolution. Three hundred years ago, a Second Agricultural Revolution was in progress as improved equipment, better farming methods, and other innovations greatly increased the productivity of European farming. The Industrial Revolution stimulated this modernization of farming and helped spread it around the world.

Over the past several decades, a **Third Agricultural Revolution** has been in progress. Also called the **Green Revolution**, this revolution occurred—and continues to develop—in the laboratory and the plant nursery, not in the fields and paddies. It is the product of the age of **biotechnology**.

The Third Agricultural Revolution may be said to have begun in the 1960s, when scientists at a research institution in the Philippines crossed a dwarf Chinese variety of rice with an Indonesian variety, and produced IR8. This "artificial" rice plant had a number of desirable properties: it developed a bigger "head" of grain and had a stronger stem that did not collapse under the added weight. IR8 yielded substantially better than either of its "parents," but the researchers were not satisfied. In 1982, they produced IR36, bred, according to a report in *Science*, from 13 parents to achieve genetic resistance against 15 pests and a growing cycle of 110 days under warm conditions, thus allowing three crops per year. By 1992, IR36 was the most widely grown crop variety on Earth.

In September 1994, scientists announced yet another breakthrough; the development of a strain of rice substantially more productive even than IR36. Still greater achievements may lie ahead: researchers at the international Rice Research Institute are reported to be working to breed a "super rice" that will not have to be transplanted as seedlings, but can be seeded directly in the paddy soil. It will have the virtues of its predecessors but, it is anticipated, will yield nearly twice as much rice per acre than is average for strains in current use. The charting of the genome of rice (the 12 chromosomes that carry all of the plant's characteristics) is under way, and so it will also be possible to transform rice genetically so that it will continuously acquire more desirable properties. Not only will it yield better: it also will be increasingly resistant to diseases and pests.

Other crops, from wheat and corn to tomatoes and bananas, already have benefited from research in biotechnology. Advances in this field have produced methods to fatten livestock faster and to improve the appearance of fruits. The results of the ongoing revolution in agriculture already are evident: the disastrous famines of the past have abated despite the growth of humanity, the result of increased yields of grains since the 1960s. Scientists now talk of the possibility that entirely artificial crops and animals may some day be created in their laboratories. The Third Agricultural Revolution may transform the world in ways not yet imaginable.

From the Field Notes

❝ The technology of refrigeration has kept pace with the containerization of seaborne freight traffic. When we sailed into the port of Dunedin, New Zealand, I was unsure of just what those red boxes were. Closer inspection revealed that they are refrigeration units, to which incoming containers are attached. Meats and other perishables can thus be kept frozen until they are transferred to a refrigerator ship. ❞

vest the grain. Rice continues to be grown on small plots and is labor-intensive, so that subsistence and export-production (at least in Southeast Asia) occur side by side. Significant rice exports notwithstanding, the majority of Southeast Asia's farmers are subsistence farmers. Since the map, at this scale, must generalize, Southeast Asia appears as a dominantly subsistence grain-growing area. Here, the benefits of recent "Green Revolution" developments are especially evident (see box, "The Third Agricultural Revolution").

Even a cursory glance at Figure 28-1 reveals the wide distribution of, and large areas devoted to, **livestock** ranching (12). The raising of cattle for meat and of sheep for meat and wool developed, as the map suggests, in the wake of European colonization. In addition to the large cattle-ranching areas in

the United States, Canada, and Mexico, much of eastern Brazil and Argentina are devoted to it, along with large tracts of Australia and New Zealand, as well as South Africa. You may see a Thünian pattern here: livestock ranching on the periphery, with the consumers concentrated in the great cities of the eastern United States and Western Europe. Refrigeration has overcome the perishability problem, and volume has lowered the unit cost of transporting beef, lamb, and other animal products. Much of the land devoted to this form of extensive commercial agriculture is unsuitable for cultivation (see the map of world climate, Figure 2-3) because it is arid or semiarid. But the natural vegetation in these areas cannot always sustain the herds, especially during prolonged droughts. This leads to ecological damage and, in some

areas, to desertification. In recent years, the surging popularity of fast-food chains that serve hamburgers had led to the deforestation of wooded areas in order to open up additional pastures for beef cattle, notably in Central and South America.

Only one form of agriculture mentioned in the legend of Figure 28-1 refers to a particular climate: **Mediterranean agriculture** (6). As the map shows, this kind of specialized farming occurs in areas where the dry-summer Mediterranean climate prevails: along the Mediterranean's shores, in part of California, in central Chile, at South Africa's Cape, and in parts of southwestern and southern Australia. Here grows a special combination of crops: grapes, olives, citrus fruits, figs, certain vegetables, dates, and others. From these areas come many of the world's wines; these and other commodities flow to distant markets because Mediterranean products tend to be popular and command high prices.

Numerous factors have shaped, and continue to influence, the world distribution of subsistence and commercial agricultural systems. As we have noted, history and tradition play their roles, as do environment and technology. Many governments encourage their people to limit the number of offspring because the universal desire is to lift the population above the subsistence level. Some governments, notably the former Soviet Union's and Maoist China's, tried to control agricultural output by expropriating all private farms and creating collective farms and agricultural communes, a giant experiment that resulted in untold hardship, tens of millions of deaths, and mixed results in terms of output. Today, reprivatization is under way in both countries, and the profit motive is again driving agriculture.

Most of all, the map carries the

imprints of what von Thünen saw in the first place: the capacity of the market to control the land and its farmers. The range and variety of products familiar to us on the shelves of city supermarkets still is uncommon in this world of simple meals and often inadequately balanced diets. A global network of farm production is oriented to that one-fifth of the world's population that is highly urbanized, wealthy, and powerful, and that lives in the developed realms of the world. The farmers in distant lands may even be less able to make decisions on the use of their land than those in von Thünen's Isolated State, for the developed world continues to decide what will be bought at what price, and it is the wealthy countries that have the choices, not the poor. The colonial age may have

come to an end, but, as Figure 28-1 reminds us, the age of dependence has not.

KEY TERMS

Biotechnology
Coffee
Commercial Agriculture
Cotton
Dairying
Green Revolution
Livestock
Luxury Crops
Mediterranean Agriculture
Plantation Agriculture
Rice
Rubber
Tea
Third Agricultural Revolution
Wheat

29

FARM AND VILLAGE: RURAL SETTLEMENT FORMS

In the first two chapters of Part 9, we have viewed farming from the earliest times to the present, in subsistence and commercial contexts, and as a global system dominated by the wealthier countries of the Northern Hemisphere's Middle Latitudes. We noted humankind's growing capacity to overcome environmental limitations and to create higher-yielding varieties of crops through research in biotechnology. In our modern world, high-tech agriculture still coexists with slash-and-burn cultivation.

Such variations are reflected in the dwellings and villages of farmers. These components of the cultural landscape can tell us much about the well-being, inventiveness, natural environments, and even problems and fears of their occupants. In this chapter, we survey the homes and villages of the world's diverse countrysides.

Geographica

- **Nearly half the world's population still resides in rural villages, hamlets, and dispersed dwellings.**

- **The forms, functions, materials, and spacing of rural dwellings reveal much about region and culture, including social and economic opportunities and needs, natural environments, and traditions.**

- **Wattle, wood, brick, and stone are among building materials that give regional expression to domestic architecture.**

- **Village forms reflect historical circumstances, physiographic conditions, and prevailing necessity, and vary from linear and clustered to circular and grid-patterned.**

DWELLINGS AND VILLAGES

Shelter ranks high on the list of human needs. Throughout the world, in the coldest regions as well as in the warmest, in the rainiest areas as well as in deserts, people build dwellings that are the focal points of their daily lives. These dwellings have several functions, and protection against cold, wind, and

From the Field Notes

❝ I drove northward from Bergen, Norway, and then inland. Roads narrowed from four lanes to two, then to one, and turned from asphalt to dirt. Houses became simpler. Here, near Stalheim, is a house that well represents the area, where the building materials are in ample supply. Wood forms the walls; large slabs of slate create the roof. ❞

precipitation is only one of them. In residential quarters people find privacy, a certain degree of comfort, a place to store accumulated belongings, and even an opportunity to display their values and achievements.

Geographers have many reasons to be interested in the housing and settlements of the world's human population. A house reveals much about a region and culture: the building materials that are available, the social and economic needs and the cultural traditions of the occupants, and the natural environment that the house must withstand. In the *form* of houses, we can sometimes see one culture give way to another. If you were to take a trip southward on a Nile riverboat, you could observe that the square, flat-roofed Arab houses of Egypt and northern Sudan yield to the round, steep-roofed African houses of southern Sudan and Uganda. House types can be valuable indicators of

cultural traditions and transitions. In the layout and *function* of houses, we get an impression of social values and economic needs: in areas of rural Eastern Europe, for example, people and some of their livestock live under the same roof, so that the building is part house and part barn. Consider the contrast with an "elaborate" suburban American home, in which different rooms serve different purposes such as cooking, bathing, eating, and sleeping. The *materials* used in the construction of dwellings reflect local availability and purpose. In the cold, forested areas of Northern Europe, the log cabin developed, with its thick walls and pitched roof to withstand extreme cold and heavy snowfalls. In tropical areas, cold weather is not a problem, and you will find leaves, branches, and matting used in the construction of dwellings.

We are also interested in the *spacing* of houses in various parts

of the world. There is a relationship between the density of houses and the intensity of crop cultivation, but it is necessary to generalize carefully. In the U.S. Midwest, for example, individual farmhouses lie quite far apart in what we call a **dispersed settlement** pattern: still the land is intensively cultivated, but by machine rather than by hand. In Java, the populous Indonesian island, you run into a village every half-mile or so along a rural road, and settlement here is defined as nucleated. Land use is just as intense, but the work is done by animals and by human hands. So when we consider the density of human settlement as it relates to the intensity of land use, we should keep in mind the way in which the land is cultivated.

Nucleated settlement is by far the prevalent rural residential pattern in the world's agricultural areas. When houses are grouped together in tiny clusters or *hamlets*, or in slightly larger clusters we call *villages*, their spatial arrangement also has significance. Sometimes, it is possible to identify the prevailing culture just by looking at the ground plan of a village. In parts of Africa where cattle form the dominant means of existence, the houses in a village are arranged in a circle (that of the chief or headman will be larger and somewhat separated) surrounding a central corral where the livestock are kept at night. In the low-lying areas of Western Europe, the houses of a village are often situated on a strip of higher ground (such as a dike or a levee), and when you look at the map of such a village, it is simply a row of evenly spaced units, perhaps on two sides of a road but often on only one.

In such different regions as Eastern Europe, western Nigeria, and northern Spain, the houses of older villages are not regularly arranged, but are closely clustered together, a defensive measure that included the construction of a surrounding outer wall. Whereas the need for such defenses has disappeared, the traditional village still remains on the landscape and people continue to build new compact villages reminiscent of those of bygone centuries. The arrangement of houses in villages therefore takes many different forms. Tradition, political domination, physiographic limitation, and many other factors underlie the development of the villages we see today.

HOUSING AND LANDSCAPE

In the most recent centuries of human history, the basic functional social group has been the nuclear family, and when we discuss houses and villages, we tend to think of these in terms of the single-family unit. There is some evidence that the family is breaking down in some cultures, including our own. It is also likely that the family was not yet the fundamental human group when people first began to build shelters. Thus we may assume that our distant ancestors lived in groups the size of bands, containing from a dozen to 50 or 60 individuals, which moved from place to place, setting up campsites for temporary residence when the opportunity presented itself. We can only speculate on the appearance of these campsites, because nothing very permanent was built there. Perhaps holes were dug into the ground and covered with branches and leaves to serve as shelters. Later, these burrows may have been improved and enlarged, with posts to support rafters across the roof. In any case, it is unlikely that the cave was humanity's earliest dwelling, as we might be led to believe. Our ancestors lived in many areas of the world, including those where no convenient natural housing was available. Various efforts to construct shelters undoubtedly occurred wherever

the earliest human communities clustered.

Such communal living (of which there are now several modern versions) gave way to family structures as human society developed, and dwellings came to accommodate single families, rather than other groups. As the capacity to domesticate animals, grow crops, and store food increased, so did the size and complexity of human groupings. Communities emerged that were larger and more highly organized than those of early bands, and among their adopted rules were those governing marriage, inheritance, food allocation, domestic duties, and so on. It also became necessary to construct buildings other than those used for living. (The chief or headman's residence must appear more imposing than others, and facilities were needed for the storage of food and implements, for guest quarters, and for the sheltering of livestock.) Thus we begin to see some functional differentiation in buildings. Even to-

day, we can observe human groups whose lifestyles and dwellings must resemble those of many thousands of years ago. In the Kalahari Desert of Southern Africa, some San communities are bands that probably resemble those of the distant past: their shelters are often mere windbreaks made of a few branches across which an animal skin is stretched. Campsites are occupied only temporarily, for the people must hunt wandering animals in their constant struggle for survival. Elsewhere in Africa, villages are permanent, and larger communities build the kinds of centralized facilities that give evidence of the differentiation and increasing complexity of society, as in the case of the cattle-raising peoples in the eastern highlands.

There is ample evidence that human communities existed in widely separated areas even 100,000 years ago, occupying warm as well as cold regions, moist as well as dry zones, coastal as well as interior locations, and river valleys as well as

From the Field Notes

66 Between the Tana River and the Somali border, the bush becomes thinner and building materials are less easy to come by. Still, some houses here are very substantial, requiring a large amount of wood for their frames. This house not far from Ijara is ready for roofing (thatch will be used) and wall construction. The walls are made of a mixture of pebbles and soil mixed with termite-mound clay, dried and hardened by the sun. 99

uplands. Early migrations propelled human groups from familiar habitats into unfamiliar environments, and conflict and war drove others away from known surroundings into new and sometimes difficult situations. Variable environmental conditions—floods, storms, severe cold, and heavy winter snows—confronted people from the beginning, and as soon as communities began to build shelters, the struggle to adapt to—and protect against—the elements advanced. Thus the physical structure built by ancient human groups differed from the very beginning in form, content, appearance and function, initiating traditions which have in some cases survived for thousands of years. People in flood-prone areas learned to construct stilt houses. Where heavy snow prevailed, the steep-sided roof proved to be a protection against the enormous weight of a winter's accumulation. Nomadic peoples needing lightweight, transportable shelters developed various kinds of tents. Among the truly amazing adaptations was the invention of the igloo by Inuit peoples in the frozen northlands, using as building material the very snow and ice against which protection was sought.

Thus the diversity of dwellings around the world has ancient origins. The distribution pattern was further complicated by human movement and migration, processes that diffused building practices along numerous routes. Sometimes, the introduction of new ideas in construction led to the abandonment or modification of indigenous practices. Acculturation during the period of European colonial expansion had such an effect in many parts of the Americas, Africa, and Asia. In other cases, societies continued their building methods even when they were displaced. Some builders of stilt houses, for instance, continued to construct elevated dwellings even after they had been

relocated to areas where floods were not a threat. Building on stilts had become an integral part of their culture, not to be quickly replaced by other technologies.

Cultural geographers have tried to reconstruct the diffusion of building forms, a task that has at times proved to be extremely difficult. Barns and other outbuildings, and even fences, have been the subjects of such studies, and influences have been traced halfway around the world. (For example, historical linkages from Western Europe to New England to California, and ultimately to Hawaii, have been verified). The dynamic geography of **domestic architecture** is a field full of fascination—and countless complexities.

CHANGING RESIDENTIAL TRADITIONS

Although cultural traditions promote continuity and permanence in building types and styles, time does bring change. In certain parts of the world—areas of Arab culture, for example, dwellings appear much as they did centuries ago. In portions of Africa, too, dwellings in rural areas and even in some cities are still built according to centuries-old principles. You can walk some of the streets of Kano, Nigeria, and readily imagine that you are in another age. On the other hand, the effects of modernization can be seen even in the remote African bush, where many a house builder now substitutes corrugated metal sheeting for the thatch formerly used on the roof. Today, the floor plan of the house may remain the same, but the building materials are no longer exclusively those of the region. Thus it is appropriate to recognize four groups of dwellings:

unchanged-traditional, modified-traditional, modernized-traditional (where change affects both building materials and floor plan), and modern.

UNCHANGED-TRADITIONAL DWELLINGS

Unchanged-traditional houses (permanent and temporary) are those in which layout, construction, and appearance have not been significantly altered by external influences. Certainly, such traditional houses and other dwellings are modified over time—but as a result of internal cultural development, not external borrowing or acculturation. Such is the domestic architecture that gives character to distinctive cultural landscapes in Arab towns, African villages, rural settlements in China, and other places remote from or resistant to foreign influences. Villages all over the world contain a mixture of traditional and modified housing, but unchanged-traditional dwellings do survive. These range from wood-framed, mat-walled, thatch-roofed Micronesian houses to rough stone structures in Native American areas of Andean South America; also included are mud-walled houses in China, log cabins in Northern Europe, and cloth tents in North Africa.

Traditional houses of European and other Western cultures also belong in this category of domestic architecture. Log houses with sod-protected roofs in Scandinavia, single-story stone houses with thatched roofs in Ireland, and barrel-tiled, whitewashed houses in Spain all represent local or regional traditions. In North America, also, parallel traditions can be recognized. In Canada, domestic architecture is chiefly represented by two types of houses, the French-Canadian house of Quebec and the British-Canadian house of

Ontario. The French-Canadian house tends to be more elaborate, with characteristically curved roof lines, attic or dormer windows, and a raised balcony across the front; attached to one side is a summer kitchen closed off during the severe Canadian winter. The British-Canadian house occurs most commonly in Ontario, and it is rather more compact and austere. Stone and brick are used in the construction of these two traditional Canadian house types.

In the United States, three types of traditional houses can be identified: the New England, Middle Atlantic, and Southern styles. The New England house, unlike its Canadian counterparts, consists of wood-frame construction. This style dates from colonial times (the Cape Cod type developed later), and it diffused from its source area across the northern United States to Michigan, Wisconsin, and beyond (see Fig. 29-1). The Middle Atlantic style originated as a one-room log cabin with a stone chimney and fireplace at one end. Later, additional rooms, a porch, and a second floor were added. In the South, the size and construction of (mostly wood-frame) houses reflected the modest means of most of their builders and the comparative warmth of the climate. Smaller than New England houses, Southern dwellings were of the single-story variety (sometimes with a small attic room) and possessed a characteristic porch. Often, the house was built on a raised platform to reduce interior heat. In low-lying areas, houses were built on raised stone foundations to guard against flood damage.

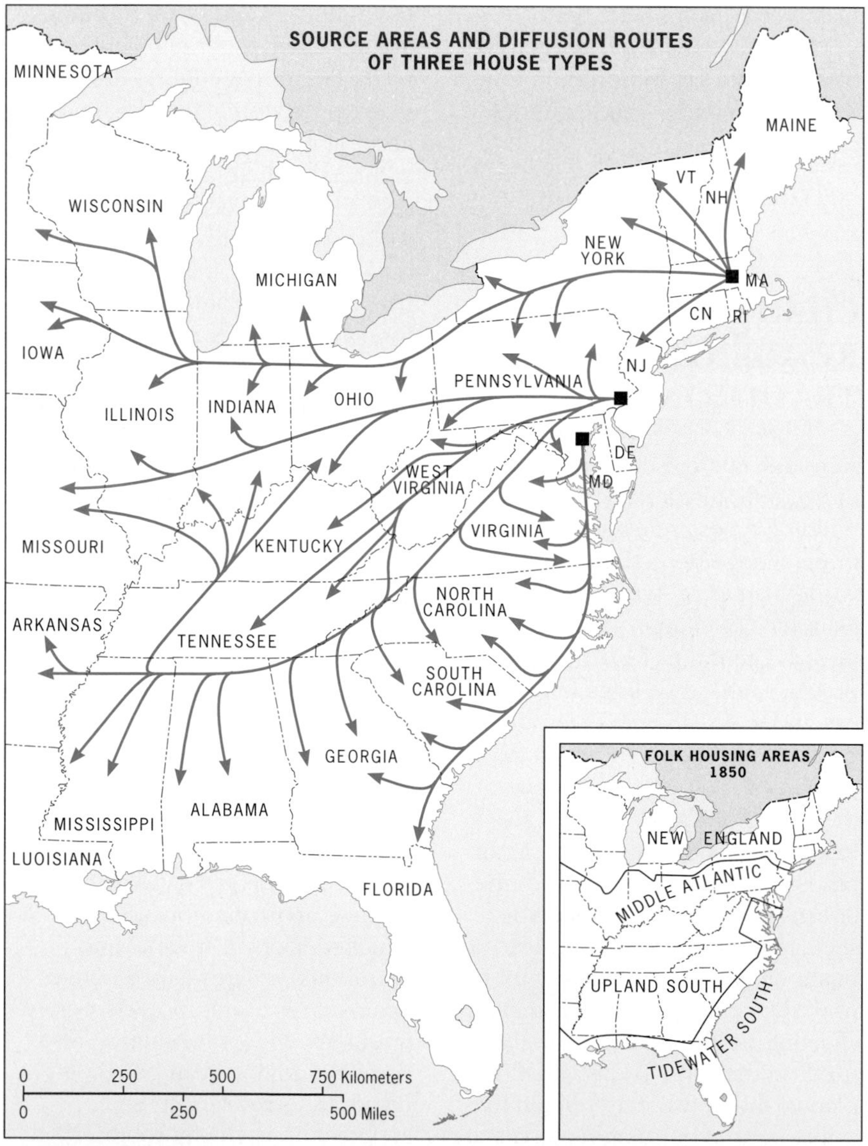

MODIFIED-TRADITIONAL DWELLINGS

As noted previously, traditional houses the world over have been modified in many ways. The second category, modified-traditional, refers to dwellings for which change has come in the form of new building materials, or with the addition of elements that do not fundamentally alter their original structure or layout. The use of corrugated iron panels as a roofing material, for example, has diffused to many areas of the world and has affected housing everywhere. From Polynesia to West Africa, traditional thatch-roofed dwellings stand adjacent to houses with corrugated-iron roofs. Certainly, this does not improve the aesthetics of the cultural landscape, because the iron sheeting is subject to ugly rusting. However, the iron roof, although hot, protects better against rain and moisture, does not accommodate disease-carrying vermin, and often serves as a catchment for much-needed fresh water.

Other modifications of traditional houses include the introduction of shuttered openings (to serve as

FIGURE 29–1 New England, Middle Atlantic, and Southern house styles and their diffusion. From F.B. Kniffen, "Folk Housing: Key to Diffusion," *Annals* of the AAG 55 (1965), p. 560.

windows) in formerly solid walls, and the provision of wooden doors where something less durable once served. The wall openings are especially important in village houses in Africa, where fires burn inside closed dwellings and smoke-related diseases (especially glaucoma, an affliction of the eyes) are prevalent. Improved air circulation helps reduce the negative effects of the smoke, which is especially important for the health of the newborn and young children. Another modification of traditional dwellings is the raised floor. Without changing the basic structure, the practice of raising the floor has the effect of reducing the moisture level inside the dwelling, further inhibiting discomfort and disease. Colonial governments (not only the Europeans in Africa and Asia, but also the Japanese in the Pacific) encouraged the raising of floors by builders of traditional dwellings. Still other improvements are less obvious, yet important. Thatched roofs were improved through the introduction of wire mesh and superior metal ties. Walls made of sun-dried brick were coated with mortar rather than smeared with mud. While these did not materially change the appearance of the traditional dwelling, they did result in better protection and greater durability.

MODERNIZED-TRADITIONAL DWELLINGS

In the case of modern-traditional house types, the modifications are more far-reaching, involving not only the materials used in building but also the floor plan and general layout. Elements of the traditional house persist, but modernization has overtaken tradition. When the New England house type emerged (from European traditions), it had no two-car garage, a single bathroom quite unlike those of today, and almost none of the interior specialization that characterizes

From the Field Notes

❝ A large number of buildings in the town of Torshavn (Faroe Islands) display a characteristic Scandinavian feature: a sod-covered roof. It conserves warmth during the cold winter, but it does present rot problems (judging by the repairs under way all over town) in the supporting wood. ❞

modern versions. Remnants of traditional styles continue to exist—for example, in the Cape-Dutch facades of South Africa, upturned roof lines of Japan, and "Mediterranean" forms in Central and South America—but these are mere vestiges of the originals. European styles have also changed traditional housing in former colonies, where the idea of multiple rooms and specialized facilities has produced imitations of Western houses displaying a mixture of modern and traditional forms and building materials.

MODERN DWELLINGS

The United States undoubtedly displays the modern house type most ubiquitously. This dwelling category has itself become an American tradition, a reflection of U.S. technology, upward mobility, practicality, comfort, and hygiene—and massive suburbanization. There was a time when the two-story house reflected a family's socioeconomic

status and well-being, but the practical advantages of the ranch-style house (once called the "California bungalow") overtook such considerations. From the designs of Elbert Hubbard in Buffalo and Frank Lloyd Wright and his associates in Oak Park, outside Chicago, the ranch-style house took root in southern California and diffused in various forms to suburbs where it was patently less practical, with its low-angle roof, screened porches and patios, pool and deck, barbecue pit, and other space-demanding, energy-consuming qualities. Aesthetic properties are not among the leading attributes of modern domestic architecture in the United States, but there are compensations. With its plumbing and electrical systems, temperature- and humidity-control mechanisms, unparalleled kitchen and bathroom facilities, and automated equipment, ranging from garage-door openers to pool-maintenance devices, the modern American house makes up in technology for what it lacks in style.

Modern domestic architecture everywhere tends to sacrifice traditional in favor of practicality and efficiency. Modern house types in and around Tokyo, Sydney, Nairobi, São Paulo, and Vancouver are far more similar to each other than to the traditional houses in the regions these cities represent. Clearly, tradition remains strongest in the domestic architecture of rural areas.

STRUCTURE AND MATERIALS

Dwellings may also be studied from the viewpoint of their physical structure, the degree of their complexity, and the materials from which they are constructed. Cultural geographers formally differentiate among dwelling types by classifying combinations of these criteria. At one end of the scale, there is the cave dwelling (people still live in caves in many areas of the world), the windbreak of the wandering, food-gathering peoples, the pit dwelling (built and modified as long as human societies have existed), and the simplest of "huts" (little more than stacked-up sticks, branches, grass, and leaves). At the other end, there are complex and imposing mansions in the wealthy suburban areas of Western cities, as well as millions of single-family homes of simpler character that are nonetheless also a world away from those most rudimentary dwellings of the underdeveloped world. Between these ends of the continuum, there are dozens of intermediate dwelling types, ranging from the beehive-shaped Zulu house (an elaboration of "hut" construction) to the quite substantial and complex houses of several cultures of

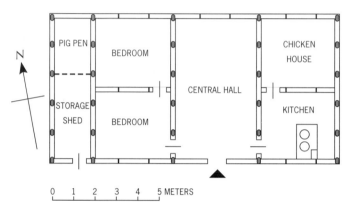

FIGURE 29–2 A traditional house from Jiangsu Province, China. From R.G. Knapp, *China's Traditional Architecture* (Honolulu: University of Hawaii Press, 1986), p. 80.

South, Southeast, and East Asia.

Maps of the distribution of dwelling-structure types would show regions where particular characteristics prevail (Fig. 29-2). In China, for example, farmhouses as well as village houses are now most often built of baked-mud walls and thatch roofs, but older villages contain houses with walls of brick and roofs made of tile. Such older villages are especially concentrated in the Chang (Yangtze) Jiang's middle basin, in the hinterland of Shanghai. China's numerous less durable dwellings reflect the scarcity of building materials and the explosive population growth of recent times, which created widespread housing shortages. In Africa, the transition

from the Arab dwelling of the north to the traditional African house of mid-continent is a significant indicator of the overall passage from one geographic realm to another. The intermittent existence of Arab and African structures side by side within the heart of the transition zone reveals the interpenetration of the two culture regions in still another way.

In South America, a map of house structures would reveal not only the diffusion of modern and modernized-traditional forms, but also the persistence of older styles, such as the rough-stone houses of the Andean Indians, the mud-walled dwellings of the west and south, and the Amazonian Indians' structures of branches and leaves. Maps of this kind have been drawn for local regions, but not for entire geographic realms. However, as in the case of indigenous languages, it is often difficult to discern the truly traditional from the introduced—the original from the modified.

BUILDING RESOURCES

A particularly useful way to approach the world geographic study of dwellings involved the materials from which they are constructed. Houses made principally of *wood* still show some regional association with the world distribution of forests, although wood as a building material is, of course, shipped to all world areas today. The log house, which probably originated in the cold forest zones of Northern Europe, became a haven for the early European settlers of northern North America, where the forests were plentiful and the cold at least as severe. Comparatively few log houses are still being constructed. These days, log cabins are built in remote areas as recreational, rather than as year-round residential structures. You could build a log house or cabin with an ax, but modern sawmills now produce cut lumber that makes building with wood even easier. Thus the frame house became commonplace in and near forested areas. In this type of structure, walls and ceilings are attached to a frame of cut lumber. The walls may be constructed of wooden planks or board, and the ceilings of paper; both products are derived from trees. The roof is normally made of wood as well, with a protective layer of tarpaper, shingles, or tiles.

Houses made primarily of wood occur in a zone across Eurasia that extends from central Scandinavia and Eastern Europe through Russia to the Pacific coast, including Korea and Japan as well. Wood-frame houses prevail throughout North America from New England to California, and from Florida to Alaska. In South America, wood is the primary building material for houses in southern Chile and southeastern Brazil, which are both areas where this commodity is available from local forests. Wood also figures prominently in domestic architecture in Australia and New Zealand.

Where wood is not so readily available, houses are likely to be built of *brick*. We tend to define a brick by what is familiar to use: a hard, cement and oven-baked block of various standard sizes. However, elsewhere in the world, bricks are made of the Earth itself. In the Middle East (and nearer home, in the southwestern United States and Mexico), wet mud is poured into wooden frames, allowed to dry briefly, and then placed in the sun to harden. These bricks are then used in wall construction, more moist mud forming the mortar, and after the newly built structure dries out, the walls are smeared with mud as well. For the roof, a frame of sticks, branches, and straw is covered with mud. In arid regions, such dwellings are adequate protection against both heat and cold; when infrequent heavy rain occurs, it raises havoc, because the sun-baked mud bricks never become as hard as the oven-baked bricks and tiles used in the Western world. Variations of the method just described occur in many parts of the world.

Sun-dried brick is widely used as a building material. It is the main component of traditional dwellings, not only in the Middle East and the Arab culture realm generally, but also in much of Middle and South America (especially west of the Andes and south of Brazil), the savannalands of Africa, and northern India. Also, the mud-brick house is a common form in timber-poor, fairly dry northern China, and it is thought by some scholars that the homebuilding method used there may have diffused from the Middle East. The fired or baked brick, a more modern innovation, has become a major element of modern construction all over the world. Traditional houses in a Mexican village are made of sun-dried brick, but in the towns and cities, homes are built with oven-baked bricks. So it is in the cities of the Arab realm, Africa, and South America (although traditional dwellings cluster on the outskirts of the modern town sectors). In a few areas of the world, notably in Southern Africa and central China, the use of fired brick had developed as a traditional building method before modern building technologies were introduced.

Houses also are built of natural *stone*. In the high Andes of Peru, house-builders pile rough stones on top of each other, without mortar, caulk the remaining openings with mud, and fashion a thatched roof.

Traditional European homes, such as English cottages, also are made of natural stone with cement mortar, and have thatched roofs. Southern and interior Egypt, where natural building stone is plentiful, is another area where stone houses are widely built. Building with available stone developed as **traditional architecture** in central and southern India, Xizang (Tibet) and neighboring areas of western China, Yucatan and adjacents parts of Maya-influenced Mexico, and south-central Africa (where the great ruins of Zimbabwe evince the higher level of technology achieved in stone building). Overall, however, wood and mud brick are far more common building materials. In the United States and other Western countries, natural stone is also sometimes used as a decorative building material to adorn homes already constructed mainly of wood and brick.

For want of a better term, we identify as *wattle* those numerous houses built from poles and sticks, woven into a tight network, and then plastered with mud. In fact, these dwellings are built of a combination of wood (the poles and sticks) and the same material from which mud bricks are made. Many African houses are constructed this way, with a thick thatched roof to protect against the occasionally heavy rains.

Regions where poles, sticks, bamboo, bark, leaves, and similar materials are used for building purposes obviously correspond to zones where these are readily available. In terms of population numbers, Southeast Asia is undoubtedly the leading region in this category, as the traditional houses of populous Indonesia, the Philippines, and the mainland countries south of China and east of India are made of wattle. In Africa, this dwelling-material type prevails along the west coast and throughout the lowland basin at whose heart lies Zaïre. And in South America, the sparsely populated Amazon Basin provides ample building material for its traditional, Native American settlements.

Between the wattle dwellings of the equatorial rainforest areas and the earthen construction of the subtropical drier zones lie the low-latitude regions where *grass and brush* form principal building materials. The African savannalands, including interior West Africa south of the Sahel, East Africa's highlands, and drier South Africa's veld, form the major region of this type, but many traditional dwellings on the Africa savanna also contain sun-dried mud. Grass-and-brush construction also prevails in the Brazilian and Venezuelan highlands poleward of the forested Amazon Basin. Northern Australia's indigenous peoples also build their simple dwellings from the savanna's vegetation.

From the Field Notes

Our enumeration of building materials is by no means complete. The Zulu's beehive-shaped dwellings are made almost exclusively of African tall grass. The tents of nomadic peoples are made of cloth or skins. Even blocks of ice, as noted, are used as building materials. Bamboo serves in parts of Southeast Asia. In northernmost Europe, sod may be piled on the roof to enhance insulation, and in summer you can see goats grazing on the new grass that grows up there. People live permanently on boats and in trailers. Again, the variations are almost infinite, and comprehensive regionalization is a prodigious task, which cultural geographers have hardly begun to tackle.

❝ ❝ Wood continues to serve as a building material for private homes in many areas of the world. The two–story house in Bergen, Norway (left) reflects the environment there: large windows for maximum light on the many cloudy days, and a high–pitched roof of tile to cope with weight from snowfalls. Wood is as plentiful in Scandinavia as stone is in the Transcaucasus. A typical house in Armenia (right) is built of stone, as are the outbuildings and fences; the metal roof has a low pitch, and windows are small. ❞ ❞

DIFFUSION OF HOUSE TYPES

The houses of the world's numerous cultures display great variety in form and layout. When people migrate, they carry with them notions of how a home should be planned and constructed, but in new environments, those ideas become modified. Differences in available materials and new environmental conditions cause changes that contribute to the development of new styles.

A good example of this process comes from the eastern seaboard of the United States. Professor Fred Kniffen, who for many years researched house types and their diffusion in North America, concluded that three principal house types appeared, more or less simultaneously, in the east-coastal United States: in New England, in the Middle Atlantic region, and in the "Tidewater South" of lower Chesapeake Bay (Fig. 29-1). From these sources, the diverse building styles diffused westward and southward in several parallel streams, creating, by the middle of the nineteenth century, three distinct **folk-housing regions** (see the inset in Figure 29-1).

We have only to look around us to see how things have changed since about 1850. In the Midwest and the South and elsewhere, we still encounter many single-family houses that are structural variations of the Atlantic-coast types described by Professor Kniffen. However, we also find L-shaped ranch houses, T-shaped homes with the bedrooms

From the Field Notes

❝ In almost every village houses were in need of repair, and stacks of mudbricks were ready for use. The bricks (top photo) look sturdy when fresh, but it is evident that they do not withstand the ravages of time very well. They are made from a porridge of clayey mud mixed with batches of straw cut into four-inch-thick pieces. In the (bottom) photograph of the village, taken in the Chinese province of Yunnan, the mud-plaster that is smeared over the brick walls can be seen to be eroding, and the bricks are exposed, the (also mud) mortar failing. Note that some of the houses have traditional thatch roofs, while others have barrel tiles. ❞

separated in the two wings of the T, and U-shaped houses with a patio and perhaps a pool in the enclosed courtyard.

The present cultural landscape thus is a composite of older and newer forms. Figure 29-1 shows the **diffusion routes** of the three original types into the U.S. interior. Note that the New England house type remained confined to a northern corridor, whereas the Middle Atlantic and Lower Chesapeake types spread more widely into the heartland. What the map does not show is the eastward diffusion of ranch-style houses from the West. This house style evolved during the 1920s in California and became a cultural symbol of a lifestyle. Expansion diffusion had carried Eastern styles westward, but now western styles diffused in the opposite direction, first along the Sunbelt corridor and then more widely. But the ranch house is designed for a balmy climate and outdoor living; its single-story, open construction is not really suitable for climates with considerable extremes. Nevertheless, ranch houses now are found virtually everywhere in the United States, even in areas where they are not appropriate. This results from a period of **maladaptive diffusion**; image and symbol took precedence over practicality. This is only one of many examples; the New England style diffused as far as Hawaii, where clusters of these houses still stand—strangely out of place in a tropical environment.

VILLAGES

We now turn our attention from individual dwellings to *settlements*: purposely grouped, organized clusters of houses and nonresidential buildings. The smallest such clusters are known as **hamlets**, which may contain only about a dozen such buildings. The largest clustered settlements, of course, are the world's great cities, the topic of Part 10 of our study. Our present interest is in the smallest of settlements—hamlets, and **villages**.

Before proceeding, we should note that the definition of a village varies. We all have a mental picture of a village as a small settlement without high-rise buildings or large commercial enterprises, but it is difficult to be precise. What is the upper limit of population? When does a village become a town? In Canada, that limit, by official decision, is 1000 people; in the United States, 2500. In India, a place can have up to 5000 residents and still be classified officially as a village. And in Japan, a settlement cannot be called an "urban" place until it has 30,000 inhabitants or more. International statistics reporting "rural" (village) and "urban" (city) populations, therefore, must be standardized, or they will be meaningless.

VILLAGE FORMS

Rural settlements, in any case, tend to be comparatively small. People who live in them either farm the surrounding land or provide services to those who do the farming. Thus they are the settlement clusters most closely and directly connected to the land, and most of their inhabitants' livelihoods depend, directly or indirectly, on the cultivation of nearby farmland. As such, they tend to reflect historical circumstances or prevailing necessity. Japanese farming villages, for example, are so tightly packed together that only the narrowest passageways remain between the houses. This reflects the need to allocate every possible square foot of land to farming; villages must not spill over where crops could grow.

In the hilly regions of Europe, you will frequently see villages clustered on hillslopes, leaving the level land for farming. Often, an old castle sits atop the hill, and so the site had two advantages: protection as well as land conservation. In many low-lying areas of Western Europe, villages are positioned on dikes and levees, so that they often take on *linear* characteristics (Fig. 29-3A). Where there is space, the house and outbuildings may be sur-

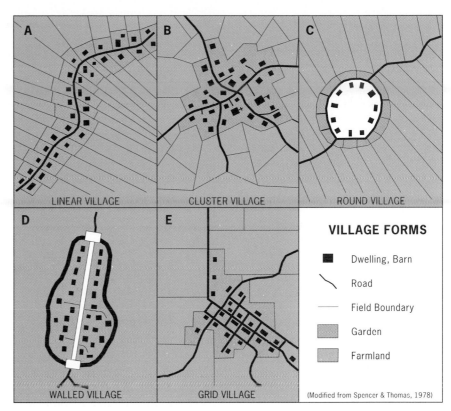

FIGURE 29–3 Representative village layouts. From J.E. Spencer and W.H. Thomas, *Introducing Cultural Geography* (New York: Wiley, 1978), p. 154.

rounded by a small garden; the farms and pasturelands lie just beyond. Where no such terrain limitations exist, the village may attain *cluster* characteristics (Fig. 29-3B). It may have begun as a small hamlet at the intersection of two roads, and then developed by accretion. The European version of the East African circular village, with its central cattle corral, is the *round* village or *rundling* (Fig. 29-3C). This layout was first used by Slavic farmer-herdsmen in Eastern Europe, and later modified by Germanic settlers.

In many parts of the world, farm villages were fortified to protect against the invasion of marauders. Ten thousand years ago, the first farmers in the Middle East's Fertile Crescent faced attacks from the horsemen of Asia's steppes and clustered together to ward off this danger. In Nigeria's Yorubaland, the

farmers would go out into the surrounding fields by day, but retreat to the protection of walled villages at night. Villages, as well as larger towns and cities in Europe, were frequently walled and moated. When the population became so large that people had to build houses outside the original wall, a new wall would be built to protect them as well. *Walled* villages (Fig. 29-3D) still exist in the rural landscape of many countries, reminders of a turbulent past. More modern villages, notably planned rural settlements, may display their origins by a *grid* pattern (Fig. 29-3E). This is not, however, a twentieth-century novelty. The Spanish invaders of Middle America laid out grid villages and towns centuries ago, as did other colonial powers elsewhere in the world, as they organized their acquired possessions. In urban Africa, as we will see in Part 10, this is a pervasive colonial imprint.

Although the twentieth century has witnessed unprecedented urban growth throughout the world, the majority of the world's people still reside in villages and rural areas. In China alone, more than 800 million people (in a country of over 1.2 billion) inhabit villages and hamlets. In India, with a population exceeding 940 million, three of four persons live in villages. Small rural settlements are home to most of the inhabitants of Indonesia, Bangladesh, Pakistan, and a host of other developing countries, including all of those in Africa. Thus the agrarian (farm) village remains the most common form of settlement on Earth today, industrial and technological revolutions notwithstanding. The pulse of village life is still the main human experience.

REGIONAL CONTRASTS

Regionally, village life is indeed a variable experience. It is a far cry from the modern comforts of a farm village in Wisconsin, with its paved streets, electricity, water supply, and other urban amenities, to the poverty-ridden, dusty, isolated, single-well village of central India. In the developed world, modernization has penetrated all but the remotest rural areas, and on most of the farmlands, mechanization prevails. In the underdeveloped world, farm villages lie far removed from the sources of change, backs are bent to the soil, and material comforts are few. In South Asia, there may be as many as 1 million farm villages, most with fewer than 1000 inhabitants. From a distance, many appear picturesque, rising from emerald-green ricefields or clinging to rocky Deccan slopes. However, walk the paths and see the poorly fed, underdressed children, the open sores, the insects, the absence of sanitation, the inadequate housing, and you will marvel at these

people's capacity to cope and to face an always difficult and uncertain future.

It is therefore not easy to generalize about village life in a worldwide context. Villages where subsistence modes of life prevail share certain qualities, whether they lie in South Asia, sub-Saharan Africa, or Middle America. Karl Marx once remarked that such places confine the human mind within the narrowest possible compass, but he failed to understand that inner strength is what sustains the people—their secure relationship with God or Allah, their knowledge that this is but one step on the road to ultimate salvation. Villages in regions of commercial agriculture share a more materialistic orientation, whether they exist in Western Europe, Japan, or the U.S. Midwest. Villages, too, may be viewed as lying along a continuum, extending from the most communal (the multiple-family "long-house" communities of some Pacific, Native American and Asian cultures) to the most private and individualistic (in affluent rural North America). Between these extremes are the collective farm experiments of communist societies (such as the *kolkhoz* of the former Soviet Union), other forms of communal agrarian living (Israel's *kibbutzim*), closely knit farm villages in Asian, African, or Native American society, and looser clusters in rural Europe.

However, villages everywhere do display certain common qualities, including evidence of social stratification and the fundamental differentiation of buildings. Social stratification is reflected by the range in size and quality of village houses, representing their owners' wealth and stature within the community. Material well-being is the chief determinant in Western commercial agricultural regions, where prosperity translates into more elaborate homes. In Africa, a higher social position in the community is

associated with a more impressive house than those of lower-status residents. The house of the chief or headman may not only be superior to others but may also stand in a more prominent location. In India, caste still determines the overall quality of daily life, including village housing; the manors of landlords, often comprising large walled compounds, stand in striking contrast to the modest houses of domestic servants, farm workers, carpenters, and craftspeople. The poorest people of the lowest castes live in small one-room, wattle-and-thatch dwellings, which are mere huts without even the barest of amenities.

FUNCTIONS

The functional differentiation of buildings in farm villages is also a worldwide phenomenon, and again, it is more elaborate in certain societies than in others. The protective accommodation of livestock and the storage of harvested crops are primary functions of farm villages, and in many a village where subsistence is the rule, the storage place for grains and other food is constructed with as much care as the best-built house. Moisture and vermin must be kept away from stored food; containers of grain often stand on stilts, under the most meticulously thatched roof or behind walls made of carefully maintained sun-dried mud. In India's villages, the paddy-bin made of mud (in which rice is stored) often stands inside the living quarters of the house, to afford maximum protection. Similarly, livestock pens are often attached to houses or, as in the familiar African pattern, dwellings are built in a circle to surround the interior corral or kraal.

The functional differentiation of buildings is most fully developed in Western cultures, where a single farmstead may contain as many buildings as an entire hamlet elsewhere in the world. A prosperous North American farm is likely to include a two-story farmhouse, a stable, a barn, and various outbuildings, including a garage for motorized equipment, a workshop, a shed for tools, and a silo for grain storage. The space these structures occupy often exceeds that used by entire villages in Japan, China, and other space-conserving agrarian regions. In the United States, such farmsteads often lie separated from each other in a characteristic dispersed pattern of rural land occupance; this spatial configuration results from the **township-and-range system**, a rectangular land-division scheme designed by Thomas Jefferson and his associates before 1800 in order to disperse settlers evenly across farmlands of the U.S interior, producing in the process the largest area of planned rural settlement anywhere on Earth. Even when farms are oriented toward a more nucleated settlement pattern in the United States or Europe, they are much more elaborate than they are in underdeveloped areas. Comparative permanence and tradition can be deduced from the architectural styles of farmhouses, barn structures, and even fence and field patterns. The geographer who remains alert to such detail is rewarded by enlightening insights into the making of rural cultural landscapes.

Thus villages display an enormous variety of sizes and spatial forms. Their unifying quality is their agricultural orientation: the great majority of residents make their living by farming, and these settlements typically contain barns, storage sheds, and other buildings of similar purpose. Villages are also likely to include a place of worship, perhaps a medical clinic, a school, and a public gathering place; larger villages may accommodate such professional people as teachers, doctors, and ministers, as well as shopkeepers and repair mechanics. However, all of these people serve a population whose major tie is to the surrounding land.

Although village life remains the principal form of existence in the world's most populous geographic realms (East and South Asia), in Africa, and in large regions of Middle and South America, people in the developing countries are beginning to migrate toward larger settlements in increasingly significant numbers. In Europe, North America, Japan, and Australia, the majority of the population already reside in towns and cities. We now shift our attention to these urbanized areas, which are becoming ever more important on the world scene in the closing years of the twentieth century.

KEY TERMS

Building Resources
Diffusion Routes
Dispersed Settlement
Domestic Architecture
Folk-Housing Region
Hamlet
Maladaptive Diffusion
Nucleated Settlement
Township-and-Range System
Traditional Architecture
Village

Overcrowded, congested—and yet a magnet for millions. Belem, Brazil

PART TEN

THE URBANIZING WORLD

At Issue

Ours is the age of urbanization—but at what horrifying social cost! True, cities are the crucibles of culture, the engines of society, the centers of power, the harbingers of hope for those in search of opportunity. But for hundreds of millions of residents crowded in squatter camps from Cape Town to Karachi, life in the city is a nightmare of deprivation and discomfort, and, increasingly, risk. The swelling numbers of squatters in the urban perimeters form a ready target for diseases old and new (the recent cholera outbreak in Peru began in the slums of Lima and became an American epidemic). From Brazil to South Africa and from Mexico to India the issue is the same: How can the tide of migrants from countryside to city be stemmed without the tactics used by totalitarian regimes to do so?

30

CIVILIZATION AND URBANIZATION

In March 1994, newspapers and television newscasts carried a brief report on a momentous milestone. Statistics and projections indicated, this report said, that the world's urban population had just exceeded 50 percent of the total. From 1994 onward, more people would live in cities and towns than in rural areas. During the twenty-first century, projections suggested, the world would become two thirds urbanized. The end of the twentieth century thus witnessed the end of a human condition that had prevailed for as long as humanity existed. Ours is now an urbanized world.

But urbanization is not evenly distributed around the globe. In Western Europe, the United States, Canada, and Japan, four out of five citizens live in cities or towns. But in India and China, the figure is closer to three out of ten. But even where urbanization still is low, people are moving to the towns and cities. China's city of Shenzhen was the world's fastest-growing urban area during the second half of the twentieth century, its population increasing from about 20,000 to 2.5 million in three decades. When a major development project was an-

nounced in Shanghai, nearly 3 million people rushed to the area, hoping to find work. Two of the world's fastest-growing cities, Cal-

cutta and Bombay in India, also rank among the ten largest. The world's cities beckon as never before.

Geographica

- Urbanization and state formation transformed egalitarian society into stratified, functionally specialized society; this process occurred independently in several regions of the world, probably first in the Fertile Crescent.

- The ancient Greeks assimilated concepts of urban life from Mesopotamia as well as Minoa, and produced the most highly urbanized society on Earth during their time, 2500 years ago.

- The ancient Romans combined domestic as well as Greek traditions in building an urban system that extended spatially from Britain to Mesopotamia, its hierarchy centered on dominant Rome; all urban centers were linked by a network of land and water routes.

- Greek and Roman concepts of urbanization diffused into Western Europe, but Europe's preindustrial cities, even those inherited from the Romans, were poorly organized, unsanitary, overcrowded, and uncomfortable places to live for the majority of their inhabitants.

- Cities evolve in stages. The traders' mercantile city gave way to the factory-dominated manufacturing center, and the automobile enabled the evolution of the suburbanized modern city; today's "postmodern" cities reflect the age of high technology.

Cities are the centers of political power and industrial might, higher education and technological innovation, artistic achievement and medical advances. They are the great markets of today, the hubs of specialization and interaction, the sources of news and information, the suppliers of services, the providers of sports and entertainment. In short, cities are the crucibles of civilization.

Aurhor's Video Link
↓
1
Geographically
Speaking Urban
Geography

It is therefore difficult to think of a human world without cities. Cities are the anchors of culture: the urban system and its spokes form the structural skeleton of society. And

yet, there *was* human society before there were cities, and not even very long ago. The rise of the city is a very recent phenomenon in human history. If human communities have existed for 200,000 years, they did not cluster into towns for more than 190,000 years. Humans migrated far and wide, glaciations came and went, and climates warmed and cooled. But not until about 8000 years ago did some human settlements begin to grow into larger places.

In Part 10, we trace the evolution of urbanization in geographic context, identify the factors that influenced the location and growth (or decline) of cities, investigate the internal structure of cities in various cultural settings, and note the serious problems rapid urban growth has brought to modern society. We begin by looking back at the beginnings of urbanization.

From the Field Notes

❝ The stone ruins of Zimbabwe mark the rise of an early African city, but the functions of its many buildings still are a mystery. They have been interpreted as fortifications, as religious structures, and as political symbols. Visit Zimbabwe, and you will quickly fall under the spell of this unique African place. Many questions come to mind: Where were the stones quarried? Who planned these enormous structures? What did the many decorations signify? There is no doubt that when this center arose, whatever its role, African society in this area changed dramatically. ❞

ANCIENT CITIES AND EARLY CIVILIZATIONS

In earlier chapters, we noted the beginnings of the diffusion of agriculture, between 10,000 and 12,000 years ago. Population numbers grew and people migrated outward from the early agricultural hearths, carrying their farming knowledge with them. Settlements became more sedentary than had been possible previously; languages diffused and diversified.

But for several thousand years, the settlements in regions of developing agriculture remained true villages. These were small, there was not much variation in their sizes, and the households they contained had about the same amount of possessions and status (i.e., the limited wealth was rather evenly distributed). Anthropologists report that there appears to have been no governmental authority beyond the village, no network of control. There were no public buildings and no workshops. An **egalitarian society** prevailed and remained so long after agriculture was introduced.

Scholars can be fairly certain that this was the situation in the region of the Fertile Crescent and the areas into which agricultural innovations diffused, because there is evidence that the same conditions prevailed in other later hearths of agricultural innovation. In Southwest Asia, things began to change about 6000 B.P. (Before Present). Archeological research provides evidence that social inequality was developing. The sizes of houses began to vary. Some people had more property than others and were buried with the best of their earthly belongings. Specialization developed as some people remained farmers, but others were craftspeople, and some became involved in government; government buildings and workshops appeared.

None of this made a city out of a village, but now an important political development occurred. As some villages grew larger (while others did not), groups of these settlements came under the control of a central authority. It was the beginning of the formation of the **state**, a process that was to lead to the rise of ancient Egypt, Greece, the Roman Empire, and ultimately, the modern state of today.

The rise of the earliest states is closely linked to the evolution of the first cities. But when did a group of villages, controlled by a central government, become a state? Anthropologists Henry Wright and Gregory Johnson, in an article published in 1975, proposed that the existence of an early state was verified by the presence of a centralized political hierarchy with at least three levels of administration. These levels could be discerned, they argued, from the settlement hierarchy (among other pieces of evidence). To prove their point, Professors Wright and Johnson analyzed the ancient geography of an area in the southwest of present-day Iran. This area contained evidence of more than four dozen settlements. The great majority of these were small villages, but four larger "towns" could be identified, and one center was even larger than these towns. So there was a dominant urban center, the probable capital, where the power probably was concentrated, and two levels of settlement below it. That suggests that a state had arisen there, more than 5000 B.P.

The period between about 7000 B.P. and 5000 B.P. is called the **formative era** of both state development and urbanization—the two obviously went hand in hand—in Southwest Asia. Toward the end of that period, there was a large state in the lower basin of the Tigris-Euphrates (Mesopotamia) with a number of cities, among which was Ur. Sumer's cities had impressive temples positioned on high, artificial mounds of Earth, imposing

public buildings, army barracks, numerous workshops, and dwellings of various sizes. The egalitarian society had become a **stratified society**. Now there were priests, merchants, administrators, soldiers, farmers, craftspeople, and slaves. The city had become the focus of state culture, the nexus of civilization.

FUNCTION AND LOCATION

As such, the ancient city also was the organizational focus of the state. Agriculture had to be planned so that the inflow of food staples would be guaranteed—a task that became even more complicated when irrigation systems developed.

Some scholars believe that the earliest true cities and civilizations were products of the organizational need that arose when irrigation was invented. Furthermore, the collection of taxes and tribute from an expanding region under the city's control had to be organized, administered, and maintained. The city soon needed physical protection against enemies, which required such collective action as the construction of fortified walls.

Hence the geographic advantages of certain locations, as well as the internal organization of the clustered community, played roles in the growth of ancient towns and cities. Not only proximity to productive farmlands, but also the

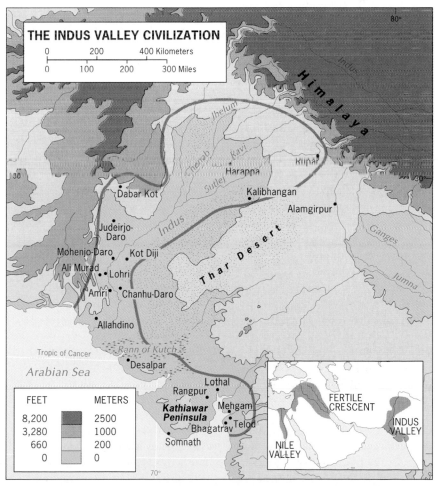

FIGURE 30–1 The Indus Basin was a crucible, a hearth of culture whose innovations diffused into India.

availability of water from surface or underground sources, and the defensibility of the settlement's site, contributed to the durability of certain towns. On the flanks of the Fertile Crescent, towns in Mesopotamia enjoyed secure food supplies (see Fig. 5-2). In the Indus Basin, the first cities were served by carefully constructed and maintained stone-lined wells to tap groundwater supplies (see Harappa and Mohenjo-Daro in Fig. 30-1). Also significant was the position of towns on ancient routes of travel and trade. Where such routes converged on an urban place, there were contact, interaction, and growth. Less accessible, more isolated places were at a comparative disadvantage.

Urban growth tested the ingenuity of the town's leading citizens. Food must not only be acquired and stored, but also distributed. Essential to such a system of allocation, of course, was a body of decision makers and organizers, people who controlled the lives of others: an **urban elite**. Such an urban-based elite could afford the luxury of leisure and devote time to religion and philosophy. Out of such pursuits came the concept of writing and record-keeping, an essential ingredient in the rise of urbanization. Writing made possible the codification of laws and the confirmation of traditions. It was a crucial element in the development of systematic administration in urbanizing Mesopotamia, and in the evolution of its religious-political ideology. The rulers in the cities were both priests and kings, and the harvest the peasants brought to be stored in the urban granaries was a tribute, as well as a tax.

Thus ancient cities had several functions (see box, "The Ancient Mesopotamian City"). As centers of power, they became political foci, the headquarters of the first state-like entities the world had seen. As religious centers, their authority was

THE ANCIENT MESOPOTAMIAN CITY

The ancient Mesopotamian city was usually protected by an earthen wall that surrounded the entire community, or, sometimes, the cluster of temples and shrines at its center. Temples dominated the urban landscape, not only because they were the largest structures in town, but also because they were built on artificial mounds often over 100 feet (30 meters) high, which towered above the townscape.

Priests and other authorities resided in substantial buildings, many of which might be called palaces, but ordinary citizens lived in a jumble of mud-walled houses packed closely together and separated only by narrow lanes; there was no vehicular traffic. Facing these lanes were shops and the workplaces of craftspeople. On the outskirts of this compact city were the quarters of the poorest inhabitants, often made of mud-smeared reed walls, little more than tiny huts. Slaves were held in communal, prison-like accommodations, sometimes outside the city wall.

In the general absence of waste-disposal or sewage facilities, ancient cities were far from sanitary. Mesopotamians threw their garbage and refuse into the streets and other open spaces, to the extent that layers of this waste accumulated to a depth of several yards, requiring modification of doorways of houses! In a way this was fortunate, because archeologists have been able to sift through the garbage for clues to life in the ancient city. Not surprisingly, disease was among the reasons why the ancient cities' populations remained comparatively small. The towns of the Indus and Nile Valleys appear to have been somewhat cleaner.

augmented by the pressure of the clergy and by temples and shrines. Ancient cities in many areas of the world were **theocratic centers**, where rulers were deemed to have divine authority and were, in effect, god-kings. In the Americas the great structures of Yucatan, Guatemala, and Honduras built by the ancient Maya Indians (including Tikal, Chichén-Itak, Uxmal, and Copán) exemplify such places (Fig. 30-2). As economic centers, they were the chief markets, the bases from which wealthy merchants, land and livestock owners, and traders operated. As educational centers, they included among their residents respected teachers and philosophers. They also had their handicraft industries, which attracted the best craftspeople and inventors. Therefore, ancient cities were the anchors of culture and so-

ciety, the focal points of power, authority, and change.

The formative era of urbanization did not, as noted previously, occur simultaneously in all culture hearths. Figure 30-3 is an approximation that suggests the primacy of Mesopotamia and neighboring areas; the Nile Valley witnessed a formative era less than a millennium later. City formation in China and in the Indus Valley may have been approximately coincidental. European and West African urbanization came later still. In Mesoamerica, the formative era probably began during the middle of the third millennium B.P.

The earliest towns probably experienced the same growth conditions that later sustained the modern rise of such cities as Paris and London: as the principal centers, crossroads, markets, places of

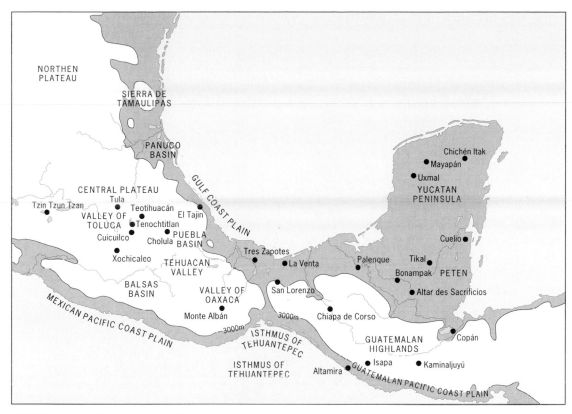

FIGURE 30–2 Early centers of culture in Maya and Aztec America.

authority, and religious headquarters, they drew the talents, trade, and travelers from far around. Where should the beginnings of metallurgy have been based but in these incipient cities? Where would a traveler, a tradesman, a priest, or a pilgrim rest before continuing the journey? Towns had to have facilities that would not be found in farm villages: buildings to house the visitors, store the food, treat raw materials, worship, and accommodate those charged with protection and defense.

How large were the ancient cities? We only have estimates, because it is impossible to conclude from excavated ruins the total dimensions of a city at its height, or the number of people that might have occupied each residential unit. However, it seems that at least by modern standards, the ancient cities were not large. The cities of Mesopotamia and the Nile Valley may

have had between 10,000 and 15,000 inhabitants after nearly 2000 years of growth and development. That, scholars conclude, is about the maximum size that could have been sustained by existing systems of food gathering and distribution, and by social organization. So these urban places were just islands, geographical exceptions in an overwhelmingly rural society. Urbanized societies such as we know today did not emerge until several thousand years later.

DIFFUSION TO GREECE

Concepts of urbanization spread from Mesopotamia in several directions. Whether cities emerged in the Nile Valley as a result of expansion diffusion or by independent invention is uncertain. No doubt exists, however, regarding the early devel-

opment of urban traditions on the Mediterranean island of Crete, where Knossos was the cornerstone of a system of towns of the Minoan civilization, more than 3500 years ago. Ideas about city life may therefore have reached Greece from several directions. During the third millennium B.P., Greece became one of the most highly urbanized areas on Earth.

Whatever the sources of the stimuli, the urbanization of ancient Greece ushered in a new stage of city evolution. By the middle of the third millennium B.P. (600 to 500 B.P.), Greece had acquired an urban network of more than 500 cities and towns, not only on the mainland but also on the many Greek islands. Greek seafarers connected these urban places with trade routes and carried the notion of urban life far and wide into the Mediterranean region. Athens and Sparta, often vying with each other for power,

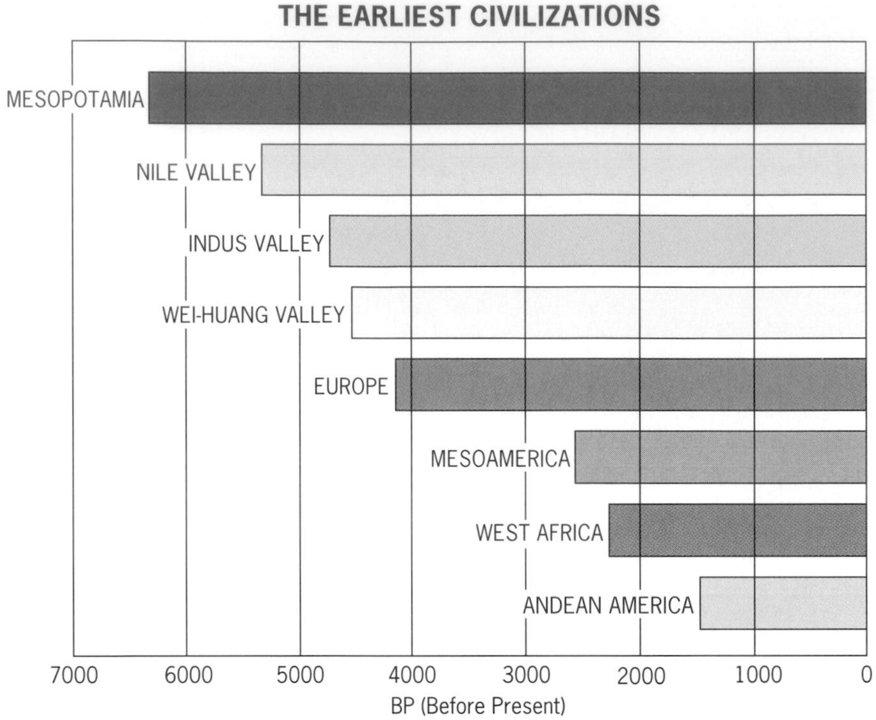

THE EARLIEST CIVILIZATIONS

FIGURE 30–3 Approximate dates of birth of the world's early civilizations.

and interacted socially. As time went on, the **agora** (the word means market) also became the focus of commercial activity, a development decried by conservatives.

Greece's cities also were endowed with excellent theaters, another innovation transmitted to the Romans—who elaborated on it by creating huge stadiums. But while the aristocracy and the privileged attended plays and listened to philosophical discourses, life for many people in the Greek cities was miserable. Housing for ordinary people was no better than it was in the Mesopotamian cities millennia older. Sanitation was poor and health conditions were no better. And hundreds of thousands of slaves languished in bondage, organized to build much of the grandeur designed by Greece's urban planners.

were Greece's leading cities. Athens may have been the largest city in the world at the time, with an estimated 250,000 inhabitants.

We should remember that urbanization, 2500 years ago, was proceeding in several other parts of the world: in China, where an impressive urban tradition was developing, in South Asia, and in Mesoamerica, where the formative era had begun. But the developments in ancient Greece were to have global, not just regional, impact. Greece inherited Southwest Asia innovations. It transmitted its own urban traditions to the Roman empire, and Roman urban culture diffused to Western Europe. From there, "Western" concepts of city life were disseminated around the world on the wings of colonialism and imperialism. From Washington, D.C. to Canberra, Australia, Greco-Roman imprints persist in the urban landscape.

In hilly Greece, there was no need to build earthen mounds upon which to perch temples: nature provided spectacular, commanding sites. Every city had its **acropolis** (acro = high point; polis = city), upon which the most impressive structures were built. The Parthenon of Athens remains the most famous of all, surviving to this day, despite nearly 2500 years of war, earth tremors, vandalism, and environmental impact. This magnificent columned structure, designed by the Athenian architect-engineer Phidias, was begun in 447 B.C.; its rows of tapering columns have inspired designers ever since.

Like the older Southwest Asian cities, Greece's cities also had public places. In the Southwest Asian towns, these seem to have been rather cramped, crowded, and bustling with activity, but in ancient Greece, they were open, spacious squares, often in a low part of town and flanked by steps leading down to them. On these steps, the Greeks debated, lectured, judged each other, planned military campaigns,

THE ROMAN URBAN SYSTEM

The great majority of Greece's cities and towns fringed the Mediterranean Sea, linking peninsulas and islands. When the Romans succeeded the Greeks as rulers of the region, their empire incorporated not only the Mediterranean littoral, but also a large part of interior Europe and North Africa (Fig. 30-4). The **urban system** of the Roman Empire was in every way the largest yet developed anywhere on Earth. The great capital, Rome, lay at the apex of a hierarchy of settlements ranging from small villages to large cities. A **transport network** linked these places by road, sea, and river. Roman regional planners displayed a remarkable capacity for identifying suitable locales for the placement of settlements. They also chose surface routes, many of which serve European motorists

From the Field Notes

❝ ❝ The Greek island of Delos is a window on a time when this was a pivotal place in the Aegean Sea, and indeed in a much larger maritime region. Delos was the Hong Kong of the Mediterranean, a place of magnificent temples, sculptures, theaters, and aqueducts. It had a bustling harbor at least 3,000 years ago, an entrepot that housed and transferred slaves, wild animals, and goods from Africa and Asia. Delos fell to the Greeks and later to the Romans, and for a time was a free port. But the foci of trade in the region changed, and Delos collapsed. All this happened before the birth of Christ; later, this magnificent site was quarried for building stone by, among others, Venetians and Turks. Today Delos is a national monument, uninhabited, to preserve what remains of a creative and turbulent past. ❞ ❞

today. Efficiency was a Roman hallmark: urban places were positioned a modest distance from each other, so that they could be reached in limited travel time. Roman road builders created a grid of communications to integrate the empire.

In Chapter 19, we followed the diffusion of architectural innovations from Greece to Rome and onward, noting that the Romans were better adapters than innovators. There already was an urban tradition on the Italian peninsula, however, before Rome emerged. The Etruscans, predecessors of the Romans, built cities that were centered on prominently sited temples. These cities, still not well known or understood by researchers, served as nodes for a thriving agricultural

and commercial civilization. The number and distribution of these Etruscan cities still is under investigation, but they extended from present-day Tuscany into the valley of the Po River, so that the Etruscan state occupied much of what was to become the heart of the Roman Empire. The Romans, therefore, had a domestic as well as foreign tradition on which to build.

Greek imprints on the layout of Roman cities are unmistakable. The Greeks had learned to plan their colonial cities in a rectangular grid pattern (early cities of mainland Greece were jumbled and congested), a plan that was adopted by the Romans where the surface made it possible. The notion of an open market found expression in

the Roman city's *forum*, the focus of public life. The Romans expanded on the Greek city's theater to build the world's first great *stadium*, the Colosseum in Rome. (All Roman cities of any size had such an arena in which competitions, war games, ceremonies, and other public events took place.) Wild animals imported from Africa were slaughtered there. (The Spanish "sport" of bullfighting is a derivative of such spectacles.) Following the diffusion of Christianity to Rome, Christians were forced into the Colosseum's pit to be attacked and eaten by hungry lions as crowds watched.

The Roman city was a place of cultural contrasts: of great monumental buildings (see Chapter 19), impressive villas and spacious avenues, ingenious aqueducts and baths, and sewage systems built of stone and pipe. But the Roman city also was home to the most wretchedly poor, who were crammed into overcrowded tenements where the amenities enjoyed by the privileged were absent. Even worse off were the slaves, many from North Africa, who were in ample supply and whose lives were distressingly expendable. The Roman city, like the city of today, mirrored society's accomplishments as well as its excesses.

POST-ROMAN DECLINE

The collapse of the Roman Empire was accompanied by the disintegration of its urban system and the decay of many of its cities. Trade and transport networks broke down, the social order fell apart, and once-vibrant cities went to ruin. Between about 500 A.D. and 1000 A.D., little was left of the urban tradition Rome had bequeathed to its empire. The now-fragmented realm's weakness was confirmed by the successful invasion of Iberia by

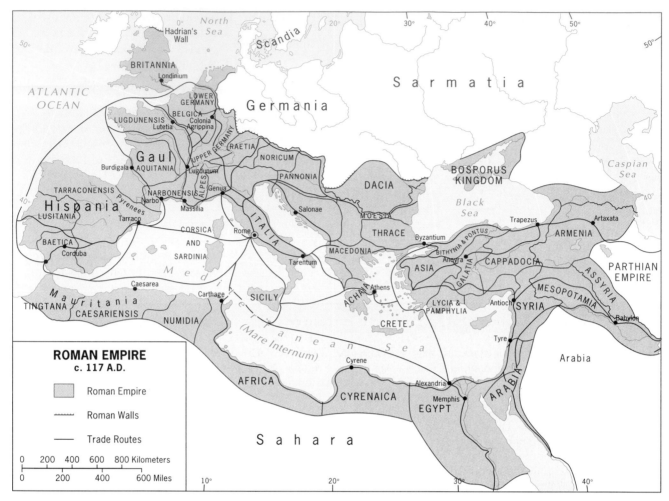

FIGURE 30–4 The Romans established a system of cities linked by a network of land and sea routes. Many of the Roman cities have grown into modern metropolises.

the armies of the Moorish Empire of North Africa, who brought order, new architectural and scientific ideas, and Islam into what had been one of Rome's principal provinces.

GROWTH ELSEWHERE

Elsewhere in the world, however (including the expanding Islamic realm), the growth of cities was proceeding vigorously. Xian in China was known as the Rome of East Asia, and China's urban system was developing rapidly. In West Africa, a tier of trading cities was developing along the southern margin of the Sahara. By 1350,

Timbuktu was a city of major consequence, a seat of government, a university town, a market, and a religious center. In the upper valley of the Nile River, Meroë was a leading center of metallurgy, specializing in the smelting of iron and the manufacture of weapons. Trade routes from a wide region focused on this populous city.

In the Americas, significant urban growth was now taking place. In the Yucatan Peninsula and adjacent areas (Mexico and Guatemala), Maya urbanization proceeded. On the Mexican Plateau to the northwest, even larger urban centers emerged. Mexico's largest pre-Colombian city, the Aztecs' capital of

Teotihuacan, may have had more than 100,000 inhabitants and was growing vigorously while many European cities lay in ruins.

PREINDUSTRIAL EUROPE

The Roman-European urban traditions were weakened, but they were not extinguished. The Muslim invasion helped galvanize Europeans into action; the invaders were halted as they were about to penetrate southern Italy and southern France, and the Christian counter-thrust began. Soon the Crusades carried the battle to the very heartland of Islamic power, and old trade routes were reopened. Medieval Europe was stirring, and the colonial era was about to begin.

In the dormant cities, these events had quick expression. The pulse of commerce picked up again, there was work to be had, and population growth resumed. Paris, Amsterdam, Antwerp, Lisbon, Venice, Naples, and many other cities and towns were revived. It is important again to keep a perspective on the sizes of the cities we are talking about: London, by the middle of the fifteenth century, had perhaps 80,000 inhabitants; Paris had 120,000. While colonies were secured and riches poured into Europe, London, around the beginning of the nineteenth century, still

had fewer than 1 million residents, and Paris only 670,000.

URBAN ENVIRONMENTS

What were the preindustrial cities like as places to live and work? Well, the adage of the "good old days" hardly applies. If today's cities are no bargain for many of their residents, neither were preindustrial Ghent, Manchester, or Warsaw. With more efficient weaponry and the invention of gunpowder, cities faced threats not confronted before: walls and moats could no longer withstand armies. So cities developed into veritable fortifications just at a time when they were also required to accommodate growing numbers of people. Those fortifications could not simply be moved outward; once built, they more or

less marked the confines of the place. Thus the only way people could be housed in greater numbers was by building not outward, but upward, and four- and five-story tenements began to appear.

By the seventeenth century, European cities were generally slum-ridden, unsanitary, and depressing. Epidemics, disastrous fires, rampant crime, and social dislocation prevailed. Yes, the picturesque, four-story merchants' homes did overlook the sparkling canals of Amsterdam and the lush green parks of London. However, their residents were the fortunate few who were in a position to manipulate the labor force in the city and control the lucrative overseas commerce. For the ordinary people, the over-crowded cities, more often than not, were no place to be.

From the Field Notes

❝ From the Eiffel Tower, one can see why Paris is one of the world's best-defined primate cities. The historic old city contains numerous military, political, and religious icons. Several of these can be seen on this photograph, notably the Arc de Triomphe rising above the townscape. ❞

Many decided accordingly when the chance came to leave for America, Australia, and other parts of the world.

MODELS

Obviously, preindustrial cities of Renaissance Europe were quite different from preindustrial cities in India or China, and despite their common preindustrial character, the cities of Roman Europe differed from those of medieval times. Historical geographers and other scholars have tried to develop a general model of preindustrial urbanism that would account for the different properties of cities at various times in history and in various societies. Among the most effective generalizations was that proposed by Gideon Sjoberg in his book, *The Preindustrial City: Past and Present* (1960). Sjoberg argued that cities should be viewed as products of their societies and that the levels could be divided into four categories: (1) **folk-preliterate**; (2) **feudal**; (3) **preindustrial**; and (4) **urban-industrial**.

Durable cities develop along a continuum, representing their societies at each stage and retaining imprints from previous forms and functions in their spatial structures. Thus a European city during feudal times was little more than a town, its houses modest and its streets unpaved. The estates of the landlords and the monasteries of the church were more imposing. Medieval revival brought the first stage in the rise of the preindustrial European city. The consolidation of political power and the expansion of states were reflected in the growth of the cities, now the foci of a new order. Architecture and the arts, as well as commerce and trade, moved forward, but the dominant aspect of the preindustrial city, as we saw in Chapter 19, was the imposing complex of religious and governmental structures at its heart. Much later,

"LAW" OF THE PRIMATE CITY

Great cities have always reflected regional cultures. In 1939, geographer Mark Jefferson published an article entitled "The Law of the Primate City." in which he described the dominant city much as Sjoberg did later—as a place that reflects the essence of the culture at whose focus it lies. The "law" states that "a country's leading city is always disproportionately large and exceptionally expressive of national capacity and feeling." It refers, obviously, to cities of the twentieth century representing national cultures of modern times, but the notion can be extended to earlier periods, too. As Sjoberg stated, cities of preindustrial, feudal, and preliterate societies were also products as well as reflections of their cultures.

Although Jefferson's notion is rather imprecise, it is supported by numerous cases, past and present: Kyoto as the primate city reflective of old Japan, and Tokyo of the new; Paris as the personification of France; and London, where the culture and history of a nation and empire are so deeply etched in the urban landscape. These are primate cities indeed! In Europe, such cities as Athens, Lisbon, Prague, and Amsterdam may no longer in every case be disproportionately large, but they remain exceptionally expressive of the cultures they represent. Beijing in China, Lahore in Pakistan, Ibadan in Nigeria, and Mexico City are also examples of primate cities—in some cases, no longer the largest regionally, but quintessentially representative of national capacity and feeling. Jefferson's generalization, like Sjoberg's, might be adapted to conform to stages in a culture's growth. Thus Beijing is the primate city of the old China, Shanghai (now China's largest) of the new; Rio de Janeiro reflects Brazil's historic evolution, whereas São Paulo represents the vigor of its contemporary society.

Today, the primate city also exists prominently in: (1) countries with dominantly agriculture-based economies, such as Bangladesh, Indonesia, and Ethiopia; (2) countries with a recent history of colonial subjugation, including Kenya, Zimbabwe, and Senegal; and (3) less-developed countries such as Sri Lanka, Liberia, and Nicaragua. In many of these cases, only part of Jefferson's thesis is fulfilled: the cities are disproportionately large, but they do not necessarily express national capacity and feeling, having a foreign-influenced past.

when Europe entered its urban-industrial age, the high-rise buildings of financial and commercial organization took over the dominant position in its burgeoning urban cores.

Focusing on the preindustrial city around the world, Sjoberg suggested that virtually all cities prior to the industrial age shared essential structural characteristics. Whether in medieval Europe, West Africa, East Asia, the Islamic culture realm, or the Americas, preindustrial cities were similar in form, function, and atmosphere. They

truly represented the evolving **primate city** (see box, " 'Law' of the Primate City"), expressing, most of all, the culture and ideology of their societies. By modern standards, they were not large, but they were certainly dominant, their influence underscored by the cluster of religious and/or governmental buildings at their center (whether cathedral, mosque, temple, or shrine) and the spaciousness and wealth associated with this urban centrality. Close identification with the center of influence and power was valued, and so the wealthy and powerful had homes nearby. The center of the city may also have been viewed as desirable because of its comparative safety. Toward the outskirts, and sometimes even beyond the safety of the city's protective walls, lived the less privileged, the poor and the misfits, who were segregated from both the elite and the mass of commoners.

This set of generalizations about preindustrial cities is open to debate, and Sjoberg's thesis certainly generated it. Not all preindustrial cities were structured as Sjoberg suggested. In Muslim cities, with their impressive central mosques, the surrounding housing is of less variable quality than in Europe's preindustrial cities, and commerce and crafts are concentrated within a bazaar that is without equivalent. In the theocratic states of Middle America, the city centers, with their great temples, served as ceremonial sites where thousands of people were present during rituals, but were vacant (and not a part of the functional city) at other times. In black Africa, no religious or governmental structures dominated the townscape in ways comparable to the preindustrial European or Muslim city. Nevertheless, Sjoberg's thesis provides a useful basis for comparison.

Author's Video Link

4

Hong Kong

Another viewpoint holds that the term "preindustrial" represents an inaccuracy, because so-called preindustrial cities of various historic periods (Roman, medieval European) and in various world realms (Africa, South Asia, China) were so different in form that they cannot properly be grouped together under the same rubric. In the first place, "preindustrial" cities had industries.

These were not the modern manufacturing industries of the past two centuries, but were industries nevertheless. The old urban places of Japan and India, for example, contained much handicraft industry. Thus the preindustrial city's morphology *was* shaped by activity of an industrial type: the dimensions of the industries were small, but their numbers often were quite large. Some geographers, therefore, avoid the adjective "preindustrial" entirely; others use it only in reference to the Western city before the advent of the Industrial Revolution.

EVOLUTION OF THE MODERN WESTERN CITY

Much of the remainder of Part 10 is devoted to the geographic study of the Western city. In Chapter 19, we

noted some of the characteristics of the medieval and **mercantile cities**, the urban centers revived by Europe's colonial expansion. During the sixteenth and seventeenth centuries, mercantile cities such as Amsterdam, Antwerp, Copenhagen, London, Lisbon, and others became the nodes of a global network of regional, national, and international commerce. The power of trading companies and wealthy merchants was so great that they were able to establish settlements in distant lands, from America to Indonesia. The earliest colonial cities in North America were products of this period, as were Dakar, Cape Town, and Lourenço Marques (now Maputo) in Africa, Madras and Hong Kong in Asia, and many other mostly coastal settlements.

Therefore, when the Industrial Revolution made its impact during the last quarter of the eighteenth century, many European cities were no longer moribund. But none was prepared for what lay ahead: an av-

From the Field Notes

❝ This is probably not the popular image of San Francisco, but it *is* the modern imprint on an old city. Coupled with this modernization of the city center is the suburbanization of the urban population, a process that has transformed the Western City model in the United States. ❞

alanche of changes that ripped the fabric of urban life. Cities had to adapt to the mushrooming of factories and supply facilities, the expansion of transport systems, and the construction of tenements for the growing labor force. They bulged—and sometimes broke—at the seams. The **manufacturing city** now emerged, first in the British Midlands and soon in Western Europe, where the ripples of the Industrial Revolution spread. The historic centers of many European cities were totally or partially destroyed as the walls of manufacturing plants and their smokestacks rose above the townscape. Cities became unregulated jumbles of activity. Private homes were engulfed by factories. Open spaces became refuse dumps. Elegant housing was converted into overcrowded slums. Ugly railroad tracks knifed through long-stable neighborhoods. Sanitation systems failed, and water supply was inadequate and often polluted, so that the manufacturing city was a ready market for diseases.

And yet, people migrated to the manufacturing cities, not only in Europe but wherever factory towns emerged. Living conditions were known to be dreadful for the workers, and working conditions were shocking. Children worked 12-hour shifts in textile mills. Health conditions were worse than they had been in medieval times; acrid, polluted air and contaminated water ensured it. The English Midland cities were appropriately called the "black towns," grimy and soot-covered as they were.

In time, the excesses of the capital-driven transformation of the European manufacturing city were tempered by government intervention, legislation, the introduction of city planning and zoning, and the recognition of workers' rights. Many manufacturing cities in the New World never suffered the fate of their European predecessors, although living and working conditions for factory workers (and "blue collar" workers generally) were far from satisfactory. During the late nineteenth and early twentieth centuries, the American manufacturing city still carried some of the earmarks of its European forerunners.

The modernization of the manufacturing city in America was a late nineteenth-century phenomenon, and it resulted from one of the products of the Industrial Revolution: innovation in transportation. The introduction of the electric trolley, in the words of Professor James Vance, transformed the geographical pattern of cities. In a chapter entitled "Geography and Human Mobility: the Perpetual Revolution in Transportation" (1988), Professor Vance states that the trolley created "public mass transit to the edge of the built-up city, and, importantly, for the first time the transit system was circumferential as well as radial in its pattern. It became possible to work in factories in the older industrial satellites embedded within the suburban band, to shop in the central business district, and to patronize clusters of shops sited at the junction points where several trolley lines converged." The suburbanization of the **modern city** had begun, to be augmented by what Professor Vance calls the "revolution of the 1920s," the introduction of the affordable automobile.

The modern city of the twentieth century is the city as we know it: the sprawling, expanding urban region of many parts and functions, from "downtown" to suburb, from shopping mall to business park. It is the epitome of entrepreneurial culture, a showplace of technology. But the modern city has not stabilized. The era of postindustrial high technology is reflected by what some urban geographers see as **postmodernism** in the urban scene of highly developed societies. We turn next to this very topic: the structuring and spacing of urban centers on the eve of the twenty-first century.

KEY TERMS

Acropolis
Agora
Egalitarian Society
Feudal City
Folk-Preliterate City
Formative Era
Manufacturing City
Mercantile City
Modern City
Postmodernism
Preindustrial City
Primate City
State
Stratified Society
Theocratic Center
Transport Network
Urban Elite
Urban-Industrial City
Urban System

31

URBANIZATION AND LOCATION

When the medieval and mercantile cities of Europe were torn asunder by the forces of the Industrial Revolution, a new map was in the making. For all its famous cities from Athens to Amsterdam, Europe's population around 1800 was overwhelmingly (probably more than 85 percent) rural. Less than two centuries later, Western Europe is about 85 percent urban, an astonishing transformation. It was the vanguard of a worldwide process set in motion by colonialism and its attendant diffusion of the new industrial know-how. The growth of **urbanization** in Western Europe and in the world as a whole is charted in Figure 31-1. The increase in urbanization in Western Europe (Fig. 31-1A) shows that as recently as 1950, only slightly more than 50 percent of Western Europeans lived in cities and towns of 5000 inhabitants or more. Urbanization has raced ahead over the past half century there.

By some measures, as noted above, Western Europe is even more highly urbanized than Figure 31-1A suggests. This is so because, as we noted in Chapter 29, various countries use different criteria when

Geographica

- An urban center's situation (or relative location) strongly influences its fortunes over time; its linkages with and economic domination in a large and productive hinterland can ensure its well-being.

- An urban center's site (or physical base) may have played a key role in its origin and early survival, for example, as a defensive locale; but in modern times that same site may limit its growth and expansion.

- World urbanization as a percentage of total population still is highest in Western Europe, North America, Japan, and Australia, but it is gaining rapidly elsewhere; urbanization is increasing most rapidly in the world's least-urbanized realm, Africa.

- Megalopolitan coalescence marks several of the world's great urban complexes, notably in eastern North America, Western Europe, and Japan; the fastest-growing megacities, however, lie in South and East Asia.

- Despite wretched urban living conditions for many, the cities continue to attract new residents by the millions; cities today are the crucibles of culture and acculturation.

they publish statistical reports on their urban residents. Some regard almost any clustered settlement, even a village of a few hundred people, as urbanized. Others put the limit higher. Still others use the type of employment in which people are engaged as the chief criterion. Since the criteria vary, so do the regional estimates. Figure 31-1A uses the limit of 5000, which gives a regional estimate of urbanization of

385

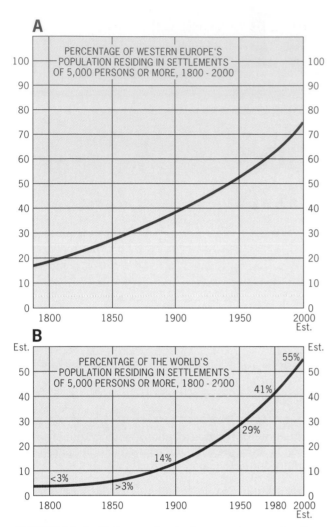

FIGURE 31–1 Data on urbanization vary by country; the level of 5000 residents for a settlement to qualify as urban is arbitrary.

agglomeration, the spatial process of clustering by commercial enterprises for mutual advantage and benefit.

The cities in the hearth of the Industrial Revolution also went through a phase of **specialization**. Certain industries grew to dominate the manufacturing sector in such cities to such a degree that their products and the names of the cities became almost synonymous. Today, such associations are fading from memory, but not long ago, Manchester textiles, Sheffield silver, and Birmingham steel were virtual redundancies. (We commemorate such connections by accusing someone of carrying "coals to Newcastle" or rooting for the Pittsburgh Steelers.) This stage of specialization passed, however, and most industrial cities today have a diversified manufacturing base.

In this chapter, we view the process of urbanization in a global context and the phenomenon of the city in a spatial perspective. As we will find, there are areas in the world where large cities are coalescing into giant metropolitan complexes that are taking on the characteristics of urban regions. Yet the fate of cities is still bound up with some old geographic principles that bestow advantage or disadvantage in this competitive, changing world.

URBAN GEOGRAPHY

In the previous chapter, we traced the evolution of cities from their Southwest Asian origins to modern times, combining cultural geography and historical geography in the process. But the study of the ways cities function, their internal systems and structures and their external influences, is the field of **urban geography**. Urban geographers want to know how cities work, how their circulation systems

about 75 percent. By other calculations, urbanization in Western Europe exceeds 85 percent.

The same caveat applies to Figure 31-1B, which shows the growth of urbanization worldwide. As we noted in Chapter 30, the world has just reached the level Western Europe did 50 years ago: one in two world citizens now lives in an urban setting.

In Britain and mainland Europe, the process of industrialization brought far-reaching change to existing cities, but not all cities were affected in the same way. Relative location played a major role: some cities were fortuitously located with

respect to resources and other essentials, and burgeoned. Others had lesser spatial advantage and could not keep pace; some even declined under the withering competition industrialization brought.

In the growing manufacturing cities, raw materials were consumed at prodigious rates, and products poured forth from the factories in ever greater quantities. Competing industrialists found that there was an advantage in sharing the services of raw-material suppliers, transporters, builders, glassmakers, and other businesses, and these providers in turn found ready markets for their specialties. Thus cities grew by

function, how commuting patterns develop and change, how and why people move from one part of a city to another. What is it that attracts millions of people to the cities every year, even while millions of others "escape" the city to the suburbs?

Cities, too, display spatial variation; that is, they possess internal regional contrasts. Urban regions (such as the "downtown" or the "inner city") can be better understood if they are clearly delineated, so that urban geographers perform detailed studies on economic, cultural, political, and other aspects of the human geography of cities. Using consistent criteria, we find that the layout of Western cities contrasts quite sharply with that of East Asian, African, or South American cities. Later in Part 10, we bring these contrasts into focus.

RANKING URBAN CENTERS

Before proceeding, we should confront a problem of terminology that turns out to be much more than semantic. Terms such as "city," "town," "village," and even "urban" do not have consistent, universally adopted meanings. Inconsistent usage can lead to confusion and invalid comparisons.

Take, for example, the term *urban*. Earlier, we compared the dispersed settlements of rural areas to clustered urban settlements. If clustering is the hallmark of urbanization, even a hamlet is an urban settlement, although it may contain just 100 residents or so. But when does a hamlet become a village, and a village a town, and a town a city?

One way to view urbanization of different dimensions is to use the notion of **urban hierarchy** and to consider the *functions* of clustered

settlements in addition to their size. Take the case of that hamlet again. If a hamlet (usually a settlement of fewer than 100 people) is made up of a group of farmers' dwellings, it offers no services, such as a gas station, general store, or coffee shop—in short, it has no **urban function**. But if a hamlet does provide some basic services for the people living there and some of those nearby, then it is an urban place on the bottom step of the urban hierarchy.

A village, the next larger urban settlement, is likely to offer several dozen services, and the key is specialization. Stores sell certain goods, gas stations sell competing brands. As an urban center, the village serves a larger area and more people than a hamlet.

A town generally is not simply larger than a village; its functions reveal a higher level of specialization. Bank and postal services, medical services, educational institutions (school, library), and stores selling such goods as furniture, appliances, and hardware are among town functions. Rather than relying solely on population size, we define a town as a place where a certain assemblage of goods and services is available, with a **hinterland** (surrounding service area) that includes the smaller service areas of villages and hamlets. The hinterland reveals the *economic reach* of each settlement, the maximum distance from the town or village where people still are attracted to it for business purposes. A settlement's functions plus its economic reach produce a measure of its *centrality*, its economic power among competitors.

A city comes next in the urban hierarchy. Not only does a city have more functional specialization than a town, but it has a larger hinterland and greater centrality. To distinguish between town and city, we also should look at the urban layout. A city has a well-defined commercial center, a so-called

central business district or, in urban-geographic parlance, a CBD. A town may merely have outskirts; a city has *suburbs*. Suburbs, as the term suggests, are subsidiary urban areas surrounding and connected to the central city. Many are exclusively residential, but other suburbs have their own comparatively small commercial centers or shopping malls.

Urban areas larger than cities have various names. To designate urban agglomerations even bigger than cities, the term "metropolis" is sometimes used, and on television newscasts you may hear the term "metropolitan area" when weather forecasts are given. In many areas of the world, neighboring large metropolises are coalescing into megacities called **megalopolises**. One such megalopolis stretches along the U.S. East Coast from Boston to beyond Washington, D.C.—the so-called Bosnywash megalopolis. Its economic reach, obviously, is not just regional but global.

PLACE AND LOCATION

In the southern province of China named Guangdong there is a city named Shenzhen. Just two decades ago, Shenzhen was a fishing village with perhaps 20,000 inhabitants and few services. Thatch houses and duck ponds marked the distinctly nonurban scene. Today, Shenzhen has a population of 2.5 million and is the world's fastest-growing urban area (Fig. 31-2). The thatch houses are long gone; skyscrapers tower over the townscape.

URBAN SITUATION

What has propelled Shenzhen to megacity status? The answer is geography. Shenzhen happens to lie across the border from one of the world's most successful economic centers, Hong Kong. It benefits

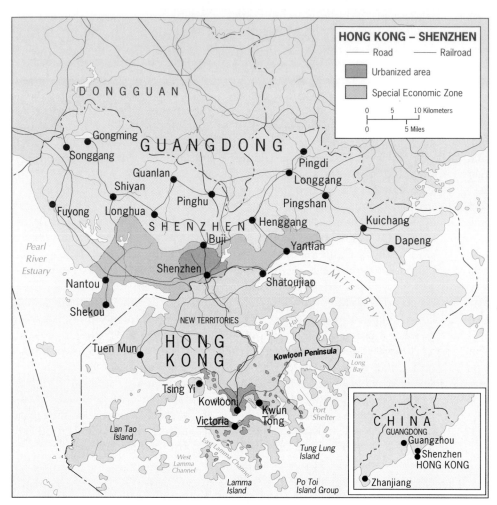

FIGURE 31–2 Shenzhen, China's most successful Special Economic Zone, lies adjacent to Hong Kong, one of the economic "tigers" on the Pacific Rim. This proximity has propelled Shenzhen's SEZ ahead of all others. SOURCE: From a map in H.J. de Blij and P.O. Muller, *Geography: Realms, Regions, and Concepts*, 7th ed. (New York: Wiley, 1994), p. 243.

from this proximity in numerous ways, but these benefits could only accrue when the once-closed border between China and Hong Kong became porous. Today, that is the case, and Shenzhen's relative location—its **situation**, as urban geographers call it—has helped make it the growth pole of a vast region.

When it comes to explaining the growth and success of certain cities over others, situation often is the key. A city's situation describes its position relative to much-traveled transport routes, productive farmlands, manufacturing complexes,

other towns and cities—in short, its near and distant surroundings. Indeed, the size, growth, and character of a city are in themselves reflections of its situation.

Importantly, a city's situation can change. The world's largest and most durable cities have seen their situation improve with the times: take the example of Paris, the capital of France. Settlement there may have begun in pre-Roman times, long before the Seine River became a major transport route and before the Seine Basin became one of Europe's most productive areas. Over time the situational advantage of

Paris grew. As its hinterland prospered, so did the city. Paris became an increasingly multifunctional city, a religious center, a cultural crucible, a political capital, an industrial giant, a high-technology focus. Centrally situated not only to the prosperous Seine Basin but also to the country as a whole, Paris eclipsed every other city in France. Today, Paris (population 10 million) is a **megacity**, a vast metropolitan area (Fig. 31-3). The next-largest city in France, Lyon, is only one-seventh the size of the City of Light.

Closer to home, we can observe

FIGURE 31–3 From a map drawn for the second edition of *Geography: Regions and Concepts* (New York: Wiley, 1978) by Rand McNally.

the effect of a long-term favorable situation on the growth of the Chicago urban area. Chicago lies at the landward end of the Great Lakes waterway, where it meets the water routes of the Mississippi system; it lies where the western end of the country's largest manufacturing belt yields to the vast farmlands of one of the world's most productive agricultural zones; it is situated at the convergence of rail, road, and air routes; and it has major natural resources in its vast and populous hinterland. Chicago has long been the dominant city of the North American interior, a place with unparalleled situational advantages.

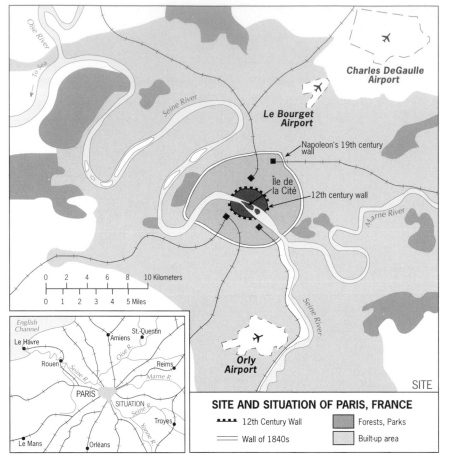

FIGURE 31–4   The Ile de la Cité was— and remains—at the heart of Paris.

URBAN SITE

A second locational factor affecting the development of cities and towns is their **site**. This term refers to the actual physical qualities of the place a city occupies: whether it lies in a confining valley, on a coastal plain, on the edge of a plateau, or perhaps on an island. It was site, not situation, the led to the founding of Paris: the first settlement was built on an island in the middle of the Seine River where there was security and easy defense, where the river could be easily crossed—and the cross traffic controlled. The *Ile de la Cité*, where Paris began, was endowed with the great Notre Dame Cathedral, but the island soon proved to be too small, and Paris spread onto both banks of the Seine (Fig. 31-4).

Paris was fortunate: no physical obstacles stood in the way of the city's expansion. Other cities have seen their growth stunted by site problems of various kinds or have experienced such severe environmental deterioration resulting in

A city's situation can improve; it can also deteriorate. When parts of the U.S. northeastern manufacturing belt began to decline, many cities and towns soon reflected this downturn. Resource exhaustion, agricultural failure, climatic change, and political developments all can change a city's situation, and historical geographers cite numerous examples. Berlin suffered severely not only from its destruction during the Second World War, but also from the subsequent division of Germany, which deprived the city of much of its hinterland. At a different level of scale, note what happens to the busy commercial center of a small town when a new expressway bypasses it. Gasoline stations, restaurants, and other services feel the effects as connectivity patterns change and traffic declines.

From the Field Notes

❝ A canalfront store on one of Bangkok's numerous *khlongs* displayed a wide range of goods, including one with a familiar logo. But the site of canal–riddled Bangkok is presenting serious problems: it is sinking relative to sealevel. Already, waterfront structures are showing signs of deterioration and flooding. The future of the 'Venice of Southeast Asia' is in doubt. ❞

part from site factors that urban development has been affected. The world's second largest urban area, Mexico City, lies in a mountain-flanked basin at an elevation of more than 2100 m (7000 feet). Underlain by the now-dry bed of a former lake, the city is vulnerable to earthquakes, is chronically short of water, cannot dispose of its wastes effectively, and has smog-choked air. Once one of the most gracious and attractive cities in the Americas, with magnificent public and private buildings and tree-lined avenues, Mexico City today is a noisy, crowded, high-rise–dominated, traffic-congested central city encircled by about 500 slums, beyond which lies a ring of the most

squalid squatter camps in the world. It is probably true that no physical site could have adequately accommodated Mexico City's rapid growth (the city receives about 1000 immigrants each day to add to a natural increase of similar dimensions, creating an annual total growth of about 750,000 inhabitants). But Mexico City's site has made things worse than is sometimes imaginable.

Other fast-growing cities in developing countries confront site problems of various kinds. Bangkok (9 million), the capital of Thailand, lies on the delta of the Chao Phraya, the major river in this part of the country. Fresh water is in short supply here, and numerous

wells provide it. But all the pumping has contributed to a serious site problem: southern Bangkok is sinking into the Gulf of Thailand at more than 2 cm (nearly 1 in.) per year. Already the city is honey-combed by countless canals that form, in effect, the city's second network of streets: millions of people stand to lose their homes if the subsidence continues. Add to this the fact that Bangkok's air on an average day is even more polluted than that of Mexico City (by some measures Bangkok today is the world's most environmentally blighted city), and it is clear that life here entails serious risks.

The role of site in the development of cities obviously has

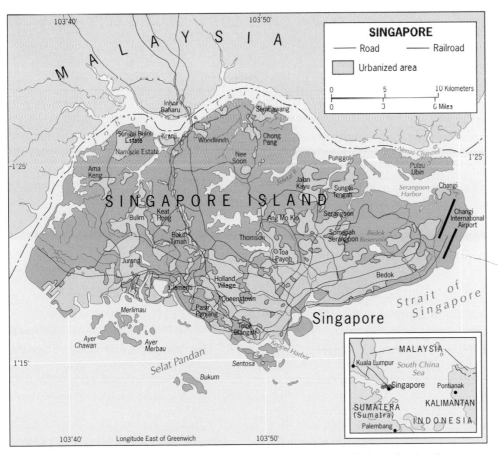

FIGURE 31–5 Singapore's physiographic separation from the Malayan Peninsula facilitated its secession from the Malaysian Federation. The city-state's relative location (inset) helped boost its economy. SOURCE: From a map in H.J. de Blij and P.O. Muller, *Geography: Realms, Regions, and Concepts*, 7th ed. (New York: Wiley, 1994), p. 246.

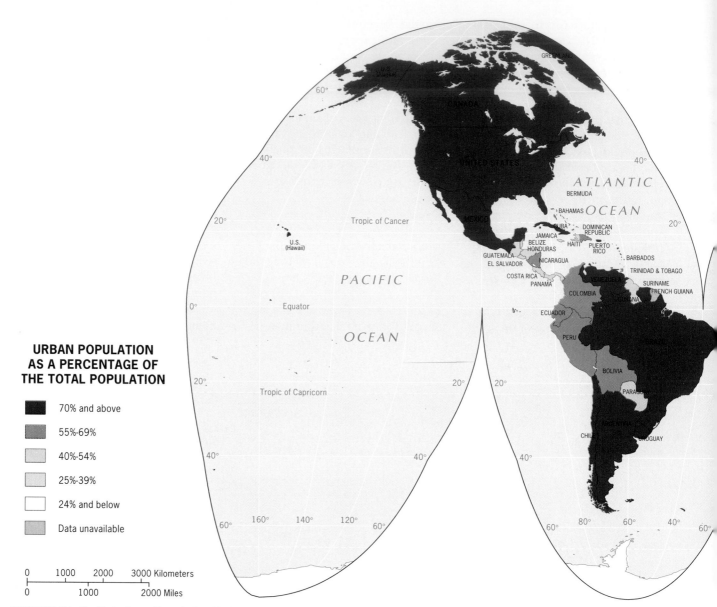

FIGURE 31–6 Data from Population Reference Bureau, *World Population Data Sheet 1995*, Washington, D.C.: 1994.

URBAN POPULATION AS A PERCENTAGE OF THE TOTAL POPULATION

- 70% and above
- 55%-69%
- 40%-54%
- 25%-39%
- 24% and below
- Data unavailable

```
0    1000   2000   3000 Kilometers
0         1000        2000 Miles
```

changed over time. The ancient Romans, who founded many of Europe's cities, often chose a site for its defensibility; that function is no longer relevant. Still, a city's site can play a role even in today's political struggles. Geographers often use Singapore to illustrate the advantages of a city's favorable situation; Singapore has parlayed its situational advantages into a status as one of the successful "economic tigers" on the Pacific Rim. But in 1965, when Chinese-dominated

Singapore opted to secede from Malay-dominated Malaysia, it was Singapore's insular site that helped make this step feasible. Singapore lies entirely on an island, separated cleanly from the Malaysian mainland by the Johore Strait (Fig. 31-5). That clear site definition created geographic identity; without it, Singapore's secession is unlikely to have occurred. Whenever we study a major city, therefore, site as well as situation should be investigated for clues to its development.

URBANIZATION IN THE 1990S

The map of urban population of the world as a percentage of the total population, by country, reveals not only the high level of urbanization in Western Europe, North America, Australia, and Japan, but also the remarkably high percentages of several of the world's less-developed countries (Fig. 31-6). Taking 70 percent and higher as the highest category, we find Mexico

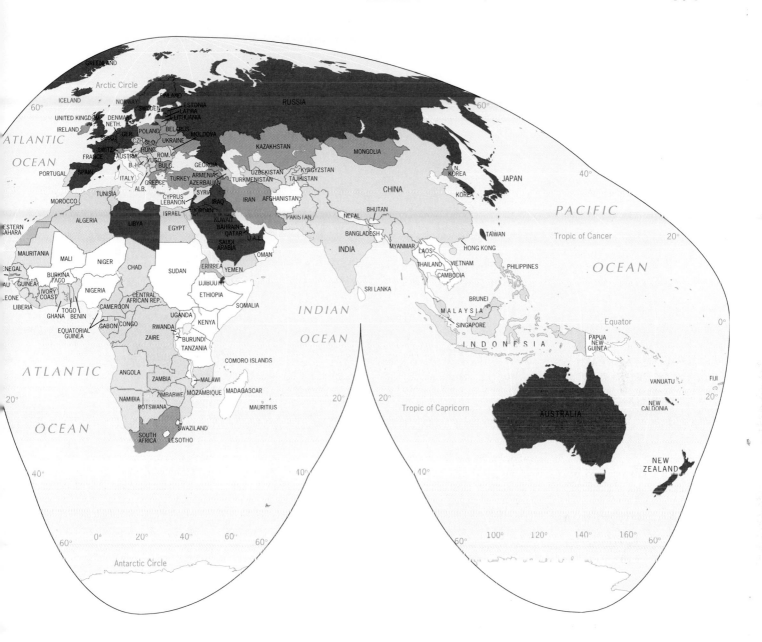

and Cuba on a par with France. In fact, Mexico's level of urbanization is higher than that of several Eastern European countries.

Seventy years of communist rule and associated industrialization raised levels of urbanization throughout most of the former Soviet Union. Today, Russia's population is nearly 75 percent urbanized; in Ukraine the figure is just below 70 percent. In Transcaucasia urbanization exceeds 55 percent, although Armenia is well ahead of Georgia and Azerbaijan.

As would be expected, the former Soviet colonial domain in Central Asia is least urbanized, ranging from 57 percent in strongly Russified Kazakhstan to a mere 31 percent in remote and severely underdeveloped Tajikistan.

The progress of urbanization in South America is also obvious from the map. Not only the three countries of the South American "cone" (Argentina, Chile, and Uruguay) are highly urbanized, but Brazil and Venezuela also rank high. In the mid-1990s, only the landlocked

countries (Paraguay and Bolivia) lagged well behind their neighbors; the lowest levels of urbanization in the realm were reported by the three countries on the north coast, Guyana, Suriname, and French Guiana. These "three Guianas" with their Caribbean (and otherwise non-Iberian) cultural characteristics stand apart from the rest of South America in other geographic ways as well.

In the mid-1990s the black African geographic realm continued to include countries with some of the

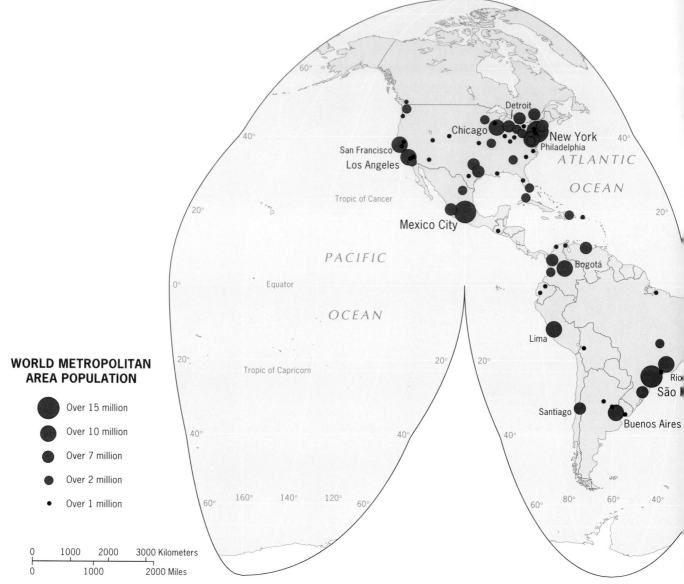

**WORLD METROPOLITAN
AREA POPULATION**

⬤ Over 15 million

⬤ Over 10 million

● Over 7 million

● Over 2 million

· Over 1 million

0   1000   2000   3000 Kilometers

0   1000   2000 Miles

FIGURE 31–7   Based on data from numerous sources: data on urban centers often are inconsistent. From United Nations, U.S. Census, Encyclopaedia Britannica Yearbooks, World Bank, Statesman's Yearbook, and other often contradictory sources.

world's lowest levels of urbanization, reminding us of the livelihoods of most African families. Nigeria, the realm's giant, in 1995 was just 16 percent urban. Even lower percentages were reported by Malawi in Southern Africa and Uganda in East Africa. In tropical Africa, only Zambia, with its northern mining towns, had close to a majority (49 percent) urban population. Only South Africa had a level

of urbanization above 50 percent, but that figure should be seen in light of that country's strong regional diversity. South Africa's mining-industrial heartland is highly urbanized, approaching Western European levels, but beyond this core area the country is dominantly rural and resembles tropical Africa in this context.

The culturally and economically diverse realm of Southwest Asia and

North Africa displays remarkable variation in national levels of urbanization, a variation related to differences in economies and cultures. Much of what may be considered the core of the realm (the Middle East and the Arabian Peninsula) is quite highly urbanized. **Nucleation** occasioned by the oil industry has much to do with this situation, although it does not explain the urbanization of Jordan.

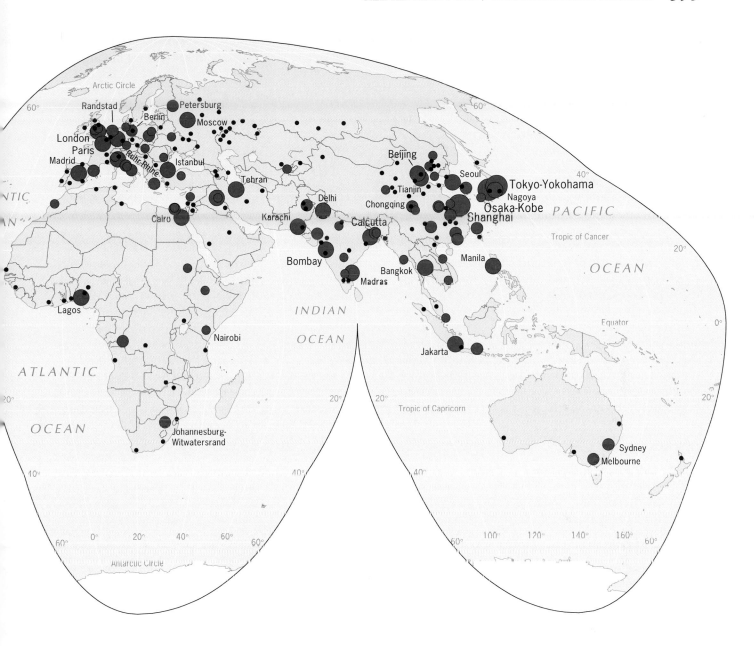

At the southern end of the Arabian Peninsula, urbanization has not reached high levels because modernization (and the exploitation of energy resources) has not affected the lives of a majority of the inhabitants as it has in Iraq and Saudi Arabia. To the east and west, the variations have similar backgrounds; note the low level of urbanization in resource-poor Afghanistan and the high level in oil-rich Libya.

Great cities such as Bombay and Calcutta notwithstanding, urbaniza-tion in South Asia remains low. For the realm as a whole, urbanization remains well below 30 percent. India today is about 26 percent ur-banized, Pakistan 32 percent, and populous Bangladesh, one of the world's least-urbanized countries, 17 percent. As we noted earlier, farming (including subsistence farming) remains the dominant way of life in this realm, and this condi-tion is reflected in the level of urbanization.

Southeast Asia has the distinction of incorporating the only country in the world that is 100 percent urban: the city-state of Singapore. But overall, this geographic realm is marked by low levels of urbaniza-tion, as the map underscores. In addition to Singapore, Brunei, the ministate on the Island of Borneo, and Malaysia were more than 50 percent urbanized by 1995; else-where, the figures were more characteristic of the still-developing world: Myanmar (25 percent), Viet-nam (21), and Thailand (19). Indonesia, the fourth most popu-lous country in the world, remains only 31 percent urbanized today.

These days we hear a great deal about the rapid rate of economic growth on the western Pacific Rim and the explosive growth of urban centers there (such as Shenzhen). And yet only Japan, South Korea, and Taiwan are highly urbanized countries. As a whole, East Asia is only about 35 percent urbanized, and China, despite its great cities, such as Shanghai and Beijing, has barely over one in four citizens living in urban centers. Shanghai and Beijing between them have about 25 million inhabitants, and China has many other large cities, but their total populations must be seen against China's 1.2 billion inhabitants. Urbanization in China is destined to proceed slowly. Should China experience an uncontrolled migration to the ciites, the country's future would be in the balance.

THE GREAT CITIES

It is useful to compare Figure 31-6 to a map showing the distribution of the world's over 300 cities with populations over 1 million (Fig. 31-7). The latter map immediately shows the concentration of large urban agglomerations in eastern North America, Western Europe, and East Asia, notably Japan. Africa's low urbanization level also is reflected clearly.

In North America, the anchors of several emerging megalopolitan regions are shown, including the Boston–Washington D.C., Chicago–Detroit–Pittsburgh, San Francisco–Los Angeles–San Diego, and Montreal–Toronto–Windsor conurbations. Yet another, in peninsular Florida, is still marked only as a set of discrete, comparatively small cities, but recent population growth in the state has been rapid: a regional megalopolis is developing quickly, centered on Miami–Fort Lauderdale–West Palm Beach,

growing northward along the Atlantic coast toward Jacksonville and westward across the burgeoning Orlando and Tampa areas of central Florida.

Author's Video Link
↓
6
Bosnywash

In Europe, England's conurbations are approaching megalopolitan unification: London and its immediate environs lie at the center of an expanding population cluster of nearly 20 million, and the industrial cities of South Wales and the Midlands are now just a short distance away. On the European mainland, a major urban complex is emerging in western Germany, In the Ruhr–Rhine zone that includes such cities as Düsseldorf, Essen, and Cologne. In the Netherlands, planning for a triangular megalopolis (Amsterdam–Rotterdam–The Hague) is a matter of leading national priority. An attempt is being made to guide this megalopolis, already being called *Randstad* ("ring-city"), into a twenty-first-century megacity showcase, complete with parks, spacious housing, good communications and public transportation, and optionally distributed social services. Belgium, too, is experiencing the development of a coalescing urban complex, with Brussels and Antwerp as the twin foci.

Other major urban agglomerations in Europe include the region centered on Paris, the rapidly developing Po Plain of northern Italy, and the Central European complex that extends from Germany's Saxony to Poland's Silesia. Elsewhere, there are major individual cities, such as Moscow, Saint Petersburg, and Madrid, but not yet a true polycentric, multicity urban region. Of

course, we should keep the *dimensions* of developments in Europe in perspective. The whole urbanized area, from Britain's Midlands to Germany's Ruhr–Rhine region, extends over an area not much larger than North America's megalopolis. Yet Europe's historic political fragmentation and cultural diversity lead us to identify discrete urban units by country within its vast multination urban core.

Large-scale megalopolitan development outside North America and Western Europe is occurring only in Japan. The Tokyo–Yokohama and Osaka–Kobe–Kyoto conurbations are of enormous dimensions, and they are growing toward each other along Honshu Island's Pacific coast. This is not to suggest that the urbanizing trend that has generated the "Bosnywash" megalopolis and Randstad–Holland is not being experienced in other areas of the world. Johannesburg in South Africa, for example, lies at the center of a smaller-scale megalopolis that includes several medium-size cities of the Witwatersrand region. However, in general, conurbanization outside Europe, the United States, and Japan has not yet reached comparable proportions. A high percentage of urbanization is not necessarily a corollary of conurbation, as the widely spaced, singular cities of Australia and Argentina reveal.

PRESENT AND FUTURE MEGACITIES

As Table 31-1 shows, many of the world's most populous cities lie in countries with poorer economies. These great human agglomerations stand alone in their vast rural hinterlands. Mexico City, Shanghai, Calcutta, Bombay, and Cairo rank in this group, and Bangkok, Lima-Callao, and Saigon-Cholon are not

TABLE 31–1 Populations of the World's Largest Conurbations from 1990 to 2000[a] (in millions)

Rank 1990	Rank 2000	Urban Area	1990	1995	2000
1	2	Tokyo–Yokohama–Kawasaki, *Japan*	27.1	27.9	28.7
2	1	Mexico City, *Mexico*	20.9	24.5	29.6
3	3	São Paulo, *Brazil*	18.1	21.7	26.1
4	4	Seoul, *South Korea*	16.7	19.4	22.4
5	8	New York–New Jersey, *U.S.A.*	14.6	14.7	14.7
6	9	Osaka–Kobe–Kyoto, *Japan*	13.8	14.1	14.5
7	7	Shanghai, *China*	13.0	14.0	15.2
8	5	Calcutta, *India*	11.7	13.1	15.9
9	6	Bombay, *India*	11.7	13.0	15.3
10	12	Buenos Aires, *Argentina*	11.5	12.2	12.9
11	10	Rio de Janeiro, *Brazil*	11.4	12.8	14.3
12	13	Moscow, *Russia*	10.4	10.7	11.1
13	14	Los Angeles Area, *U.S.A.*	10.0	10.4	10.7
14	11	Cairo, *Egypt*	10.0	11.2	13.2

[a]Reports and estimates of urban-area populations vary quite widely. Various sources may cite different figures.

far behind. By the year 2025, United Nations studies suggest, there may be as many as 15 cities with populations in excess of 20 million inhabitants, and some (Mexico City, São Paulo, and Shanghai) may have close to 30 million. Thus several of these huge urban areas will have more people than some of the megalopolitan conurbations in the developed world. This prediction suggests that the greatest challenges posed by the urban spiral still lie ahead.

Table 31-1 also indicates how fast the stand-alone cities in the poorer countries are growing, as opposed to conurbations in the richer countries. By the year 2000, the New York–New Jersey conurbation will have dropped from 5th to 8th largest in the world, and the Osaka–Kobe–Kyoto megalopolis from 6th to 9th. On the other hand, Calcutta will move from 8th place to 5th, and Bombay from 9th to 6th. Between them, Calcutta and Bombay will gain 8 million people during the decade of the 1990s; Tokyo and New York less than 2 million.

As we noted in Part 3, people continue to migrate to cities on the basis of pull factors that are more imaginary than real; their expectations of a better life mostly fail to materialize. Particularly in the less-developed realms, but in the industrial cities of developed regions as well, the new arrivals (and many long-term residents, too) are crowded together in overpopulated apartment buildings, dismal tenements, and teeming slums. Such arrivals come from other cities and towns and from the rural countryside, often as large families; they add to the cities' already-substantial rate of natural population growth. No housing expansion can keep up with this massive inflow. Huge areas of new shantytowns develop almost overnight, mostly without the barest amenities. However, immigration is not deterred, and multiplying millions of people will spend their entire lives in urban housing of wretched quality.

Miserable living conditions for urban immigrants notwithstanding, the world's cities—even Calcutta and Lagos—continue to beckon. In the mid-1990s, Africa had the world's fastest-growing cities, followed by those in South Asia and mainland East Asia and tropical South and Middle America. In contrast, the cities of North America, southern South America, and Australia were growing slowly, and those of Western Europe were barely growing at all. Figure 31-7 will therefore show much change in the developing world and relatively little in the developed world. In underdeveloped countries, villages are becoming towns, towns are growing into cities, and cities are expanding into metropolises. There was a time when New York was the world's largest city, its skyline of skyscrapers a symbol of the economic power of the Western world. Then Tokyo's urban area overtook New York in terms of numbers. And now Mexico City is poised to become the world's most populous city, an agglomeration of slums and squatter settlements encircling a deteriorating central city. By 2025, New York will no longer rank among the world's 10 largest cities.

It is impractical to generalize about the urban geography of the fast-growing cities in the developing world because they reveal much regional variation. China's Shanghai and India's Calcutta, for example, are both river-mouth cities with colonial imprints in their waterfront townscapes; the British built prominent landmarks along both the Huang Po and the Hooghly Rivers. Although the Chinese have decided to preserve the colonial frontage along the famous Bund of Shanghai, much of the urban legacy of colonialism in the city is disappearing under a relentless urban-renewal program. In addition, China's government has designated a triangle of land between the Huang Po and Chang (Yangtze) Rivers as a zone for special economic development, and this zone, called Pudong, has been almost totally razed of older, traditional Chinese urban and rural dwellings. When word of the jobs available in Pudong and in Shanghai's redevelopment program spread into the hinterland, 3 million job-seekers converged on the city. Those who did not take jobs found themselves speedily sent away. Such decisions can be made and implemented more easily in non-democratic China than in India, where individual rights are stronger. As a result, Shanghai is enormously overcrowded, but neither encircled nor pocked by squatter settlements as is the case in Calcutta; and Shanghai does not have countless thousands of people living under bridges, in cardboard boxes, even in drainpipes. The deprivation that is a hallmark of Calcutta's cultural landscape is not immediately evident in Shanghai.

If cities in the underdeveloped world share a characteristic, it may result from an absence of enforceable **zoning** regulations. Zoning laws determine the use to which urban land may be put, and zoning ordinances are drawn up to ensure the orderly use of space. Thus a fast-food franchise could not occupy a corner lot in a leafy suburb, because all the lots in that suburban block would be zoned exclusively for single-family residences. In all the cities of the less-developed world, zoning practices are inadequate, ineffective, or unenforced. In Madras and other cities of India, open space between high-rise buildings (sometimes luxury high-rise buildings) often is occupied by squatter settlements. In Bangkok, elementary schools and noisy, pollutant-belching factories stand side by side. In Nairobi (Kenya) hillside villas overlook some of Africa's worst slums. Over time, such incongruities are likely to lessen if not disappear, as is happening now to many cities on the fast-developing Pacific Rim of East Asia. Rising land values and associated demand for enforced zoning regulations are helping transform the central cities there as hotels and apartment buildings rise above the townscape. But in South Asia, sub-Saharan Africa,

From the Field Notes

❝ From atop one of the tallest hotels in central Cairo, the city's townscape is reminiscent of a Mediterranean–European scene. But a bus ride to the outskirts gave us quite another view of this metropolis: Asphalt roads gave way to dusty tracks, apartments to tenements and then to shacks. Parched, poor, garbage–strewn outer Cairo is a world away from the elegance and comfort of the center. ❞

Southwest Asia and North Africa, and Middle and South America, the megacities reflect their helter-skelter growth in various dysfunctional ways.

Perhaps the most obvious of all the characteristics of the growing, developing-world megacities lies in the stark contrasts they display. Stand on the roof of the Nile Hilton Hotel in Cairo, Egypt, and overlook the square and avenues leading into it, and you get the impression of a modern, almost Mediterranean-European metropolis. But get on a bus and ride it toward the city's outskirts, and that impression fades almost immediately as hard-surface streets give way to dusty alleys, apartment buildings give way to harsh tenements, sidewalk coffee shops yield to broken doors and windows. Traffic-choked, garbage-strewn, searingly polluted Cairo is home to an estimated 12 million people, about one-fifth of Egypt's population, a city bursting at the seams. And still the people continue to arrive, hoping for the better life that pulls countless migrants from the countryside year after year.

CITY AND CULTURE

All the world's great cities today are crucibles of culture, arenas of trans-culturation and often difficult accommodation. The many millions who are drawn to the cities (or forced off their land) represent countless histories and traditions, habits and practices. We acknowl-edge this multiculturalism geographically by identifying such urban regions as "Chinatown," "Little Havana," and "the French Quarter."

From the Algerian sectors of

From the Field Notes

66 Nearly twenty-five years ago, when I was doing field work for my book *Mombasa: An African City*, this was a quiet, calm, almost sedate town. When I walked the same streets again in 1992, I found Mombasa transformed: its population quadrupled, its neighborhoods overcrowded, its social services strained, its infrastructure suffering. Yet Mombasa now has a vitality and energy it lacked before. In the Old Town, near Fort Jesus, was a sight you would not have seen in the '60s. 99

Paris and the Turkish neighborhoods of Frankfurt to the (Asian) Indian suburbs of Durban and the Chinese quarters of Bangkok, cities the world over have been regionalized culturally. New arrivals tend to seek living space among those whose background they share, so that parts of the city become ethnic and cultural entities. In many African cities such as Lagos (Nigeria), Mombasa (Kenya), and Johannesburg (South Africa), the residential areas, ranging from established suburbs to still-growing squatter camps, incorporate a wide range of cultures from within their respective countries and beyond.

To understand the city better, we must investigate its spatial layout and discover the influences that have gone into the map it now presents. In the next chapter we begin by studying the kind of city most familiar to us, the North American version. Later, we expand our horizons to South America, Asia, and Africa.

KEY TERMS

Agglomeration
Hinterland
Megacity
Megalopolis
Nucleation
Site
Situation
Specialization
Urban Function
Urban Geography
Urban Hierarchy
Urbanization
Zoning

32

URBAN PATTERN
AND STRUCTURE

The study of urban settlements in human geography encompasses a broad range of approaches and interests. We have already noted the application of the cultural landscape concept to urban areas, because the "townscape" in many ways reflects and represents the culture that generates it. Earlier in this century, Professor Carl Sauer proposed a view of urban places as manifestations of the relationship between human societies and natural landscapes. Culture was the *factor*, the natural landscape was the *medium*, and urban plan and structure were the *forms*. This raised questions about the resulting cityscape. How did the actual, physical place where a city grew affect its development? A city might have begun as a settlement on an island, where protection was provided by nature, but later that same island might lose its protective advantage and be the source of severe space limitations. How did the relative location of a city—its regional position vis-à-vis other settlements—influence its growth and development? Some cities emerged as focal points for large prosperous regions, with little competition from

Geographica

- In the United States, the urban system evolved through five stages of development extending over two centuries, each stage determined by prevailing modes of transport and industry; today's high-technology epoch, still in the process of transforming the modern city, dates from the 1970s.

- Every urban center has an economic base, with workers employed in basic (that is, goods-producing) and nonbasic (service) jobs; this employment structure reveals the primary functions a city performs.

- Central place theory helps explain why, under ideal circumstances, small urban places such as villages lie close together, while larger cities lie far apart.

- Models of urban structure reveal how the forces that shape the internal layout of cities have changed, transforming the single-center city with one dominant downtown into the now-common polycentric metropolis with several competing downtowns.

other nearby urban centers. Certain other cities found themselves in less favored locations, perhaps marginal to productive regions or overshadowed by more successful competitors. Our understanding of the influences of site and situation helps explain these contrasts.

Interactive relationships between cities and surrounding countrysides can be measured and mapped. Every city and town has an adjacent region, large or small, for which it forms the focus and where its influence is paramount. Farmers in that region sell many of their products

401

on the city's markets, and customers from smaller towns and villages come to shop for certain goods and to conduct other business in the city's commercial areas; the city's newspapers are read and its television stations are watched in this zone. In many other ways, also, the city's dominance can be recorded and its interconnections charted. The term **hinterland**, a German word meaning, literally, the land "behind" the city, came into use to designate such a subsidiary region, and many geographic studies have confirmed the tangible and intangible influences of the central city over it.

When two (or more) cities lie some distance apart, where does the hinterland of one end and that of the other begin? That question leads us to investigate the factors that influence the *spacing* of cities.

In general, large cities tend to lie farther apart than smaller ones; towns lie even closer together, and villages are separated by even shorter distances. What forces influence the evolution of this pattern? Can von Thünen's method of model building be used to interpret what we see?

These are the questions to be addressed in this chapter, and as we will see, they lead quite naturally to the anatomy of the city itself, its internal structure and functions. A city's spatial organization can reveal much about its efficiency and productivity, and hence its capacity to compete not only for dominance over a large immediate hinterland, but also for more distant linkages. As we will note, the spatial layout of the modern city has changed quite dramatically over the past decades, and it still is evolving.

INTERURBAN SPATIAL ORGANIZATION

In the United States, the Industrial Revolution occurred almost a century after Europe's, but when it finally did cross the North Atlantic in the 1870s, it took hold so successfully and advanced so robustly that only 50 years later, America was surpassing Europe as the world's mightiest industrial power. Thus the far-reaching economic, demographic, and societal changes experienced in Europe's industrializing countries were greatly accelerated in the United States, fueled further by the arrival of more than 25 million European immigrants who were overwhelmingly concentrated in the major manufacturing centers. The impact of industrial urbanization occurred simultaneously at two levels of generalization. At the national level, or *macroscale*, a network or system of new cities rapidly emerged, specializing in the collection, processing, and distribution of raw materials and manufactured goods, linked together by an ever more efficient web of long-distance and local transport routes. Within that urban system, at the *microscale*, individual cities prospered in their new roles as manufacturing centers, generating a wholly new internal structure that still forms the spatial framework of most of the industrialized cities to invest in a bigger local infrastructure of private and public services, as well as housing, and thereby convert each round of industrial expansion into a new stage of urban development. Moreover, this whole process unfolded so quickly that planning was impossible, and almost literally, America awoke one morning near the turn of the twentieth century to discover it had built a number of large cities. This rise of the national urban system, unintended though it may have been, was a necessary by-

From the Field Notes

❝ In many U.S. cities, only vestiges of the steel-rail epoch remain. But in a few places, the tram still services—or rather, serves again—on limited routes linking the downtown to nearby areas. This surface version of the elevated 'people mover' in Portland, Oregon, is a reminder of a bygone era. ❞

product of industrialization, without which rapid U.S. economic development could not have taken place. This far-flung hierarchy of cities and towns now blanketed the whole continent, and came to serve its local populations with the conveniences of modern life.

EVOLUTION OF THE AMERICAN URBAN SYSTEM

Even though it first emerged during the Industrial Revolution of the period from 1870 to 1910, the U.S. urban system was in the process of formation for several decades preceding the Civil War. The human geographer John Borchert conceptualized the evolutionary sequence of the American urban system in an article entitled "American Metropolitan Evolution" (1967). A four-stage model summarizes two centuries of urban development, which Professor Borchert based on key changes in transportation technology and industrial energy.

The first stage was the preindustrial *Sail-Wagon Epoch* (1790–1830), when interaction was limited by slow and primitive overland and waterway movements. The leading cities of the time were the landfall settlements of the northeast, such as Boston, New York, and Philadelphia, which were at least as heavily oriented to the European overseas trade as they were to their still rather inaccessible western hinterlands (although the Erie Canal was opened as this epoch came to a close).

Next came the *Iron Horse Epoch* (1830–1870), dominated by the arrival and diffusion of the steam-powered railroad, which steadily expanded its network from east to west until the first transcontinental line was completed as the epoch ended. Accordingly, a nationwide transport system had been forged, coal-mining centers boomed (to keep locomotives running), and,

From the Field Notes

❝ Rapid-transit is a symbol of the high-technology epoch in American cities. The idea is to persuade people to park and to ride into the city center, leaving the highways less crowded. But, as in the case of Miami's Metro, seen here from the University of Miami station, routes often do not connect the most appropriate hubs of activity. Miami's Metro parallels South Dixie Highway (far right), but it does not link downtown Coral Gables nor (until now) the sprawl-encircled Miami International Airport to Miami's CBD, nor to each other. ❞

aided by the easier and cheaper movement of raw materials, small-scale urban manufacturing began to spread outward from its New England hearth, to which the factory-system innovation had been transplanted from Britain in the early 1800s. The national urban system started to take shape as New York advanced to become the primate city by 1850, and the next level in the hierarchy was increasingly occupied by such booming new industrial centers as Pittsburgh, Detroit, and Chicago.

This economic-urban development process crystallized during the third stage, the *Steel-Rail Epoch* (1870–1920), which coincided with the American Industrial Revolution. Among the massive forces now shaping the growth and full establishment of the national metro-

politan system were the rise and swift dominance of the all important steel industry along the Chicago-Detroit-Pittsburgh axis (as well as its coal and iron ore supply areas in the northern Appalachians and Lake Superior district, respectively), the increasing scale of manufacturing that necessitated greater agglomeration in the most favored raw material and market locations for industry, and the steel-related improvements of the railroads: much more durable tracks of steel (which replaced iron), more powerful steam locomotives, and heavier and larger (also refrigerated) freight cars, which permitted significantly higher speeds, longer hauls of bulk commodities, and the more effective linking of hitherto distant rail nodes.

The *Auto-Air-Amenity Epoch*

(1920–1970) comprised the latest stage of American industrial urbanization and maturation of the national urban hierarchy. The key innovation was the gasoline-powered internal combustion engine, which underwrote ever greater automobile- and truck-based regional and metropolitan dispersal. Furthermore, as technological advances in manufacturing spawned the increasing automation of blue-collar jobs, the U.S. labor force steadily shifted toward a new emphasis on white-collar personal and professional services to manage the industrial economy—a productive activity that responded less to traditional cost- and distance-based location forces and ever more strongly to the amenities (pleasant environments) available in suburbia, as well as in the southern-tier Sunbelt states, in a nation now fully interconnected by jet travel and long-distance communication networks.

Although Professor Borchert's model extends to 1970, the innovations that propelled its last stage continue to shape the country's urban framework today. Intercity commuting no longer is a rarity (some residents of Santa Fe, New Mexico, commute weekly to jobs in Los Angeles, for example), and the decline of "Rustbelt" cities continues. But there are signs that a *High-Technology Epoch* is in the offing, a time when service and information industries, with their growing capacity to operate efficiently from nonurban bases, will stimulate an even greater dispersal of city populations than is already the case. Might the city, accordion-like, have gone through its maximum concentration, eventually to send its people back into the countryside, far beyond suburbia, to repopulate with high-tech specialists the very rural areas it once depopulated by offering factory jobs?

URBAN SPATIAL STRUCTURE

When we look at an atlas map of the United States or Canada, or at a road map of a state or province, we see an array of places, larger and smaller, longer and shorter distances apart. The map looks like a jumble, and yet, each place is where it is because of some decision, some perception of the site or its situation, or perhaps some incident that led to settlement.

Even from such a general map, it is possible to get an impression of the sizes of the places on it. There are many villages with unfamiliar names, a number of towns named in larger print and situated on highways, several cities upon which radial systems of routes converge, and perhaps one familiar, dominant city. We conclude that the larger the places become, the fewer there are: there is only one largest metropolis, several large cities, a greater number of towns, and many villages. Not only do we discern the hierarchy of urban places, but also the so-called **rank-size rule**. The rank-size rule holds that in a model urban hierarchy, the population of a city or town will be inversely proportional to its rank in the hierarchy. For example, if the largest city has 12 million people, the second city will have about 6 million (i.e., half of the largest); the third city will have 4 million (one-third of the leader), the fourth city will have 3 million, and so on. Note that the differences between cities lower on the hierarchy become less: the tenth-largest city would have 1.2 million.

The rank-size rule does not apply in all countries, especially not in countries with dominant primate cities, such as France or Mexico. But long-diversified, complex economies do seem to approximate it (the United States is an example). Although our map conveys these impressions of rank and frequency, however, it tells us little about the reasons behind the distribution of places at various levels in the hierarchy. We can use our knowledge of site and situation to speculate on the dominance of Boston compared to, say, Portland (Maine). But what governs the distances from city to city in about the same rank, or from village to village?

FUNCTIONS

Before we try to answer this question, we should take note of the functions cities and other urban places perform. Every city and town has an **economic base**. Geographers divide the activities of workers in cities on the grounds of their purpose: a percentage of workers produce goods or services to satisfy demand in the hinterland or in external markets even farther away, while other workers do things that keep the city itself going. For example, workers in a manufacturing plant that produces microwave ovens (the first category) are in the city's **basic sector**; their work results in exports and generates an inflow of money. On the other hand, workers who maintain city streets, clerks who work in offices, and teachers in city schools are responsible for the functioning of the city itself, and they constitute the **nonbasic sector** (also called the *service* sector). Many who work in a city, of course, do some of each. An attorney may serve clients from a village in the city's hinterland, where there is no lawyer's office, but also serve city residents.

The ratio of basic to nonbasic workers, therefore, gives geographers an impression of the economic base of a city. The number of nonbasic workers always is greater than the number of basic workers, and this ratio tends to increase as a city grows in overall size. And therein lies a danger: when the products or services exported from the basic sector fail to find a market and basic-sector jobs are lost, many more nonbasic-sector jobs are affected.

From data on the number of people employed in various basic and nonbasic jobs (the **employment structure**) we can discern the primary functions a city performs. Note that the emphasis is on the plural: all cities have multiple functions, and the larger the city, the larger the number of functions. As we noted at the beginning of this chapter, however, the functions of some cities are dominated by one activity. This **functional specialization** was a characteristic of European cities even before the Industrial Revolution, but the Industrial Revolution gave it new meaning. To most of us the associations have little relevance today, but there was a time when the English city of Sheffield and the commodity of stainless steel were simply synonymous, as were Leicester and leather footwear, Manchester and textiles, and Leeds and woolens. The United States, too, saw the growth of cities that were closely identified with certain products (Pittsburgh steel, Detroit automobiles). But even when automobile production dominated Detroit's economic base, other functions already contributed significantly as well.

What was the situation about the middle of the twentieth century? We are fortunate that the geographer Chauncy Harris published a detailed study of the distribution of U.S. cities according to their dominant functions. In an article entitled "A Functional Classification of Cities in the United States" (1943), Harris revealed the northeastern concentration of manufacturing-dominated cities, the wide dispersal (with a central U.S. concentration) of retail centers, and the western diffusion of cities already so diversified that no primary or dominant function could be established from the employment data (Fig. 32-1). He also mapped cities with other functional characteristics, but the three maps included in Figure 32-1 are representative of a situation that now, more than 50 years later, no longer exists. Only slightly more than a dozen northeastern cities could still be mapped as manufacturing centers, including such cities as Flint, Michigan, Gary, Indiana, and Wil-

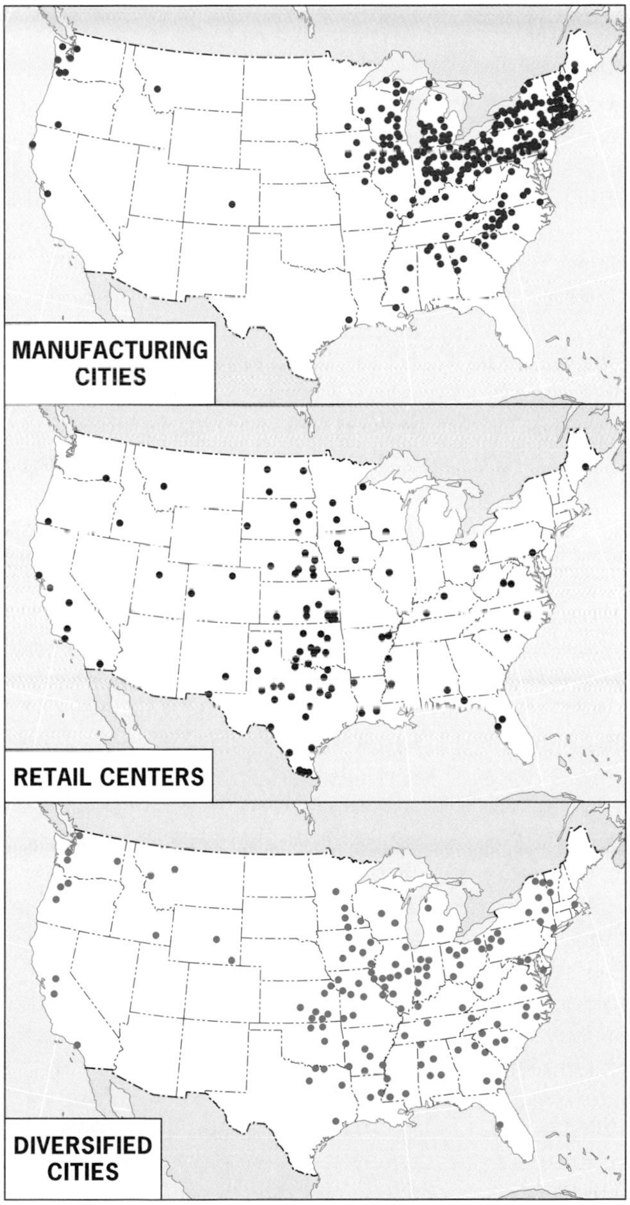

FIGURE 32–1 The distribution of cities according to function: manufacturing, retail-dominated, and diversified cities in the early 1940s. From C. Harris, "A Functional Classification of Cities in the United States," *The Geographical Review* 33 (1943), p. 88.

mington, Delaware; most of the others mapped by Harris have become diversified centers. Retail-dominated cities are fewer still, including Phoenix, Arizona, San Antonio, Texas, and Orlando, Florida. With growing size has come greater diversification.

This is not to suggest that specialization no longer exists. As we noted at the beginning of this chapter, we can still recognize educational centers (college towns), gambling cities (Las Vegas, Atlantic City), resort and retirement towns (Vero Beach, Florida), government headquarters (Augusta, Maine), and mining centers (Wheeling, West Virginia). But many of these places remain small—or the industry is exceptionally dominant. As urban centers grow, they tend to lose their functional specialization.

Another implication of urban growth lies in the ratio between workers in the basic sector and those in the nonbasic sector. This ratio is about the same (1 to 2) for large cities. When, therefore, a business is established with 50 production (basic) workers, it adds 100 nonbasic workers to the work force. Economic expansion of this kind therefore has a **multiplier effect**, not only in terms of the work force, but also on the urban population as a whole, because most workers bring dependents to the city. These dependents are additional consumers of goods and services.

CENTRAL PLACES

Earlier we encountered the notion of a *hierarchy* of urban settlements ranging from hamlets to metropolises, based not only on their population numbers but on the functions and services they offer. These functions and services attract consumers not just from the urban areas themselves, but also from surrounding areas beyond the urban limits, so that all urban centers have a certain **economic reach** that, in turn, is a measure of its centrality.

Centrality is a situational property that is crucial to the development and persistence of urban places and their concomitant service areas. To these hinterlands, towns and cities function as *central places*; even a village is a central place to its small tributary area. How, then, do all these service areas relate to each other? Do they overlap? Do towns of approximately the same size lie about the same distance away from each other? What rules govern the arrangement of urban places on the landscape? These are critical questions if we are to understand the structuring of urban hierarchies. Geographers have discovered many answers, and this inquiry constitutes some of the most significant theoretical work in human geography to date. Let us take a closer look.

CENTRAL PLACE THEORY

In 1933, an economic geographer named Walter Christaller published a book entitled *The Central Places of Southern Germany*. In this volume, which was not translated into English until the 1950s, Christaller laid the groundwork for the **central place theory**. Addressing questions such as those we have just raised, he attempted to develop a model that would show how and where central places in the hierarchy (hamlets, villages, towns, and cities) would be functionally and spatially distributed with respect to one another. In his effort to discover the laws that govern this distribution, Christaller began with a set of simplifying assumptions. The surface of the ideal, laboratory-like region would be flat and without physical barriers. Soils would have equal, unvarying fertility. He also assumed an even distribution of population and purchasing power and a uniform transport network that permitted direct travel from each settlement to the other. Finally, Christaller assumed that a constant maximum distance or range for the sale of any good or service produced in a town would prevail in all directions from that urban center.

Christaller's idea was to calculate the nature of the central place system that would develop under such idealized circumstances and then to compare that model to real-world situations, explaining variations and exceptions. Some places, he realized, would have more centrality than others. The central functions of larger towns would cover regions within which several smaller places with lesser central functions and service areas are nested. What was needed, Christaller reasoned, was a means to calculate the *degree* of centrality of various places. In order to do this, Christaller identified *central goods and services* as those provided only at a central place. These would be the goods and services that a central place would make available to its consumers in a surrounding region—as opposed to services that might be available anywhere (without local focus), and unlike those that are produced for distant and even foreign markets and are therefore of no relevance to the local consumers. Next came the question of the range of sale of such central goods and services: the distance people would be willing to travel to acquire them. The limit would lie halfway between one central place and the next place where the same product was sold at the same price, because under the assumptions Christaller used, a person would not be expected to travel 11 miles to one place to buy an item if it were possible to go only 9 miles to purchase it at another place.

HEXAGONAL HINTERLANDS

In Christaller's **urban model** each central place, therefore, has a surrounding *complementary region*, an exclusive hinterland, within which the town has a monopoly on the sale of certain goods, since it alone can provide such goods at a given price and within a certain range of travel. From what we have just said, it would seem that such complementary regions would be circular in shape. However, when we construct the model on that basis, problems arise: either the circles adjoin and leave unserved areas, or they overlap, and when they do there is no longer a condition of monopoly. These two problems and their resolution—a system of perfectly fitted hexagonal regions—are sketched in Figure 32-2.

The logical extension of this conclusion is shown in Figure 32-3. If the hexagonal complementary region shown in Figure 32-2 is centered on a hamlet, where the fewest goods and services are available, then that hamlet and its region must form a part of the larger complementary region of a village. And the village and its complementary region would be a part of a town's larger and still hexagonal complementary region. The central place system, therefore, reveals a *nesting* (region-within-region) pattern; each larger complementary region is centered on a higher-order urban place.

Like von Thünen, whose economic-geographic model also was based on a series of assumptions, Christaller knew that the real world would not present the conditions he had postulated. But his model yielded a number of important conclusions that had practical applicability. First, he established that the ranks of urban places we saw on that atlas map in fact represent an orderly hierarchy of central places in spatial balance. Disturb that balance by eliminating one component of it, and the whole system will move toward a new equilibrium. Second, Christaller's model implied that places of the same size and number of functions would be spaced the same distance

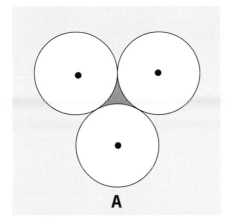

A

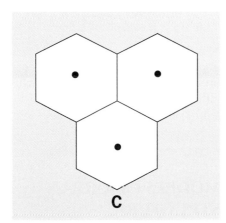

B

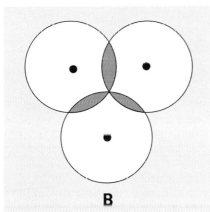

C

FIGURE 32–2 Constructing Christaller's hexagonal trade areas surrounding urban centers: (*A*) unserved areas shown in orange; (*B*) orange areas indicate places where the conditions of monopoly would not be fulfilled; and (*C*) hexagons completely fill an area without overlap.

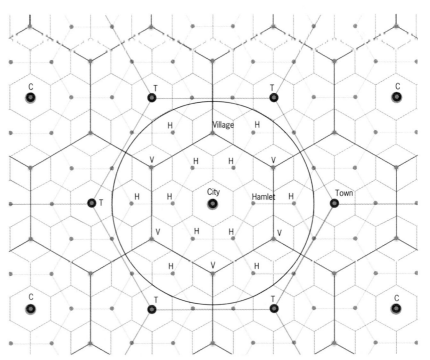

FIGURE 32–3 Christaller's interlocking model of a hierarchy of settlements and their service areas. T = town; C = city; H = hamlet; V = village.

apart. Third, larger cities would be spaced farther from each other than smaller towns or villages. What the model confirmed, therefore, was that the general pattern on the map is the result *not* of accident, but of forces that tend to create rank-size regularity.

THE REAL WORLD

Fly over the actual rural landscape of southern Germany or any other countryside, and you are reminded that Christaller's proposed hexagonal pattern is a model, not reality. Physical barriers, resource distributions, and other factors serve to distort the model's regularity. Geographers were divided on the relevance of the model. Some saw hexagonal systems everywhere; others saw none at all. Soon there were attempts to alter the Christaller model and to relate it to various areas of the world. Christaller himself joined the debate: in 1950, he published a new article entitled "The Foundations of Spatial Organization in Europe," in which he insisted that he had been correct all along, writing,

When we connect the metropolitan areas with each other through lines, and draw such a network of systems of the map of Europe, it indeed becomes eminently clear how the metropolitan areas everywhere lie in hexagonal arrangements.

Christaller received support from the research of geographers who applied his ideas empirically to regions in Europe, North America, and elsewhere. In China, the North China Plain and the Sichuan Basin both display the kind of uninterrupted flatness Christaller's model assumed. When G. William Skinner examined the distribution of villages, towns, and cities there, he found a spatial pattern closely resembling that predicted by Christaller's model. Studies in the U.S. Midwest suggested that

THREE CLASSIC MODELS OF URBAN STRUCTURE

The three models of **urban structure** shown in Figure 32-4 display not only three obvious alternative interpretations of the layout of cities, but also the progression of urban-structural complexity over time. The *concentric zone model* (Fig. 32-4*a*) resulted from sociologist Ernest Burgess's study of Chicago in the 1920s. He recognized five concentric functional zones, including the CBD (1), itself subdivided into several subdistricts (financial, retail, theater, etc.). The zone of transition (2), in Burgess's time was one of residential deterioration, marked by the encroachment of business and light manufacturing. Zone 3 was a ring of closely built but adequate homes of the blue-collar labor force. Zone 4 consisted of middle-class residences, and zone 5 represented the suburban ring around Chicago. Burgess described his model as dynamic: as the city grew, inner zones encroached on outer ones, so that CBD functions invaded zone 2 and the problems of zone 2 affected the inner margins of zone 3.

In the late 1930s Homer Hoyt published his *sector model* (Fig. 32-4*b*) in part as an answer to the inadequacies of the Burgess model. Arterial routes and their frontages, Hoyt argued, created a pie-shaped urban structure. From the concentric zone model we would conclude that rent paid for residential use would increase steadily from the tenements of zone 2 to the suburbs of zone 5. But in reality, Hoyt discovered, a low-rent area could extend all the way from the CBD to the city's outer edge, as in sector 3; the same could be true for a high-rent sector (1). Transport (5) and industrial (6) sectors also did not reflect the concentricity Burgess had proposed.

In fact, we can recognize elements of concentric as well as sector layout in the urban structure of many cities. Arguing that neither model adequately reflected city structure, Chauncy Harris and Edward Ullman in the 1940s proposed the *multiple nuclei model* (Fig. 32-4*c*). This model was based on the notion that the CBD was losing its dominant position as the undisputed nucleus of the urban area; several of the urban regions shown have their own subsidiary but competing "nuclei."

while the square layout of the Township-and-Range System imposed a different kind of regularity on the landscape, the spatial forces at work tended to confirm Christaller's fundamental theory.

The important contribution by Christaller to human geography was the stimulus he gave to urban and economic geography in general, and to location theory in particular. If you look at the professional literature in geography, you will see a large number of articles published since the 1950s in which geographers have attempted to unravel complexities inherent in Christaller's model, its assumptions, and its applications. In the process, our

understanding of the functioning of urban places, and of the forces that influence their distribution on the land, has been strengthened.

MODELS OF URBAN STRUCTURE

Cities are not simply random agglomerations of buildings and people. They exhibit **functional structure**: they are spatially organized to perform their functions as places of commerce, production, education, and much more. Just as Christaller developed generaliza-

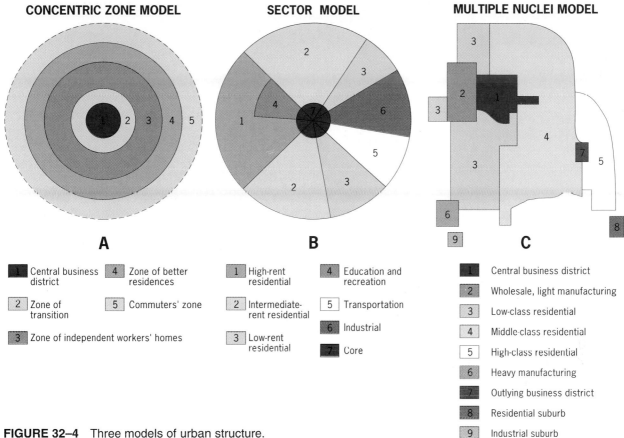

CONCENTRIC ZONE MODEL

A

1	Central business district	4	Zone of better residences
2	Zone of transition	5	Commuters' zone
3	Zone of independent workers' homes		

SECTOR MODEL

B

1	High-rent residential	4	Education and recreation
2	Intermediate-rent residential	5	Transportation
3	Low-rent residential	6	Industrial
		7	Core

MULTIPLE NUCLEI MODEL

C

1	Central business district
2	Wholesale, light manufacturing
3	Low-class residential
4	Middle-class residential
5	High-class residential
6	Heavy manufacturing
7	Outlying business district
8	Residential suburb
9	Industrial suburb

FIGURE 32–4 Three models of urban structure.

tions about the spacing of cities and towns, we could prepare an idealized model of the internal layout of the metropolitan city. How and where are the various residential and nonresidential components of the city positioned with respect to each other? If there are forces that govern the distribution of central places on the landscape, then surely there are forces that affect the way cities are internally organized. It is not difficult to think of one of these forces: the price of land. This tends to be highest in the central city downtown, and then declines irregularly outward, so one would not look for a spacious residential area in the central business district.

Before we proceed, let us define some terms commonly used to denote regions of the city. The **central business district (CBD)** is the core, the nucleus, the heart of the city, called the downtown in

American parlance. High land values, tall buildings, busy traffic, converging highways and mass transit systems mark the American CBD. An urban *zone* is a sector of a city within which land use is relatively uniform (an industrial or residential zone, for example). The term **central city** is often used to denote that part of an urban area lying within the outer ring of residential suburbs that encircles modern cities. In effect, it refers to the older city, as opposed to the newer suburbs. A **suburb** is an outlying, functionally uniform part of an urban area, often (but not always) contiguous to the central city. Most suburbs are residential, but some have other land uses.

Just by using such terms as residential area and central business district, we reveal our awareness of the existence of a regional structure within cities. When you refer to downtown, or to the airport, or to

the municipal zoo, you are in fact referring to urban regions where certain functions prevail (business activity, transportation, and recreation, in the three just mentioned). All of these urban regions or zones, of course, lie near or adjacent to each other and together make up the total metropolis. But how are they arranged? Is there any regularity or recurrent pattern to the alignment of the various zones of the city, perhaps reflecting certain prevailing growth processes? In other words, do the city's regions constitute the elements of a metropolitan structuring that can be recognized in every urban concentration, perhaps with modifications related to such features as a city's particular site, size, shape, and relief?

One way to attack this problem is to study the layout of a large number of cities, compare resulting maps, and determine which features recur. In very general terms, we would soon conclude that cities have *central zones*, consisting mainly of the CBD, and *outer zones*, where lower-density suburbs and their new business and shopping centers lie. Between the central and outer zones, it is often possible to discern a *middle zone*, an ill-defined, often rather mixed and disorganized area; in this zone, change is frequently observed, as in the aging of housing and the development of slums within its deteriorating inner salient.

Throughout the past century, urban geographers have attempted to construct models that would account for the geographic layout of cities (see box, "Three Classic Models of Urban Structure"). But as manufacturing cities became modern cities, and as modern cities began to display the trappings of postmodernism, this task became more complicated. Today, urban geographers see superregions they call urban realms, and they create models that show cities within cities.

URBAN REALMS

Even the multiple nuclei model (see box, "Three Classic Models of Urban Structure") fails to account for all the spatial-structural complexities of the contemporary American metropolis. Although this model accurately reflects the decentralization and nucleation of certain urban functions, much has changed since 1945. In the early postwar period, as Professor James Vance documented in a study of the San Francisco Bay Area, rapid population dispersal to the outer suburbs not only created distant nuclei, but also reduced the volume and level of interaction between the central city and these emerging suburban cities. This situation strengthened the self-sufficiency of the new *outer cities* of the suburban ring, where locational advantages produced an

ever-greater range of retailing and employment activity. By the 1970s, outer cities were becoming increasingly independent of the CBD to which these former suburbs had once been closely tied, and they began to duplicate—and even overtake—certain high-order functions of the central city. In the 1980s, the increasingly complex American metropolitan area revealed combinations of the classic models described previously, plus a new redistribution of activities and zones in the urban fringe. Regional shopping centers in the suburban zone were becoming the CBDs of the outer nuclei. Business and industrial parks were locating outside the central city as well (Fig. 32-5). The term **urban realms** came into use

to describe the metropolis of the 1990s, each a separate and distinct economic, social, and political entity within the larger urban framework.

Los Angeles
A good idea of the utility of the urban realms model can be seen in its application to metropolitan Los Angeles, where the realm structure is readily apparent. Five discrete urban realms have emerged around the central city (Fig. 32-6), creating a suburban ring that extends as far as 50 miles (80 kilometers) from the CBD. Clockwise from the west, these are: (1) the *West Realm*, typified by Santa Monica, Beverly Hills, and the coast-facing ribbon extending toward Santa Barbara along the

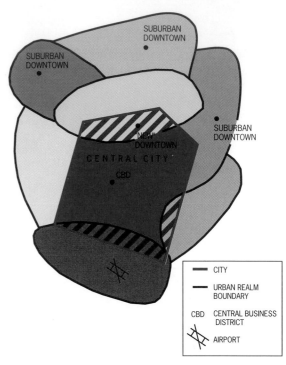

URBAN REALMS MODEL

FIGURE 32–5 The Urban Realms Model. SOURCE: From T. Hartshorn and P. O. Muller, "Suburban Downtowns and the Transformation of Metropolitan Atlanta's Business Landscape," *Urban Geography* 10 (1989), p. 375. Reproduced by permission of *Urban Geography*.

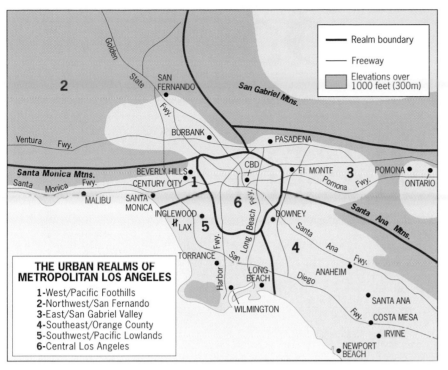

FIGURE 32–6 From a map in H. J. de Blij and P. O. Muller, *Geography: Regions and Concepts*, 5th ed. (New York: Wiley, 1988), p. 220, designed by P. O. Muller.

Santa Monica Freeway; (2) the *Northwest Realm*, essentially the San Fernando Valley between the Santa Monica and the San Gabriel Mountains; (3) the *East Realm*, which follows the San Gabriel Valley eastward to the desert margin; (4) the *Southeast Realm*, Orange County, one of America's fastest growing urban areas, centered on Costa Mesa and Anaheim; and (5) the *Southwest Realm*, straddling the San Diego Freeway from near Inglewood in the north to Long Beach in the south, and dominated economically by L.A. International Airport (LAX) and aerospace activities. Approximately in the middle lies the sixth urban realm of this vast metropolitan complex, *Central Los Angeles*, at the hub of the freeway network, but serving more as a crossroads than as a regional core. The CBD itself does contain a cluster of high-rise commercial buildings and a group of cultural and sports facili-

ties, but it is overshadowed in many categories of economic power by just one of the five surrounding realms, Orange County.

The growth of the outer cities has been the hallmark of American urbanization since the 1960s. As early as 1973, American suburbs surpassed the central cities in total employment. By the mid-1980s, even some major metropolises in the Sunbelt were experiencing the suburbanization of a critical mass of jobs (greater than 50 percent of the urban-area total).

As the outer city grew rapidly and its functional independence increased, new suburban downtowns were spawned after about 1970 to serve their new local economies, with the leading concentrations located near key freeway intersections. These multipurpose activity nodes mainly developed around big regional shopping centers, with prestigious images that attracted

scores of industrial parks, office companies, hotels, restaurants, entertainment facilities, and even major league sports stadiums. As these new downtowns of the outer city flourish in the 1990s, they are attracting tens of thousands of nearby suburbanites to organize their lives around them—offering workplaces, shopping, leisure activities, and all of the other elements of a complete urban environment—thereby loosening remaining ties not only to the central city, but to other portions of suburbia as well.

Thus the urban realms model constitutes the latest step forward in the geographical interpretation of urban structure. It clearly demonstrates that today's outer cities are not satellites of the central city—they have become mighty, coequal partners in the shaping of the decidedly polycentric metropolis of the late twentieth century.

This discussion has viewed the city anatomically and has dissected its parts. It remains now to consider spatial aspects and real-world, practical problems of life in the changing city, and to widen our perspective again to the urban world beyond North America.

KEY TERMS

Basic Sector
Central Business District (CBD)
Central City
Centrality
Central Place Theory
Economic Base
Economic Reach
Employment Structure
Functional Specialization
Functional Structure
Hinterland
Multiplier Effect
Nonbasic Sector
Rank-Size Rule
Suburb
Urban Model
Urban Realm
Urban Structure

33

CHANGING CITIES IN A MODERNIZING WORLD

The cultural geography of the modern world is affected by urban influences as never before. Two centuries ago, demographers estimate, less than 5 percent of the world's population was urbanized. Today the figure exceeds 50 percent. In some countries, such as Germany, Spain, and Belgium, 90 percent of the people now live in cities and towns. In the developed world, megalopolises are evolving from formerly separate cities. In the less developed world, megacities are rising with populations that exceed those of many entire countries.

This concluding chapter of Part 10 discusses these regional changes and focuses on several of the critical problems rapid urbanization has produced. We do this by considering the circumstances of life in some zones of the modern city: the inner city in America, the shanty-towns of Africa, and the central city in India. As we will find, the problems of large cities are cross-cultural; they differ in degree, not kind. Cities all over the world suffer from pollution, inadequate sanita-

Geographica

- **The problems of urban America are especially severe in the inner cities and in the older central business districts, where deglomeration is in progress.**

- **Suburbanization has expanded the American city far into the surrounding countryside, has contributed to the impoverishment of the central cities, and has had a major, not always positive, impact on community life.**

- **European cities have not yet experienced the dispersal of their U.S. counterparts, and remain more compact and clustered; modern CBDs have emerged adjacent to preserved historic cores of these cities.**

- **South American, Southeast Asian, and Subsaharan African cities reflect their colonial beginnings as well as more recent domestic developments; disamenity sectors are large and populous.**

tion, substandard housing, congestion, crime, and other ills. Such conditions stand in sharp contrast to the modernity and energy that characterize cities as well. Softening and reducing those contrasts is the great challenge facing cities and their governments today.

PROBLEMS IN URBAN AMERICA

The American metropolis is a place of contradictions. While urban sprawl continues and cities are coalescing (Fig. 33-1), people by the millions have left the inner cities

From the Field Notes

❝ Flying into any major U.S. city, you can see the outward sprawl of suburbs. Individual developments such as this one near Miami use artificial canals and waterways to create the separation suburbanites often desire. ❞

live with this discomfort and who cannot escape the vicious cycle that put them there.

AUTHOR'S VIDEO LINK
↓
5
Brooklyn

Yet there is something of value that remains in many of the aging, stressed neighborhoods of New York and other "Manufacturing Belt" cities. In the squalid poverty of ghetto and slum life, there persists a sense of neighborhood, social structure, and continuity. Urban renewal in the form of anonymous high-rises and the relocation of the people may so disrupt this sense of community that the liabilities ultimately outweigh the assets. Drug abuse, crime, vandalism, and other social pathologies afflict newer areas of the inner city, often engulfing the old. Relationships between communities and law enforcement officers usually are tense, a single incident can set off massive and self-destructive rioting.

During the 1990s, the deterioration of the American central city became a major issue of public debate. Many CBDs lie surrounded by the sickest sectors of American cities. Is the central city worth saving? Let us remember that the downtown area still contains many of a city's crucial assets. If many establishments and businesses have joined the move to suburbia, others have not, at least not yet. Great museums, research libraries, world-renowned orchestras, leading universities, attractive recreational facilities, and other amenities still grace the centers of American cities. Crowds still fill the sidewalks each business day, and traffic jams evince the continuing vitality of these original metropolitan foci. But this is a different sort of vigor than the kind that first made the down-

and have moved to the outer cities, the suburbs. No longer the dominant metropolitan-wide center for urban goods and services, the **central business district (CBD)** is being reduced to serving the less affluent residents of the innermost realm and those working there. As core-area manufacturing employment has declined precipitously during the last two decades, many large cities have adapted successfully by promoting a shift toward the growing service industries. Beyond the CBDs of many cities, however, the vast **inner cities** remain problem-ridden domains of low- and moderate-income people, most of whom live there because they have no alternative place to go. Financially ailing big-city governments are unable to fund adequate schools, crime-prevention

programs, public housing, and sufficient social services, and the downward spiral, including abandonment in the old industrial cities, continues unabated in the 1990s.

In the older industrial cities, the inner city has become a landscape of inadequate housing, substandard living, and widespread decay. New York City typifies the situation: here nearly 3 million persons (plus another million or so illegal aliens who are not officially tabulated in the census), mainly representing minorities, are crowded into apartment buildings averaging five stories high that were built as walkups 75 to 100 years ago. Most of these buildings are now simply too old, worn out, and unsanitary; many suffer from rodent infestations. Yet these apartments are overfilled with people who must

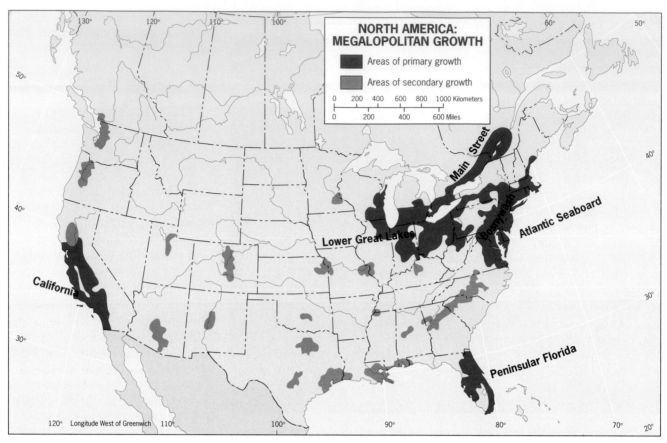

FIGURE 33–1 Evolving megalopolises in North America. SOURCE: From a map in H. J. de Blij and P. O. Muller, *Geography: Realms, Regions, and Concepts*, 7th ed. (New York: Wiley, 1994), p. 187.

town the heart of the city. It is in many ways a residual, but now intermittent, vitality that is engendered by activities and facilities still based in or immediately adjacent to the CBD. Central banks, old educational institutions, major museums, governmental agencies, and large hotels are among organizations that remain, often because their physical facilities are not transferable or replaceable. But former advantages of agglomeration are fast becoming nonessential. Publishing companies, for example, shared the pool of specialized services available in Manhattan, but now many of those services can be done anywhere in the country and transmitted electronically. The high cost of a downtown location is overtaking the advantages of agglomeration, and publishing

companies have relocated from New York as far away as Florida and Texas. Geographers call this process **deglomeration**, and it affects older downtowns everywhere in America.

REVITALIZING THE CENTER

In recent years, city governments have taken a number of steps to counter the deterioration of the urban core. One of these involves new **residential construction** in the hope of luring middle- and upper-class residents (and their taxes and spending) back to the heart of the city. But the number of people who have actually moved back downtown is comparatively small. Most of the reinvestment was undertaken by people already residing

in the central city, so that a hoped-for "return to the city" movement by disaffected suburbanites never really materialized.

Residential construction within and near the downtown has created some attractive high-rise buildings with modern amenities and advantageous locations, but it has not reversed the net outward flow of the urban population. Another effort has done better: the **gentrification** of run-down areas of the inner city. Gentrification is the rehabilitation of deteriorated, often abandoned housing of low-income inner-city residents, chosen because of its favorable location relative to the CBD and central-city places of employment. The growing interest in such inner-city housing results in part from the changing character of American society: the proportion of childless couples and single people in the population is growing, and for these urbanites, the suburbs do not look so attractive. Living within walking distance of the workplace, and very near the cultural and recreational amenities the central city still offers, attracts more residents every year. For them, the gentrified neighborhood is a good choice.

Still another program for inner-city revival is the **commercialization** of part of the downtown. Several cities, including Miami, New York, and Baltimore, have created waterfront "theme" developments to attract visitors. Such ventures have been successful in attracting tourists and generating business, but have not substantially revived the downtowns because they cannot secure what the core of the city needs most: permanent inhabitants with a stake in its future.

Does it matter over the long term? Sweeping changes have affected cities for 200 years now, so if the time of downtown prosperity has come and gone, why try to stem the tide? Apparently, our culture's collective answer is that it does not matter enough to change either investment priorities or habits. The office towers of Denver, Houston, and other cities contain thousands of suburban commuters whose only contact with the city below is the short drive between the freeway exit and their building's parking garage. Again, the shining skyscrapers that were built to attract businesses (or keep them) downtown have not had a major effect on the social fabric of the CBD, and they have actually contributed to the abandonment of older commercial buildings, thus adding to the region's blight. Even more significantly, the federal government's financial support has not been nearly enough to help the major cities reverse their slide into insolvency. As a result, services are being reduced, staff and workers in

the nonbasic sector are being laid off, and the city's essential functions (sanitation, maintenance, security, transportation, and education) are suffering, affecting the downtown severely. And so, the livability of the core of the city declines, its role and relevance in America's urban culture diminished by a changing geography.

THE SUBURBAN CITY

The attraction of country life with city amenities, reinforced by the discomforts of living in the heart of many central cities, has for many decades propelled those who could afford to move to the suburbs and more distant urban fringes. In postwar times, the automobile made mass commuting possible from suburban residences to downtown workplaces, and the kind of suburbanization familiar to North

Americans and other Westerners is a characteristic of urbanization in the most mobile of developed societies.

Suburbanization holds special interest for human geographers, because it involves the transformation of large areas of land from rural to urban uses, affects large numbers of people who can afford to express their spatial preferences, and rapidly creates distinct urban regions complete with industrial, commercial, and educational, as well as residential, components. In a sense, the suburbs reveal their occupants' idealized living patterns more accurately than any other urban zone, because their layout can be planned in response to choice and demand; elsewhere in the metropolis, there are too many constraints imposed by preexisting land-use arrangements. In his book, *Suburban Growth* (1974), editor J. H. Johnson

SUBURB AND COMMUNITY

The United States has become the land of suburbia, and suburban life is celebrated as an escape from the city, an attainment of freedom of space and status. But in this process of dispersal, community life in urban settings largely went by the board. For centuries, indeed for millennia, we had learned to live in close proximity, and even during the streetcar era walking was a major part of daily routines. Sidewalks were the ribbons of activity that connected people and places, the arenas of interactions.

All this was left behind in a few short years. Front lawns replaced sidewalks, driveways replaced front doors as functional outlets. The automobile came to dominate life-styles. Workers began to spend hours commuting—hours that should be spent with families.

Youngsters depended on wheels to meet their peers, and many grew up bored and disconnected. Shopping became a car trip to the mall, not an interactive walk down Main Street. Oldsters no longer able to drive found themselves isolated in their houses or forced into nursing homes; in the city their useful lives would have been much longer. Bars disgorged patrons who would have been no danger walking home, but who killed countless people while driving impaired. In an ultimate misconception, some observers described the suburb-splitting four-lane highway as the new "Main Street U.S.A."

Suburban life has its positives: privacy, comparatively clean air, lawns and gardens, barbecues. But this space- and resources-consuming phenomenon, for all its current popularity, is a new experience. We have built suburbia, but we have yet to invest it with a sense of community.

suggests that in the suburbs, "life and landscape are in much closer adjustment" than in the older parts of the urban area, providing geographers with a direct expression of the behavior of contemporary urban society and, therein, some important clues about the nature of the urban future. Not all signs of this future are positive (see box, "Suburb and Community").

The overall importance of suburban life in the United States is underscored by the results of the 1990 census, which indicated that no less than 46 percent of the entire American population resided in the suburbs (up from 37 percent in 1970); the remaining 54 percent of the American people were divided between the central cities (31 percent) and nonmetropolitan or rural areas (23 percent). Of the population living in metropolitan areas, 60 percent resided in the suburbs, which in 1990 counted 115 million inhabitants, whereas the central cities totaled 78 million. Another indication of the importance of suburbia comes from regional growth-rate figures: during the 1980s, the country's suburban population grew by 15.2 percent; the central cities grew by only 6.6 percent (+4.8 million on a base of 73 million). Thus the suburbs have unmistakably become the essence of the late-twentieth-century American city (see box, "Atlanta: Capital of the New South").

THE CANADIAN CITY

Fly into Toronto, Canada's largest city, and you may get the impression that Canadian and American cities are pretty much the same. A cluster of skyscrapers creates an impressive CBD. Arterial highways carry busy traffic. Tree-lined streets mark suburban neighborhoods. Groups of high-rises near major intersections mark incipient suburban downtowns.

The impression, however, would be mistaken. Canada's major cities

---

ATLANTA: CAPITAL OF THE NEW SOUTH

Atlanta today is in the vanguard of American cities. A half century ago, Atlanta was a nearly perfect example of the Burgess and Hoyt models, showing a well-developed concentricity around its dominant CBD with some sector development. Today, Atlanta is a polycentric metropolis, a real-life manifestation of the urban realms model. Emerging downtowns lie scattered across the urban area in what geographers Truman Hartshorn and Peter Muller have called a "pepperoni-pizza pattern."

Atlanta, like other U.S. cities, suffers from inner-city neighborhood deterioration, crime, and dislocation. But Atlanta also is the destination, rather than the source, of relocating companies. Its economic vitality has helped mitigate the social problems all urban centers confront.

Atlanta is the largest metropolitan area in a huge triangle extending from the southern end of Bosnywash to South Florida to Texas. With more than 3 million inhabitants, the city is growing faster, as a percentage of total population, than any other large metropolitan area in the country. It now extends over an area that incorporates 20 counties, and it has the largest toll-free telephone dialing area in the world.

Numerous multinational firms have established their corporate headquarters in Atlanta's "edge cities," the burgeoning centers on the urban perimeter. Today, the original downtown no longer serves as either the primary retail center or corporate headquarters location: the CBD now is mainly a government, hotel, entertainment, sports, and ceremonial center.

Atlanta began as a railroad junction; today it is one of the world's busiest airport hubs, with over 300 international flights to 23 countries. It has become a truly international city, with more than 40 foreign consulates. At the same time, Atlanta is becoming a truly multicultural community. The Asian population has grown by more than 300 percent since 1980; the Hispanic population approaches 70,000. In 1995, a Buddhist monastery was under construction in the city.

Atlanta's international image is strengthened daily by its telecommunications role. The world's first global television network, CNN, is based here. And the city has taken the lead in creating a fiberoptic cable system: in 1995 more than 100,000 miles of fiberoptics were in place. High-tech companies have been attracted to Atlanta as a result.

Unlike the coalescing cities of megalopolis, Atlanta is a single center that has grown outward and spun off its own satellites, some of which overshadow the old city center. Centrally positioned to the South, it reflects the new vitality of the region.

AUTHOR'S VIDEO LINK
↓
6
Atlanta

---

suffer far less from the problems that beset their American counterparts. Large as the Toronto urban area may seem, for example, it is much less dispersed than an American city with the same population. Urban densities are higher; multiple-family dwellings are more common; and most importantly, suburbanization has not gone nearly as far as it has in the United States. This means that far more high- and middle-income workers have remained in the central city, resulting in a stronger tax base and, generally, better services, ranging from public transit to police protection.

Downtown Toronto still is the functional heart of the Toronto urban area (and the same is true for Montreal, Vancouver, Calgary, Winnipeg, and other Canadian cities); no suburban downtowns threaten its primacy despite the few clusters of high-rise buildings (mostly apartments) seen from the airplane window. The kinds of urban amenities that make a central city attractive have not relocated to the outer ring of suburbs; in general, those suburbs that have developed are neither as wealthy nor as far from downtown as their American counterparts. The harsh deterioration of inner-city, low-income housing that marks so many American cities is not in evidence in urban Canada, despite the fact that Canada, too, has substantial minority populations and ethnic neighborhoods in its cities. Indeed, Canadian cities do not display the sharp contrasts in wealth so evident in American cities.

All this should not suggest that Toronto or other Canadian cities do not share in some of the problems affecting American urban areas. The integration of foreign-born residents has not always gone smoothly in Canada's cities. Violent crime, while much less serious than it is in the United States, is rising in Canada's cities, too. Intra-urban circulation, while eased by the general use of mass transit, reflects inadequate road building in several cities. But the overriding reality is that Canada's cities have not (at least not yet) devolved into competitive urban realms. Stability and cohesion have translated into a Canadian urban model now beyond the reach of politically and socially fragmented American cities.

THE EUROPEAN CITY

European cities are older than North American cities, but they, too, were transformed by the Industrial Revolution. Indeed, industrialization struck many of Europe's dormant medieval towns and vibrant mercantile cities like a landslide. But has the European experience paralleled the American?

In terms of population numbers, the great European cities are in the same class as major North American cities. London (6.4 million) and Paris (10.2 million), like Rome, Berlin, Madrid, and Athens, are megacities by world standards. These, however, are among Europe's many historic urban centers, affected but not engulfed by the industrial tide. The cities of the British Midlands and the megalopolis of Germany's Ruhr are more representative of the manufacturing era. Individually, these cities are smaller, but in their regional context, they constitute major urban complexes.

The industrial cities have lost much of their historic heritage, but in Europe's largest cities the legacy of the past is better preserved. Disproportionately large and dominant cities, such as Paris, Athens, and Lisbon (many of them *primate* cities under Jefferson's "law"), proved to be the most durable in the face of the impact of the Industrial Age. Wars, of course, have taken their toll: in the London CBD, historic and modern buildings vie for space in the congested core. Many of the modern structures stand on sites where historic buildings were destroyed during the *blitz* of the Second World War. In Paris, Madrid, Rome, and Lisbon, on the other hand, the historic cores are

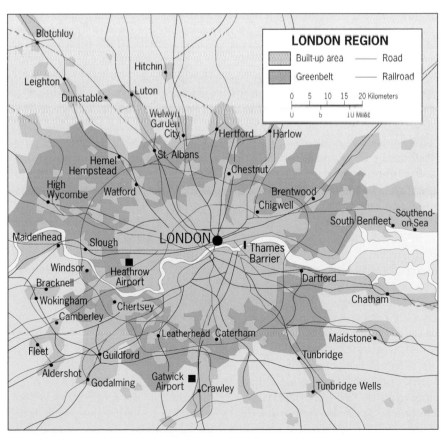

FIGURE 33–2 London's greenbelt and the built-up area adjacent. SOURCE: From a map in H. J. de Blij and P. O. Muller, *Geography: Realms, Regions, and Concepts*, 7th ed. (New York: Wiley, 1994), p. 72.

From the Field Notes

❝ Despite the ravages of war and the destruction of religious treasures ordered by Stalin during the Soviet period, St. Petersburg still is a city of great architectural riches. The tsars' winter palace (the Hermitage) is among many magnificient buildings that stand in sharp contrast to the drab styles of the communist era. On the public square in front of the Hermitage, fateful history was made, and standing here you can almost hear the echoes of the crowd surging through the gate (right) across from the palace, and the gunfire that followed. ❞

well preserved and protected against encroachment. The central city of London, immediately adjacent to—and indeed intertwined with—the CBD, contains residential sectors of varying quality and class, radiating outward. It also contains the city's main industrial zones. But unlike American cities, the central city of London is not ringed by a zone of expanding suburbs. Indeed, the central city today is about the same size as it was in the early 1960s. The reason for this is the so-called Metropolitan Greenbelt, a zone of open country averaging more than 30 km (20 miles) wide, which is studded with scattered small towns but is otherwise open forest-and-farm country. This planning triumph had the effect of containing London's built-up area within its 1960 limit throughout the period of rapid suburbanization in the United States. Although some

settlement exists within the greenbelt, suburbanization has had to proceed beyond it—a long train ride away from the CBD (Fig. 33-2).

The greenbelt phenomenon is not unique to London; many European cities have a version of it. This preservation of near-urban open space is a legacy of governments' reaction to the destructive impact of the Industrial Revolution on cities during the nineteenth century. It has had the effect not only of limiting urban sprawl, but also of containing the unrestrained suburbanization that marks American cities. Beyond the greenbelt, suburbs are impractically far away from the CBD. Furthermore, since the cost of gasoline is as much as three times that in the United States, it persuades people to use rapid transit. To do this, it is more practical to cluster homes closely together, so the suburbs of European cities tend

to be high-density villages or towns set in open countryside.

The Americanization of the European urban scene, therefore, has yet to gain momentum. Cities in Western Europe tend to be more compact (more so even than the Canadian model). Highway penetration and beltway development also lag far behind, with mixed results: the central cities are automobile-clogged, but mass transit, bicycles, and walking are the primary modes of getting to work. Zoning rules are restrictive and strictly observed. As a result, the European city remains clustered and crowded—with good consequences for the financial health of its CBD.

Note that we referred to *Western* Europe here. Just as there are significant differences between the American and Canadian city, so the cities of Europe show regional con-

From the Field Notes

❝ It was not easy to gain permission to go to the roof of the building overlooking Lima's Plaza de San Martin, one of the Peruvian capital's most impressive public squares. The political situation was tense; the orange tent on the grass was a police post. Only in the company of an armed guard was I able to survey the square, which if flanked by some of the city's architectural treasures, several of them recently restored. The great plazas of Middle and South America's major cities often are named (as this one is) after revolutionary heroes and are flanked by cathedrals and churches as well as public buildings. ❞

trasts. The cities of Eastern Europe, many of them old primate cities, were afflicted by socialist planning that tended to neglect their cultural and historic heritage in favor of a reorganization of urban life into so-called **microdistricts**. This reorganization entailed the creation of a huge, dominant, central-city square and wide, radiating avenues fronted by architecturally ugly apartment blocks. Assemblages of these apartment blocks, generally 7 to 11 stories high, were designed to form microdistricts with workplaces, schools, recreational facilities, stores, and other amenities either within or nearby. Thus there was no need for a large CBD, as districts were designed to be largely self-sufficient. Neither would there be suburbanization, mass commuting, class contrasts in

neighborhoods, or traffic congestion. The emptiness of those vast, multilane avenues was always a hallmark of the "socialist city."

In Eastern Europe, the impact of socialist city planning varied. Prague and Budapest were less severely affected than Bucharest (Romania), where the communist regime destroyed much of the ancient city's historic townscape and replaced it with the faceless apartment blocks that make socialist cities so monotonous and dull. Today, the cities of Eastern Europe are undergoing still another transformation as often-incongruous glass towers of capitalism rise above the townscape.

In the cities of the former Soviet Union the socialist-communist urban model was most extensively imposed. Russia's original primate

city, Saint Petersburg, was heavily damaged during the Second World War, and its open spaces were laid out in accordance with communist planning. Fortunately, the great city's still-standing historic buildings were repaired and renovated, so that the urban landscape became a study in stark contrasts. Moscow fared better in the war, but grew faster afterward, to about 11 million inhabitants today. One logical consequence of communist urban planning was the absence of a high-rise CBD, and apart from some dominant Soviet-era buildings (such as the main tower of Moscow University) nothing resembling an American skyline developed. Moscow's growing population, meanwhile, was accommodated in hundreds of microdistricts along avenues radiating outward from Red Square.

How will the postcommunist era be imprinted on the Soviet city? It is too early to tell. Already, high-rise hotels and modern apartment buildings stand above the townscape, symbolizing the new age. But a half century of communist planning will not be erased overnight.

THE IBERO-AMERICAN CITY

South and Middle America are among the world's most rapidly urbanizing realms today, and the largest cities are growing in the "Latin" portions of those realms—the regions where Iberian cultures dominate. There, the urban population grew from 41 percent to 70 percent between 1950 and 1990. Although the urban experience has been a varied one within Middle and South America—a function of diverse historical, cultural, and economic influences—there are many common threads that have prompted geographers to search for

A GENERALIZED MODEL OF LATIN AMERICAN CITY STRUCTURE

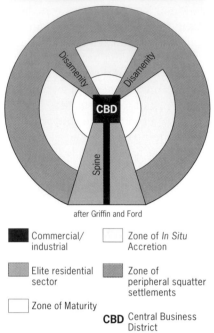

after Griffin and Ford

- ■ Commercial/ industrial
- □ Zone of *In Situ* Accretion
- ▨ Elite residential sector
- ▨ Zone of peripheral squatter settlements
- □ Zone of Maturity
- **CBD** Central Business District

FIGURE 33–3 From E. Griffin and L. Ford, "A Model of Latin American City Structure," *The Geographical Review* 70 (1980), p. 406.

A GENERALIZED MODEL OF LAND USE AREAS IN THE LARGE SOUTHEAST ASIAN CITY

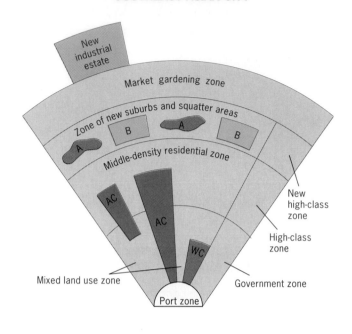

A	Squatter areas
B	Suburbs
AC	Alien commercial zone
WC	Western commercial zone

FIGURE 33–4 A model of land use in the large Southeast Asian city. SOURCE: From T. G. McGee, *The Southeast Asian City* (London: Bell, 1967), p. 128. Reprinted by permission of the publisher.

meaningful generalizations. One of the more successful is the model of the intra-urban spatial structure of the Latin American city proposed by Professors Ernst Griffin and Larry Ford (Fig. 33-3), which may well have even wider applications to cities throughout the developing world.

The basic spatial framework of city structure, which blends traditional elements of Latin American culture with modernization forces now reshaping that urban scene, is a composite of radial sectors and concentric zones. Anchoring the model is the thriving CBD, which, like its European (but increasingly unlike its North American) counterpart, remains the primary business, employment, and entertainment focus of the surrounding metropolitan agglomeration. Decent public transit systems and nearby residential concentrations of the affluent assure

the dominance of the CBD, the landscape of which increasingly exhibits modern high-rise buildings. Emanating outward from the urban core along the city's most prestigious axis is the *commercial spine*, which is surrounded by the *elite residential sector*. This widening corridor is essentially an extension of the CBD, featuring offices, shopping, high-quality housing for the upper- and upper-middle classes, restaurants, theaters, and such amenities as parks, zoos, and golf courses which give way to wealthy suburbs that carry the elite sector beyond the city limits.

The three remaining concentric zones are home to the less fortunate residents of the city (who constitute the great majority of the urban population), with socioeconomic levels and housing quality decreasing markedly as distance from the city center increases. The zone of *maturity* in the inner city contains the best housing outside the spine sector, attracting the middle classes, who invest sufficiently to keep their solidly built but aging dwellings from deteriorating. The adjacent zone of *in situ accretion* is one of much more modest housing, interspersed with unkempt areas, which represent a transition from inner-ring affluence to outer-ring poverty. The residential density of this zone is usually quite high, reflecting the uneven assimilation of its occupants into the social and economic fabric of the city. The outermost *zone of peripheral squatter settlements* is home to the impoverished and unskilled. Although housing in this ring mainly consists of teeming, high-density shantytowns, residents here are surprisingly optimistic about finding work and eventually bettering their living conditions—a realistic aspiration documented by researchers, who confirm a process of gradual upgrading as squatter communities mature. A final structural element of many Latin American cities is the **disamenity sector**, which contains relatively unchanging slums, known as *barrios* or *favelas*; the worst of these poverty-stricken areas often include sizable numbers of people who are so poor that they are forced, literally, to live in the streets.

To what extent is the Griffin-Ford model a representative depiction of the Ibero-American city? In truth, the cities of South and Middle America display so much diversity that no simple model will encompass all aspects. Elements of sector development can be seen in many large South American cities, for example, and the concentricity the model suggests seems to be breaking down. Nevertheless, this model remains a useful abstraction of the "Latin" American city.

THE SOUTHEAST ASIAN CITY

When we think of urbanization in Southeast Asia, we sometimes tend to focus on Singapore as the prime example. But other cities in this geographic realm also are growing and modernizing, and some of

them are surpassing Singapore in certain respects. Anyone who has not seen Kuala Lumpur, the capital of Malaysia, in recent years is in for a surprise: the city is a complex of high-rise development and manu-

facturing, a Hong Kong on the Malaysian Peninsula.

Urban centers in Southeast Asia are growing at a rapid rate. Between 1950 and the mid-1990s, the realm's urban population doubled

From the Field Notes

❝ Cities in the developing world often seem to be a jumble of inadequate housing and poorly maintained (or absent) facilities. But despite their appearance, clusters of housing such as those shown in this photo are far superior to the rudimentary shacks of newly arrived squatters on the outskirts. This view over a part of Lagos, Nigeria, was just two blocks from the port and on the very edge of the city center. High-rise development was overtaking this area, reflecting the dual geographies of so many urban centers in such countries. This group of houses was occupied by a set of extended families; recent arrivals had been accommodated among them. ❞

in relative size (from 15 to more than 29 percent) and increased five-fold in absolute numbers (26 million to 132 million). Foreign influences and investments (notably from the Japanese, also from overseas Chinese who may be citizens of their respective countries but are still regarded as Chinese) continue to play a major role in urban development. Urban growth has focused on the realm's large coastal cities (or cities connected by water to the open ocean); Ho Chi Minh City, the largest city in Vietnam, for example, now contains more than 10 percent of the country's population of 75 million.

Urban geographers studying the growth of Southeast Asia's cities report that, from one end of the realm to the other, these cities exhibit similar land use patterns. These patterns were identified and summarized in a model by T. G. McGee as long ago as 1967 in his book *The Southeast Asian City* (Fig. 33-4). The old colonial port zone, its functions renewed in the postcolonial period, is the city's focus, together with the largely commercial district that surrounds it. Although no formal central business district is evident, its elements are present as separate clusters within the land use belt beyond the port: the government zone, the Western commercial zone (a colonialist remnant, which is practically a CBD by itself), the alien commercial zone, usually dominated by Chinese merchants whose residences are attached to their places of business, and the mixed land-use zone that contains miscellaneous economic activities, including light industry. The other nonresidential areas are the market-gardening zone at the urban periphery and, still farther from the city, an industrial park, or "estate," of recent vintage. The residential zones in McGee's construct are quite reminiscent of the Griffin-Ford model of the Latin American city (Fig. 33-3). Among

the similarities between the two are the hybrid sectoring framework, an elite residential sector that includes new suburbanization, an inner-city zone of comfortable, middle-income housing (with new suburban offshoots in the McGee schema), and peripheral concentrations of low-income squatter settlements. The differences are relatively minor and can partly be accounted for by local cultural and historical variations.

THE AFRICAN CITY

Africa south of the Sahara is today the least urbanized *and* the fastest urbanizing realm in the world. As yet no city in black Africa has reached the dimensions of a Shanghai or a Calcutta, or even a Cairo. But the quickening pace of urbanization virtually throughout the realm presages an urban transformation.

As in Southeast Asia, the colonial imprint remains pervasive in the

structures of many African cities. In Africa, the traditional city can be seen mainly in the west, in the Muslim zone anchored by northern Nigeria. Kano, Kaduna, Zaria, and other cities in this zone retain their precolonial structures in part because of their remoteness from the European colonial invasion routes.

But it was the colonialists who laid out such prominent urban centers as Kinshasa, Nairobi, and Harare in the interior, and Dakar, Abidjan, Luanda, Maputo, and other ports along the coast. Africa even has cities that are neither traditional nor colonial. South Africa's major urban centers (Johannesburg, Cape Town, and Durban) are essentially Western, exhibiting elements of European as well as American models, including high-rise CBDs and sprawling outer suburbs.

As a result of this diversity, it is difficult to formulate a model African city that would account for all or even most of what we see. Studies of African cities indicate that the central city often consists of not one, but three CBDs (Fig. 33-5): a

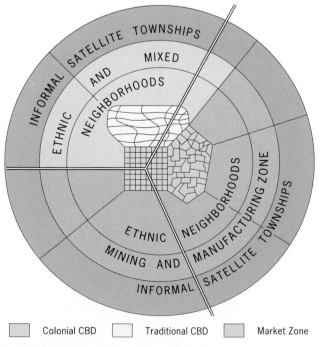

THE MODEL AFRICAN CITY

| Colonial CBD | Traditional CBD | Market Zone |

FIGURE 33–5   One model of the African city.

remnant of the colonial CBD, an informal and sometimes periodic market zone, and a transitional business center where commerce is conducted from curbside, stalls, or other storefront facilities. The ex-colonial CBD exhibits the city's main vertical development; the traditional business center usually is a zone of single-story buildings with some traditional architecture; and the market zone tends to be open-air, informal, but not inconsequential. Sector development marks the encircling zone of ethnic and mixed neighborhoods (these neighborhoods often are characterized by strong ethnic identities and even animosities), and parts of this zone abut against manufacturing or mining operations. Finally, African cities from Dakar to Durban and from Kano to Cape Town are now ringed by what the model calls satellite townships; these are, in effect, squatter settlements. In this outer zone lies the evidence of Africa's spiraling urbanization.

In Part 10, we have viewed the evolution and maturation of the city from ancient to modern times, and it was evident that the Industrial Revolution brought the most far-reaching transformation to the cities it affected. Coupled with this urban transformation was an economic one: not just cities but entire regions underwent metamorphoses. Raw materials that previously had no relevance or value became critical resources. Countries that had been remote, traditional entities found themselves in possession of fossil-fuel and mineral reserves over which powerful empires would fight wars. We turn next to the industrial and technological transformation of the world, and the regions and landscapes it has generated.

KEY TERMS

Central Business District (CBD)
Commercialization
Deglomeration
Disamenity Sector
Gentrification
Inner City
Microdistrict
Residential Construction
Suburbanization

Environment Friendly

SUNRISE ZINC LTD

Producing zinc through innovative technology

A global concern: the impact of industry on environment. India.

PART ELEVEN

CULTURES, LANDSCAPES, AND REGIONS OF INDUSTRY

At Issue

What price development? The Industrial Revolution propelled the world into a new age, and its environmental impacts reach from the ocean floors to the stratosphere. When the Iron Curtain lifted, the full measure of ecological damage to streams, forests, pastures, and groundwater caused by unchecked industrial activity in Eastern Europe became evident. Following the collapse of the Soviet Union, environmental damage ranging from nuclear waste pollution in the Arctic Ocean to radiation contamination in Siberia was found to be widespread. At issue is responsibility: in the formerly communist countries, state-owned enterprises created ecological disasters. But in Western countries, environmental laws failed to forestall oil and chemical spills and other devastation. Should a global security system be established to prepare for, and cope with, industrial accidents?

34

CONCEPTS AND CULTURES OF DEVELOPMENT

In Japan in 1993, the per capita **gross national product** (GNP) in U.S. dollars was $31,450. In the United States it was 24,750. In Western Europe it averaged $23,310. But in India it was $290, in Nigeria $310, and in Indonesia, demographically the world's fourth-largest country, $730. This enormous range reflects the often searing contrasts between the rich world and the poor (Table 34-1).

The economic and social geographies of the contemporary world remain a patchwork of almost inconceivable contrasts. On the crude fields of shifting cultivators in equatorial American and African forests, root crops still are grown according to ancient practices and with the most rudimentary of tools—while modern machines plow the land, seed the grain, and harvest the wheat, hundreds of acres at a time, on the Great Plains of North America, in Ukraine, and in eastern Australia. Toolmakers in the villages of Papua New Guinea still fashion their implements by hand, as they did many centuries ago, while the factories of Japan disgorge automobiles by the shipload for dis-

tribution to markets thousands of miles away. Between these extremes, the range and variety of productive activities are virtually endless.

Notwithstanding the globe-girdling impact of the Industrial Revolution, there are even areas within the industrialized countries

where change is coming only slowly. Parts of the rural South in the United States still experience significant poverty and remain comparatively remote from the effects of U.S. economic growth. In areas of northern Japan, life has changed little during the dramatic century of Japan's modernization. In industrial-

Geographica

- **Development and underdevelopment are measured by national statistics, but the geography of development reveals regional disparities in virtually all countries and regions, developed as well as underdeveloped.**

- **Development is a cultural and political as well as an economic phenomenon: traditions, attitudes, capacities, as well as leadership, all play crucial roles**

- **States, according to models of development, pass through distinct stages of economic growth; as the twenty-first century approaches, some states still are tradition-bound and subsistence-based while others are in the "takeoff" stage.**

- **Rapid development is taking place under widely different political systems; while democratic principles appear to be optimal, growth also is occurring today under communist as well as noncommunist dictatorships.**

427

TABLE 34–1   Per Capita GNP for Selected Countries, 1993 (In U.S. $)

Europe		South Asia	
United Kingdom	17,970	India	290
Sweden	24,830	Bangladesh	220
France	22,360	Pakistan	430
Germany	23,560	Sri Lanka	600
Hungary	3,330	Southeast Asia	
Italy	19,620	Indonesia	730
Spain	13,650	Malaysia	3,160
Greece	7,390	Singapore	19,310
North America		Thailand	2,040
Canada	20,670	Southwest Asia-North Africa	
United States	24,750	Egypt	660
Middle America		Morocco	1,030
Mexico	3,750	Saudi Arabia	7,780
Costa Rica	2,160	United Arab Emirates	22,470
Nicaragua	360	Subsaharan Africa	
Haiti	380*	Nigeria	310
South America		Ethiopia	100
Argentina	7,290	Kenya	270
Brazil	3,020	Moçambique	80
Bolivia	770	Gabon	4,050
Guyana	350	Sierra Leone	140
Peru	1,490	South Africa	2,900
East Asia	75		
China	490		
Japan	31,450	SOURCE: *Population Reference Bureau,*	
Hong Kong	17,860	*World Population Data Sheet 1995.*	
South Korea	7,670	*(1992)	

izing Europe, there remain several areas of isolation and stagnation. Conversely, there are places in poorer, less-industrialized countries where isolated industries have emerged, where productive urban growth is taking place, and where local conditions differ sharply from those prevailing in surrounding areas. Recent economic growth on the Pacific Rim of East Asia has created huge **regional disparities** between parts of certain coastal provinces of China and distant interior provinces. Such regionally contrasting economic development has significant social as well as political consequences, and China is by no means the only country thus affected. Throughout the world, the economic relief map is showing higher peaks and deeper valleys.

CONCEPTS OF DEVELOPMENT

Countries that have achieved high levels of urbanization and industrialization and enjoy high material standards of living are routinely referred to as the **developed countries (DCs)**. But the concept of **development** is a complicated one, and there is more to it than cities and industries. Even the GNP index has its shortcomings, and not just because it conceals variations within countries. Consider, for example, the GNP data for such countries as Kuwait and the United Arab Emirates (UAR). In 1993, Kuwait's per capita GNP exceeded $23,000; the UAR's, $22,000. These figures exceed those of many countries regarded as part of the

developed world, including several European countries. Also note the high per capita GNPs for such countries as Saudi Arabia and Libya. Are these "developed" countries in the economic and social sense? The answer is that large amounts of money, derived from the sale of a single product (in this case oil), do not automatically or even quickly result in overall national development.

Even when the source of national income is not as one-sided as in Kuwait or Saudi Arabia, indexes of development can be misleading. The bare figures give us no hint of the degree of participation of minorities in the success of a country's overall economy. National statistics on the economy (like those on population, as we learned earlier) can conceal enormous regional and demographic diversity.

If there are developed countries, such as Canada, the United States, France, and New Zealand, then there must also be **underdeveloped countries (UDCs)**, where progress and prosperity are lower. For a severe case of such **underdevelopment**, we do not have to leave the Western Hemisphere. Our Caribbean neighbor, Haiti, is one of the world's poorest and most underdeveloped countries. The data in Table 34-1 suggest that there are a number of African and Asian countries in a similar condition.

The indexes on which measures of development are based (see box, "Measures of Development") do not produce a clear dividing line between developed and underdeveloped countries. Instead, UDCs and DCs lie along a development continuum from the poorest to the richest, and any division between them is arbitrary. The continuum can also be divided into three segments: underdeveloped, "developing," and developed economies, for example. The **developing countries** would, in this conceptualization, be countries that show evidence of progress, which, if sustained, would eventually bring them into the developed category. Such countries are sometimes referred to as being in the *takeoff* stage of development.

FOUR CATEGORIES

The World Bank, a Washington, D.C.-based agency that monitors development and assists countries with various development projects, uses not three but four categories in grouping states, based on income:

Low-income economies
Lower-middle-income economies
Upper-middle-income economies
High-income economies

MEASURES OF DEVELOPMENT

What distinguishes a developed economy from an underdeveloped one? Obviously, it is necessary to compare countries on the basis of certain measures; the question cannot be answered simply by subjective judgment. No country is totally developed, and no economy is completely underdeveloped. We are comparing *degrees* of development when we identify DCs (developed countries) and UDCs (underdeveloped countries). Our division into developed and underdeveloped economies is arbitrary, and the dividing line is always a topic of debate. There is also the problem of data. Statistics for many countries are inadequate, unreliable, incompatible with those of others or simply unavailable.

The following list of measures is normally used to gauge levels of economic development:

1. **National Product per Person** This figure is determined by taking the sum of all incomes achieved in a year by a country's citizens and dividing it by the total population. Figures for all countries are then converted to a single currency index for purposes of comparison. In DCs, the index can exceed $10,000; in some UDCs, it is as low as $100. The World Bank, in its 1993 *Report*, used U.S $650 as the upper limit for low-income countries (the most severely underdeveloped countries).

2. **Occupational Structure of the Labor Force** This statistic is given as the percentage of workers employed in various sectors of the economy. A high percentage of laborers engaged in the production of food staples, for instance, signals a low overall level of development.

3. **Productivity per Worker** This figure is the sum of production over the period of a year, divided by the total number of persons making up the labor force.

4. **Consumption of Energy per Person** The greater the use of electricity and other forms of power, the higher the level of national development. These data, however, must be viewed to some extent in the context of climate.

5. **Transportation and Communications Facilities per Person** This measure reduces railway, road, airline connections, telephone, radio, television, and so forth to a per capita index. The higher the index, the higher the level of development.

6. **Consumption of Manufactured Metals per Person** A strong indicator of development levels is the quantity of iron and steel, copper, aluminum, and other metals utilized by a population during a given year.

7. **Rates** A number of additional measures are employed, including literacy rates, caloric intake per person, percentage of family income spent on food, and the amount of savings per capita.

This grouping is represented cartographically in Figure 34-1. As the map indicates, the low-income countries are concentrated in Africa and in South, Southeast, and East Asia. In the mid-1990s, the countries with the world's lowest incomes were Bangladesh in Asia, and Moçambique, Ethiopia, Tanzania, and Somalia in Africa. In all, 40 of the world's countries still are designated as low-income states; only one of them, Haiti, lies in the Western Hemisphere.

It is encouraging that middle-income countries outnumber the poorer states substantially. According to World Bank statistics, there are 65 middle-income countries, including many Middle and South American countries. The lower-middle-income group numbers 43, and the upper middle-income group includes 22 countries.

Both groups are quite diverse, and some economic geographers question the inclusion of such economies as Congo and Angola in the lower-middle-income group (which also contains Turkey and Argentina).

The high-income economies include oil-rich Southwest Asian states as well as prosperous Western European countries. When Figure 34-1 is compared to Table 34-1, some inconsistencies seem to arise. But remember that per capita GNP (Table 34-1) is only *one* criterion for development, whereas Figure 34-1 is based on a wider range of indicators. Development is measured by various means, as the box reminds us.

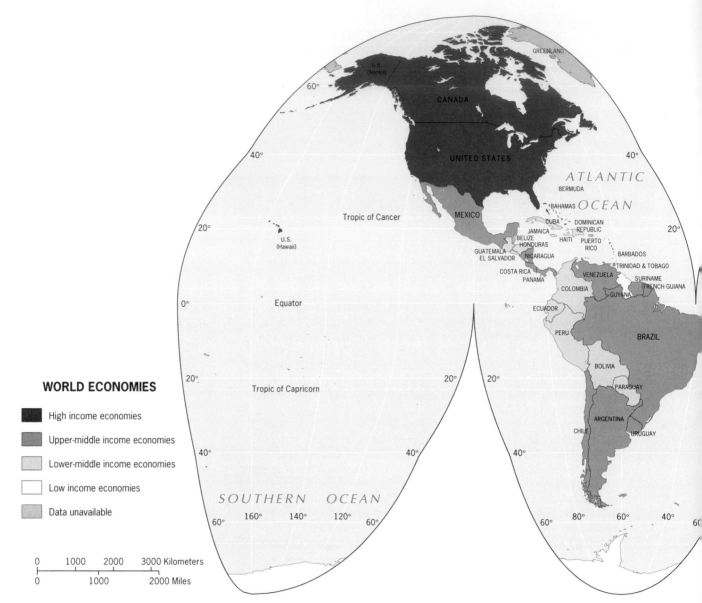

WORLD ECONOMIES

High income economies

Upper-middle income economies

Lower-middle income economies

Low income economies

Data unavailable

0   1000   2000   3000 Kilometers

0   1000   2000 Miles

FIGURE 34–1   SOURCE: Based on data from the World Bank, *World Development Report 1993* (Oxford: Oxford University Press, 1994), pp. 238, 239.

CULTURE AND DEVELOPMENT

If development is a problematic concept in technical ways, it also has emotional connotations. People from "underdeveloped" countries sometimes argue that "developing" or "less-developed" countries (LDCs) are more appropriate, less pejorative terms. Their sensitivities are understandable when it is realized that ideas and classifications involving the development concept

tend to come from scholars in the wealthier countries. Moreover, terms such as "developed" and "underdeveloped" also mean rich and poor, haves and have-nots, and, perhaps most appropriately, advantaged and disadvantaged. Producers and workers in the underdeveloped countries often work on the terms of decision makers in the developed countries. For some products, the economists of the developed countries (the wealthy markets) even assign quotas, telling underde-

veloped countries how much of their produce they may sell there. The plight of the disadvantaged countries can be an emotional issue indeed.

Figure 34-1 is in large measure a reflection of the course of history and the realities of historical economic geography. The sequence of events that led to the present division of our world began long before the Industrial Revolution occurred. Europe, even by the middle of the eighteenth century, had laid

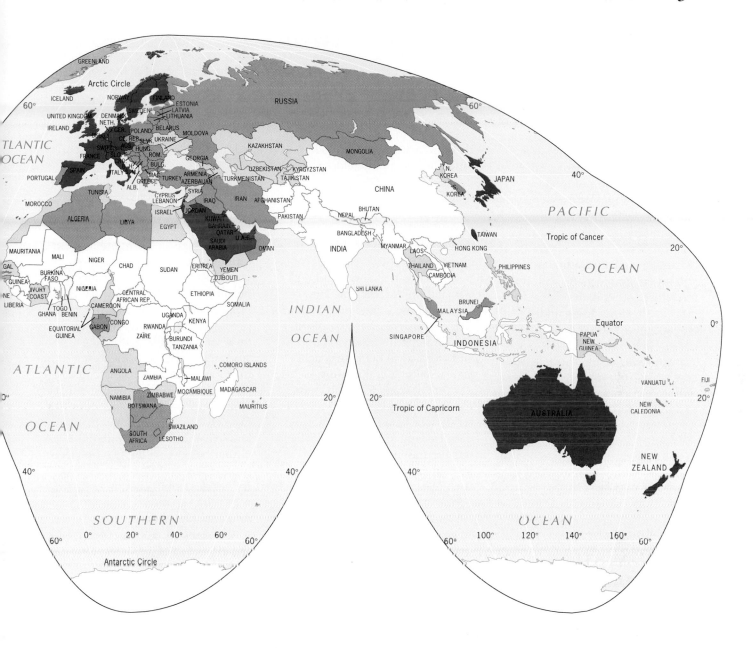

the foundations for its colonial expansion. The Industrial Revolution magnified Europe's demands for raw materials, while its products increased the efficiency of its imperial control. While Western countries gained an enormous head start, colonial dependencies remained suppliers of resources and consumers of the products of Western industries. Thus a system of international exchange was born, along with a capital flow that really changed little when the age of colonialism came to an end in the middle of the twentieth century.

Underdeveloped countries, well aware of their predicament, accuse the developed world of perpetuating its advantage through **neocolonialism**—the entrenchment of the old system under a new guise.

There can be no doubt that the world economic system works to the disadvantage of the underprivileged countries, but, sadly, it is not the only obstacle that the poorer countries face. Political instability, corruptible leaderships and elites, misdirected priorities, misuse of aid, and traditionalism are among the

circumstances that further inhibit development.

Some scholars regard such human failings—and not the distribution or availability of resources—as the critical determinant of development and economic growth. The economist Roger Leroy Miller, in his book, *Economics Today* (1973), quotes a corporation president involved in providing capital to developing areas:

I am . . . forced to the conclusion that economic development or lack of it is primarily due to differences in people—in their attitudes, customs, traditions and the consequent differences in their political, social and religious institutions.

This may overstate the case, but examples of the role of culture in development abound. Along the Pacific Rim, from Japan to Singapore, the adoption of modern innovations in industrial technology has set societies on a course toward rapid modernization. With only a fraction of China's resources, Japan became a world industrial power and an economic giant; with no resources (other than relative location) at all, Hong Kong and Singapore organized their human resources to achieve development. Taiwan today is an economic success story—but not because it is rich in resources. These cases seem to confirm classical economist Adam Smith's observation that a nation's prosperity is determined mainly "by the skill, dexterity, and judgment with which its labor is generally applied."

SYMPTOMS OF UNDERDEVELOPMENT

The disadvantaged countries suffer from numerous demographic, economic, and social ills. Their populations tend to display high birthrates and moderate to high death rates, and life expectancy at birth is comparatively low (see Part Three). A large percentage of the population (as much as half) is 15 years old or younger. Infant mortality is high. Nutrition is inadequate, and diets are not well balanced; protein deficiency is a common problem. The incidence of disease is high; health-care facilities are inadequate. There is an excessively high number of persons per available doctor; hospital beds are too few in number. Sanitation is poor.

Substantial numbers of school-age children do not go to school; illiteracy rates are high.

Rural areas are overcrowded and suffer from poor surface communications. Men and women do not share fairly in the work that must be done; women's work loads are much heavier, and children are pressed into the labor force. Landholdings are often excessively fragmented, and the small plots are farmed with outdated, inefficient tools and equipment. The main crops tend to be cereals and roots; protein output is low because its demand on the available land is higher. There is little production for the local market, because distribution systems are poorly organized and weak local markets generate low demand. On the farms, yields per unit area are low, subsistence modes of life prevail, and the specter of debt hangs constantly over the peasant family. These unchanging circumstances preclude investment of money and time in such luxuries as fertilizers and soil conservation methods. As a result, soil erosion and land denudation scar the rural landscapes of most underdeveloped countries. Where areas of larger-scale, modernized agriculture have developed, these produce for foreign markets, and their impact on domestic conditions is minimal.

In the urban areas, overcrowding, poor housing, inadequate sanitation, and a general lack of services prevail. Employment opportunities are insufficient and unemployment is high. (Yet rural conditions are perceived to be so much worse that accelerating cityward migrations have marked many underdeveloped countries since 1975.) Per capita income remains low, savings per person are minimal, and credit facilities are poor. Families spend a very large portion of their income on food and basic necessities. The middle class remains small, and not infrequently, a

substantial segment of the middle class consists of foreign immigrants.

These are some of the conditions that signal underdevelopment, and this enumeration is far from complete. Geographically, underdeveloped countries tend to be marked by severe regional disparities. In UDCs, local exceptions to the national condition can be especially strong. Thus the capital city may appear as a skyscrapered symbol of urban modernization, with thriving farms in the immediate surroundings and factories on the outskirts. Road and rail connect to a bustling port, where luxury automobiles are unloaded for use by the privileged elite. Here in the country's core area, the rush of "progress" may be evident, but travel a few miles into the countryside beyond and you will find that almost nothing has changed. Just as the rich countries become richer and leave the poorer countries even farther behind, so the gap between progressing and stagnant regions *within* developing countries grows wider. It is an intensifying problem of global dimensions.

Obviously, the levels of industrialization of the DCs differ from those of the UDCs, as noted previously. Certainly some industries exist in virtually all UDCs, however modest and local; it is in the *kinds* of industries, their prevalence and dimensions, that the differences between DCs and UDCs lie. As we noted, among indicators to gauge the level of development in a country are the productivity per worker in the labor force, the consumption of energy per person, the quantity of metal used, and the transport facilities that have been developed. These indicators also reflect a country's industrialization, because the output per worker goes up when industry becomes increasingly mechanized, commercial energy is consumed in greater quantities by industries, metals play a leading role in manufacturing, and transport

From the Field Notes

❝❝ The name Hong Kong (soon to change to Xanggang) has for decades been a synonym for development. In the streets of Kowloon, businesses and their advertisements vie for space and attention. What made Hong Kong an economic success was not resources, not initially, skilled labor, nor security. A combination of geography (as communist China's "back door") and political and economic culture (a laissez-faire environment) created here a core of development whose influence diffused far beyond the borders of the colony. ❞❞

networks reflect the geographic scale and exchange character of an economy.

Small wonder, then, that some countries whose governments seek to accelerate their economic development have tried to go the route of massive industrialization. In the pre-*perestroika* Soviet Union, planners poured massive quantities of that country's resources into a determined program to industrialize. (Underdeveloped countries from Indonesia to Egypt have wanted their

own steel mills and national airlines as symbols of "progress").

However, not all developing countries have made this decision. The more enlightened governments of such UDCs realized that the criteria by which development is measured—and achieved—are not only those of industrial growth, but also the transformation of an entire society. A domestic steel mill or some other symbolic industry will do little to speed that transformation, and remains little more than

an alien anomaly, a costly producer of misleading statistics. Some governments, therefore, made agriculture, not secondary industry, their priority. Sadly, the ideological struggle between the then-First and Second Worlds led certain Third-World governments to impose communist models of farming for which local circumstances were not appropriate. (Tanzania and Ethiopia, for example, suffered setbacks as a result).

Whatever the course chosen by

national governments toward development goals (see box, "Tourism: Boon or Bane?"), all UDCs in the 1990s continue to face enormous obstacles, arising not only from their own internal circumstances (such as excessive population growth, limited capital, etc.), but also from global economic conditions over which they have no control. The developed countries constitute two-thirds of the market for all the products of the UDCs combined, but market prices, tariffs, demand, and other conditions can change quickly and, for some UDCs, disastrously. When oil costs rose during the 1970s, the UDCs suffered severely. When inflation rose in the developed world, the UDCs' exports were severely affected. And now the foreign debt crisis is further afflicting the prospects for the low- and middle-income countries.

A MODEL OF DEVELOPMENT

How do countries progress toward development? Various attempts have been made to improve our understanding of the development process. One global model was formulated by the economist Walt Rostow in the 1960s and is still relevant. Rostow's model suggests that all developing countries follow an essentially similar path through five interrelated growth stages.

In the first of these stages, society is **traditional** and the dominant activity is subsistence farming. The social structure is rigid and unchanging, and there is much resistance to technological change.

The second stage brings the **preconditions for takeoff**. The model suggests that a progressive leadership now moves the country toward greater flexibility, openness, and diversification. Old ways are abandoned by many people, birthrates begin to decline, products other than farm produce make their

TOURISM: BOON OR BANE?

Underdeveloped countries in the Caribbean region of Middle America and in other areas of the world have become leading destinations for millions of tourists from richer nations. However, the tourist industry, in general, contributes little to those countries' development—and its costs in terms of cultural degeneration are sometimes quite high.

With respect to economic geography, the investment that must be made by the "host" country is substantial. Often, the required imports of building materials and equipment strains the country's entire supply system, and funds are diverted to hotel construction that should be spent on the other local needs (such as ordinary housing for citizens). Furthermore, many hotels and other tourist facilities are not owned by the host country, but by large multinational corporations, which control huge chains of tourist accommodations. These corporations, therefore, earn enormous profits, which flow out of the very countries in which the tourist attractions lie.

Certainly there are countries that do earn substantial income from tourism: Kenya, Barbados, and Fiji, among others. However, such income does not constitute a real and fundamental benefit to local economies. On the contrary, some of this income may result from the diversion to tourist consumption of scarce commodities such as food, water, and electricity. Much of it must be reinvested in the construction of airport, cruise-port, transport, and other tourist-serving amenities. As for the creation of employment, neither the number nor the nature of jobs in the tourist industry is encouraging. Tourism frequently strains the fabric of local communities. The invasion of materially poor communities by wealthier visitors leads at times to hostility and even actual antagonism among the hosts. For some local residents, tourists have a "demonstration effect" that leads these lo-

appearance in the domestic economy, and transportation improves. A sense of national unity and purpose may accompany these developments.

This, in turn, will lead to the third stage, **takeoff**. Now the country experiences something akin to an industrial revolution, and sustained growth takes hold. Urbanization increases, industrialization proceeds, and technological and mass-production breakthroughs occur.

Next, the economy enters the fourth stage, **drive to maturity**. Technologies diffuse nationwide, industrial specialization occurs, and international trade expands. Modernization is evident in the core areas of the country; population growth is now in one of the lower categories.

Some countries reach the final stage in the model, that of **high mass consumption**, marked by high incomes, the widespread production of many goods and services, and a majority of workers in the tertiary and quaternary sectors of the economy.

Much has changed in the world since Rostow's model was first published, but there is no doubt that some societies do remain traditional and economically stagnant, that others are at the takeoff stage, and that still others are in the final phase. The largest cluster of countries still in the traditional stage lies in Africa, and many of the countries in the takeoff stage lie in South America and East Asia. But we should not forget that the Rostow model depicts a continuum, and countries that by some criteria have

cals to behave in ways that may please or interest the visitors, but is disapproved of by the larger community. Free-spending, sometimes raucous tourists contribute to anger and resentment. Moreover, tourism can have the effect of debasing local culture, which is adapted to suit the visitors' taste; anyone who has witnessed hotel-staged "culture" shows has seen this process at work. Many workers say that employment in the tourist industry is especially dehumanizing, because expatriate managers demand displays of friendliness and servitude that locals find insulting to sustain.

A flood of affluent tourists may be appealing to the government of an underdeveloped country (whose elite may have a financial stake in the opulent hotels where they too can share the pleasures of the wealthy), but local entrepreneurs usually take a different view. The powerful multinational corporations and the government may intervene to limit the opportunities of local, small-scale operators in favor of mass, prearranged tour promotions that isolate the tourist from local society.

The cultural landscape of tourism is a study in harsh contrasts: gleaming hotels tower over modest, often poor housing; luxury liners glide past poverty-stricken villages; opulent meals are served where, down the street, children suffer from malnutrition. If the tourist industry offered real prospects for economic progress in underdeveloped countries, such circumstances might be viewed as the temporary, unfortunate by-products of the upward struggle. However, the evidence indicates otherwise.

Nevertheless, tourist travel heightens knowledge and awareness, and can promote intercultural contact and understanding. "Ecotourism" aims to inform about the natural environment; "Geotourism" involves scholars in the tourists' travel experience. Such initiatives help improve the image of what is sometimes called the "irritant industry."

---

reached stage 3 are, by other criteria, still in stage 2. The model's assessments are subjective and should be viewed as such.

A CHANGING WORLD

Ours remains a divided world, but change marks it almost everywhere. And in general, the change is toward development. In many countries such change continues to be localized, so that "national" statistics suggesting overall progress mask growing regional inequalities. Nevertheless, there are grounds for optimism. Significant indicators— rates of population growth, levels of education, percentages of workers in nonagricultural jobs—in many countries are showing im-

provement. About 20 years ago the biologist P. Ehrlich, in a book entitled *Population, Resources, Environment* (1976), characterized UDCs as "never-to-be-developed" countries. Since then the lesson has been: when it comes to development, never say never.

One reason for the upsurge of development and the achievement of "takeoff" levels by important countries such as Mexico, Brazil, Thailand, and Malaysia lies in the breakdown of the long-term political-economic division of the world. Until the end of the 1980s, our bipolar political world was a tripolar economic world: a capitalist First World, a communist Second World, and an uncommitted (usually mixed-economy tending toward state control) Third World. Second World countries, following Soviet

and Chinese communist economic models, influenced Third World countries to adopt such models too. But when communist models of development were adopted by Third World countries, they had a high rate of failure, even long before the Soviet system failed in the Soviet Union itself. By the late 1980s, Third World countries from tropical Africa to Southeast Asia were seeking alternatives to Marxist economics. When the Soviet Union collapsed after 75 years of communist doctrine and its 15 constituent republics opted for freer market economics, other socialist-communist countries around the world looked for alternatives as well. The result has been a difficult and sometimes tumultuous transition whose outcome is yet uncertain. It has, however, changed the economic geography of the world. The old distinctions arising from the bipolar political world no longer apply, and "Third World" is a relic notion today.

If communist economics failed in the Soviet Union and Eastern Europe, the same cannot yet be said of China. The East Asian bulwark of communism, in the mid-1990s, remained a bastion of socialist planning, having overcome the political challenge of democratization by military force in 1989. In China, unlike Tanzania or Ethiopia, the collectivization of agriculture brought success in the war against famine, and unlike the Soviet Union, the 1980s did not bring a steadily worsening economic situation. So while communism was abandoned in Russia and its neighbors, China became the ideology's last stronghold, with only North Korea and Cuba in its camp.

The current fervor toward free-market practices notwithstanding, let us remember that the routes to development are many. Just as there always were hard-line communist states (such as Albania and North Korea) and less rigid systems (as in Yugoslavia and Hungary), so capitalism displays variations. The economic systems of, say, Sweden and New Zealand may be closely tied in the Western world and are essentially capitalist, but many of the principles of socialism prevail there as well. This is less true in the Netherlands and the United Kingdom, and still less true in the United States and Japan.

Politics and economics are closely intertwined. In the Soviet Union, the end of Communist Party domination was a precondition for economic as well as political change. In South Africa, the end of *apartheid* and a changing political order will be followed by an economic transformation, perhaps in an opposite direction. But the key question may well be this: Can China prove that communist political systems are able to coexist with capitalist economic practices? If the authoritarianism of China's political system survives the economic transition now under way, other countries may conclude that such a combination (under whatever ideological guise) constitutes a model worth emulating. In that case the world would be polarized all over again.

KEY TERMS

Developed Country (DC)
Developing Country
Development
Drive to Maturity
Gross National Product (GNP)
High Mass Consumption
Neocolonialism
Preconditions for Takeoff
Regional Disparity
Takeoff Stage
Traditional Stage
Underdeveloped Country (UDC)
Underdevelopment

35

INDUSTRIAL ACTIVITY AND GEOGRAPHIC LOCATION

In Chapter 27 we noted that eco nomic activities can be categorized according to their purpose, their relationship to the natural resources on which they are based, and their degree of complexity. The primary industries the *extractive* industries—exist to feed and to supply, and they occur where the resources are: the soils to be farmed, the minerals to be mined, the forests to be cut. The secondary and tertiary and later types of economic activity, however, function to convert and to facilitate—to convert raw materials into finished products and to facilitate trade and other interactive relationships between producers and consumers. Not only are these manufacturing and service industries more complex than primary industries, they also are much less closely tied to the location of natural resources. Hong Kong during the second half of the twentieth century developed one of the world's most powerful economies based on secondary and tertiary industries. It could never have done so on the basis of a primary industry.

Geographica

- **Location theory helps explain the spatial positioning of industries and their success or failure; Weber spatially modeled the secondary industries as von Thünen accounted for agriculture, a primary industry.**

- **Transportation costs are key in the industrial location decision: raw-material acquisition and finished-product distribution determine the options.**

- **Factors influencing the location of industries also include labor costs, energy availability, and infrastructure.**

- **The growth or decline of the secondary industries is also influenced by factors not accounted for by models, including political changes and environmental fluctuations.**

- **The tertiary industries, also known as the service industries, do not produce tangible products but employ more workers than the primary and secondary industries combined, and they locate far more capriciously; they often are called the "footloose" industries.**

Economic geographers investigate the reasons behind the location of economic activity. What was it that made Hong Kong the economic tiger it became? Nearby lay the Portuguese colony of Macau, but Macau never came close to matching Hong Kong's meteoric rise. Today, the world is a vast panorama of primary economic activity within which are set clusters of secondary industries, symbolized by the great manufacturing belts of Japan, the United States, Europe, and Russia, plus growing complexes elsewhere (notably on the Pacific Rim). What geographic factors brought about this layout? What will happen next?

Answers to such questions come from the field of **location theory**, of which that student of primary industry, von Thünen, was a pioneer. But before we look into the future, let us take note of the past. The modern map of world industries carries imprints of history—of a time, long before the onset of the Industrial Revolution, when manufacturing centers had already become established in many parts of the world.

THE "PREINDUSTRIAL" WORLD

It is accurate to describe our modern age as one of *industrial intensification*, because industrial development did not begin with the Industrial Revolution. Instead, it accelerated and diffused from certain areas of innovation to other parts of the world during that period. Long before the momentous events of the second half of the eighteenth century, when the foundations for mass production were laid, industries already existed in many parts of the world, and trade in their products was widespread. In the towns and villages of India, workshops produced metal goods of iron, gold, silver, and brass. India's carpenters were artists as well as artisans, and their work was in demand wherever it could be bought. India's textiles, made on individual spinning wheels and hand looms, were acknowledged to be the best in the world. These industries were sustained not only by the patronage of

local Indian aristocracies, but also by trade on international markets. So good were India's textiles that British textile makers rioted in 1721, demanding legislative protection against the Indian competition that was overwhelming local British markets.

China, too, possessed a substantial industrial base long before the modern Industrial Revolution, and so did Japan. Even European industries, from the textile makers of Flanders and Britain to the iron smelters of Thüringen, had developed considerably, but in terms of price and quality, Europe's products could not match those of other parts of the world.

What European manufacturing products lacked in finesse, Europe's merchants and their representatives more than made up for in aggressiveness and power. Europe's commercial companies (such as the Dutch and British East India Companies) laid the groundwork for the colonial expansion of Europe. They gained control over local industries in India, Indonesia, and elsewhere, profited from the political chaos they precipitated, and played off allies against enemies. British merchants could import about as many tons of raw fiber for the textile industries as they wanted, and all they needed to do, they knew, was to find ways to mass-produce these raw materials into finished products. They would then bury the remaining local industries in Asia and Africa under growing volumes and declining prices. Even China, where local manufactures long prevailed over inferior and more expensive European goods, would eventually succumb.

INDUSTRIAL REVOLUTION

During the eighteenth century, European domestic markets were growing, and there was not enough labor to keep pace with either the local trade or the overseas poten-

tial. Machines capable of greater production were urgently needed, especially improved spinning and weaving equipment. The first steps in the **Industrial Revolution** were not so revolutionary, for the larger spinning and weaving machines that were built were driven by the old source of power: water running downslope. However, James Watt and others who were trying to develop a steam-driven engine succeeded (1765–1788), and this new invention was adapted for various uses. At about the same time, it was realized that coal could be transformed into high-carbon coke, a far superior substitute for charcoal in the smelting of iron.

These momentous innovations had a rapid effect. The power loom revolutionized the weaving industry. Freed from their dependence on charcoal from dwindling wood supplies in the remaining forests, iron smelters could now be concentrated near the British coalfields—the same fields that supplied fuel for the new textile mills. One invention led to another, with each innovation having practical application to more and more industries. Pumps could now keep water out of the flood-prone mines. Engines could move power looms, as well as prototype locomotives and ships. As for the capital required, there was plenty available for investment. British industrialists had been getting rich from the overseas empire for many years.

Thus the Industrial Revolution also had its effects on transportation and communications. The first railroad in England was opened in 1825. In 1830, the city of Manchester was connected by rail to the nearby port of Liverpool, and in the next several decades, thousands of miles of first iron and then steel track were laid. Ocean shipping likewise entered a new age as the first steam-powered vessel crossed the Atlantic in 1819. Now England enjoyed even greater advantages

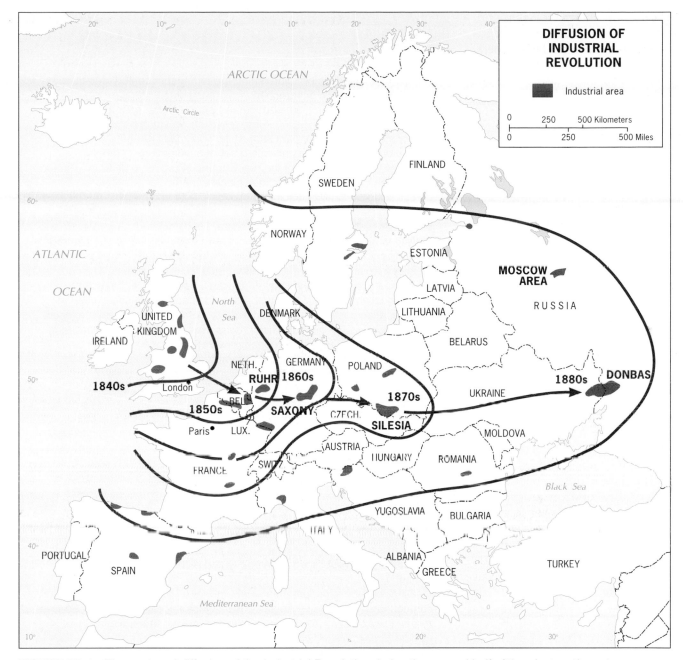

FIGURE 35–1 The eastward diffusion of the Industrial Revolution during the second half of the nineteenth century.

than those with which it entered the period of the Industrial Revolution. Not only did England hold a monopoly over products that were in world demand, but Britain alone possessed the skills necessary to make the machines that manufactured them. Europe and America wanted railroads and locomotives; England had the know-how, the experience, and the capital to supply them. Soon the fruits of the Industrial Revolution were being exported, and British influence around the world was reaching its peak.

Meanwhile, the spatial pattern of modern industrial Europe began to take shape. In Britain, industrial regions, densely populated and heavily urbanized, developed in the "Black Country" near the coalfields. The largest complex was (and remains) positioned in the Midlands of north-central England. In mainland Europe, a belt of major coalfields extends from west to east, roughly along the southern margins of the North European Lowland—due eastward from southern England, across northern France and southern Belgium, the Netherlands, the German Ruhr, western Bohemia in Czech Republic, and Silesia in Poland. Iron ore is dispersed within a broadly similar belt, and the industrial map of Europe reflects the resulting concentrations of economic activity (Fig. 35-1). Nowhere on the continent, however, were the coalfields, the iron ores, and the coastal ports located in such proximity as they were in Britain.

As Figure 35-1 shows, the eastward diffusion of the Industrial Revolution proceeded rapidly, a process that presaged a worldwide spread. Some industrial regions emerged because of their raw material combinations (such as the Ruhr, Saxony, Silesia, and the Donbas); others were based on large urban centers that constituted enormous markets (such as the London and Paris areas). These urban agglomerations attracted industries for reasons other than available resources, and they remain important industrial complexes today.

The Industrial Revolution transformed the world's economic map, but while it had dramatic impact in certain areas, it totally bypassed others. Understanding the forces and factors that shaped the world's industrial layout is a prime objective of economic geographers.

THE LOCATION DECISION

Industrial activity takes place in certain locations and not in others. We already have accounted for the spatial character of the primary industries: the location of the resource base is the determining factor. But **secondary industries** are less dependent on resource location. Raw materials can be transported to distant locations for conversion to manufactured prod-

INDUSTRIAL LOCATION THEORY

Europe's rapid industrialization during the nineteenth century attracted the attention of economic geographers at an early stage. What processes channeled Europe's industrialization and produced the patterns that were developing? Much of this pioneering research was incorporated into Alfred Weber's book, *Theory of the Location of Industries* (1909). Like von Thünen before him, Weber began with a set of assumptions in order to minimize the complexities of the real Europe. However, unlike von Thünen, Weber dealt with activities that took place at particular points, rather than across large areas. Manufacturing plants, mines, and markets are located at specific places, so Weber created a model region marked by sets of points where these activities would occur. He eliminated labor mobility and varying wage rates, and this enabled him to calculate the "pulls" exerted on each point in his theoretical region.

In the process, Weber discerned various factors that affected industrial location, and defined these in various ways. For example, he recognized what he called "general" factors that would affect all industries, such as transportation costs for raw materials and finished products, and "special" factors, such as the perishability of foods. He also differentiated between "regional" factors (transport and labor costs) and "local" factors. Local factors, Weber argued, involved agglomerative (concentrative) and deglomerative forces. Thus the advantages of clustering drew manufacturing plants to large existing urban centers, thereby perpetuating their growth.

Weber singled out transportation costs as the critical determinant of regional industrial location, and suggested that the site of least transportation cost is the place where it would be least expensive to bring raw materials to the point of production, and from which finished products could be distributed to consumers. However, economic geographers following Weber have concluded that some of Weber's assumptions seriously weakened the usefulness of his conclusions, especially in his notions concerning markets and consumer demand. Consumption does not take place at a single location, but over a wide (in some cases a worldwide) area. Nonetheless, practically all modern analytical studies of industrial location have a direct relationship to Weber's work, and he was a pioneer in a class with von Thünen.

Other economic geographers later extended Weber's theories. A major contribution was made by August Lösch, whose book, *The Spatial Structure of the Economy* (1940), was published in English translation in 1954 as *The Economics of Location*. Lösch countered Weber's studies of least-cost location by seeking ways to determine maximum-profit locations. He inserted the spatial influence of consumer demand, as well as production costs, into his calculations, a major step forward in the effort to discern the factors shaping the economic landscape.

ucts—if the associated costs are overcome by adequate profits.

Any attempt to establish a model for the location of secondary industry runs into complications much greater than those confronting von Thünen (who dealt with primary in-

dustries only). The location of secondary industries depends to a larger extent on human behavior and decision making, on cultural and political as well as economic factors, even on intuition or whim. Since models must be based on assumptions, economic geographers have to assume that decision makers are trying to maximize their advantages over competitors when they choose a location, that they want to make as much profit as possible, and that they will weigh the **variable costs**, such as energy supply, transport expenses, labor costs, and other needs.

WEBER'S MODEL

The German economic geographer Alfred Weber (1868–1958) did for the secondary industries what von Thünen had done earlier for agriculture: he developed a model for the location of manufacturing establishments. Weber's **least cost theory** accounted for the location of a manufacturing plant in terms of the minimization of three critical expenses. The first and most important of these was transportation: the choice of site must entail the lowest possible cost of moving raw materials to the factory and finished products to the market. The second cost was that of labor. Rising labor costs cut the margin of profit, so that a factory might do better farther from raw materials and markets—if cheap labor makes up for added transport costs. (The current economic boom on East Asia's Pacific Rim is based substantially on low labor costs, so that industries are relocating from Japan and Taiwan to areas where labor is cheap in China and Vietnam).

The third factor in Weber's model was a condition he called **agglomeration**. When a substantial number of enterprises cluster in the same area, as happens in a large industrial city, they can provide assistance to each other through shared talents, services, and facilities. All manufacturers need office furniture and equipment; the presence of one or more producers in a large city satisfies this need for all. Thus a certain advantage of big-city location accrues from agglomeration, perhaps overcoming some increase in transport and labor costs. Of course, excessive agglomeration leads to high rents, rising wages, circulation problems resulting in increased transport costs and loss of efficiency, and other problems. These may eventually negate the original advantages of agglomeration. (Such factors have much to do with the departure of many industries from the crowded urban centers of the U.S. eastern megalopolis to other locations).

Like von Thünen's model, Weber's least cost theory gave rise to a long and spirited debate among economic geographers. Some argued that Weber's model did not adequately account for variations in costs over time; for example, when relative labor costs decline (as they sometimes do) or when land rent goes down, the enterprise can sustain an increase in transport costs. While the Weber model might indicate that a location had become unprofitable, this **substitution principle** suggests otherwise. Also, the model would suggest that one particular site would be optimal for a manufacturer's location, while such an enterprise might be quite profitable within a larger area. And other factors not accounted for by the model, such as taxation policies, also complicate the picture. Despite all these (and other) caveats, Alfred Weber set into motion a debate over the spatial aspects of economic activity that continues in the geographic literature today (see box, "Industrial Location Theory").

FACTORS OF LOCATION

Our discussion of models and theories of industrial location is based on circumstances prevailing in commercial economies, that is, in economies guided by market mechanisms and by relationships between supply and demand that are determined by prices and profits. Later, when we view the outcome of all the processes and decisions that shape the world's economic layout, we will note that the market mechanism was not universal in its application. Several of the world's major industrial regions evolved under the rules of state planning, which tolerated large losses in the interest of greater national objectives. As we saw earlier, the Industrial Revolution reached Ukraine and Russia before the Soviet Union was created, so that the economic-geographic map of 1917 had arisen from market forces. But subsequent Soviet economic policy changed the direction of industrial growth, and the map at the end of the Soviet era (1989) was a mixture of the old commercial era and the later planned one. Today the market rules again in Russia, but the Soviet framework persists—and inhibits reform.

One of the first decisions faced by the capitalists who built the great iron works of Europe had to do with the need to move either coal to the iron ores or iron ore to the coalfields. As you will see from any map of the time, the iron smelters were built near the coalfields of the British Midlands (the Black Towns were aptly named for the soot that hung permanently in the air and coated the entire cultural landscape). That practice of moving the iron to the coal spread throughout Europe's industrial axis, but it is one of three options: the other two are (1) to move the coal to the iron ore reserves or (2) to transport both to an intermediate location. (In the former Soviet Union's planned economy, still another option was exercised: steel mills were built on the coalfields as well as on the iron ore reserves; trains carried coal in one direction and iron ore in the other). In commercial economies, iron ore is transported most frequently to the coalfields, often after the partial elimination of waste and impurities. But there are exceptions. For example, coal is transported in large quantities to France's iron-rich Lorraine region, where coal is scarce. When an industrial complex develops near a coalfield and the coal supplies become exhausted, it may be less expensive to start importing coal from elsewhere than to relocate the factories. Even when both coal and iron ore are shipped over large distances to some intermediate site, the iron ore usually travels the farthest.

RAW MATERIALS

Numerous considerations enter into such decisions, and these questions are of prime interest to economic geographers who want to know what the processes are whereby manufacturing activity organizes and adjusts economic space. Obviously, the resources involved—the **raw materials**—play a major role. One example is the coastal orientation of the steel industry along the U.S. northeastern seaboard. Those industrial facilities are there, in large measure, because they long used iron ore shipped from Venezuela, Labrador, Liberia, and other overseas sources. Instead of transferring these materials from oceangoing ships onto trains and transporting them inland, the ores are used right where they arrive—practically at the point of unloading at such huge steel-mill complexes as Sparrows Point, near Baltimore, and Fairless, near Philadelphia. So in this case, faraway ore deposits had much to do with the location of industry in the United States. Thus transport costs affect the location of industry in important ways. (Transportation is discussed in a separate section because this factor involves finished products as well as raw materials.)

In the case of raw materials, we have already noted the spatial rela-

tionships between Europe's zone of coalfields and iron ores and the spread of manufacturing throughout the region. However, not all of the world's great industrial regions lie near major sources of raw materials. Japan's massive industries must import their raw materials from distant sources, because Japan's domestic resource base is quite limited. This situation has not prevented Japan from developing into one of the world's great industrial nations, but it does present particular problems of availability and cost to Japanese manufacturers. Japan's early industrial progress was based on its own indigenous manufacturing traditions and, initially, on a set of comparatively minor domestic resources. The rapid depletion of these local raw materials was among the motives that led Japan to embark on its expansion into East Asia, where Korea and Northeast China became Japanese dependencies and sources of additional industrial resources.

Even after Japan lost its colonial empire, its industrial might continued, sustained by its large, highly skilled, and initially cheap labor force (rising wages in Japan have recently hurt its manufacturers). Japanese products dominated markets around the world, and from the proceeds Japanese enterprises could purchase needed raw materials virtually anywhere. Australia, for example, has become one of Japan's leading suppliers.

For many decades, European industrialized countries also controlled the sources of raw materials they needed, because they had colonized the countries where these resources existed (Britain's example had much to do with Japan's colonial expansion for similar purposes). In the postcolonial era, the flow of commodities has linked the underdeveloped countries that are the suppliers to the manufacturers in the developed countries, in many cases former colonial powers. This not-so-new pattern of trade

spells disadvantage for the underdeveloped countries, because they must sell their raw materials in order to secure foreign capital even when commodity prices fall through oversupply or recession. The developed countries, on the other hand, can keep prices low by moving their business from one supplier to another. When an underdeveloped country loses customers for its raw materials, the effect on its economy may be disastrous.

Underdeveloped countries have tried to band together in cartels in order to control vital commodities the developed countries need, but such efforts have not succeeded. Usually the buyers are in a stronger position than the sellers, because they can find alternative sources for their needs (including countries that have not joined the cartels). In the 1970s, when OPEC (the Organization of Petroleum Exporting Countries) took control of world oil supplies, it succeeded in creating an oil crisis and in driving up the price of petroleum. But countries that did not join OPEC increased their production and gave the developed countries a chance to break OPEC's hold; the world supply recovered, prices collapsed, and the producers—not the consumers—were again the losers.

LABOR

Weber regarded **labor** as one of the three fundamentals of his least cost model, and in recent years we have seen what the availability of cheap and semiskilled labor means in regional industrial development. Even in this day of automated assembly lines and computerized processing, the prospect of a large, low-wage, trainable labor force attracts manufacturers as it did when children were pressed into 12-hour workdays in industrializing Britain two centuries ago.

From the Field Notes

❝ Mining is one of the primary, extractive industries. Its impact on the environment can be staggering. Near Queenstown in western Tasmania we saw a landscape, once forested and verdant, transformed by mining operations. Gaping open-pit mines, slag heaps, and denuded slopes reached as far as the eye could see. ❞

Japan's postwar success on international markets, we noted earlier, was based in large measure on the skills *and* the low wages of its labor force, allowing manufacturers to flood foreign markets with low-priced goods. Into the 1950s, Japanese goods had little reputation for quality but were known for their affordability; but then Japan's factories began to excel in quality as well. This in turn led to higher prices, higher wages, and, inevitably, competition from countries where cheaper labor could be found. Taiwan and South Korea competed with Japan with goods ranging from electronics to automobiles, and in the mid-1990s Japan was in a deep recession while Taiwan and South Korea boomed. But the next stage of economic transformation on the Pacific Rim was already under way in the 1980s: the entry of China with its huge labor force. In March 1994 the daily wage of a factory worker in Shanghai's Pudong district was one-fortieth that of a Japanese worker in a similar job and one-thirtieth that of a Taiwanese worker. Coupled with advantageous tax regulations, such numbers are attracting thousands of enterprises to China's Special Economic Zones, where cities and towns are being transformed as Europe's were during the early decades of the Industrial Revolution.

What is happening on China's Pacific Rim today is nothing new (similar developments are affecting Thailand and Malaysia), and China, like South Korea and Japan before it, also will feel the effects of still-cheaper labor when Vietnam enters the picture. Nor is this exclusively an Asian phenomenon. One of the most powerful points of debate during the period before the United States, Canada, and Mexico joined in the North American Free Trade Agreement (NAFTA) on January 1, 1994, had to do with industrial relocation—relocation from the U.S. across the border to Mexico, where wages were lower and where profits would be larger. The cost of labor still looms large in the location of industry.

✓ TRANSPORTATION

Transportation facilities and costs, as Weber noted, are crucial in industrial location. A huge market may exist for a given product, but if that market is not served by an efficient transportation system, much of the associated advantage is lost. The maps in the next chapter underscore that highly developed industrial areas are also the places served most effectively by transportation facilities. Industrialization and the development of modern circulation systems go hand in hand and, in a sense, the Industrial Revolution was a transportation revolution—a transformation that is still going on. Every year, more freight is carried by air, and in the United States, trucks more frequently haul goods formerly carried on trains.

For industry, efficient transportation systems enable manufacturers to purchase raw materials from distant sources and to distribute finished products to a dispersed population of consumers. Manufacturers desire maximum transport effectiveness at the lowest possible level of costs. Their location decision-making will also consider the availability of alternative systems in the event of emergencies (e.g., truck routes when rail service is interrupted). Among the significant recent innovations in bulk transport is the development of container systems that facilitate the transfer of goods from one type of carrier to another (from rail to ship and ship to truck). This has lowered costs and increased flexibility, permitting many manufacturers to pay less attention to transportation in their location decisions.

It has long been known that for most goods, it is cheapest to transport by truck over short distances. Alternatively, railroads are cheapest over medium distances, and ships are cheapest over the longest distances. However, when decisions are made relating to the location of industries, numerous aspects of transportation must be taken into account, and no single generalization can do justice to the complexities of the problem. For example, when goods are hauled, costs are incurred at the terminal where trucks, trains, and ships are unloaded. These costs vary and are much higher for ships than for trucks. Then, of course, there is the actual cost of transportation itself, which increases with distance, but at a decreasing rate, making long-distance transportation cheaper per mile. Such long-haul economies make it possible for a manufacturer to reach out to distant suppliers of raw materials and also to sell to faraway customers. Still another factor has to do with the weight and volume of the freight. Certain goods may be of light weight, but may occupy a lot of space inside railroad cars or ships' holds, and may thus still be expensive to transport. Consider just these few aspects of transportation—and remember that transportation is only one factor among a number of others affecting industrial location!

✓ INFRASTRUCTURE

When Weber alluded to the notion of agglomeration and its positive as well as negative connotations, he could not foresee the dimensions of urban areas or industrial complexes a century hence. In his time, world population was about the size of China's today; cities with more than 1 million inhabitants were comparatively few. Today's numbers are very different—and so are the problems and benefits of agglomeration. If you were to build a factory in Shanghai or elsewhere in Pacific Rim China to make use of that low-cost labor mentioned earlier, you would have many needs, ranging from transportation facilities to Chinese and overseas markets to telephones and utilities such as electricity and water supply. All these facilities, also including banks, postal and messenger services, hotels, and social services, are collectively referred to as **infrastructure**. Airports, roads, docks, railways, and taxis all are part of it.

Available infrastructure constitutes an important criterion among factors influencing the industrial location decision. One reason the communist Chinese regime in Beijing has tried to slow the rate of economic development and industrialization along its Pacific Rim lies in the inadequacy of the local and regional infrastructures: the demand for such facilities as telephones and administrative assistance far exceeds what is available. Factories are having difficulty importing raw materials; market distribution systems cannot yet fill the need. Public utilities prove inadequate (Shanghai in 1994 brought on-line a major new coal-burning power plant, but projected requirements will overtake the supply in a few years).

Given such shortcomings in infrastructures, why does the influx of enterprises continue? The answer lies in part in one of those areas for which no economic-geographic model can account: the perception of future disadvantage. The rush is on, and not to have a stake in the new industrial frontier is to risk falling behind in the future. So the Chinese economic hot spots continue to burgeon, even in the face of inadequate infrastructures.

Compared to China, Vietnam (regarded by some observers as the next economic "tiger" on the Pacific Rim) has an even weaker infrastructure. For all its advantages (self-sufficiency in food, good relative location, a large educated labor force, a domestic market of nearly 80 million), Vietnam has problems in its infrastructure that will not soon be overcome. Inadequate power and water supply and a poor

From the Field Notes

❝ Approaching Saigon on the Saigon River in mid-1995, we could observe many infrastructure improvements as we neared the city. This gas storage and distribution facility was built on the riverfront immediately adjacent to the new Economic Development Zone (background), designed to attract foreign investment, for which land was being cleared. Energy availability is a key factor in the location of industry. ❞

surface transportation network are just some of these weaknesses.

Author's Video Link
↓
➐
"Vietnam"

In many Western cities, the disadvantages of excessive agglomeration are driving firms away from crowded and deteriorating urban areas, notwithstanding the massive capacities of their infrastructures. In non-Western cities, industries are entering in anticipation of improved infrastructures. The **economic landscape** constantly shifts, and another surge of change is under way in Asia today.

ENERGY

Another factor in the location of industry is the availability of an **energy** supply. This factor used to be much more important than it is today. The early British textile mills,

because they depended on water rushing down hillsides to drive the looms, had few locational alternatives. However, these days power comes from different sources, and can even be transmitted via high-voltage electrical lines over long distances. Manufacturers are therefore able to locate primarily on the basis of considerations other than power, except when an industry needs exceptionally large amounts of energy—for example, certain metallurgical (aluminum and copper processing) and chemical industries (fertilizer production). Such industries are attracted to sites where abundant energy is available, as is the case near hydroelectric plants. In the United States, the growth of aluminum production in the Pacific Northwest and in the Tennessee Valley is mainly based on the ready availability of cheap electricity, as is also the case in Canada's Saint Maurice and Saguenay River Basins.

The role of power supply as a factor in industrial location has changed over time. Whereas manu-

facturing plants of the Industrial Revolution often were established on or near coalfields, we do not see modern-era clustering of major industrial complexes near oil fields. Instead, a huge system of pipelines and tankers delivers oil and natural gas to existing manufacturing regions (and to individual consumers throughout the developed world).

For some time during and after the OPEC-induced global oil crises of the 1970s, fears of future rises in oil costs led some industries that require large amounts of electricity to move to sites where the environment is moderate, keeping heating and air-conditioning costs at a minimum. But such moves were comparatively few, and national energy-conservation goals were soon modified. In the United States, reliance on foreign energy resources in the mid-1990s exceeded that prevailing when the energy crises of the 1970s struck. Just as energy supply has become a less significant factor in industrial location, so energy security is off the national priority list today.

OTHER FACTORS

Factors other than those we have already identified may also influence industrial location. If several plants have already located in a certain area, others might be influenced to do the same—not only because of the advantages of the site, but because of a certain clustering or agglomeration effect that comes into play. Had those already established plants not been there, the more newly located industries might have been positioned elsewhere (this factor is especially pertinent for tertiary industries; see box, "The Tertiary Industries"). There is also a factor of political stability and receptiveness to investment. Industries are frightened away if there are signs of

THE TERTIARY INDUSTRIES

The **tertiary industries** do not (as the primary and secondary industries do) generate an actual, tangible product. Tertiary industries include services, such as transportation and communications, financial services (banking is such an industry), retailing, recreation, teaching, even government. Here the measure of worth is not the quantity of a commodity produced, but the quality and effectiveness with which the particular service is performed.

Although tertiary industries do not produce tangible commodities, they *do* employ large numbers of people. In the United States, for example, the service industries employ more workers than the primary and secondary industries combined. This should not surprise us: primary industries such as farming and mining no longer employ large numbers of people, and the manufacturing industries of the secondary economic sector are becoming increasingly mechanized. So the main task now is to bring the producer and the consumer together—through advertising, transportation, selling, installing, servicing, lending money, and so forth. Moreover, as the economies of the most advanced countries achieve "postindustrial" status, the information (quaternary) sector becomes increasingly important, and, by some measures, already is the single largest employment sector in the United States in the 1990s.

Tertiary industries are often quite small, so that, in number, they outrank both primary and secondary establishments. In terms of location, these are the most directly people-oriented of all industries, so that almost any map showing population clusters is a good indicator of the world distribution of tertiary economic activities. Tertiary industries, quite logically, tend to be concentrated in cities and towns. Unlike the primary industries, they are not tied to the location of raw materials, nor are they as closely governed by locational factors as are the secondary industries. Indeed, certain tertiary industries today are often called *footloose* industries, because their range of locational choices is so wide.

a rivermouth trading port there was little to suggest its phenomenal growth to come. Then China was ostracized for its role in the Korean War, and Hong Kong's links to the mainland were cut; manufacturers had to look for new products and markets, and textiles were the answer. The political situation ensured a huge supply of labor at low wages, and the textile industry boomed, based on imported raw materials and exported clothing. The money made in the textile industries was invested in the development of other manufactures, and the rest is—geography.

But Hong Kong would not have achieved what it did without another advantage. China, isolated as it was, needed a back door to the outside world, a route along which to funnel finances, crucial imports, and messages. That route lay through Hong Kong, and the British colony benefited incalculably from its geographic situation. As the door opened wider, Hong Kong prospered and spawned a "twin" in Shenzhen across the border.

Explaining industrial location and predicting its growth are complex matters, as the regional maps in Chapter 36 will confirm.

uncertainty in the political future of a country, or when a government gives indications that it intends to nationalize industries owned by foreigners. Taxation policies can also play a role, and some countries try to attract industries by offering huge tax exemptions over long time periods. Sometimes, influential industrialists can simply decide to locate a major plant in some area for personal reasons, thereby signaling that they can afford to ignore the principles of industrial location. The directors of global (multinational) corporations can affect the course of regional industrial development in many countries almost at

will. Furthermore, some industries are located where they are because of environmental conditions. The film industry has been strongly concentrated in Southern California because of the large number of clear, cloudless days there—a climatic advantage that also has attracted aircraft manufacturers, who need good weather for flight-testing new planes.

Much as we may theorize, therefore, the location and success of industries may depend on unanticipated, even unaccountable factors as well. We now explain Hong Kong's success with available hindsight, but when the colony was just

KEY TERMS

Agglomeration
Economic Landscape
Energy
Industrial Revolution
Infrastructure
Labor
Least Cost Theory
Location Theory
Raw Materials
Secondary Industries
Substitution Principle
Tertiary Industries
Transportation
Variable Costs

36

WORLD INDUSTRIAL REGIONS

When the victorious Bolsheviks took control of the Russian empire, they found themselves in charge of a vast, underdeveloped realm with a dominantly agricultural economy. The **Industrial Revolution** had penetrated the Soviet Union, but in only a few areas could its impact be seen in the landscape. The Donbas region on both sides of the Russian-Ukrainian border was such a place, and the Moscow and (then) Leningrad areas also had attracted secondary industries. But there was nothing in the Soviet Union of the 1920s to rival what was happening in Europe or North America.

Soviet communist rulers were determined to change this. They wanted to transform the Soviet economy into an industrial one, with which they intended to out-compete their ideological adversaries in the capitalist world. To accomplish this, the dictator Josef Stalin ordered the expropriation of land and the collectivization of agriculture, so that labor would be freed for manufacturing jobs and capital could be diverted from farm to factory. The human cost of this

Geographica

- The world today displays four major industrial regions, all in the Northern Hemisphere: Western and Central Europe, Eastern North America, Russia-Ukraine, and Eastern Asia; each consists of core areas with subsidiary clusters.

- The location of Europe's primary industrial regions still reflects the spatial diffusion of the Industrial Revolution; an axis of manufacturing extends from Britain to Poland and the Czech Republic, and on to Ukraine.

- North America's manufacturing complex is the largest in the world today, anchored by the American Manufacturing Belt.

- Despite Ukraine's political separation from the former Soviet Union and hence from Russia, Ukrainian and Russian industries are interdependent; Ukraine needs Russian fuels and Russia needs Ukrainian raw materials.

- Industrial regions in East Asia are the world's fastest-growing today; the Asian Pacific Rim, from Japan to Indonesia, includes several of the most successful economies including Taiwan and Singapore, but the juggernaut is China.

giant communist scheme was dreadful: millions of farmers were executed or starved to death when they failed to comply or were sus-pected of opposition (as countless Ukrainians were). But the transformation Moscow's despotic regime envisaged did take place. The

447

Soviet Union became a major industrial power with vast manufacturing complexes that produced enough material to defeat the German armies during World War II, less than 20 years after Lenin's death. In the 1950s, Soviet prowess was confirmed when the USSR launched and orbited the world's first artificial satellite, and a Soviet cosmonaut became the first human being in space. In the early 1960s a Soviet ruler visiting America pounded his fist on his hosts' table and bellowed, "We will bury you!" Back home, his industries were pouring out products ranging from toys to tanks, and confidence in the superiority of communist planning was at an all-time high. Moscow and Leningrad (now renamed St. Petersburg) lay at the center of major industrial complexes. The old Donbas region had rivals to the east as far away as Lake Baykal. The Soviet Union had taken the Industrial Revolution a giant step further.

While the Soviets were forging their **planned industrial economy, industrial development** took a very different course elsewhere. Market forces, not state planning, had propelled the Industrial Revolution in Europe and in North America, and industrial economies on both sides of the Atlantic Ocean rose to global prominence. After World War II, the Soviets for more than four decades imposed their ideology on Eastern Europe's industrial development, so that Eastern Europe's economic geography displayed a hybrid character—a layout begun through free enterprise later constrained by communist planning. But Western Europe's industrial growth proceeded more freely, and in the postwar period Japan, Taiwan, and South Korea industrialized under free-enterprise rules as well. China, on the other hand, followed a modified Soviet model, collectivizing its farming and putting its industries under state control.

Whatever the ideological basis (market-commercial, communist-state, or some combination), the world map of major regional-industrial development reveals that only a small minority of the world's countries have become major industrial economies. Many factors (resource endowment, relative location, political circumstances, economic leadership, labor-force capacity) are involved, but the map is changing. The legacy of the Industrial Revolution still is evident, and many of the older industrial complexes (Germany's Ruhr, Poland's Silesia, Ukraine's Donbas) still prevail. But industrial centers of consequence are emerging far beyond this original zone of industrial diffusion, in such countries as India and Brazil, not to mention a revitalized and burgeoning China. What follows, therefore, is a picture of a fast-changing world in which new competitors are challenging the old economic order.

When industrial concentrations are mapped, four **primary industrial regions** stand out.

1. Western and Central Europe
2. Eastern North America
3. Russia and Ukraine
4. Eastern Asia

Each of these industrial regions consists of one or more core areas of industrial development with subsidiary clusters some distance away. As we will note, while the older manufacturing regions are quite entrenched, notable shifts are nevertheless occurring. This dispersal is especially evident today in East Asia, where Japan's virtual monopoly is changing to a primacy challenged by what economic geographers call the "Four Tigers" of East Asia. In Europe, the Ruhr is being affected by a southward shift of German industry. In North America, the old eastern core of industries is still dominating,

but the balance is shifting toward subsidiary clusters to the west and south. The map is changing as we read.

EUROPE'S MANUFACTURING REGIONS

It is appropriate to begin with Europe, for it is here that the Industrial Revolution was launched. The manufacturing regions of Europe (Fig. 36-1) largely constitute the European heartland, the focus of the evolving European Union.

As noted previously, Britain's coal-fired industries produced a pattern of areal functional specialization that, for a time, had no equal in the world. Today, much of that pattern is lost, diluted by diversification, relocation, and failure. Britain has failed to keep up with modern technological developments. Plants that at one time were the epitome of industrial modernization still operate today—aging, comparatively inefficient, expensive to run, slow, and wasteful. With the relative decline of the manufacturing cities of the *Midlands* and northern England, there is a tendency for those industrial enterprises that can afford to, and are able to do so, to relocate near the historic focal point of Britain: *London*. This still is the greatest domestic market of the British Isles, and, increasingly, that market is of importance to local manufacturers, as the competition for markets from elsewhere intensifies. All this reflects the decreasing importance of coal in the energy-supply picture (which is changing toward nuclear power), the desire to start afresh with up-to-date machinery, and a realization that London, in addition to forming a huge domestic market, is also a good port through which to import raw materials. So London,

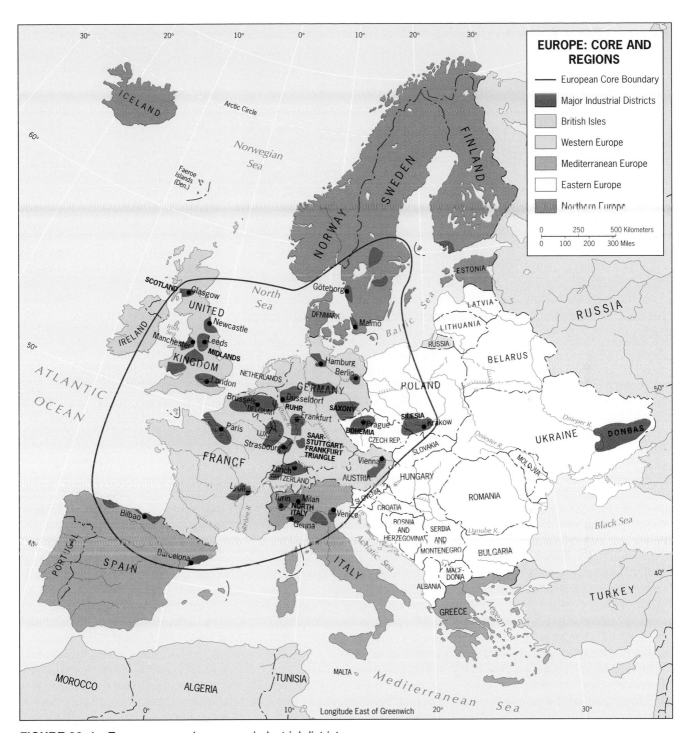

FIGURE 36–1 Europe: core, urban areas, industrial districts.

too, shows up in Figure 36-1 as a key industrial district within the European region, and Paris does as well.

When the Industrial Revolution diffused onto the mainland, *Paris* was already continental Europe's

greatest city—but Paris did not (as London did not) have coal or iron deposits in its immediate vicinity. Nevertheless, Paris was the largest existing local market for manufacturers for hundreds of miles around, and when a railroad system was

added to the existing network of road and waterway connections, the city's centrality was further strengthened. As in the case of London, Paris soon began to attract major industries, and the city, long a center for the manufacturing of

From the Field Notes

❝ Paris and the Paris Basin form the industrial as well as agricultural heart of France. The city and region are served by the Seine River, along which lies a string of ports from Le Havre at the mouth to Rouen at the head of navigation for ocean-going ships. Rouen has become a vital center on France's industrial map. As we approached on the river, you could see the famous cathedral and the city's historic cultural landscape to the left (north), but on the right bank lay a major industrial complex including coal-fired power facilities (although France leads Europe in nuclear energy), petrochemical plants, and oil installations. It is all part of the industrial region centered on Paris. ❞

TABLE 36–1	World Steel Production, 1993 (Millions of Metric Tons)
Japan	101,373
China	88,482
Russia[a]	86,184
United States	86,099
Germany	37,846
South Korea	32,576
Italy	25,892
Brazil	25,069
India	18,542
France	17,377
United Kingdom	16,820
Canada	15,848
Taiwan	14,949
Poland	9,919
Czech Republic	9,908

[a]Estimate. Russian steel production has declined greatly since 1990, and the figure given here may be high.
Sources: Organization for Economic Cooperation and Development, *Annual Steel Market Report 1995*, United Nations International Iron and Steel Institute, 1994.

luxury items (jewelry, perfumes, and fashions), experienced substantial growth in such industries as automobile manufacturing and assembly, metallurgy, and chemical manufacturing. With a ready labor force, an ideal regional position for the distribution of finished products, the presence of governmental agencies, a nearby ocean port (Le Havre), and France's largest domestic market, the development of Paris as a major industrial center was no accident.

Europe's coal deposits, however, lie in a belt across northern France, Belgium, north-central Germany, the northwestern Czech Republic, and southern Poland—and it was along this zone that mainland Europe's primary concentrations of heavy industry developed. Three major manufacturing districts lay in Germany: the mighty *Ruhr*, based on the Westphalian coalfield, the

Saxony district, near the border of the former Czechoslovakia, and *Silesia* (now part of Poland). Among these, the Ruhr became the greatest industrial complex of Europe. Today, Germany still ranks among the world's leading producers of both coal and steel and remains Europe's leading industrial power (Table 36-1).

The Ruhr, named after a small tributary of the Rhine River, reveals the combined advantages of high-quality resources, good accessibility, and proximity to large markets. When local iron ore reserves became depleted, replacement ores could be brought in from overseas with only a single transshipment. Since the 1870s, the Ruhr has poured forth the products of heavy industry. Its tanks and other weapons of war enabled Hitler's armies to challenge for world power.

Saxony, on the other hand, was always skill and quality oriented, known for such products as optical equipment and cameras, refined textiles, and ceramics. Leipzig and Dresden were the urban anchors of the Saxony district, which suffered from its incorporation into now-defunct East Germany. The region's revival is a prime objective of reunified Germany's economic planners.

Farther eastward, the industrial district of Silesia was also first developed by the Germans, although it now lies in Poland and extends into the Czech Republic (Fig. 36-1). The Saxony–Bohemia–Silesia axis of industry evolved on high-quality coal resources and lesser iron ores that were later supplemented by imports from Ukraine.

Europe's industrial success was based not only on such raw materials, however: the skills of its labor forces and the high degree of specialization achieved in various industrial zones led to intensive exchange of products. This exchange was facilitated by Europe's natural transport routes, augmented by artificial ones. Thus the industrial imperative diffused far from the original sources to such areas as northern Italy, now one of Europe's major industrial hearths, Catalonia (anchored by Barcelona) and northern Spain, southern Sweden, and southern Finland. These and other European industrial zones not mentioned here are just districts within the continent's massive industrial structure; each would stand out as a first-order cluster of manufacturing activity in most other parts of the world.

EASTERN NORTH AMERICA'S MANUFACTURING REGIONS

The European Union's industrial achievement notwithstanding, North America's manufacturing complex has no rival in the world today. In North America, the eastern regions of industry led the way. Served by a wide array of natural resources and supported by networks of natural as well as artificial transportation systems, remote from the devastation wrought by wars in other industrial regions, and on the doorstep of the world's richest market, North American manufacturing developed rapidly and highly successfully. Ample capital, mass production, areal specialization, and diversification marked the robust growth of this region, which enjoyed ample available energy (see box, "Industry and Energy").

The bulk of American manufacturing in the United States and Canada is concentrated in the rectangular-shaped region delimited in Figure 36-3, the *American Manu-*

INDUSTRY AND ENERGY

North America's industrial prowess has been based in part on a large and varied regional resource base, and sustained by its capacity to acquire needed raw materials from overseas sources. While coal remained the chief fuel for the industries that helped achieve this primacy, there was no threat of a domestic energy shortage: U.S. coal reserves are among the world's largest. Coalfields in the United States are widely distributed, moreover, from Appalachian Pennsylvania to the northwestern Great Plains (Fig. 36-2). Still today, the United States vies with China as the world's largest coal producer, but the situation with respect to another energy source—petroleum—is quite different. The story of industrial and transportation development in the United States during the twentieth century has been one of increasing dependence on fossil fuels that are no longer nearly as plentiful in local reserves as coal: oil and natural gas.

United States consumption of petroleum and natural gas today is about 27 percent and 37 percent, respectively, of the annual world total. In the early 1990s, the United States required no fewer than 17 million barrels of petroleum *per day* to keep its power plants, machinery, vehicles, aircraft, and ships functioning. However, U.S. production of oil in recent years has averaged about 18 percent of the world total, and, even including the known Alaskan potential, U.S. reserves of oil are estimated to amount to only about 4 percent of the world total. That underscores this country's present and future dependence on foreign oil supplies, with all the uncertainties involved.

Petroleum is not the only energy source for which the United States leads world demand and consumption. As Figure 36-2 shows, accumulations of natural gas often occur in general association with oil deposits. The use of natural gas has increased enormously since World War II. In the 1990s, the United States annually consumed about 37 percent of the natural gas used in the world, and even this was barely enough to satisfy demand. One result of this intensification of natural gas use is the proliferation of pipelines shown in Figure 36-2. In North America in 1995, there were over 2.5 million miles (4 million kilometers) of pipeline carrying gas from sources to consumers, including parts of a new pipeline designed to carry Alaskan natural gas across Canada to the U.S. market.

Dependence on external supplies of fuels affects three of the four world industrial regions discussed in this chapter. Europe's North Sea discoveries of oil and gas notwithstanding, foreign shipments of petroleum remain critical necessities. The United States has two neighbors with substantial fossil fuel reserves (Mexico's oil and gas may rank among the world's largest), but its domestic potential remains rather limited. Japan is almost totally dependent on distant oil suppliers.

---

facturing Belt, which extends from the northeastern seaboard to Iowa, and from the St. Lawrence Valley to the confluence of the Ohio and Mississippi Rivers.

Manufacturing in North America began in *New England* as early as late colonial times, but these northeastern states are not especially rich in mineral resources. Still, this old-

est manufacturing district continues to produce high-quality light manufactures.

Another district of early importance in America centers on *New York,* at the very heart of the megalopolis today and still the locus of tens of thousands of industrial establishments. An early start, large urban growth, and agglomeration

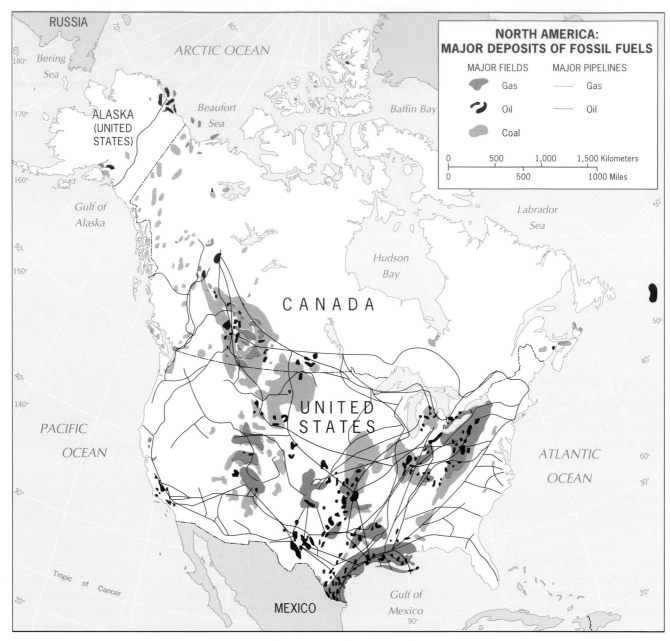

FIGURE 36–2 The world's largest energy consumer is also endowed with substantial energy resources.

played roles in this development; the New York area is not especially well endowed with mineral resources. It does constitute a large market (like Paris and London), has a huge skilled and semiskilled labor force, is the focus of an intensive transport network, and has long been one of the world's great ports, a major **break-of-bulk** location. Break-of-bulk refers to the transfer of transported cargo from one kind

of carrier (e.g., a ship) to another (truck or train). Such transfers generate much activity.

Southward, the light industries of New England and New York give way to heavier manufacturing. Here lies the *Southeast Pennsylvania* district, centered on metropolitan Philadelphia and encompassing the Baltimore area. Iron ores shipped from distant locations (Canada, South America) are smelted right on

the waterfront in tidewater steel mills. Major chemical industries (notably in northern Delaware), pharmaceutical industries, and lighter manufacturing plants have been established there.

Farther west lies the well-defined *Upstate New York* district, extending from the environs of Albany, on the Hudson River, to Buffalo, on the shore of Lake Erie. Growth there was originally stimulated by the old

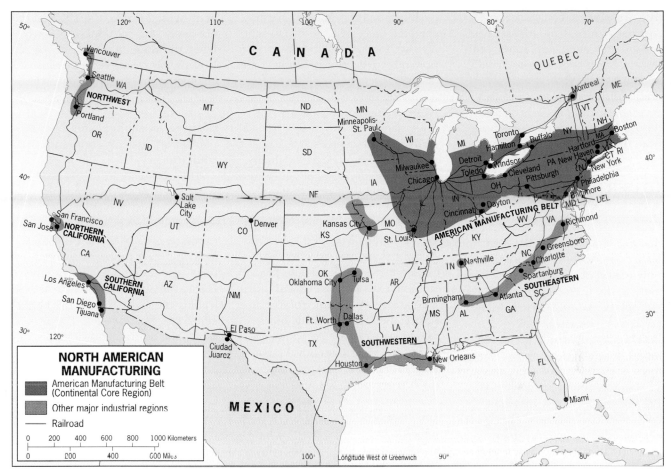

FIGURE 36–3 North American manufacturing has dispersed westward and southward, but the eastern core area remains dominant.

Lake Erie Canal, dug in the early nineteenth century to connect the East Coast to the Great Lakes, but industrial decline has affected this district since about 1970. In some ways, both this historic sequence and local specialization are reminiscent of what happened in Britain. Rochester was long known for its cameras and optical products, Schenectady for electrical appliances, and Buffalo for its steel. But times have changed, and so have the fortunes of this district.

Canada's *Southern Ontario* district extends from the western end of Lake Ontario to the industrial zone that envelops the western end of Lake Erie. As Figure 36-3 shows, this district links two parts of the U.S. manufacturing belt anchored

by Buffalo and Detroit; the most direct route between these two industrial cities is through Ontario.

Canadian and U.S. manufacturing complexes meet in two great horseshoe-shaped zones around the western ends of Lakes Ontario and Erie. In the northeast is the so-called "Golden Horseshoe" that curls from automobile-producing Oshawa through diversified Toronto and steel-producing Hamilton to Buffalo. Westward, around the western end of Lake Erie, is the "Erie Horseshoe" that extends from Windsor in Ontario through Detroit and Toledo to Cleveland. The first of these zones is mainly Canadian and the second is largely American, but the effect of the **North American Free Trade Agreement**

(NAFTA) is diminishing the political partition and enhancing economic interconnection.

As Figure 36-3 shows, the Montreal area along the upper St. Lawrence River also forms part of the Canadian industrial zone. This area is no match for the Ontario district, but it has one big advantage: cheap hydroelectric power. This is what aluminum-refining and paper-making industries need, and they are there.

Westward lies the great *interior* industrial district, with nodes such as the Pittsburgh–Cleveland area, the Detroit–Southeast Michigan area, Chicago–Gary–Milwaukee, and smaller areas centered on Minneapolis, St. Louis, Cincinnati, and other areas. There industrial power truly transforms the landscape, as Appalachian coal and Mesabi iron ore are converted, and autos, bulldozers, harvesters, armored cars, and tanks roll off the assembly lines. Refrigerators, televisions, toys, cornflakes, and pills—these and thousands of other products pour from the factories of the Midwest.

OTHER NORTH AMERICAN REGIONS

Figure 36-3 reminds us, however, that this industrial heartland we have been discussing is not the only region of significant development in the United States. A region we call the *Southeastern* district extends from the vicinity of Birmingham, Alabama, to Richmond, Virginia. Birmingham is a name long associated with iron and steel in this country as well as in Britain, and local raw materials have sustained this now rapidly declining industry here for many years. Atlanta, rapidly rising as the South's regionwide focus, has a growing industrial base. High-tech industries are changing the industrial structure of this region, but older activities still prevail. Cotton and tobacco rank high in this district's array of products, and furniture is an important product, too.

Author's Video Link
↓
6
"Atlanta"

On the Gulf of Mexico, a *southwestern* district is emerging, centered on the thriving urban areas of Houston and the Dallas–Forth Worth "Metroplex," and extending along the Gulf coast to New Orleans. The oil fields generate a major petrochemical industry here, but a wide range of other activities (including meat

packing and flour milling) are also centered here. Also, aerospace and high-tech industries contribute importantly to the development of this district.

Among industrial districts in the western half of the United States, three stand out. The *Southern California* district, centered on Los Angeles and San Diego, originally emerged on the basis of agricultural products and their processing, packaging, and shipment; but today this is a vast industrial complex with a highly diversified base. The *Northern California* district, anchored by San Francisco and San Jose but extending westward of San Francisco Bay, is home to Silicon Valley, the manufacturing and research leader in the computer industry and a vanguard of postindustrial America. And the *Northwest* district, extending from Seattle northward to Vancouver, Canada, and southward to Portland, Oregon, long has been the focus of America's aerospace industry, led by Boeing, maker of aircraft used by airlines around the world. The three West Coast districts shown in Figure 36-3 represent the U.S. presence on the burgeoning Pacific Rim, and already this geographic reality is boosting their growth and prospects.

As we noted earlier, political decisions as well as economic forces can change the map. Long before NAFTA took effect (on January 1, 1994), a manufacturing zone was developing in northern Mexico's border zone with the United States. These **maquiladora** plants, owned mainly by large U.S. companies, transform imported, duty-free components or raw materials into finished industrial products. At least 80 percent of these goods are then reexported to the United States, whose import tariffs are limited to the value added to the products during the Mexican fabrication stage.

Although the maquiladora pro-

gram started during the 1960s, it did not really take off until the 1980s, when the wage differences between U.S. and Mexican workers, plus changed political conditions, stimulated it. Today about 2000 assembly plants employ more than 600,000 workers, constituting well over 20 percent of Mexico's entire industrial labor force.

The maquiladora plants produce such goods as electronic equipment, electrical appliances, automobiles, textiles, plastics, and furniture; tertiary sector industries, including data-processing operations, also are relocating from the U.S. to Mexico. Two districts are leading the rush: Tijuana on the Pacific coast, linked to San Diego across the border, and Ciudad Juarez on the Rio Grande across from El Paso, Texas. These incipient Mexican manufacturing districts are as yet no match for those discussed earlier, but they remind us that the factors governing industrial location are changing.

RUSSIA'S AND UKRAINE'S MANUFACTURING REGIONS

When the Soviet Union collapsed and 15 independent countries emerged from it, Russia remained the political and economic giant. Political and economic geographers had to revise their views in the post-Soviet era: a new Eastern Europe was in the making. New alignments were in the offing for such long-suppressed countries as Estonia, Lithuania, and Moldova.

Undoubtedly, the most important country detached from the Soviet-Russian empire was Ukraine. In the new Europe, Ukraine would be the largest territorial state and one of the most populous. As we saw pre-

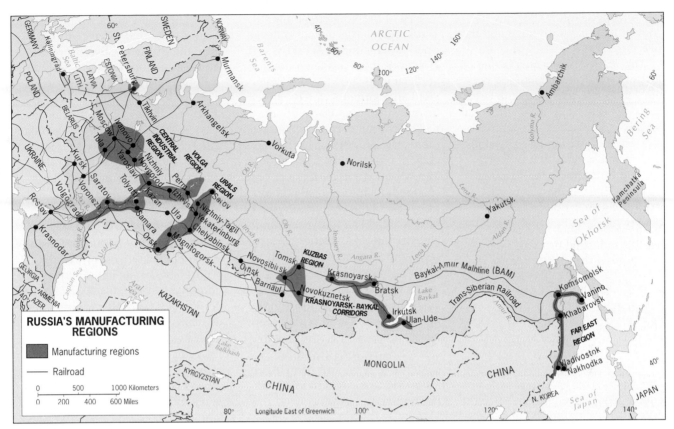

FIGURE 36–4 The major manufacturing regions of Russia reflect the dominance of the west in the country's economic geography. SOURCE: From a map in H. J. de Blij and P. O. Muller, *Geography: Realms, Regions, and Concepts,* 7th ed. (New York: Wiley, 1994), p. 152.

viously, Ukraine prior to its annexation into the Soviet empire had been strongly affected by the Industrial Revolution; its Donetsk Basin (Donbas) was a major producer of heavy-industry manufactures before the end of the nineteenth century. Afterward, Ukraine produced as much as 90 percent of all the coal mined in the then Soviet Union and, with iron ores from the Krivoy Rog reserve and later from Russia's Kursk Magnetic Anomaly, grew into one of the world's largest manufacturing complexes. The integration of eastern Ukraine and southern Russia was nearly complete: electrical transmission lines, roads, railroads, pipelines for oil and gas, and other facilities crossed the border as though it did not exist. To the minds of Soviet planners, that was

the case: in 1954, Soviet premier Khrushchev arbitrarily transferred the largely Russian-peopled Crimean Peninsula from Russian to Ukrainian jurisdiction.

Today Ukraine is a divided country with a largely agrarian, fervently nationalist west and a strongly Russified, industrial east. The map, however, leaves no doubt: the heart of industrialization in this area lies on the Ukrainian side of the border. Ukraine's industries need Russian raw materials and energy supplies, and Russia needs Ukrainian products, including foods, but what lies on the Russian side of the boundary is no match for what lies in Ukraine. When Ukraine became independent, Russia lost one of its key industrial heartlands, and with it a substantial Russian population living in Ukraine. In the mid-1990s

this situation clouded the future of relations between the two giants of the former Soviet empire.

Russia's economic geography (minus Ukraine) reflects both the arrival of the Industrial Revolution in precommunist times and the planned economy dating from the Soviet era, as well as the eastward shift of industry that occurred during the Second World War, when Russia was invaded from the west. The *Central* industrial region is anchored by Moscow, where industry first clustered for the same reasons it did near London and Paris: the large local market, converging transport routes, major labor force, and strong centrality (Fig. 36-4). Light manufacturing dominated in this region during tsarist times, but under communist rule heavy industries were added. Nizhni Novgorod (then named Gorkiy) became the "Soviet Detroit," with huge automobile factories.

The *St. Petersburg* area is one of Russia's oldest manufacturing centers, chosen by tsar Peter the Great not only to serve as Russia's capital but also to become the country's modern industrial focus. The skills and specializations that Peter the Great nurtured with the help of Western European artisans still mark the area's industries: high-quality machine building, optical products, and medical equipment are among local activities. But St. Petersburg has become a large metropolis, and industries such as shipbuilding, chemical production, food processing, and textile making are part of the complex.

Two elongated regions lie to the east of the Central Industrial region (Fig. 36-4). The *Volga* has experienced major development since the mid-1930s. With the Ukraine and Moscow areas threatened by the German armies, whole industrial plants were dismantled and reassembled in Volga cities, protected from the war by distance. Samara (formerly Kuibyshev) even served as the Soviet capital for a time during World War II. Then, after the war, the progress that was set in motion continued. A series of dams were constructed on the Volga, and electrical power became plentiful. Oil and natural gas proved to exist in quantities larger than anywhere else in the former USSR. Canals linked the Volga to both Moscow and the Don River, making the importing of raw materials easy. The cities lining the Volga, spaced at remarkably regular intervals, were assigned particular industrial functions in the state-planned economy. Samara became an oil refinery center, Saratov acquired a chemical industry, and Volgograd was known for its metallurgical industries. The Volga district's contribution to the now-Russian economy is still rising rapidly.

East of the Volga region lies the *Urals* region. This area also developed rapidly during World War II. However, there has been nothing artificial in its growth. The Urals yield an enormous variety of metallic ores, including iron, copper, nickel, chromite, bauxite, and many more. The only serious problem is coal, of which there is not enough, and what is there does not have the required quality. So coal is shipped in by rail all the way from reserves near Novosibirsk to the east. In the cities of the Urals district, metals, metal products, and machinery are fabricated in great quantities. Together with the Siberian centers, the Urals district now produces more than half of all the iron and steel made in Russia. It is a sign of the eastward march of the country's center of gravity, and permanent testimony to the communist planners' grand design.

THE EASTERN INTERIOR

Three industrial regions are developing in Siberia. About 1900 kilometers (1200 miles) east-southeast of the Urals is the *Kuznetsk Basin*, or *Kuzbas*. In the 1930s, this area was developed as a supplier of raw materials, especially coal for the Urals, but this function has steadily diminished in importance as local industrial growth has accelerated. The original plan was to move coal from the Kuzbas to the Urals, and to let returning trains carry iron ore to the coalfields but, subsequently, good iron ores were discovered in the area of the Kuznetsk Basin itself. As the resource-based Kuzbas industries grew, so did its urban centers: Novosibirsk (with nearly 2 million inhabitants) stands on the Trans-Siberian Railroad at the crossing of the Ob River as the symbol of Russian enterprise in the vast Siberian interior. To the northeast lies Tomsk, one of the oldest Russian

Siberian towns in the whole eastern region, founded three centuries before the Bolshevik takeover and now caught up in the modern development of the Kuznetsk area. Southeast of Novosibirsk lies Novokuznetsk, a city of nearly 1 million people specializing in the manufacture of such heavy engineering products as rolling stock for the railroads. Aluminum products, using Urals bauxite, are also fabricated here.

Between the Kuzbas and Lake Baykal lies the *Krasnoyarsk-Baykal Corridors* region. Served by the Trans-Siberian Railroad and several important rivers, this 1600 kilometer-long (1000 mile-long) region contains impressive resources including coal, timber, and water. Large hydroelectric facilities at Krasnoyarsk, Irkutsk, and Bratsk supply power to factories producing mining equipment, chemicals, aircraft, and railway rolling stock. Weaknesses of the region include a lack of local petroleum, distance from Russia's major population center, and underinvestment in the development infrastructure.

Finally, there is the *Far East* region, long focused on the Pacific port of Vladivostok (and more recently on the new port of Nakhodka) but also growing in the hinterlands of such cities as Komsomolsk (the first steel producer in the region) and Khabarovsk, now the leading center in the Russian Far East (with metal and chemical industries). The remote Far East is finally beginning to yield its rich raw materials, and there is enormous potential for development beyond the low-grade coal and iron ore found to date. Already the zinc and tin deposits mined here constitute Russia's largest sources of these metals. Development of this region, Russia's window on the Pacific Rim and on the doorstep of China, should be a leading objective of Russia's reformers in Moscow, 10 time zones away.

MANUFACTURING REGIONS OF EASTERN ASIA

Two centuries after the onset of the Industrial Revolution, East Asia is the cauldron of **industrialization**. From Japan to Guangdong and from South Korea to Singapore, the islands, countries, provinces, and cities fronting the Pacific Ocean are caught up in a frenzy of industrialization that has made the geographic term **Pacific Rim** synonymous with economic opportunity. If you want to relive the days when the British Midland cities were caught up in the first wave of the Industrial Revolution, visit the front lines of industrialization in cities such as Dalian, Shanghai, Zhuhai, Xiamen, or Shenzhen. Pollution-belching smokestacks rise above smog-choked townscapes. Streets are jammed with traffic ranging from animal-drawn carts and overloaded bicycles to trucks and buses. Bulldozers are sweeping away vestiges of the old China, cottages with porches and tile roofs fronting streets on the outskirts of the expanding city that must make way for faceless, gray tenements. Children labor in the waste, salvaging anything of value from the rubble of urban "renewal": bricks, pipes, wood. Decaying vestiges of the old city stand amid glass-encased towers that symbolize the new economic order and await demolition.

Not all of East Asia's Pacific Rim displays such symptoms. At present, China's coastal provinces are industrializing, but the process already has run its course in Japan and Singapore. Taiwan and South Korea are at an intermediate stage, and Vietnam lags behind China. But the signs are clear: taken as a whole, East Asia is becoming the world's most productive cluster of industrial regions. Already, China's economy ranks as the world's third largest (after the United States and Japan). So successful are the economies of South Korea, Taiwan, Hong Kong, and Singapore that these have been called the **"Four Tigers"** of the Pacific Rim (see box, "The Four Tigers"). The real tigers, though, are Japan and China.

JAPAN

Japan lies a world removed from the hearth of the Industrial Revolution, but in less than a century it became one of the world's leading industrial nations. This is all the more remarkable when it is realized that Japan has a very limited domestic natural resource base. Much of what Japan manufactures is made from raw materials purchased all over the world and imported to its small archipelago (island chain) off the East Asian coast. Japan's national territory is just one twenty-fifth the size of the United States, and its population is less than half the U.S. total. Its transformation into the world's second largest economy has rightfully been described as a miracle.

Japan gave notice of its capacities long before its current success. During the second half of the nineteenth century, Japan embarked on a campaign of modernization and colonization that thrust it into the forefront of Pacific affairs. A group of reformers, under the banner of the Meiji Restoration, modernized Japan's domestic industries, moved the capital from the interior to the coast, organized its armed forces, and borrowed British talent to advise them on issues ranging from education to transportation (which is why the Japanese drive on the left side of the road to this day). The Japanese also took a page from the book of British colonialism, and soon raw materials were flowing to Japan's growing industries from an expanding colonial empire in Korea, Taiwan, and mainland China.

The Second World War brought triumph and disaster: triumph in the form of a military campaign that included a surprise attack on Pearl Harbor in Hawaii and vast conquests in the Pacific, East Asia, and Southeast Asia, and disaster when Japanese forces were driven back with great loss of life and the war was ended with the destruction of two Japanese cities by atomic bombs. When U.S. forces took control of shattered Japan in 1945, there was little to presage the country's revival. Yet decades later Japan had not only recovered but achieved with its economy what it had been denied by the war: a global empire. And so far the second time in little more than a century, Japan had converted chaos into conquest.

Japan has a very small domestic raw-material base, so that its industries depend on external sources of supply. This (plus Japan's mountainous topography) impelled the coastal location for its manufacturing plants, the more so because most goods produced by the factories are exported.

As Figure 36-5 shows, Japan's dominant region of industrialization and urbanization (along with highly productive farming nearby) is the *Kanto Plain*, which contains about one-third of the Japanese population and is focused on the Tokyo–Yokohama–Kawasaki metropolitan area (27 million). This gigantic cluster of cities and suburbs (the world's largest urban agglomeration), interspersed with intensively cultivated farmlands, forms the eastern anchor of the country's elongated and fragmented core area. Besides its flatness, the Kanto Plain possesses other advantages: its fine natural harbor at Yokohama, its relatively mild and moist climate, and its central location with respect to the country as a whole. It has also benefited from Tokyo's designation as the modern capital, which coincided with Japan's embarkation on its planned course of economic development. Many industries and businesses chose Tokyo as their headquarters in view of the advantages of proximity to the government's decision makers.

The Tokyo–Yokohama-Kawasaki conurbation has become Japan's leading manufacturing complex, producing more than 20 percent of the country's annual output. The raw materials for all this industry, however, come from far away. For example, the Tokyo area is among the chief steel producers in Japan, using iron ores from the Philippines, Malaysia, Australia, India, and even Africa; most of the coal is imported from Australia and North America, and the petroleum from Southwest Asia and Indonesia. The Kanto Plain cannot produce nearly enough food for its massive resident population. Imports must come from Canada, the United States, and Australia as well as from other areas in Japan. Thus Tokyo depends completely on its external trade for all things ranging from food to energy.

Japan's second-largest industrial complex extends from the eastern end of the Seto Inland Sea to the Nagoya area and includes the Kobe–Kyoto–Osaka triangle. This, the *Kansai* District, comes close to rivaling the Kanto area: it is a vast industrial region with steel mills, a major chemical industry, automobile manufacturing, shipbuilding, textile factories, and many other types of production. The urban agglomeration developing here is often called the *Tokaido* megalopolis.

The Seto Inland Sea is Japan's pivotal waterway, and the Kansai District has benefited from its location at the eastern end of it: during the nineteenth century, raw materials from Korea and later northeast China moved in volume along this route. At the western entrance to the sea lies the focus of Japan's

THE "FOUR TIGERS"

Until about two decades ago, Japan's dominance in the industrial geography of East Asia was beyond doubt. Other nodes of manufacturing existed, but these were no threat, and certainly no match, for Japan's industrial might.

Over the past 20 years, however, Japan has been challenged. Although Japan remains the undisputed leader, it now faces growing competition from the so-called "Four Tigers" of East and Southeast Asia: South Korea, Taiwan, Hong Kong, and Singapore. Among these, populous and productive *South Korea* is a formidable industrial rival. Three major manufacturing districts export products ranging from automobiles and grand pianos to calculators and computers: one is centered on the capital, Seoul (18 million people), and the two others lie at the southern end of the peninsula, anchored by Pusan and Kwangju, respectively (Fig. 36-5). Should the two Koreas be united, the combination of the North's heavy industries and the South's major manufacturing would create a formidable industrial power just a few miles from Japan. As it is, South Korea is a growing challenge to Japan's hegemony.

To the south lies *Taiwan*, another growing industrial power along the "Pacific Rim." The island is neither large nor populous (21 million people, compared to 46 million in South Korea), but it produces prodigiously. Taiwan's economic planners in recent years have been moving the secondary sector away from labor-intensive manufacturing toward high-technology industries, thus meeting Japanese competition head-on. Personal computers, telecommunications equipment, precision electronic instruments, and other high-tech products flow from Taiwanese plants, evincing the advantages of a skilled labor force and reducing the need for massive raw-material imports from faraway markets. The capital, Taipei (7 million people), is the focus of the country's industrial complex, situated on the northern and northwestern zone of the island.

Just a trading colony five decades ago, *Hong Kong* exploded onto the world economic scene during the 1950s with textiles and light manufactures. The success of these industries, based on plentiful and cheap labor, was followed by a growing production of electrical equipment, appliances, and other household products. Site limitations constrict crowded Hong Kong, but situational advantages have contributed enormously to its fortunes. The colony became mainland China's gateway to the world, a bustling port, financial center, break-of-bulk point—and coveted prize. In 1997, China will take over the government of Hong Kong from the British, and one of the world's showplaces of capitalism will come under communist control (barring another democratic revolution in China). The future of this third "Tiger" is in doubt.

third industrial district, called *Kitakyushu*, a conurbation of five northern Kyushu Island cities. Located there were Japan's first coal mines, and there the first steel mills of modernizing Japan were built, which for many years remained the largest the country had. Look for this district to develop even faster than it has should the trade normal-

ization with China continue to expand. No place in Japan is better located to do business with mainland Asia. Presently, heavy industries dominate there, with shipbuilding and steel making in the lead, supplemented by a large chemical industry and numerous lighter manufacturing plants.

Only one Japanese manufactur-

The industrial growth of *Singapore* also can be attributed, in considerable measure, to geography. Strategically located at the tip of the Malayan Peninsula, Singapore is but a small island populated by under 3 million dominantly ethnic Chinese people (with Malay and Indian minorities). Forty years ago, Singapore was mainly an **entrepôt** (transshipment point) for such products as rubber, timber, and oil, but today, the bulk of its foreign revenues come from the export of manufactures, and increasingly from high-technology products. Singapore also is a center for the quaternary industries, selling services and expertise to a global market.

Japan was challenged by the Four Tigers; today, these economic powerhouses are themselves in a contest for their primacy, resulting from rising labor and production costs. From China's mushrooming industrial complexes to those of Malaysia and Thailand (and, in the future, Indonesia and Vietnam), the economic geography of East and Southeast Asia is rapidly changing.

ing district in the area depicted by our map lies outside the belt extending from Tokyo in the east to Kitakyushu in the west: the secondary district centered on Toyama, on the Sea of Japan. The advantage there is cheap electricity from nearby hydroelectric stations, and the cluster of industries reflects it: paper manufacturing, chemical industries, and textile plants have located there. Of course, our map gives an inadequate picture of the variety and range of industries that exist throughout Japan, many of them oriented to local (and not insignificant) markets. Thousands of manufacturing plants operate in cities and towns other than those shown on the map, even on the cold northern island of Hokkaido. As we did in the case of Europe, North America, Russia, and Ukraine, we have focused here only on the truly outstanding manufacturing districts of Japan.

CHINA

Although some industrial growth occurred in China during its period of European colonial influence, and later during the Japanese occupation, the major industrial expansion seen today was achieved during the communist period. When the com-

munist planners took over in Beijing in 1949, one of their leading priorities was to develop China's own resources and industries as rapidly as possible.

China is a very large country, and it is likely that some of its natural resources have yet to be discovered. Even so, China has already proved to possess a substantial domestic resource base. In terms of coal, there is hardly a limit on industrialization in China: the quality is good, the quantity enormous, and many of the deposits are near the surface and easily extracted. China's iron ores are not so productive and are generally of rather low grade, but new finds are frequently made and the picture has improved steadily. This is also true of China's oil potential. In recent years, China, with the aid of Western companies, has intensified its search for oil reserves, and in two areas—the western interior and the continental shelf—the effort has achieved some good results. (China is laying claim to large sectors of

FIGURE 36–5 For decades, the Northeast was China's most rapidly growing industrial area. Now the Chang District is taking the lead.

From the Field Notes

❝ On the right bank of the Huang Pu, across from Shanghai's famous waterfront Bund and its Victorian buildings, one of the world's greatest development projects is under way. An entire section of the city has been leveled to make way for an industrial zone that will, China's planners say, eclipse even Hong Kong and Shenzhen. Billboards and unfinished structures now dot a townscape that will soon transform eastern China's industrial map. But, as I learned during a visit in 1995, a serious problem looms. The weight of all the new construction, plus the increased drawing of water from beneath the city, is causing a measurable subsidence of the ground—in a part of the delta where the surface already is barely above sealevel. ❞

the South China Sea for these purposes). Nonetheless, the energy picture as far as oil and natural gas are concerned remains uncertain. In the mid-1990s, China's known reserves amounted to about 4 percent of the world total.

China's communist-era industrial development, aided until the early 1960s by Soviet planners, was spatially constrained by the location of raw materials, by the development that had taken place before the

1949 communist takeover, by the pattern of long-term urbanization in the country, by the existing transport network, and by the eastern clustering of the population. Like their Soviet allies, China's rulers were determined to speed the industrialization of the economy, and their decisions created several major and lesser industrial districts. Under state-planning rules, the *Northeast* district (formerly known as Manchuria and called *Dongbei* in

China today) became China's industrial heartland, a complex of heavy industries based on the region's coal and iron deposits located in the basin of the Liao River. Shenyang, with a population of 5 million, became the "Chinese Pittsburgh," with metallurgical, machine-making, engineering, and other large factories. Anshan, to the south, emerged as China's leading iron- and steel-producing center. Harbin to the north (China's northernmost large city, with more than 2 million inhabitants) produced textiles, farm equipment, and light manufactures of many kinds (Fig. 36-5).

Around the capital and its major port, Tianjin, the *Northern* industrial district was established, but although it benefited from nearby coalfields, an ample labor force, and large agricultural production, this district did not match the Northeast in any respect. Heavy industry was placed in the Tianjin area, and textile-making and food-processing plants handled local products.

The second-largest industrial region in China developed in and around the country's biggest city, Shanghai. The communist planners never allowed Shanghai to attain its full potential, often favoring the Beijing-Tianjin complex over the great port at the mouth of the Chang (formerly Yangtze) River. Nevertheless, the twin-focused district along the Chang River (the interior sector centers on the great conurbation of Wuhan) rose to prominence and, by some mea-

sures, the *Chang* district exceeded the Northeast as a contributor to the national economy. As Figure 36-5 shows, still another industrial complex developed farther upstream along the Chang River, focused on the city of Chongqing. Whether we view the Chang district as one industrial zone or three, it is a pacesetter for Chinese industrial growth, if not in terms of iron and steel production, then in terms of its diversified production and its local specializations. Railroad cars, ships, books, foods, chemicals—an endless variety of products comes from the burgeoning Chang districts.

In the south, the *Guangdong* industrial district remained in fourth place under communist state planning. Beijing's rulers tended to favor northern provinces over southern ones in their allocation of priorities, and Guangzhou (the city formerly called Canton) never was a favorite. China's uneasy relationship with free-enterprise Hong Kong, located on the estuary of Guangzhou's Pearl River, further diminished Beijing's interest in the south. In the absence of major min

eral or fuel resources, the Guangdong industrial zone could not rival the complexes of the north.

Author's Video Link
↓
6
"Hong Kong"

Note that the foregoing paragraphs are written in the past tense. Today, economic policies in China are very different. The communist regime still is in control, but China's rulers have opted for a market-driven economic course. Moreover, they have opened certain cities and areas facing the Pacific coast as **Special Economic Zones (SEZs)**, "Open Cities," and "Open Coastal Areas" to encourage foreign investment. Shanghai is no longer shackled: a gigantic development project is transforming the right bank of the Huangpu (River Pu) into an industrial complex (named Pudong) that is expected to rival Hong Kong. In the meantime, one of the SEZs, Shenzhen, across the

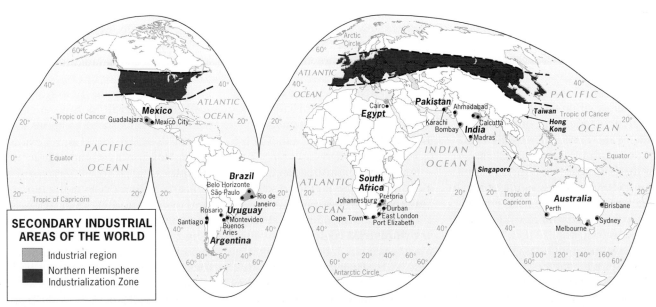

FIGURE 36–6 The concentration of industrialization is in the Northern Hemisphere. Among secondary industrial regions, those in Mexico and Brazil may expand most rapidly in the decade ahead.

border from Hong Kong, has become the world's fastest-growing urban area with massive industrialization. Once-dormant Guangdong Province has become the largest contributor by value to China's export economy; after China's takeover of Hong Kong, the Shenzhen–Hong Kong–Guangdong complex will be China's answer to Japan and the three remaining "Tigers." Concurrently, the Northeast has become China's rustbelt, many of its state-run factories sold, closed, or operating below capacity; unemployment is high, and growth has stopped. Eventually, the Northeast is likely to recover, because its resources and its geography favor it. But under the new economic policies, the dynamic eastern and southern provinces are producing their own industrial revolution, in the process changing the map of this part of the Pacific Rim.

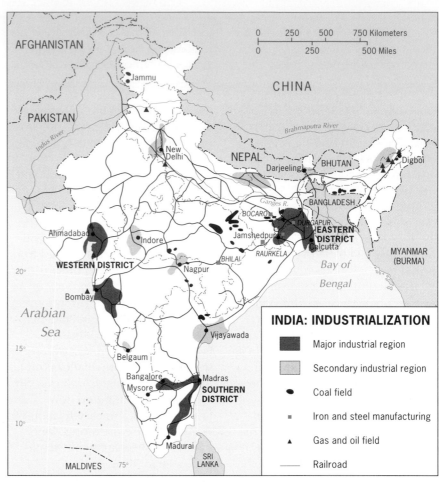

FIGURE 36–7 India's widely dispersed industrial areas. India has large coal deposits, but its oil reserves are small.

INDUSTRIALIZATION ELSEWHERE

As this chapter has underscored, major industrialization in this world has taken place in a globe-girdling, Northern Hemisphere, resource-rich zone that extends eastward from Britain, across the heart of Europe, through Ukraine and along the southern margins of Russia, through northern China, and, on the other side of the Pacific, across the U.S. Midwest and East. Industrialization of the kind that transformed central Europe and its cities did not fully reach the other side of the world until China's communist rulers decided to industrialize their country—not much less than two centuries after the first stirrings of the Industrial Revolution.

But we have learned another lesson. The rules of industrialization are changing. Japan did it without a domestic raw-material base of any size. Guangdong (with limited natural resources) is thriving, while China's once formidable Northeast is failing. Economic geographers call the tertiary industries the footloose industries, but secondary industries, too, are less tethered by the old rules today.

At present, industrial development beyond the regions discussed here remains comparatively limited and lies in a discontinuous **secondary industrial region** south of the world's primary industrial region (Fig. 36-6). Thailand, Malaysia, Indonesia, and Vietnam (and possibly the Philippines) are likely to share in Pacific Rim developments, but elsewhere, industrialization proceeds slowly. In the Western Hemisphere, only Brazil and Mexico have substantial manufacturing industries: Brazil in the São Paulo–Rio de Janeiro–Belo Horizonte triangle (with output ranging from automobiles and weapons to chemicals and textiles) and Mexico in the Mexico City–Guadalajara complex (Fig. 36-6). In Africa, some industrialization exists in the hinterland of Cairo and in South Africa, principally in the PWV (Pretoria-Witwatersrand–Vereeniging) complex. Australia's smaller industries lie near the local urban markets.

More significant is the industrial development taking place in India (Fig. 36-7). Although small in context of India's huge territorial size and enormous population, India's overall economy now ranks as the tenth largest in the world, and industrialization is expanding as a result of recently changed economic policies. Industrialization in India still reflects its colonial beginnings, but major complexes are developing centered on Calcutta (the *Eastern* district, with engineering, chemical, cotton, and jute industries, plus iron and steel based on the Chota Nagpur reserves), on Bombay (the *Western* district, where cheap electricity helps the cotton and chemical industries), and Madras (the *Southern* district, with an emphasis on light engineering and textiles).

India suffers from a lack of major oil reserves, so that the country must spend heavily on energy every year. On the other hand, India has much hydroelectric potential (some of which has been realized); it has ample coal, and its Bihar and Karnataka iron ores may be among the largest reserves in the world. With a large labor force and a relative location midway between Europe and the Pacific Rim, India may yet take its place as a participant in the last wave of the Industrial Revolution.

From what we have learned in Part 11, it would seem that economic development and political progress toward democracy go hand in hand. Most of the world's true democracies are developed countries; most undemocratic countries are economically underdeveloped.

But it is not that simple. The coming of democracy to Russia, for example, has been accompanied by economic setbacks so severe that the democratic reforms may be at risk. China's rapid economic development over the past decade has not been matched by political progress toward democracy. Some developed countries, notably Singapore, are not fully democratic and restrict the freedoms of their citizens. And one of the world's most severely underdeveloped countries, India, has managed to sustain its fragile democracy in the face of numerous economic, social, and political pressures.

It is appropriate, therefore, to conclude our journey through geography by turning to the world of politics. Economic growth produces national vitality, which in turn can generate power—economic power in the world at large and political power to influence the behavior of other countries. The final chapters of *Human Geography* focus on the spatial manifestations of political behavior. Much of this behavior, we will find, involves efforts to achieve competitive advantage not just in the political arena, but in the economic sphere as well. Political activity often has economic goals.

KEY TERMS

Break-of-Bulk

Entrepôt

"Four Tigers"

Industrial Development

Industrialization

Industrial Revolution

Maquiladora

North American Free Trade Agreement (NAFTA)

Pacific Rim

Planned Industrial Economy

Primary Industrial Region

Secondary Industrial Region

Special Economic Zone (SEZ)

Rising red star: a symbol of China's takeover in Hong Kong, 1997

PART TWELVE

THE POLITICAL IMPRINT

At Issue

The political world is in transition. A new world order looms, but its outlines are unclear. Some scholars envisage a multipolar world in which the United States, a unified Europe, Russia, and China constitute four power cores balanced to ensure a stable global system. In the late 1990s, however, the United States was the dominant superpower, Europe's unification was on hold, Russia was in disarray, and China was in ascendancy but not yet a world force. In the United States, a key issue involved China's human rights record. In 1994, the White House decided to "decouple" U.S. trade relations with China from China's treatment of political dissidents. Both sides benefited economically from this decision, but it also served to expose the ideological gap between the two countries. In 1995, China displayed its self-assurance by backing North Korea in its nuclear dispute with the United Nations, by continuing to deny Taiwan its place in the community of nations, and by claiming regions of the South China Sea far beyond its legal limits. Rather than a four-power balance, the twenty-first century may see a contest between a rising China and a stable, mature United States of America—a two-power world in which China has replaced the former Soviet Union. The key issue is how to guide this contest in peaceful channels.

37

POLITICAL CULTURE AND THE EVOLVING STATE

Of all the geographies we encounter in this book, **political geography** in many ways is the most consequential. Political activity is as basic an ingredient of human culture as is food production or religion. Political activity undoubtedly began as soon as communal life began, when individuals asserted themselves as leaders of village or clan, when competition (for such leadership roles, for territorial rights, or for other individual or communal goals) became a part of life. Ever since, political behavior by individuals, groups, communities, and nations has expressed the human desire for power and influence in the pursuit of personal and public goals. All of us are caught up in these processes, whose effects range from the composition of school boards to the conduct of war.

Since political activity has spatial expression and focus, its outcome is revealed on the map. The present-day layout of the world political map is a product of humanity's endless politico-geographic accommodation and adjustment, a mosaic

Geographica

- The world's living space is divided today into nearly 200 states ranging in territorial size from microstates to subcontinental giants; a minority of these states are nation-states.

- The European state model was exported to the world at large through migration and colonialism, but the model's applicability and relevance in the non-Western world have been inconsistent.

- State territory varies in terms of morphology as well as size; the spatial forms of states are among factors that influence their functioning and cohesion.

- State territories are defined by international boundaries that mark the limits of national jurisdiction; boundary lines on the ground mark the position of vertical planes that separate states and that cut through airspace as well as subsoil.

- The functions of boundaries have changed over time, and few boundaries today have a defensive function; the performance of boundaries may relate to such factors as their genesis and their morphology.

of more than 200 countries and territories separated by boundaries that make the world look like a jigsaw puzzle (Fig. 37-1). In a sense, the map reveals a process gone awry: it displays the inequality of countries even in terms of sheer territory (certain countries are hundreds of times as large as others) and relative location (some

467

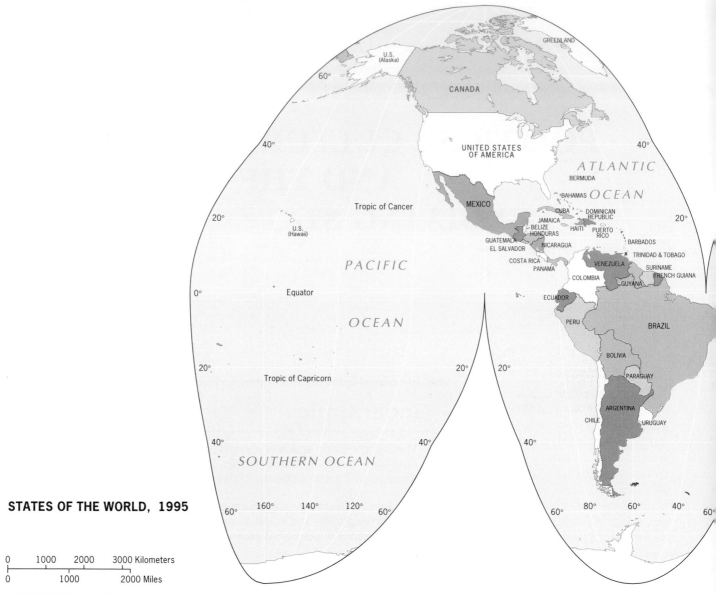

STATES OF THE WORLD, 1995

```
0    1000    2000    3000 Kilometers
0         1000        2000 Miles
```

FIGURE 37–1 The political-geographical fragmentation of the world, 1995. Only the smallest (micro-) states are not shown.

countries are **landlocked**, without coasts on the open sea, while the majority benefit from coastal frontage).

Political geographers study the spatial manifestations of political processes at various levels of scale. As we will find, the functioning of individual countries as political regions has been a long-term preoccupation, and from this research we have learned how countries are organized, how they overcome (or fail to overcome) internally divisive forces, how their boundaries perform, how their capital cities serve, and much more. Today we are witnessing the collapse of the empires spawned by some of those countries, and the problems confronted by recently independent entities in the postcolonial era have taken political geography in new directions. In the meantime, some countries are banding together in international alliances, associations, and unions designed to further their joint objectives—even as certain participants in this process are facing disintegration.

POLITICAL CULTURE

Political geography, therefore, is a field of contrasts and contradictions. From Congressional district boundaries to international borders, the

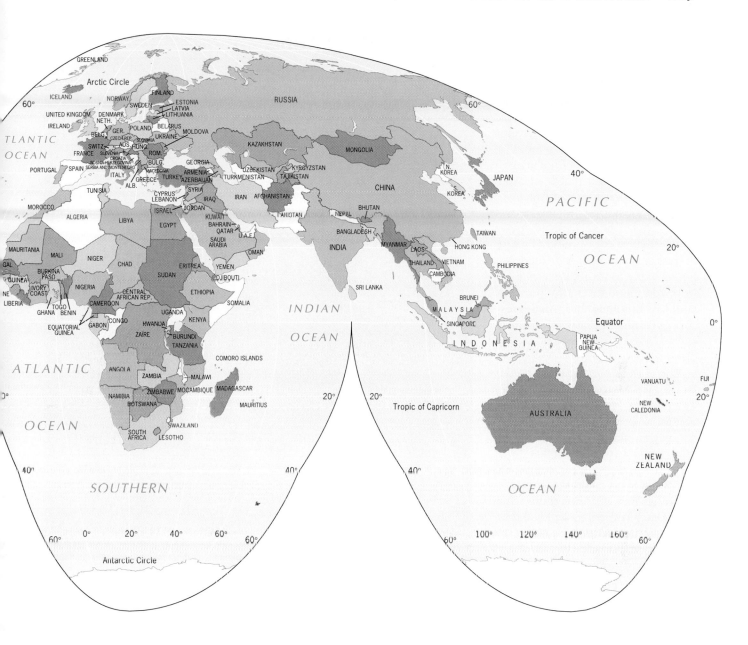

maps we draw form a manifestation of **political culture**. And across the world, political cultures vary. People adhere to political ideas just as they profess a religion and speak a mother tongue. Today, many political systems are designed to keep religion and politics separate, but other states are virtual **theocracies**, their leaders deemed to be under divine guidance, their actions representing the will of God or Allah.

If the world's political cultures have a common element, it lies in their attachment to territory, an animal instinct that, some scholars suggest, characterizes humans as well. In his book *The Territorial Imperative* (1966), Robert Ardrey argued that humans are territorial animals, acting individually and collectively to defend territory. The way people and their governments organize themselves to do this, Ardrey suggested, produced the current map—from fortified international boundaries such as the Korean Armistice Line to fenced backyards of private homes.

Not all scholars agree, but territorial possessiveness certainly is a part of political culture. The trait manifests itself in different ways. At the village level, for example, land is held communally in some cultures and individually in others. Such differences also mark larger groups and even entire nations. Attitudes toward land and territory differ from society to society and from country to country.

Few issues, however, can agitate a people as a perceived violation of territory can. A neighbor's annexation of even the smallest piece of land is likely to unify even the most fractious society in opposition. Conversely, the prospect of having to yield any area over which a government has jurisdiction can cause violent opposition among otherwise peaceable citizens. Governments use this element of political culture to further their aims. A divided nation is likely to forget its disputes if its government raises the specter of land loss to a neighbor. An aggressive government knows that it will cause disarray next door by laying claim to "lost" territory.

The current contest over the Golan Heights forms a good example. The territory has been under Israeli control since the 1967 War, when it was captured from Syria. The prospect of its return to Syria has created deep division in Israeli society. But if Syria sought to annex any other part of Israel, there would be no such division, and Israelis would be unified in opposition. The territorial imperative remains a strong motivator in the modern world.

STATE AND NATION

Until this chapter, we have referred to national political entities as *countries*, a word that has a comfortable neutrality. The word "country" derives from the Latin *contra*, which actually means "against" or, more geographically, "on the opposite side." That seems a rather strange derivation for a term that presently denotes a political unit inhabited by a people of common nationality, but the meaning of words, as we noted in Chapter 22, often changes over time.

From the Field Notes

❝ Walking up embassy row in the outskirts of Colombo, capital of Sri Lanka, I came across evidence of Palestinian efforts to establish the trappings of a state in the international community. There is as yet no Palestinian nation-state, but here in Colombo the non-state has an embassy. ❞

Political geographers prefer to call individual countries **states**, a word that comes from the Latin *status*, for "standing." This leads to a problem: certain countries are partitioned into internal divisions also called states, as in the United States of America. The solution is to capitalize *State* when it refers to such an internal division, such as the State of Michigan or the State of Uttar Pradesh (India).

The terms "country" and "state," therefore, are interchangeable, but the same is not true for **nation** and state or country. This is one of the most common geographic errors you will see in the press and popular literature, and it is understandable because people in a state have a shared nationality. The term "nation," however, has historic, ethnic, and often linguistic and religious connotations. It refers to a people's sense of belonging to such an entity. Sometimes, a nation is even larger than the state that gave birth to it; the French form a nation, but many French-speaking and French-cultured people living outside France feel that they are part of the French nation. But Yugoslavia

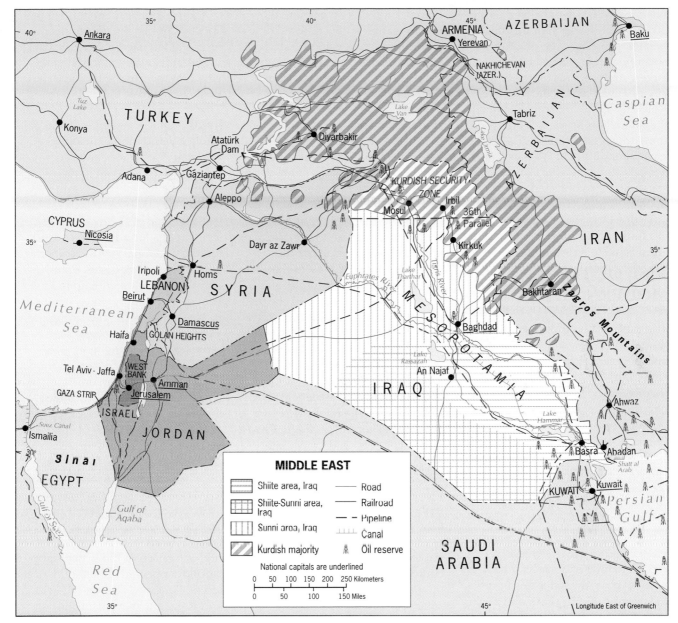

FIGURE 37–2   The territory of a stateless nation: Kurdistan, a land divided under six flags. SOURCE: From a map in H. J. de Blij and P. O. Muller, *Geography: Realms, Regions, and Concepts*, 7th ed. (New York: Wiley, 1994), p. 385.

never achieved nationhood in that sense. Millions of people of Yugoslav nationality (in the legal sense) always felt themselves to be ethnic Slovenes, Croats, Serbs, or other group members first, in the emotional sense. Yugoslavia was a *state* but never a *nation*; and eventually the state system collapsed under this contradiction. Many other countries of the world are states but not nations.

Stateless Nations

Still another complication on the world political map is that some nations are *stateless*; that is, they do not possess a national territory even within a larger multinational state. The Palestinian Arabs in 1994 were on the verge of acquiring control over fragments of territory that may form the foundations of a future state, but most of the 6.5 million Palestinians remained domiciled in a

dozen countries, including Jordan (2.1 million), Lebanon (400,000), and Syria (350,000), in addition to Israel. A much larger stateless nation is that of the Kurds, who number in excess of 20 million, living in a nearly contiguous area covering parts of six states (Fig. 37-2). In the aftermath of the 1991 Gulf War, the United Nations established a Kurdish Security Zone north of the 36th parallel in Iraq, but subsequent events have dashed any Kurdish hopes that this might become the core area of a future sovereign state. The Kurds form the largest minority in Turkey, and the city of Diyarbakir is the unofficial Kurdish capital; relations between the 10 million Kurds in Turkey and the Turkish government in Ankara have been difficult. Without Turkish acquiescence, no Kurdish national state will be established anywhere in "Kurdistan."

RISE OF THE MODERN STATE

The state is the modern manifestation of the political goals of nations and peoples. In the modern political world, the state must promote the objectives and aspirations of its citizens. Nations depend on their governments to represent them in the competitive international arena, whether to secure needed resources (oil, over which wars still are fought, for example), to create and protect markets for their products, or to join in alliances to enhance their security. Of course, governments are not always wholly representative of a state's inhabitants. (There are still states under the control of minorities and oligarchies.) In such instances, the state primarily serves the interests of a ruling class (sometimes a racial minority). Outwardly, the state functions as any other, but its internal politics are likely to reflect stress resulting from divisive forces, a topic to be discussed later.

THE EUROPEAN MODEL

In previous chapters, we traced the evolution of the earliest states and the diffusion of the state idea to Greece and later to Rome, from where concepts of statehood spread into Europe. There, in the post-Roman period of stagnation, they lay dormant—until a renewal of political progress came about. Several early developments mark this renewal. The Norman invasion of England in 1066 is perhaps the most prominent benchmark: the Normans invaded, destroyed the Anglo-Saxon nobility, created a whole new political order, and achieved great national strength under William the Conqueror. On the European mainland, the continuity of dynastic rule and the strength of certain rulers began to produce national cohesiveness in the more stable domains. In present-day Germany, France, and Spain, sizable states existed, and some of the trespass lines of the twelfth century were to become modern-day political boundaries (e.g., the border between France and Spanish Aragon along the Pyrenees). At the same time, Europe experienced something of an economic revival, and internal as well as foreign trade increased. Ports and other cities came to life after lengthy dormancies, and while the wealth went to the nobility and the rich merchants, more people than ever were drawn from a subsistence life-style into the new economic order. Now the Muslim invaders in southern Spain could be repelled, and Crusades to the Middle East could be financed. Crucial technological innovations occurred, presaging the Industrial Revolution. The horse collar, for example, enormously increased the efficiency of that domestic animal for plowing, transport, and other work. Windmills dotted the European countryside, evincing Europe's progress toward the harnessing of energy. The Dark Ages were over, and a new Europe was emerging.

Author's Video Link
↓
1
"Holland-Netherlands"

From a political-geographic perspective, it may be appropriate to refer to the Peace of Westphalia as the seminal moment in the emergence of the European state. The treaties signed at the end of the Thirty Years' War (1648) contained fundamentals of statehood and nationhood and mutual recognition, boundary definition, and security guarantees. Such commitments eventually were broken (and they continue to be broken today), but the language of the treaties lays the foundations for a Europe constituted by national states. Spain, the Dutch United Provinces, France, and the Holy Roman Empire thus sought to secure regional stability. In Western Europe, the strong prevailing monarchies began to represent something more than mere authority. Increasingly, they became centers of an emerging national consciousness and pride. At the same time, Europe's chronic political fragmentation of central authority gave way to the recapture of breakaway feudal territories; royal alliances and marriages consolidated national territories. The aristocracies, which had strongly opposed monarchical rule, were placed under control. Parliamentary representation of the general population reappeared, albeit in modest terms. Renewed interest in Greek and Roman achievements, in politics as well as the sciences, prevailed. It was, indeed, Europe's *Renaissance*, celebrated (as we saw) in architecture, the arts, and literature.

POWER AND PRIMACY

Europe's rebirth would not be painless. The new political nationalism was paralleled by policies of economic nationalism expressed as mercantilism, the promotion of the acquisition of wealth through plunder, colonization, and the protection of home industries and foreign markets. Rivalry and competition, in Europe as well as abroad, intensified. Superimposed on these conflicts was a series of religious wars that constituted a reaction to the new secular values of the Renaissance and that ravaged Europe for many years. Catholicism and Protestantism, Reformation and Counter-Reformation fired the conflicts that devastated not only Europe's towns and cities, but also the parliaments and assemblies that had become a part of political life. In the end, the monarchies benefited most, and absolutism emerged once again—a despotism reminiscent of the Dark Ages. Louis XIV of France was the personification of this despotic rule. All the while, the confrontation between organized religion and the state continued to erode society.

Thus the politico-geographical map of Europe was slow in taking shape. In the mid-seventeenth century, such states as the Republic of Venice, Brandenburg, the Papal States of central Italy, the Kingdom of Hungary, and several minor German states were all part of an enormously fragmented and complicated patchwork of political entities, many with poorly defined boundaries. Powerful competing royal families struggled for primacy in Eastern and Southern Europe. Instability was the rule, and strife occurred frequently. Repressive government prevailed. Europe was still far from achieving the realization of the nation-state, the state of and for the people.

Ultimately, Europe's growing economic power proved to be the undoing of monarchical absolutism and its system of patronage. It was the city-based merchants who gained wealth and prestige, not the nobility. Money and influence were concentrated more and more in the cities, and the traditional measure of affluence—land—began to lose its relevance in that changing situation. The merchants and businessmen demanded political

recognition and began to exert pressure to get it. In the 1780s, a series of upheavals commenced that would change the sociopolitical face of the continent. Overshadowing these events was the French Revolution (1789–1795), but this

momentous event was only one in a series. The consequences of Europe's political revolution were felt by every monarchy on the continent, and the revolution continued into the twentieth century. It may not be over, even now.

From the Field Notes

❝ The majority of European states abolished their monarchies, but some, such as the United Kingdom and the Netherlands, became parliamentary democracies while retaining their monarchs as titular heads of state. In those monarchies, the royal palaces remain icons in the cultural landscape, as are Buckingham Palace and, shown here, the Royal Palace overlooking the historic Dam Square at the heart of Amsterdam, Netherlands. ❞

THE NATION-STATE

As Europe evolved politically and politico-geographically, its influence in the rest of the world deepened and intensified. In the process, the European states were enriched as their colonial acquisitions produced wealth in various forms: as sources of raw materials and as markets for European products. England, benefiting from its political stability and its growing maritime power, gained an empire that spanned the world. While Europe's political evolution continued, Europe's powers transformed the world.

Europe's own politico-geographical evolution was to have enormous significance, because the European model of the state—the **nation-state**—would eventually be adopted around the world. Emerging from Europe's agricultural, industrial, and political revolutions was a modern state in which democratic principles prevailed. To be sure, this ideal was not achieved everywhere. Autocratic rule persisted and some monarchies managed to retain old-style powers. However, a certain maturing occurred in many states. While some, such as France and Italy, abolished the monarchy altogether, others, including the United Kingdom and the Netherlands, became parliamentary democracies with the monarch remaining as titular head of state. Almost everywhere, the sense of nationhood strengthened, as an allegiance to flag and country replaced attachments to region and royalty.

Europe's nation-states thus unified and nationalized comparatively large populations, and they did so within well-established, clearly defined national territories. The modern map of Europe still displays considerable fragmentation, but much less than was the case in the 1600s. Furthermore, states were now bounded clearly. National territories were delimited by boundaries, not separated by uncertain frontiers or vague trespass lines. They achieved unprecedented organization in numerous spheres, including not only politics and government, but also education, health, and the military. They possessed varying degrees of power, which enabled them not only to assert themselves in Europe, but also to engage in colonial campaigns.

These qualities (a population that considers itself to be a nation, a substantial and defined territory, well-developed organization, and a measure of power) sometimes are called the "four pillars" of the nation-state (see box, "The Model Nation-State"). On the map, they are expressed by the state's external and internal boundary systems, its core area and surface communications networks, and its capital city. Other manifestations of the nation-state appear on thematic maps revealing resources and their exploitation, land use patterns, military installations, and other attributes. To many peoples the world over, the modern European nation-state became a national objective. During the middle period of the nineteenth century, Japan undertook a major reorganization to emulate European achievements, even moving its capital from an-

THE MODEL NATION-STATE

As Europe went through its periods of rebirth and revolutionary change, the politico-geographical map was transformed. Smaller entities were absorbed into larger units, conflicts resolved (by force as well as negotiation), boundaries defined, and internal divisions reorganized. European nation-states were in the making.

What is a nation-state and what is not? The question centers in part on the definition of the term *nation*. The definition usually involves measures of homogeneity: a nation should speak a single language, have a common long-range history, share the same ethnic background, and be united by common political institutions. Accepted definitions of the term suggest that many states are not nation-states, because their populations are divided in one or more important ways.

However, cultural homogeneity may not be as important as a more intangible "national spirit" or emotional commitment to the state and what it stands for. One of Europe's oldest states, Switzerland, has a population that is divided along linguistic, religious, and historical lines, but Switzerland has proved a durable nation-state nevertheless. Therefore, a nation-state may be defined as a political unit comprising a clearly delineated territory and inhabited by a substantial population, sufficiently well organized to possess a certain measure of power, the people considering themselves to be a nation, with certain emotional and other ties that are expressed in their most tangible form in the state's legal institutions, political system, and ideological strength.

This definition essentially identifies the European model that emerged in the course of the region's long period of evolution and revolutionary change. France is often cited as the best example among Europe's nation-states, but Italy, the United Kingdom, Germany (before World War I), Spain, Poland, Hungary, and Sweden are also among countries that satisfy the terms of the definition to a great extent. European states that cannot at present be designated as nation-states include Moldova and Belgium.

cient interior Kyoto to coastal Edo, which was renamed Tokyo. Later, when colonial empires disintegrated, the goal of liberated peoples was to achieve the nation-state on the European model: to forge nations from still-divided peoples, to secure the national territory, to develop economic (as well as other) systems of organization, and to assert national strength—sometimes, unfortunately, through inordinate spending on military equipment and forces. On the map, former colonial provinces emerged as embryonic national states, with their administrative borders suddenly elevated to international boundary status. Colonial administrative towns became national capitals, skyscrapers rising above the townscape evincing their new position. London and Paris were symbols of national progress and power in Europe, and so would be the headquarters of the newly emergent states. In countless ways, the European state became the world model.

GEOGRAPHIC PROPERTIES OF STATES

Even an outline map such as Figure 37-1 underscores that all states are not alike. There may be a perceived "European model" of the nation-state, but even in Europe, states differ in as many ways as they are similar. In terms of territorial size and morphology, demography, organizational structures, resources, development, power, and in a host of other ways, states vary. We live in a world where one state has nearly 17 million square kilometers of territory (6.6 million sq mi) and several others exceed 7.5 million sq km (3 million sq mi), while others do not even have 1000 square kilometers (400 sq mi). In terms of

population, too, the contrasts are huge. China has over 1.2 billion people; Iceland 0.25 million.

The state is an infinitely complex system of many interacting parts. It is far more than a piece of the Earth's territory and a number of people: it is a region of cities, towns, and hinterlands, railroad and road networks, administrative subdivisions, schools, and hospitals. It is a maze of circulation and movement: of people, raw materials, finished products, foodstuffs, money, and ideas. It exists for the people and demands their taxes, their adherence to the law, and often their service in the armed forces. To succeed, it must foster a sense of national unity and pride. The system functions to serve the nation.

As noted in the box regarding the "model" nation-state, the incorporation of a body of people within a political boundary does not automatically make those people members of a nation. The evolution of a nation involves an intangible but vitally important process: the development of a national attitude and an emotional attachment to the country and what it stands for. Such a posture can be fostered in various ways; many states engage in programmed education and propaganda to encourage it. Periods of adversity or war can also strengthen national resolve. On the other hand, the spirit of nationhood is fragile and can be damaged by divisive issues. In the United States, the Indochina War of the 1960s and early 1970s had a long-lasting and in some ways permanent impact on the nation. In Canada, the issue of Quebec's separatism has frayed the national fabric. In Argentina, the costly invasion of Britain's Falkland Islands leads observers to this day to talk of the "troubled" soul of the nation.

The world politico-geographical map reveals that certain states' boundaries enclose true nations, or

very nearly so. France is often cited as a nation-state; outside Europe, Egypt, Japan, and Uruguay also are identified as such. However, more often than not, the world's boundary framework has the effect of separating and dividing peoples with cultural affinities and throwing diverse peoples together. The language map of Europe (Fig. 21-3) reminds us of the former; the colonial map of Africa is evidence of the latter. As will be noted later, boundaries often were established not by those people they affect most directly, but by outside forces. Imperial campaigns in Europe and colonial operations in Africa and Asia created oft-discordant boundary frameworks.

The European model of the nation-state may have evolved as the guidepost for many states elsewhere, but the model has proven difficult to emulate (even in Europe itself, where exceptions exist from Belgium to Moldova). Nevertheless, a large majority of today's states do possess all four of the European model's tangible ingredients: a clearly defined territory, a substantial population, certain organizational structures, and a measure of power. We focus next on these geographic properties of states.

TERRITORY AND THE STATE

No state can exist without territory, although the United Nations has set the precedent for the recognition of stateless nations through its admission of the Palestinians. Within the state's territory lie the resources, human and material, that the state must develop. When we examine the political-geographic map of the world, three aspects of territory—**territorial morphology**—present themselves immediately: (1) size or total area, (2) shape or morphology, and (3) relative location.

SIZE

It is tempting to assume that the more territory a state owns, the better off it is in all respects, especially in terms of raw materials. But this is not necessarily the case. True, a state with several million square miles of territory has a greater chance of having a wide range of environments and resources exist within its borders than does a small state. However, much also depends on location with reference to the Earth's known mineral resources.

The range of sizes among the world's approximately 200 states is so great as to defy generalization. Even after the loss of its 14 colonies, Russia remains the world's giant, more than twice the size of Canada or China. At the other end of the spectrum lie states so tiny that they are referred to as **microstates**, such as Liechtenstein, Andorra, and San Marino. The existence of such microstates might be of little more than anecdotal interest were it not for the admission of many of them to the United Nations and other international bodies, where they can exert an influence far beyond their collective territorial (or demographic) dimensions.

SHAPE

A second quality of states' territories that is evident from the world political map is their shape, or spatial form. Some states, such as the Philippines, lie on a group of islands, their territories broken by extensive waters. Other states (e.g., Chile) consist of a long, narrow strip of land. When at first we look at the map, there appear to be so many different kinds of territorial forms that classification seems impossible. However, when the states of the world are examined carefully, a typology does emerge. The Philip-

pines and Chile suggest two types, and there are others as well.

Many states—Belgium, Uruguay, Kenya, and Cambodia, among others—have territories that are shaped somewhere between round and rectangular. There are no islands, peninsulas, or major indentations such as bays or estuaries. These states' territories are **compact**, which means that the distance from the geometric center of the area to any point on the boundary does not vary greatly (Fig. 37-3). The compact state encloses a maximum of territory within a minimum length of boundary, which is an obvious asset. As Figure 37-3 shows, Hungary's compactness is related to the physiography of this sector of the basin of the Danube River, which traverses the country from north to south. Unlike Uruguay, Hungary's capital (Budapest) lies well within the national territory, and not in a peripheral location. Also, note that for a compact and comparatively small country, Hungary has a large number of neighbors (five); Cambodia has three, and Uruguay only two.

Quite the opposite situation prevails in the case we mentioned, the Philippines, and in Indonesia, Japan, and Malaysia. In those states, the territory is **fragmented** into numerous pieces, and it is possible to go from one part to the other only by water or air (Fig. 37-3). We can recognize three different kinds of fragmented states: those with national territory that lies entirely on islands (Japan, the Philippines), those with territory that lies partly on a continental landmass and partly on islands (Malaysia, Italy), and those with major territorial units lying on the mainland, separated by the territory of another state (the United States, with its state of Alaska, which cannot be reached overland from the conterminous states except through Canada).

Fragmented states have problems

of internal circulation and contact, and often suffer in other ways from the friction of distance. Far-flung Malaysia, for example, was incapable of accommodating the strong forces of secession in Singapore. After years of rising tension, East Pakistan broke away from West Pakistan and became the independent state of Bangladesh. The government of Indonesia is based on the most populous island of that state, Djawa, and it has had difficulties pacifying distant islands. The state of the Philippines has faced similar problems: the capital is on Luzon, the country's largest island, but there is a Muslim minority on Mindanao, another major island far to the south. The government has found it difficult to cope with the sporadic opposition mounted on Mindanao and in the Sulu Archipelago in the distant southwest. The Philippines' national territory consists of more than 7000 islands, but the majority of the country's 70 million inhabitants live on Luzon and on the islands facing the Visayan Sea (Fig. 37-3). At least part of the Philippines' recent problem of division and conflict relates to the country's particular regional geography.

Still another spatial form is represented by Chile, Norway, Malawi, Panama, and Vietnam. The territory of these states is **elongated**. Such elongation (or *attenuation*, as it is sometimes called) also presents certain difficulties. If such a state also has a large territory, or if it lies astride a cultural transition zone, its elongated shape may endow it with strong internal regionalism. An example of the latter is Togo in West Africa, not a very large state but extending inland from the coast, across the rainforest and savanna, to the drier Muslim-influenced interior. In Italy, which is an elongated as well as a fragmented state, there are north-south contrasts that are related to the different exposures of those two regions to European

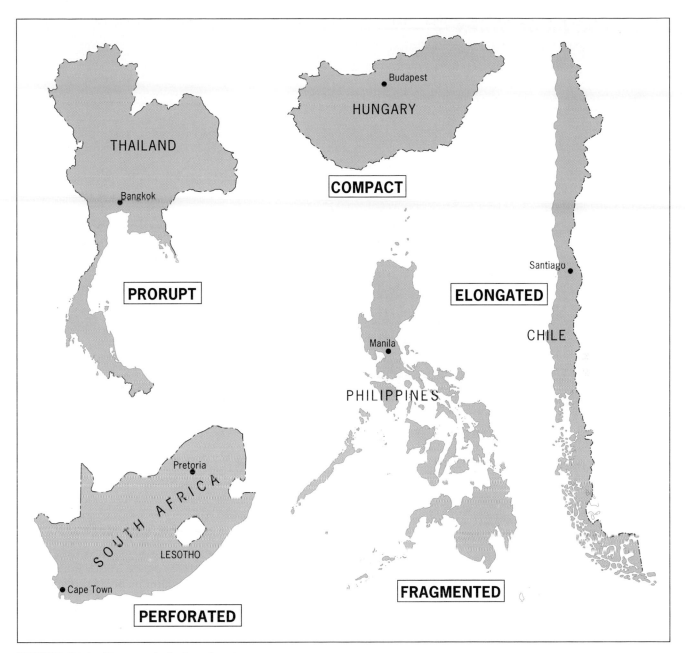

FIGURE 37–3 The morphologies of states.

mainstreams of change. In Norway, the distant frigid north, inhabited by Sami, is another world from the south, where the capital city and the country's core area are positioned. Chile, of course, provides the classic example of environmental—if not cultural—contrast (Fig. 37-3). Northern Chile is desert country, the barren Atacama prevailing there. Central Chile has a large area of Mediterranean climatic conditions, and here the majority of the people are clustered. Southern Chile is dominated by a cooler, more rain-producing climate, and by rugged topography. The effects of distance and isolation are very evident in the far desert north and in the remote south. In many ways, Chile *is* that central area between the two, the rest of the country still awaiting effective integration into the state.

An entirely different situation is presented by Thailand. Thailand would be a compact-state, except for one peculiarity: from its main body of territory a long peninsula extends several hundred miles southward to the boundary with Malaysia (Fig. 37-3). In fact, Thailand's neighbor Myanmar (Burma) exhibits the same feature, except that its southward extension is a bit shorter. This spatial form is called

From the Field Notes

❝ Standing in this vineyard south of Santiago, you look eastward and there, where the permanent snow marks the Andes Mountains' crestline, lies Chile's boundary with Argentina. Turn around, and you see the ocean in the distance. You are reminded that Chile is a mere sliver of land, the classic elongated state. ❞

prorupt (sometimes called *extended*), and any time you see such a situation on the map, a little investigation is warranted. Proruptions often have noteworthy histories. They also create special problems: in the case of Thailand, those border areas near Malaysia are nearly 1000 kilometers (600 miles) away from the capital, Bangkok, farther than any other area is removed from the government's headquarters. However, at least there is a railroad along the Thai proruption. Not so in Myanmar: the railroad southward from the capital ends 500 kilometers (300 miles) short of the southern border, and for the last 240 km (150 mi) there is not even a good all-weather road!

One other spatial form should be mentioned, although its significance hardly matches that of the other four. In rare instances, the territory of a state completely surrounds that of another state. The larger state, then, is **perforated** by the surrounded country. A look at the map of South Africa will make this clear: the country of Lesotho is entirely surrounded by South Africa. Lesotho is about the size of Belgium, so it takes a substantial piece of territory out of the heart of South Africa. Elsewhere, perforators are smaller, as in the case of San Marino and Vatican City, both of which perforate Italy.

Exclaves and Enclaves

Some states, through accidents of history, possess comparatively small outliers of territory not large enough to make them fragmented states. When such a small part of a state is separated from the main territory by land belonging to another state, that part is referred to as an **exclave**.

Many exclaves lie on coasts, for example, the territory of Cabinda, an exclave of Angola, and the small settlements of Ceuta and Melilla, two Spanish exclaves across the Mediterranean Sea in Morocco. But others are landlocked, so that they become **enclaves** completely surrounded by the separating country. Figure 37-4 shows one of the world's most embattled enclaves, Nagorno-Karabakh, an exclave of Christian Armenia totally within Muslim Azerbaijan. This situation was created by Soviet political planners, whose habit it was to award sizable ethnic or cultural minorities

SPATIAL RELATIONSHIPS IN TRANSCAUCASIA

FIGURE 37–4 Spatial relationships in Transcaucasia. SOURCE: From a map in H. J. de Blij and P. O. Muller, *Geography: Realms, Regions, and Concepts*, 7th ed. (New York: Wiley, 1994), p. 165.

in the communist empire with designated homelands. Christian Armenia was made a republic in the Soviet scheme, and so was Muslim Azerbaijan. The problem of a large cluster of Christian Armenians within Azjerbaijan was solved by awarding the Armenians their own territory but also by giving Azerbaijan the right to administer it.

Author's Video Link
↓
4
"Central Asia"

All this worked while Soviet rule kept the lid on potential conflict, but when the USSR collapsed, old animosities got free reign. The Republic of Armenia openly demanded the incorporation of Nagorno-Karabakh into its territory, if need be by a corridor linking the exclave to the main territory (only about 16 kilometers, or 10 miles, of mountainous terrain separate them). Meanwhile, Armenians living in

Azerbaijan cities, such as Baku and Sumgait, were attacked and driven out. Many fled to the Nagorno-Karabakh, where nearly 200,000 Armenians were defending themselves against Azeri aggression. Soon Armenia and Azerbaijan were in a full-scale conflict, and by early 1994 the Armenians not only had created their corridor to Nagorno-Karabakh but had occupied about one-quarter of the Republic of Azerbaijan. In late 1994 peace negotiations were under way, mediated by Turkey and Iran; but it seemed that only a permanent boundary change could stave off future conflict.

As Figure 37-4 shows, Nagorno-Karabakh is not the only exclave in this region. Azerbaijan itself has a sizable exclave, Nakhichevan, separated from it by Armenian territory. But note that Nakhichevan is *not* an enclave; that is, it is not completely surrounded by one country. Nakhichevan has borders on Armenia to the north and on Iran to the south.

LOCATION

The third geographic property of states is their location, specifically their relative location. Earlier we noted that some states have coasts on the open oceans and seas, while others are landlocked. To assess the significance of a landlocked location, factors of physical as well as human geography come into play. Bolivia, for example, is a notorious case of landlocked isolation; Andean highlands separate the country from ports along the Pacific coast (historically, Bolivia had rights to those outlets, lost during an ill advised war with its neighbors). The Czech Republic is also landlocked, but its isolation is far less serious as it is well connected by waterways and surface transport routes to the outside world. In Asia, Mongolia and Nepal are severely landlocked, with distance, terrain, and extant communications all contributing to their condition. In Africa, the realm with the most landlocked states of all, the resulting problems are especially severe. West Africa's Sahel states are poorly linked to coastal entry points; in East Africa, Uganda has a rail link to the coast but Rwanda and Burundi are among the world's most isolated places. In Southern Africa, Zimbabwe has exit options via South Africa and Moçambique, but Zambia and Malawi suffer from poor connections *and* political instability in their coastal neighbors.

Location also should be seen in context of what we know about environmental zones and mineral resource belts of the Earth. Russia's enormous territorial size, an apparent advantage in terms of mineral potential, is moderated by its high-latitude situation, which makes much of the vast country unlivable. Sudan is more than seven times as large as Germany, but Germany lies on the raw-material belt that underpinned the Industrial Revolution, and Sudan has few natural resources by comparison.

Location with reference to global mainstreams of activity and change also favors certain countries and disadvantages others. Singapore is often described as the "country made great by geography," a small city-state positioned at the crossroads of some of the world's busiest shipping routes and now an important economy on the burgeoning Pacific Rim. Hong Kong, too, owes its success in part to location. Conversely, isolation inhibits progress. Sierra Leone, Yemen, Myanmar, and Suriname are among countries whose location is coastal, but not touched by major routes of activity, not even of the tourist industry. Their remoteness from the paths of diffusion of goods, ideas, and technologies translates into disadvantage.

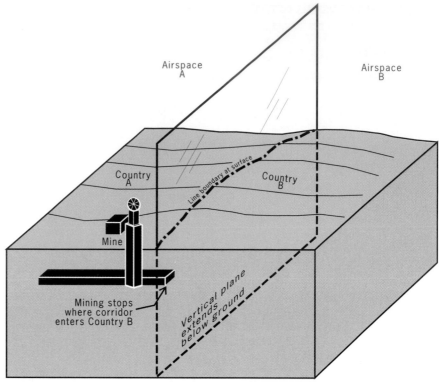

FIGURE 37–5   A political boundary is a vertical plane, not merely a line on the ground.

LAND BOUNDARIES OF STATES

We are able to judge the size, shape, and location of states because the world's states are outlined on the map by *international boundaries*. Great stretches of boundaries twist and turn to conform to the bends of rivers and the curves of hills and valleys. But a boundary is more than a line, far more than a fence or wall on the ground. A **boundary** between states is a vertical *plane* that cuts through the rocks below (called the **subsoil** in legal papers when countries argue about it) and the airspace above (Fig. 37-5). Only where this vertical plane intersects the Earth's surface (on land or at sea) does it form the line we see on the map.

When boundaries were established, the resources below the surface were much less well-known than they are today. As a result, coal seams extend from one country to another, oil reserves are split between adjacent states, and gas reserves are shared as well. Take the case of coal: the coal reserves that fired the Industrial Revolution in mainland Europe extend from Belgium underneath the Netherlands and on into Germany. Soon after mining began, these three neighbors began to accuse each other of theft, of mining coal that did not lie directly below their own national territories. (In truth, the underground surveys that were available were too inaccurate to pinpoint the ownership of each coal seam.)

More recently, Germany and the Netherlands disputed their joint exploitation of a gas reserve that lies across their boundary. The Germans argued that the Dutch were withdrawing so much natural gas that the gas was flowing from beneath German land to the Dutch side of the border. The Germans wanted compensation for their "lost" gas. And we all know that a major issue between Iraq and Kuwait, leading up to Iraq's 1990 invasion, was the oil in the Rumaylah reserve, a reserve that lies across the boundary between the two states underneath the desert. The Iraqis not only asserted that the Kuwaitis were drilling too many wells and draining the reserve too quickly; they also alleged that the Kuwaitis were drilling *oblique* boreholes, thus penetrating the vertical plane that cuts the oil field in half. But at the time the Iraq–Kuwait border was established, no one knew that this giant oil reserve lay in the subsoil, or that it would help cause an international crisis (Fig. 37-6).

Author's Video Link
↓
6
"Kuwait"

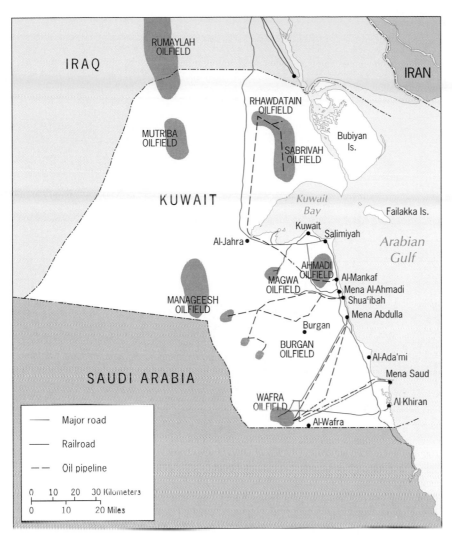

FIGURE 37–6 Relative location of Kuwait. The country's northern boundary was redefined and delimited by a United Nations boundary commission; it was demarcated by a series of concrete pillars 2 km (1.24 mi) apart.

boundary is involved, points of latitude and longitude). Next cartographers, using large-scale maps and referring to the boundary line as defined, put the boundary on the map in a process called **delimitation**. If either or both of the states so desire, the boundary is actually marked on the ground by steel posts, concrete pillars, fences (sometimes even a wall), or some other visible means. That final state is the **demarcation** of the boundary. By no means are all boundaries on the world map demarcated. There are thousands of miles where you could cross from one state into another without knowing it. Demarcating a lengthy boundary by any means at all is expensive, and it is hardly worth it in inhospitable mountains, vast deserts, frigid polar lands, or other places where there is virtually no permanent human population.

BOUNDARY TYPES

Even the most casual glance at the world's boundary framework leads us to realize that boundaries differ morphologically. Some conform to lines of latitude or longitude (Egypt literally occupies Africa's northeastern corner!), others conform to natural features such as rivers, and still others separate societies of contrasting ethnic backgrounds or cultural properties. Political geographers use the term **geometric boundary** to identify straight-line boundaries such as that between the United States and Canada west of the Great Lakes. Such boundaries are totally unrelated to any aspects of the cultural or physical landscape. As the world map shows, the colonial powers made considerable use of such boundary making in Africa.

Certain boundaries conform to physiographic features in the landscape, such as rivers or the crests of mountain ranges. These are named

Above the ground, too, the boundary-as-plane interpretation has serious implications. A state's "airspace" is defined by the atmosphere above its land area as marked by its boundaries and by what lies beyond, at higher altitudes. But how high? States that insist on controlling the airline traffic over their territories have not (yet) done so with space satellites, but that time may come. And the mobile atmosphere circulates from one airspace to another, often carrying the pollutants of one state across the vertical plane to another. Acid rain knows no political boundaries, but it can cause serious political disputes.

BOUNDARY EVOLUTION

In ideal circumstances, boundaries evolve through three stages. Imagine a frontier area, about to be divided between two states. First, agreement is reached on the rough positioning of the border. Then the exact location is established through the process of **definition**, whereby a treatylike, legal-sounding document is drawn up in which actual points in the landscape are described (or, where a straight-line

GENETIC POLITICAL BOUNDARY TYPES

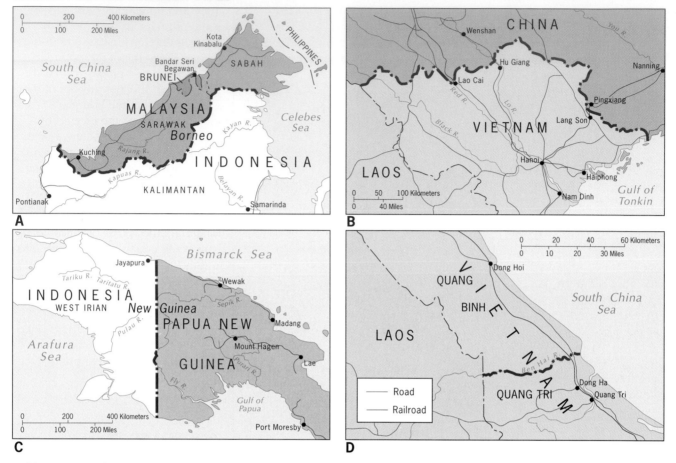

FIGURE 37–7 Genetic political boundary types: (*A*) antecedent, (*B*) subsequent, (*C*) superimposed, and (*D*) relict. SOURCE: From a map in H. J. de Blij and P. O. Muller, *Geography: Realms, Regions, and Concepts*, 7th ed. (New York: Wiley, 1994), p. 559.

physical-political or sometimes **natural-political boundaries**, and many of them are modern versions of old trespass lines, lines nature seemed to provide to delimit human activity. The Rio Grande is an important physical-political boundary between the United States and Mexico; an older border follows crest lines of the Pyrenees between Spain and France. Lakes sometimes serve as boundaries as well—for example, four of the five Great Lakes of North America (between the U.S. and Canada) and several of the Great Lakes of East Africa (between Zaïre and its eastern neighbors). At first, national jurisdiction extended to the banks of rivers and the shores of lakes, but today, the waters themselves are di-

vided between riparian and littoral states.

Boundaries that mark breaks in the human landscape formerly were called anthropo-geographic boundaries, but a simpler term would be **cultural-political boundaries**. When the communist planners of the Soviet empire laid out their grand design for the Soviet Union, they tried to create a patchwork of nationalities, delimiting many miles of cultural-political boundaries in the process. For example, the boundary between Christian Armenia and Muslim Azerbaijan (mentioned earlier in this chapter) was such a cultural-political boundary. The map of European languages and political borders (Fig. 21-3) suggests how common

such boundaries still are. But cultural breaks in the human landscape tend to shift over time, which is one reason why cultural-political boundaries often lead to conflict. Nevertheless, when peacemakers tried to draw a new map of Bosnia to help end the conflict among Serbs, Croats, and Muslims there, their attempts were based on cultural-political boundary principles. The Muslim "safe zones" were to be, essentially, cultural enclaves.

ORIGIN-BASED CLASSIFICATION

Another way to view boundaries has to do with their evolution or genesis. This *genetic boundary classification* was established by Richard Hartshorne (1899–1992), a leading American political geographer. Hartshorne reasoned that certain boundaries were defined and delimited before the present-day human landscape developed. Although Hartshorne used mainly Western examples to illustrate this idea, its applicability is also illustrated elsewhere, for example, in Southeast Asia. In Figure 37-7*A*, the boundary between Malaysia and Indonesia on the island of Borneo is an example of this **antecedent boundary** type. Most of this border passes through sparsely inhabited tropical rainforest, and the break in settlement can even be detected on the world population map (Fig. 6-1). A second category of boundaries evolved as the cultural landscape of an area took shape. These **subsequent boundaries** are exemplified by the map in Figure 37-7*B*, which shows the border between China and Vietnam, the result of a long-term process of adjustment and modification.

Some boundaries are forcibly drawn across a unified cultural landscape. Such a **superimposed boundary** exists in the center of the island of New Guinea and separates Indonesia's West Irian from the country of Papua New Guinea (Fig. 37-7*C*). West Irian, which is peopled mostly by ethnic Papuans, was part of the Netherlands East Indies that did not receive independence as Indonesia in 1949. After many tension-filled years, the Indonesians finally invaded this territory in 1962 to drive out the remaining Dutch; following UN mediation and an eventual plebiscite, West Irian was formally attached to Indonesia in 1969—thereby perpetuating the boundary that the colonial administrators had originally superimposed on New Guinea in the early nineteenth century. The fourth genetic boundary type is the **relict boundary**—a border that has ceased to function, but whose imprints are still evident on the cul-

tural landscape. The boundary between former North Vietnam and South Vietnam (Fig. 37-7*D*), is a classic example: once demarcated militarily, it has had relict status since 1976 following the reunification of Vietnam in the aftermath of the Indochina War (1964–1975).

From the Field Notes

❝ For many years, the boundary between Hong Kong and the People's Republic of China, on land, was among the world's most strongly demarcated. In 1974 I stood on a hill on the Hong Kong side to see the fenced and barbed-wired border, brightly lit at night and patrolled continuously. But in 1992, when I visited the same lookout point much had changed. The patrols were infrequent. The area adjacent to the fence no longer was a vacuum. With unification approaching, the 'Berlin Wall' of southeast China was becoming permeable. ❞

FRONTIERS

The term **frontier** is misused almost as much as *nation*. Often, nongeographers use "boundary" and "frontier" interchangeably, as though they were synonyms; but they are not. A frontier is (and throughout human history has been) a zone of separation, an area between communities, clusters, groups, and states, a territorial cushion that keeps rivals apart, so that distance decay might reduce the intensity of their conflicts. Such frontiers were swamplands, vast and nearly impenetrable forests, wide deserts or other environmental obstacles, mountain ranges, or river basins. Before the now-familiar world boundary framework jelled, many societies remained separated by such natural frontiers. Eventually, even the most remote reaches of the planet were appropriated, and boundaries were drawn through the last frontiers—even in Antarctica, the Earth's last land frontier, and, as we will see later, the seas and oceans.

BOUNDARY FUNCTIONS

There was a time when states and empires built walls to fortify their borders, to keep adversaries out, and, sometimes, to keep locals from wandering too far from the seat of authority. China's Great Wall and Britain's Hadrian's Wall (built by the Romans) still stand as evidence of such intentions. Indeed, the notion that boundaries could serve as fortifications endured into the mid-twentieth century; the Second World War witnessed several attempts at it. And boundaries continue to be reinforced to stop people from moving across them without authorization. The infamous Berlin Wall was built to keep East Germans from crossing into the Western enclave of West Berlin, there to seek asylum from communist rule. More recently, the border between Mexico and the United States was walled and fenced to reduce illegal migration. Boundaries still have their defensive functions, although in a different context.

Today, boundaries mark the limit of state jurisdiction. They serve as symbols of state inviolability; states often display maps of their national territories on the front pages of newspapers, on school books, on stamps, and even on flags. This contributes to the building of a national consciousness, a sense of inclusion that fosters **nationalism**.

In practical terms, the state territory as outlined by its boundaries is the region within which its laws prevail, its taxes are collected, its armed forces are recruited or drafted, its language(s) must be used, its educational curricula are implemented, and, in certain countries, the state religion is practiced. Boundaries, therefore, do much to keep this world divided—and not just politically.

INTERNAL BOUNDARIES

For administrative purposes, and sometimes to accommodate cultural regionalism within the state, it is necessary to divide countries internally. The United States consists of 50 States that are in turn divided into counties (except Louisiana, which is divided into parishes). Canada is divided into 10 provinces, 2 federal territories, and 1 self-governing homeland set aside for Inuit residents of the country. One of Canada's provinces, Quebec, is itself a homeland for Francophone Canadians, although Quebec's borders do not coincide with the area in which French speakers live. India, with nearly four times as many inhabitants as the U.S., has 25 States and 7 Union Territories, and some of the States have more people than most countries of the world. Cross from the State of Maharashtra into Karnataka, and be prepared to speak a different language. India's internal boundaries represent more cultural variation than do many international boundaries elsewhere.

Political geographers take note of another kind of internal boundary, a kind that does not show up on an administrative map. Numerous countries are culturally divided, but the administrative map only hints at the situation. Take the case of the former Yugoslavia: although there were internal "republics" for the country's Serbian, Croatian, Slovenian, Macedonian, and other major cultural components in the population, this administrative structure was no match for the real situation. There were Serbs in Croatia, Croatians in Bosnia, and so on. Figure 37-8 is actually a simplification of the cultural mosaic of Yugoslavia just at the time things fell apart there.

Such internal, nonadministrative boundaries can be seen in Belgium, Cyprus, Sri Lanka, Malaysia, Moldova, and a host of other countries, including several African states. It is a global phenomenon and, as we note later, one that puts great stress on state systems all over the world.

BOUNDARY DISPUTES

Nations, like families and individuals, can become very territorial when they feel that their space has been violated. In suburban areas in the United States, quarrels over fence lines and surveys rank high among social disputes that must be solved by legal means.

So it is with states. The boundary we see as a line on an atlas map is the product of a complex series of legal steps that begins with a written description of the border. Sometimes that legal description is old and imprecise. Sometimes it has a history of inequality, that is, it was dictated by a stronger power now less dominant, giving the weaker neighbor a reason to argue for change. At other times the geography of the borderland has actually

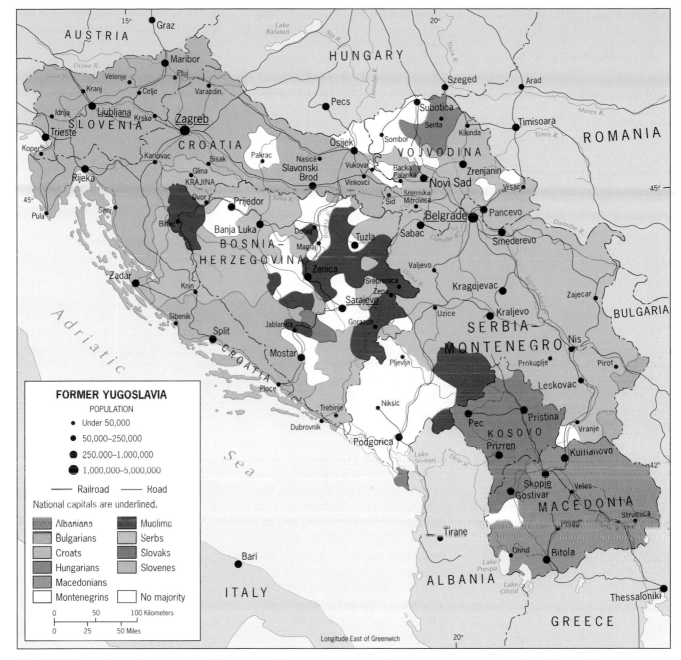

FIGURE 37–8 The ethnic mosaic of the former Yugoslavia. SOURCE: Based on maps drawn in the Office of the Geographer of the U.S. Department of State, Washington, D.C., 1991.

changed: the river that was to mark the boundary may have changed course, or a meander has been cut off. Resources discovered to lie astride a boundary can lead to conflict. In short, states dispute their boundaries often. Thousands of kilometers of boundary are in contention today.

Boundary disputes take four principal forms: definitional, locational, operational, and allocational.

Definitional boundary disputes focus on the legal language of the boundary agreement. For example, a boundary definition may stipulate that the border will be marked by the median line of a river. That

would seem clear enough, but rivers' water levels vary. If the valley is asymmetrical, the median line will move back and forth between low-water and high-water stages of the stream. This may involve hundreds of meters of movement—not very much, it would seem, but enough to cause serious argument, just as a few inches do in the suburbs. Solution: refine the definition to suit both parties.

Locational boundary disputes center on the delimitation and possibly the subsequent demarcation of the border. Thus the definition is not in dispute, but its interpretation is. The language of boundary treaties sometimes is sufficiently vague to allow mapmakers to delimit the line variously. When the colonial powers defined their respective empires in Africa and Asia, they defined their international boundaries rather carefully. But when they drew internal boundaries for administrative purposes, this often was done without strict definition. When those internal boundaries become the boundaries of independent, sovereign states, there was plenty of room for argument.

In a few instances, locational disputes arise because no joint definition of the boundary exists at all. A potentially important case involves Saudi Arabia and Yemen, whose potentially oil-rich border area is not served by a treaty.

Operational boundary disputes involve neighbors who differ over the way their joint boundary should function. When two adjoining countries agree that cross-border migration should be controlled, the boundary functions satisfactorily. But if one state wants to limit migration while the other does not, a dispute may arise. Again, the interdiction of contraband sometimes leads to operational disputes when one state's efforts in this regard are not matched (or are possibly even sabotaged) by its neighbor's. In areas where nomadic lifeways still prevail, the movement of people and their livestock across international borders can lead to conflict.

Allocational disputes of the kind described earlier, involving the Netherlands and Germany over natural gas and Iraq and Kuwait over oil are becoming more common as the search for resources intensifies. Today, many allocational disputes focus on international boundaries at sea, to be discussed later. Oil reserves beneath coastal waters, under the seafloor, sometimes lie in the very area where states meet at sea, and where exact boundary delimitation may be difficult or subject to definitional debate. Another growing area of allocational dispute lies in water supplies: The Tigris, Nile, Colorado, and other rivers are subject to this. When a river crosses an international boundary, the rights of the upstream and the downstream users of the river often are the subject of dispute.

In Chapter 37 we have examined various geographic aspects of the territory of states, including its morphology and its spatial limits. As we noted, the territorial endowments of states vary widely, and so do their comparative advantages of relative location. Whatever their territorial attributes, however, states achieve strength, durability, and power through the organization of the assets at their disposal. Some states have overcome severe geographic disadvantage to attain prosperity and security; others, with apparent opportunities, have failed to capitalize. We turn next to the role of spatial organization in the well-being of states.

KEY TERMS

Antecedent Boundary
Boundary
Boundary Definition
Boundary Delimitation
Boundary Demarcation
Boundary Dispute
Compact State
Cultural-Political Boundary
Elongated State
Enclave
Exclave
Fragmented State
Frontier
Geometric Boundary
Landlocked State
Microstate
Nation
Nationalism
Nation-State
Natural-Political Boundary
Physical-Political Boundary
Perforated State
Prorupt State
Political Culture
Political Geography
Relict Boundary
State
Subsequent Boundary
Subsoil
Superimposed Boundary
Territorial Morphology
Theocracy

38

STATE ORGANIZATION
AND NATIONS' POWER

Political geographers predict that the number of independent states will surpass 200 in the near future—200 countries on the surface of a small planet over two-thirds of which is covered by water or ice! With such a large number of entities, some of which are large and others very small, it is inevitable that equality will remain a mirage. Not only are there large as well as small states: there are well-endowed and poor states, advantaged and disadvantaged states, developed and underdeveloped states.

In previous chapters we noted that size, resources, and location relative to mainstreams of innovation were among factors influencing the strength of states in this competitive world. In this chapter we investigate the human and organizational dimension.

ORGANIZING THE STATE

For several years now we have been witnessing China's fast-paced economic growth. While developed

---

Geographica

- **A well-developed primary core area and a mature capital city form the heart and brain of the state, and are essential components of a satisfactorily functioning state system.**

- **The European state model had a centralized, unitary framework, and alternative federal systems were developed in the New World and in overseas dependencies elsewhere.**

- **All states are held together by such centripetal forces as nationalism, education, circulation, and the institutions of government; but no state escapes centrifugal forces in the form of ethnic disunity, cultural differences, or regional disparities.**

- **Geopolitics, a century-old field of political geography, studies the power relationships among states; current developments in the Asia-Pacific Rimland fuel an old debate on Eurasian power relationships.**

---

economies are experiencing growth of 1 to 3 percent annually, China is reporting growth of 9 to 13 percent—growth so fast that Chinese rulers are trying to hold it down for fear of uncontrolled inflation, infrastructure failure, and, as a Chinese economic geographer recently put it, "implosion." China's economy in the early 1990s took third place, be-

hind those of the United States and Japan, for sheer size.

And yet, the Chinese people in 1995 were earning just a tiny fraction per capita of what Americans or Japanese earn. On the development map, China still ranks in the lower category by many measures. Why is this so? The answer lies in large measure in China's population numbers. With over 1.2 billion people, and adding 16 million every year, every measure of individual (material) progress must be divided by twelve hundred million. No matter how fast an economy grows, that kind of arithmetic will long depress per capita indices.

Economic success and political power are closely linked. When Western Europe's leading states acquired colonial empires, they were able to do so because they already were economically successful; Japan, too, used its economic reforms to mount a campaign of territorial expansion. The colonial acquisitions produced a multiplier effect that enabled small European countries to become imperial powers, controlling human numbers far in excess of their domestic populations.

Today, the fragments of those colonial empires are nominally independent states. Earlier we noted the range of territorial sizes marking the world's states; in terms of population, the range is even greater. Over half the world's states (and soon-to-be states) have populations below 5 million; nearly 50 have fewer than 1 million citizens. These smallest "real" states are called **ministates** (unlike the *microstates*, which do not have all the elements of statehood), and they seem destined to remain powerless in a world where decisions are made by their larger neighbors (Singapore is one of very few exceptions), although they have been given disproportionately strong representation in various international agencies, including, as noted earlier, the United Nations.

Experience has shown that there is no "ideal" or model population size for a state of given territorial properties. Japan has achieved, on a Montana-sized territory, what giant Brazil has not. "Overpopulated" Singapore thrives, while Liberia fractures. The European model nation-state rightfully stipulates no population size.

From the Field Notes

❝ Singapore, a ministate that also is a city-state, is the product of organization as well as location. With an area of just 240 square miles (622 sq km) and a population of nearly 3 million, Singapore, the world's most urbanized state, has to be organized strictly in order to function. With the largest port in the world (in terms of number of ships served) and the third-largest oil refinery complex, Singapore is one of the Pacific Rim's economic tigers. This view, from the 68th floor of Asia's tallest hotel, shows Singapore's still-evolving skyline, a reflection of its success. ❞

The model does, however, speak of organization and thus of people's capacities for organization. As Japan, Hong Kong, and now Guangdong have proven, the abilities of the labor force to learn and to adapt to changing technologies is a greater resource than the largest iron reserve in the world. The map—even at a small scale—reflects state organization and productivity. Urbanization, transport routes, and production centers indicate the level of a state's organization and strength. One of the indicators is the state's core area; another is the size and functions of its capital city.

CORE AREAS

The model European state grew over many centuries from a heartland, a **core area**, expanding into a regional entity and absorbing territory in receding frontiers; eventually, its expansion was halted when neighboring entities blocked it, boundaries were defined and internal organization matured.

The original nucleus in many European states still forms the focus of the modern core area. Many countries elsewhere in the world also have well-defined core areas, even though they are often much younger than their European counterparts. You can discern core areas even on a small-scale atlas map: here lie a country's major cities, usually including the capital, its largest and densest population cluster, its most intensive transport networks, and often its most intensively cultivated farmlands. Here the national economy is best developed; circulation is at its most efficient. Travel away from the core area, and you see smaller towns, fewer factories, less-productive farms, more open land.

Japan's Tokyo-centered Kanto

Plain is one of the world's leading national cores, including Japan's unrivaled primate city. Note that intensive agriculture still plays a role in this highly urbanized heartland. France's Paris Basin is another, but more ancient, core area, centered on one of Europe's greatest primate cities. In Egypt, the Cairo-Alexandria axis and the Nile Delta form the national core, and in Chile, Santiago lies in what the Chileans themselves call their country's *nucleo central.*

Is a well-developed core area essential for a well-functioning state? The map would suggest that it is. Countries without recognizable cores (Zaïre, Chad, Mongolia, Bangladesh) may have notable capitals, but these alone do not ensure a well-functioning, complete state system.

Some states possess more than one core area, and such multicore states confront particular problems. If the primary core area is dominant, as in the United States, such problems may be slight. In the U.S., the core area still lies in the East and Northeast, corresponding approximately with the economic region mapped in Figure 36-3, and includes the federal capital. Subsidiary core areas are not competitive, or regionally divisive, in this country. In Nigeria, on the other hand, three core areas mark ethnically and culturally diverse parts of the state, and none is truly dominant (Fig. 38-1). Nigeria's northern core area represents the Muslim heart of the country; the two southern cores center on two of its major population clusters.

CAPITAL CITIES

The core area is the heart of the state; the **capital city** is the brain. This is the nerve center of the country, the national headquarters, seat of government, site of crucial decision making, source and symbol of power, center of national life. We recognize this special status by

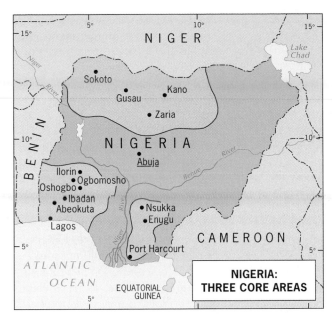

FIGURE 38–1 Nigeria is a multicore state; its northern core area lies in the Muslim realm, while the southern core areas lie in Christian-influenced Africa. Nigeria's political survival is a major African political achievement. But pressures on Nigeria are rising, and devolution remains a threat.

using the name of a country's capital interchangeably with that of the state itself; for example, a news report may say that "London's position has changed" or "Moscow is at odds with Ukraine."

Capitals nurture national memories and emotions. The primacy of the capital is yet another manifestation of the European state model, one that has diffused worldwide. After they had gained independence, many developing countries spent lavishly on their capitals, not because this was essential to political or economic success, but because the European image, drawn from London or Paris or Lisbon or Brussels, compelled it.

Some newly independent states decided to relocate their capital cities, again at enormous expense. Several did so for internal reasons, to move the capital from a peripheral situation to a more central one. Nigeria's colonial capital, Lagos, lies on the coast in the southwest of the country. For years now, a new capital has been under construction at

Abuja, nearer the geographic center of the state. Malawi moved its capital from deep-south Zomba to centrally positioned Lilongwe. In Asia, a significant capital relocation occurred in Pakistan, where the colonial headquarters of Karachi was vacated in favor of a far northern city called Islamabad.

Capital cities are of interest to cultural as well as political geographers because they are occasionally used to focus a society's attention on a national objective. In Pakistan's case, the two-step transfer of the capital's functions to Islamabad (indeed an appropriate name for the capital of an Islamic republic) was part of a plan to orient the nation toward its historic focus in the interior and toward the contested north where the country narrows between Kashmir, China, and Afghanistan. In Brazil, the decision to move the capital from historic Rio de Janeiro to Brasília was made, in large part, to direct the nation's attention toward the huge, underpopulated, yet ineffectively integrated, interior. We have already noted Japan's significant transfer of its capital functions from Kyoto to Tokyo, also with specific national objectives. The capital city, therefore, can be used as a device to achieve national aims, to spearhead change. Geographers sometimes refer to such cities as **forward capitals**.

Berlin, the old and now the reestablished capital of newly reunified Germany, once served as such a forward capital. During the nineteenth century, when the German state was forming, its western boundaries (with the Netherlands, Belgium, and, until 1870, France) were relatively stable. To the east, however, lay Germany's frontier: there, the Germans confronted the Poles and other Slavic nations, and the growing empire expanded into much of what is today Poland.

This eastward march was underpinned by the choice of Berlin as the capital. Berlin lies not far from the Oder River, whose basin, until the 1860s, was Germany's easternmost territory. Most of Germany lay to the west of Berlin, but the capital confirmed Germany's eastern orientation.

A century later, Germany lay defeated and divided. West Germany chose a new capital, Bonn; East Germany, under Soviet control, was governed from East Berlin. The German empire had lost all its eastern frontier and more: Poland now extended to the Oder River, on Berlin's doorstep.

When Germany was reunified in 1990, the world watched as Germans deliberated the choice of their new capital. Many favored Bonn, located near the country's western border and symbolic of its new role in Europe. Many others preferred a return to Berlin, now less a forward than a peripheral capital. Still others wanted to put the past behind them and argued for a totally new choice, such as Hannover, near the spatial center of the country. In the end,

Berlin was selected—raising fears among some who remembered the capital and its role during times of aggression and war.

Author's Video Link
↓
2
"German Unification"

In general, the capital city is the pride of the state, and its layout, prominent architectural landmarks, public art, historic buildings and monuments, and often its religious structures reflect the society's values and priorities. It may be employed as a unifying force, a binding element; it can assert a state's posture internally, as well as externally. It is the focus of the state as a political functional region.

UNITARY AND FEDERAL SYSTEMS

The well-functioning state system consists of a stable, clearly bounded territory served by an adequate infrastructure, an effective administrative framework, a productive core area, and a prominent capital. All states, however, confront divisive forces—some strong enough to threaten the very survival of the system. The question is how best to adjust the workings of the system to ensure its continuity.

When the nation-state evolved in Europe, this was not a serious problem. Democracy as we know it today had not yet matured; governments were powerful and could suppress dissent by forceful means. Most European governments were highly centralized; the capital city represented authority that stretched to the limits of the state. These limits, more often than not, also marked the margins of the national culture, so that a strong sense of unity and identity characterized Europe's nations. There seemed to be

no need to accommodate minorities or outlying regions where the sense of national identity might be a bit weaker. Europe's nation-states were **unitary states**, and their administrative frameworks were designed to ensure the central government's authority over all the parts. France, for example, was divided *after* its "democratic" revolution of 1789 into more than 80 *départements*, whose representatives came to Paris less to express regional concerns than to implement governmental decisions back home.

European notions of statecraft diffused to much of the rest of the world on the wings of colonialism and imperialism, but in the New World, these notions did not always work well. Where Europeans freed themselves of European dominance, they found that conditions did not lend themselves to unitary systems of government—not, at least, in areas occupied by Western Europeans. In the United States, Canada, and Australia the newness of the culture, the absence of an old

From the Field Notes

❝ This license plate, seen along a street in Oman, made me think for a moment—what Arabian Peninsula country was this? The answer: one of the most interesting post-colonial federations, the United Arab Emirates, a federal state consisting of seven sheikdoms. License plates here generally are in Arabic and English, signifying this area's colonial past and modernizing present. ❞

primate city, the incipient nature of the core area, the vastness of the national territory, and the emergence of regionalism all required something other than highly centralized government. In Europe itself, some political philosophers had already theorized about alternatives to the unitary system, and regionalism in Scotland and Wales had become a concern in London. So the emergence of the **federal state** had strong underpinnings. Federalism made possible the accommodation of regional interests by awarding considerable power to the provinces, States, or other regional units comprising the national entity. The Australian geographer K. W. Robinson described federation as "the most geographically expressive of all political systems, based as it is on the existence and accommodation of regional differences . . . federation does not create unity out of diversity; rather, it enables the two to coexist."

FIGURE 38–2   The new 22-region France (not shown: Corsica). SOURCE: From a map in H. J. de Blij and P. O. Muller, *Geography: Realms, Regions, and Concepts*, 7th ed. (New York: Wiley, 1994), p. 80.

In Europe, the only genuine, long-term federation was multicultural Switzerland, but circumstances in that unique country were not sufficiently similar to those in the New World to permit a transfer of the experience. For example, the choice of a capital city was a challenge for many federations. Given the competitiveness of the regions, none would yield to another to allow the national capital to be designated there. As a result, federations often created new capitals, built specifically for the purpose on federal territories carved from one or more States. Thus the U.S. capital became neither New York nor Philadelphia, but Washington, built on a federal territory initially taken from Maryland and Virginia. The Australian capital became neither Sydney nor Melbourne (both contenders for the honor) but Canberra, established on federal territory taken from the State of New South Wales.

Federalism spread even to countries whose European settlers came from highly centralized unitary states. In Europe, few states were more strongly centralized than Spain and Portugal, and yet Mexico and Brazil established federal systems (Brazil moved its capital functions from the primate city, Rio de Janeiro, to interior Brasília as recently as the 1950s).

While the European colonial powers retained control over their empires in Africa and Asia, colonial rule mirrored the unitary system—only more so. Overseas domains were autocratically run, with little or no consideration for local or regional cultural variation. But when the colonial era came to an end, the federal idea seemed to hold promise for newly independent, ethnically and culturally divided countries. The British particularly attempted to create belated federal frameworks as the end of the empire approached. Undoubtedly their most spectacular success was India, where the transition to independence *and* the subsequent survival

ELECTORAL GEOGRAPHY

"All politics is local," it is often said, and in truth a voter's most direct and most consequential contact with his or her government is at the local level. Voters who feel that they can have but little impact on national elections but who clearly have a voice in local elections still have a sense of participation in the system. This can be a crucial factor in building a sense of commitment to the nation and what it stands for.

The subfield of **electoral geography** deals with various spatial aspects of voting systems, voting behavior, and voter representation. Various countries use different voting systems to elect their governments, and in the 1994 South African election we could observe how the leaders of that plural society formulated a system that would provide majority rule while awarding certain power to each of nine newly formulated regions. The overall effect was to protect, to some extent, the rights of minorities in those regions. In the United States, proportional representation prevails in the House of Representatives (Congress) while the rights of States with small populations are protected in the Senate.

The geographic study of voting behavior is especially interesting because it relates the way people vote to their geographic environments. Maps of voting patterns often produce surprises that can be explained by other maps, and GIS technology has raised this kind of analysis to new levels. Church affiliation, income level, ethnic background, education level, and numerous other social factors are invoked to learn why voters voted the way they did.

Probably the most practical area of interest in electoral geography is what may be called the geography of representation. When there is a certain fixed number of seats for representatives in an elected legislature (such as the 435 congressional seats in the U.S. House of Representatives), then there must be a fixed number of electoral districts from which those representatives are elected. Since the congressional seats are based on State population totals, it is up to each State to draw a map of

of the state may be attributed in large part to the federal framework achieved by British and Indian negotiators during the 1940s. Several failures in Africa did not invalidate the notion; the delicate mechanisms of federation were put in place too hastily (for example, in Nigeria and Uganda) and did not have time to stabilize.

Today, the divisive forces of regionalism are affecting not only recently formulated federations but also the older, established unitary states of Europe (this topic is discussed in more detail later). In response, European states are reconstructing their administrative frameworks; France, for example, has recognized 22 "regions" (count-

ing the island of Corsica, not shown on the map), which consist of groupings of the 96 *départements* dating back to the time of Napoleon (Fig. 38-2). These regions are geographic evidence of France's attempt to decentralize governmental control from Paris. In similar ways, Spain, Italy, the United Kingdom, and other older unitary states are adjusting to new political-geographical circumstances—new to Europe, but well-known to federal governments elsewhere.

OPPOSING FORCES

Adjusting the internal organization of the state is one way to reduce the divisive forces that put stress on

congressional districts from which representatives will be elected.

Or is it? Can the States be trusted to draw their districting maps fairly, giving minorities an opportunity to elect their own representatives? After all, if a State has a population that is 80 percent white, 10 percent African-American, and 10 percent Hispanic, an electoral districting map could easily result in white majorities in all districts and no minority representatives at all. The U.S. government, following the 1990 census, instructed all States with substantial minority populations that might be disenfranchised to construct so-called majority-minority districts (meaning, literally, districts within which a minority would have the majority of the voters). In the hypothetical State described here, this districting would lead to the election of at least one African-American and one Hispanic representative from among 10 districts.

Reapportionment of the number of representatives to States goes on all the time because the population shifts: some States gain seats, others lose. As a result, redistricting also occurs after every census, and within States (for State legislatures) more frequently than that. Ideally, a State's congressional districts would, on the map, look relatively compact and contain roughly the same numbers of voters. In reality, our plural society requires the construction of some oddly shaped districts in order to adhere to the majority-minority rule (Fig. 38-3).

Strange-looking districts constructed to attain certain political ends are nothing new in American politics, of course. In 1812, Governor Elbridge Gerry (pronounced with a hard *G*) of Massachusetts signed into law a district designed to advantage his (Republican) party—a district that looked so odd to artist Gilbert Stuart that he drew it with a head, wings, and claws. Stuart called it the "salamander district," but a colleague immortalized it by naming it a **gerrymander**. Ever since, the term "gerrymandering" has been used to describe "redistricting for advantage." And certainly many of the districts now on the U.S. electoral map may be seen as gerrymanders, but for a cause that is important to the nation: to provide representation to minorities who, without it, would not be as effectively represented in the nation's capital.

---

it. By manipulating the system, many countries have managed to enhance the **centripetal**, or binding, **forces** that promote national unity. This may involve changing the administrative structure of the state either to strengthen the hand of central authority or to assign more power to the provinces or regions. Although India is often cited as the prime example of success through nearly continuous manipulation of the federal framework, the case of Nigeria also merits attention. When Nigeria became independent in 1960, after centuries of British colonial rule, it was endowed with a federal framework of three regions, based on the core areas shown in Figure 38-1.

Soon a fourth region was added, but this was not enough to stave off a disastrous war of secession fought by the Eastern Region between 1967 and 1971. After that war, it was clear to Nigerian leaders that the original regions had been too large; they were large enough to regard themselves as national entities capable of going it alone. It was decided to redivide Nigeria into a larger number of regions (and to rename these States, not regions). The smaller States would be less able to mount separatist campaigns. Today, on paper, Nigeria is still a federation of 30 States, although successive military regimes have eroded their power and centralized the government. Given the religious division of Nigeria between a Muslim north and a non-Muslim south, the country's cultural fragmentation into 200 peoples, and economic troubles arising from the drop in price of its leading export commodity (oil), Nigeria's continued cohesion is noteworthy.

Manipulating the system, however, may not be enough; it has recently failed in the Soviet Union, in Yugoslavia, and in Czechoslovakia. Governments, therefore, seek to foster unity in other ways as well. Being a citizen of a country and carrying its passport are not manifestations of an emotional commitment to the ideals for which the state stands. Such commitment is expressed as a sense of **nationalism**, an allegiance and loyalty that transcend other feelings of attachment that a citizen inevitably has. In a multicultural state such as South Africa, loyalties are divided: many people feel greater allegiance to their own ethnic group than to the state as a whole. In newly independent countries throughout Africa, *tribalism* has been an immediate threat to "national" unity. Governments everywhere, therefore, seek to nurture nationalism to help overcome more local loyalties. One important way to accomplish this is by ensuring that minorities are represented in government (see box, "Electoral Geography").

Author's Video Link
↓
4
"Redistricting"

Another centripetal force may be embodied in the *leadership* of an especially charismatic individual, who personifies the state and captures the population's imagination (the origin of the word *charisma* lies in a Greek expression that means "divine gift"). At times such charismatic qualities can spur nationalism powerfully, as Perón did

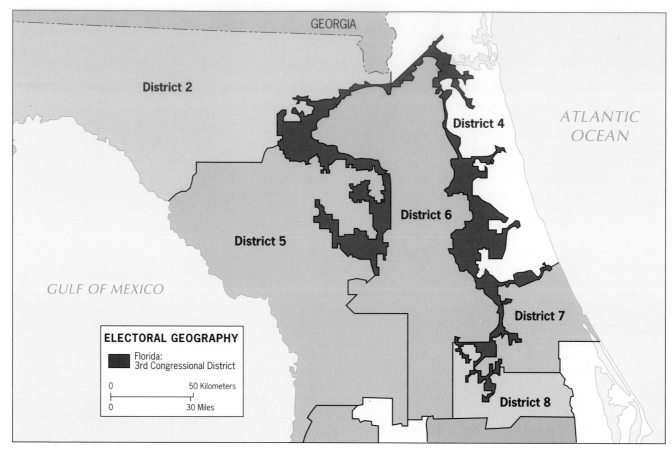

FIGURE 38–3 Florida Congressional District No. 3, an example of the spatial manipulation necessary to create majority-minority districts. In 1990, District 3 had about 310,000 African-American residents, 240,000 whites, and 16,000 Hispanics. In places, District 3 is no wider than U.S. Highway 90. SOURCE: Map and data provided by Tanya de Blij, Geographer/Analyst for the Florida House of Representatives.

in Argentina, de Gaulle in France, and Tito in Yugoslavia. Conversely, the demise of such a leader may be followed by a weakening of nationalist sentiment.

Still another unifying force can come from a real or perceived *external threat.* When a country is confronted by an aggressive neighbor, or by the loss of something vital (a critical resource or an open exit route, for example), the people are likely to rally to the national flag. Some governments have used this reality as a technique to divert attention from internal problems, artificially creating an international crisis to rally the nation.

More durable building blocks of nationalism come from *education* and from other national institutions, including, in some countries, the

church. In all countries, much of what is taught in the schools focuses on the home turf, its history and geography, its symbols and songs, its traditions and values. This universal practice builds the sense of belonging that later translates into nationalism. Where the church still dominates life, as in many Muslim countries and in some Roman Catholic societies, its contribution to national cohesion can be enormous.

Directly related to this institutional centripetal force is what we may refer to as national *ideology.* Nazism was a powerful ideological force that rallied the German nation during the 1930s; communism fired the emotions of hundreds of millions of people for nearly 80 years beginning early in this century.

Communist ideology unified disparate peoples, caused them to abandon (although temporarily as it turned out) their narrow tribalisms, persuaded them to make terrible sacrifices, and blinded them to dreadful excesses carried out under its banner. Indoctrination, not education, made communism the cornerstone of national culture. Those who took control of states from Poland to Cuba and from Albania to North Korea made ideology the strongest centripetal force.

Communist states were walled off (literally in some instances) from the rest of the world, and when cracks opened in those walls, communist ideology alone was not enough to withstand the flow of ideas from the outside world. This situation underscores that one of

From the Field Notes

❝ The king of Thailand personifies the state, is above politics, and performs the key functions of leadership to bind his sometimes fractious country. His image is everywhere in view, in poses ranging from the formal to the casual, and in costumes ranging from the regal to the informal. When you leave the grounds of Bangkok's Grand Palace, there is the king, his likeness protected by a gold-embroidered umbrella. ❞

used by a substantial percentage of the population and will be regarded generally as part of the national culture. Low mobility, on the other hand, reinforces the separateness imposed by different languages.

Centrifugal Forces

All states confront divisive, or **centrifugal forces**. When these centrifugal forces outweigh the centripetal ones, the state will collapse. In recent times we have witnessed the disintegration of the world's largest colonial empires, including, in the late 1980s, the Soviet Union. We have seen the collapse of Yugoslavia, where a quasi-federal system failed to withstand the forces of division. Czechoslovakia has broken up into two countries. Cyprus is divided; Eritrea has separated from Ethiopia. In the late twentieth century, centrifugal forces seem to be on the rampage.

In the concluding chapter of this book we consider several of the forces that are splintering states, even older European states that should serve as models of durability. For the moment, we should note that geography itself is a powerful factor: regionalism and real or perceived regional inequality are strong centrifugal forces. When, in multicultural states, regionalism marks religious or linguistic or other cultural contrast, the threat to state and nation is enhanced.

the most significant of all nation-building factors is best summarized by the term *circulation*. When a population is mobile, moving to and from various parts of a country and diffusing national norms in the process, regionalism and separatism decline. Stagnant, isolated, dis-

affected regions in a state are potentially divisive. Integration with the nation as a whole through effective circulation and communication systems reduces this threat. In a multilingual country, circulation enhances the likelihood that each language will be known and

POWER RELATIONSHIPS

Just as some states are large and others small, some rich and others poor, and some developed while others are underdeveloped, so there are powerful states and weak states. Measuring the relative **power** of states is a complex and imprecise business best left to political scientists who specialize in **power**

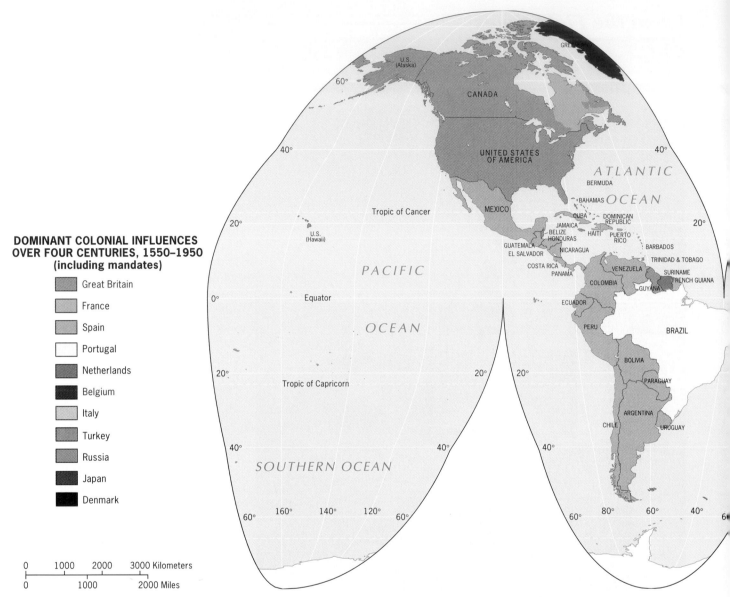

DOMINANT COLONIAL INFLUENCES OVER FOUR CENTURIES, 1550–1950 (including mandates)

- Great Britain
- France
- Spain
- Portugal
- Netherlands
- Belgium
- Italy
- Turkey
- Russia
- Japan
- Denmark

FIGURE 38–4 Many areas of the world were under more than one colonial power. This map depicts the *dominant* colonial imprint over the four-century period 1550–1950.

analysis. There can be no doubt, however, that a state's power—however it is measured—relates directly to its capacity for organization.

In his book *The Might of Nations* (1961), J. G. Stoessinger defines power as "the capacity of a nation to use its tangible and intangible resources in such a way as to affect the behavior of other nations." Again, this does not mean solely or even primarily by military presence or threat; rather, it involves possess-ing and producing in economic spheres. A state can win conces-sions or reciprocal agreements with other states through its economic strength. It can outbid other states in the competition for exploitation rights in the territories of less-devel-oped countries by being able to offer superior conditions. Growth and development require organiza-tion, and organization generates power.

The might of imperial nations, as we noted earlier, projected Euro-pean power into the non-European world. The height of European **colonialism** came during the eigh-teenth and nineteenth centuries, when the British, French, Spanish, Portuguese, Dutch, and Belgians consolidated their holdings (the Germans and Italians were compar-ative latecomers on the colonial scene). (Fig. 38-4). Spain and Portu-gal lost their American possessions even before the Berlin Conference laid out the colonial map of Africa, and early in the twentieth century it

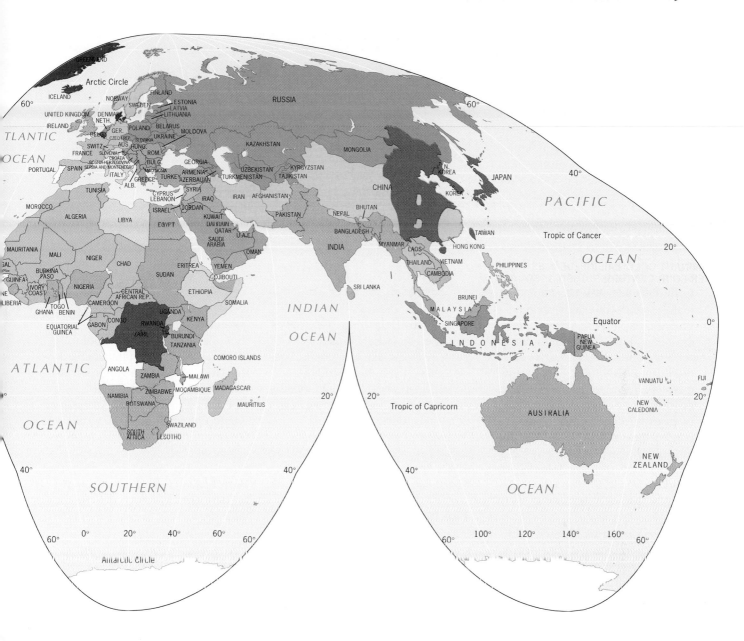

was evident that small European countries would not be able to control large, distant empires forever.

Elsewhere in the world, two other colonial powers built major empires: Russia and Japan. The Russian empire was vast and, unlike others, contiguous: only in what is today Alaska did Russia acquire an "overseas" domain—sold in 1867 to the United States. Japan came late to the colonial stage, but in a few decades seized major holdings in East Asia.

The colonial powers were able to gain control over their empires

by virtue of their economic, political, and military organization; when that organization failed, they lost their advantage. Russia's internal weaknesses were exposed by the losses in its Far East (Japan decisively defeated the Russian armies in 1905). But during the heyday of colonialism, the imperial powers exercised ruthless control over their domains and organized them for maximum exploitation. The capacity to install the infrastructures necessary for such efficient profiteering is itself evidence of the power relationships involved: entire

populations were regimented in the service of the colonial ruler. Systems of raw-material flow were instituted for the benefit of the colonial power, and the tangible evidence (mines, railroads, ports, plantations) is still on the map. Moreover, these economic systems have survived decolonization. Raw-material flow is much as it was before the colonial era came to an end. And while the former colonies are now independent states, the influence of their former rulers continues in many, notably in the former French empire.

GEOPOLITICS

Just as economic, cultural, and urban geographers have attempted to recognize general principles governing locational behavior and processes in their subfields, political geographers have sought to understand the complex political world. The first political geographer who studied the state and its power relationships in detail was Friedrich Ratzel (1844–1904), with a particular emphasis on the behavioral dynamics of states. He postulated that the state resembles a biological organism whose life cycle extends from birth through the attainment of maturity and, ultimately, degeneration and expiration. To prolong its existence, Ratzel argued, the state requires nourishment, just as an organism needs food. Such nourishment is equivalent to the periodic acquisition of a less powerful competitor's territory and its cultural contents. Confine a state within permanent and static boundaries and deprive it of overseas domains, argued Ratzel, and it will inevitably atrophy. Space is the state's essential, life-giving force.

Ratzel's **organic theory** held that a nation, being constituted by an aggregate of organisms (human beings), would itself function and behave as an organism. This idea constituted an extreme form of the environmental determinism that was to dominate human geography for decades to come, but it was so speculative that it would probably have soon been forgotten—except for its conversion into a subfield of political geography called **geopolitics**. Some of Ratzel's students translated his abstract writings into practical national policies, and this lineage led directly to the Nazi expansionist philosophies of the 1930s. One of Hitler's associates was a political geographer named Karl Haushofer, who had learned his geopolitics in the school of which Ratzel was the unwitting founder.

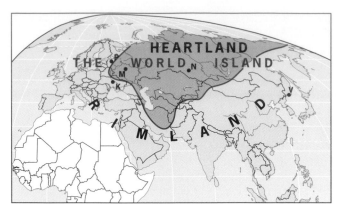

FIGURE 38–5 Eurasia = "World Island" divided into Heartland and Rimland.

For some decades following World War II, the term "geopolitics" remained so closely linked to its perverted past that few political geographers, even those studying power relationships, would identify themselves as students of geopolitics. Time, along with more balanced perspectives, has reinstated geopolitics as an appropriate rubric for the study of power relationships past, present, and future.

The Heartland Theory

Ratzel was not alone as a political geographer in late-nineteenth-century Europe, although his was undoubtedly the most conceptual orientation. Other geographers trying to find order in the class of Europe's modern evolution were more specific, relating their conclusions to the fortunes of existing states. Prominent among these practical political geographers was Sir Halford Mackinder (1861–1947), who, in 1904, published an article entitled "The Geographical Pivot of History" in the Royal Geographical Society's *Geographical Journal*—an article that became one of the most intensely debated geographic publications of all time.

Mackinder, too, was concerned with power relationships, at a time when Britain had acquired a global empire through its primacy on the oceans. To many of his contemporaries, the oceans—avenues of colonial conquest—formed the key to world domination, but not to Mackinder. He carefully weighed the prospects for the various contenders and concluded that a land-based power, not a sea power, would ultimately rule the world. His famous article contained a lengthy appraisal of the largest and most populous landmass on Earth, at the heart of which, he argued, lay an impregnable, resource-rich "pivot area" extending from Eastern Europe to eastern Siberia (Fig. 38-5). This would become the base for world conquest, and the key to it, Mackinder asserted, was Eastern Europe.

Mackinder later renamed his "pivot area" the *heartland*, and his notion became known as the **heartland theory**. In his book *Democratic Ideals and Reality* (1919) he stated the theory as follows:

Who rules East Europe commands the Heartland
Who rules the Heartland commands the World Island
Who rules the World Island commands the World

When Mackinder proposed his heartland theory, there was little to presage the rise of a superpower in the heartland. Russia was in disarray, losing a war against Japan and facing revolution. Eastern Europe was fractured politico-geographically. Germany, not Russia, was ascending. But when the Soviet Union succeeded tsarist Russia and the Second World War bequeathed Moscow with control over much of Eastern Europe, the heartland theory drew renewed attention.

Not all political geographers agreed with Mackinder regarding his inventory and assessment of the heartland. One of Mackinder's critics, Nicholas Spykman, coined a geographic term more than 50 years ago that is still in use today: **rimland**. Spykman argued that the Eurasian rim, not its heart, held the key to global power. In a book entitled *The Geography of the Peace* (1944) Spykman parodied Mackinder:

Who controls the Rimland rules
   Eurasia
Who rules Eurasia controls the
   destinies of the world

As Figure 38-5 shows, the rimland is a zone of much political-geographical fragmentation, unlikely to fall under the sway of one superpower as the heartland might. Spykman, who was more of a pragmatist than a theorist, saw a divided rimland as a key to the world's balance of power. Today, the rimland is still divided, but a significant part of it forms the stage for the rise of a future superpower: China.

A Multipolar World—Again?
We return in Chapter 40 to the topic of global geopolitics, but it is appropriate here to reflect on the evolving power relationships that will shape the twenty-first-century world. When Mackinder foresaw a world dominated by a single superpower, that notion, too, was revolutionary. The nineteenth century had produced (or was in the process of producing) a substantial

number of states aspiring to global influence: Britain (correctly, the United Kingdom), France, recently unified Germany, imperial Russia, the emerging United States, and colonializing Japan among them. This was a world of many power poles, a *multipolar* world soon engulfed in a global war (1914–1918) and then another (1939–1945). The First World War was global as a result of the colonial empires of the combatants; German and Allied forces fought battles in East Africa and elsewhere. The Second World War was global for additional reasons: it spilled southward and eastward beyond the confines of Europe, and it involved the United States and Japan.

Out of the Second World War came two newly strengthened powers, the United States and the Soviet Union, and several diminished older powers based in a devastated Europe, losing their colonies, and in political and economic disarray. While the United States aided Europe through its Marshall Plan and Japan through its enlightened postwar administration, no European or Asian power regained its former status. In the aftermath of the Second World War there were two clear superpowers, a *bipolar* world divided into capitalist and communist camps. The Soviet Union dominated almost all of the heartland as Mackinder had defined it. The United States proved that Mackinder had underestimated the capacities of the world beyond his "world island" Eurasia.

In the mid-1990s, following the disintegration of the Soviet Union, the United States found itself the surviving superpower, but constrained by the unprecedented worldwide diffusion of weapons, including nuclear weapons. Briefly after the Second World War, the United States, which used nuclear bombs to end that conflict, was alone in possession of the armaments that could have endowed it

with global supremacy. Today, after the collapse of the Soviet Union in 1991, the United States again is the dominant force in world affairs. But again this dominance is likely to be short-lived, because the outlines of a new multipolar world are forming.

What are these outlines? Both Mackinder and Spykman might claim vindication: a multipolar world in which the heartland *and* the rimland are represented by power cores. The potential superpowers on the "world island" are (1) Russia, in disarray following the collapse of communism but still in possession of an enormous military complex and major resources; (2) Europe, if this fractious realm can find a way to sustain its drive toward integration and unification; (3) China, the rimland power now energized by the spectacular economic growth of its eastern provinces; and (4) the United States, facing China across a Pacific that has become a highway of trade and diffusion. And so, the world to some degree resembles that of Mackinder's time, an unstable multipolar world with much potential for conflict.

KEY TERMS

Capital City
Centrifugal Force
Centripetal Force
Colonialism
Core Area
Electoral Geography
Federal State
Forward Capital
Geopolitics
Gerrymander
Heartland Theory
Ministate
Nationalism
Organic Theory
Power
Power Analysis
Rimland
Unitary State

39

MULTINATIONALISM
ON THE MAP

Ours is a world of contradictions. On television we see Quebecers demand independence from Canada even as Canada joins the United States in NAFTA (North American Free Trade Agreement). At a soccer game in Scotland, fans drown out "God Save the Queen" with a thunderous rendition of "Flower of Scotland," while the British Parliament in London debates the European Union (EU). We are reminded at every turn of the interconnectedness of nations, states, regions, and realms of our world, and yet people seem intent on separatism and autonomy. In the 1990s we appear to be in a race between forces of division and forces of unification.

In this chapter we look at the positive side: the progress made in various spheres of unification. Hardly a country exists today that is not involved in some multinational association. There is ample proof that such association is advantageous to the partners and that being left out can have serious negative effects on state and nation.

Geographica

- **Supranational unions range from global organizations such as the United Nations and its predecessor, the League of Nations, to regional associations such as the European Union; all signify the failure of the state system to satisfy national needs.**

- **The imposition of international sanctions and the mobilization of peacekeeping operations are among the crucial functions of the United Nations; today, the UN is active militarily in more than a dozen countries.**

- **The United Nations has channeled the extension of national claims over the high seas; the UN Law of the Sea is one of the organization's leading achievements.**

- **Among many regional multinational associations, the European Union is the most complex and advanced; its 15 member states are likely to be joined by others within a decade.**

- **Economic, military, cultural, and political forces underpin the frameworks of more than 60 major international organizations in this final decade of the twentieth century; economic prosperity and a shared military threat are the strongest factors promoting international cooperation.**

SUPRANATIONALISM

The phenomenon of interstate cooperation is quite old (in the days of ancient Greece, city-states formed leagues to protect and promote common advantage, a practice imitated many centuries later by the cities of Europe's Hanseatic League), but the degree to which this idea has taken root in the modern world is unprecedented. The twentieth century has witnessed the establishment of numerous international associations in political, economic, cultural, and military spheres, and the term **supranationalism** defines this phenomenon. Technically, supranationalism refers to efforts by *three* or more states to forge associations for common advantage and in pursuit of common goals. Today, some 60 major supranational organizations exist, many consisting of subsidiaries that bring the total to more than 100. The more states are enmeshed in such multilateral associations, the less likely are they to act unilaterally, that is, alone and in pursuit of a self-interest that might put them at odds with neighbors.

International Sanctions

These days we hear a great deal about **international sanctions** to induce states to change their behavior. Sanctions are designed to isolate a country that behaves in a way deemed inappropriate by the international community, and such isolation can be very costly. Sanctions against South Africa, for example, were implemented to speed the end of that country's minority government *apartheid* policies. Foreign firms left South Africa; foreign investment almost dried up. How much the sanctions contributed to the ending of *apartheid* is still debated, but of their impact on the economy there is no doubt. When the government of Haiti defied international demands for the reinstatement of its democratically elected president, sanctions were imposed. When North Korea defied international inspection of its nuclear programs, sanctions were threatened. For sanctions to succeed, international agreement is needed, and such

agreement is itself a manifestation of supranationalism at work.

FROM LEAGUE TO UNITED NATIONS

The modern beginnings of the supranational movement came with the conferences that followed the end of World War I. The concept of an international organization that would include all the states of the world became a flawed reality in 1919 with the creation of the **League of Nations**; the United States, however, was among the countries that did not join this organization. In all, 63 states participated in the League, although the total membership at any single time never reached that figure. Costa Rica and Brazil left the League even before 1930; Germany departed in 1933, shortly before the Soviet Union joined in 1934. The League was born of a worldwide desire to repudiate any future aggressor, but the failure of the United States to join dealt the organization a severe blow. Then, in the mid-1930s, the League had its big opportunity to stand on principle when Ethiopia's Haile Selassie made a dramatic appeal for help in the face of an invasion by Italy, a member state until 1937. However, the League failed to take action, and, in the chaos of the beginning of World War II, it collapsed.

Nonetheless, the interwar period witnessed significant progress in the domain of interstate cooperation. The League of Nations spawned other international organizations; a prominent one was the Permanent Court of International Justice, created to adjudicate legal issues between states, such as boundary disputes and fishing rights.

The League of Nations also initiated international negotiations on a matter that was to become critical in the second half of the twentieth century: maritime boundaries and

related aspects of the law of the sea. The conferences organized by the League laid groundwork that proved to be indispensable when, decades later, the states of the world convened once more to address this pressing problem.

THE UNITED NATIONS ORGANIZATION

After the end of World War II, the international community once again formed an organization designed to foster international security and cooperation: the **United Nations**. Just as the United Nations in many ways was a renewal of the League of Nations, so its International Court of Justice succeeded the Permanent Court of the interwar period.

The representation of countries in the United Nations has been more universal than that of the League (Fig. 39-1). A handful of states, for various reasons, did not belong to the United Nations in the mid-1990s, but the admission of the People's Republic of China in 1971 gave the organization unprecedented constituency; in 1995, the United Nations had 185 member states. The UN's General Assembly and Security Council, the newsmaking units, have overshadowed the cooperative efforts of numerous less visible but enormously productive subsidiaries, such as the FAO (Food and Agriculture Organization), UNESCO (United Nations Educational, Social, and Cultural Organization), and WHO (World Health Organization). Membership in these organizations is less complete than in the parent body, but their work has been of benefit to all humankind.

Participation in the United Nations also serves the useful purpose of committing states to standards of behavior endorsed by

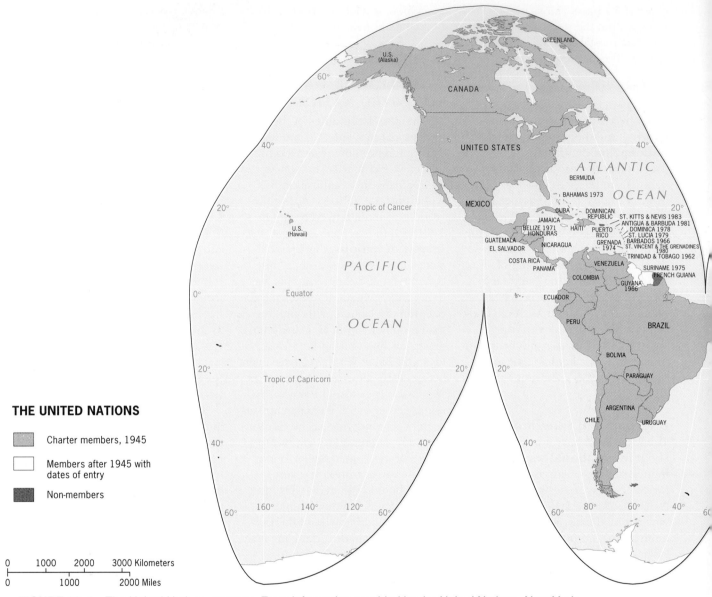

THE UNITED NATIONS

Charter members, 1945

Members after 1945 with dates of entry

Non-members

0   1000   2000   3000 Kilometers

0   1000   2000 Miles

FIGURE 39–1   The United Nations. SOURCE: From information provided by the United Nations, New York.

the international community. Many states still violate these standards, embodied in the UN Charter, but such violations can lead to collective action, for example, in the cases of South Africa, Iraq, and North Korea recently. It is noteworthy that states, even when censured or subjected to UN-sponsored military action, do not withdraw from the organization. Membership is too valuable to lose; thus national governments develop an understanding of the advantages of international cooperation.

PEACEKEEPING OPERATIONS

The United Nations is not a world government, and member states participate voluntarily in the organization. Although member states do not yield any sovereignty to the UN, they may agree to abide by specific UN decisions, for example, those made by the International Court of Justice or those involving the law of the sea. In recent years, individual states have also asked the United Nations to intervene in internal conflicts, to monitor elections, and to provide for refugees.

Among these (and numerous other) functions, peacekeeping has become a costly and controversial UN responsibility. The United Nations does not have its own armed force; any UN army or police

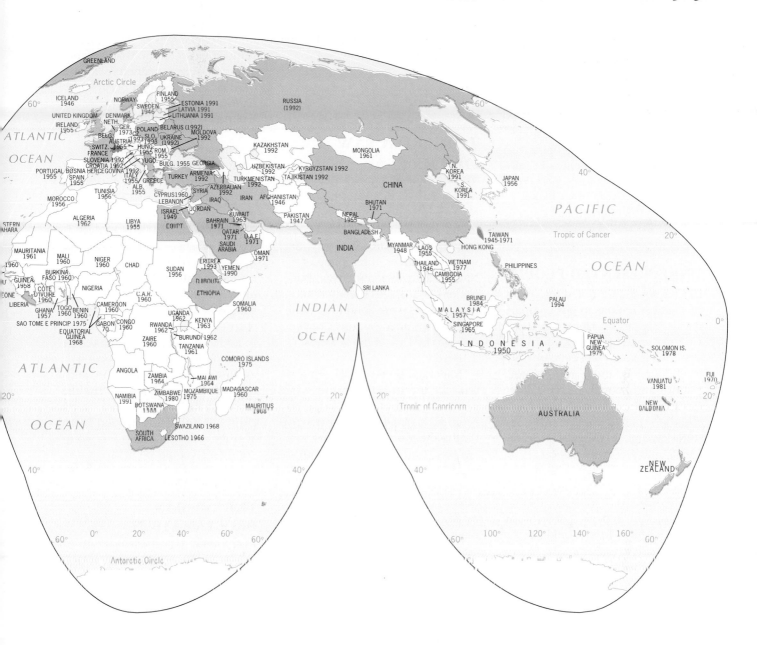

force consists of soldiers assigned to UN duty by member states. This situation can lead to disputes over leadership. A multinational UN army consists of national forces, each commanded by its own officers. These officers, however, are under the command of a UN-appointed general. Disagreements over tactics may lead to unilateral action by individual officers in contravention of the UN command. When a UN force consisting of United States, Pakistani, and Italian soldiers attempted to alleviate hun-

ger in Somalia, the mission changed from humanitarian to political—and there were costly disagreements over tactics that led to many casualties among the UN peacekeepers. During 1994 and 1995, UN **peacekeeping operations** faced their most difficult challenge in the former Yugoslavia, where a civil war among Serbs, Croats, and Muslims, chiefly in Bosnia, defied UN efforts to relieve the crisis. Eventually, a fragmented UN force of more than 20,000 peacekeepers found itself in an untenable position, its members

attacked and even taken hostage, and the mission failed.

Author's Video Link
↓
④
"Somalia"

Despite these problems, the United Nations' peacekeeping role has continued to grow, and its successes have far outweighed its failures. In early 1995, more than

70,000 peacekeepers from some 70 UN member states served in Angola, Bosnia, Cyprus, El Salvador, Georgia, Haiti, Kashmir, Lebanon, Liberia, Macedonia, various parts of the Middle East, Rwanda, and Western Sahara. Considering the small size of most UN peacekeeping contingents and the enormity of their tasks, the organization's peacekeeping function constitutes a major benefit to the international community.

UNREPRESENTED PEOPLES

In Chapter 37, we noted the plight of stateless nations in our compartmentalized world. Here, too, the United Nations provides a forum and thus relieves tensions. In 1991, the UN created the Unrepresented Nations and Peoples Organization (UNPO), which by 1995 had 43 members and 17 applicants. Four former members (Armenia, Estonia, Latvia, and Georgia), having achieved full UN membership, no longer needed UNPO's help.

The roster of UNPO membership, and the appeals that arrive at UNPO's offices from would-be members, form a barometer of the world's political condition. Albanians in Greece, Tatars of the Crimea, Ogoni in Nigeria, the Ka Lahui Hawai'i (Hawai'i's indigenous nation seeking a stronger voice), North Dakota's Lakota Nation, Abkhazians in Georgia, Tibetans under China's rule, Zanzibaris hoping for independence from Tanzania, Basques in Spain, and dozens of other peoples seeking some form of redress, approach UNPO for assistance.

To be sure, UNPO cannot by itself solve the problems of stateless or otherwise "unheard" peoples, but it can and does provide them a platform. In addition, UNPO ensures that appeals from its members, applicants, and others are channeled to appropriate agencies and not lost in the UN bureaucracy. In so doing, UNPO already has cleared up misunderstandings and

has forestalled conflict, another major contribution to the world's stability.

TOWARD A LAW OF THE SEA

Another arena in which the United Nations has accomplished much lies in the establishment of a comprehensive **law of the sea** treaty. As we noted earlier, the League of Nations actually led the way, but under UN auspices the international negotiations were continued until, in 1982, a United Nations Convention on the Law of the Sea was achieved.

National claims to adjacent waters (the **territorial sea**) are centuries old and originated in Europe. An Italian legal scholar active during the fourteenth century is credited with the first formal proposal that states should be awarded sovereignty over a strip of water next to their coastlines; this proposal led to a lengthy legal debate over the width of that offshore zone. Among various suggestions was one holding that this width should be determined by the distance a shore-based cannon could fire a cannonball; once within cannon-shot range, a ship would be in territorial waters.

Not surprisingly (given the lack of international coordination), various states chose different widths. Western European countries liked a 3-mile territorial sea (maritime distances are measured in *nautical miles*; about 1.15 statute mile equals 1 nautical mile). Scandinavian countries preferred 4 nautical miles. Mediterranean states chose a 6-mile limit to sovereignty.

Some countries during the sixteenth and seventeenth centuries tried to broaden their maritime jurisdictions by closing off large bays with *baselines* and by claiming fishing grounds far from shore. But

until the meetings of the League of Nations between the world wars, territorial seas remained relatively narrow, and the open oceans remained open or, to use the technical language, remained "high seas."

The League did get a hint of what lay ahead. The Soviet Union proposed widening the territorial sea to an unheard-of 12 nautical miles, which would mean that many straits could be closed off by the littoral states and bays up to 24 miles wide could be closed as well. And the matter of delimitation—exactly how maritime boundaries should be constructed on the map—also received much attention. In addition, participating states expressed the need for protection against smuggling, pollution, and other threats from the sea (not the least of which was concern over security). But then the Second World War intervened, and no follow-up conference could be held.

THE TRUMAN PROCLAMATION

Even before the newly formed United Nations could address these issues again, a critical event occurred. In September 1945, President Truman issued two proclamations. The first of these stated that the United States would henceforth regulate fisheries' activities in areas of the high seas adjacent to its coastlines, but that in other respects, these maritime regions would continue to function as free and open high seas. The second proclamation had much greater impact. It announced, in part, that

the Government of the United States regards the natural resources of the subsoil and seabed of the continental shelf beneath the high seas but contiguous to the coasts of the United States as appertaining to the United States, subject to its jurisdiction and control. . . .

The **Truman Proclamation**, as this pronouncement has since become known, specified that United States jurisdiction over the continental shelf and its contents would be limited to the region within the 600-foot *isobath* (line connecting points of equal depth). It also reconfirmed that the high seas above the continental shelf would remain open.

The Truman Proclamation focused world attention on the potential of the continental shelves, and it also served to underscore the unequal allocation of shelf areas among the world's coastal countries. With its large eastern continental shelf, the United States gained more than 2.5 million square kilometers (900,000 square miles) of offshore territory. Neighboring Mexico, which shares the continental shelf off North America with the United States, was among the better-endowed countries, and it immediately followed the Truman example by claiming this region. Next Argentina announced, in 1946, that it claimed not only its wide continental shelf but also the waters lying above it. This was a significant step, because it closed an enormous area of high seas and made them territorial waters instead.

WIDENING MARITIME CLAIMS

States without extensive continental shelves now began to follow Argentina's example, claiming as much as 200 miles of territorial sea. In 1947, Chile and Peru took the lead, proclaiming that their seaward boundaries henceforth lay 200 miles into the Pacific Ocean. This had the effect of closing the rich fishing grounds of the Humboldt (Peru) Current to the ships of countries other than Chile and Peru, and soon Peru confirmed its primacy in its new maritime sphere by arresting fishing vessels and fining the companies and countries where they were based.

Thus the economic motive has been the driving force behind the maritime expansion of coastal states, and undoubtedly the era of decolonization played its role in complicating the situation as well. Countries that had long suffered colonial occupation and had been forced to adhere to colonial stipulations could make their own decisions after independence. Not unnaturally, many of them concluded that if narrow territorial waters were advantageous to the colonial powers, then wider territorial seas would serve their own interests better. They were encouraged in this by the former Soviet Union and by China, both countries claiming 12 miles when 3 miles was still the general rule.

THE UNCLOS PROCESS

This was the chaotic situation faced by the first United Nations Conference on the Law of the Sea (UNCLOS I) when it convened in 1958, and, although some technical matters were resolved during this meeting, key issues, such as the width of the territorial sea and the exclusive use of fishing grounds, remained unsettled. UNCLOS II met just 2 years later and it, too, was unsuccessful. But then came UNCLOS III, beginning in 1973 and ending in 1982 with a convention opposed by only four countries (the United States among them) and signed by 157 states within 2 years of its completion. While the United Nations had not yet established an enforceable law of the sea, it had created a consensus on what that law should contain. The key provisions were the following:

1. *The Territorial Sea.* The convention permits states to delimit their territorial seas up to 12 nautical miles (just under 14 statute miles) from their shorelines. State sovereignty in all its forms extends over this zone. Ships of other flags, however, have the

right of innocent passage through such territorial seas, so that narrow straits remain open to transit.

2. *The Exclusive Economic Zone (EEZ).* The convention recognizes a state's economic rights up to 200 nautical miles (just over 230 statute miles) from shore. Here the coastal state has the right to control exploration and exploitation of natural resources in the water, seabed, and subsoil below. All resources—fish, minerals on the seafloor, oil in the continental shelf—are the property of the coastal state and may be used or sold to foreign interests. If the continental shelf extends beyond 200 nautical miles from shore, the coastal state has exclusive rights to the resources it contains up to 350 nautical miles (400 statute miles) away.

Another provision, this one having to do with the remaining high seas and what lies beneath them, caused the United States not to sign or ratify the UNCLOS III Treaty. According to this clause, mineral resources beneath the high seas constitute a "common heritage of humankind," and their exploitation is subject to UN management. The notion behind this clause, in part, was to give some benefit of the Earth's marine resources to states without any coasts at all (the world's landlocked states are part of a UN group called the "Geographically Disadvantaged States"). The United States and three other countries opined that a UN bureaucracy set up for this purpose might inhibit exploitation of such deep-sea resources by the only countries that could actually mine them, the technologically advanced states.

The United States during the (Democratic) Carter administration played a leading role in UNCLOS III, but the convention was not completed until the (Republican)

FIGURE 39–2 The 200-mile EEZ dramatically reduces the Earth's high seas. SOURCE: Based on a map prepared by the Office of the Geographer of the U.S. Department of State, 1980.

Reagan administration had taken over in Washington. The new administration decided against ratifying the treaty, which cannot become law until 1 year after 60 states have ratified it. Following the installation of the Clinton (Democratic) administration, the prospect of ratification improved, and in June 1994, following modification of the seabed provision, the treaty was accepted.

MEDIAN LINES

Although the UNCLOS III Treaty is not yet an instrument of international law, its provisions have been generally adopted in international relations. Figure 39-2 shows the effect of the 200-mile EEZ on the high seas: huge expanses of ocean have been assigned to coastal countries, some of them mere specks of islands.

What happens when countries lie closer than 400 nautical miles to each other, so that neither can have a full 200-mile EEZ? In such cases (for example, in the Caribbean,

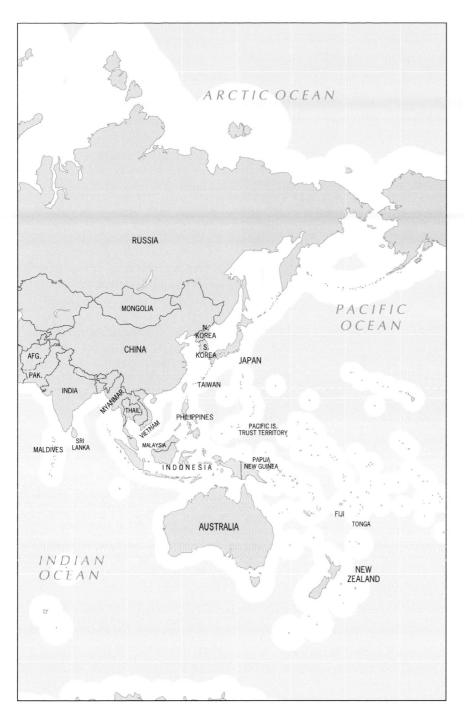

North, Baltic, and Mediterranean Seas) the **median-line principle** takes effect. States on opposite coasts divide the waters separating them, creating an intricate system of maritime geometric boundaries. Often such boundaries cross resource-rich zones, for example, in the North Sea between Norway and Britain, and allocational boundary disputes may follow.

The effect of EEZ delimitations and median-line calculations can be seen on a map of Southeast Asia (Fig. 39-3), which also reminds us that the UNCLOS III Treaty may represent broad consensus but cannot prevent disputes. The South China Sea, in particular, is a problematic maritime region. The black line shows China's share of the South China Sea based on its possession of numerous small islands there, including the Paracels. The red line represents China's published claims to the region, based on "historic" association with it. One key geographic element is the Spratly Islands, potentially oil rich and claimed by China and no fewer than *five* other states!

This type of problem, however, is the exception, not the rule. The UN-sponsored conferences that led to the 1982 treaty rank among the great achievements in international

From the Field Notes

❝ As we sailed from the port of Invergordon, Scotland, we could see a row of oil-drilling platforms under construction, in repair, or being towed out into the North Sea. The shallow, oil- and gas-rich North Sea subsoil has made it necessary to divide this maritime region through median lines. The wealth of energy resources off the Scottish coast has been a factor in the rise of Scottish nationalism and notions of greater autonomy or even independence. ❞

diplomacy and stand as an example of what can be accomplished when states choose to cooperate for the common good.

REGIONAL MULTINATIONAL UNIONS

The League of Nations and the United Nations constitute global manifestations of a twentieth-century phenomenon that is expressed even more strongly at the regional level. This century has been a period of cross-national ideologies, growing cultural-regional awareness and assertiveness, and intensifying economic competition. States have begun to join together to further their shared political ideologies, their economic objectives, and their strategic goals. In 1995, about 60 such **multinational unions** existed, many of them with subsidiaries designed to focus on particular issues or areas. Today, interstate cooperation is so widespread around the world that a new era has clearly arrived.

The first major experiments in interstate cooperation were undertaken in Europe, with the three small Low Countries—the Netherlands, Belgium, and Luxembourg—leading the way. It had long been thought that all three might benefit from mutual agreements that would reduce the divisiveness of their po-litical boundaries. Certainly, they have much in common. Residents of northwestern Belgium speak Flemish, a language very close to Dutch, and residents of Luxembourg speak French, as do those of southeastern Belgium. Even more importantly, these countries have considerable economic complementarity. Dutch farm products sell widely on Belgian markets, and Belgian industrial goods go to the Netherlands and Luxembourg. Would it not be reasonable to create common tariffs, to eliminate import licenses and quotas? Representatives of **Benelux** (as the organization came to be called) thought so, and even before the end of World War II they met in London to sign an agreement of cooperation. Other European countries watched the experiment with great interest, and soon there was talk of larger, more comprehensive economic unions.

This movement proved to be crucial to the reconstruction of early postwar Europe, and it was given an enormous boost in 1947 when U.S. Secretary of State George Marshall proposed that the United States finance a European recovery program. A committee representing 16 Western European states plus (then) West Germany presented the U.S. Congress with a joint program for economic rehabilitation, and Congress approved it. From 1948 to 1952, the United States gave Europe about $12 billion under what became known as the Marshall Plan. This investment not only revived European national economies, it also constituted a crucial push toward international cooperation among European states.

TOWARD EUROPEAN UNION

Out of that original committee of 16 was born the Organization for European Economic Cooperation

FIGURE 39–3 The potential for conflict over maritime claims in the seas of Southeast Asia remains strong. SOURCE: From U.N., U.S., and Chinese maps as well as press reports.

(OEEC), and this body in turn gave rise to other cooperative organizations. Soon after the OEEC was established, France proposed the creation of a European Coal and Steel Community (ECSC), with the principal objective of lifting the restrictions and obstacles that impeded the flow of coal, iron ore, and steel among the mainland's six primary producers: France, (then) West Germany, Italy, and the three Benelux countries. This proposal was also implemented, but the six participants did not stop there.

Gradually, through negotiations and agreement, they enlarged their sphere of cooperation to include reductions and even eliminations of certain tariffs and a freer flow of labor, capital, and nonsteel commodities. This led, in 1958, to the creation of the European Economic Community (EEC), also called the **Common Market**.

The success of the EEC induced other countries to apply for membership. The United Kingdom (which had initially declined to participate and formed EFTA, the European Free Trade Agreement), Denmark, and Ireland joined in 1973, Greece in 1981, and Spain and Portugal in 1986. The organization became known as the **European Community** (EC) because it was envisaged not only as an economic union but, in effect, as a future United States of Europe. Eventually, the EC reached a membership of 12: the three giants (Germany, France, and the United Kingdom); the four southern countries (Italy, Spain, Portugal, and Greece); and the five small states (the Netherlands, Belgium, Luxembourg, Denmark, and Ireland). These 12 EC members initiated a concerted program of cooperation and unification that would lead, in 1992, to the formal establishment of a **European Union**.

Author's Video Link
↓
7
"European Union"

This program involved the yielding of power and authority by the member states to the Union's central authority, and not all member countries were equally supportive of it. One major stumbling block had to do with money: if the European Union were to have a single currency, other currencies would eventually have to be abandoned.

Imagine France without its franc, the United Kingdom without its pound, Germany without a mark! Many voters in the constituent countries were reluctant to let go of such national symbols; others did not wish to see their national parliaments subservient to that of the European Union. But the program of unification continued, and the European Union evolved into something far beyond what the original Benelux members had envisioned.

EUROPEAN SUPRANATIONALISM'S FUTURE

The gestation of the European Union is the most significant development of its kind in the world today. It is a process of considerable difficulty in which the projected advantages cannot be attained by sometimes painful adjustments within the participant states. For example, agricultural practices and policies have always varied widely (just imagine the contrasts between Portuguese and Dutch farming). Yet some general policy must govern agriculture throughout the European Union if the Community is to have real meaning. Individual states have found these adjustments problematic, and the EU parliament has had to devise policies that accommodate regional contrasts and delays in implementation.

Another concern relates to the dominance of Germany in the European Union. Germany is by far the most populous and most productive of the Union states, and will undoubtedly dominate Union politics as well. Memories of two world wars and fears of German preponderance are among potential centrifugal forces in the European Union. For all its convergence, the Union still, and for a very long time to come, will be a patchwork of

states with ethnic traditions and histories of conflict and competition. Economic success and growing well-being tend to submerge such differences, but should the European Union face difficult economic or social times, these divisive forces will again emerge.

Such concerns have created strong division over EU membership in the United Kingdom. Whereas other countries have held referendums allowing all eligible citizens to vote on participation (Denmark at first voted no, then yes in a second round), the issue has not been put to a vote in Britain. Polls suggest that British voters would turn down EU membership, but the government has decided to let the people's representatives in Parliament choose. There, EU membership enjoys majority support, but the Conservative government of the early 1990s failed to represent British interests adequately in the evolving Union. As a result, the EU prospect has divided rather than united the population of what should be one of the Union's powerful and effective cornerstones.

Expansion

Still another problematic issue relates to the desire on the part of many countries to join the Union at some future time. As long as these potential members are economically strong and politically stable, no insurmountable difficulties loom. But as the EU expands eastward, perhaps some day to incorporate such states as Slovakia and Bulgaria and possibly Turkey, there will be powerful strains on the organization.

In late 1994, four states voted on membership: Austria, Finland, Sweden, and Norway. In the first three, voters approved of entry into the European Union. But in Norway, a substantial majority opposed membership in the EU. Norway's citizens apparently felt that they might lose control over their North Sea oil and gas resources and over their lucra-

From the Field Notes

❝ No place in Europe displays the flag of the European Union as liberally as does the City of Maastricht, where the European Union Treaty of 1991 was signed. The flag, seen here at City Hall, shows twelve yellow stars (representing the signatories to the Treaty) against a blue background. Although three additional states joined the EU in 1995, and others may join later, the flag will remain as is, and will not, as the U.S. flag does, change to reflect changing times. ❞

tive fishing grounds. These assets, polls revealed, gave Norwegians confidence that membership in the EU would not enhance their economic prospects. On January 1, 1995, therefore, The Twelve became The Fifteen (Fig. 39-4).

Already, other would-be members are knocking on the EU's door. Poland, the Czech Republic, Slovakia, Hungary, Romania, and Bulgaria have announced their intention to seek membership, and other Eastern European states are

likely to follow their lead. Under the rules of the EU, the richer countries must subsidize the poorer ones, and the entry of Eastern European states will add to the burden which this rule imposes on the wealthier Western and Northern European members. But an even more difficult problem will involve Turkey. Several Western European countries would like to see Turkey join the EU, thereby widening the organization's reach into the Muslim world. Turkey has indicated its interest in joining, but a referendum in Greece showed that more than 90 percent of voters there are opposed to Turkey's admission. Other EU members expressed concern over Turkey's human rights record, specifically its treatment of the Kurdish minority, which would not meet the standards set by the Union.

Even as the debate over expansion goes on, the very center of the EU is being buffeted by other stresses. Many of the goals set optimistically in Maastricht in 1992 are proving to be elusive; enthusiasm for the Union is fading in key countries, notably France. But progress toward supranational goals tends to be cyclic. Visions of a political United States of Europe may be sustained by the maturing of a European Parliament and the anointing of a European capital (Brussels or Strasbourg), but the engine of European unification is fueled by economics. When economic times are good, supranationalism flourishes. And until recently, Europe (especially the old EEC countries) prospered. When times became more difficult, so did the path toward further integration.

SUPRANATIONALISM ELSEWHERE

The great supranational experiment of our time is the European Union, but the notion of international asso-

FIGURE 39–4   European supranationlism. SOURCE: From a map in H. J. de Blij and P. O. Muller, *Geography: Realms, Regions, and Concepts,* 7th ed. (New York: Wiley, 1994), p. 68.

ciation for mutual benefit is a worldwide phenomenon. As we noted earlier, the EU evolved from *economic* common ground to embrace other objectives. Economic prospects lay behind the formation of the original North American Free Trade Agreement (NAFTA), formal-ized on January 1, 1994 to join Canada, the United States, and Mexico in an economic community. Before the year was out, Chile had been invited to join, and NAFTA became an outdated acronym. The goals of its successor, the Free Trade Agreement of the Americas (FTAA) however, are far more modest than those of the EU. The lowering and eventual elimination of trade barriers is but one of the many goals of EU; the free flow of labor, a common currency, and a common agricultural policy are others. FTAA has no comparable financial or political dimensions; and it does not look forward to an FTAA parliament or a single monetary unit.

Nevertheless, the Americas today form an action sphere of supranationalism. The majority of the Caribbean island-states, with Belize in Middle America and Guyana in South America, are linked in the Caribbean Community (CARICOM), an evolving common market in the region. In 1995, CARICOM was growing into an organization called the Association of Caribbean States (ACS), which incorporated not just Belize and Guyana but all interested states around the Caribbean perimeter. Also developing is the Central American Common Market, with seven members extending from Guatemala to Panama.

In South America, two major supranational groups are maturing: the Andean Group and the Southern Cone Community Market (MERCOSUR). The Andean Group links Venezuela, Colombia, Ecuador, Peru, and Bolivia. Shared economic objectives are the key; open markets are the mechanism. MERCOSUR consists of giant Brazil, powerful Argentina, comparatively prosperous Uruguay, and underdeveloped Paraguay. Chile and Bolivia may join MERCOSUR, which is on track to become a full-fledged customs union early in the twenty-first century.

Economic objectives also were key in the formation of ECOWAS, the Economic Community of West African States. With far fewer assets and many more liabilities than most multinational organizations, ECOWAS nevertheless supports economic cooperation and integration, joint development efforts, and a reduction in tariff and other barriers in West Africa generally. ECOWAS played an important role in 1990, when Liberia was engulfed in civil war. Several West African states organized and sent a multinational peacekeeping force to

Liberia, and thus helped end this costly conflict.

So numerous are the various economic unions that they clearly represent a new and apparently permanent force on the world map. From APEC (Asia-Pacific Economic Council) to CIS (Commonwealth of Independent States, a Russian attempt to integrate its former colonies), countries are joining, treaties are being drawn up, and new associations are emerging. Not all these alliances are successful, of course; OPEC, the cartel of oil exporting states, has lost the advantages it once held. But economic supranationalism is a sign of the times, a grand experiment still in progress.

OTHER FORMS OF SUPRANATIONALISM

Economic motives are in the forefront of supranational cooperation, but these are not the only bases for international association. Often, the formation of one supranational union stimulates the creation of another (either a rival or a cooperative one). The development of economic supranationalism in Europe was paralleled by the formation of a **military alliance**, the North Atlantic Treaty Organization (NATO). This, in turn, led to the creation of the communist Warsaw Treaty, which combined the USSR and its Eastern European satellites into an opposing military alliance. Today, the Warsaw Treaty is defunct, and NATO faces demands from formerly communist East European countries for inclusion or, at least, for some form of association. Like economic unions, military alliances come and go. Among those no longer extant are the Baghdad Pact, a Western-oriented alliance based on Middle Eastern conditions that no longer exist, and SEATO (Southeast Asia Treaty Organization), also a victim of changing national policies.

Military alliances are especially significant because they normally require member states to allow foreign participant forces the reciprocal use of bases and facilities, which involves a certain surrender of sovereignty in the common interest. This is a more consequential dimension of current trends toward supranationalism even than economic cooperation; military forces symbolize power and intrusion, and their presence on allied soil, even in a common cause, can easily raise sensitivities.

Other supranational organizations are based on *cultural* objectives, although the distinction between cultural and political goals is sometimes blurred. The Organization of African Unity (OAU) is often cited as a cultural alliance to promote shared African goals and to mitigate intra-African disputes, but the OAU also has had very clear political objectives (among which was the ending of *apartheid* in South Africa). Most African states are members of the OAU. Another **cultural organization** with political overtones is the Arab League, a multinational alliance of Muslim states in the geographic realm of North Africa and Southwest Asia, founded in 1945 and still a major force in regional affairs.

Some supranational organizations are primarily *political* in nature; Europe's Parliament is the political manifestation of this Union's overall unification effort. Without economic underpinnings, though, **political unions** tend to be short-lived or inconsequential. The Commonwealth of Nations (successor to the British Commonwealth) is little more than a relic of Britain's imperial past, a discussion group, its economic benefits weakened by the United Kingdom's involvement in the European Union. The French Community also has lost much of its political (if not cultural) relevance. The Federation of the West Indies is long forgotten.

Nothing in the political arena matches the economic unions functioning today.

The many manifestations of supranationalism all point to one important reality: the individual state no longer meets the requirements imposed on its people in modern times. We still recognize the state as the highest manifestation of politico-geographical organization; international interaction at the highest level means at the national level. All over the world, however, states are joining supranationalism unions of various kinds to further their aims, economic, strategic, or other. This reflects a loss of confidence in the state as the bastion of security and prosperity. Has the state system run its course, and will something else replace it? It is too early to tell, but on the answer depends the shape of the coming New World Order.

KEY TERMS

Benelux	Median-Line Principle
Common Market	Military Alliance
Cultural Organization	Multinational Union
European Community	Peacekeeping Operation
European Union	Political Union
Exclusive Economic Zone (EEZ)	Supranationalism
International Sanctions	Territorial Sea
Law of the Sea	Truman Proclamation
League of Nations	United Nations

40

POLITICAL GEOGRAPHY AND A NEW WORLD ORDER

As the twentieth century draws to a close, consider how the world has changed since 1900: its human population has quadrupled; hundreds of thousands of species of animals and plants have become extinct; two World Wars have been fought; weapons of mass destruction have been invented; colonial empires have collapsed; the United States has risen to superpower status; the great communist experiment of the Soviet Union has failed; Europe has unified; Japan has achieved economic dominance; the Pacific Rim has emerged as a new force in world affairs. Add to these developments the countless breakthroughs in science (notably the beginning of space travel) and medicine, and it is no exaggeration to say that the past century has seen our world transformed.

But what has happened to the world of political geography? During the 1990s, consequent to the breakdown of the Soviet Union and the end of the bipolar world we had known for so long, there was optimistic talk of a **New World**

Geographica

- **Devolution, the process of state disintegration along regional lines, afflicts a growing number of countries old and young, large and small, developed and underdeveloped.**

- **Visions of local or regional autonomy, notions of democracy and participation, and concepts of religious fundamentalism are changing the map of the modern world.**

- **The changing world today is burdened by a weakening state system and an antiquated boundary framework.**

- **A New World Order is in the making following the end of the Cold War, but its geographic outlines cannot yet be discerned; it is likely to involve a multipolar rather than a bipolar configuration.**

Order, a world in which the balance of nuclear terror between two superpowers would no longer determine the destinies of states. This New World Order would be shaped by forces that interconnect nations and states, by supranational blocs that balance the power of major powers, by multinational action should any state violate rules of communal conduct. The risks of nuclear war would recede, and negotiation, not confrontation, would mitigate any geopolitical crisis that might arise. When Iraq was driven out of Kuwait by a UN coalition of states led by the United States in 1991, the framework of a New World Order seemed visible. Russia, which a few years earlier might have led the Soviet Union in support of Iraq, endorsed the UN operation. Arab as well as non-Arab forces helped repel the Iraqi invaders.

Soon, however, doubts and uncertainties began to cloud hopes for a New World Order. Although the states of the world were more closely linked to each other than ever before, national self-interest still proved to be a powerful centrifugal force. For all its faults, the state remained the critical building block in the new global framework. Yet states may vary too widely to serve this purpose: not only do they range enormously in size, population, economic development, culture, and traditions, but they also differ in terms of degree of democracy, treatment of minorities, respect for human rights, and in many other ways. Even as these diverse states tried to join their interests in supranational unions, individual ones among them collapsed in chaos. As we noted earlier, ours is a world of contradictions.

DEVOLUTION

The number of states in the world today is approaching 200, and an astonishingly large number of these states are afflicted by internal centrifugal forces so strong as to endanger their future, if not immediately, then over the long term. The counterforce to supranationalism is **devolution**, the process through which regions or peoples within states demand and gain strength and sometimes **autonomy** at the expense of the center, through negotiation or active rebellion. Devolution is affecting many countries in the world today, destabilizing regional political frameworks from Europe to Southeast Asia and from South America to Africa. As long as devolutionary

forces threaten the very states that must form the building blocks of the New World Order, no such order will be attainable.

DEVOLUTION IN EUROPE

We might assume that devolutionary forces are strongest in youthful states, recently decolonized countries where ethnic or other centrifugal strains remain strong. In fact, devolution is buffeting older as well as younger states, larger as well as smaller ones. For example, it presently affects several states in Europe, including the United Kingdom (Fig. 40-1). In the United Kingdom, the revival of regional separatism is something of a geographic irony. The United Kingdom functions as a unitary state, but it consists of four geographic entities: England, Wales, Scotland, and Northern Ireland. The most populous, powerful, and dominant entity, of course, is England, the British Isles' historic core area. The English conquered Wales in the Middle Ages, and Scotland was politically tied to England during the seventeenth century. Ireland was also acquired, but after a very difficult colonial occupation, the Irish achieved independence in 1921—except Northern Ireland, a substantially Protestant corner of the overwhelmingly Catholic island, which remained part of the United Kingdom (Fig. 40-1).

Time has failed to submerge **regionalism** in the United Kingdom, notwithstanding the results (in terms of development) of the Industrial Revolution and the period of empire and comparative wealth. During the 1960s and 1970s, London was forced to confront a virtual civil war in Northern Ireland, as well as a rising tide of separatism in Scotland and Wales. Scottish and Welsh nationalism proved to be potent forces in British politics, and the government responded by giving the nationalists the opportunity

to vote in favor of their own assemblies with (initially) limited legislative and executive powers. This would, in effect, have moved the United Kingdom toward a federal form of organization, but in 1979, that proposal was defeated (on a technicality in Scotland, where a majority *did* vote in favor of it). This had the effect of keeping separatists and their opponents on a collision course, and the devolution process in Britain is far from over.

Author's Video Link
↓
4
"Scotland"

The emergence and strength of regionalism in the United Kingdom, one of Europe's most durable states, underscores the potential impact of devolution elsewhere. In light of what we have learned about Europe's efforts to unify, Figure 40-1 comes as something of a shock: three of the original Common Market countries are subject today to devolutionary stresses! The following summary reflects Europe's devolutionary problems.

1. *Yugoslavia.* The breakup of Yugoslavia was the great human tragedy of Europe in the second half of the twentieth century. Long-dormant, long-contained centrifugal forces broke apart a multinational, multicultural state that had survived seven decades of turmoil and war. Yugoslavia ("Land of the South Slavs") lay between the Adriatic Sea to the west and Romania to the east, and between Austria and Hungary to the north and Bulgaria and Greece to the south. This was a country thrown together on maps after World War I, a land of 7 major and 17 smaller eth-

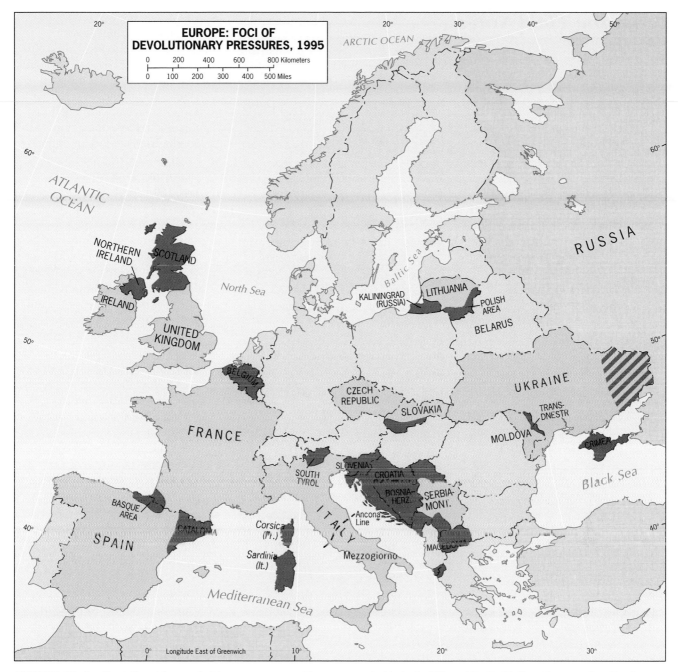

FIGURE 40–1 Centrifugal forces in Europe. SOURCE: From a map in H. J. de Blij and P. O. Muller, *Geography: Realms, Regions, and Concepts*, 7th ed. (New York: Wiley, 1994), p. 68.

nic and cultural groups. The north, where Slovenes and Croats prevailed, was Roman Catholic; the south, Serbian Orthodox. Several million Muslims lived in Christian-surrounded enclaves. Two alphabets were in use.

No Yugoslav nation existed except in the legal sense. This was a zone of ancient animosities first held together by the Royal House of Serbia and later by communist dictatorship personified by one man, the war hero Marshal Tito. But when they got the chance, the Yugoslavs fought each other:

Nazi-supporting Croats against anti-Hitler Serbs during World War II, Muslims against non-Muslims after the communist system collapsed. Here in what used to be Yugoslavia, people think of themselves first and foremost as Serbs, Croats, Slovenes, Muslims, Macedonians,

From the Field Notes

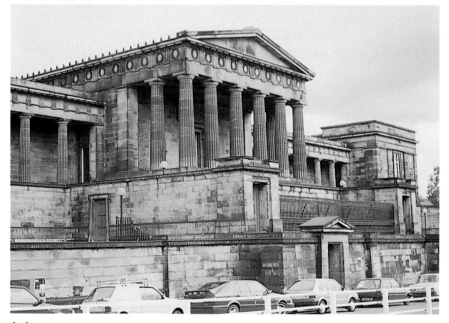

❝ The people in the kiosk were busy gathering signatures and funds in support of their campaign to promote Scottish independence. They told me that the gray, rather drab building nearby looked 'beautiful' to them; this would be the Assembly Hall, seat of the first modern Scottish parliament should their drive succeed. It was peaceful devolution in progress. ❞

or members of other, smaller cultural groups.

As a result, Yugoslavia is no more. When the communists ruled the country, they divided it into six internal "republics" on the Soviet model, each dominated (except Bosnia) by one major group. Now these republics are independent countries and we must learn the outlines of a new map still taking shape. Out of the collapse of Yugoslavia have come the newly recognized states of Slovenia, Croatia, Bosnia, Serbia-Montenegro (called Yugoslavia by diehard Serbs), and Macedonia (whose independence and name, also that of a Greek province, impelled the Greeks to close their port of Salonika to Macedonian traffic).

In early 1995, the tragedy of devolving Yugoslavia was centered in Bosnia. As Figure 40-1 shows, Bosnia's spatial morphology is triangular, with one of its points just barely touching the sea; for all intents and purposes, Bosnia is landlocked. Internally, about 44 percent of Bosnia's population of 4.4 million is Muslim; 31 percent adhere to the Serbian Orthodox Church and are culturally Serbs; 17 percent are culturally Croats and follow the Croatian Catholic Church. In the civil war, Muslim Bosnians and Catholic Croats together fought against the Bosnian Serbs, who were aided directly and indirectly by the Serbs in Serbia proper (capital Belgrade). When a stalemate occurred in late 1994, the Serbs had gained supremacy over about 70 percent of Bosnia, and the Muslims were in the majority over a fragmented territory west of their capital, Sarajevo. More than 20,000 United Nations peacekeeping soldiers were unable to stem the tide of conflict.

And the list of casualties arising from Yugoslavia's disintegration may grow longer still. Potential problems exist in Hungarian-dominated Vojvodina in Serbia's north and in Muslim-majority Kosovo in the south. The ultimate outcome of Yugoslavia's collapse is far from clear.

2. *Albania.* Although Albania's population is dominantly ethnic Albanian (and 70 percent Muslim), the country's southeastern corner is inhabited by a substantial Greek minority. Greek irredentism in the region has intensified during the breakdown of order in the former Yugoslavia, and Albania's Greek minority has responded by seeking greater autonomy.

3. **Greece.** While Greece may not confront a risk of fragmentation, and while more than 95 percent of Greece's more than 10 million are of Greek ancestry, the country's minorities are regionally concentrated in the west and in the proruption toward Turkey in the east. In the border area where Greece meets Albania and Macedonia, ethnic and cultural problems prevail. Tens of thousands of Albanians have spilled over the boundary into Greece, and ethnic Greeks, as noted, form a small but significant minority in southern Albania. Albania is a dominantly Muslim state, and Greece has a long history of conflict with Muslim Turks to the east. Add to this the Greek opposition to an independent state named Macedonia, and the potential exists for geopolitical conflict here. Ever since the civil war in the former Yugoslavia began, there has been fear that this conflict would spill over into Albania, Macedonia, and Greece, and might possibly involve the Turks. That risk has not yet been eliminated.

4. **Spain.** Another European state attempting to adjust to strong regional forces is Spain, where demands for local autonomy have not been confined to the Basque province of Vascongadas. In 1979, the Spanish government signed autonomy agreements with leaders of the Basque region and the northeastern province of Catalonia, giving both areas their own parliaments, recognizing their languages as equal to Spanish and establishing their official status, and transferring powers of local taxation and education. However, these measures did not satisfy the more extreme of the independence-seeking Basques, whose intermittent campaign of terrorism continued into the mid-1990s.

5. **Italy.** A less publicized but persistent movement demands autonomy for the neighboring island of Sardinia, which is part of Italy. And Italy faces another secessionist movement in South Tyrol, where Austria, Switzerland, and Italy meet. Tyrol is an embattled area whose historic ethnic-political problems gave rise to the term **irredentism**. The area occupied by Italian Tyrol's German minority was, from neighboring Austria's viewpoint, *terra irredenta*, "land unredeemed." Austria actively supported the Tyrolean Germans in their aspirations to autonomy, an irredentist policy practiced by many governments and nations since. Today, in the new Europe of which Italy is (and Austria hopes to be) a part, Austria's support for the South Tyroleans is muted. But the Tyroleans themselves have not abandoned their secessionist hopes. Another devolutionary force may ultimately affect Italy far more severely: the growing regional disparity between north and south. The poorer, lagging Mezzogiorno lies across the Ancona Line (an imaginary border extending from Rome to the Adriatic coast at the city of Ancona) from the richer, politically much more conservative north. The potential for fragmentation is rising.

6. **Belgium.** Earlier we noted Belgium's language schism: 6 million northerners (in the region of Flanders) speak Flemish, a derivative of Dutch, while 4 million southerners (in the region of Wallonia) speak French. A small minority of Belgians along the eastern border speak German. This linguistic partition is also a historic and a cultural one, and even the economic landscape changes across it. Belgium has long felt the strains of devolution, although the country came into existence as a kingdom and thus a unitary state. But in 1970 the Belgians adopted a system they called "federalization without federalism," creating four language-based regions (including multilingual Brussels). The system never worked well, and by the 1990s Flanders was a hotbed of separatism and political conservatism, adding still more distance to relationships with Wallonia. Belgium, a founding member of Benelux and the original EEC, and now a charter member of the EU, may not survive the century in one piece.

7. **France.** Even France, the model nation-state, has not escaped the forces of devolution. As we noted in Chapter 38, France has superimposed a framework of 22 province-level regions on its 96 *départements* as part of a major decentralization of government control from Paris. These regions have their own governing councils with considerable autonomy. All this, however, has not been enough to subdue a separatist movement in one of these regions, the island of Corsica.

8. **Slovakia.** The fragmentation of former Czechoslovakia into two states, the Czech Republic and Slovakia, may not signal the end of the devolutionary process here. A large Hungar-

ian minority along Slovakia's southern boundary, comprising more than 11 percent of the state's population, has separatist tendencies and is subject to Hungarian irredentism.

From the Field Notes

❝ This monument to the struggle for independence stands in the capital of Latvia, Riga. My visit was a learning experience as a large demonstration nearby displayed not only written signs denouncing lingering Russian influence in Latvia, but also maps that equated Latvia with internal Russian republics such as Karelia and Chechnya. ❞

9. **Lithuania.** Although the issue is not in the forefront as Lithuania moves forward from Soviet "republic" to independent, democratic state, the small country's ethnic mix has a regional dimension. The capital, Vilnius, lies in its southeastern, "Polish" corner. A potential for separatism also exists in the Russian exclave of Kaliningrad.

10. **Moldova.** About 65% of the population of the former Soviet republic of Moldavia (now named Moldova) is ethnic Romanian, but 14 percent is Ukrainian and 13 percent is Russian. The Russian minority is concentrated in a strip of land between the Dnestr River and the eastern border, and there a secessionist movement has developed with a "Trans-Dnestr Republic" as its devolutionary goal.

11. **Ukraine.** More than 22 percent of Ukraine's 52 million inhabitants are Russians, and most of this large Russian minority is concentrated in the Crimea Peninsula. This peninsula was transferred from Russian to Ukrainian authority by Soviet decree in 1954, when there was no prospect of Ukrainian sovereignty. The events of the late 1980s and early 1990s created just such a situation, leaving more than 10 million Russians under Ukrainian government. Strong devolutionary pressures exist here, and Crimean secession or reabsorption by Russia may lie ahead.

DEVOLUTION OF THE SOVIET UNION

The late 1980s witnessed an explosion of centrifugal forces in the former Soviet Union, then still one of the world's two superpowers. The transition from old-style communist domination to a more open, flexible society was made possible by Mikhail Gorbachev, who succeeded the last of the dogmatists, Konstantin Chernenko, in 1985 as general secretary of the Communist party, then the USSR's most powerful political post. He moved the society toward greater openness (*glasnost*) and restructuring (*perestroika*) and made possible the end of Soviet domination over Eastern Europe. The consequences abroad were far-reaching: the Berlin Wall, symbol of communist oppression, came down, communist-ruled East Germany was freed and reunited with West Germany, and communist parties from Poland to Bulgaria lost their primacy.

The most consequential developments, however, occurred in the Soviet Union itself. Devolutionary forces grew rapidly throughout the empire, and the component parts of the devolving Soviet Union (on paper a federal state but in fact ruled as a unitary entity) asserted their independence (Fig. 40-2). For a time, Gorbachev tried to channel these forces toward a new union structure that would combine elements of the old as well as the new, but events spun out of his (and his party's) control. As the republics of the USSR organized their own internal elections and voted new leaders into office, the Soviet Union became irrelevant and the proposed new Union was not a satisfactory substitute.

As individual Soviet republics declared their independence, the end of the Soviet Union (and communist empire) grew nearer. In December 1991 the Russian Republic's leader, Boris Yeltsin, sought to replace the USSR with a voluntary supranational entity called the Commonwealth of Independent States (CIS). The headquarters of this organization would be in Mensk (capital of Belarus) to balance Moscow's supremacy. After some initial hesitation, all but the

three Baltic states and Georgia joined the CIS (and Georgia was later forced to join after Russia helped it end a civil war). But when the Soviet flag was lowered for the last time on Christmas Day 1991, the CIS was but a skeleton organization to replace what had been a cohesive empire.

The process of devolution did not stop here. While the 15 Soviet republics had become independent states, each of them also confronted centrifugal forces arising from ethnic, historic, cultural, and economic circumstances. Few geographers believed that the hastily constructed Commonwealth of Independent States would withstand these divisive pressures. But more ominously, the individual republics faced economic hard times while trying to adjust politically. Large ethnic Russian minorities remained in each republic, as did armed forces, including Russian soldiers. Minorities that had been exiled by communist dictators demanded to be allowed to return home—where others had taken their homes and land. Old animosities between ethnic groups surged to the surface. Soon, Muslim Azerbaijan and Christian Armenia, both in the region called Transcaucasia (between the Black and Caspian Seas), were in a state of armed conflict.

The Near-Abroad

The presence of as many as 25 million Russians in the former Soviet Republics along Russia's rim, combined with political instability and even armed conflict there, created a sphere of involvement the Russians came to call their **Near-Abroad**. The implication of the term is that Russia's national interest extends throughout the former Soviet empire, and Russia has given substance to that notion by intervening in several countries of its Near-Abroad. In Georgia, like Azerbaijan and Armenia a part of the Transcaucasian region, a political

crisis soon after independence led to a civil war. Even as this conflict raged, a separatist movement seized the opportunity in the internal "republic" of Abkhazia in Georgia's northwest to proclaim independence. In the costly and bitter struggle that followed, Georgia's government was compelled to ask for Russian help. This help came at a price: a permanent Russian military presence on Georgian soil.

Not only the Transcaucasus but also Turkestan produced reasons for Russian intervention. In the republics of the former Soviet Central Asia (this region is again called Turkestan, its pre-Soviet name), Russian interests were challenged on several fronts. The most serious crisis arose in Tajikistan, where Russian forces sustained considerable losses trying to protect a pro-Russian government against insurgents from across the border in Afghanistan.

The international community has appeared to recognize Russia's primacy in the Near-Abroad, in part because Moscow's problems there were caused by the Soviet communists whose system the Russians have rejected. The Soviet planners had bequeathed their enormous realm not only with an economic system doomed to failure, but also with a political framework destined to collapse. Boundaries were superimposed on a complex cultural landscape, and the friction these boundaries would create was ruthlessly suppressed. Within Russia itself, 16 so-called Autonomous Soviet Socialist Republics had been designed to give territorial embodiment to minorities—but only *some* minorities (Fig. 40-2). As times changed, and economic development occurred, population shifts took place. The Soviet national planners in Moscow kept modifying the system, sometimes on the whim of the incumbent dictator. Boundaries were shifted to reward, to punish, to control. Boundaries that

FIGURE 40–2 Devolution of the Soviet Union. SOURCE: From a map in H. J. de Blij and P. O. Muller, *Geography: Realms, Regions, and Concepts*, 7th ed. (New York: Wiley, 1994), pp. 136–137.

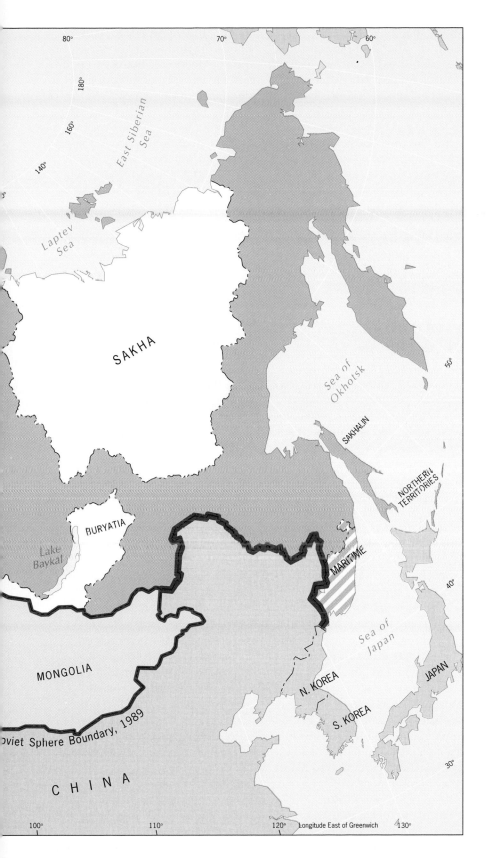

Author's Video Link
6
"Year in Review 1994"

should have been established (for example, between the Russian Kazakh parts of Kazakhstan) were not. The Soviets left their empire with a politico-geographic legacy that will prove problematic—and worse—for generations to come.

Devolution of Russia

Not only the Near-Abroad, but also Russia itself was burdened by a political-geographic system that was bound to present difficulties for the new democratic government in Moscow. Soon after the Russian tricolor replaced the Soviet hammer and sickle above the Kremlin, leaders of the internal "republics" began to demand more autonomy, more control over their "own" resources and facilities, and, in some instances, more territory. When the Soviet Union was dissolved, there were 16 such republics within Russia, but immediately other entities announced their demand for similar status. Within 4 years, the Russian Parliament had agreed to recognize five additional republics (one, Chechno-Ingushetia, fragmented into two republics, Chechnya and Ingushetia). In late 1993, when President Yeltsin dissolved the Parliament and precipitated a violent confrontation in Moscow, two additional republics demanded recognition (see Fig. 40-2 for the location of these).

The map suggests one reason for the strength of devolutionary forces in Russia: the country's vastness and the isolation of many of its population clusters. One of the two "proclaimed" republics, the Maritime Republic, lies centered on the Pacific port of Vladivostok; local sentiment is that the bureaucrats in

Moscow are inhibiting the Russian Far East from participating in the economic opportunities arising from Pacific Rim development. Greater autonomy is seen as the solution.

When the Russian federation was formalized, some of its internal republics refused initially to acknowledge their place in the new system. Tatarstan, with a substantial Muslim population and located amid a cluster of republics east of Moscow, at first demanded a status equal to that of republics outside Russia in the Near-Abroad, such as newly independent Latvia, Moldova, and Uzbekistan.

Eventually, the Tatar Republic yielded to Moscow's pressure, but a more serious problem arose in a more difficult geographic region: on the flanks of Transcaucasia, farther from Moscow and less well integrated into the Russian core. After the Republic of Chechno-Ingushetia split in two, the new Republic of Chechnya declared its independence and asserted that it would not be governed from Moscow. For nearly three years Moscow, preoccupied with other problems, failed to act in response. But in late 1994, after intermittent negotiations had failed, Russian forces entered Chechnya in order to impose Moscow's authority. It was a fateful moment: there was opposition to this action in Moscow and in the Russian armed forces as well as in Chechnya, whose Muslim population had suffered severely at Russian and Soviet hands over nearly two centuries. The extent to which this crisis would affect Russian federalism and democracy remained uncertain in early 1995, but as evidence of devolutionary pressures, Chechnya was Russia's most serious challenge.

While notions of independence drive nationalism in the realm's republics, large and small, and ethnic tensions long suppressed now explode in conflict, the geographic reality is that the ex-Soviet republics need each other economically. Even giant Russia cannot go it alone: it needs food and raw materials from its neighbors (especially Ukraine), and it needs nearby markets for its products (oil and natural gas are two of its most valuable exports). Ukraine could become a self-sufficient country, but not Belarus, Turkmenistan, or Armenia. When the apparently inevitable strife in the aftermath of the Soviet empire ebbs, this geographic reality will still be there. Then, perhaps, a new multinational state will rise from the ashes of the old.

DEVOLUTION IN THE AMERICAS

If devolutionary forces can afflict old European nation-states, no state is immune. All three of the largest states in the Americas—Canada, the United States, and Brazil—are experiencing devolution in the 1990s.

The case of Canada undoubtedly is the most consequential, and here the process has gone furthest. At issue is the relationship between Canada's largest province, dominantly French-speaking Quebec, and the federation's other nine provinces.

Modern, prosperous Canada would seem to have it all: a vast territory (only Russia is larger), a wealth of resources, a small, slow-growing population, a modern economy with high incomes by world standards, and a carefully balanced, federal system of government that should be able to accommodate the regionalisms its huge area may stimulate. Canada's provinces are accustomed to a degree of autonomy of which Russian republics could only dream. And yet Canada in recent years has come to the brink of disintegration.

Canada is a **plural society**, a society consisting of more than one ethnic and/or cultural group, and includes people with British, French, Native American, Eastern European, and other ancestries. But the key division is between English- and French-speaking "nations." Under the British North America Act of 1867 (which established the Canadian federation), Ontario and Quebec became the two key provinces of a still-expanding union (Fig. 40-3). Ontario ("Upper Canada") was the British core area; Quebec ("Lower Canada") was French Canada. Quebec was given important guarantees: the French civil code of law was left unchanged, and the French language was protected in Parliament and in the courts.

Author's Video Link
↓
❷
"Quebec"

Time has not submerged the differences between French and British Canada. Polls indicate that Quebecers regard themselves as second-class citizens in their own country, that bilingualism means that French speakers have to learn English but not vice versa, and that Quebec is not getting its share of the wealth of Canada. In the 1980s, matters came to a head; to stave off a crisis, Quebec was asked to present its terms for continued membership in the Canadian federation. Its key demand was recognition as a "distinct society" within Canada.

Although the prime ministers of all of Canada's 10 provinces agreed to Quebec's terms, the parliaments of two provinces failed to ratify that agreement. Quebec had reason to feel rejected, and demands for a referendum on secession arose immediately.

In the meantime, ethnic issues in Quebec, especially those involving language, reached unprecedented intensity. More than 85 percent of

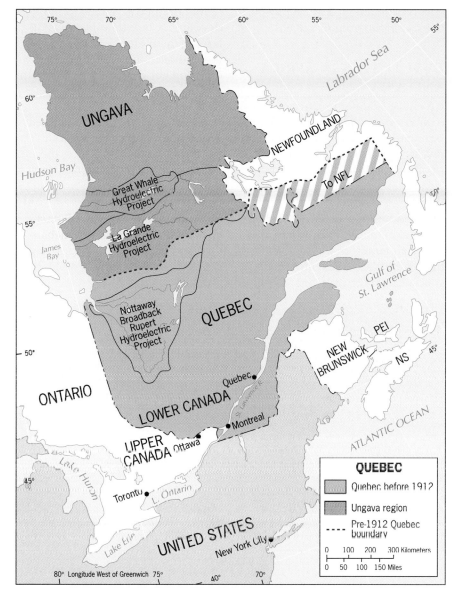

FIGURE 40–3 Quebec: secession ahead? SOURCE: From a map in H. J. de Blij and P. O. Muller, *Geography: Realms, Regions, and Concepts*, 7th ed. (New York: Wiley, 1994), p. 257.

reconsidered the costs of bilingualism. If English could be treated as it was within Quebec, should French be accorded its rightful equality under the law in, say, Alberta or Saskatchewan?

In the mid-1990s, the devolution of Canada remains possible, despite the fact that Quebec's role and position in the federation, compared to that of so many minorities in so many countries of the world has been very favorable. On average, people in Quebec earn nearly as much as Canadians nationwide. Quebecans have served as federal prime ministers for 30 of the past 44 years. Few, if any, countries have been as diligent in enforcing bilingualism in their schools and agencies. Quebec's grievances have been heard and have been resolved, from unfair taxation to proportional appropriation. It has not been enough to ward off divisive forces that may yet fracture the federation.

Devolutionary Pressures on the United States

The United States has not experienced devolutionary forces of the kind now affecting Canada, but this country is not immune. It is not inconceivable that the interests of States in the West (notably the Northwest) might diverge from those of the East, where national power may still be concentrated. Occasionally, the notion of a "Cascadia," consisting of Oregon, Washington, and the Canadian province of British Columbia, comes to public notice through the press.

The first real brush with devolution, however, may come in the State of Hawai'i. When, in early 1993, the hundred-year anniversary of the U.S. annexation of Hawai'i was commemorated, a vocal minority of native Hawai'ians and their sympathizers demanded the return of land rights lost during the "occupation." These demands included

Quebec's more than 7 million people speak French at home, but that still leaves a substantial minority of non-French speakers. In 1977, the Quebec Parliament passed a law that compelled all business in the province to demonstrate that they functioned in French. This led to an exodus of businesses and individuals to Ontario. Canada's Supreme Court ruled against Quebec's language legislation, but this ruling only emboldened the provincial lawmakers. In 1988, Quebec enacted a law that not only reinstated the legislation the Supreme Court had invalidated, but added a regulation that made it illegal to exhibit any outdoor commercial sign in a language other than French within the entire province of Quebec.

Predictably, such actions caused counterreactions elsewhere in Canada. With fewer than 700,000 French-speaking Canadians living outside Quebec, other provinces

the right to reestablish a Hawai'ian state (Hawai'i before the annexation was a Polynesian kingdom ruled, at the time, by Queen Liliuokalani) on several smaller islands of the archipelago. Ultimately, the island of Kauai would become a component of this parallel Hawai'ian state, or at least a significant part of that island deemed to be ancestral land.

At present, the native Hawai'ians do not have the numbers, resources, or influence to achieve their secessionist aims. There is potential, however, for a separation between Hawai'i and mainland United States. The political geographer S. B. Cohen theorizes that political entities situated in border zones between geopolitical power cores may become **gateway states**, absorbing and assimilating diverse cultures and traditions and emerging as new entities, no longer dominated by one or the other. Hawai'i, he suggests, is a candidate.

Author's Video Link
↓
2
"Puerto Rico"

Brazil

In South America, Brazil is experiencing its first impact of devolutionary forces in modern times. Brazil's "European" south in many ways resembles South America's southern cone (Uruguay, Argentina, and Chile) rather than the bulk of this tropical, Afro-Lusitanian country. A still-small but vocal separatist movement has formed in Brazil's three southernmost States of Rio Grande do Sul, Santa Catarina, and Parana. Driven by disregard for the allegedly corrupt and inefficient government in Brasília, leaders of the southern independence movement argue that their three territories possess the population, resources, and infrastructure to enable the formation of

a viable country at least as prosperous as neighboring Uruguay.

DEVOLUTION IN AFRICA AND ASIA

Given the manner in which colonial realms were acquired, the way boundaries were defined (or ill defined), and the custom of moving people around to suit imperial objectives, it is remarkable that devolutionary forces have not sundered more ex-colonial states than they have. One of Africa's most costly experiences with devolution, the Biafra secessionist movement, was successfully overcome by Nige-

ria (where, today, a new form of devolution, based on religious differences, threatens). Those geographers and others who predicted major changes in the African and Asian boundary frameworks were wrong.

Devolution, nevertheless, threatens a number of states on both landmasses today. In Africa, the most powerful devolutionary fault line parallels the Muslim front that crosses the continent from West Africa to Somalia. Not only Nigeria but other states in this zone are threatened; in the Horn of Africa, devolution is changing the map (Fig. 40-4).

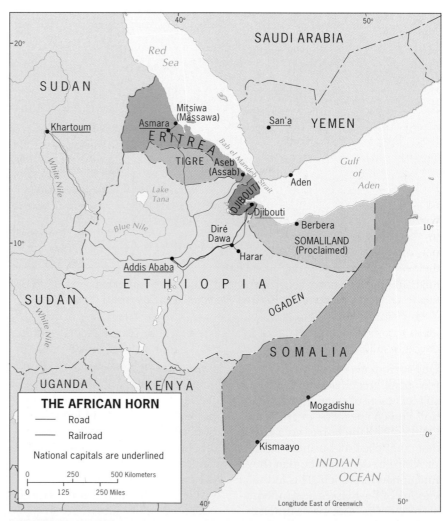

FIGURE 40–4 Africa's Changing Horn. SOURCE: From a map in H. J. de Blij and P. O. Muller, *Geography: Realms, Regions, and Concepts*, 7th ed. (New York: Wiley, 1994), p. 468.

In Ethiopia, a long and costly civil war ended with the secession of the newly independent state of Eritrea. As the map shows, the independence of Muslim Eritrea from Christian Ethiopia has significant spatial consequences: Ethiopia, the region's giant (population: 56 million) is landlocked as a result. Ethiopia now must use either Djibouti or the ports of its secessionist neighbor for international trade, a situation that contains the seeds of future conflict. Also note the Ethiopian province of Tigre outlined in Figure 40-4. Tigre mounted its own separatist campaign during the war, and the politico-geographical future of Ethiopia is not yet secure.

Author's Video Link
↓
③
"Ethiopia's Geopolitics"

The map also shows two Somali states: Somalia and Somaliland. While the state of Somalia officially continues to incorporate Somaliland, the latter's proclamation of secession has never been officially withdrawn. The northerners made use of the chaos in the southern part of the country to announce their separation, reconstructing the relict colonial boundary between former British and Italian Somalilands as their border. This action may eventually be nullified, but the devolutionary forces that propelled it will not. The Horn of Africa remains an unstable region.

North Africa and Southwest Asia

In the geographic realm of North Africa and Southwest Asia, we already have noted the devolutionary forces inherent in the accommodation of major stateless nations, such as the Kurds and the Palestinians. Another country that has fallen to centrifugal stresses of this kind is

From the Field Notes

❝ The Tamil neighborhood of Colombo, capital of Sri Lanka, has been the scene of serious civil disorder resulting from the secessionist war waged by the Tamil Tigers in the country's north and east. During my visit in March, 1995, armed forces and police controlled major intersections, but things were quiet and negotiations were under way. In April, the uneasy peace collapsed again and the conflict in the north resumed. This Colombo neighborhood, once again, braced for trouble. ❞

Cyprus, the island state near Turkey in the eastern Mediterranean Sea. Populated by Greeks (nearly 80 percent) and Turks, Cyprus seemed on a path toward stability when, in 1964, the fragile order broke down and civil war engulfed the island. Out of that conflict has come an island divided between Turks (to the north of the "Green Line" boundary) and Greeks (who control about 60 percent of it to the south). In 1983 the Turkish north proclaimed itself the Turkish Republic of Northern Cyprus, and while this action has not received international sanction, devolution has claimed yet another plural state.

In the mid-1990s, a political crisis bordering on civil war, complete with devolutionary portents, afflicted Algeria. What was essentially a power struggle between secular and Islamist sectors of Algerian society took on devolutionary dimensions when leaders of the country's Berbers (descendants of pre-Arab peoples who now constitute about one-quarter of Algeria's population of nearly 30 million) began to call for political autonomy. The area in question is called Kabylia, and it lies in the northeast corner of Algeria, extending from the Aures Mountains to the Mediterranean Sea as well as to the

Tunisian border. The ultimate cost of Algeria's internal strife may well be the dismemberment of the country.

South and East Asia

In Asia, Singapore stands as a monument to peaceful and successful devolution of the state of Malaysia, but other processes have not been so smooth. In the borderlands of Thailand and Myanmar (Burma), minority peoples are waging wars of secession against the powers in the national core areas. In Sri Lanka, the future of the state is threatened by a classic devolutionary conflict.

Sri Lanka (population: 18 million) lies just a few miles off the tip of India's Dravidian-peopled southern peninsula. The majority (about 70 percent) of Sri Lankans are not Dravidian, however, but are of Aryan origin with a historical link to ancient northern India. After the fifth century B.C., their ancestors began to migrate to Ceylon, a relocation that took several centuries to complete and brought to this southern island the advanced culture of the northwestern portion of the subcontinent. Part of that culture was the Buddhist religion; another component was the knowledge of irrigation techniques. Today, the descendants of these early invaders, the *Sinhalese*, speak a language (Sinhala) belonging to the Indo-European linguistic family of northern India.

The darker-skinned Dravidians from southern India never came in sufficient numbers to challenge the Sinhalese. They introduced the Hindu way of life, brought the Tamil language to northern Sri Lanka, and eventually came to constitute a substantial minority (now 18 percent) of the country's population. Their numbers were markedly strengthened during the second half of the nineteenth century when the British brought hundreds of thousands of Tamils from the adjacent mainland to work on the

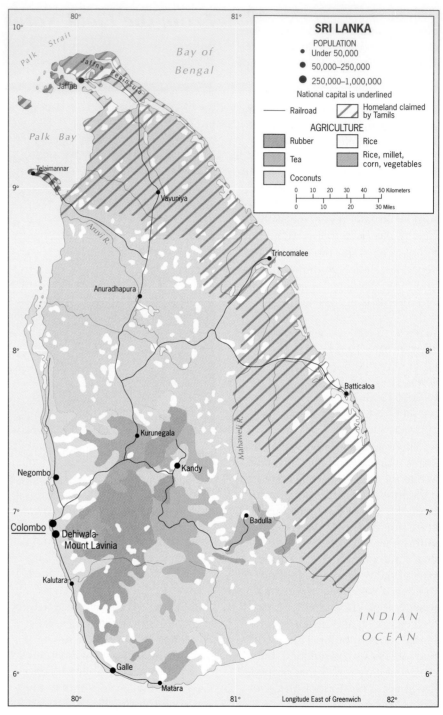

FIGURE 40–5 Sri Lanka in Transition. SOURCE: From a map in H. J. de Blij and P. O. Muller, *Geography: Realms, Regions, and Concepts*, 7th ed. (New York: Wiley, 1994), p. 499.

plantations that were being laid out. Sri Lanka has sought the repatriation of this ethnic element in its population, and an agreement to that effect was even signed with India. In 1978, however, Tamil was granted the status of a national language of Sri Lanka.

In the early 1980s, conflict erupted between the Sinhalese majority and the Tamils of the north and east. The Tamils argued that they were unable to achieve equal rights in education, employment, landownership, or political representation, and they demanded a Cyprus-like partitioning of the island that would create an independent state they called Eelam (see the striped area in Fig. 40-5). Since 1984 their war of independence has caused tens of thousands of casualties and has severely damaged Sri Lanka's economy. In the mid-1990s the strife had abated somewhat, but in the past such inactivity has been followed by renewed violence. Devolution has placed an incalculable burden on one of Britain's more promising former colonies.

Since dozens of the world's states are in devolution at a time when a New World Order must be in the making, it is premature to assume that the state as we know it today will ultimately be the fundamental building block of that order. Some political geographers are suggesting that a world of 300 or even more states lies ahead, most of them fragments of larger states. Even China, the last surviving empire, may not be immune to devolution; the regional inequalities generated by its Pacific coast economic growth may not be accommodated by the communist system still in place. The devolution of eternal China may be difficult to envisage, but in the recent past we have been compelled to contemplate the unimaginable.

TOWARD A NEW WORLD ORDER

Devolution is the direct result of a vision that has diffused worldwide: the vision among subnational groups of people, bound by ties of ethnicity or culture, or greater autonomy or independence to overcome real or perceived threats to their well-being or security. From

native Hawai'ians to New Zealand's Maori, from Canada's Cree to Australia's aboriginal peoples, communities are stirred by previously unimagined rights and freedoms. National governments often misjudge the power of such movements, or have no adequate mechanisms to deal with them. The "window" for negotiation may be very small, and once a demand translates into violent action, the cycle of conflict may not be reversible.

Other global visions also appear to be at work:

1. *Notions of Democracy.* Definition and practice may vary, but the idea and ideal of **democracy** is globe girdling. Visions of a democratic China led to the disastrous Tienanmen Square massacre in June 1989, when Beijing's communist authorities crushed the prodemocracy movement of students and workers. A desire to leave Hong Kong's population with better representation when China takes over in 1997 led the British governor of the colony to democratize the political system there, a belated conversion that had the effect of insulting the Chinese. South Africa achieved a triumph for democracy with its universal elections of April 1994, soon after the dismantling of *apartheid*. From Malawi to Taiwan and from Fiji to Argentina, a global democracy movement is under way. Not all regions of the world are equally affected: representative government has made only halting progress in the North African-Southwest Asian realm.

When it comes to democracy, vision and practice are two different things. Some African ruling elites still see no contradiction in the term "one-party democracy," arguing that the multiple parties in many Western countries cover a narrower polit-

ical spectrum than many a single African party does. Elsewhere those in control seek to constrain democratic practice, as in Singapore. But even in countries where little progress toward representative government has been made (Indonesia, Saudi Arabia, Zaïre) the idea of democracy still stirs the hopes of millions.

Even well-functioning democracies have voters or groups of voters who feel underrepresented or even disenfranchised. Such voters do not believe that, as members of minorities, their votes can affect the course of affairs. There are ways, however, to empower such voters in state and local elections (see box, "Electoral Geography" in Chapter 38). By manipulating the system, a national government can ensure that state and local elections give minority voters an opportunity to influence the outcome. This is a crucial feature of a well-functioning democracy that has the effect of involving voters who otherwise might feel alienated.

2. *Growing Influence of Religion.* Another global phenomenon with major implications for a future World Order is the revival of religion. In Chapter 25 we noted the continuing diffusion of the major faiths, especially Islam, and the renaissance of the Russian Christian churches in the post-Soviet era. This is another contrast in our world of contradictions: even in this era of science and secularism, millions are turning to the fundamentals of religion to make sense of their lives and goals.

Religious fundamentalism constitutes an alternative for people in societies where prospects for democracy are dim or where oppression seems otherwise inescapable. A burst of Shiite fundamentalism, led by an exiled *ayatollah*, ousted the Shah of Iran and transformed the political geography of a wider region. In Algeria, as noted, Islamic fundamentalists were poised to gain majority rule through democratic elections in 1992, and the country faced the prospect that a resulting Islamic republic would void democracy. The elections were canceled, and Algeria has been in violent disarray ever since. In Egypt, Islamic fundamentalists decry what they regard as the godless excesses and the oppression of the government and seek to destabilize the state by destroying its tourist industry. In Sudan, the Islamic regime extends Islam's brutal *sharia* criminal law across Muslim and non-Muslim communities alike, and a devolutionary conflict follows. In Malaysia, calls for the implementation of *sharia* law are heard in Parliament.

None of this should lead us to conclude that such a renewal of fundamentalism is exclusively or even primarily an Islamic phenomenon. Undoubtedly, the youngest of the major religions also is the most energetic today, but the attraction of a return to basics can be observed among Christians, Hindus, Buddhists, and other believers virtually everywhere. In the United States, the evidence can be seen at the doors of abortion clinics and on the political convention floor, where the "religious right" has become a potent force. In India, the emergence of the political party that openly promotes Hindu fundamentalism (the Bharatiya Janata party) is a significant development. In Russia, the revival of the Christian churches suppressed during communism's seven decades of official atheism is contributing to the resurgence of political conservatism and nationalism as

DOMINO THEORY

During the Indochina War (1964–1975), it was United States policy to contain communist expansion by supporting the efforts of the government of South Vietnam to defeat communist insurgents. Soon, the war engulfed North Vietnam as U.S. bombers attacked targets north of the border between North and South. And in the later phases of the war, conflict spilled over into Laos and Cambodia. In addition, U.S. warplanes took off from bases in Thailand. Like dominoes, one country after another fell to the ravages of the war or was threatened.

Some scholars warned that this domino effect could eventually affect not only Thailand but also Malaysia, Indonesia, and Burma (today Myanmar): the whole Southeast Asian realm, they predicted, could be destabilized. But, as we know, that did not happen. The war remained confined to Indochina. And the domino "theory" seemed invalid.

But is the theory totally without merit? Unfortunately, some political geographers to this day make the mistake of defining this idea in terms of communist activity. Communist insurgency, though, is only one way in which a country may be destabilized (as is happening today in Peru). But right-wing rebellion (Nicaragua's Contras), ethnic conflict (Bosnia-Herzegovina), religious extremism (Algeria), and even economic and environmental causes can create havoc in a country. Properly defined, the **domino theory** holds that destabilization from any cause in one country can result in the collapse of order in a neighboring country, starting a chain of events that can affect a series of contiguous states in turn.

In fact, any visitor to Laos and especially to Cambodia will see that disastrous long-term impact of the "Vietnam" war on these countries and societies; these dominoes certainly fell. Today, Indochina is relatively stable (although Cambodia suffers from sporadic strife). Now, the dominoes are falling in another shatter belt, Eastern Europe. Look at the map again: the struggle in former Yugoslavia has moved from Slovenia to Croatia, on to Bosnia-Herzegovina and Serbia-Montenegro, and threatens to engulf Kosovo, Macedonia, Albania, and perhaps even Greece and Turkey. In 1994–1995, it was U.S. and UN policy to attempt to contain ex-Yugoslavia's conflicts and prevent them from spreading to Kosovo and beyond. There may be something to the domino theory after all.

well. Even China is affected by an incipient religious revival as controls over proselytizing have been relaxed.

REDEFINING THE MAP

To summarize: the New World Order must come about while subnational groups invisage independence, while notions of democracy in various forms infuse peoples everywhere, and while religious forces affect the course of events. These conditions in one way or another, all reflect *weak-*

nesses of the state system, a major impediment to the achievement of a future stable world. Both supranationalism and devolution betray a search for alternatives, but neither process promises a satisfactory alternative. Most supranational unions remain weak and require little yielding of state sovereignty. The products of devolution (Slovakia, Croatia, Eritrea, Moldova) in most cases do not constitute superior alternatives to the state as we know it.

Another factor affecting our course toward a New World Order is the *antiquated boundary framework* with which the world has been bequeathed. We are entering the twenty-first century with a boundary system rooted in the nineteenth, which is a recipe for disorder. Changes in the social and economic geographies of entire regions have made inherited boundaries irrelevant or worse. Decolonization and the demise of Soviet communism elevated administrative borders of convenience into international boundaries, without regard for their capacity to function as such. Many cannot, but in this geopolitical world we seem to be wedded to the notion that conflicts must be resolved "within established borders." Our territorial imperative stands in the way of the New World Order.

We have already noted the impact of cross-border migrations, the media-driven flow of ideas and images, and the role of irredentism on the world's politico-geographic framework. Still another influence comes from what has become known as the *domino effect*, a theory that holds states' proximity responsible for regional destabilization (see box, "Domino Theory"). Also significant is the incessant and voluminous *flow of weapons* and the diffusion of nuclear arms in the modern world. During the Cold War, both superpowers flooded their allies with weaponry, and numerous smaller arms manufacturers contributed further to the dissemination of the means to wage war. As a result, there is no shortage of weapons when a subnational group wishes to pursue its political goals by violent means. From the clans of Somalia to the rebels of Abkhazia, from the religious fanatics in Lebanon to the street gangs of Los Angeles, the acquisition of arms and ammunition poses no problem. This, obviously, creates a grave threat to any future World Order; a failure of consensus can quickly degenerate into armed conflict.

Even more critical is the ongoing *diffusion of nuclear arms technology*. Nuclear weapons endow even small states with the capacity to inflict massive damage to larger and distant adversaries. Combined with missile technology, this undoubtedly is the most serious danger the world faces, which is why the United Nations insisted on the dismantling of Iraq's nuclear capacity following the 1991 war and why the apparent progress by North Korea in the nuclear arms arena in the mid-1990s caused President Clinton to issue a preemptive-strike threat. While it was always known that the former Soviet Union and several Western powers possessed nuclear bombs and the missiles to deliver them to enemy targets, the nuclear capabilities of other countries are carefully guarded secrets and not well-known. When, in 1977, intelligence reports regarding Iraq's nuclear program reached Israel, the Israelis launched a preemptive strike. But Israel itself is believed to possess a nuclear arsenal; South Africa during the *apartheid* period was working toward one; India and Pakistan appear to be joining the nuclear club even as the Kashmir dispute embroils them; and there are concerns over Iran's potential as a nuclear power. As nuclear weapons became smaller and "tactical" nuclear arms made their appearance, the threat of nuclear-weapons sales, for example, from post-Soviet inventories, had to be taken seriously. It is now possible for a belligerent state to purchase the power with which to blackmail the world.

The foregoing underscores the risks should a New World Order come about by any means other than consensus. Earlier we recorded the outlines of a four-cornered New World Order in which the United States, a united Europe, a stable Russia, and a developing China might find themselves in a mutually beneficial balance of power. At present, only the United States, among these four, is not in a major transition. Whether supranationalism in Europe will eventually generate a United States of Europe is uncertain. The Russian federation also has an unclear future, still a superpower in terms of armaments but dangerously weak at the center. Nor is the fate of China beyond doubt: the failure of communist rule or the breakdown of stability resulting from regional economic disparities may set it back. Expectations of a four-power New World Order in the twenty-first century may, therefore, be premature.

We live on a small, crowded, environmentally changing, economically disparate, politically unstable planet. To understand the fundamentals of its geography is to marvel at its diversity, capacity, and continuity. Five billion years ago, the Earth was about to be born. Five million years ago, our ancestral lineage had been set. Five thousand years ago, the first cities worthy of the name, and the first complex states, had come into existence. Five hundred years ago, Europe made its fateful contact with the Americas. Fifty years ago, the world emerged from its most devastating war. Five years ago, the world's largest empire collapsed. Where will the world be five years from now, when a new century begins?

Still, we may expect, searching for a just and durable World Order.

KEY TERMS

Autonomy
Democracy
Devolution
Domino Theory
Irredentism
Gateway State
Near-Abroad
New World Order
Plural Society
Regionalism
Religious Fundamentalism

Resource A

MAPS

The geographer's greatest ally is the map. Maps can present enormous amounts of information very effectively, and can be used to establish theories and solve problems. Furthermore, maps often are simply fascinating, revealing things no other medium can. It has been said that if a picture is worth a thousand words, then a map is worth a million. Alfred Wegener, nearly a century ago, drew his notion of a fragmenting supercontinent on an amateurish set of four maps purporting to show how continental drift happened. He is no longer cited, but that set of maps, which at a glance summarize his entire hypothesis, continues to be reproduced in many books around the world (Fig. R-1).

Maps can be fascinating, but they often do not get the attention they deserve. You may spend 20 minutes carefully reading a page of text, but how often have you spent 20 minutes with a page-size map, studying what it reveals? No caption and no paragraph of text can begin to summarize what a map may show; it is up to the reader to make the best use of it. For example, in the chapters on population issues

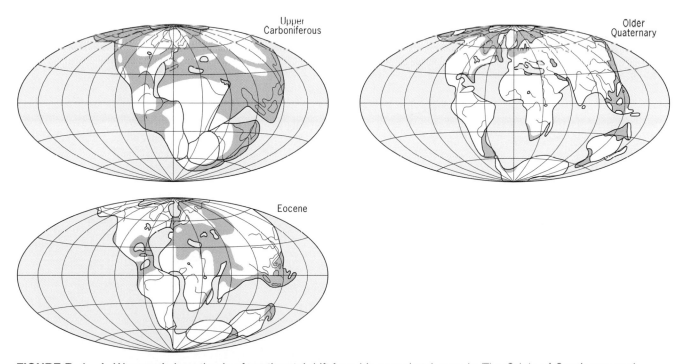

FIGURE R–1   A. Wegener's hypothesis of continental drift from his own sketch map in *The Origin of Continents and Oceans* (1914).

we study several maps that depict the human condition by country, in terms of birth and death rates, infant mortality, calorie intake, life expectancy, and so on. In the text, we can refer only to highlights (and low points) on those maps. But make a point of looking beyond the main issue to get a sense of the global distributions these maps represent. It is part of an intangible but important process: to enhance your mental map of this world.

While on the topic of maps, we should remind ourselves that a map—any map—is an incomplete representation of reality. In the first place, the map is smaller than the real world it represents. Secondly, it must depict the curved surface of our world on a flat plane, for example, a page of this book. And thirdly, it must contain symbols to convey the information that must be transmitted to the reader. These are the three fundamental properties of all maps: scale, projection, and symbols.

Understanding these basics helps us interpret maps while avoiding their pitfalls. Some maps look so convincing that we may not question them as we would a paragraph of text. Yet maps, by their very nature, to some extent distort reality. Most of the time, such distortion is necessary and does not invalidate the map's message. But some maps are drawn deliberately to mislead. Propaganda maps, for example, may exaggerate or distort reality to promote political aims. We should be alert to cartographic mistakes when we read maps. The proper use of scale, projection, and symbolization ensures that a map is as accurate as it can be made.

MAP SCALE

The *scale* of a map reveals how much the real world has been reduced to fit on the page or screen on which it appears. It is the ratio between an actual distance on the

FIGURE R–2 The layout of a major city can be shown in considerable detail at this scale.

ground and the length given to that distance on the map, using the same units of measurement. This ratio is often represented as a fraction (e.g., 1:10,000 or 1/10,000). This means that one unit on the map represents 10,000 such units in the real world. If the unit is 1 inch, then an inch on the map represents 10,000 inches on the ground, or slightly more than 833 feet. (The metric system certainly makes things easier. One centimeter on the map would actually represent 10,000 cm or 100 meters). Such a scale would be useful when mapping a city's downtown area, but it would be much too large for the map of an entire state. As the real-world area we want to map gets larger, we must make our map

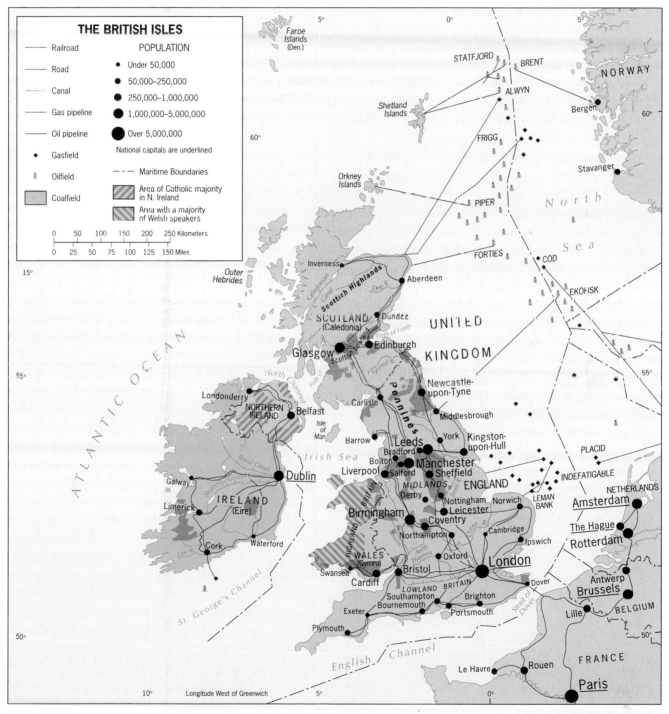

FIGURE R–3 Smaller scale allows display of larger area, but with less local detail.

scale smaller. As small as the fraction 1/10,000 seems, it still is 10 times as large as 1/100,000, and 100 times as large as 1/1,000,000. If the world maps in this book had fractional scales, they would be even smaller. A large-scale map can contain much more detail and be far more representative of the real world than a small-scale map. Look at it this way: when we devote almost a full page of this book to a map of a major city (Fig. R-2), we are able to represent the layout of that city in considerable detail. But if the entire continental realm in which that city is located must be represented on a single page, the city becomes just a large dot on that small-scale map, and the detail is lost in favor of larger-area coverage (Fig. R-3). So the selection of scale depends on the objective of the map.

But when you examine the maps in this book, you will note that most, if not all, of them have scales that are not given as ratios or fractions, but in graphic form. This method of representing map scale is convenient from several viewpoints. Using the edge of a piece of paper and marking the scale bar's length, the map reader can quickly—without calculation—determine approximate distances. And if a map is enlarged or reduced in reproduction, the scale bar is enlarged or reduced with it and remains accurate. That, of course, is not true of a ratio or fractional scale. Graphic scales, therefore, are preferred in this book.

MAP PROJECTIONS

For centuries cartographers have faced the challenge of map projection—the representation of the spherical Earth, or part of it, on a flat surface. To get the job done, there had to be a frame of reference on the globe itself, a grid system that could be transferred to the flat page. Any modern globe shows that system: a set of horizontal lines, usually at 10-degree intervals north and south from the equator, called *parallels*, and another set of vertical lines, converging on the poles, often shown at 15-degree intervals and called *meridians* (see box, "Numbering the Grid Lines"). On the spherical globe, parallels and meridians intersect at right angles (Fig. R-4).

But what happens when these lines of latitude (parallels) and longitude (meridians) are drawn to intersect at right angles on a flat piece of paper? At the equator, the representation of the real world is relatively accurate. But go toward the poles, and distortion grows with every degree until, in the northern and southern higher latitudes, the continents appear not only stretched out but also misshaped (Fig. R-5). Because the meridians cannot be made to converge in the polar areas, this projection makes Antarctica look like a giant, globe-girdling landmass.

Looking at this representation of the world, you might believe that it could serve no useful purpose. But in fact, the *Mercator* projection, invented in 1569 by Gerardus Mercator, the Flemish cartographer, had (and has) a very particular function. Because parallels and me-

NUMBERING THE GRID LINES

When cartographers girdled the globe with their imaginary grid lines, they had to identify each line by number, that is, by *degree.* For the (horizontal) latitude lines, that was easy: the equator, which bisects the Earth midway between the poles, was designated as 0° (zero degree) Latitude, and all parallels north and south of the equator were designated by their angular position (Fig. R-4). The parallel midway between the equator and the pole, thus, is 45° North Latitude in the Northern Hemisphere, and 45° South Latitude in the Southern Hemisphere.

But the (vertical) longitude lines presented no such easy solution. Among the parallels, the equator is the only one to divide the Earth into equal halves, but *all* meridians do this. During the second half of the nineteenth century, maps with conflicting numbers multiplied, and it was clear that a solution was needed. The most powerful country at the time was Britain, and in 1884, international agreement was reached whereby the meridian drawn through the Royal Observatory in Greenwich, England, would be the *prime meridian*, 0° (zero degree) Longitude. All meridians east and west of the prime meridian could now be designated by number, from 0° to 180° East and West Longitude.

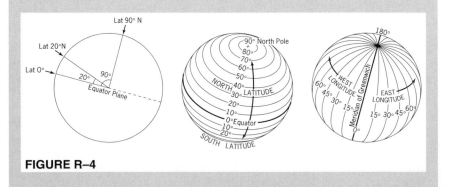

FIGURE R-4

ridians cross (as they do on the spherical globe's grid) at right angles, direction is true everywhere on this map. Thus the Mercator projection enabled navigators to maintain an accurate course at sea simply by adhering to compass directions and plotting straight lines. It is used for that purpose to this day.

The spatial distortion of the Mercator projection serves to remind us that scale and projection are interconnected. What scale fraction or graphic scale bar could be used here? A scale that would be accurate at the equator on a Mercator map would be quite inaccurate at higher latitudes. So the distortion that is an inevitable by-product of any map projection also affects map scales.

One might imagine that the spatial (areal) distortion of the Mercator projection is so obvious that no one would use it to represent the world's countries. But in fact, many popular atlas maps (Mercator also introduced the term *atlas* to describe a collection of maps) and wall maps still use a Mercator for such purposes. The National Geographic Society published its world maps on a Mercator projection until 1988, when it finally abandoned the practice in favor of a projection developed by the American cartographer Arthur Robinson (Fig. R-6). During the news conference at which the change was announced, a questioner rose to pursue a point: Why had the Soci-

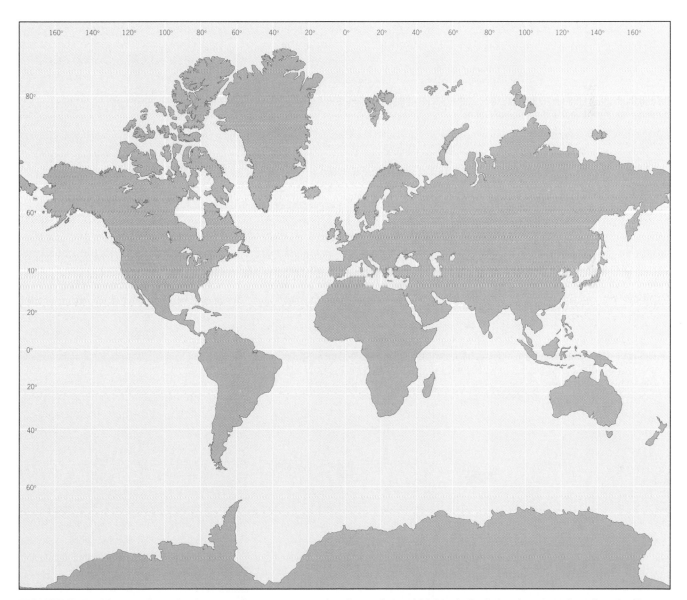

FIGURE R–5 Mercator's projection greatly exaggerates the dimensions of higher-latitude landmasses, but direction is true everywhere on this map.

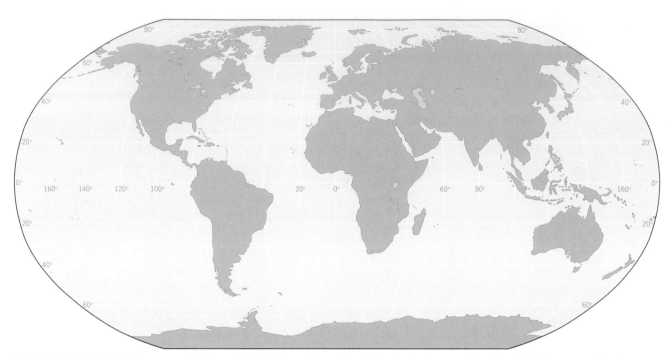

FIGURE R–6   The Robinson projection substantially reduces the latitudinal size magnification. It better approximates dimension, but it lacks directional utility.

ety waited so long to make this change? Was it because the distortion inherent in the Mercator projection made American and European middle-latitude countries large, compared to tropical countries in Africa and elsewhere? Of course there was no such intent, but that questioner obviously understood the misleading subtleties inherent even in so apparently neutral a device as a map projection.

The Mercator projection is one of a group of projections called *cylindrical* projections. Imagine the globe's lines of latitude and longitude represented by a wire grid, at the center of which we place a bright light. Wrap a piece of photographic paper around the wire grid, extending it well beyond the north and south poles, flash the bulb, and the photographic image will be that of a Mercator projection (Fig. R-7).

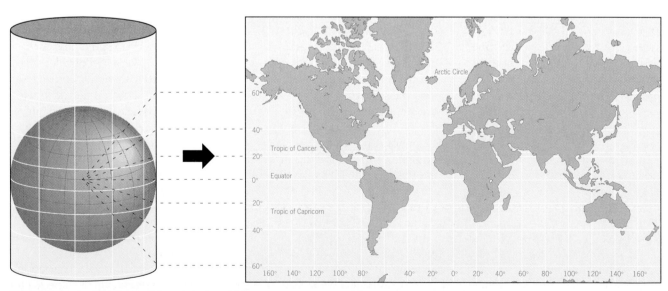

FIGURE R–7   Shadows of the globe's grid lines on wraparound paper: a cylindrical projection results.

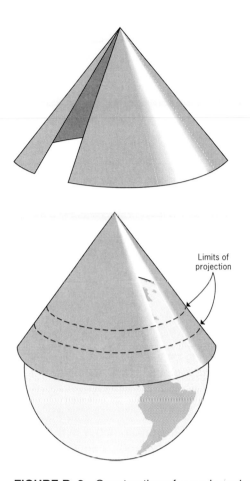

FIGURE R–8 Construction of a conic projection.

We could do the same after placing a cone-shaped piece of paper over each hemisphere, touching the grid, say, at the 40th parallel north and south; the result would be a *conic* projection (Fig. R-8). If we wanted a map of North America or Europe, a form of conic projection would be appropriate. Now the meridians do approach each other toward the poles (unlike the Mercator projection), and there is much less shape and size distortion. And if we needed a map of Arctic and Antarctic regions, we would place the photographic paper as a flat sheet against the North and South Poles. Now the photographic image would show a set of diverging lines, as the meridians do from each pole, and the parallels would appear as circles (Fig. R-9). Such a *planar* projection is a good choice for a map of the Arctic Ocean or the Antarctic continent.

Projections are chosen for various purposes. Just as the Mercator is appropriate for navigation because direction is true, other projections are designed to preserve areal size, keep distances real, or maintain the outlines (shapes) of landmasses and countries. Projections can be manipulated for many needs. In this book, we examine global distributions of various phenomena. The world map that forms the base for these displays is one that is designed to give prominence to land areas at the expense of the oceans. This is achieved by "interrupting" the projection where loss of territory (in this case water area) is not problematic.

When a map is planned, therefore, the choice of projection is an important part of the process. Sometimes, an inappropriate selection weakens the effectiveness of a map and may even lead to erroneous interpretations. Of course, the problem diminishes when the area to be mapped is smaller and the scale larger. We may consider various alternatives when it comes to a map of all of North America, but a map of a single state presents far fewer potential problems of distortion. And for a city map—even of a large city such as Chicago—the projection problem virtually disappears.

The old problem of how to represent the round Earth on a flat surface has been attacked for centuries, and there is no single best solution. What has been learned in the process, however, will be useful in fields of endeavor other than

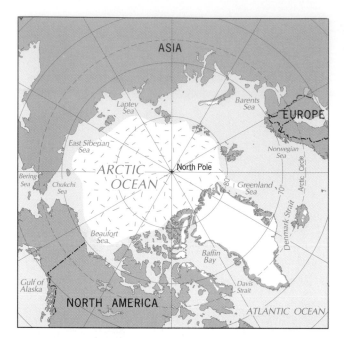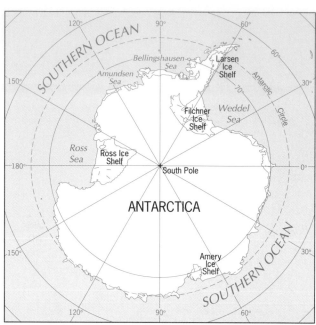

FIGURE R–9   Planar projection: now the light at the center of the globe projects diverging longitude lines on a flat sheet of paper placed over the North Pole (left) and the South Pole.

Earthly geography. As the age of planetary exploration dawns, and our space probes send back images of the surfaces of the Moon, mars, Jupiter, and other components of our solar system, we will have to agree once again on grids, equators, and prime meridians. What has been learned in our efforts to map and represent the Earth will be useful in depicting the universe beyond.

SYMBOLS ON MAPS

The third fundamental property of a map is its symbolization. Maps represent the real world, and this can be done only through the use of symbols. Anyone who has used an atlas map is familiar with some of these symbols: prominent dots (perhaps black or red) for cities; a large dot with a circle around it, or a star, for capitals; red lines for roads (double lines for four-lane highways), black lines for railroads; and patterns or colors for areas of water,

forest, or farmland. Notice that these symbols respectively represent points, lines, and areas on the ground. For our purposes, we need not go further into map symbolization, which can become a very complex topic when it comes to highly specialized cartography in such fields as geology and meteorology. Nevertheless, it is useful to know why symbols such as those used on the maps in this book were chosen.

Point symbols, as we noted, are used to show individual features or places. On a large-scale map of a city block, dots can represent individual houses. But on a small-scale map, a dot has to represent an entire "city." Still, cities have various sizes, and those size differences can be put in categories and mapped accordingly (Fig. R-10). Thus New York, Chicago, and Los Angeles still appear as dots on the map, but their dots are larger than those representing Tucson, Milwaukee, or Denver. A dimensional scale is added to the map's graphic scale, and at a glance we can see the rela-

tive sizes of major cities in the United States and Canada.

Line symbols include not only roads and railroads, but also political and administrative boundaries, rivers, and other linear features. Again scale plays its crucial role: on a large-scale map, it is possible to represent the fenced boundaries of a single farm, but on a small-scale map, such detail cannot be shown.

Some lines on maps do not actually exist on the ground. When physical geographers do their field work they use *contour* maps, lines that represent a certain consistent height above mean sealevel (Fig. R-11). All points on such a contour line thus are at the same elevation. The spacing between contour lines immediately reveals the nature of the local topography (the natural landsurface). When the contour lines at a given interval (e.g., 100 feet) are spaced closely together, the slope of the ground is steep. When they are widely separated, the landsurface slopes gently. Of course contour lines cannot be found in the real world, and neither

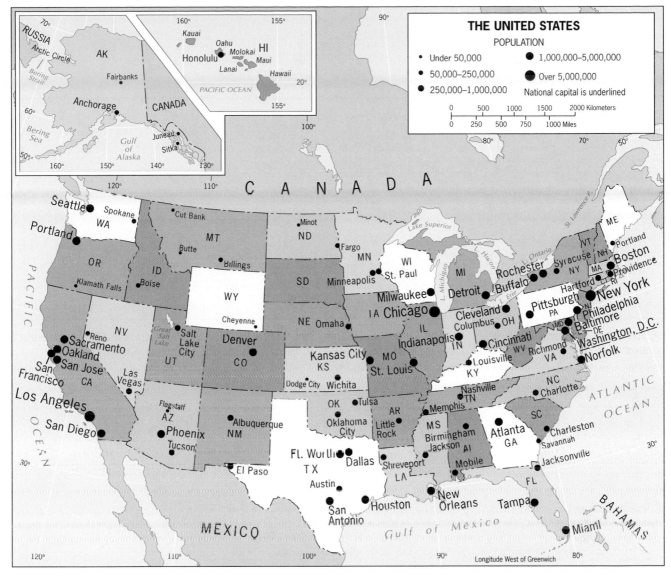

FIGURE R–10 This map uses dot symbols to indicate size categories of cities in the United States.

can the lines drawn on the weather maps in our daily newspaper. These lines connect points of equal pressure (isobars) and temperature (isotherms) and show the development of weather systems. Note that the letters *iso* (meaning "the same") appear in these terms. Invisible lines of this kind are collectively known as **isolines**, lines of equal or constant value. These are abstract constructions, but they can be of great value in geographic research and representation.

Area symbols take many forms,

and we will see some of them on the maps in this book. Area symbols are used in various ways to represent distributions and magnitudes. Maps showing distributions (of such phenomena as regionally dominant languages or religions in human geography, and climates or soils in physical geography) show the world, or parts of it, divided into areas shaded or colored in contrasting hues. But be careful: those sharp dividing lines are likely to be transition zones in the real world, and a dominant language or reli-

gion does not imply the exclusion of all others. So distribution maps, and there are many in this book, tend to be small-scale generalizations of much more complex patterns than they can reveal. Again, maps showing magnitudes also must be read with care. Here the objective is to reveal *how much* of a phenomenon prevails in one unit (e.g., country) on the map, compared to others. The maps on population in Part 2 are examples of such maps. The important cartographic decision has to do with

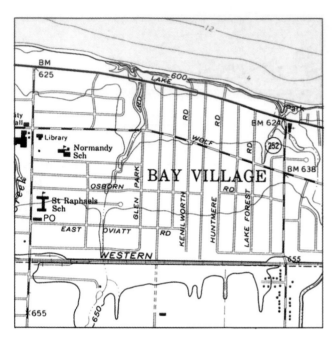 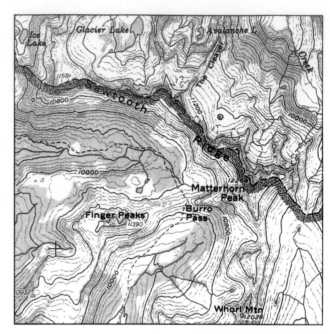

FIGURE R–11   Contour lines reflecting low relief (left) and high relief (right). The map at left is part of the U.S.G.S. North Olmstead Quadrangle, Ohio; the map at right is part of the U.S.G.S. Matterhorn Peak Quadrangle, California.

color (or, in black and white, gray-tones). Darker should mean more, and lighter implies less. That is relatively easily done when the dominant color is the same. But on a multicolored map, the use of reds, greens, and yellows can be confusing, and first impressions may have to be revised upon examination of the key.

Some students who are first drawn to the discipline of geography go on to become professional cartographers, and their work is seen in atlases, foldout magazine maps, books, and many other venues. Although cartographic technology is changing, the world's great atlases and maps still are designed and produced by researchers, compilers, draughts-people, and other specialists working in such offices as the Cartographic Division of the National Geographic Society, the Cartographic and Design Division of Rand McNally & Company, the Cartographic Laboratory of Hammond, Incorporated, and other map producers, including Mapping Specialists, cartographers for *Human Geography.*

Resource B

CITATIONS AND BIBLIOGRAPHIC SOURCES

Chapter 1 INTRODUCTION: GEOGRAPHY AND HUMAN GEOGRAPHY

Abler, R., et al., eds. *Human Geography in a Shrinking World* (North Scituate, Mass.: Duxbury Press, 1975).

Abler, R., et al. *Spatial Organization: The Geographer's View of the World* (Englewood Cliffs, N.J.: Prentice-Hall, 1971).

Amedeo, D., & Golledge, R. *An Introduction to Scientific Reasoning in Geography* (New York: John Wiley & Sons, 1975).

Bruhnes, J. *Human Geography* (London: George Harrap, trans. E. Row, 1952).

Campbell, J. *Map Use and Analysis* (Dubuque, Iowa: Wm. C. Brown, 1991).

Davis, W. M. *Geographical Essays* (New York: Dover, 1957).

de Blij, H., & Muller, P. *Geography: Regions and Concepts* (New York: John Wiley & Sons, 7th rev. ed., 1994).

de Terra, H. *The Life and Times of Alexander Von Humboldt, 1769–1859* (New York: Knopf, 1955).

Dent, B. *Principles of Thematic Map Design* (Reading, Mass.: Addison-Wesley, 1984).

Espenshade, E. B., Jr., ed. Goode's *World Atlas* (Chicago: Rand McNally, 18th rev. ed., 1990).

Geography and International Knowledge (Report) (Washington, D.C.: Association of American Geographers, Committee on Geography and International Studies, 1982).

Glassner, M., & de Blij, H. *Systematic Political Geography* (New York: John Wiley & Sons, 4th rev. ed., 1987).

Gold, J. *An Introduction to Behavioral Geography* (New York: Oxford University Press, 1980).

Gould, P. *The Geographer at Work* (London: Routledge & Kegan Paul, 1985).

Gould, P., & White, R. *Mental Maps* (Harmondsworth, U.K.: Penguin Books, 2nd rev. ed., 1982).

Harris, C. D., ed. *A Geographical Bibliography for American Libraries* (Washington, D.C.: Association of American Geographers and the National Geographic Society, 1985).

Hartshorne, R. *The Nature of Geography* (Washington, D.C.: Association of American Geographers, 1939).

Hartshorne, R. *Perspective on the Nature of Geography* (Chicago: Rand McNally, 1959).

James, P. E., & Jones, C. F., eds. *American Geography: Inventory and Prospect* (Syracuse, N.Y.: Syracuse University Press, 1954).

James, P. E., & Martin, G. *All Possible Worlds: A History of Geographical Ideas* (New York: John Wiley & Sons, 2nd rev. ed., 1981).

Johnston, R. *The Nature of Human Geography* (Oxford, U.K.: Basil Blackwell, 1985).

Johnston, R., et al., eds. *The Dictionary of Human Geography* (Oxford, U.K.: Basil Blackwell, 1981).

Keates, J. S. *Cartographic Design and Production* (Essex, U.K.: Longmans, 1989).

Larkin, R., & Peters, G., eds. *Dictionary of Concepts in Human Geography* (Westport, Conn.: Greenwood Press, 1983).

Massey, D., & Allen, J., eds. *Geography Matters! A Reader* (New York: Cambridge University Press, 1985).

Michener, J. "The Mature Social Studies Teacher," *Social Education*, November 1970, pp. 760–766.

Monmonier, M. S. *Computer-Assisted Cartography: Principles and Prospects* (Englewood Cliffs, N.J.: Prentice-Hall, 1982).

Monmonier, M. S. *How to Lie with Maps* (Chicago: University of Chicago Press, 1990).

Monmonier, M. S. *Mapping It Out: Expository Cartography for the Humanities and Social Sciences* (Chicago: University of Chicago Press, 1993).

Monmonier, M. S. *Maps with the News* (Chicago: University of Chicago Press, 1989).

National Geographic Society. *Atlas of the World* (Washington, D.C.: National Geographic Society, 6th rev. ed., 1990).

National Geographic Society. *Historical Atlas of the United States* (Washington, D.C.: National Geographic Society, 1988).

Pattison, W. "The Four Traditions of Geography," *Journal of Geography* 63 (1964), 211–216.

Rand McNally & Co. *The New International Atlas* (Chicago: Rand McNally, 2nd rev. ed., 1984).

Robinson, Arthur H., et al. *Elements of Cartography* (New York: John Wiley & Sons, 6th rev. ed., 1990).

Strahler, A. N., & Strahler, A. H. *Modern Physical Geography* (New York: John Wiley & Sons, 4th rev. ed., 1992).

Thomas, W., ed. *Man's Role in Changing the Face of the Earth* (Chicago: University of Chicago Press, 1956).

Tufte, Edward R. *Envisioning Information* (Chesire, Conn.: Graphics Press, 1990).

Wegener, A. *The Origin of Continents and Oceans* (New York: Dover, trans. J. Biram, 1966).

Wheeler, J., & Muller, P. *Economic Geography* (New York: John Wiley & Sons, 2nd rev. ed., 1986).

Part One   ENVIRONMENT AND HUMANITY

Ackerman, S. "European Prehistory Gets Even Older," *Science*, 6 October 1989, pp. 28–30.

Bailey, R., ed. *The True State of the Planet* (New York: The Free Press, 1995).

Bradley, R. S. *Quaternary Paleoclimatology: Methods of Paleoclimatological Reconstruction* (Boston: Allen & Unwin, 1985).

Campbell, B., ed. *Humankind Emerging* (Glenville, Ill.: Scott, Foresman, 5th rev. ed., 1988).

Ciochon, R. L., & Fleagle, J. G., eds. *Primate Evolution and Human Origins* (Hawthorne, N.Y.: Aldine & de Gruyter, 1987).

Colinvaux, P. A. "The Past and Future Amazon," *Scientific American*, May 1989, pp. 102–108.

Connah, G. *African Civilizations* (Cambridge, U.K.: Cambridge University Press, 1987).

Ember, C. R., & Ember, M. E. *Anthropology* (Englewood Cliffs, N.J.: Prentice-Hall, 6th rev. ed., 1990).

Fagan, B. *In the Beginning: An Introduction to Archaeology* (Boston: Little, Brown, 1988).

Fagan, B. M. *People of the Earth: An Introduction to World Prehistory* (Glenville, Ill.: Scott, Foresman, 1989).

Feder, K. L., & Park, M. A. *Human Antiquity: An Introduction to Physical Anthropology and Archaeology* (Mountain View, Calif.: Mayfield, 1989).

Gibbons, A. "First Hominid Finds from Ethiopia in a Decade," *Science*, 22 March 1991, p. 1428.

Graedel, T. E., & Crutzen, P. J. *Atmosphere, Climate and Change* (New York: Scientific American Library, 1995).

Holz, R., ed. *The Surveillant Science: Remote Sensing of the Environment* (New York: John Wiley & Sons, 2nd rev. ed, 1984).

Janus, C. *The Search for Peking Man* (New York: Macmillan, 1975).

Jellicoe, G., & Jellicoe, S. *The Landscape of Man: Shaping the Environment from Prehistory to the Present Day* (London: Thomas & Hudson, 1975).

Johanson, D., & Edey, M. *Lucy: The Beginnings of Humankind* (New York: Simon & Schuster, 1981).

Jurmain, R., Nelson, H., & Turnbaugh, W. A. *Understanding Physical Anthropology and Archaeology* (St. Paul, Minn.: West, 1947).

Hoffman, M. "Hand Ax Throws Light on European Prehistory," *Science*, 2 August 1991, p. 515.

Larsen, C. S., & Matter, R. M. *Human Origins: The Fossil Record* (Prospect Heights, Ill.: Waveland Press, 1985).

Leakey, R. E. *The Making of Mankind* (New York: Dutton, 1981).

Leakey, R. E., & Walker, A. "A Fossil Skeleton 1,600,000 Years Old: Homo Erectus Unearthed," *National Geographic* 168: 5 (1985), 624–629.

Levenson, T. *Ice Time: Climate, Science and Life on Earth* (New York: Harper & Row, 1989).

Lewin, R. "A New Toolmaker in the Hominid Record?," *Science*, 6 May 1988, pp. 724–725.

Lewin, R. "Species Question in Modern Human Origins," *Science*, 31 March 1989, pp. 1666–1667.

Maunder, W. J. *The Human Impact of Climate Uncertainty* (New York: Routledge, Chapman & Hall, 1989).

Phillipson, D. W. *African Archaeology* (Cambridge, U.K.: Cambridge University Press, 1981).

Pielou, E. C. *After the Ice Age: The Return of Life to Glaciated North America* (Chicago: University of Chicago Press, 1991).

Roberts, Neil. *The Holocene: An Environmental History* (New York: Basil Blackwell, 1989).

Schneider, S. H. *Global Warming: Are We Entering the Greenhouse Century?* (New York: Vintage Books, 1990).

Shapiro, H. L. *Peking Man* (New York: Simon & Schuster, 1974).

Sheffield, C. *Man on Earth: How Civilization and Technology Changed the Face of the World—A Survey from Space* (New York: Macmillan, 1983).

Simons, E. L. "Human Origin," *Science*, 22 September 1989, pp. 133–135.

Strahler, A. N., & Strahler, A. H. *Modern Physical Geography* (New York: John Wiley & Sons, 3rd rev. ed., 1988). Definition on p. 476.

Trinkhaus, E., & Howells, W. W. "The Neanderthals," *Scientific American*, December 1979, pp. 118–133.

Vigilant, L., et al. "African Populations and the Evolution of Human Mitochondrial DNA," *Science*, 27 September 1991, pp. 1503–1507.

Walker, A., & Teaford, M. "The Hunt for Proconsul," *Scientific American*, January 1989, pp. 76–82.

Weaver, K. "The Search for Our Ancestors," *National Geographic*, November 1985, pp. 560–623.

Wenke, R. J. *Patterns in Prehistory: Humankind's First Three Million Years* (New York: Oxford University Press, 3rd rev. ed., 1990).

Whittle, A. *Neolithic Europe: A Survey* (Cambridge, U.K.: Cambridge University Press, 1985).

Part Two   POPULATION AND SPACE

Alonso, W., & Starr, P., eds. *The Politics of Numbers* (New York: Russell Sage, 1987).

Bennett, D. G. *World Population Problems* (Delray Beach, Fla.: Park Press, 1984).

Berardi, G. M., ed. *World Food, Population and Development* (Totowa, N.J.: Rowman & Allanheld, 1985).

Boserup, E. *Population and Technological Change* (Chicago: University of Chicago Press, 1981).

Brown, L., & Wolf, E. *Soil Erosion: Quiet Crisis in the World Economy* (Washington, D.C., Paper No. 60, 1984).

Brown, L. R., et al. *State of the World* (New York: W. W. Norton & Co., Annual).

Butzer, K. *Environment and Archaeology: An Introduction to Pleistocene Geography* (Chicago: Aldine, 1964).

Clarke, J., ed. *Geography and Population: Approaches and Applications* (Elmsford, N.Y.: Pergamon Press, 1984).

Ehrlich, P., & Ehrlich, A. *The Population Explosion* (New York: Simon & Schuster, 1990).

Ehrlich, P., & Ehrlich, A. *Healing the Planet: Strategies for Resolving the Environmental Crisis* (Reading, Mass.: Addison-Wesley Publishing Co., 1991).

Heer, D. M., & Grigsby, J. S. *Society and Population* (Englewood Cliffs, N.J.: Prentice Hall, 2nd ed., 1992).

Hornby, W., & Jones, M. *An Introduction to Population Geography* (New York: Cambridge University Press, 1980).

Johnson, S. P. *World Population and the United Nations: Challenge and Response* (Cambridge, U.K.: Cambridge University Press, 1987).

Kleinman, D. *Human Adaptation and Population Growth: A Non-Malthusian Perspective* (Totowa, N.J.: Rowman & Allanheld, 1980).

Lydolph, P. *The Climate of the Earth* (Totowa, N.J.: Rowman & Allanheld, 1985).

Newman, J., & Matzke, G. *Population: Patterns, Dynamics, and Prospects* (Englewood Cliffs, N.J.: Prentice-Hall, 1984).

Peters, G., & Larkin, R. *Population Geography: Problems, Concepts, and Prospects* (Dubuque, Iowa: Kendall Hunt, 1979).

Population Reference Bureau. *1995 World Population Data Sheet* (Washington, D.C., 1995).

Preston, S. H., ed. *World Population: Approaching the Year 2000.* Special edition of the *Annals of the American Academy of Political and Social Science*, July 1990, Vol. 510.

Roberts, G. *Population Policy: Contemporary Issues* (New York: Praeger, 1990).

Schnell, G., & Monmonier, M. *The Study of Population: Elements, Patterns and Processes* (Columbus, Ohio: Charles E. Merrill, 1983).

Teitelbaum, M. S., & Winter, J. M., eds. *Population and Resources in Western Intellectual Traditions* (Cambridge, U.K.: Cambridge University Press, 1989).

United Nations. *World Population Prospects, 1988* (New York: United Nations, 1989).

United Nations. *World Population: Trends and Policies* (New York: United Nations, 1988).

Woods, R. *Theoretical Population Geography* (London and New York: Longman, 1982).

World Bank. *World Development Report 1994* (New York: Oxford University Press, 1994).

World Bank. *World Development Report 1990: Poverty* (New York: Oxford University Press, 1990).

Wrigley, E., & Schofield, R. *The Population History of England, 1541–1871: A Reconstruction* (London, U.K.: Edward Arnold, 1981).

Zopf, P. E. *Population: An Introduction to Social Geography* (Palo Alto, Calif.: Mayfield Publishing Co., 1984).

Part Three   STREAMS OF HUMAN MOBILITY

Boswell, T., & Curtis, J. *The Cuban-American Experience: Culture, Images, and Perspectives* (Totowa, N.J.: Rowman & Allanheld, 1984).

Clarke, G. *Interregional Migration: National Policy and Social Justice* (Totowa, N.J.: Rowman & Allanheld, 1983).

Clarke, J., & Kosinski, L., eds. *Redistribution of Population in Africa* (Exeter, N.H.: Heinemann Educational Books, 1982).

Curtin, P. D. *Death by Migration: Europe's Encounter with the Tropical World in the Nineteenth Century* (New York: Cambridge University Press, 1989).

Drake, C. *National Integration in Indonesia: Patterns and Policies* (Honolulu: University of Hawaii Press, 1989).

Fuchs, R., & Demko, G., eds. *Population Distribution Policies in Development Planning* (New York: United Nations, Department of International Economic and Social Affairs, 1981).

Grossman, J. R. *Land of Hope: Black Southerners and the Great Migration* (Chicago: University of Chicago Press, 1989).

Gugler, J., ed. *The Urbanization of the Third World* (New York: Oxford University Press, 1988).

Jones, R., ed. *Patterns of Undocumented Migration in Mexico and the United States* (Totowa, N.J.: Rowman & Allanheld, 1984).

Kane, H. *The Hour of Departure: The Forces that Create Refugees and Migrants* (Washington, D.C.: Worldwatch Institute, 1995).

Lewis, G. *Human Migration: A Geographical Perspective* (New York: St. Martin's Press, 1982).

Ley, D. *A Social Geography of the City* (New York: Harper & Row, 1983).

Lisansky, J. *Migrants to Amazonia: Spontaneous Colonization in the Brazilian Frontier* (Boulder, Colo.: Westview Press, 1990).

McKee, J., ed. *Ethnicity in Contemporary America: A Geographical Appraisal* (Dubuque, Iowa: Kendall/Hunt, 1985).

Mortimore, M. *Adapting to Drought: Farmers, Famines, and Desertification in West Africa* (Cambridge, U.K.: Cambridge University Press, 1989).

Ogden, P. *Migration and Geographical Change* (New York: Cambridge University Press, 1984).

Prothero, R. M. *Migrants and Malaria in Africa* (London, U.K.: Longmans, Green, 1965).

Pryor, R., ed. *Migration and Development in Southeast Asia: A Demographic Perspective* (Kuala Lumpur, Malaysia: Oxford University Press, 1979).

Ravenstein, E. "The Laws of Migration, I and II," *Journal of the Royal Statistical Society* 48 (1885), 167–235; 52 (1889), 241–305.

Richardson, B. *Caribbean Migrants: Environment and Human Survival on St. Kitts and Nevis* (Knoxville, Tenn.: University of Tennessee Press, 1983).

Rogge, J. *Too Many Too Long: Sudan's Twenty-Year Refugee Dilemma* (Totowa, N.J.: Rowman & Allanheld, 1985).

Roseman, C. "Cities in Flux: Migration, Mobility, and Political Change," in Christian, C., & Harper, R., eds., *Modern Metropolitan Systems* (Columbus, Ohio: Charles E. Merrill, 1982), pp. 277–298.

Simon, R., & Brettell, C., eds. *International Migration: The Female Experience* (Totowa, N.J.: Rowman & Allanheld, 1986).

Swann, M. M. *Migrants in the Mexican North: Mobility, Economy, and Society in a Colonial World* (Boulder, Colo., Westview Press, 1989).

Thomas, R., & Hunter, J., eds. *International Migration Systems in the Developing World* (Cambridge, Mass.: Schenkman, 1980).

White, P., & Woods, R., eds. *The Geographical Impact of Migration* (London and New York: Longman, 1980).

Zegeye, A., & Ishemo, S., eds. *Forced Labor Migration: Movement within Africa* (London: Hans Zell Publishers, 1989).

Part Four   PATTERNS OF NUTRITION AND HEALTH

Barnett, T., & Blaikie, P. *AIDS in Africa: Its Present and Future Impact* (New York: Guilford Press, 1992).

Brown, L. R. *The Changing World Food Prospects: The Nineties and Beyond* (Washington, D.C.: Worldwatch Institute, 1988).

Brown, L. R. *Full House: Reassessing the Earth's Population Carrying Capacity* (Washington, D.C.: Worldwatch Institute, 1994).

Cherfas, J. "New Hope for Vaccine Against Schistosomiasis," *Science*, 8 February 1991, pp. 630–631.

Cliff, A., & Haggett, P. *Atlas of Disease Distribution* (Oxford, U.K.: Basil Blackwell, 1989).

Cliff, A., et al. *Spatial Diffusion: An Historical Geography of Epidemics in an Island Community* (London, U.K.: Cambridge University Press, 1981).

Currey, B., & Hugo, G., eds. *Famines As a Geographical Phenomenon* (Boston: D. Reidel, 1984).

Dando, W. *The Geography of Famine* (Silver Spring, Md.: V. H. Winston/Halsted Press, 1980).

Dawson, A. *The Land Problem in the Developed Economy* (Totowa, N.J.: Barnes & Noble, 1984).

Delaporte, F. *The History of Yellow Fever* (Cambridge, Mass.: MIT Press, trans. A. Goldhammer, 1991).

Dumont, R., & Mottin, M. *Stranglehold on Africa* (Totowa, N.J.: Barnes & Noble, 1984).

Eyles, J., & Woods, K. *The Social Geography of Medicine and Health* (New York: St. Martin's Press, 1983).

Fee, E., & Fox, D. M., eds. *AIDS: the Burdens of History* (Berkeley: University of California Press, 1988).

Franke, R., & Chasin, B. *Seeds of Famine: Ecological Destruction and the Development Dilemma in the West African Sahel* (Montclair, N.J.: Allanheld, Osmun, 1980).

Gesler, W. *Health Care in Developing Countries* (Washington, D.C.: Association of American Geographers, Resource Publications in Geography, 1984).

Gould, P. *The Slow Plague: A Geography of the Aids Pandemic* (Oxford: Basil Blackwell, 1993).

Hunter, J., ed. *The Geography of Health and Disease* (Chapel Hill, N.C.: University of North Carolina, Department of Geography, Studies in Geography, No. 6, 1974).

Joseph, A., & Phillips, D. *Accessibility and Utilization: Geographic Perspectives on Health Care Delivery* (New York: Harper & Row, 1984).

Katz, M., et al. *Parasitic Diseases* (New York: Springer-Verlag, 2nd rev. ed., 1990).

Learmonth, A. *Patterns of Disease and Hunger: A Study in Medical Geography* (North Pomfret, Vt.: David & Charles, 1978).

McGlashan, N., & Blunden, J., eds., *Geographical Aspects of Health* (New York: Academic Press, 1983).

Meade, M., ed. *Conceptual and Methodological Issues in Medical Geography* (Chapel Hill, N.C.: Department of Geography, 1980).

Meade, M. S., et al. *Medical Geography* (New York: Guilford Press, 1988).

Palca, J. "The Sobering Geography of AIDS," *Science*, 19 April 1991, pp. 372–373.

Phillips, D. R. *Health and Health Care in the Third World* (Essex, U.K.: Longmans, 1990).

Pimental, D., & Pimental, M. *Food, Energy, and Society* (New York: Wiley-Halsted, 1979).

Pyle, G. *Applied Medical Geography* (Silver Spring, Md.: V. H. Winston/Halsted Press, 1979).

Pyle, G. *The Diffusion of Influenza: Patterns and Paradigms* (Totowa, N.J.: Rowman & Allanheld, 1986).

Roberts, L. "Disease and Death in the New World," *Science*, 8 December 1989, pp. 1245–1247.

Sachs, C. *The Invisible Farmers: Women in Agricultural Production* (Totowa, N.J.: Rowman & Allanheld, 1983).

Shannon, G. W., et al. *The Geography of AIDS* (New York: Guilford Press, 1991).

Smith, C., & Hanham, R. *Alcohol Abuse: Geographical Perspectives* (Washington, D.C.: Association of American Geographers, Resource Publications in Geography, 1982).

Stamp, L. D. *The Geography of Life and Death* (Ithaca, N.Y.: Cornell University Press, 1964).

Tarrant, J. *Food Policies* (New York: John Wiley & Sons, 1980).

Part Five   PATTERNS OF RACE AND GENDER

Anonymous "Women's Value, Men's Worth," *The Economist*, 10 November 1991, p. 54.

Bagchi, D. "Rural Energy and the Role of Women," in J. Momsen, & J. Townsend, eds. *Geography of Gender in the Third World* (Albany, N.Y.: SUNY Press, 1987).

Brooks, G. *Nine Parts of Desire: The Hidden World of Islamic Women* (New York: Anchor Books/Doubleday, 1994).

Brown, B. J., & LaPrairie, L. A. *Shades of Opportunity and Access: Ethnic and Gender Minority Issues in America with Global Reflections* (Boulder, Colo.: Department of Geography, University of Colorado, 1989).

Constantino, R. F., & Desharnais, R. A. *Population Dynamics* (New York: Springer-Verlag, 1991).

Garn, S. M. *Human Races* (Springfield, Ill.: Thomas, 1971).

Gibson, A., & Fast, T. *Women's Atlas of the United States* (New York: Facts on File Publications, 1986).

Grundfest, E. "Geographic Perspectives on Women," in G. L. Gaile, & C. J. Willmott, eds., *Geography in America* (Columbus, Ohio: Merrill, 1990).

Hartl, D. L., & Clark, A. G. *Principles of Population Genetics* (Sunderland, Mass.: Sinauer Associates, 1989).

Holcomb, B. "Women in the City," *Urban Geography* (5) 1984, 247–254.

Lee, D. *Women in Geography: A Comprehensive Bibliography* (Boca Raton: Florida Atlantic University, 1988).

Lieberson, S., & Waters, M. C. *From Many Strands: Ethnic and Racial Groups in Contemporary America* (New York: Russell Sage Foundation, 1988).

Lloyd, B. S., Rengert, A. C., & Monk, J. J. "Landscapes of the Home," in A. C. Rengert, & J. J. Monk, eds. *Women and Spatial Change: Learning Resources for Social Science Courses* (Dubuque, Iowa: Kendall-Hunt, 1982).

Momsen, J. H., & Townsend, J., eds. *Geography of Gender in the Third World* (Albany, N.Y.: SUNY Press, 1987).

Monk, J., & Hanson, S., "On Not Excluding Half of the Human in Human Geography," *The Professional Geographer* 34 (1982), 11–23.

Montagu, A. *Man's Most Dangerous Myth: The Fallacy of Race* (Cleveland: World, 4th rev. ed., 1964).

Rengert, A. C., & Monk, J. J., eds. *Women and Spatial Change: Learning Resources for Social Science Courses* (Dubuque, Iowa: Kendall-Hunt, 1982).

Seager, J., & Olson, A. *Women in the World: An International Atlas* (New York: Simon & Schuster, 1986).

Herrnstein, R. J., & Murray, C. *The Bell Curve: Intelligence and Class Structure in American Life* (New York: The Free Press, 1994).

Shipman, P. *The Evolution of Racism* (New York: Simon & Schuster, 1994).

Shortridge, B. G. *Atlas on American Women* (New York: Macmillan, 1987).

Singer, M., & Berg, P. *Genes and Genomes: A Changing Perspective* (Mill Valley, Calif.: University Science Books, 1990).

Sivard, R. Leger. *Women: A World Survey* (Washington, D.C.: World Priorities, 1985).

Sowell, T. *Race and Culture: A World View* (New York: Basic Books, 1994).

Stini, W. A. *Ecology and Human Adaptation* (Dubuque, Iowa: Wm. C. Brown, 1975).

UNICEF. *The Lesser Child: The Girl in India* (Geneva: United Nations, 1990).

United Nations. *The World's Women, 1970–1990* (New York: United Nations, 1991).

Weaver, R. F. "Changing Life's Genetic Blueprint," *National Geographic*, December 1984, pp. 818–847.

Part Six   LANDSCAPE AND THE GEOGRAPHY OF CULTURE

Ardrey, R. *The Territorial Imperative* (New York: Atheneum, 1966).

Brown, L. *Innovation Diffusion: A New Perspective* (London and New York: Methuen, 1981).

Clay, G. *Close-Up: How to Read the American City* (Chicago: University of Chicago Press [reprint of 1973 original], 1980).

Fleming, R., & von Tscharner, R. *Place Makers: Public Art That Tells You Where You Are* (Cambridge, U.K.: Townscape Institute/Hastings House, 1981).

Gould, P., & White, R. *Mental Maps* (Harmondsworth, U.K.: Penguin Books, 2nd rev. ed., 1982).

Hägerstrand, T. *Innovation Diffusion as a Spatial Process* (Chicago: University of Chicago Press, trans. A. Pred, 1967).

Harris, M. *Culture, Man, and Nature* (New York: Thomas Y. Crowell, 1971).

Higuchi, T. *The Visual and Spatial Structure of Landscapes* (Cambridge, Mass.: MIT Press, 1983).

Jackson, J. B. *Discovering the Vernacular Landscape* (New Haven, Conn.: Yale University Press, 1984).

Jakle, J. A., et al. *Common Houses in America's Small Towns: The Atlantic Seaboard to the Mississippi Valley* (Athens: University of Georgia Press, 1989).

Jordan, T. "Perceptual Regions in Texas," *Geographical Review* 68 (1978), 293–307.

Jordan, T., & Rowntree, L. *The Human Mosaic: A Thematic Introduction to Cultural Geography* (New York: Harper & Row, 4th rev. ed., 1986).

Kazin, A. *A Writer's America: Landscape in Literature* (New York: Alfred A. Knopf, 1988).

Knapp, R. G. *China's Vernacular Architecture* (Honolulu: University of Hawaii Press, 1989).

Kroeber, A., & Luckhohn, C. "Culture: A Critical Review of Concepts and Definitions," *Papers of the Peabody Museum of American Archaeology and Ethnology* 47 (1952), entire issue.

Leighly, J., ed. *Land and Life: a Selection from the Writings of Carol Ortwin Sauer* (Berkeley and Los Angeles: University of California Press, 1963).

Meinig, D. "The Mormon Culture Region: Strategies and Patterns in the Geography of the American West, 1847–1964," *Annals of the Association of American Geographers* 55 (1965), 191–220.

Meinig, D. W. *The Shaping of America: A Geographical Perspective on 500 Years of History, Vol. 1: Atlantic America, 1492–1800* (New Haven, Conn.: Yale University Press, 1988).

Pounds, N. J. G. *Hearth and Home: A History of Material Culture* (Bloomington: Indiana University Press, 1989).

Relph, E. *Rational Landscapes and Humanistic Geography* (Totowa, N.J.: Barnes & Noble, 1981).

Richardson, M., ed. *The Human Mirror: Material and Spatial Images of Man* (Baton Rouge, La.: Louisiana State University Press, 1974).

Rogers, E. *Diffusion of Innovations* (New York: Free Press, 3rd rev. ed., 1983).

Rooney, J., et al., eds. *This Remarkable Continent: An Atlas of United States and Canadian Societies and Culture* (College Station, Tex.: Texas A & M University Press, 1982).

Salter, C., ed. *The Cultural Landscape* (Belmont, Calif.: Wadsworth, 1971).

Sauer, C. O. *Agricultural Origins and Dispersals* (New York: American Geographical Society, 1952).

Shortridge, J. R. *The Middle West: Its Meaning in American Culture* (Lawrence: University Press of Kansas, 1989).

Spencer, J., & Horvath, R. "How Does an Agricultural Region Originate?" *Annals of the Association of American Geographers* 53 (1963), 74–92.

Stilgoe, J. *Common Landscape of America: 1580–1845* (New Haven, Conn.: Yale University Press, 1982).

Swartz, M., & Jordan, D. *Culture: The Anthropological Perspective* (New York: John Wiley & Sons, 1980).

Thomas, W., ed. *Man's Role in Changing the Face of the Earth* (Chicago: University of Chicago Press, 1956).

Tuan, Y.-F. *Landscapes of Fear* (New York: Pantheon Books, 1979).

Tuan, Y.-F. *Topophilia: A Study of Environmental Perception, Attitudes and Values* (Englewood Cliffs, N.J.: Prentice-Hall, 1974).

Wilson, P. J. *The Domestication of the Human Species* (New Haven, Conn.: Yale University Press, 1988).

The World Atlas of Architecture (Boston: G. K. Hall, 1981).

Zelinsky, W. *The Cultural Geography of the United States* (Englewood Cliffs, N.J.: Prentice-Hall, 1973).

Zelinsky, W. "North America's Vernacular Regions," *Annals of the Association of American Geographers* 70(1980), 1–16.

Part Seven   PATTERNS OF LANGUAGE

Bellwood, P. "Austronesian Dispersal and the Origin of Languages," *Scientific American*, July 1991, pp. 88–93.

Cavalli-Sforza, L. L. "Genes, Peoples and Languages," *Scientific American*, November 1991, pp. 104–110.

de Carvalho, C. "The Geography of Languages," in P. Wagner, & M. Mikesell, eds., *Readings in Cultural Geography* (Chicago: University of Chicago Press, 1962), pp. 75–93.

Dixon, R.M.W. *Searching for Aboriginal Languages* (Chicago: University of Chicago Press, 1989).

Dugdale, J. *The Linguistic Map of Europe* (London: Hutchinson University Library, 1969).

Eastman, C. *Aspects of Language and Culture* (San Francisco: Chandler & Sharp, 1975).

Fishman, J., et al., eds. *Language Loyalty in the United States: The Maintenance and Perpetuation of Non-English Mother Tongues by American Ethnic and Religious Groups* (The Hague, Netherlands: Mouton, 1966).

Gamkrelidze, T. V., & Ivanov, V. V. "The Early History of Indo-European Languages," *Scientific American*, March 1990, pp. 110–116.

Greenberg, J. *The Languages of Africa* (Bloomington: Indiana University Press, 1963).

Greenberg, J. *Languages in the Americas* (Bloomington: Indiana University Press, 1987).

Hymes, D. *Language in Culture and Society* (New York: Harper & Row, 1964).

Katzner, K. *The Languages of the World* (New York: Funk & Wagnalls, 1975).

Kirk, J., et al., eds. *Studies in Linguistic Geography* (Dover, N.J.: Longwood, 1985).

Krantz, G. S. *Geographical Development of European Languages* (New York: Peter Lang, 1988).

Kurath, H. *The Word Geography of the Eastern United States* (Ann Arbor: University of Michigan Press, 1949).

Laird, C. *Language in America* (Cleveland: World, 1970).

Lewin, R. "American Indian Language Dispute," *Science*, 23 December 1988, pp. 1632–1633.

Lewin, R. "Ancestral Voices at War," *New Scientist*, 16 June 1990, pp. 42–44.

McCrone, J. *The Ape That Spoke* (New York: William Morrow, 1991).

McDavid, R., Jr., & O'Cain, R., eds., *Linguistic Atlas of the Middle and South Atlantic States* (Chicago: University of Chicago Press, 1980).

Murphy, A. B. *The Regional Dynamics of Language Differentiation in Belgium: A Study in Cultural-Political Geography* (Chicago: University of Chicago Geographical Research Paper No. 227, 1988).

Renfrew, C. *Archaeology and Language: The Puzzle of Indo-European Origins* (Cambridge, Cambridge University Press, 1988).

Renfrew, C. "The Origins of Indo-European Languages," *Scientific American*, October 1989, pp. 106–114.

Ross, P. E. "Hard Words," *Scientific American*, April 1991, pp. 138–146.

Schwartzberg, J. *An Historical Atlas of South Asia* (Chicago: University of Chicago Press, 1978).

Sopher, D., ed. *An Exploration of India: Geographical Perspectives on Society and Culture* (Ithaca, N.Y.: Cornell University Press, 1980).

Stewart, G. *Names on the Globe* (New York: Oxford University Press, 1975).

Stewart, G. *Names on the Land: A Historical Account of Place-Naming in the United States* (Boston: Houghton Mifflin, 2nd rev. ed., 1958).

Trudgill, P. "Linguistic Geography and Geographical Linguistics," in C. Board et al., eds., *Progress in Geography*, Vol. 7 (New York: St. Martin's Press, 1975), pp. 227–252.

von Grunebaum, G., ed. *Islam: Essays on the Nature and Growth of a Cultural Tradition* (London: Routledge & Kegan Paul, 1955).

Wurm, S., & Hattori, S., eds. *Linguistic Atlas of the Pacific Area* (Canberra, Austr.: Australian Academy of the Humanities, 1982).

Part Eight   GEOGRAPHY OF RELIGION

al Faruqi, I., & Sopher, D., eds. *Historical Atlas of the Religions of the World* (New York: Macmillan, 1974).

Barakat, H. *The Arab World: Society, Culture, and State* (Berkeley: University of California Press, 1993).

Bhardwaj, S. *Hindu Places of Pilgrimage in India: A Study in Cultural Geography* (Berkeley and Los Angeles: University of California Press, 1973).

Bjorklund, E. "Ideology and Culture Exemplified in Southwestern Michigan," *Annals of the Association of American Geographers* 54 (1964), 227–241.

Carroll, J., et al. *Religion in America: 1950 to the Present* (New York: Harper & Row, 1979).

de Blij, H. J. "Islam in South Africa," in J. Kritzeck, & W. H. Lewis, eds., *Islam in Africa* (New York: Van Nostrand, 1970).

Dumont, L. *Homo Hierarchus: The Caste System and Its Implications* (Chicago: University of Chicago Press, 1980).

Eliade, M. *The Sacred and the Profane: The Nature of Religion* (New York: Harcourt, Brace & World, 1959).

Ewing, S. *Man, Religion and Environment* (Dubuque, Iowa: Kendall/Hunt, 1975).

Gaustad, E. *Historical Atlas of Religion in America* (New York: Harper & Row, 1962).

Glacken, C. *Traces on the Rhodian Shore: Nature and Culture in Western Thought from Ancient Times to the End of the Eighteenth Century* (Berkeley and Los Angeles: University of California Press, 1967).

Halvorson, P., & Newman, W. *Atlas of Religious Change in America, 1952–1971* (Washington, D.C.: Glenmary Research Center, 1978).

Halvorson, P., & Newman, W. *Patterns in Pluralism: A Portrait of American Religion* (Washington, D.C.: Glenmary Research Center, 1980).

Hill, S. S. Jr., *The South and the North in American Religion* (Athens: University of Georgia Press, 1980).

Isaac, E. "The Pilgrimage to Mecca," *Geographical Review* 63 (1973), 405–409.

Lewis, B., ed. *The World of Islam: Faith, People, Culture* (London, U.K.: Thames & Hudson, 1976).

Marty, M. E. *Pilgrims in Their Own Land: 500 Years of Religion in America* (Boston: Little, Brown, 1984).

Mitchell, G. *The Hindu Temple: An Introduction to Its Meaning and Forms* (New York: Harper & Row, 1977).

Noble, A. G., & Efrat, E. "Geography of the Intifada," *The Geographical Review*, July 1990, pp. 288–307.

Schwartzberg, J. *An Historical Atlas of South Asia* (Chicago: University of Chicago Press, 1970).

Sopher, D., ed. *An Exploration of India: Geographical Perspectives on Society and Culture* (Ithaca, N.Y.: Cornell University Press, 1980).

Sowell, T. *Ethnic America: A History* (New York: Basic Books, 1981).

Swartz, M. J. *The Way the World Is* (Berkeley: University of California Press, 1991).

Thernstrom, S., ed. *Harvard Encyclopedia of American Ethnic Groups* (Cambridge, Mass.: Belknap-Harvard University Press, 1980).

Voeks, R. "Sacred Leaves of a Brazilian Candomble," *The Geographical Review*, April 1990, pp. 118–131.

Weekes, R., ed. *Muslim Peoples: A World Ethnographic Survey* (Westport, Conn.: Greenwood Press, 2 vols., 1984).

Wurm, S., & Hattori, S., eds. *Linguistic Atlas of the Pacific Area* (Canberra: Australian Academy of the Humanities, 1982).

Zelinsky, W. "An Approach to the Religious Geography of the United States," *Annals of the Association of American Geographers* 51 (1961), 139–167.

Part Nine CULTURAL LANDSCAPES OF FARMING

Alexander, J. W., & Hartshorn, T. *Economic Geography* (Englewood Cliffs, N.J.: Prentice-Hall, 3rd rev. ed., 1986).

Berleant-Schiller, R., & Shanklin, E., eds. *The Keeping of Animals: Adaptation and Social Relations in Livestock-Producing Communities* (Totowa, N.J.: Rowman & Allanheld, 1983).

Boserup, E. *The Conditions of Agricultural Growth: The Economics of Agrarian Change under Population Pressure* (Chicago: Aldine, 1966).

Dalal-Clayton, D., ed. *Black's Agricultural Dictionary* (Totowa, N.J.: Barnes & Noble, 2nd rev. ed., 1986).

de Blij, H. *Wine: A Geographic Appreciation* (Totowa, N.J.: Rowman & Allanheld, 1983).

de Blij, H. *Wine Regions of the Southern Hemisphere* (Totowa, N.J.: Rowman & Allanheld, 1985).

de Souza, A. *World Space-Economy* (Columbus, Ohio: Charles E. Merrill, 2nd rev. ed., 1989).

Duckham, A., & Masefield, G. *Farming Systems of the World* (New York: Praeger, 1970).

Gourou, P. *The Tropical World: Its Social and Economic Conditions and Its Future Status* (London and New York: Longman, 5th rev. ed., trans. S. Beaver, 1980).

Grigg, D. *An Introduction to Agricultural Geography* (London, U.K.: Hutchinson University Library, 1984).

Grigg, D. *Population Growth and Agrarian Change* (London, U.K.: Cambridge University Press, 1980).

Gritzner, J. A. *The West African Sahel: Human Agency and Environmental Change* (Chicago: University of Chicago Geography Research Paper No. 226, 1988).

Harris, D., ed. *Human Ecology in Savanna Environments* (New York and London: Academic Press, 1980).

Hart, J. F. *The Land That Feeds Us* (New York: Norton, 1991).

Heiser, C., Jr. *Seed to Civilization: The Story of Food* (San Francisco: W. H. Freeman, 2nd rev. ed., 1981).

Horvath, R. "Von Thünen's Isolated State and the Area Around Addis Ababa, Ethiopia," *Annals of the Association of American Geographers* 59 (1969). 308–323.

Jumper, S., et al. *Economic Growth and Disparities: A World View* (Englewood Cliffs, N.J.: Prentice-Hall, 1980).

Keen, E. A. *Ownership and Productivity of Marine Fishery Resources* (Blacksburg, Va.: McDonald & Woodward, 1988).

Klee, G., ed. *World Systems of Traditional Resource Management* (New York: Halsted Press N.H. Winston, 1980).

Levi, J., & Havinden, M. *Economics of African Agriculture* (Harlow, U.K.: Longman, 1982).

Lipton, M. *Progress and Poverty* (Brighton, U.K.: Institute of Development Studies, University of Sussex, 1991).

Moris, J. R., & Thom, D. J. *Irrigation Development in Africa: Lessons of Experience* (Boulder, Colo.: Westview Press, 1990).

Pacione, M., ed. *Progress in Rural Geography* (Totowa, N.J.: Barnes & Noble, 1983).

Sauer, C. O. *Agricultural Origins and Dispersals* (Cambridge, Mass.: MIT Press, 2nd rev. ed., 1969).

Spencer, J., & Horvath, R. "How Does an Agricultural Region Originate?" *Annals of the Association of American Geographers* 53 (1963), 74–82.

Spencer, J., & Thomas, W. *Cultural Geography: An Evolutionary Introduction to Our Humanized Earth* (New York: John Wiley & Sons, 1969).

Von Thünen, J. H. *Der Isolierte Staat.* Translated by C. M. Wartenberg. In P. Hall, ed. *Von Thünen's Isolated State* (Elmsford, N.Y.: Pergamon, 1966).

Yellen, J. E., "The Transformation of the Kalahari !Kung," *Scientific American*, April 1990, pp. 96–105.

Part Ten THE URBANIZING WORLD

Abbott, C. *The New Urban America: Growth and Politics in Sunbelt Cities* (Chapel Hill: University of North Carolina Press, 1981).

Adams, J., ed. *Contemporary Metropolitan America* (Cambridge, Mass.: Ballinger, 4 vols., 1976).

Agnew, J., et al., eds. *The City in Cultural Context* (Winchester, Mass.: Allen & Unwin, 1984).

Bairoch, P. *Cities and Economic Development* (Chicago: University of Chicago Press, trans. C. Braider, 1989).

Berry, B.J.L. *Comparative Urbanization: Divergent Paths in the Twentieth Century* (New York: St. Martin's Press, 2nd rev. ed., 1981).

Borchert, J. "American Metropolitan Evolution," *Geographical Review* 57 (1967), 301–332.

Bourne, L., ed. *Internal Structure of the City: Readings on Urban Form, Growth, and Policy* (New York: Oxford University Press, 2nd rev. ed., 1982).

Bourne, L., et al., ed. *Urbanization and Settlement Systems: International Perspectives* (New York: Oxford University Press, 1984).

Brunn, S., & Wheeler, J., eds. *The American Metropolitan System: Present and Future* (New York: Wiley N. H. Winston, 1980).

Brunn, S., & Williams, J., eds. *Cities of the World: World Regional Urban Development* (New York: Harper & Row, 1983).

Burgess, E. "The Growth of the City," in R. Park et al., eds., *The City* (Chicago: University of Chicago Press, 1925), pp. 47–62.

Burnett, J. A. *A Social History of Housing, 1815–1970* (North Pomfret, Vt.: David & Charles, 1978).

Butzer, K. *Early Hydraulic Civilization in Egypt: A Study in Cultural Ecology* (Chicago: University of Chicago Press, 1976).

Castells, M., ed. *High Technology Space and Society* (Beverly Hills, Calif.: Sage Publications, 1985).

Choldin, H. *Cities and Suburbs* (New York: McGraw-Hill, 1985).

Christaller, W. *Central Places in Southern Germany* (Englewood Cliffs, N.J.: Prentice-Hall, trans. C. Baskin, 1966 [originally published 1933]).

Christaller, W. "The Foundations of Spatial Organization in Europe," *Frankfurter Geographische Hefte* 24 (1950).

Christian, C., & Harper, M., eds. *Modern Metropolitan Systems* (Columbus, Ohio: Charles E. Merrill, 1982).

Chudacoff, H. *The Evolution of Urban American Society* (Englewood Cliffs, N.J.: Prentice-Hall, 3rd rev. ed., 1985).

Clark, D. *Post-Industrial America: A Geographical Perspective* (New York and London: Methuen, 1985).

Clay, G. *Close-Up: How to Read the American City* (Chicago: University of Chicago Press, 1980 [reprint of 1973 original]).

Costa, F. J., et al. *Asian Urbanization: Problems and Processes* (Berlin: Gebruder Borntraeger, 1988).

de Blij, H. J. *Mombasa: An African City* (Evanston, Ill.: Northwestern University Press, 1968).

Gilbert, A., & Gugler, J. *Cities, Poverty and Development: Urbanization in the Third World* (New York: Oxford University Press, 1982).

Glassie, H. *Pattern in the Material Folk Culture of the Eastern United States* (Philadelphia: University of Pennsylvania Press, 1969).

Gottman, J. *Megalopolis: The Urbanized Northeastern Seaboard of the United States* (New York: Twentieth Century Fund, 1961).

Griffin, E., & Ford, L. "A Model of Latin American City Structure," *Geographical Review* 70 (1980), 387–422.

Gugler, J., ed. *The Urbanization of the Third World* (New York: Oxford University Press, 1988).

Guldin, G. E., ed. *Urbanizing China* (Westport, Conn.: Greenwood Press, 1992).

Hall, P. *The World Cities* (New York: St. Martin's Press, 3rd rev. ed., 1984).

Hall, P., & Markusen, A., eds., *Silicon Landscapes* (Winchester, Mass.: Allen & Unwin, 1985).

Hallman, H. *Neighborhoods: Their Place in Urban Life* (Beverly Hills, Calif.: Sage Publications, 1984).

Harris, C. "A Functional Classification of Cities in the United States," *Geographical Review* 33 (1943), 86–99.

Harris, C. D., & Ullman, E. L. "The Nature of Cities," *Annals of the American Academy of Political and Social Science* 242 (1945), 7–17.

Hartshorn, T. *Interpreting the City: An Urban Geography* (New York: John Wiley & Sons, 3rd rev. ed., 1992).

Hoyt, H. *The Structure and Growth of Residential Neighborhoods in American Cities* (Washington, D.C.: U.S. Federal Housing Administration, 1939).

Jackson, K. *Crabgrass Frontier: The Suburbanization of the United States* (New York: Oxford University Press, 1985).

Jakle, J. *The American Small Town* (Hamden, Conn.: Shoestring Press, 1982).

Jefferson, M. "The Law of the Primate City," *Geographical Review* 29 (1939), 226–232.

Johnson, J. H., ed. *Suburban Growth: Geographical Processes at the Edge of the Western City* (London: John Wiley & Sons, 1974).

King, L. *Central Place Theory* (Beverly Hills, Calif.: Sage Publications, 1984).

Kniffen, F. B. "Folk Housing: Key to Diffusion," *Annals of the Association of American Geographers* 55 (1965), 549–577.

Knox, P. L. *Urbanization: An Introduction to Urban Geography* (Englewood Cliffs, N.J.: Prentice-Hall, 1994).

Leinbach, T., & Ulack, R. "Cities of Southeast Asia," in S. Brunn and J. Williams, eds., *Cities of the World: World Regional Urban Development* (New York: Harper & Row, 1983), pp. 370–407.

Lewis, G. *Rural Communities* (North Pomfret, Vt.: David & Charles, 1979).

Ley, D. *A Social Geography of the City* (New York: Harper & Row, 1983).

McAlester, V., & McAlester, L. *A Field Guide to American Houses* (New York: Knopf, 1984).

McGee, T. G. *The Southeast Asian City: A Social Geography* (New York: Praeger, 1967).

Meinig, D., ed. *The Interpretation of Ordinary Landscapes: Geographical Essays* (New York: Oxford University Press, 1979).

Mitchell, R., & Groves, P., eds. *The Shaping of North America: An Historical Geography* (Totowa, N.J.: Rowman & Allanheld, 1986).

Mohl, R. *The New City: Urban America in the Industrial Age, 1860–1920* (Arlington Heights, Ill.: Harlan Davidson, 1985).

Muller, P. *Contemporary Suburban America* (Englewood Cliffs, N.J.: Prentice-Hall, 1981).

Mumford, L. *The City in History: Its Origins, Its Transformations, and Its Prospects* (New York: Harcourt, Brace, 1961).

Noble, A. *Wood, Brick, and Stone: The North American Settlement Landscape* (Amherst: University of Massachusetts Press, 1984).

Palm, R. *The Geography of American Cities* (New York: Oxford University Press, 1981).

Rapoport, A. *House Form and Culture* (Englewood Cliffs, N.J.: Prentice-Hall, 1969).

Sjoberg, G. *The Preindustrial City: Past, and Present* (Glencoe, Ill.: Free Press, 1960).

Skinner, G. W. "Marketing and Social Structure in Rural China," *Journal of Asian Studies* 24 (1964–1965), 3–44, 195–228, 363–400.

Smailes, A. *The Geography of Towns* (London, U.K.: Hutchinson University Library, 1953).

Stilgoe, J. R. *Borderland: Origins of the American Suburb, 1820–1939* (New Haven, Conn.: Yale University Press, 1988).

Stren, R. E., & White, R. R., eds. *African Cities in Crisis: Managing Rapid Urban Growth* (Boulder, Colo.: Westview Press, 1989).

Vance, J. E., Jr. *This Scene of Man: The Role and Structure of the City in the Geography of Western Civilization* (New York: Harper's College Press, 1977).

Walmsley, D. J. *Urban Living: The Individual in the City* (New York: John Wiley & Sons, 1988).

Ward, D. *Poverty, Ethnicity, and the American City, 1840–1925: Conceptions of the Slum and the Ghetto* (New York: Cambridge University Press, 1989).

Western, J. *Outcast Cape Town* (Minneapolis: University of Minnesota Press, 1981).

Wheatley, P. *The Pivot of the Four Quarters: A Preliminary Enquiry Into the Origins and Character of the Ancient Chinese City* (Chicago: Aldine, 1971).

Wright, H. T., & Johnson, G. A. "Population, Exchange, and Early State Formation in Southwestern Iran," *American Anthropologist* 77 (1975), 267–277.

United Nations. Population Division. *World Urbanization Prospects, 1950–2025* (1992 revision, New York: United Nations, 1993).

Yeates, M. *Main Street: Windsor to Quebec City* (Toronto: Macmillan, 1975).

Zelinsky, W. *The Cultural Geography of the United States* (Englewood Cliffs, N.J.: Prentice-Hall, 1973).

Part Eleven   CULTURES, LANDSCAPES, AND REGIONS OF INDUSTRY

Birdsall, S. S., & Florin, J. W. *Regional Landscapes of the United States and Canada*, 4th ed. (New York: John Wiley & Sons, 1992).

Blakely, E. J., & Stimson, R. J., eds. *New Cities of the Pacific Rim*, Monograph 43 (Berkeley: University of California, Institute of Urban and Regional Development, 1992).

Blouet, B. W., & Blouet, O. M., eds. *Latin America and the Caribbean: A Systematic and Regional Survey*, 2d ed. (New York: John Wiley & Sons, 1993).

Borthwick, M. *Pacific Century: The Emergence of Modern Pacific Asia* (Boulder, Colo.: Westview Press, 1992).

Boserup, E. *Economic and Demographic Relationships in Development* (Baltimore: Johns Hopkins University Press, 1990).

Burks, A. W. *Japan: A Postindustrial Power*, 3rd ed. (Boulder, Colo.: Westview Press, 1991).

Chapman, G. P., & Baker, K. M., eds. *The Changing Geography of Asia* (New York: Routledge, 1992).

Chowdhury, A., & Islam, I. *The Newly Industrializing Economies of East Asia* (New York: Routledge, 1993).

Clout, H. D. *Western Europe: Geographical Perspectives*, 3rd ed. (New York: John Wiley & Sons, 1994).

Cole, J. P., & Cole, F. J. *The Geography of the European Community* (New York: Routledge, 1993).

de Souza, P. *Territorial Production Complexes in the Soviet Union—With Special Focus on Siberia* (Gothenburg, Sweden: University of Gothenburg, 1989).

Drakakis-Smith, D. *Pacific Asia* (New York: Routledge, 1992).

Drakakis-Smith, D., & Dixon, Chris, eds. *Economic and Social Development in Pacific Asia* (New York: Routledge, 1993).

Freeman, M. *Atlas of the World Economy* (New York: Simon & Schuster, 1991).

Gleave, M. B., ed. *Tropical African Development: Geographical Perspectives* (New York: Wiley/Longman, 1992).

Hamilton, I., ed. *Resources and Industry* (New York: Oxford University Press, 1992).

Hanink, D. M. *The International Economy: A Geographical Perspective* (New York: John Wiley & Sons, 1994).

Hussey, A. "Rapid Industrialization in Thailand, 1986–1991," *Geographical Review* 83 (1993), 14–28.

Kotler, P., et al. *Marketing Places: Attracting Investment, Industry, and Tourism to Cities, States, and Nations* (New York: Free Press, 1993).

Leeming, F. *The Changing Geography of China* (Cambridge, Mass.: Blackwell, 1993).

Lewis, R. A., ed. *Geographic Perspectives on Soviet Central Asia* (New York: Routledge, 1992).

Linge, G.T.R., & van der Knapp, G. A., eds. *Labour, Environment, and Industrial Change* (New York: Routledge, 1989).

Lockhart, D. G., et al., eds. *The Development Process in Small Island States* (New York: Routledge, 1993).

Losch, A. *The Economics of Location.* Translated by W. Woglom & W. Stolper (New York: Wiley Science Editions, 1967); originally published in 1940.

McKnight, T. L. *Regional Geography of the United States and Canada* (Englewood Cliffs, N.J.: Prentice-Hall, 1992).

Ogawa, N., et al., eds. *Human Resources in Development along the Asia-Pacific Rim* (Singapore: Oxford University Press, 1993).

Phillips, D. R. *Health and Health Care in the Third World* (Essex, U.K.: Longmans, 1990).

Pick, J. B., & Butler, Edward W. *The Mexico Handbook: Economic and Demographic Maps and Statistics* (Boulder, Colo.: Westview Press, 1993).

Pounds, N.J.G. *An Historical Geography of Europe, 1800–1914* (New York: Cambridge University Press, 1985).

Rodwin, L., & Sazanami, H. *Industrial Change and Regional Economic Transformation: The Experience of Western Europe* (New York: Harper Collins Academic, 1991).

Rostow, W. W. *The Stages of Economic Growth*, 2d ed. (New York: Cambridge University Press, 1971).

Smith, D. M. *Industrial Location: An Economic Geographical Analysis*, 2nd ed. (New York: John Wiley & Sons, 1981).

Songqiao, Z. *Geography of China: Environment, Resources, and Development* (New York: John Wiley & Sons, 1994).

Stewart, J. M., ed. *The Soviet Environment: Problems, Policies and Politics* (New York: Cambridge University Press, 1992).

Vogel, E. F. *The Four Little Dragons: The Spread of Industrialization in East Asia* (Cambridge, Mass.: Harvard University Press, 1991).

Warren, K. *The American Steel Industry 1850–1970: A Geographical Interpretation* (Pittsburgh, Pa.: University of Pittsburgh Press, 1989).

Weber, A. *Theory of the Location of Industries.* Translated by C. Friedrich (Chicago: University of Chicago Press, 1929; originally published in 1909).

Wheeler, J. O., Muller, P. O., & Thrall, G. I. *Economic Geography*, 3rd ed. (New York: John Wiley & Sons, 1995).

World Bank. *World Development Report, 1990: Poverty* (New York: Oxford University Press, 1990).

Yeung, Yue-Man, & Hu, Xu-Wei, eds. *China's Coastal Cities: Catalysts for Modernization* (Honolulu: University of Honolulu Press, 1992).

Part Twelve   THE POLITICAL IMPRINT

Barakat, H. *The Arab World: Society, Culture, and State* (Berkeley: University of California Press, 1993).

Booth, J. A., & Walker, T. W. *Understanding Central America*, 2d ed. (Boulder, Colo.: Westview Press, 1993).

Boyd, A. *An Atlas of World Affairs*, 9th ed. (New York: Routledge, 1992).

Cohen, L. J. *Broken Bonds: The Rise and Fall of Yugoslavia* (Boulder, Colo.: Westview Press, 1993).

Crossette, B. *India: Facing the Twenty-First Century* (Bloomington: Indiana University Press, 1993).

Davidson, B. *The Black Man's Burden: Africa and the Curse of the Nation-State* (New York: Time Books/Random House, 1992).

Dawson, A. H. *The Geography of European Integration: A Common European Home?* (New York: Belhaven, 1993).

Dink, N., & Karatnycky, A. *New Nations Rising: The Fall of the Soviets and the Challenge of Independence* (New York: John Wiley & Sons, 1993).

Esposito, J. L. *The Islamic Threat: Myth or Reality?* (New York: Oxford University Press, 1992).

Finkelstein, N. *The Separation of Quebec and the Constitution of Canada* (North York, Ontario: York University Centre for Public Law and Public Policy, 1992).

Fournier, P. *A Meech Lake Post-Mortem: Is Quebec Sovereignty Inevitable?* (Montreal: McGill-Queens University Press, 1991).

Freeman-Grenville, G.S.P. *The New Atlas of African History* (New York: Simon & Schuster, 1991).

Glassner, M. I. *Neptune's Domain: A Political Geography of the Sea* (Winchester, Mass.: Unwin Hyman, 1990).

Glassner, M. I. *Political Geography* (New York: John Wiley & Sons, 1993).

Hancock, M. D., & Welsh, H., eds., *German Unification: Process and Outcomes* (Boulder, Colo.: Westview Press, 1993).

Held, C. C. *Middle East Patterns: Places, Peoples, and Politics*, 2nd ed. (Boulder, Colo.: Westview Press, 1993).

Ingham, K. *Politics in Modern Africa: The Uneven Tribal Dimension* (London: Routledge, 1990).

Joffé, G., ed. *North Africa: Nation, State and Region* (London: Routledge, 1993).

Johnston, R. J. *Geography and the State: An Essay in Political Geography* (New York: St. Martin's Press, 1983).

Johnston, R. J., Knight, D. B., & Kofman, E., eds. *Nationalism, Self-Determination, and Political Geography* (New York: Croom & Helm, 1988).

Johnston, R. J., Shelley, F. M., & Taylor, P. J. *Developments in Electoral Geography* (New York: Routledge, 1990).

Lewis, R. A., ed. *Geographic Perspectives on Soviet Central Asia* (New York: Routledge, 1992).

Mackinder, H. J. *Democratic Ideals and Reality: A Study in the Politics of Reconstruction* (New York: Holt, 1909).

Mackinder, H. J. "The Geographical Pivot of History," *Geographical Journal* 23 (1904), 421–444.

Mellor, R.E.H. *Nation, State, and Territory: A Political Geography* (New York: Routledge, Chapman & Hall, 1989).

Muni, S. D. *Pangs of Proximity: India and Sri Lanka's Ethnic Crisis* (Newbury Park, Calif.: Sage Publications, 1993).

Nahaylo, B., & Swoboda, V. *Soviet Disunion: A History of the Nationalities Problem in the USSR* (New York: Free Press, 1990).

Nijman, J. *The Geopolitics of Power and Conflict: Superpowers in the International System, 1945–1992* (London: Belhaven, 1993).

Noble, A. G., ed. *To Build in a New Land: Ethnic Landscapes in North America* (Baltimore: Johns Hopkins University Press, 1992).

O'Loughlin, J. V., & Van der Wusten, H., eds. *The New Political Geography of Eastern Europe* (New York: Belhaven/Wiley, 1993).

Prescott, J.R.V. *Political Frontiers and Boundaries* (London: Allen & Unwin, 1987).

Ratzel, F. "Laws of the Spatial Growth of States." In Roger E. Kasperson & Julian Minghi, eds., *The Structure of Political Geography.* Translated by R. L. Bolin (Chicago: Aldine, 1969).

Robinson, K. W. "Sixty Years of Federation in Australia," *Geographical Review* 51 (1961), 1–20.

Rumley, D., & Minghi, J. V., eds. *The Geography of Border Landscapes* (New York: Routledge, 1991).

Slowe, P. O. *Geography and Political Power: The Geography of Nations and States* (New York: Routledge, Chapman & Hall, 1990).

Spykman, N. J. *The Geography of the Peace* (New York: Harcourt, Brace, 1944).

Stoessinger, J. *The Might of Nations* (New York: Random House, 1967).

Taylor, P. *Political Geography: World-Economy, Nation-State, and Locality*, 2d ed. (New York: John Wiley & Sons, 1993).

Taylor, P. J., ed. *Political Geography of the Twentieth Century: A Global Analysis* (New York: Halsted Press, 1993).

Taylor, P., & House, J., eds. *Political Geography: Recent Advances and Future Directions* (Totowa, N.J.: Barnes & Noble, 1984).

Turnock, D. *Eastern Europe: An Economic and Political Geography* (New York: Routledge, 1989).

Van Dyke, J. M., et al. *Freedom for the Seas in the 21st Century: Ocean Governance and Environmental Harmony* (Washington, D.C.: Island Press, 1993).

Vasciannie, S. C. *Landlocked and Geographically Disadvantaged States in the International Law of the Sea* (New York: Oxford University Press, 1990).

William, C. H., ed. *The Political Geography of the New World Order* (New York: Halsted Press, 1993).

Resource C

1995
WORLD POPULATION
DATA SHEET

	Population mid-1995 (millions)	Birth Rate per 1000 pop.	Death Rate per 1000 pop.	Natural Increase (annual, %)	"Doubling Time" in Years at Current Rate	Projected Population (millions)		Infant Mortality Rate[a]	Total Fertility Rate[b]	% Age		Life Expectancy at Birth (years)			% Urban	Per Capita GNP, 1993 (US$)
						2010	2025			<15	65+	T	M	F		
WORLD	5,702	24	9	1.5	45	7,024	8,312	62	3.1	32	6	66	64	68	43	$ 4,500
MORE DEVELOPED	1,169	12	10	0.2	432	1,232	1,271	10	1.6	20	13	74	70	78	74	17,270
LESS DEVELOPED	4,533	28	9	1.9	36	5,791	7,041	67	3.5	35	5	64	62	65	35	1,030
LESS DEVELOPED (Excl. China)	3,314	31	9	2.2	32	4,406	5,518	72	4.0	38	4	62	60	63	38	1,250
AFRICA	720	41	13	2.8	24	1,069	1,510	90	5.8	45	3	55	53	56	31	660
SUB-SAHARAN AFRICA	586	44	14	3.0	23	892	1,290	95	6.2	46	3	52	51	54	27	560
NORTHERN AFRICA	162	32	8	2.4	29	219	279	63	4.4	41	3	64	63	65	45	1,040
Algeria	28.4	30	6	2.4	29	38.0	47.2	55	4.4	39	4	67	66	68	50	2,650
Egypt	61.9	30	8	2.3	31	80.7	97.9	62	3.9	40	4	64	62	65	44	660
Libya	5.2	42	8	3.4	21	8.9	14.4	68	6.4	48	3	63	62	65	85	—
Morocco	29.2	28	6	2.2	32	38.4	47.4	57	4.0	40	4	69	67	71	47	1,030
Sudan	28.1	41	12	3.0	23	41.5	58.4	77	5.9	46	2	55	54	56	27	—
Tunisia	8.9	25	6	1.9	36	11.2	13.3	43	3.4	37	5	68	67	69	60	1,780
Western Sahara	0.2	47	18	2.8	24	0.3	0.4	—	—	—	—	—	—	—	—	—
WEST AFRICA	199	45	14	3.1	22	311	467	86	6.4	46	3	53	52	55	23	370
Benin	5.4	49	18	3.1	22	8.3	12.3	86	7.1	47	3	48	46	49	30	420
Burkina Faso	10.4	47	19	2.8	24	14.5	20.9	94	6.9	48	3	45	44	46	15	300
Cape Verde	0.4	36	9	2.8	25	0.6	0.7	50	4.3	45	6	65	64	66	44	870
Côte d'Ivoire	14.3	50	15	3.5	20	23.1	36.8	92	7.4	47	2	51	50	52	39	630
Gambia	1.1	48	21	2.7	26	1.5	2.1	90	5.9	45	2	45	43	47	26	360

	Population mid-1995 (millions)	Birth Rate per 1000 pop.	Death Rate per 1000 pop.	Natural Increase (annual, %)	"Doubling Time" in Years at *Current* Rate	Projected Population (millions) 2010	2025	Infant Mortality Rate[a]	Total Fertility Rate[b]	% Age <15	65+	Life Expectancy at Birth (years) T	M	F	% Urban	Per Capita GNP, 1993 (US$)
Ghana	17.5	42	12	3.0	23	26.6	38.0	81	5.5	45	3	56	54	58	36	430
Guinea	6.5	44	19	2.4	29	9.3	12.9	143	5.8	44	3	44	42	47	29	510
Guinea-Bissau	1.1	43	21	2.1	32	1.5	2.0	140	5.8	43	3	44	42	45	22	220
Liberia	3.0	47	14	3.3	21	4.8	7.2	126	6.8	46	4	55	54	57	44	—
Mali	9.4	51	20	3.2	22	15.0	23.7	104	7.3	46	4	47	45	48	22	300
Mauritania	2.3	40	14	2.5	27	3.3	4.4	101	5.4	45	4	52	50	53	39	510
Niger	9.2	53	19	3.4	21	14.8	22.4	123	7.4	49	3	47	45	48	15	270
Nigeria	101.2	43	12	3.1	22	162.0	246.0	72	6.3	45	3	56	55	58	16	310
Senegal	8.3	43	16	2.7	26	12.2	16.9	68	6.0	45	3	49	48	50	39	730
Sierra Leone	4.5	46	19	2.7	26	6.4	8.7	143	6.2	44	3	46	44	47	35	140
Togo	4.4	47	11	3.6	19	7.4	11.7	86	6.9	49	2	58	56	60	30	330
EASTERN AFRICA	**266**	**46**	**15**	**3.0**	**23**	**345**	**491**	**106**	**6.4**	**47**	**3**	**50**	**48**	**52**	**21**	**210**
Burundi	6.4	46	16	3.0	23	9.5	13.5	102	6.6	46	4	50	48	52	6	180
Comoros	0.5	46	11	3.6	20	0.9	1.4	79	6.8	48	3	58	56	60	29	520
Djibouti	0.6	38	16	2.2	32	0.8	1.1	115	5.8	41	2	48	47	50	77	780
Eritrea	3.5	42	16	2.6	27	5.2	7.0	—	—	—	—	—	—	—	—	—
Ethiopia	56.0	46	16	3.1	23	90.0	129.7	120	7.0	49	3	50	48	52	15	100
Kenya	28.3	45	12	3.3	21	43.6	63.6	69	5.7	48	3	56	54	57	27	270
Madagascar	14.8	44	12	3.2	22	23.3	34.4	93	6.1	46	3	57	55	58	22	240
Malawi	9.7	47	20	2.7	25	14.7	21.3	134	6.7	48	3	45	44	45	17	220
Mauritius	1.1	21	7	1.5	47	1.3	1.5	18.5	2.4	30	6	69	65	73	44	2,980
Mozambique	17.4	45	19	2.7	26	26.9	38.3	148	6.5	46	2	46	45	48	33	80
Reunion	0.7	23	6	1.8	40	0.8	0.9	8	2.3	31	6	73	69	77	73	
Rwanda	7.8	40	17	2.3	30	10.4	12.8	117	6.2	48	3	46	45	48	5	200
Seychelles	0.1	23	7	1.5	46	0.1	0.1	*11.9*	2.7	32	7	70	68	73	50	6,370
Somalia	9.3	50	19	3.2	22	14.5	21.3	122	7.0	48	3	47	45	49	24	—
Tanzania	28.5	45	15	3.0	23	42.8	58.6	92	6.3	47	3	49	47	50	21	100
Uganda	21.3	52	19	3.3	21	32.3	48.1	115	7.3	47	3	45	44	46	11	190
Zambia	9.1	47	17	3.1	23	13.0	17.1	107	6.5	50	2	48	47	49	42	370
Zimbabwe	11.3	39	12	2.7	26	15.3	19.6	53	4.4	44	3	54	52	55	27	540
MIDDLE AFRICA	**83**	**46**	**16**	**2.9**	**24**	**127**	**191**	**107**	**6.3**	**46**	**3**	**49**	**47**	**51**	**33**	**—**
Angola	11.5	47	20	2.7	26	17.6	24.7	137	6.4	45	3	46	44	48	37	—
Cameroon	13.5	40	11	2.9	24	21.2	32.6	65	5.9	44	3	58	56	60	41	770
Central African Republic	3.2	42	22	2.0	34	3.9	5.2	136	5.3	43	4	41	40	43	39	390
Chad	6.4	44	18	2.6	27	9.3	12.9	122	5.9	41	3	48	46	49	22	200
Congo	2.5	40	17	2.3	31	3.2	4.2	109	5.2	44	3	46	44	48	58	920
Equatorial Guinea	0.4	40	14	2.6	27	0.6	0.9	99	5.3	43	4	53	51	56	37	360
Gabon	1.3	37	16	2.2	32	1.9	2.7	94	4.0	39	6	54	52	55	73	4,050
Sao Tome and Principe	0.1	35	9	2.6	27	0.2	0.2	61.8	4.4	47	4	64	62	66	46	330
Zaire	44.1	48	16	3.2	22	69.1	107.6	108	6.6	48	3	48	46	50	29	—

	Population mid-1995 (millions)	Birth Rate per 1000 pop.	Death Rate per 1000 pop.	Natural Increase (annual, %)	"Doubling Time" in Years at Current Rate	Projected Population (millions) 2010	Projected Population (millions) 2025	Infant Mortality Rate[a]	Total Fertility Rate[b]	% Age <15	% Age 65+	Life Expectancy at Birth (years) T	Life Expectancy at Birth (years) M	Life Expectancy at Birth (years) F	% Urban	Per Capita GNP, 1993 (US$)
SOUTHERN AFRICA	50	31	8	2.3	30	67	83	49	4.2	38	4	65	62	67	59	2,720
Botswana	1.5	31	7	2.3	30	2.2	3.0	39	4.2	43	3	64	60	66	27	2,590
Lesotho	2.1	31	12	1.9	36	3.0	4.2	79	5.2	41	4	61	58	63	22	660
Namibia	1.5	37	10	2.7	26	2.2	3.0	57	5.4	42	4	59	58	60	32	1,660
South Africa	43.5	31	8	2.3	30	57.5	70.1	46	4.1	37	5	66	63	68	63	2,900
Swaziland	1.0	43	11	3.2	22	1.6	2.5	90	6.1	46	2	57	53	61	30	1,050
NORTH AMERICA	293	15	9	0.7	105	334	375	8	2.0	22	13	76	72	79	75	24,340
Canada	29.6	14	7	0.7	102	33.6	36.6	7.0	1.7	21	12	78	74	81	77	20,670
United States	263.2	15	9	0.7	105	300.4	338.3	8.0	2.0	22	13	76	72	79	75	24,750
SOUTH AND MIDDLE AMERICA	481	26	7	1.9	36	601	706	44	3.1	34	5	69	66	72	70	3,040
CENTRAL AMERICA	126	29	5	2.3	30	163	196	37	3.5	37	4	71	68	74	65	3,090
Belize	0.2	38	5	3.3	21	0.3	0.4	34	4.5	44	4	68	67	71	48	2,440
Costa Rica	3.3	26	4	2.2	32	4.4	5.5	13.7	3.1	35	5	76	74	79	49	2,160
El Salvador	5.9	32	6	2.6	27	7.6	9.4	41	3.8	40	4	68	65	70	46	1,320
Guatemala	10.6	39	8	3.1	22	15.8	21.7	48	5.4	45	3	65	62	67	38	1,110
Honduras	5.5	34	6	2.8	25	7.6	9.7	50	5.2	47	4	68	66	71	46	580
Mexico	93.7	27	5	2.2	34	117.7	136.6	34	3.1	36	4	72	70	76	71	3,750
Nicaragua	4.4	33	6	2.7	26	6.7	9.1	49	4.6	46	3	65	62	68	62	360
Panama	2.6	29	8	2.1	33	3.3	3.8	28	3.0	34	5	72	69	75	54	2,580
CARIBBEAN	36	23	8	1.5	46	43	50	39	2.9	31	7	70	67	72	60	—
Antigua and Barbuda	0.1	18	6	1.2	58	0.1	0.1	*18*	1.7	25	6	73	71	75	31	6,390
Bahamas	0.3	20	5	1.5	47	0.3	0.4	23.8	2.0	29	5	73	69	78	84	11,500
Barbados	0.3	16	9	0.7	98	0.3	0.3	*9.1*	1.8	24	12	76	73	78	38	6,240
Cuba	11.2	14	7	0.7	102	12.3	12.9	9.4	1.8	22	9	75	72	78	74	—
Dominica	0.1	20	7	1.3	55	0.1	0.1	*18.4*	2.5	29	8	77	74	80	—	2,680
Dominican Republic	7.8	27	6	2.1	32	9.7	11.2	42	3.3	35	4	70	68	72	61	1,080
Grenada	0.1	29	6	2.4	29	0.1	0.2	*12*	3.8	43	5	71	68	73	—	2,410
Guadeloupe	0.4	18	6	1.2	56	0.5	0.5	10.3	2.0	26	8	75	71	78	48	—
Haiti	7.2	35	12	2.3	30	9.8	13.1	74	4.8	40	4	57	55	58	31	—
Jamaica	2.4	25	6	2.0	35	2.8	3.3	13.2	2.4	33	8	74	71	76	53	1,390
Martinique	0.4	17	6	1.1	62	0.4	0.5	*8*	2.0	23	10	76	73	79	81	—
Netherlands Antilles	0.2	19	6	1.3	55	0.2	0.2	*6.3*	2.0	26	7	76	74	79	92	—
Puerto Rico	3.7	18	8	1.0	67	4.1	4.6	12.7	2.2	27	10	74	70	79	73	7,020
St. Kitts-Nevis	0.04	23	9	1.4	50	0.1	0.1	*19*	2.5	32	9	69	66	71	42	4,470
Saint Lucia	0.1	27	6	2.0	34	0.2	0.2	18.5	3.1	37	7	72	68	75	48	3,040
St. Vincent & the Grenadines	0.1	25	7	1.8	38	0.1	0.2	*16*	3.1	37	6	73	71	74	25	2,130
Trinidad and Tobago	1.3	17	7	1.1	64	1.6	1.8	10.5	2.7	31	6	71	68	73	65	3,730
SOUTH AMERICA	319	25	7	1.8	38	395	460	47	3.0	33	5	68	65	71	73	3,020
Argentina	34.6	21	8	1.3	55	40.8	46.1	23.6	2.8	30	9	71	68	75	87	7,290
Bolivia	7.4	36	10	2.6	27	10.2	13.1	71	4.8	41	4	60	59	62	58	770

	Population mid-1995 (millions)	Birth Rate per 1000 pop.	Death Rate per 1000 pop.	Natural Increase (annual, %)	"Doubling Time" in Years at *Current* Rate	Projected Population (millions) 2010	Projected Population (millions) 2025	Infant Mortality Rate[a]	Total Fertility Rate[b]	% Age <15	% Age 65+	Life Expectancy at Birth (years) T	Life Expectancy at Birth (years) M	Life Expectancy at Birth (years) F	% Urban	Per Capita GNP, 1993 (US$)
Brazil	157.8	25	8	1.7	41	194.4	224.6	58	2.9	32	5	66	64	69	77	3,020
Chile	14.3	22	6	1.7	41	17.3	20.1	14.6	2.5	31	6	72	69	76	85	3,070
Colombia	37.7	24	6	1.8	39	46.1	53.0	37	2.7	33	5	69	66	72	50	1,400
Ecuador	11.5	28	6	2.2	31	14.9	17.8	50	3.5	38	4	69	66	71	58	1,170
Guyana	0.8	25	7	1.8	39	1.0	1.1	48	2.6	32	4	65	62	68	33	350
Paraguay	5.0	33	6	2.8	25	7.0	9.0	38	4.3	40	4	70	68	72	51	1,500
Peru	24.0	29	7	2.1	33	30.3	35.9	60	3.5	36	4	66	64	68	70	1,490
Suriname	0.4	25	6	2.0	36	0.5	0.6	28	2.7	35	5	70	68	73	49	1,210
Uruguay	3.2	17	10	0.7	102	3.5	3.7	18.6	2.3	26	12	73	69	76	90	3,910
Venezuela	21.8	30	5	2.6	27	28.7	34.8	20.2	3.6	38	4	72	69	75	84	2,840
ASIA	**3,451**	**24**	**8**	**1.7**	**42**	**4,242**	**4,939**	**62**	**2.9**	**33**	**5**	**65**	**64**	**67**	**33**	**1,980**
ASIA (EXCL. CHINA)	**2,232**	**28**	**9**	**1.9**	**36**	**2,857**	**3,416**	**68**	**3.5**	**36**	**5**	**63**	**62**	**64**	**35**	**2,860**
WESTERN ASIA	**168**	**31**	**7**	**2.4**	**29**	**242**	**329**	**51**	**4.3**	**39**	**4**	**67**	**65**	**69**	**58**	**—**
Armenia	3.7	16	7	0.8	83	4.2	4.3	17	2.0	31	7	71	68	74	68	660
Azerbaijan	7.3	23	7	1.6	43	9.0	10.3	26	2.5	33	5	71	66	75	54	730
Bahrain	0.6	29	4	2.5	28	0.8	1.1	25	3.7	32	2	74	71	76	88	7,870
Cyprus	0.7	17	8	0.9	76	0.8	0.9	9	2.3	25	11	77	75	79	68	10,380
Gaza	0.9	52	6	4.6	15	1.8	2.8	34	8.1	50	4	69	68	69	94	—
Georgia	5.4	12	10	0.2	462	5.7	6.0	18	1.5	25	10	73	69	76	56	560
Iraq	20.6	43	7	3.7	19	34.5	52.6	62	6.6	47	3	66	65	67	70	—
Israel	5.5	21	6	1.5	47	6.9	8.0	7.0	2.8	30	9	77	75	79	90	13,760
Jordan	4.1	38	4	3.3	21	6.2	8.3	32	5.6	43	3	72	70	74	68	1,190
Kuwait	1.5	25	2	2.2	31	2.5	3.6	12	4.0	34	2	75	73	77	—	23,350
Lebanon	3.7	25	5	2.0	34	5.0	6.1	28	2.9	33	5	75	73	78	86	—
Oman	2.2	53	4	4.9	14	3.7	6.0	24	6.9	36	3	71	70	72	12	5,600
Qatar	0.5	19	2	1.8	39	0.6	0.7	13	3.8	30	1	73	70	75	91	15,140
Saudi Arabia	18.5	36	4	3.2	22	30.0	48.2	24	5.5	43	2	70	69	72	79	*7,780*
Syria	14.7	41	6	3.5	20	23.6	33.5	39	5.9	49	4	66	65	67	51	—
Turkey	61.4	23	7	1.6	44	79.2	95.6	53	2.7	33	4	67	64	70	51	2,120
United Arab Emirates	1.9	23	4	1.9	36	2.5	3.0	23	4.1	32	1	72	70	74	82	22,470
West Bank	1.5	41	7	3.4	20	2.7	3.8	38	5.7	46	4	68	68	68	—	—
Yemen	13.2	50	14	3.6	19	21.9	34.5	109	7.7	52	3	52	52	53	25	—
SOUTH CENTRAL ASIA	**1,355**	**31**	**10**	**2.1**	**33**	**1,772**	**2,138**	**79**	**3.8**	**38**	**4**	**60**	**60**	**61**	**27**	**420**
Afghanistan	18.4	50	22	2.8	24	31.1	41.4	163	6.9	41	3	43	43	44	18	—
Bangladesh	119.2	36	12	2.4	29	160.8	194.1	108	4.3	42	3	55	56	55	17	220
Bhutan	0.8	39	15	2.3	30	1.1	1.5	138	6.2	39	4	51	51	50	13	170
India	930.6	29	9	1.9	36	1,182.7	1,384.6	74	3.4	36	4	60	60	60	26	290
Iran	61.3	36	7	2.9	24	83.7	106.1	56	5.0	44	3	67	66	68	57	*2,230*
Kazakhstan	16.9	19	9	0.9	74	18.4	20.5	28	2.3	31	6	69	64	73	57	1,540
Kyrgyzstan	4.4	26	8	1.8	38	5.6	7.0	33	3.3	38	5	68	64	72	36	830

	Population mid-1995 (millions)	Birth Rate per 1000 pop.	Death Rate per 1000 pop.	Natural Increase (annual, %)	"Doubling Time" in Years at Current Rate	Projected Population (millions) 2010	Projected Population (millions) 2025	Infant Mortality Rate[a]	Total Fertility Rate[b]	% Age <15	% Age 65+	Life Expectancy at Birth (years) T	M	F	% Urban	Per Capita GNP, 1993 (US$)
Maldives	0.3	43	7	3.6	19	0.4	0.6	52	6.2	47	3	65	64	67	26	820
Nepal	22.6	38	14	2.4	29	32.2	43.3	102	5.8	42	3	54	56	53	10	160
Pakistan	129.7	39	10	2.9	24	187.7	251.8	91	5.6	41	3	61	61	61	32	430
Sri Lanka	18.2	21	6	1.5	46	21.0	24.0	19.4	2.3	35	4	73	70	75	22	600
Tajikistan	5.8	33	9	2.4	29	9.2	13.1	47	4.3	43	4	70	68	73	31	470
Turkmenistan	4.5	33	8	2.5	28	5.9	7.9	44	4.0	41	4	66	63	70	45	*1,380*
Uzbekistan	22.7	31	7	2.5	28	31.9	42.3	37	3.8	41	4	69	66	72	41	960
SOUTHEAST ASIA	**485**	**26**	**8**	**1.9**	**37**	**601**	**704**	**53**	**3.2**	**37**	**4**	**64**	**62**	**66**	**31**	**1,070**
Brunei	0.3	27	3	2.4	29	0.4	0.4	7.0	3.1	36	3	74	73	76	67	—
Cambodia	10.6	44	16	2.8	25	15.7	22.8	108	5.8	46	3	50	48	51	13	—
Indonesia	198.4	24	8	1.6	43	240.6	276.5	64	2.8	37	4	63	61	65	31	730
Laos	4.8	42	14	2.8	25	7.2	9.8	98	6.0	45	3	52	51	54	19	290
Malaysia	19.9	29	5	2.4	29	27.5	34.5	12	3.3	36	4	71	69	74	51	3,160
Myanmar (Burma)	44.8	28	9	1.9	36	57.3	69.3	48	3.6	36	4	60	58	63	25	—
Philippines	68.4	30	9	2.1	33	87.2	102.7	49	4.1	40	3	65	63	66	49	830
Singapore	3.0	17	5	1.2	56	3.6	4.0	4.7	1.8	23	7	74	72	77	100	19,310
Thailand	60.2	20	6	1.4	48	68.7	75.4	35	2.2	31	4	70	68	72	19	2,040
Viet Nam	75.0	30	7	2.3	30	92.5	108.1	42	3.7	39	5	65	63	67	21	170
EAST ASIA	**1,442**	**17**	**6**	**1.0**	**66**	**1,628**	**1,768**	**40**	**1.8**	**26**	**7**	**70**	**68**	**72**	**35**	**3,570**
China	1,218.8	18	6	1.1	62	1,385.5	1,522.8	44	1.9	27	6	69	67	70	28	490
Hong Kong	6.0	12	5	0.7	99	6.4	6.3	4.8	1.2	20	9	78	75	81	—	17,860
Japan	125.2	10	7	0.3	277	130.4	125.8	4.3	1.5	16	14	79	76	83	77	31,450
Korea, North	23.5	23	6	1.8	40	28.5	32.1	26	2.4	30	4	70	67	73	61	—
Korea, South	44.9	15	6	1.0	72	49.7	50.8	11	1.6	24	5	72	68	76	74	7,670
Macao	0.4	16	4	1.2	57	0.5	0.6	9	1.6	24	7	—	—	—	97	—
Mongolia	2.3	22	8	1.4	51	3.0	3.6	61	3.8	40	4	64	62	65	55	400
Taiwan	21.2	16	5	1.0	67	24.0	25.5	5.6	1.8	25	7	74	72	77	75	—
EUROPE	**729**	**11**	**12**	**-0.1**	**—**	**743**	**743**	**11**	**1.5**	**20**	**13**	**73**	**68**	**77**	**72**	**11,870**
NORTHERN EUROPE	**94**	**13**	**11**	**0.2**	**443**	**97**	**99**	**71**	**1.8**	**30**	**15**	**76**	**73**	**79**	**85**	**18,020**
Denmark	5.2	13	12	0.1	770	5.3	5.3	5.7	1.8	17	15	75	73	78	85	26,510
Estonia	1.5	9	14	-0.5	—	1.4	1.4	16	1.3	21	13	70	64	75	71	3,040
Finland	5.1	13	10	0.3	227	5.2	5.2	4.4	1.8	19	14	76	72	79	64	18,970
Iceland	0.3	17	7	1.1	64	0.3	0.3	*4.8*	2.2	25	11	79	77	81	91	23,620
Ireland	3.6	14	9	0.5	139	3.5	3.5	6.0	2.0	26	11	75	73	78	57	12,580
Latvia	2.5	10	15	-0.5	—	2.4	2.4	16	1.5	21	13	68	62	74	69	2,030
Lithuania	3.7	13	12	0.0	6,931	3.8	3.9	16	1.7	22	12	71	65	76	68	1,310
Norway	4.3	14	11	0.3	224	4.7	5.0	5.8	1.9	19	16	77	74	80	73	26,340
Sweden	8.9	13	12	0.1	990	9.2	9.6	4.8	1.9	19	18	78	76	81	83	24,830
United Kingdom	58.6	13	11	0.2	385	61.0	62.1	6.6	1.8	19	16	76	74	79	92	17,970

	Population mid-1995 (millions)	Birth Rate per 1000 pop.	Death Rate per 1000 pop.	Natural Increase (annual, %)	"Doubling Time" in Years at Current Rate	Projected Population (millions) 2010	2025	Infant Mortality Rate[a]	Total Fertility Rate[b]	% Age <15	% Age 65+	Life Exp. T	M	F	% Urban	Per Capita GNP, 1993 (US$)
WESTERN EUROPE	181	11	10	0.1	741	187	184	6	1.5	18	15	77	73	80	81	23,310
Austria	8.1	12	10	0.1	533	8.3	8.3	6.2	1.4	18	15	77	73	80	54	23,120
Belgium	10.2	12	11	0.1	578	10.4	10.5	7.6	1.6	18	16	77	73	80	97	21,210
France	58.1	12	9	0.3	217	61.7	63.6	6.1	1.7	20	15	78	74	82	74	22,360
Germany	81.7	10	11	-0.1	—	81.2	76.1	5.8	1.3	16	15	76	73	79	85	23,560
Liechtenstein	0.03	12	6	0.6	108	0.03	0.04	10.7	1.4	19	10	—	—	—	—	—
Luxembourg	0.4	13	10	0.4	193	0.4	0.4	6.0	1.7	18	14	76	73	79	86	35,850
Netherlands	15.5	13	9	0.4	182	16.9	17.6	5.9	1.6	18	13	77	74	80	89	20,710
Switzerland	7.0	12	9	0.3	224	7.6	7.5	5.6	1.5	16	15	78	75	81	68	36,410
EASTERN EUROPE	310	10	14	-0.3	—	315	320	17	1.5	22	12	68	62	73	68	2,180
Belarus	10.3	11	13	-0.2	—	10.9	11.3	13	1.5	22	12	69	64	74	68	2,840
Bulgaria	8.5	10	13	-0.3	—	7.9	7.5	15.5	1.4	19	14	71	68	74	67	1,160
Czech Republic	10.4	12	11	0.0	2,310	10.5	10.7	8.5	1.7	21	10	73	69	77	75	2,730
Hungary	10.2	12	14	-0.3	—	9.9	9.3	11.6	1.7	19	14	69	65	74	63	3,330
Moldova	4.3	15	12	0.4	193	4.8	5.1	22	2.1	28	9	68	64	72	47	1,180
Poland	38.6	12	10	0.2	301	40.2	41.7	13.7	1.8	24	11	72	67	76	62	2,270
Romania	22.7	11	12	-0.1	—	22.2	21.6	23.3	1.4	22	11	70	66	73	55	1,120
Russia	147.5	9	16	-0.6	—	149.5	153.1	19	1.4	22	11	65	59	72	73	2,350
Slovakia	5.4	14	10	0.4	178	5.7	6.0	15.6	1.9	25	11	71	67	75	57	1,900
Ukraine	52.0	11	14	-0.4	—	53.0	54.0	15	1.6	21	13	69	64	74	68	1,910
SOUTHERN EUROPE	144	11	9	0.1	516	144	139	11	1.4	18	14	76	73	79	60	14,720
Albania	3.5	23	5	1.8	39	4.1	4.7	32.9	2.9	33	5	72	69	75	37	340
Bosnia-Herzegovina	3.5	14	7	0.7	95	4.4	4.5	15.3	1.6	23	7	72	70	75	34	—
Croatia	4.6	10	11	0.1		4.4	4.2	11.6	1.4	10	13	70	66	75	54	
Greece	10.5	10	9	0.0	1,733	10.2	10.0	8.3	1.4	19	14	77	75	80	63	7,390
Italy	57.7	9	10	-0.0	—	56.5	52.8	7.4	1.2	16	16	77	74	80	68	19,620
Macedonia	2.1	16	8	0.8	85	2.3	2.5	24.4	2.2	26	7	72	70	74	58	780
Malta	0.4	14	7	0.7	102	0.4	0.4	9.3	2.0	23	11	75	73	78	85	—
Portugal	9.9	12	11	0.1	866	9.9	9.8	8.6	1.5	18	14	75	71	78	34	7,890
San Marino	0.03	10	6	0.4	169	0.03	0.03	9.3	1.1	15	14	76	73	79	90	—
Slovenia	2.0	10	10	0.1	1,386	2.0	1.9	6.6	1.3	19	12	73	69	77	50	6,310
Spain	39.1	10	9	0.1	578	39.0	37.1	7.6	1.2	17	15	77	73	81	64	13,650
Yugoslavia[c]	10.8	13	10	0.3	204	11.1	11.5	18.4	2.0	23	10	72	69	75	47	—
PACIFIC	28	19	8	1.2	60	34	39	24	2.5	26	10	73	71	76	71	13,540
Australia	18.0	15	7	0.8	91	20.8	23.1	6.1	1.9	22	12	78	75	81	85	17,510
Federated States of Micronesia	0.1	38	8	3.0	23	0.1	0.1	52	5.6	46	4	68	66	70	26	—
Fiji	0.8	25	5	2.0	35	0.9	1.1	19	3.0	38	3	63	61	65	39	2,140
French Polynesia	0.2	26	5	2.1	34	0.3	0.4	12	3.1	36	3	70	68	72	57	—
Guam	0.2	30	4	2.6	27	0.2	0.2	9.8	3.3	30	4	74	72	76	38	—
Marshall Islands	0.1	49	9	4.0	17	0.1	0.2	63	7.2	51	3	63	62	65	65	—

	Population mid-1995 (millions)	Birth Rate per 1000 pop.	Death Rate per 1000 pop.	Natural Increase (annual, %)	"Doubling Time" in Years at *Current* Rate	Projected Population (millions) 2010	Projected Population (millions) 2025	Infant Mortality Rate[a]	Total Fertility Rate[b]	% Age <15	% Age 65+	Life Expectancy at Birth (years) T	Life Expectancy at Birth (years) M	Life Expectancy at Birth (years) F	% Urban	Per Capita GNP, 1993 (US$)
New Caledonia	0.2	26	6	2.0	34	0.2	0.3	21	3.3	33	5	74	71	77	70	—
New Zealand	3.5	16	8	0.9	81	4.1	4.5	6.9	2.0	23	12	76	73	79	85	12,900
Palau	0.02	220	8	1.4	50	0.03	0.03	*25*	3.1	30	6	67	—	—	60	—
Papua-New Guinea	4.1	33	10	2.3	30	5.7	7.3	63	4.7	40	4	57	56	58	15	1,230
Solomon Islands	0.4	44	7	3.7	19	0.6	0.8	43	5.8	47	3	61	—	—	13	750
Vanuatu	0.2	38	9	2.9	24	0.2	0.3	45	5.3	46	3	63	—	—	18	1,230
Western Samoa	0.2	34	8	2.6	27	0.2	0.3	21	4.2	41	4	65	—	—	21	980
	Pop. 1995	Birth Rate	Death Rate	Natural Increase	Doubling Time	Pop. 2010	Pop. 2025	Infant Mort.	TFR	% <15	% 65+	Life Exp. T	Life Exp. M	Life Exp. F	% Urban	GNP p.c.

(—) indicates data unavailable or inapplicable

[a] Infant deaths per 1,000 live births

[b] Average number of children born to a woman in her lifetime

[c] On April 27, 1992, Serbia and Montenegro formed a new state, the Federal Republic of Yugoslavia

Note: This Data Sheet is published annually by the Population Reference Bureau, a Washington-based agency that assembles and disseminates information concerning population and population-related issues. As has been stated in the text, such information may vary according to source. United Nations and World Bank data, for example, differ from those published here in important respects. Note that the PRB does not agree that world urbanization has reached the 50 percent level, as is asserted by some other agencies, was widely reported by the media several years ago, and has been cited in this book.

Resource D

GLOSSARY

Absolute direction A compass direction such as north or south.

Absolute distance The physical distance between two points usually measured in miles or kilometers.

Absolute location The position or place of a certain item on the surface of the Earth as expressed in degrees, minutes, and seconds of **latitude**, 0° to 90° north or south of the equator, and **longitude**, 0° to 180° east or west of the **prime meridian** passing through Greenwich, England (a suburb of London).

Accessibility The degree of ease with which it is possible to reach a certain location from other locations. Accessibility varies from place to place and can be measured.

Acculturation Cultural modification resulting from intercultural borrowing. In cultural geography, the term is used to designate the change that occurs in the culture of indigenous peoples when contact is made with a society that is technologically more advanced.

Acid rain A growing environmental peril whereby acidified rainwater severely damages plant and animal life. Caused by the oxides of sulfur and nitrogen that are released into the atmosphere when coal, oil, and natural gas are burned, especially in major manufacturing zones.

Acropolis Literally "high point of the city". The upper fortified part of an ancient Greek city, usually devoted to religious purposes.

Activity (or **action**) **space** The space within which daily activity occurs.

Age-sex pyramid Graphic representation (profile) of a population showing the percentages of the total population by age and sex, normally in five-year groups.

Agglomerated (nucleated) settlement A compact, closely packed settlement (usually a hamlet or larger village) sharply demarcated from adjoining farmlands.

Agglomeration A process involving the clustering or concentrating of people or activities. The term often refers to manufacturing plants and businesses that benefit from close proximity because they share skilled-labor pools and technological and financial amenities.

Agrarian Relating to the use of land in rural communities or to agricultural societies in general.

Agricultural density The number of inhabitants per unit of agricultural land. As used in population geography, agricultural density excludes urban residents so that it reflects the pressure of population in rural areas. **Physiologic density** measures the total population, urban and rural, against the agricultural land.

Agricultural Revolution The revolutionary transformation of agricultural practices, systems, and production. The *First Agricultural Revolution*, dating back 10,000 years, achieved plant and animal domestication. The *Second Agricultural Revolution* dovetailed with and benefited from the *Industrial Revolution* and witnessed improved methods of cultivation, harvesting, and storage of farm produce. The *Third Agricultural Revolution*, currently in progress, is based on new high-yielding strains of grains and other crops developed by genetic engineering.

Agriculture The purposeful tending of crops and livestock in order to produce food and fiber.

Animism The belief that inanimate objects, such as hills, rocks, rivers, and other elements of the natural landscape (including trees), possess souls and can help as well as hinder human efforts on Earth.

Antecedent boundary A political boundary that existed before the **cultural landscape** emerged and stayed in place while people moved in to occupy the surrounding area. An example is the 49th parallel boundary, dividing the United States and Canada between the Pacific Ocean and Lake of the Woods in northernmost Minnesota.

Anthropogeographic boundaries Political boundaries that coincide substantially with cultural discontinuities in the human landscape, such as religious or linguistic transitions.

Apartheid Literally, "apartness". The Afrikaans term given to the policies of racial separation once practiced in South Africa and to the highly segregated sociogeographical patterns they produced—a system now being dismantled.

Aquaculture The use of a river segment or an artificial body of water such as a pond for the raising and harvesting of food products, including fish, shellfish, and even seaweed. Japan is among the world's leaders in aquaculture.

Arable Literally, cultivable. Land fit for cultivation by one farming method or another.

Area A term that refers to a part of the Earth's surface with less specificity than **region**. For example, urban area alludes very generally to a place where urban development has taken place, whereas urban region requires certain specific criteria on which a delimitation is based (e.g., the spatial extent of commuting or the built townscape).

Area symbols Portray two-dimensional spaces on a map, with colors or black-and-white areal patterns representing specific quantitative ranges (which are identified in the map legend).

Areal interdependence A term related to **functional specialization**. When one area produces certain goods or has certain raw materials or resources and another area has a different set of resources and produces different goods, their needs may be complementary; by exchanging raw materials and products, they can satisfy each other's requirements. The concepts of areal interdependence and **complementarity** are related: both have to do with exchange opportunities between regions.

Arithmetic density A country's population, expressed as an average per unit area (square mile or square kilometer), without regard for its distribution or the limits of **arable** land. See also **physiologic density**.

Aryan From the Sanskrit Arya ("noble"), a name applied to an ancient people who spoke an Indo-European language and who moved into northern India from the northwest. Although properly a language-related term, Aryan has assumed additional meanings, especially racial ones.

Austrasia New name for the western Pacific Rim where a significant regional realignment is now taking place. Includes rapidly-developing countries and parts of countries lining the Pacific from Japan's Hokkaido in the north to New Zealand in the south.

Autocratic An autocratic government holds absolute power; rule is often by one person or a small group of persons who control the country by despotic means.

Babylon A capital of Mesopotamia and one of the largest and most powerful cities between 4100 and 2000 B.P.

Balkanization The fragmentation of a region into smaller, often hostile political units.

Basic activities Economic activities whose products are exported beyond a region's limits. Nonbasic, or service, activities involve production and consumption within the region.

Bergmann's Rule A principle holding that the lower the mean annual temperature, the higher a population's mean body weight.

Birth rate The crude birth rate is expressed as the annual number of live births per 1000 individuals within a given population.

Brahman A Hindu of the highest caste, most often a priest, a person believed to possess sacred knowledge and to be of the greatest purity. Brahmans (or Brahmins) alone are believed capable of carrying out particular religious rituals and tasks. In India, Brahmans have for many centuries been religious, intellectual, and even political leaders.

Break-of-bulk point A location along a transport route where goods must be transferred from one carrier to another. In a port, the cargoes of oceangoing ships are unloaded and put on trains, trucks, or perhaps smaller riverboats for inland distribution.

Buffer zone A set of countries separating ideological or political adversaries. In southern Asia, Afghanistan, Nepal, and Bhutan were parts of a buffer zone between British and Russian-Chinese imperial spheres. Thailand was a buffer state between British and French colonial domains in mainland Southeast Asia.

Cartel An international syndicate formed to promote common interests in some economic sphere through the formulation of joint pricing policies and the limitation of market options for consumers. The Organization of Petroleum Exporting Countries (OPEC) is a classic example.

Cartography The art and science of making maps, including data compilation, layout, and design. Also concerned with the interpretation of mapped patterns.

Caste system The strict social segregation of people—specifically in India's Hindu society—on the basis of ancestry and occupation.

Cenozoic The era of recent life on the geologic time scale extending from 65 million years ago to the present; subdivided into the Tertiary and Quaternary periods.

Census A periodic and official count of a country's population.

Central business district (CBD) The downtown heart of a central city, the CBD is marked by high land values, a concentration of business and commerce, and the clustering of the tallest buildings.

Central place Any point or place in the urban hierarchy, such as a town or city, having a certain economic reach or **hinterland**.

Central place theory Theory proposed by Walter Christaller that explains how and where central places in the urban hierarchy would be functionally and spatially distributed with respect to one another.

Centrality The strength of an urban center in its capacity to attract producers and consumers to its facilities; a city's "reach" into the surrounding region.

Centrifugal forces A term employed to designate forces that tend to divide a country—such as internal religious, linguistic, ethnic, or ideological differences.

Centripetal forces Forces that unite and bind a country together—such as a strong national culture, shared ideological objectives, and a common faith.

Child mortality rate The number of children who die between the ages of 1 and 5 for every 1000 children in that age group.

Circulation In political geography, the system of integration and movement through language, education, transportation, and communications.

City-state An independent political entity consisting of a single city with (and sometimes without) an immediate **hinterland**. The ancient city-states of Greece have their modern equivalent in Singapore.

Civilization An advanced state of a society possessing historical and cultural unity whose attributes include plant and animal domestication, metallurgy, occupational specialization, writing, and cities.

Climatic optimum Period of maximal warmth during the Holocene interglaciation epoch, experienced between 7000 and 5000 years ago.

Clovis culture Culture of the earliest inhabitants in the Americas.

Colonialism See **imperialism**.

Compact state A politico-geographical term to describe a state that possesses a roughly circular, oval, or rectangular territory in which the distance from the geometric center to any point on the boundary exhibits little variance. Cambodia, Uruguay, and Poland are examples of this shape category.

Complementarity Regional complementarity exists when two regions, through an exchange of raw materials and/or finished products, can specifically satisfy each other's demands.

Concentric zone model A structural model of the American central city that suggests the existence of five concentric land-use rings arranged around a common center.

Condominium In political geography, this denotes the shared administration of a territory by two governments.

Connectivity The degree of direct linkage between one particular location and other locations in a transport network.

Conservation The careful management and use of natural resources, the achievement of significant social benefits from them, and the preservation of the natural environment.

Contagious diffusion The distance-controlled spreading of an idea, innovation, or some other item through a local population by contact from person to person—analogous to the communication of a contagious illness.

Continental drift The notion hypothesized by Alfred Wegener concerning the fragmentation of Pangaea and the slow movement of the modern continents away from this core supercontinent.

Continental shelf The gently sloping, relatively shallow, submerged plain just off the coast of a continent, extending to a depth of around 180 meters (600 feet/1000 fathoms).

Conurbation General term used to identify large, multimetropolitan complexes formed by the coalescence of two or more major urban areas. The Boston– Washington **megalopolis** along the U.S. northeastern seaboard is an outstanding example.

Core area   In geography, a term with several connotations. Core refers to the center, heart, or focus. The core area of a **nation-state** is constituted by the national heartland—the largest population cluster, the most productive region, the area with greatest **centrality** and **accessibility**, probably containing the capital city as well.

Core-periphery relationships   The contrasting spatial characteristics of, and linkages between, the have (core) and have-not (periphery) components of a national or regional system.

Corridor   In general, refers to a spatial entity in which human activity is organized in a linear manner, as along a major transport route or in a valley confined by highlands. Specific meaning in politico-geographical context is a land extension that connects an otherwise **landlocked** state to the sea. History has seen several such corridors come and go. Poland once had a corridor (it now has a lengthy coastline); Bolivia lost a corridor to the Pacific Ocean between Peru and Chile.

Creole   Ethnic term first applied in the Caribbean region to the native-born descendants of the Spanish conquerors and their local consorts.

Creole language   A language that began as a *pidgin* but was later adopted as the mother tongue by a people in place of the mother tongue.

Cultural diffusion   The process of spreading and adoption of a cultural element, from its place of origin across a wider area.

Cultural ecology   The multiple interactions and relationships between a culture and its natural environment.

Cultural landscape   The forms and artifacts sequentially placed on the physical landscape by the activities of various human occupants. By this progressive imprinting of the human presence, the physical landscape is modified into the cultural landscape, forming an interacting unity between the two.

Cultural pluralism   A society in which two or more population groups, each practicing its own **culture**, live adjacent to one another without mixing inside a single **state**.

Cultural-political boundaries   Political boundaries that coincide with cultural breaks in the landscape, such as language, religion, and ethnicity.

Cultural revival   The process of continuous reinvigoration of cultural traits and behavior into communities geographically separated from their original source area.

Culture   The sum total of the knowledge, attitudes, and habitual behavior patterns shared and transmitted by the members of a society. This is anthropologist Ralph Linton's definition; hundreds of others exist.

Culture area   A distinct, culturally discrete spatial unit; a region within which certain cultural norms prevail.

Culture complex   A related set of culture traits, such as prevailing dress codes and cooking and eating utensils.

Culture-environment tradition   One of the four major areas of geographic research and teaching; the relationships between human societies and their natural environments.

Culture hearth   Heartland, source area, innovation center; place of origin of a major culture.

Culture realm   A cluster of regions in which related culture systems prevail. In North America, the United States and Canada form a culture realm, but Mexico belongs to a different culture realm.

Culture region   A region within which common cultural characteristics prevail.

Culture trait   A single element of normal practice in a culture, such as the wearing of a turban.

Cyclical movement   Movement—for example, nomadic migration—that has a closed route repeated annually or seasonally.

Death rate   The crude death rate is expressed as the annual number of deaths per 1000 individuals within a given population.

Definition   In political geography, the written legal description (in a treatylike document) of a boundary between two countries or territories. See also **delimitation**.

Deforestation   See **tropical deforestation**.

Deglomeration   The process of industrial deconcentration in response to technological advances and/or increasing costs due to congestion and competition.

Delimitation   In political geography, the translation of the written terms of a boundary treaty (the **definition**) into an official cartographic representation.

Demarcation   In political geography, the actual placing of a political boundary on the landscape by means of barriers, fences, walls, or other markers.

Demographic transition model   Multistage model, based on Western Europe's experience, of changes in population growth exhibited by countries undergoing industrialization. High birth rates and death rates are followed by plunging death rates, producing a huge net population gain; this is followed by the convergence of birth rates and death rates at a low overall level.

Demographic variables   Births (fertility), deaths (mortality), and migration are the three basic demographic variables.

Demography   The interdisciplinary study of population—especially **birth rates** and **death rates**, growth patterns, longevity, migration, and related characteristics.

Density of population   The number of people per unit area. Also see **arithmetic density** and **physiologic density** measures.

Desertification   The encroachment of desert conditions on moister zones along the desert margins, where plant cover and soils are threatened by desiccation—through overuse, in part by humans and their domestic animals, and, possibly, in part because of inexorable shifts in the Earth's environmental zones.

Determinism   See **environmental determinism**.

Development   The economic, social, and institutional growth of national states.

Devolution   The process whereby regions within a **state** demand and gain political strength and growing autonomy at the expense of the central government.

Diffusion   The spatial spreading or dissemination of a culture element (such as a technological innovation) or some other phenomenon (e.g., a disease outbreak). See also **contagious, expansion, hierarchical,** and **relocation diffusion**.

Dispersed settlement   In contrast to **agglomerated** or **nucleated** settlement, dispersed settlement is characterized by a much lower **density of population** and the wide spacing of individual homesteads (especially in rural North America).

Distance decay   The various degenerative effects of distance on human spatial structures and interactions.

Divided capital   In political geography, a country whose administrative functions are carried out in more than one city is said to have divided capitals.

Domestication   The transformation of a wild animal or wild plant into a domesticated animal or a cultivated crop to gain control over food production. A necessary evolutionary step in the development of humankind—the invention of **agriculture**.

Domino theory   The belief that political destabilization in one country can result in the collapse of order in a neighboring state, starting a chain reaction of collapse.

Double cropping   The planting, cultivation, and harvesting of two crops successively within a single year on the same plot of farmland.

Doubling time   The time required for a population to double in size.

Drive to maturity   Fourth state in the Rostow model of development, characterized by industrial specialization and the expansion of international trade and technology.

Dualism   The division of geography into broad categories: "human" and "physical"; and "regional" and "systematic."

Earth-science tradition One of the four major areas of geographic research and teaching; also known as **physical (natural) geography**.

Ecology Strictly speaking, the study of the many interrelationships between all forms of life and the natural environments in which they have evolved and continue to develop. The study of ecosystems focuses on the interactions between specific organisms and their environments. See also **cultural ecology**.

Economic reach The maximum distance people can be from a central place and still be attracted to it for business purposes. See also **hinterland**.

Economic tiger One of the burgeoning beehive countries of the Pacific Rim of Australasia. Using postwar Japan as a model, these countries have experienced significant modernization, industrialization, and Western-style economic growth since 1980. The four leading economic tigers are South Korea, Taiwan, Hong Kong, and Singapore.

Economies of scale The savings that accrue from large-scale production whereby the unit cost of manufacturing decreases as the level of operation enlarges. Supermarkets operate on this principle and are able to charge lower prices than small grocery stores.

Ecosystem A linkage of plants or animals to their environment in an open system as far as energy is concerned.

Ecumene The portion of the world's land surface that is permanently settled by human beings.

El Niño A periodic, large-scale, abnormal warming of the sea surface in the low latitudes of the eastern Pacific Ocean that produces a (temporary) reversal of surface ocean currents and airflows throughout the equatorial Pacific; these regional events have global implications, disturbing normal weather patterns in many parts of the world.

Electoral geography Subfield of geography that deals with various spatial aspects of voting systems, voting behavior, and voter representation.

Elongated state A **state** whose territory is decidedly long and narrow in that its length is at least six times greater than its average width. Chile and Vietnam are two classic examples on the world political map.

Emigrant A person migrating away from a country or area; an out-migrant.

Empirical Relating to the real world, as opposed to theoretical abstraction.

Enclave A piece of territory that is surrounded by another political unit of which it is not a part.

Endemic A disease that is particular to a locality or region.

ENSO Acronym for El Niño Southern Oscillation; the reversal of the flow of ocean currents and prevailing winds in the equatorial Pacific Ocean that disturbs global weather patterns.

Entrepôt A place, usually a port city, where goods are imported, stored, and transshipped; a **break-of-bulk point**.

Environmental determinism The view that the natural environment has a controlling influence over various aspects of human life, including cultural development. Also referred to as environmentalism.

Environmental perception The total impression individuals have of their surroundings which create a mental map.

Environmental stress The threat to environmental security by human action such as atmospheric and groundwater pollution, deforestation, oil spills, and ocean dumping.

Esperanto An artificial Latin-based language, which its European proponents in the early twentieth century hoped would become a global language.

Ethnic The combination of a people's culture (traditions, customs, language, and religion) and racial ancestry.

Ethnic cleansing The slaughter and/or forced removal of one ethnic group from its homes and lands by another ethnic group.

Eugenic population policy Government policy designed to favor one racial sector over others.

Eugenic Protection Act Policy enacted by the Japanese government in 1948 that legalized abortion for social, medical, and economic reasons.

European state model A **state** consisting of a legally defined territory inhabited by a population governed from a capital city by a representative government.

Eve theory Theory that postulates that early modern humans derived from a single woman who lived in Africa about 200,000 years ago.

Exclave A bounded (nonisland) piece of territory that is part of a particular state but lies separated from it by the territory of another state.

Exclusive economic zone (EEZ) An oceanic zone extending up to 200 nautical miles form a shoreline, within which the coastal state can control fishing, mineral exploration, and additional activities by all other countries.

Expansion diffusion The spread of an innovation or an idea through a population in an area in such a way that the number of those influenced grows continuously larger, resulting in an expanding area of dissemination.

Expansive population policy Government policy that encourages large families and raises the rate of population growth.

Exponential growth Cumulative or compound growth (of a population) over a given time period.

External migration Migration across an international border.

Extractive sector See **primary economic activity**.

Extraterritoriality Politico-geographical concept suggesting that the property of one **state** lying within the boundaries of another actually forms an extension of the first state.

Favela Shantytown on the outskirts or even well within an urban area in Brazil.

Federal state A political framework wherein a central government represents the various entities within a **nation-state** where they have common interests—defense, foreign affairs, and the like—yet allows these various entities to retain their own identities and to have their own laws, policies, and customs in certain spheres.

Federation See **federal state**.

Feng Shui The ancient Chinese belief that powerful spirits of ancestors, dragons, tigers, and other beings occupy natural phenomena such as mountains, rivers, and trees, and that to disturb them would incur their wrath.

Fertile Crescent Crescent-shaped zone of productive lands extending from near the southeastern Mediterranean coast through Lebanon and Syria to the alluvial lowlands of Mesopotamia (in Iraq). Once more fertile than today, this is one of the world's great source areas of agricultural and other innovations.

Feudalism Prevailing politico-geographical system in Europe during the Middle Ages when land was owned by the nobility and was worked by peasants and serfs. Feudalism also existed in other parts of the world, and the system persisted into this century in Ethiopia and Iran, among other places.

Folk culture Cultural traits such as dress modes, dwellings, traditions, and institutions of usually small, relatively changeless, tradition-bound communities.

Food web (food chain) All plants and animals are in some way connected to this organic sequence in which each life-form consumes the form below and, at the same time, is consumed by the form above. Plant life constitutes the foundation of the food web; the meat-eating animals (carnivores) stand at the top.

Forced migration Human **migration** flows in which the movers have no choice but to relocate.

Formal region A type of region marked by a certain degree of homogeneity in one or more phenomena; also called uniform region or homogeneous region.

Forward capital Capital city positioned in actually or potentially contested territory, usually near an international border; it confirms the **state**'s determination to maintain its presence in the region in contention.

Fragmented state A state whose territory consists of several separated parts, not a contiguous whole. The individual parts may be isolated from each other by the land area of other states or by international waters.

Francophone Describes a country or region where other languages are also spoken, but where French is the **lingua franca**, or the language of the elite. Quebec is Francophone Canada.

Frontier Zone of advance penetration, usually of contention; an area not yet fully integrated into a national **state**.

Functional region A region marked less by its sameness than its dynamic internal structure; because it usually focuses on a central node, also called nodal or focal region.

Functional specialization The production of particular goods or services as a dominant activity in a particular location.

Gateway state A state, by virtue of its border location between geopolitical power cores, that abosrbs and assimilates cultures and traditions of its neighbors without being dominated by them.

Gender gap The differences in levels of health, education, income, opportunity and participation in politics and public life that exist between males and females.

Gentrification The rehabilitation of deteriorated, often abandoned, housing of low-income inner-city residents.

Geographic information system (GIS) A collection of computer hardware and software that permits spatial data to be collected, recorded, stored, retrieved, manipulated, analyzed, and displayed to the user.

Geographic realm The basic **spatial** unit in our world regionalization scheme. Each realm is defined in terms of a synthesis of its total human geography—a composite of its leading cultural, economic, historical, political, and appropriate environmental features.

Geography Literally means "Earth Description." As a modern academic discipline, it is concerned with the explanation of the physical and human characteristics of the Earth's surface. "Why are things located where they are?" is the central question that geographical scholarship seeks to answer.

Geologic time scale The standard timetable or chronicle of Earth history used by scientists; the sequential organization of geologic time units, whose dates continue to be refined by ongoing research.

Geometric boundaries Political boundaries **defined** and **delimited** (and occasionally **demarcated**) as straight lines or arcs.

Geopolitics (Geopolitik) A school of political geography that involved the use of quasi-academic research to encourage a national policy of expansionism and imperialism.

Gerrymandering Redistricting for advantage, or the practice of dividing areas into electoral districts to give one political party an electoral majority in a large number of districts while concentrating the voting strength of the opposition in as few districts as possible.

Ghetto An urban region marked by particular ethnic, racial, religious, and economic properties, usually (but not always) a low-income area.

Glaciation A period of global cooling during which continental ice sheets and mountain glaciers expand.

Gondwana The southern portion of the primeval supercontinent, Pangaea.

Gravity model A mathematical prediction of the interaction of places, the interaction being a function of population size of the respective places and the distance between them.

Green Revolution The successful recent development of higher-yield, fast-growing varieties of rice and other cereals in certain developing countries, which led to increased production per unit area and a temporary narrowing of the gap between population growth and food needs.

Greenhouse effect The widely used analogy describing the blanketlike effect of the atmosphere in the heating of the Earth's surface; shortwave insolation passes through the "glass" of the atmospheric "greenhouse," heats the surface, is converted to long-wave radiation that cannot penetrate the "glass," and thereby results in trapping heat, which raises the temperature inside the "greenhouse."

Gross national product (GNP) The total value of all goods and services produced in a country during a given year.

Growing season The number of days between the last frost in the spring and the first frost of the fall.

Growth pole An urban center with certain attributes that, if augmented by a measure of investment support, will stimulate regional economic development in its **hinterland**.

Heartland theory The hypothesis, proposed by British geographer Halford Mackinder during the first two decades of this century, that any political power based in the heart of Eurasia could gain sufficient strength to eventually dominate the world. Furthermore, since Eastern Europe controlled access to the Eurasian interior, its ruler would command the vast "heartland" to the east.

Hegemony The political dominance of a country (or even a region) by another country. The former Soviet Union's postwar grip on Eastern Europe, which lasted from 1945 to 1990, was a classic example.

Hierarchical diffusion A form of **diffusion** in which an idea or innovation spreads by trickling down from larger to smaller adoption units. An **urban hierarchy** is usually involved, encouraging the leapfrogging of innovations over wide areas, with geographic distance a less important influence.

Hierarchy An order or gradation of phenomena, with each level or rank subordinate to the one above it and superior to the one below. The levels in a national urban hierarchy are constituted by hamlets, villages, towns, cities, and (frequently) the **primate city**.

High seas Areas of the oceans away from land, beyond national jurisdiction, open and free for all to use.

Hinterland Literally, "country behind," a term that applies to a surrounding area served by an urban center. That center is the focus of goods and services produced for its hinterland and is its dominant urban influence as well. In the case of a port city, the hinterland also includes the inland area whose trade flows through that port.

Holocene The current interglaciation epoch, extending from 10,000 years ago to the present on the geologic time scale.

Human geography One of the two major divisions of systematic geography; the spatial analysis of human population, their cultures, and activities.

Hydrologic cycle The system of exchange involving water in its various forms as it continually circulates among the **atmosphere**, the oceans, and above and below the land surface.

Ice age A stretch of geologic time during which the Earth's average atmospheric temperature is lowered; causes the expansion of glacial ice in the high latitudes and the growth of mountain glaciers in lower latitudes.

Ice cap A regional mass of ice smaller than a continent-size ice sheet; while the Laurentide ice sheet covered much of North America east of the Rocky Mountains, an ice cap covered the Rockies themselves.

Ice sheet A large and thick layer of ice that flows outward in all directions from a central area where continuous accumulation of snow and thickening of ice occur. Also called continental ice sheet or continental glacier.

Iconography The identity of a region as expressed through its cherished symbols; its particular **cultural landscape** and personality.

Ideology A set of beliefs, values, assertions, and preferences about how society should be organized and focused.

Imam The political head of the Muslim community or the person who leads prayer services. In **Shiite** Islam the imam is immune from sin or error.

Immigrant A person migrating into a particular country or area; an in-migrant.

Imperialism The drive toward the creation and expansion of a colonial empire and, once established, its perpetuation.

Industrial Revolution The term applied to the social and economic changes in agriculture, commerce and manufacturing that resulted from technological innovations and specialization in late eighteenth-century Europe.

Infant mortality rate The annual number of deaths of infants under age 1 year per 1000 live births.

Infrastructure The foundations of a society: urban centers, transport networks, communications, energy distribution systems, farms, factories, mines, and such facilities as schools, hospitals, postal services, and police and armed forces.

Insurgent state Territorial embodiment of a successful guerrilla movement. The establishment by anti-government insurgents of a territorial base in which they exercise full control; thus, a state within a **state**.

Interactive mapping In geographic information systems (GIS) methodology, the constant dialogue via computer demands and feedback to queries between the map user and the map.

Interglaciation A period of warmer global temperatures between the most recent deglaciation and the onset of the next glaciation.

Internal migration Migration flow within a **nation-state**, such as ongoing westward and southward movements in the United States.

International migration **Migration** flow involving movement across international boundaries.

Intervening opportunity The presence of a nearer opportunity that greatly diminishes the attractiveness of sites farther away.

Irredentism A policy of cultural extension and potential political expansion aimed at a national group living in a neighboring country.

Irrigation The artificial watering of croplands. In Egypt's Nile valley, *basin irrigation* is an ancient method that involved the use of floodwaters that were trapped in basins on the floodplain and released in stages to augment rainfall. Today's *perennial irrigation* requires the construction of dams and irrigation canals for year-round water supply.

Isogloss A geographic boundary within which a particular linguistic feature occurs.

Karma In Hinduism and Buddhism, the force generated by a person's actions that affects transmigrations into a future existence, determining conditions and position in the next earthly stage of life.

K/T boundary Boundary between the Mesozoic and Cenozoic eras marking the extinction of many plants and animals, including the great dinosaurs.

Land bridge A narrow isthmian link between two large landmasses. They are temporary features—at least in terms of geologic time—subject to appearance and disappearance as the land or sea-level rises and falls.

Landlocked An interior country or **state** that is surrounded by land. Without coasts, a landlocked state is at a disadvantage in a number of ways—in terms of **accessibility** to international trade routes and in the scramble for possession of areas of the **continental shelf** and control of the **exclusive economic zone** beyond.

Late Cenozoic Ice Age The last great ice age that ended 10,000 years ago; spanned the entire Pleistocene epoch (2 million to 10,000 years ago) plus the latter portion of the preceding Plio-

cene epoch, possibly beginning as far back as 3.5 million years ago.

Latitude The angular distance, measured in degrees north or south, of a point along a parallel from the equator.

Law of the Sea The United Nations Convention on the Law of the Sea (UNCLOS), signed by 157 states (but not including the United States) in 1982; established states' rights and responsibilities concerning the ownership and use of the Earth's seas and oceans and their resources.

League of Nations A global (supranational) organization established by the victors of World War I to preserve peace and security and to promote economic and social cooperation among its members.

Least cost theory Model developed by Alfred Weber according to which the location of manufacturing establishments is determined by the minimization of three critical expenses: labor, transportation, and agglomeration.

Lingua franca The term derives from "Frankish language," and applied to a tongue spoken in ancient Mediterranean ports that consisted of a mixture of Italian, French, Greek, Spanish, and even some Arabic. Today it refers to a "common language," a second language that can be spoken and understood by many peoples, although they speak other languages at home.

Little Ice Age The period of decidedly cooler global temperatures that prevailed from 1430 to 1850 (averaging ca. 1.5°Celsius [3.7° Fahrenheit] lower than in the 1940s); during these four centuries, glaciers in most parts of the world expanded considerably.

Location theory A logical attempt to explain the locational pattern of an economic activity and the manner in which its producing areas are interrelated. The agricultural location theory contained in the **von Thünen model** is a leading example.

Loess Deposit of very fine silt or dust that is laid down after having been windborne for a considerable distance. Loess is notable for its fertility under **irrigation** and its ability to stand in steep vertical walls when **eroded** by a river or (as in China's Loess Plateau) excavated for cave-type human dwellings.

Longevity gap The difference in the average length of life between males and females.

Longitude The angular distance, measured in degrees east or west, of a point along a meridian from the prime meridian.

Main Street Canada's dominant **conurbation** that is home to more than 60 percent of the country's inhabitants; stretches southwestward from Quebec City in the middle St. Lawrence valley to Windsor on the Detroit River.

Malnutrition Condition of ill health resulting from the deficiency or improper balance of essential foodstuffs in the diet, usually proteins, vitamins, and minerals. Two common forms of malnutrition among children in the world's poorer countries are *kwashiorkor*, a protein-deficient disorder, and *marasmus*, which results from insufficient protein and calories.

Malthusian Designates the early nineteenth-century viewpoint of Thomas Malthus, who argued that population growth was outrunning the Earth's capacity to produce sufficient food. Neo-Malthusian refers to those who subscribe to such positions in modern contexts.

Map projection An orderly arrangement of meridians and parallels, produced by any systematic method, that can be used for drawing a map of the spherical Earth on a flat surface.

Maquiladora The term given to modern industrial plants in Mexico's northern (U.S.) border zone. These foreign-owned factories assemble imported components and/or raw materials and then export finished manufactures, mainly to the United States. Most import duties are minimized, bringing jobs to Mexico and the advantages of low wage rates to the foreign entrepreneurs.

Median-line principle The system of drawing a political boundary midway between two states' coastlines when the territorial seas or EEZ are narrower than twice the standard or adopted limit.

Medical geography The study of health in a geographic context; for example, the occurrence, location, and diffusion of disease.

Medieval optimum A warm phase during the tenth to the twelfth centuries, ended by the onset of the Little Ice Age.

Megalopolis Term used to designate large coalescing supercities that are forming in diverse parts of the world; formerly used specifically with an uppercase M to refer to the Boston–Washington multimetropolitan corridor on the northeastern seaboard of the United States, but now used generically with a lower-case m as a synonym for **conurbation**.

Mental map Image or picture of the way space (e.g., state or city) is organized as determined by an individual's perception, impression, and knowledge of that space.

Mercantilism Protectionist policy of European **states** during the sixteenth to the eighteenth centuries that promoted a state's economic position in the contest with other countries. The acquisition of gold and silver and the maintenance of a favorable trade balance (more exports than imports) were central to the policy.

Metropolitan area See **urban (metropolitan) area**.

Mesolithic period The Middle Stone Age, starting in Europe at the end of the last glacial period over 10,000 years ago.

Mesozoic The era of medieval life on the geologic time scale extending from 225 million years ago to 65 million years ago.

Migrant diffusion A form of relocation diffusion in which innovation adopted in distant places has lessened where it originated.

Migration A change in residence intended to be permanent. See also **forced**, **internal**, **international**, and **voluntary migration**.

Migratory movement Human relocation movement from a source to a destination without a return journey, as opposed to **cyclical movement**.

Milpa agriculture Middle and South American subsistence agriculture in which forest patches are cleared for temporary cultivation of corn and other crops.

Miracle rice A high-yielding variety of rice developed in the Philippines in the 1960s and now widely planted in Asia.

Model An idealized representation of reality built to demonstrate certain of its properties. A spatial model focuses on a geographic dimension of the real world.

Multinationals Internationally active corporations that can strongly influence the economic and political affairs of many countries they operate in.

Multiple nuclei model The Harris–Ullman model that showed the mid-twentieth-century American central city consisting of several land-use zones arranged around nuclear growth points.

Multiplier effect Expansion of economic activity caused by the growth or introduction of another economic activity. For example, a new basic industry will create jobs, directly or indirectly, in the nonbasic sector.

Multiregional Evolution Theory Theory that human phenotypes evolved in four separate regions (Africa, Australia, East Asia, and Europe) producing, respectively, the Negroid, Australoid, Mongoloid, and Caucasoid stocks.

NAFTA The North American Free Trade Agreement which took effect January 1, 1994 creating a free-trade area between the United States, Canada and Mexico; provides for the tariff-free movement of goods and products, financial services, telecommunications, investment, and patent protection within and between the signatories.

Nation Legally a term encompassing all the citizens of a **state**. Most definitions now tend to refer to a tightly knit group of people possessing bonds of language, ethnicity, religion, and other shared cultural attributes. Such homogeneity actually prevails within very few states.

Nationalism A sense of national consciousness and loyalty exalting one nation above all others and placing primary emphasis on the promotion of its culture and interests as opposed to those of other nations.

Nation-state A country whose population possesses a substantial degree of cultural homogeneity and unity. The ideal form to which most **nations** and **states** aspire—a political unit wherein the territorial state coincides with the area settled by a certain national group or people.

Natural increase rate Population growth measured as the excess of live births over deaths per 1000 individuals per year. Natural increase of a population does not reflect either **emigrant** or **immigrant** movements.

Natural-political boundaries See **physical-political boundaries**.

Natural resource Any valued element of (or means to an end using) the environment; includes minerals, water, vegetation, and soil.

Nautical mile By international agreement, the nautical mile—the standard measure at sea—is 6076.12 feet in length, equivalent to approximately 1.15 statute miles (1.85 kilometers).

Neocolonialism The entrenchment of the colonial order, such as trade and investment, under a new guise.

Neolithic period The New Stone Age marked by animal domestication, the beginnings of agriculture, the presence of crafts, and the diversification of tool-making industries.

Network (transport) The entire regional system of transportation connections and nodes through which movement can occur.

New World Order The international system resulting from the collapse of the Soviet Union in which the balance of nuclear terror theoretically no longer determines the destinies of states.

Nomadism **Cyclical movement** among a definite set of places. Nomadic peoples mostly are **pastoralists**.

Nonrenewable resource A resource that when used at a certain rate will ultimately be exhausted (metallic ores and petroleum are good examples).

Nuclear fusion The formation of an atomic nucleus by the union of two other nuclei having a lighter mass, a process that yields a huge amount of energy, which, if harnessed, may solve the world's power problems during the twenty-first century. A virtually inexhaustible source of fuel (hydrogen) exists, and the process does not produce dangerous radioactivity as nuclear fission does.

Nucleated settlement See **agglomerated settlement**.

Official language In multilingual countries the language selected, often by the educated and politically powerful elite, to promote internal cohesion; usually the language of the courts and government.

One-child policy Official policy launched by China in 1979 to induce married couples to have only one child in an effort to control population growth.

Organic theory A determinist view that states resemble biological organisms with life cycles that include stage of youth, maturity, and old age, now largely discredited.

Pacific Rim A far-flung group of countries and parts of countries (extending clockwise on the map from New Zealand to Chile) sharing the following criteria: they face the Pacific Ocean; they evince relatively high levels of economic development, industrialization, and urbanization; and their imports and exports mainly move across Pacific waters.

Paleolithic period The Old Stone Age, the earliest period of human development that is approximately coextensive with the Pleistocene epoch beginning over 2 million years ago and ending between 40,000 and 10,000 years ago, when communities subsisted on hunting and gathering and used tools of stone, bone, and ivory.

Pandemic An outbreak of a disease that spreads worldwide.

Pangaea The primeval supercontinent, hypothesized by Alfred Wegener, that broke apart and formed the continents and oceans as we know them today; consisted of two parts—a northern Laurasia and a southern **Gondwana**.

Parallel An east–west line of **latitude** that is intersected at right angles by meridians of **longitude**.

Pastoralism A form of agricultural activity that involves the raising of livestock. Many peoples described as herders actually pursue mixed **agriculture**, in that they may also fish, hunt, or even grow a few crops. But pastoral peoples' lives revolve around their animals.

Per capita Capita means *individual*. Income, production, or some other measure is often given per individual.

Perforated state A **state** whose territory completely surrounds that of another state. South Africa, which encloses Lesotho and is perforated by it, is an example.

Periodic movement A form of migration that involves intermittent but recurrent movement, such as temporary relocation for college attendance or service in the armed forces.

Physical (natural) geography One of the two major divisions of systematic geography; the spatial analysis of the structure, processes, and location of the Earth's natural phenomena such as climate, soil, plants, animals, and topography.

Physical-political (natural-political) boundaries Political boundaries that coincide with prominent physical features in the natural landscape—such as rivers or the crest ridges of mountain ranges.

Physiologic density The number of people per unit area of **arable** land.

Pidgin A **Lingua Franca** that has been simplified and modified through contact with other languages.

Plantation A large estate owned by an individual, family, or corporation and organized to produce a cash crop. Almost all plantations were established within the tropics; in recent decades, many have been divided into smaller holdings or reorganized as cooperatives.

Pleistocene The epoch that extended from about 2 million to 10,000 years ago on the geologic time scale; includes the latter half of the last great (Late Cenozoic) ice age, which began about 3.5 million years ago, as well as the emergence of humankind.

Political geography The study of the interaction of geographical area and political process; the spatial analysis of political phenomena and processes.

Pollution The release of a substance, through human activity, that chemically, physically, or biologically alters the air or water it is discharged into. Such a discharge negatively impacts the environment, with possible harmful effects on living organisms, including humans.

Popular culture Cultural traits such as dress modes, diet, and music that identify and are part of today's changeable, urban-based, media-drenched, fad-addicted society.

Population density A measurement of the number of people per given unit of land.

Population explosion The rapid growth of the world's human population during the past century, attended by ever-shorter **doubling times** and accelerating rates of increase.

Population policy Official (government) policy aimed at changing the size, composition (structure), or growth of population.

Population (age-sex) structure Graphic representation (profile) of a population according to age and sex.

Possibilism Geographic viewpoint—a response to determinism—that holds that human decision making is the crucial factor in cultural development, not environmental limitation or restricted options. Cultural heritage and learning are the key attributes in society's use of the natural environment.

Postindustrial (postmodern) economy Emerging economy, in the United States and a handful of other highly advanced countries, as traditional industry is overshadowed by a higher-technology productive complex dominated by services and information-related and managerial activities.

Power In political geography, the ability of one state to influence or change the behavior of another state by military, economic, political, or other means.

Precambrian The era that precedes the Paleozoic era of ancient life on the geologic time scale, named after the oldest period of the Paleozoic, the Cambrian; extends backward from 570 million years ago to the origin of the Earth, now estimated to be about 4.6 billion years ago.

Primary economic activity Activity engaged in the direct extraction of **natural resources** from the environment—such as mining, fishing, lumbering, and especially **agriculture**.

Primate city A country's largest city—ranking atop the **urban hierarchy**—most expressive of the national culture and usually (but not always) the capital city as well.

Prime meridian The north–south line on the Earth grid, passing through the Royal Observatory at Greenwich in London, defined as having a longitude of 0°.

Process Causal force that shapes a **spatial** pattern as it unfolds over time.

Prorupt state A type of **state** territorial shape that exhibits a narrow, elongated land extension leading away from the main body of territory. Thailand is an example.

Protectorate In Britain's system of colonial administration, the protectorate was a designation that involved the guarantee of certain rights (such as the restriction of European settlement and land alienation) to peoples who had been placed under the control of the Crown.

Proxemics The individual and collective preferences for nearness or distance as displayed by different cultures.

Pull factor Positive conditions and perceptions that effectively attract people to new locales from other areas.

Push factor Negative conditions and perceptions that induce people to leave their abode and migrate to a new locale.

Push-pull concept The idea that **migration** flows are simultaneously stimulated by conditions in the source area, which tend to drive people away, and by the perceived attractiveness of the destination.

Quaternary The second of the two periods of the Cenozoic era of recent life on the geologic time scale extending from approximately 2 million years ago to the present.

Quaternary economic activity Activity engaged in the collection, processing, and manipulation of information.

Radioactive waste Hazardous waste emitting radiation from nuclear power plants, nuclear weapons factories, and nuclear equipment in hospitals and industry.

Rank-size rule In a model urban hierarchy, the population of a city or town will be inversely proportional to its rank in the hierarchy.

Realm See **geographic realm**.

Recycling Conservation practice of reprocessing materials for reuse.

Refugee A person forced to flee his or her homeland owing to a well-founded fear of persecution for reasons of race, religion, nationality, or membership of a particular social or political group.

Region A commonly used term and a geographic concept of central importance. An **area** on the Earth's surface marked by certain properties.

Regional science Discipline that emphasizes the application of modern spatial analytical techniques to regional problems and issues.

Regionalism The consciousness and loyalty to a region considered distinct and different from the state as a whole by those who occupy it.

Relative direction A culturally determined locational reference such as the "Middle East" or "Far West."

Relative distance Distance measured, not in linear terms such as miles or kilometers, but in terms such as cost and time.

Relative location The regional position or **situation** of a place relative to the position of other places. Distance, **accessibility**, and connectivity affect relative location.

Relict boundary A political boundary that has ceased to function, but the imprint of which can still be detected on the **cultural landscape**.

Religious fundamentalism Religious movement whose objectives are to return to the foundations of the faith and to influence state policy.

Relocation diffusion Sequential **diffusion** process in which the items being diffused are transmitted by their carrier agents as they evacuate the old areas and relocate to new ones. The most common form of relocation diffusion involves the spreading of innovations by a **migrating** population.

Remote sensing A technique for imaging objects without the sensor being in immediate contact with the local scene.

Renewable resource A resource that can regenerate as it is exploited.

Restrictive population policy Government policy designed to reduce the rate of natural increase.

Rimland Term coined by Nicholas Spykman referring to the coastal rim of Eurasia, which Spykman maintained held the key to global power. A counterthesis to Mackinder's heartland thesis.

Rural density A measure that indicates the number of persons per unit area living in the rural areas of a country, outside the urban concentrations.

Sahel Semiarid zone extending across most of Africa between the southern margins of the arid Sahara and the moister tropical savanna and forest zone to the south. Chronic drought, **desertification**, and overgrazing have contributed to severe famines in this area for decades.

Scale Representation of a real-world phenomenon at a certain level of reduction or generalization. In **cartography**, the ratio of map distance to ground distance; indicated on a map as a bar graph, representative fraction, and/or verbal statement.

Secondary economic activity Activity that processes raw materials and transforms them into finished industrial products; the manufacturing sector.

Sector model A structural model of the American central city that suggests that land-use areas conform to a wedge-shaped pattern focused on the downtown core.

Secularism Secularism holds that ethical and moral standards should be formulated and adhered to for life on Earth and not to accommodate the prescriptions of a deity and promises of a comfortable afterlife. A secular state is the opposite of a **theocracy**.

Sedentary Permanently attached to a particular area; a population fixed in its location. The opposite of **nomadic**.

Sequent occupance The notion that successive societies leave their cultral imprints on a place, each contributing to the cumulative **cultural landscape**.

Service industry See **tertiary economic activity**.

Settlement density The amount of area in a country for each city with 100,000 people or more.

Shaman In traditional societies, a shaman is deemed to possess religious and mystical powers, acquired directly from supernatural sources. At times an especially strong shaman might attract a regional following; many shamans, however, remain local figures.

Shantytown Unplanned slum development on the margins of cities in the developing realms, dominated by crude dwellings and shelters mostly made of scrap wood, iron, and even pieces of cardboard.

Shatter belt Region caught between stronger, colliding external cultural-political forces, under persistent stress and often fragmented by aggressive rivals. Eastern Europe and Southeast Asia are classic examples.

Shifting agriculture Cultivation of crops in recently cut and burned tropical forest clearings, soon to be abandoned in favor of newly cleared nearby forestland. Also known as slash-and-burn agriculture.

Shiites Adherents of one of the two main divisions of Islam. Also known as Shiahs, the Shiites represent the Persian (Iranian) variation of Islam and believe in the infallibility and divine right to authority of the **Imams**, descendants of Ali.

Site The internal locational attributes of an urban center, including its local spatial organization and physical setting.

Situation The external locational attributes of an urban center; its **relative location** or regional position with reference to other nonlocal places.

Slash-and-burn agriculture See **shifting agriculture**.

Social stratification The differentiation of society into classes based on wealth, power, production, and prestige.

Southern Cone The southern, mid latitude portion of South America constituted by the countries of Chile, Argentina, and Uruguay; often included as well is the southernmost part of Brazil, south of the Tropic of Capricorn (23½° S).

Spatial Pertaining to space on the Earth's surface; synonym for geographic.

Spatial interaction See **complementarity** and **intervening opportunity**.

Standard language The language quality of a country's dominant language that is preferred by the elite and/or the state.

State A politically organized territory that is administered by a sovereign government and is recognized by a significant portion of the international community. A state must also contain a permanent resident population, an organized economy, and a functioning internal circulation system.

State capitalism Government-controlled corporations competing under free market conditions, usually in a tightly regimented society.

Stationary population level The level at which a national population ceases to grow.

Step migration Migration to a distant destination that occurs in stages, for example, from farm to nearby village, and later to town and city.

Stratification (social) In a layered or stratified society, the population is divided into a **hierarchy** of social classes. In an industrialized society, the proletariat is at the lower end: elites that possess capital and control the means of production are at the upper level. In the traditional **caste system** of Hindu India, the "untouchables" form the lowest class or caste, whereas the still-wealthy remnants of the princely class are at the top.

Subsequent boundary A political boundary that developed contemporaneously with the evolution of the major elements of the cultural landscape through which it passes.

Subsistence The state of existing on the minimum necessities to sustain life; spending most of one's time in pursuit of survival.

Subsistence agriculture Self-sufficient agriculture that is small scale and low technology and emphasizes food production for local consumption, not for trade.

Suburb A subsidiary urban area surrounding and connected to the central city. Many are exclusively residential; others have their own commercial centers or shopping malls.

Suburban downtown Significant concentration of diversified economic activities around a highly **accessible** suburban location, including retailing, light industry, and a variety of major corporate and commercial operations. Late-twentieth-century co-equal to the American central city's **central business district (CBD)**.

Sunnis Adherents to the largest branch of Muslims, called the orthodox or traditionalist. They believe in the effectiveness of family and community in the solution of life's problems, and they differ from the **Shiites** in accepting as authoritative the traditions (sunna) of Muhammad.

Superimposed boundary A political boundary placed by powerful outsiders on a developed human landscape. Usually ignores preexisting cultural-spatial patterns, such as the border that now divides North and South Korea.

Supranational   A venture involving three or more national states—political, economic, and/or cultural cooperation to promote shared objectives. Europe's Economic Community or Common Market is one such organization.

Swidden agriculture   See **shifting agriculture**.

System   Any group of objects or institutions and their mutual interactions. Geography treats systems that are expressed **spatially** such as **regions**.

Systematic geography   Topical geography: cultural, political, economic geography, and the like.

Takeoff   Economic concept to identify a stage in a country's **development** when conditions are set for a domestic Industrial Revolution, which occurred in Britain in the late eighteenth century and in Japan in the late nineteenth century following the Meiji Restoration.

Taphonomy   Study of assemblages of fossil remains and the circumstances prevailing during and after the organisms' death.

Territorial morphology   A **state**'s geographical shape, which can have a decisive impact on its spatial cohesion and political viability. A **compact** shape is most desirable; among the less efficient shapes are those exhibited by **elongated**, **fragmented**, **perforated**, and **prorupt** states.

Territorial sea   Zone of seawater adjacent to a country's coast, held to be part of the national territory and treated as a segment of the sovereign state.

Territoriality   A country's or more local community's sense of property and attachment toward its territory, as expressed by its determination to keep it inviolable and strongly defended.

Tertiary economic activity   Activity that engages in services—such as transportation, banking, retailing, education, and routine office-based jobs.

Theocracy   A **state** whose government is under the control of a ruler who is deemed to be divinely guided or under the control of a group of religious leaders, as in post-Khomeini Iran. The opposite of the theocratic state is the **secular** state.

Time-Distance decay   The declining degree of acceptance of an idea or innovation with increasing time and distance from its point of origin or source.

Toponomy (or **Toponymy**)   The etymological study of place names or associated language.

Total Fertility Rate (TFR)   The average number of children born to a woman during her lifetime, as expressed for a total population.

Totalitarian   A government whose leaders rule by absolute control, tolerating no differences of political opinion.

Township-and-Range System   A rectangular land division scheme designed by Thomas Jefferson to disperse settlers evenly across farmlands of the U.S. interior.

Toxic waste   Hazardous waste causing danger from chemicals and infectious materials.

Traditional   Term used in various contexts (e.g., traditional religion) to indicate originality within a culture or long-term part of an indigenous society. It is the opposite of modernized, superimposed, changed; it denotes continuity and historic association.

Transculturation   Cultural borrowing that occurs when different cultures of approximately equal complexity and technological level come into close contact. In **acculturation**, by contrast, an indigenous society's culture is modified by contact with a technologically superior society.

Transhumance   A seasonal periodic movement of pastoralists and their livestock between highland and lowland pastures.

Transition zone   An area of **spatial** change where the peripheries of two adjacent realms or regions join; marked by a gradual shift (rather than sharp break) in the characteristics that distinguish these neighboring geographic entities from one another.

Tropical deforestation   The clearing and destruction of tropical rainforests to make way for expanding settlement frontiers and the exploitation of new economic opportunities.

Truman Proclamation   In September 1945, President Harry Truman proclaimed the United States would regulate fisheries' activities in areas of the high seas adjacent to its coastline, and that U.S. jurisdiction over the continental shelf and its contents would be limited to the region within the 600-foot isobath.

Underdeveloped countries (UCDs)   Countries that, by various measures, suffer seriously from negative economic and social conditions, including low per capita incomes, poor nutrition, inadequate health, and related disadvantaged circumstances.

Unitary state   A **nation-state** that has a centralized government and administration that exercises power equally over all parts of the state.

United Nations   A global (supranational) organization established at the end of World War II to foster international security and cooperation.

Urban (metropolitan) area   The entire built-up, nonrural area and its population, including the most recently constructed suburban appendages. Provides a better picture of the dimensions and population of such an area than the delimited municipality (central city) that forms its heart.

Urban geography   A subfield of geography that focuses especially on urban places, their characteristics, processes of genesis and growth, their systems, relative location, and interrelationships.

Urban hierarchy   A ranking of settlements (hamlet, village, town, city, metropolis) according to their size and economic functions.

Urban realms model   A **spatial** generalization of the large, late-twentieth-century city in the United States. It is shown to be a widely dispersed, multicentered metropolis consisting of increasingly independent zones or realms, each focused on its own **suburban downtown**; the only exception is the shrunken central realm, which is focused on the **central business district**.

Urban system   The functional and **spatial** organization of towns and cities.

Urbanization   A term with several connotations. The proportion of a country's population living in urban places is its level of urbanization. The process of urbanization involves the movement of people to, and the clustering of people in towns and cities—a major force in every geographic realm today. Another kind of urbanization occurs when an expanding city absorbs rural countryside and transforms it into suburbs; in the case of cities in the developing world, this also generates peripheral **shantytowns**.

Vectored disease   A disease carried from one host to another by an intermedite host.

Volcanic winter   Winter-like conditions lasting decades and covering broad regions caused by volcanic eruptions whose dust and ash obscure the sun and lower temperatures.

Voluntary migration   Population movement in which people relocate in response to perceived opportunity, not because they are forced to move.

Von Thünen model   Explains the location of agricultural activities in a commercial, profit-making economy. A process of spatial competition allocates various farming activities into concentric rings around a central market city, with profit-earning capability the determining force in how far a crop locates from the market. The original (1826) Isolated State model now applies to the continental scale.

Wisconsinan Glaciation   The most recent glaciation of the Late Cenozoic Ice Age, consisting of early and late stages.

Ziggurat   A lofty ancient Babylonian temple tower that symbolized power and authority.

Zionism   The movement to unite the Jewish people of the Diaspora and to establish a national homeland for them in Palestine.

INDEX